TIME AND PLACE

Riley's Court, Leeds, a street of seven pairs of back-to-backs on either side (*c.* 1800) entered by a tunnel arch at each end; one of these frames the photograph. In 1869 the railway viaduct made it even more like a human warren.

Cannon Street, Leeds: a cul-de-sac halted by a property boundary. Nos. 1, 3, 5 and 7 were built back-to-back with the south side of Byron St. (Leylands) in 1827, and a tunnel connected the two streets.

TIME AND PLACE

COLLECTED ESSAYS

M.W. BERESFORD

THE HAMBLEDON
PRESS

The Hambledon Press 1984
35 Gloucester Avenue, London NW1 7AX

History Series 31

ISBN 0 907628 39 7

British Library Cataloguing in Publication Data

Beresford, Maurice
　　Time and place: collected essays.
　　— (History series; 31)
　　1. Great Britain — History
　　I. Title　　II. Series
　　942　DA30

CONTENTS

ACKNOWLEDGEMENTS

The articles collected here first appeared in the following places and are reprinted by the kind permission of the original publishers.

1   Inaugural Lecture (Leeds University Press, 1961).

2   *Agricultural History Review*, xviii (1970), Supplement, vii-xii.

3   *Agricultural History Review*, xii (1964), pt. 1, 13-27.

4   *Medieval Archaeology* iii (1959), 187-215.

5   *Économies et Sociétés au Moyen Age. Mélanges offerts à Edouard Perroy* (Publications de la Sorbonne, Paris 1973), 574-80.

6   *Medieval Archaeology* ii (1958), 171-3.

7   *Medieval Archaeology*, x (1966), 164-7.

8   *Medieval Archaeology*, xi (1967), 257-60.

9   *Transactions of the Birmingham Archaeological Society*, lxiv (1941 and 1942), 101-108.

10   *Economic History Review*, xiii (1943), 74-9.

11   *Economic History Review*, Second Series, i (1948), 34-46.

12   *Economic History Review*, xvi (1946), 130-42.

13   *Agricultural History Review*, i (1953), 9-15; *ibid.*, ii (1954), 15-29.

14   *Essays in the Economic and Social History of Tudor and Stuart England*, ed. F.J. Fisher (Cambridge, 1960), 40-69.

15   *Amateur Historian*, iii and iv (1957-8).

16   *Economic History Review*, Second Series, x (1957), 221-38.

17   *Yorkshire Bulletin of Economic and Social Research*,

20   *Urban History Yearbook* (1976), 7-14.

21   *Economic History Review*, Second Series, xxxv (1982), 373-89

22   *Northern History*, x (1975), 126-40.

23   *Rural Change and Urban Growth*, ed. C.W. Chalklin and M.A. Havind
      (Longmans, London, 1974), 281-320.

24   *Leeds and Its Region*, ed. M.W. Beresford and G.R.J. Jones
      (Leeds Local Executive Committee of the British Association for
      the Advancement of Science, Leeds, 1967), 186-97.

25   *The History of Working Class Housing*, ed. S.D. Chapman
      (David and Charles, Newton Abbot, 1971), 93-132.

TIME AND PLACE:
AN AUTOBIOGRAPHICAL FRAGMENT

In my working lifetime as an economic historian, an amateur until 1948 and an academic professional thereafter, my researches have produced both books and articles. Three major topics of Time and Place, treading delicately on the borders of History and Geography, preoccupied me for the central years: deserted medieval villages; the medieval landscape as evidenced by documents, maps, fieldwork and air photographs; and the planted town of the Middle Ages. Four books resulted: *The Lost Villages of England* (1954); *History on the Ground* (1957, revised 1971); *Medieval England: an aerial Survey* (1958, revised 1979); and *New Towns of the Middle Ages* (1967). Articles closely related to these books — such as the county studies of deserted villages — have been omitted from this collection, and although a fifth book, on the townscape of Leeds during industrialisation, is in preparation it is not intended there to reiterate what appears here as chapters 20-25.

The title of this collection, although taken from a single chapter in it, my Inaugural lecture of November 1960 [1], does boldly suggest that there is some unity in the other twenty-four. The purpose of this Introduction is to relate these seemingly disparate shorter studies to each other and to the researches embodied in full-length books. The two earliest derive from a vacation exercise of Christmas 1939 demanded by John Saltmarsh of King's College, Cambridge from members of his undergraduate seminar in economic history. Although local history was no formal part of the Historical Tripos nor indeed a term I can recall being employed by any lecturer, Saltmarsh encouraged his seminar to produce papers based on some personal interest: in my case it was the former topography of my birthplace, a residential suburb of Birmingham. By pure chance the records revealed that the medieval field-system of Sutton Coldfield exploited the poor quality soils of the parish by a system of intermittent cultivation ('infield-outfield') similar to those on the poor sands of the Norfolk breckland which Saltmarsh and H.C. Darby had recently studied.[1]

A search for local variants from the classical manorial and open field structures was then becoming fashionable particularly when

1   *Economic History* iii (1935), 30-44.

Professor Postan's lectures were emphasising how any a-typical manor and field-system destroyed the notion of economic progress deriving from a universal dissolution of classical manors with common fields, labour services and subsistence production. In this way an aspect of local history took its proper place as servant of general history and I was encouraged to submit a short article to *Economic History*. J.M. Keynes, then acting editor, was sent *Lot Acres* [10] in 1940 but the typescript was subsequently lost in a war-time fire and resurrected in 1942 for the *Economic History Review* after the demise of *Economic History*; chapter 11 had been read to an audience at the Midland Institute, Birmingham, on 10 December 1940 but also had its publication delayed by war-time printing conditions.

In my final year as an undergraduate I began to browse among the many pre-enclosure manuscript maps of Cambridgeshire and Huntingdonshire parishes in the University Library Map Room, although I can recall no attempt to compare any of these with surviving topography, for photographic copying was then extremely expensive and tracing very time-consuming. Nevertheless seeds were being sown that germinated in later years when I was working in Rugby and was able to copy open-field plans in archives at Birmingham, Warwick, Stratford on Avon, Leicester, and Northampton and compare them with the present hedged landscape and the surviving ridge and furrow beneath[11]. While still an undergraduate I had been attracted to a recent accession to the Manuscript Room of the Library, a large collection of working papers from the office of a solicitors whose predecessors had organised, as commissioners, the enclosure of many local parishes under authority of private acts of Parliament. These proceedings bridged the open field and the hedged field, the pre-enclosure map and the current Ordnance Survey map but the professional character of the commissioners' work was interesting in its own right. I recalled a typically iconoclastic remark in a lecture by Edward Welbourne of Emmanuel College, dismissing the Hammonds' strictures on the enclosing landlord as the greedy beneficiaries of enclosure, and assigning the real profits to the parliamentary counsel, the country solicitors and the surveyors involved in the promotion of legislation and the execution of the enclosure. As with open field maps, I was to find the Midland archives rich with enclosure records and the study making up chapter 12 was supplemented by an attempt at a national listing of commission records[2] and by a transcript of a

2   'Minute Books of Enclosure Commissioners', *Bulletin of the Institute of Historical Research*, xxi (1946), 59-69

Leicestershire commission minute book[3]; neither is included in this collection.

While the study of ridge and furrow demonstrated the near-ubiquity of former open fields in lowland England there were many parishes with no local enclosure act. I could find no local studies of pre-parliamentary enclosure in the Midlands and while browsing through the extensive collection of glebe terriers in the Leicester county record office, I became aware that this source not only confirmed the existence of open fields in many parishes which had no old maps but inevitably demonstrated the year or range of years of pre-Parliamentary enclosure as the laboured verbal description of the multitude of glebe selions was replaced by the curt list of fields given in compensation at enclosure.[4] And where even the earliest Elizabethan terriers recorded fields already enclosed I found myself on the edge of another earlier type of enclosure, that usually associated with conversion of arable to pasture and the depopulation of the village. An article on this topic in *Country Life* for 30 June 1949 resulted in a proposal from the Lutterworth Press for a book, and five years later in *The Lost Villages of England*.

The researches which gave rise to *Lost Villages* are directly represented only by two chapters in this collection, 7 and 8, short studies of sites with extant surveys earlier than the depopulation but indirectly the majority of the items in this collection derive from documentary sources utilised or first encountered in the course of my deserted village researches. In chapters 6, 13 and 15 I tried to demonstrate the general utility of documents in the Exchequer files at the Public Record Office related to enclosure, and many years later was enabled by a Social Science Research Council grant to organise a full listing of major records Chancery relevant to enclosure by agreement in the pre-Parliamentary period[18]. An overview of the contemporary reaction to this type of enclosure had appeared earlier as contribution to R.H. Tawney's *Festschrift* [14], small thanks for great inspiration and encouragement over the years.

My continuing interest in the physical form of settlements is represented most by my collaboration with Professor St. Joseph in the two editions of *Medieval England*: the study of medieval town

3   'The Minute Book of a Leicestershire Enclosure,' *Transactions of the Leicestershire Archaeological Society* xxiii (1947), 293-315.
4   'Glebe Terriers and Open-field Leicestershire', *Ibid.* xxiv (1948), 77-126; see also 'Glebe Terriers and Open-field Buckinghamshire'. *Records of Buckinghamshire* xv-xvi (1951-4). Material collected for Warwickshire remained unpublished in view of Dr. D. M. Barratt's *Ecclesiastical Terriers of Warwickshire Parishes* (Dugdale Society Publications, xxii (1945) and xxvii (1971).

plantation in the *New Towns* book clearly originated in local studies
made for *Medieval England*, and chapter 4 shows an early apprecation
of the possibility of moving from the particular to the general. The
documentation for the planted towns of Cornwall proved to be
particularly rich but in the Duchy records the evidence for the
topography of early fourteenth-century rural settlement lay cheek by
jowl with that for the boroughs. It gave an opportunity to display the
topography of settlement in a county virtually devoid of villages that
was too good to be missed. I am as proud of chapter 3 as of anything I
have written, even at book length. The short, speculative chapter 5 is a
departure from my usual habit of making bricks only when I detect
abundance of available straw.

The book-length study of planted medieval towns could not avoid
some research into the more numerous English boroughs with older,
organic development and I was fortunate to recruit as an ally Herbert
Finberg who had just retired from the chair of local history at
Leicester: together we published *English Medieval Boroughs: a
Hand-list* in 1973. The end of his period as research assistant in the
University of Leeds coincided with the gift of a *Festschrift* from the
Agricultural History Society, a special number of the Society's *Review*,
and a celebration dinner in a Leeds hall of residence. Chapter 2 is my
closest venture into the history of my own time, a biographical sketch
of my formidable collaborator and friend.

In the course of research on deserted villages I had been forced to
examine the vast unindexed records of the sixteenth and early
seventeenth century court of Exchequer where depopulators and
enclosing landlords had been prosecuted: inevitably the eye was caught
by other presentments for breaches of other economic legislation and
the challenge to enumerate and assess these could not be resisted. In
particular the use and abuse of the common informer, at once public
prosecuter and privateer, led from a study of a particular administrative
device to the wider implications of the animosity towards Authority in
the early Stuart period [chapter 16]: the same Exchequer records
unexpectedly disgorged lists of those licensed to retail tobacco in
another money-raising venture of Charles I [17]: material arising from
the licensing of ale-houses and wine taverns was also collected *en
passant* but remains unpublished.

The remaining items in this collection centre on Leeds in its transition
to an urban and industrial city between 1720 and 1850, the most
recent of my interests. Bibliographers may indeed notice that my first

book[5], published in 1951, was a commissioned history of a Leeds institution but it would be a false trail to try to connect this work to the later interest in Leeds housing. In 1951 my interest was still in rural history, and the commissioned work was a lucrative but impatient diversion, and at this time two newly-arrived colleagues, Gordon Rimmer and Asa Briggs, became active researchers in Leeds history from a much-better informed base than mine, and had they remained longer in Leeds than they did it is likely that I would never have become absorbed in the topography of Leeds.

In the original *Time and Place* lecture [1] I was anxious to show that a townscape could pose as interesting historical questions as a rural landscape; I already had material on medieval towns in Britain and the continent from work in progress for *New Towns* but I was keen to show the impress of former field patterns on speculative building development in Leeds, perhaps recalling some earlier work on the suburb of Halton carried out at my instigation by David Ward. It was natural to begin with the origins of Cavendish Road where the then Department of Economics was housed but I was also attracted to the meaner but ambitiously christened Prosperity Street, a creature of optimistic years in the eighteen-seventies.

The streets surrounding the University were at that time being rapidly levelled for the extension of the campus in the happy days of post-Robbins Report expansion, and access to the University's property deeds whetted my appetite for a study of street origins over the whole campus, eventually resulting in *Walks Round Red Brick* (1980) But the peopling of these fields from *c*. 1790 could only be explained by a flight from an earlier but deteriorating West End[24], and that West End by the wish to avoid an East End.

The origins of the East End [22 and 23] cried out for study and thus I stumbled on the origin of back-to-back houses, not as the low-grade product of factory masters and speculative builders, but as the homes of members of the town's first building clubs or terminating building societies[25]. Chapters 19 and 22 are commentaries on two important source materials, separated by over two centuries, but the intended study of the whole area of central Leeds was delayed (for the better) by encountering a fire insurance policy in a packet of property deeds and realising that the original policy registers of the Sun and Royal Exchange companies, which Dr. S.D. Chapman had begun to exploit for industrial buildings, could usefully augment the extant collection of property deeds. Chapter 20 attempted a general display of

5   *The Leeds Chambers of Commerce* (Leeds, 1951).

their utility, and chapter 21 offered a survey of the whole range of public, industrial and domestic buildings in Leeds through the eyes of the fire insurances taken out in the town from 1716 onwards.

Prometheus Insured, the most recent of the work collected in this volume, is in a true succession to *History on the Ground* and *Time and Place*, although it has no maps and no photographs. Its interest in the organisation of provincial agents of London-based institutions is also a reminder that the history of organisations has been as interesting to me as the history of places: from medieval tax collectors to Elizabethan informers, Stuart monopolists, and Georgian commissioners of enclosure; a reminder also of how different the contents of this volume might have been had I been favoured by an appointing committee of University College, London, seeking to fill a post in history some time in the autumn of 1947; thereby leaving me disappointed[1] but an available candidate in an adjectival sub-division of seamless History when a lectureship in economic history was advertised at Leeds a few days later.

1   The post was obtained by A.J. (later Professor) Taylor; Dr (later Professor) W. Ashworth was another unsuccessful candidate on that occasion.

Enter *Time* and *Place*.

Place in a partie-coloured roabe, lyke the brickes
    of the howse.

Time with yellowe haire and a greene roabe, and
    an hour glass not runninge, and his winges
    clipte.

Time speakes:

'Arre you redie, Place? Time is redie.'

(From a masque presented to Queen Elizabeth on
her visit to Lod Chancellor Egerton at Harefield,
1601. *Surtees Society*, xvii [1843], pp. 278-86.)

1. TIME AND PLACE: AN INAUGURAL LECTURE

A few moments ago there was a procession into this room—

> clothéd all in a livery
> Of a solemn and a great fraternity—

language which you will recognise as Chaucer's and not mine. In Chaucer's day a livery signified membership of a fraternity. Students of economic history are familiar with one fraternity-type especially, the guilds, whose main purpose was economic and whose members had in common some handicraft or trade. But a university was also a fraternity, with masters and apprentices to a craft, the craft of knowledge. The apprentices had their own badges and dress and the masters of arts had theirs, that which I wear this afternoon. When apprentices to a craft came out of their time there were initiation ceremonies. In Leeds breweries the apprentice coopers who learn to make barrels still mark the end of their time by being rolled out in a barrel. In *higher* education we have more dignity. Taking its tune perhaps from *The Mastersingers of Nuremberg*, the University demands of a new professor something like a mastersong. It commands him to make an exhibition of himself.

I suppose these public exhibitions are most useful when a new professor is a newcomer to Leeds. How economical for a stranger to be introduced to a roomful of people at once! But no amount of ceremonial dress can disguise me. I am not a stranger. I am the 3.0 o'clock on Tuesdays and the 4.0 o'clock on Thursdays man. For more than twelve years I have lectured in Economic History, more than half of those years in this very lecture room.

But what is new, and what I am honoured to initiate this afternoon, is the Chair itself. The actual study of Economic History in this University is half a century old, for when Leeds appointed John Harold Clapham as its first Professor of Economics in 1902 it gave him so few students that he had leisure to work in the field both of Economics and Economic History. Indeed, one might say that Leeds converted him: for after he left Leeds for Cambridge in 1908 his principal work *was* in Economic History, and in 1928 he became the first Professor of Economic History there. If it is the creation of professors that makes a subject respectable, the frock-coat period of Economic History has been since the end of the Second World War. One for Birmingham, one for Bristol, one for Nottingham, one for Glasgow, one for Edinburgh . . . and Leeds came tumbling after.

It might look as if we historians were getting near that specialisation and division of labour that Adam Smith noted in the pin factory. But the scope of the subject I am called to profess is rather larger than a pin head. It is concerned with all past economic behaviour. *English* Economic History alone now has a literature too bulky for any one person to know thoroughly. We even have our subspecialists: agrarian historians, business historians, transport historians, to name only the subspecies who now publish their journals.

It is not part of my task this afternoon to apologise for my subject or to take further time defining it. Definitions of subjects can have a brief notoriety as examination questions but that is about all they are good for. I would rather find historians too busy writing to have time to define their subject. I have great sympathy with the film director whom John Grierson once described: 'He demonstrated the limits of his art in the most effective way—by persistently going beyond them.' Nor do I want to demonstrate how the model Economic Historian should behave, nor to claim that all Economic Historians should be interested in what interests me. I am still enough of a newcomer from a non-professorial world to remember that professing a subject is not quite the same thing as possessing it. In so far as a year in a new environment has corrupted me, I will dare to be mildly possessive in one direction only. When the History of Technology comes to be a respectable subject in universities—and where else if not here?—I hope it will not go the way of the History of Science, i.e. to the place where the philosophers are kings. Technological change and economic change are so connected that I would regard them as already married, married as it were by repute and no marriage service necessary.

I have said earlier that this inaugural lecture invites me to make· an exhibition of myself. And now I can proceed, so long as it is clear what I am exhibiting: one of many ways of looking at the subject; one of many ways of working in it; and one of many ways of teaching it. Self-analysis, public self-analysis is a risky business, but if I have to define a Beresfordian approach to Economic History it is an emphasis on visual things. By 'visual things' I mean not only the traditional sources of historical inquiry, books and documents—they are visual enough; nor do I add merely maps, a visual summary of the real world. I add the visible real world itself, or rather those visible remains in it by which past economic activity can be detected. In this sense my profession is Time and Place.

These visible remains in the real world enter into two parts of my professional life and indeed help to weld these parts together. They help me as an inquirer, a researcher, for they suggest questions and sometimes answers. They help me also as a teacher. You may have wondered why for seven years I have lectured in this particular theatre. It is because it has the best lantern for showing slides; and this has been easier since we who teach in Leeds are aided by Mr Blackledge's department and have a photographic service which is the envy of my colleagues in Oxbridge and Redbrick alike.

I would call my approach a 'field-approach' or 'archaeo-logical approach', were it not that 'field' sounds like the country-

side and 'archaeological' sounds antique. The visibles of which
I spoke come from town as well as country and from any century. The Baines wing of this University is as much a piece of
Economic History of its day as the Man-made Fibres Building.
I shall not flinch if this gets me called a 'local' economic
historian, so long as 'local' is not a term of abuse. Visible evidences cannot help but be local. One looks at *particular* streets,
particular fields, one cannot look at England in one glance.

One of my colleagues, knowing that I am a time-and-place
man, said to me recently 'What do you do when you get to the
commercial crises and booms and slumps of the nineteenth century? Surely you cannot illustrate them with reference to places
and buildings!' Booms and slumps...commercial crises....
A short bus-ride could take us all to Tadcaster Bridge. I invite
you next time you cross it to look north upstream. You will see
the River Wharfe and a railway bridge crossing it. It looks an
ordinary railway bridge. If you walk up to it, it appears very
extraordinary: for it has no railway line; on one side there is no
sign that there ever was one, and on the other there are cuttings
which end in mid-field. This is in fact the debris of a Victorian
commercial failure, the uncompleted railway line of 1848 which
George Hudson planned to go direct from York to Leeds and
not round the two sides of a triangle—York to Church Fenton
and Church Fenton to Leeds—which a rival company's line
then followed and (alas) still follows. The documents, the plans
of the route that Hudson's line hoped to follow, can be seen in
the British Transport Commission's Record Office in York.[1] But
the real bridge in its isolation is more eloquent than the plans,
for they might suggest that the line was built. In Tadcaster
they know better, for they still have to come into Leeds by bus.

I should like to come into Leeds myself for my next illustrations. Ten minutes' walk from the University there is another
occasion for an observer to interpret time and place, and again

PLATE 1

(a) Prosperity Street, Leeds, 1960.

(b) The pattern of fields imposed on back-to-back houses.

PLATE 2

(a) Incomplete back-to-back housing at former field edge.

(b) Plan of Deggendorf on Danube, Bavaria.

the theme is nineteenth-century boom and slump. Plate I*a* shows Prosperity Street. The name of this street is itself a Victorian period piece. It matches *Hard Times*, the other side of the coin, for which the visible evidence is the Leeds Workhouse. Hard Times and Prosperity Street succeeded each other pretty regularly in the nineteenth century, and if one had to guess when Prosperity Street was built and christened one could write off half the years of the century to begin with. In which of the prosperous and optimistic Victorian years was our Prosperity Street christened? It does not appear in a Leeds directory of 1873 but it does appear in White's[2] of 1875. So it was christened in 1874 or 1875. Professor Cairncross's figures show that in 1875 there was virtually no unemployment among building workers, and residential building all over the country had been on the increase for the previous five years.[3] Artisans—like the saddlers, cabinet-makers and upholsterers who were the first occupants of Prosperity Street—were then experiencing nearly full employment. Beveridge's index[4] shows only $1\frac{1}{2}$ per cent out of work in 1874: clearly, the never-had-it-so-good situation, just the time for Prosperity Street.

But only just in time. Between 1874 and 1876 unemployment doubled and by 1879 it was nearly 11 per cent among the skilled, and obviously higher among the unskilled. One in twelve building workers was now unemployed. It was the worst unemployment figure between the Great Exhibition of 1851 and the post-war slump of 1921. The name of Prosperity Street was not changed, but what happened was that building stopped. Three houses on one side and seven on the other was the sum total of Prosperity Street until, near the peak of the next boom in 1882, ten more houses were built—filling up as far as the half-way mark, the crossing with Hawkins Place. Then the slump of 1886, the boom of 1890 and the slump of 1894 were to pass before the street was completed in 1898–1901.

I must add one bizarre footnote which will be meaningful to economists present, especially students of the trade cycle. In the directory giving the first occupants of Prosperity Street in 1876, who lives at no. 12? His surname is Macro, William Macro, brickmaker. And in the slump? In 1881 his house was empty. Macro had gone.[5]

I have not yet wrung the last drop of Economic History out of this unfortunate street. Let us now look at it and its neighbours from the air (Plate I*b*). There seems to be some pattern in the grouping of the rows of back-to-back houses. What dictated where these streets were placed?

They were laid out by speculative builders, and to build they needed land. Blocks of houses like these were determined, as Mr David Ward has recently shown, by the existing units of agricultural ownership.[6] In a city like Nottingham the late survival of open fields and common rights made it almost impossible for builders to buy up farm land near the town until after 1845, so that the houses of Nottingham remained compact and compressed.[7] But in Leeds the fields had long since been enclosed and there were no obstacles from common rights over them. Builders could buy up fields piecemeal whenever existing owners were tempted to sell. People sometimes speak dramatically of green fields drowned in a sea of building, but in terms of land ownership the part of Leeds in 1847 shown in Fig. 1 was not one continuous sea but a chain of pools, many small owners side by side. The units of purchase by builders were fields, and houses and streets had to be fitted into them. Five of the owners are indicated by different shadings.[8] You will notice that one of these grass fields was a tenter garth, a field where the frames were erected on which the cloth was stretched in the open air by local weavers. This next plan shows the back-to-back terraces as they were fitted in (Fig. 2). Mr Mortimore, who drew this plan for me, spotted an acute case of the shoe-lift process by which

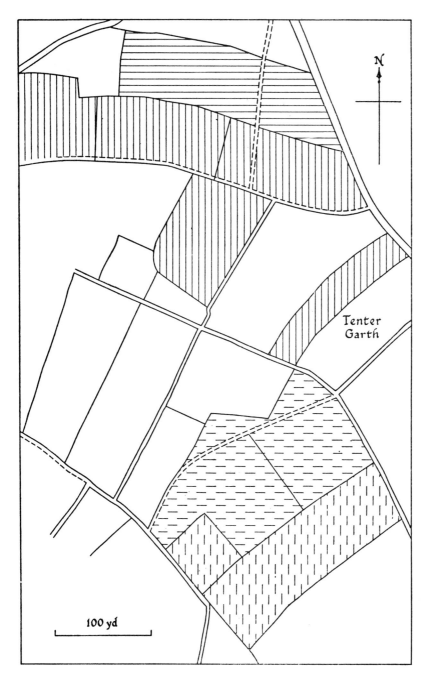

N

Tenter
Garth

100 yd

Fig. 1. Fields to south-west of Meanwood Road, Leeds, 1847. Four
different owners are shown by shading; a fifth owned the fields shown
unshaded.

Fig. 2. The area of Fig. 1 as finally filled by back-to-back houses;
the former field-boundaries emphasised.

houses were squeezed into fields. It concerns the Oxbridge area between Camp Road and Meanwood Road. You will see a curious irregularity in the length of the terraces and the placing of the open-air lavatory yards (top centre). This irregularity was dictated by the limits of the field which the builder had purchased, but to explain *why* the hedge was where it was would take me far back into the agricultural history of Leeds...where I don't propose to go at this moment. Instead I commend to you two common examples hereabouts which show the same influence of field- and property-boundaries on housing patterns. Behind Mr Austick's bookshop you will find a good example of the ship's-prow-house, shaped to fit it into the corner of a trian-gular field. Then, if you go down Elland Road (as if on your way to Leeds United) and look up to the steepnesses of Beeston Hill you will there see how rows of ordinary back-to-back houses come to an end with a single terrace, there being no room for a complete house on the land which the builder had bought. In view of the sporting locality dare I christen this phenomenon (Plate 2 *a*, right) the full back-to-back and the half-back?

Fig. 3 shows another block of Leeds fields in 1847. Some, you will see, had already been captured—not for housing arti-sans in terraces but for gentlemen with gardens, paddocks and coach-houses.9 These have been fitted into the fields but there is still plenty of green. To these fields might be applied Keynes' words: these ghosts rule us from their grave. Whose lives do these ghosts rule? The Vice-Chancellor's, the Faculty of Arts', the Department of Economics and Commerce's and so mine. One of the gentlemen's houses is now the home of the Depart-ment of Education, and the Union and University House have been fitted between the groves on the left.

In 1847 the fields in the centre of the plan, which I have shaded, all belonged to John Hillary Hebblethwaite. In 1852 he proposed to sell them off in building lots, making up a new road to be called Cavendish Road. The road was cut but there were no takers for the plots.[10] In 1859 he put them on the market again[11] and a purchaser was found for the first plot to be built upon, the present Department of Student Health (no. 3), originally the home of Joseph Horsfall, machine-maker and partner in the Victoria Foundry.[12] The two houses which now

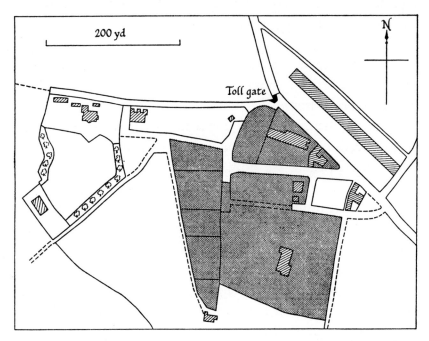

Fig. 3. Fields to the south-west of Blenheim Terrace, 1847.
The property of J. H. Hebblethwaite is shaded.

(1960) shelter most of the members of the Faculty of Economic and Social Studies were built in 1864. No. 6, the northernmost, was built by Jonathon Pulleyn, stationer and engraver.[13] This is the house where Professor Grebenik—appropriately enough for a demographer—occupies the best bedroom; while Professor Brown and I occupy the front rooms downstairs, one to dine and one to draw. No. 8 (the other half of Economics House) and no. 10 (Geology) were both built in 1864 by Miss

Matterson. Here her *Seminary for Young Ladies Day and Boarding* brought the first light of education into the precinct. She died in 1898 and in 1899 no. 10 was bought by Sydney Rumboll, the surgeon.

The houses on the south side of the Presbyterian Church, a number of which now shelter university departments, were built between 1886 and 1888 but for a different sort of customer. They have shorter back gardens with no room for coach-houses; their front gardens are narrower; and they have the family conformity of a terrace. No. 32 has no room for any back garden. If we ask why the building plots were so cabined and confined and why Tonbridge Street treads on the very heels of no. 32 we are back again among the fields which Hebblethwaite had inherited from his great-uncle in 1840. It was the Far Pasture, the Lane Close and the Low Close whose hedges determined where builders should build.

Most regnant of all the ghosts are the hedges a little to the north of Cavendish Road, those which determined the bounds of Beech Grove Terrace. It was a ghost which Messrs Lanchester and Lodge were powerless to exorcise when they designed the new Arts Block. What our architects had to do was to squeeze the building in between the two public roads which had been laid out between 1847 and 1852 on either side of what the plan of 1847 shows as 'no. 174: Lyddon's Trustees'. In this long-determined length and breadth my Arts colleagues had to be squeezed, 'a fair field full of folk'.

The theme to which I now move can also be stated in terms of Time and Place. It, too, begins in Leeds but it is far from parochial and takes us to the Danube and to the feet of the Pyrenees. I begin with two innocent questions: Why is Leeds parish church so far out of the town? Why is Briggate straight?

Strangers will need to know that Leeds parish church is neither the one in Boar Lane nor the one in upper Briggate, for these are daughter-churches, latecomers in the seventeenth and eighteenth centuries. The mother-church, the only true parish church, is St Peter's at the far (east) end of Kirkgate, tucked away behind the railway embankment which overlies part of its graveyard, its spire just visible from the city bus station. Why so remote? and why so remote from the market-place of old Leeds, which was the wide street of Briggate? Town market-places were usually *next* to their parish church. The oldest market-place in York was alongside St Sampson's; the largest market space in London was alongside St Bartholomew's church: but Briggate is not alongside St Peter's, Leeds. Why was this?

The answer was suggested in 1945 by Mr Geoffrey Woledge in a paper to the Thoresby Society. Simply, it was that the houses and yards on both sides of Briggate made up the little borough which Maurice Paynel, lord of Leeds, created in 1207. Mr Woledge argued that Paynel had not promoted the old village of Leeds into a borough but tacked a new borough alongside the old village, planting the borough in the fields (Fig. 4).[14] The village church continued to serve the borough, which had no church of its own until St John's was founded more than 400 years later at the north end of Briggate. In this view, Briggate is straight because it was laid out as a single venture in town planting, possessing the two essentials of a medieval town: sixty building plots for the houses of craftsmen and traders; and a market-place to serve the surrounding countryside each Monday.

In economic and social life a straight line is always suggestive. If you have to lay out a street in the fields and put building plots alongside it, the easiest way is to have straight streets and right-angled plots. The straight line in any period is usually a symptom of something sudden, something planned, something added, something altered. In contrast, village streets and roads-through-fields (which have grown, as it were, inch by inch, slowly and without design) tend to wriggle and to

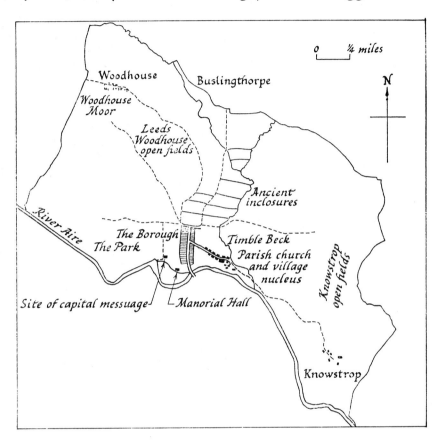

Fig. 4. Conjectural plan of Leeds borough village and fields in 1341.
(Based on *extent*, P.R.O. E. 36/176, ff. 79–87.)

wind. Compare Kirkgate or Woodhouse Lane with its double wriggle and Briggate with its set-square sides.

Straightness as the mark of the town-planner appears in many centuries and in many countries. It is the pattern of the streets of New York; it is the pattern of the boulevards which Hausmann drove through Paris between 1852 and 1870; and of the streets of Louis XIV's town of Versailles; it is the pattern, you will remember, of Prosperity Street and its neighbours.

But Versailles, Paris boulevards, New York and Prosperity Street are not of the same century as Maurice Paynel's creation of Leeds in 1207. Where can we match this? Where in medieval towns shall we find straight streets and right-angled building plots? In Hampshire is a little borough, Stockbridge, planted in the fields of King's Somborne about seven years earlier than the borough of Leeds. It has not grown in later years and its skeleton is less covered with flesh than Leeds. But there are the burgage plots (sixty-four of them by 1256) on either side of the broad market-place. The economic advantage of this site must have been thought excellent, for it was a remarkably damp place to choose. The meanders of the River Test swirl along the edge of the burgage plots, making it the most Venetian of all English boroughs. This little borough, contemporary in its foundation[15] with Leeds, is not far from Briggate even in name. In *Briggate* we have our northern form of 'bridge': and further, the original name of Stockbridge was simply *Le Strete*, and what else is the '-gate' in Briggate but the northern word for 'street'? Our borough of Leeds was simply one street also, and at the end of it was Aire bridge just as Stockbridge had its bridge.

There are medieval plantations which are not so very far (in some respects) from New York. One late thirteenth-century foundation with street-names akin to New York's was Edward I's plantation of New Winchelsea. In an early rental[16] of 1292 its streets were simply *Prima Strata, Secunda Strata*, and so on, and the very building blocks were numbered off. We may match the straightness of the streets of many North American plantations with the straightness of Gascon streets such as those of Grenade sur Garonne; or, in England, of Portsmouth, Stratford on Avon, Salisbury, Ludlow, Windsor, Bury St Edmunds and Liverpool: to name but a few of the 120 towns which were planted in England between the Norman Conquest and 1300.

In Wales about forty towns fall into the same class; in that part of France which remained English in the thirteenth century the total of English plantations is also about 120. Many of these Gascon towns were simply small market centres where the local wines were collected for shipping down river to the sea-ports of Bordeaux or Bayonne. Once a week since their foundation there have been markets in such planted towns as Sauveterre de Guyenne and Beaumont du Périgord.

I hope you will now recognise in the straightness of Briggate the evidence of its plantation and also its function as a market-place. Can the remoteness of Leeds parish church from the borough be matched in other planted towns? Is the absence of a parish church convincing evidence that a town came late on the economic scene? Visual, topographical, non-documentary evidence of this sort is necessary since so many towns have few or no documents from the period of their origin. It is exceptional to find rentals like that of Winchelsea in 1292 or of Newtown (Francheville), Isle of Wight, in the first year of its life (1257).[17]

Stratford on Avon, whose grid-pattern of streets has been mentioned, is one such town. You have to walk out of the town to find the parish church if you are in search of Shakespeare's monument. At Hull, another planted town, the walk was even longer. There is a true story of an archbishop of York in the early fourteenth century being astonished to meet a funeral procession wending its way on a stormy night along the dangerous shore of the Humber. It was on its way to the parish church of the townspeople of Hull, that of Hessle.[18] Hull had been planted in the fields of Hessle. Young Liverpool, founded in the same year as Leeds, had no parish church; nor had Borough-bridge; nor had South Zeal, Devon (Fig. 5). And all for the same reason: they were like seatless latecomers at a crowded lecture; they arrived too late.

I spent September 1960 in another part of Europe where the expanding economy of the thirteenth century induced land-

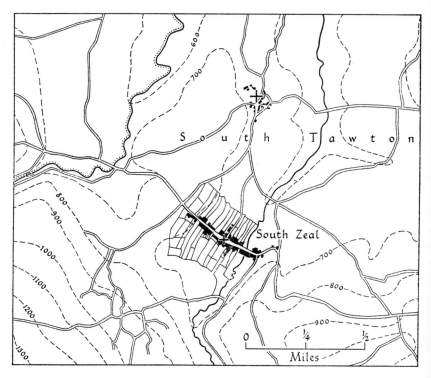

Fig. 5. The borough of South Zeal, Devon, founded *c.* 1299 in the fields of South Tawton parish. The borough has burgage plots on either side of the single broad street, like Leeds; it later acquired a chapel subordinate to South Tawton church, as St John's Briggate was subordinate to St Peter's, Leeds.

owners to speculate by planting new towns. A plan of one such town is painted inside the town gate, and it makes a dark photograph (Plate 2 *b*). But this plan of Deggendorf shows the regularity and artificiality of its shape: an oval. To the south can be seen the Danube. Deggendorf resembles Hull in having no parish church inside its walls. To find the church and town graveyard you must go outside the gate to the church of the village in whose fields Deggendorf was planted. The tall building in the market-place is not a church but the *rathaus*, the town-hall and market-hall. Until nineteenth-century improvements the Moot Hall of Leeds stood in just that position, right in the middle of Briggate, though in a less attractive style.

Fig. 6 shows the planted towns of Bavaria to match the planta-tions in England, Wales, Scotland, Ireland and Gascony. And these Bavarian towns are but a few of the hundreds of planted towns of the twelfth and thirteenth centuries along the whole moving eastern frontier of the Germanic peoples. These towns are the visible signs that new land was being colonised and new market centres called into existence. In plan, as in function, the Germanic foundations were akin to the Gascon and English *bastides*, *villes neuves* and Newtowns (Fig. 7).

Our English plantations were also part and parcel of expand-ing cultivation and expanding markets. It was not, of course, an expansion on the German scale, for England and France were not starting from scratch, even in those parts of Gascony where there had been great depopulation during the Albigensian wars. In England there were plenty of old-established towns eager for promotion. It seems to me that this makes our record of town plantation the more impressive. Our economic expan-sion found work not only for our existing stock of old towns; but also for many promotions of villages to towns; and also for all these additional ventures, the New Towns, so many of which turned out to be successes. There was room at the bottom, room in the middle and room at the top.

In Cornwall, Devon, Wales (and perhaps even York-shire) one might accept plantations as being on a frontier of colonisation. But what can be said in the face of the fact that within a forty-mile radius of Winchester, the old capital of southern England, seventeen new towns were planted along-side a good crop of old-established boroughs and promoted villages?

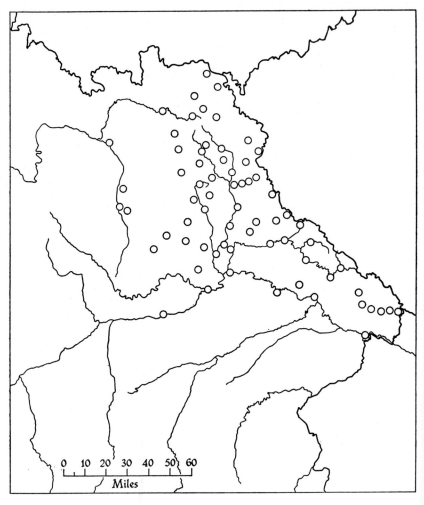

Fig. 6. *Bastide* towns in Bavaria, 1150–1350. (Plantations over the border of Czechoslovakia and East Germany are not shown.)

I must not leave you with the impression that every venture prospered. That would have made the plantations a certainty and I have rightly called them 'speculations'. Fig. 8 shows the

Straubing

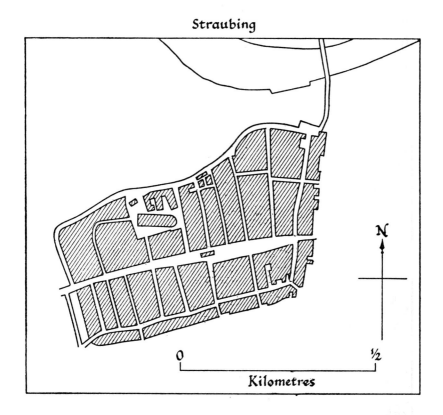

N

0 ½

Kilometres

Erbendorf

Vilseck

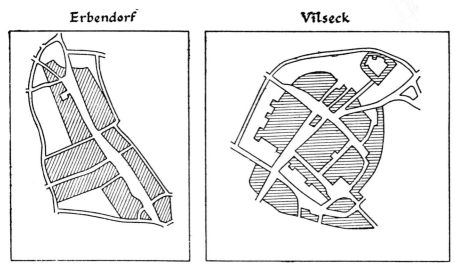

Fig. 7. Three Bavarian plantations. Straubing on the Danube is a walled town with a long central market-place; Erbendorf is of similar plan; Vilseck is walled and moated with a castle in the north-east corner.

plan of Beauregard in Gascony, its grid of streets but a shadow
of its former self. In England, Ravenserod has gone beneath
the Humber and the site of Warenmouth in Northumberland
was so little remembered that a Chancery clerk once sent its

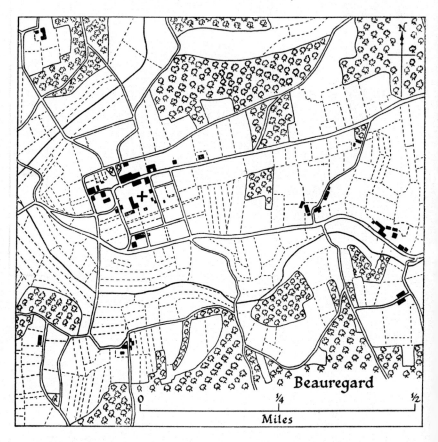

Fig. 8. The shrunken *bastide* (*sc.* plantation) of Beauregard, Dordogne,
founded by Edward I in 1286.

charter to Wearmouth. One or two of the English plantations,
such as Grampound (Cornwall) live in the history books only
as half-empty rotten boroughs of the unreformed Parliaments.
As town-planting ventures these speculations had failed.

My final example of a failure comes from a situation which

would seem to have all the geographical advantages. It was to be planted on a major road, the Fosse Way, halfway between Lincoln and Newark and well out of sight of any economic rival. Its founders were the wealthy Knights Hospitallers. Royal permission was obtained and a charter[19] issued in July 1345. All was set for the town of New Eagle. But there were never any burgesses.

Why did the speculation fail? Not because of a poor site; not through any legal snag. What, then? The timing. The town had hardly been conceived when the first plague-infected rats came ashore and England (like the rest of Europe) was swept by the pandemic of the bubonic plague. Instead of increasing population, colonisation, more villages and towns there was contraction. There was not even enough to keep all the old towns going and there was certainly no room for new ones. Perhaps the best simple commentary on the drastic change in the economic climate after 1349 is this empty field; and the knowledge that, whereas the previous 250 years in England had added at least 120 towns, there are only two foundations in the whole of the next four centuries.[20] New towns did not begin again until the spa-towns and the cotton mill-towns of the late eighteenth century.

I have almost done, and I hope that the bricks, the small pieces of local and visual evidence, have begun to make something of a building and that I have brought an aspect of urbanisation into its proper proportions.

I prefaced my lecture with no text: may I be allowed an epigraph? In 1897 the Cambridge historian Maitland delivered in Oxford those Ford lectures which were later published as *Township and Borough*. He was conscious that his Oxford audience, used to thinking of history as the decline and fall of empires, might think the walls and fields of Cambridge a petty, parochial subject. 'Will you think me ill-bred', he said, 'if I talk of the town in which I live?'[21] This afternoon I have been even more parochial. If he was ill-bred to talk of his own town in a public lecture to an academic audience, I, who have talked of my own street, must be simply disgusting.

NOTES

1. B.T.C. Record Office, York: Deposited Plans, vol. VII, p. 18.
2. 1873: Johnson's *Directory*; 1875: White's *Directory* (in a supplement of 'smaller streets').
3. A. K. Cairncross, *Home and Foreign Investment, 1870–1913* (1953), p. 149.
4. W. H. Beveridge, *Full Employment in a Free Society* (1944), p. 312.
5. Occupations and dates of completion of the street from: McCorquodale's *Directory*, 1876, 1878, 1882; White's *Directory*, 1881; Robinson's *Directory*, 1898 and 1901.
6. David Ward, unpublished M.A. thesis, Department of Geography, Leeds University, 1960.
7. J. D. Chambers, *Nottingham in the Making* (1945), pp. 5–6, with plan of 1831.
8. Drawn from the Tithe Award plan of 1847: Leeds Public Libraries, Archives Dept. RD/RT/142/1.
9. *Ibid.*
10. S. D. Martin, 'Plan of an estate...the property of J. Hebblethwaite, etc.' (1852): Thoresby Society Manuscript Plans (Bonser and Nichols, catalogue no. 126).
11. S. D. Martin, 'Plan of an estate...the property of J. B. Hebblethwaite Esq. etc.' (1859): Thoresby Society Manuscript Plans (Bonser and Nichols, no. 144).
12. University of Leeds, Deeds of Property in the Bursary: *re* nos. 3, 6, 8, 10 Cavendish Road; these take the ownership of the property back to 1788; also Charlton and Anderson's *Directory*, 1864.
13. Charlton and Anderson's *Directory*, 1864; White's *Directory*, 1866, 1870 and 1875; Kelly's *Directory*, 1867; Porter's *Directory*, 1872.

14. G. Woledge, 'The Medieval Borough of Leeds', *Proc. Thoresby Soc.* XXXVII (1945), p. 298.

15. P(ublic) R(ecord) O(ffice): C. 53/2, m. 21; C. 54/24, m. 8; C. 132/21/12; Just. Itin. 1/778, mm. 57 and 63.

16. P.R.O., SC. 11/673–4; trans. in W. D. Cooper, *History of Winchelsea* (1850), pp. 44–53.

17. Rental reproduced from original now in County Record Office, Winchester, in M. W. Beresford, 'Six New Towns of the Bishops of Winchester', *Med. Arch.* (1959), III; p. 64, fig. 76 below.

18. W. Brown, ed., *Register of [Archbishop] Corbridge* (Surtees Soc. CXXXVIII (1925)), p. 161; J. Bilson, 'Wyke-Upon-Hull in 1293', *Trans. East Riding Arch. Soc.* XXVI (1928), p. 72.

19. *Calendar of Charter Rolls*, v (1916), p. 40; T. Hugo, *The History of Eagle* (1876), pp. 14–21.

20. Queenborough, Kent (1368); Falmouth, Cornwall (1613).

21. F. W. Maitland, *Township and Borough* (1898), p. 3.

Thanks are due to Mr M. J. Mortimore who drew Figs. 1, 2, 3, 5, 7 and 8; to Mr David Ward for Fig. 4 and Plate 2a, taken from his unpublished thesis; to Mr P. M. Gulland for Fig. 6.

Plate 1b is by Aerofilms Ltd and is reproduced by permission. Plates 1a and 2b are from photographs by Mr K. J. Woolmer.

Acknowledgment is also made for help received from Mr Harold Nichols, Reference Librarian, Leeds Public Libraries; from the Acting City Archivist; and from the Bursar's staff.

2

HERBERT FINBERG: AN APPRECIATION

HERBERT PATRICK REGINALD FINBERG, we are told, was born at Rickmansworth on 21 March 1900. The fact seems as authentic as any in history, although the sprightly figure of spring 1970 taking his constitutional in Chiswick Park might seem to contradict bare chronology; and, indeed, no one would be better placed to outwit us all in a matter of dating than he who for so long pitted his wits successfully against the deceivers and the self-deceivers, the forgers and improvers of Anglo-Saxon charters.

It was provident of him to arrange to be born so neatly poised between the nineteenth and the twentieth centuries: to inherit the developed tools of nineteenth-century historical criticism and to be in time to take advantage of the motor-car—chauffeused by his wife, Joscelyne—as a means of penetrating the countryside that the charters delineated, and of arriving at distant bases from which their explorations on foot could begin. It was provident to be the son of the biographer of the artist, Turner; for, in so far as talents are inherited, he was guaranteed a lively appreciation of the significance of the painter's visual scene as well as the skill of narrative biography. It was also provident to arrange to be born at Rickmansworth, then poised between town and country: for Herbert Finberg, urbane and unmistakably a man of Town libraries, Town clubs, and Town restaurants, was destined to spend the formative years of his working life away from London in the Cotswolds and at Welwyn; and in his second life at Leicester to expound with conviction the doctrine that History is the biography of Little Places as well as of Great Men; to become Head and then Professor in a Department of English Local History set in the very middle of the grassy Midland shires, while retaining a toehold if not a foothold in West London suburbia.

This special number of THE AGRICULTURAL HISTORY REVIEW, made up of essays by Herbert Finberg's friends, colleagues, and fellow students, celebrates the seventieth birthday of an English local historian. It should be noted, however, that Finberg the historian is far from being the whole of Finberg. The 'Bibliography' that follows this 'Appreciation' gives slight clues to these other lives outside History. At Oxford he studied not History but Greats, and his earliest interests were in philosophy and literature, as the publications of 1925 and 1926 indicate; and there is said to be a manuscript of an unpublished book from this period lurking in some Chiswick cupboard. Long before the emergence into public print of Finberg the historian in 1941 and 1942, there had been another career of distinction in publishing and book production where the art interests of his father emerged again in the creative artistry of the printed page. Like Tawney and Housman before him, Finberg had been prevented from post-graduate studies by the examiners' view of his Finals papers although, like Tawney and Housman, he had the later satisfaction of contemplating the predictive quality of a Finals class from the elevated position of his own professorial Chair. Thus the young graduate found himself in a provincial workshop, the printing establishment of the Shakespeare Head Press, directed by Basil Blackwell and Bernard Newdigate, then at Stratford-upon-Avon. From Stratford he moved to Chipping Campden, and there founded his own press, the Alcuin, in a barn. His ambition was to demonstrate that one could live in the twentieth century, taking advantage of the techniques of mechanized printing, and yet achieve high and imaginative standards: from Finberg at the Alcuin Press came the Housman *Poems* in 1929, but all forms of jobbing printing were undertaken. It was at this time also that he became interested in handwriting, as the 1929 item in the 'Bibliography' indicates, achieving an elegant personal hand: on an envelope in brown ink it immediately distinguishes the sender and softens the impact of even the sharpest critical comment. In the age of typewriters one of the few pleasures remaining to a printer must be to set up a piece from Finberg in his manuscript. So far as I know, he types nothing.

In 1935 the Alcuin Press moved to Welwyn Garden City but then encountered the depression in 1936, and Finberg went to work as a director of The Broadwater Press Ltd, where he remained until 1944. In this period the Twickenham *Pope* was launched. At the end of the war he became editorial director of Burns Oates & Washbourne Ltd, no doubt attracted by the prospect of liturgical publishing for Roman Catholic use, but with a fine oecumenical toleration he also took on advisory work for Eyre & Spottiswoode Ltd, H.M. Printers, designing for them the *Coronation Service* of 1953: on the secular side he advised the then Ministry of Works from 1944 to 1948, and takes particular pride in the format of the *Post-war Building Studies: Housing Manual*. Although he ceased to be a director of Burns Oates in 1949, a connection continued, and it was from this press that his *Manual of Catholic Prayer* came in 1962, winning the *Prix Graphica Belgica* in 1965. It should not have surprised me, therefore, when Herbert Finberg visited Leeds some time in the 1950's, and I introduced him to the Brotherton Librarian as "Dr Finberg, the topographer", that I was misheard and stayed to overhear a long technical conversation between Dr Page and Dr Finberg, the typographer.

The second career, the one which this volume celebrates, begins in Dr Hart's bibliography with the short article in *Devon and Cornwall Notes and Queries* in 1941, when Finberg had already passed forty years of age. The unsuspecting agent of the transformation seems to have been Mrs Finberg. In 1933 Finberg married Joscelyne Payne, and together they became interested in the genealogy of her family. Although not published until 1956, his paper on the Gostwicks of Willington was written in 1940, and the researches had taken him—fatally, but happily for us—into the Record Office of the Bedford estate. There he encountered the massive documentation of the dukes' Tavistock Abbey properties. Holidays were taken in Devon and the assimilation of local topography began. The writing began during spells of fire-watching duties in Welwyn, and although I believe that there were no actual fires, the phoenix that arose from the flames of these long candle-watches was *Tavistock Abbey*, completed in 1949 and published in 1951. Except for the *Axel* translation of 1925 it was Finberg's first book, and there can have been few more successful late entries in the academic race. It was a book by a non-professional of which any professional would have been proud, and it must have been the main evidence on which Tawney and Stenton sponsored him in 1952 for the vacant post of Reader and Head of the Department of English Local History at the then University College of Leicester. As he himself later wrote, "what had been a private hobby thus became a professional duty." Like his first master, B. H. Newdigate, he could now be called Scholar-printer.

Finberg's predecessor at Leicester had been W. G. Hoskins. Hoskins was born in Devon, had written about Exeter, and shared many of Finberg's interests. They had begun to correspond after Finberg's early articles in *D.C.N.Q.*, met at the field outings of the Devon Association in 1946, and signalled their own working association with their *Devonshire Studies*, published in the year that Finberg went to Leicester. This volume of essays and studies is a classic, and alongside J. D. Chambers's *Nottinghamshire in the Eighteenth Century* and A. L. Rowse's *Tudor Cornwall* it marked the renaissance of English local history at a level of technique, imagination, and significance equal to that of academic history in more conventional areas of study. As might be expected from two rugged—even jagged—individualists, their collaboration derived its strength from the complementarity of their interests rather than a grand design for essays with two co-operating authors, although the reader with a keen eye may be able to detect cross-influences in the individual essays that made up the volume. The partnership was not broken when Hoskins went to Oxford, for Finberg's *Gloucestershire* of 1955 was one of a series of landscape histories initiated and edited by Hoskins, while Hoskins contributed in 1960 to the series of *Occasional Papers* of the Leicester Department which Finberg had initiated with his own first public lecture at Leicester (November 1952), and which he triumphantly edited until his retirement.

If the selectors at Leicester thought that they had appointed a desk-bound and study-bound medievalist to their academic fellowship they were to be rudely shaken. It is true that Finberg followed Hoskins's example in firmly separating the workplace from the home by the thickness of a railway timetable, but in fact his two bases were used for a double ration of historical enter-prise. At Bosworth Richard III had wondered if there were not two Richmonds in the field, but from 1952 to 1965 an observer might have been pardoned for thinking that there were even more Finbergs in the field. The 'Bibliography' shows that it was the period in which he consolidated his own reputation with his work on early charters; and it was the period when (drawing perhaps on his own observations of warfare between critical scholars and of warfare between academics and administrators) he set out to challenge the old assumption that in the Saxon invasions the victors had succeeded in annihilating the vanquished without trace. Finberg's own philosophy of local history placed little weight on the local discipline for 'illuminating' national history, a 'propaedeutic value', as he once dubbed it. "To treat it as an introduction to or a contribution to national history is to invert the true relationship between them." Yet in the historiography of the illumination of the so-called Dark Ages Finberg has assured immortality for the name of one rural Gloucestershire community, Withington.

But the 'Bibliography' which records the scholar's output in the Leicester years (1952–65) necessarily omits, or gives light emphasis to, the other side of the headship of a Department of English Local History, that of entrepreneur-ship. Here scholar, printer, publisher, and businessman were fused in a succes-sion of enterprises and initiatives. These very pages are the result of one of these enterprises: his editorship of the REVIEW after the Agricultural History Society was founded. Another enterprise, the series of *Occasional Papers of the Department of English Local History*, shows Finberg as the discerning patron of publication, the list of contributors having more than one future Reader or Professor, including the successor to his own Chair. In his *Gloucestershire Studies* (1957) he enlarged the size of the two-man partnership that had pro-duced *Devonshire Studies* five years earlier, and five years later he edited and contributed to a symposium on History itself, the Finberg element being 'The Approach to Local History'. As the diligent reader of the 'Bibliography' will also see, Finberg has never subscribed to the view that a scholar's work, once published in article form, should thereafter blush unseen: in *Lucerna*, in *Local History—Objective and Pursuit*, and latterly in *West-Country Historical Studies* he has made available within hard covers and among the 'proper books' of libraries the majority of his own historical writing that had first appeared in periodicals or become out of print.

But the greatest enterprise of these years was undoubtedly the initiation of *The Agrarian History of England and Wales*. One hopes that among Finberg's fragments of autobiography he has recorded the saga of its making. At times, confronted by the idiosyncrasies of university presses and university contri-butors he must have thought that it was easier to engineer the making of the

English landscape than the making of an Agrarian History. Yet Volume IV has shown that within a decade a grand idea could be translated into a grand reality. His friends and admirers rejoice that his current objective and pursuit, aided by the patrons of his Cambridge post-retirement fellowship and his Leverhulme Emeritus award, is to edit and also to contribute to the volume that will chronologically be the first of the *Agrarian History*.

The thirteen years at Leicester, first as Reader and then as Professor, continuing and extending the work of Hoskins, the first Head of the Department, saw Finberg—if one may paraphrase Falstaff—not only as enterprising in himself but the occasion of enterprise in others. Some of this was engendered in colleagues and graduate students. Alan Everitt, a contributor to this volume, was colleague and successor in the Chair; Joan Thirsk, another colleague of those Leicester years, was to succeed Hoskins in the Oxford Readership and Finberg in the editorship of the Agricultural History Review: and thereby to contribute to and to edit this volume of appreciative essays. As patron of younger scholars Finberg sponsored the annual John Nichols prize in English Local History, a Leicester award but competed for nationally: some fruits of this enterprise will be seen in the *Occasional Papers*. Being himself an amateur historian for so many years, Finberg still retained a close interest in training and improving the standards of amateurs in local history. His work for the Standing Conference on Local History is one aspect of this interest; the John Nichols prize, open to all comers, professional and amateur, is another; the pronouncements on the nature of local history brought together in the 1967 volume are another, an attempt to stimulate thought and action by definition and example; and alongside the solemnities (not over-solemn, however) of these public occasions, there is also that highly recommended piece of calculated and mocking didacticism, 'How Not to Write Local History'.

This particular appreciation of Herbert Finberg, historian, scholar, and friend, is confessedly less than a full appreciation of the man whose portrait faces our title-page. It has dealt only cursorily with his creative work in printing and fine book production, and it would not be appropriate in the context of this Review to treat a further aspect of his work, integral to the man, that of Roman Catholic exposition; although the 'Bibliography'—as complete as could be achieved in the semi-secrecy of a *Festschrift* project—indicates his published work in the field of liturgy and apologetics. This appreciation is also written by someone who has come to work closely with Finberg only in very recent years and who has not had the advantage of the long or intimate contact possessed by some of those who have made other contributions to this volume.

This *Festschrift*, it is intended, will be presented to Professor Finberg on 25 September 1970 at a dinner at Sadler Hall, Leeds, organized jointly by the British Agricultural History Society and the University of Leeds. Leeds is the third of Finberg's universities, where he came in retirement to a humble but honourable part-time appointment. Since my own interest in the subject of petty medieval boroughs sprang from Finberg's earlier treatment of them in Devon and Gloucestershire, it was peculiarly fitting that his retirement from Leicester in 1965 should have coincided with a moment when I was far enough advanced in my study of medieval town plantation to see that a complete hand-list of all medieval boroughs, organic and planted, would be a useful service to urban history; at that moment also I took on a stint of internal academic admini-stration, and, in some measure of compensation for my diversion from research, the University of Leeds made funds available for some assistance in compiling this handlist: and so the Doctor of Oxford and the Emeritus of Leicester be-came Part-time Research Assistant of Leeds, *serviens servientium*.

Since this 'Appreciation' has now edged itself towards the border of personal involvement, I cannot resist pointing out that the strenuous bibliographer who seems to have pursued Herbert Finberg so zealously down the corridors of time has missed one contribution to our education that is worth mentioning because it relates to another Finbergian Objective and Pursuit, the enliven-ment of provincial field work by critical examination of the cellars and tables of country inns. What is the missing reference? In the ceremonial dress of scholarly footnoting it would read, 'Raymond Postgate, ed., *The Good Food Guide, 1969–1970* (1969), p. 304, *sub* South Zeal, and see also p. 280'.

To get one's name as an approver into the footnotes of the *Good Food Guide* may seem as difficult as getting into *Who's Who*. What shall we say of a man who has succeeded not only in getting into the *Guide* twice but also in being directly quoted on the authenticity of an inn's claim to be 'twelfth-century'? It was, one must note, the historian's call of duty which clearly led H. P. R. F. to South Zeal, for is it not one of the petty medieval boroughs of Devon, with twenty burgesses *apud la Sele* in 1315?

On 25 September his hosts will acknowledge this service to the by-ways of local scholarship, for they intend to invite him to exercise this one of his many crafts, and to choose the wine for his celebration dinner.

3

DISPERSED AND GROUPED SETTLEMENT

IN MEDIEVAL CORNWALL

THE forces of cohesion that bound houses together into the compact villages of England seem—as far as they can be guessed—to have been both social and technological. Elsewhere in Europe the compact and huddled village, cut off from its fields and foes by gates and walls, emphasized different compulsions, those of fear and defence. In Provence, for example, it was only the passing of war and piracy that freed these prisoners from their hill-top fortresses and enabled them to exploit their fields from single farm-houses scattered for full convenience of working. In England the prisoners were freed from the chains of traditional nucleation by new agrarian technologies which encouraged individualism and enclosure; and, where they wished, the proprietors could set their new farms out in their newly-hedged fields.

The farmsteads that have always been out in their fields have been less the subject of study in English agrarian history, and dispersed settlement has only recently come into its own with the Devonshire studies of Dr Hoskins and Dr Finberg. In Devon, it may be broadly said, dispersed settlement has been charted as the creature of late colonization within ground that had been the outer margin of the territory of compact Anglo-Saxon villages of the traditional type. In this view, village comes first and scattered farmsteads second.

In Cornwall, on the other hand, where nucleated villages and scattered settlement also exist side by side, even on the same sheet of the 6-inch O.S. map, the accepted explanation has always been that the nucleated settlement is the later Anglo-Saxon arrival, imposed on the Celtic pattern of isolated churches and scattered farmsteads. In this view, farmsteads come first and villages second. It is not the intention of this article to challenge that view but rather to try and bring precision to the concept of scattered settlement in the light of documentary evidence from the end of the thirteenth century and the decades before the Black Death. It offers a hope of improving on descriptions of medieval settlement that are based on the Victorian Tithe Awards 450 years after the event. This short study is a by-product of an investigation of the petty boroughs of Cornwall, an even later imposition of nucleation than the Anglo-Saxon villages. Several of these boroughs were

planted in rural manors of the Duchy of Cornwall, and the documents from
five parishes have been utilized to show where the constituent farmsteads were
placed at the presumed high watermark of medieval colonization in Cornwall.

In these five parishes there were 203 separate messuages recorded in the
manorial documents, and they lay in 57 separate 'places'. The number of
messuages in each 'place' is indicated in the summary of Table VI, and the
range of sizes will show why 'place' rather than 'farm', 'hamlet', or 'village'
has been employed. The common belief that Cornish settlement was typically of isolated farmsteads is shown to be untrue in the areas studied, which
come from three different parts of the county. Indeed, only one messuage
in twenty stood absolutely alone. What does emerge as typical is the very
small cluster: half the 57 places were made up of no more than two dwellings
or, putting it another way, half of the 203 messuages lay in little communities
of up to four dwellings. The largest agglomeration achieved (outside the
boroughs, whose messuages are not counted here) were the two groups of
thirteen messuages and the one of twelve. These are the measures of dispersion in the manors for which the evidence will now be presented.

The commonest documents from which the size of fourteenth-century
settlements may be gauged derive from the royal fiscal enquiries: on the one
hand, the assessments of the lay subsidy up to 1334 (when it became conventionalized) and of the poll taxes of 1377, 1379, and 1381, especially the
first of these; on the other hand, the number of freemen and villeins recorded
in the *extents* of manors taken at the enquiry *post mortem*. In parts of England
where there is no reason to suspect non-nucleated settlement these figures,
imperfect as they are, can be taken to come as near as we are ever likely to get
to the assessment of village size. The tax documents in particular are careful
enough in their mention of hamlets and subordinate settlements, when such
do occur, for us to accept the *capita* (for example) on which four pence were
levied in 1377 as dwelling near each other in a nucleated village. The freemen
and villeins and cottars of an *extent* may likewise be assumed to be living
within a short distance of the manor house of the lord whose death has oc-
casioned the *inquisitio*.

When, in 1334, the *parochia* of Lanteglos paid its quota of 30s. and its
neighbour Advent its 20s., where were the farmsteads whose wealth was thus
assessed? When 89 heads were each assessed in Advent in 1377 to pay the
groat to the poll-tax collector, where did they dwell? Certainly not near the
churches from which so many Cornish parishes were named: for Advent and
Lanteglos churches have no village alongside them; and no earthworks have
been noted that would suggest that, as in the case of the lonely churches of

the Midlands, there has been a village but a subsequent desertion. Since in 1377 the Black Death and its associated pandemic had just passed by, the number of heads in Advent before the plagues must have been greater, perhaps half as many again. Where did they dwell? where were their fields?

It soon became obvious to me that it was little use taking the first edition of the O.S. 6-inch map or the Tithe Awards as a confident basis of reconstruction. Economic change since the early fourteenth century has both added and subtracted houses. Cornwall has seen the arrival (and some retreat) of rural industry, while turnpike roads have encouraged clusters of dwellings that have the appearance and sometimes the names of old hamlets. In Creed parish, for example, the principal medieval cluster at the manor house of Tybeste has completely gone; while at Hewas Water the cluster can be shown to have come into existence *c.* 1750. Nor is it encouraging to find that the only full-scale modern study of Cornish settlement draws its map of dispersed settlement by arbitrarily selecting the more important group of farms on the Tithe Awards of *c.* 1840. This gives a total of nine clusters in Lanteglos, Michaelstow, and Advent, when there were in fact twenty-four.

There seem to be few large-scale estate plans of Cornish estates in the early modern period from which the deficiencies of the Tithe Awards may be remedied, although it is to be hoped that the Cornish estate plans of John Norden and his son, surveyors to the Duchy, will one day emerge. In the absence of maps from this earliest period of English map-making, some kind of map must be reconstructed from documentary sources. By good fortune, the documentation for the Duchy manors is unusually good for the half century before the Black Death, and the documents are cast in such a form that they do not simply list or number the tenantry but assign them to their geographical location. Within these areas the Duchy shared the territory with no other manor and there is thus no problem of allowing for the tenants of other lords; the small size of the holdings (and in land not of the best quality) minimizes the risk that there might be additional farmsteads occupied by under-tenants about whom the documents are silent. (A close examination of the ground, such as that now being carried out by archaeologists on Bodmin Moor, should also show whether there are additional tenements to be accounted for within the parishes studied here.) In the present state of knowledge, the data assembled in the tables below and mapped in the figures are the totality of settlement in the period before the Black Death.

The tables and maps which follow are a summary of information reassembled from documents which set it out in a different form. The explanation of method and description of sources has been kept to a minimum.

Although not the earliest of the Duchy documents to be used, it is the

Assession Rolls which provide the easiest approach to early fourteenth-century settlement conditions. In these rolls each tenant's rent and services were set out, together with the size of his holding, and the location of the holding was indicated by bold lettering in the left-hand margin. The prime division of the rolls was by status of tenure, but within these divisions it was usual to place together holdings that were in the same place.

Thus, the first membrane of the entry for Trematon manor has in its left-hand margin the place-names *Netherpulle, Parva Esshe, Worfelton, Penvyntel, Oldetrematon,* and *Bradmore.* These names continue (with variant spellings) throughout subsequent rolls and then in the seventeenth- and eighteenth-century rentals. The final link in their chain of identity is afforded by the *Survey* and large-scale plan of 1819 made for the Duchy by S. Elliott. On this plan each field is numbered, and corresponding numbers appear against each farm's holding in the *Survey*. Thus the *Netherpulle* of the fourteenth century and subsequent rolls and rentals is North Pill (fields 35 to 40) of 1819; *Parva Esshe* has become Little Ash, and the plan shows it as fields 1 to 23 on the east bank of the Tamar, 98 acres in all, the old foothold of the Duchy ferry on the Devon bank. The 1819 plan can then be compared with the first edition of the 6-inch O.S. plan and thence with subsequent editions and the modern field boundaries. Some of the nameless farms on the O.S. map can be named from the Elliott survey, and holdings no longer distinguished can be delineated. Thus Elliott's plan shows that fields 481–492, south-east of Old Trematon village, made up the holding of Penfentle (35 acres in 1819), the *Penvyntel* of the first Assession Roll. Names sometimes change: a chain of references too long to print here links the holding known in 1819 as *Gripes* with the *Ivsdon* or *Insdon* of the fourteenth-century documents.

The earliest Assession Roll surviving is from 1356, and at first sight this might seem to come too late to serve our purpose of recovering the agrarian topography of the early fourteenth century, for the Black Death had intervened. Fortunately, from the period before the Black Death there survive the Caption of Seisin of 1337, another detailed survey of the Duchy tenants. Unlike the Assession Roll of 1356 it has no place-names as marginalia and the tenants are not grouped according to the location of their farms; but for each tenant the location of the messuage was still recorded, and it is simply a matter of re-sorting the entries. The areas of fields and the rents paid were also indicated, and doubtful and faded entries can be checked by these additional details. There are surprisingly few changes in either the family names or the rents paid between 1337 and 1356, and—more important—there are no place-names in 1337 which do not occur in 1356.

It is even possible to edge a little further back in time and nearer to the peak of medieval colonization by seeking the tenants of the 1337 Caption of Seisin in two other surveys, those of 1331 and 1300, which give surnames, acreages, and rents, but not the place-name of the holdings. Thus a holding of a messuage and seven acres of land held by John Nichol in 1356 for 2s. 8d. rent appears under the *Oldetrematon* rubric; in 1337 it was held for the same rent and with the same acreage by Walter Poly, the seven acres English measure being explicitly equated with a quarter-acre, *ferling*, Cornish measure; in 1331 Walter Poly appears as tenant of a *ferling* paying 2s. 8½d. rent. The survey of 1300 is more curt and more concerned with total numbers; like the manorial accounts of 1296–7 for these manors, it is principally useful in this study for solving some awkward place or surname puzzle when the later documents are torn or faded, and for confirming the values of the manorial assets to the earl.

A final check on the general compatibility of the data before and after the Black Death is afforded by counting the messuages in the three documents; the correspondence is close.

TABLE I

TOTAL MESSUAGES IN EACH MANOR, 1300, 1331, 1337, and 1356

	1300	1331	1337	1356
Helstone in Trigg		96	93	93½
Trematon		59	58	58
Tybeste	49	54	51¾	55
All manors		209	202¾	206½

The first manor to be examined, Helstone in Trigg, was the largest in area, lying between the western edge of Bodmin Moor and the sea, and centred on the Camel valley. If the landscape today seems cold and the trees stunted it is more from the exposure to winds off the sea than from moorish height: the highest point in the manor is 987 feet, and all the high ground of the adjacent Downs and Tors belonged not to Helstone but to other communities, those centred on Davidstow to the north and St Breward to the south.

The manor of Helstone took in the whole of three parishes, Lanteglos, Advent, and Michaelstow. In 1337 there were 93 messuages in these three parishes, and in addition there was the borough of Camelford planted in Lanteglos parish where the main road crossed the Camel. In 1300 there were more burgages in this new town (62) than messuages in the rest of Lanteglos parish.

In Table II the entries on the Assession Roll have been re-grouped and set out under the parishes. Fig. I shows the same data in map form. Since all the place-names of 1337 correspond to existing farms, the symbols for the free and villein messuages have been placed on the map at the site of these farms to which the six-figure National Grid reference is made. Many of these farms have the Gothic type of 'antiquities' on the O.S. map, but architectural

TABLE II

HELSTONE IN TRIGG: DISTRIBUTION OF SETTLEMENT WITHIN THE MANOR

Modern farm name or place name	Grid Reference	Free messuages	Villein messuages	Total messuages
LANTEGLOS PARISH				
Castle Goff	085825	0	1	1
Fentenwansen	076807	4	0	4
Helstone	088814	2	11	13
Hendre	091837	0	3	3
Kenstock	097811	0	2	2
Treforda	080814	1	1	2
Trefrew	109847	0	1	1
Tregoodwell	114836	3	5	8
Tremagenna	097822	0	4	4
Trevia	098836	1	8	9
Trewalder	074821	0	5	5
Trewen	088834	0	5	5
			Total	57
ADVENT PARISH				
Corndon	c. 110820?	0	1	1
Goosehill	148844	2	1	3
Pencarrow	106825	2	0	2
Tressiney	102814	3	0	3
Trethin	105819	1	1	2
			Total	11
MICHAELSTOW PARISH				
Fentonadle	084780	0	5	5
Michaelstow	080788	0	2	2
Tredarrup	078793	0	3	3
Tegawn	073788	0	4	4
Tregreenwell	075804	0	4	4
Treveighan	075795	0	5	5
Trevillic	069790	0	2	2
			Total	25
Manor total		19	74	93

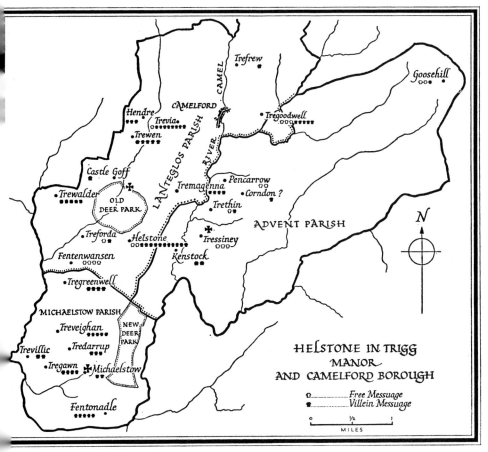

FIG. I

HELSTONE IN TRIGG MANOR

Distribution of free and villein messuages in the early fourteenth century.
(There was a turbary at Goosehill in 1296–7.)

d archaeological examination would be necessary to ascertain whether any
the existing buildings survive from the medieval farmsteads. It is signi-
ant of the conservatism of settlement here that there is no place-name of
37 that fails to reappear in Elliott's survey of 1819.

Of the three parishes in Helstone manor, Michaelstow shows the simplest
ucture, with no free holdings at all, and the villeins' messuages grouped in
ʒbules of 5, 5, 4, 4, 3, 2, and 2. Alongside the parish church was simply a
ir of houses. About one-sixth of this parish was taken up by the New Park
Helsbury which lay between the road (now the B.3266) and the river
.mel; in 1337 it had seven times as many wild animals as there were villeins
the parish.

Advent parish, with a good deal of poorer land on the Moor edge, was worse placed for arable farming than Michaelstow, all of which lay west of the Camel. Advent's eight free messuages compared with three villein may show the freedom of the frontiersmen colonists. And the holdings were ever more scattered: 3, 3, 2, 2, and 1 messuages; and none by the church.

Lanteglos was the largest, most densely settled, and most complex parish of the three. Leaving aside the borough of Camelford, it had at Helstone an agglomeration of thirteen messuages (two villein and eleven free), different from anything else in the manor of which Helstone was the *caput*. At Trevi and Tregoodwell were globules of nine and eight messuages; the rest of the pattern was 5, 5, 4, 4, 3, 2, 2, 1, and 1.

Like Advent, Lanteglos church stood alone. No rectory house is men-

TABLE III

TYBESTE: DISTRIBUTION OF SETTLEMENT WITHIN THE MANOR

	Free *messuages*	*Villein* *messuages*	*Total* *messuages*
PROBUS PARISH			
Bartilver	0	2	2
Trevilvas	0	2	2
		Total	4
CREED PARISH			
Carwinnick	2	0	2
Garlennick	2	1	3
'Garhoda' (?=Carvossa)	0	2	2
'Keuseby' (?=Pencoise)	1	0	1
'Luscoys'	3	1	4
Nancor	3¾	1	4¾
Nantellan	3	0	3
Pendenbethwy	1	0	1
Pengelly	0	1	1
Pennans	3	2	5
Trecaine	4	0	4
Treswallen	1	1	2
Trevillick	3	0	3
Trewinnow Meor (sc. Great)	2	2	4
Trewinnow Vean (sc. Little)	2	0	2
Tybeste	4	0	4
'Tybeste Vyan'	0	2	2
		Total	47¾
Manor total	34¾	17	51¾

tioned in the manorial documents although there may have been one. The houses of Helstone were half a mile away as the crow flies, and such a direct journey was impeded by the Old Park, the lord's deer-park, for the lane winds round the eastern side of the pale. The earthworks of Castle Goff by this park and of Helsbury above the other park resemble those hill-forts which Mr G. R. J. Jones has indicated near some of his centres of lordship. The name Helstone itself, like the more famous Helston in Kerrier, is half Cornish and half Saxon: it is the *tun* of the *henlis*, the settlement around the chief court-house.

The manor of Tybeste lay mainly on the east bank of the Fal, and like Helstone had running through it an important main road, that from Truro eastwards. It was this road, crossing the river by the new *grand pont*, which gave rise to the new borough of Grampound, but the importance of the river-crossing even before the bridge is suggested by the small part of the manor (two pairs of messuages) which lay on the west bank. This segment is now in Probus parish, but most of the manor lies in Creed. (Manor and parish are not now coterminous, for a rectangular projection of about one square mile at the south-east corner contains no names corresponding to any Duchy messuages.) The manorial centre at Tybeste is now deserted; the church of Creed stands aloof from either manor or borough. (Fig. II.)

In 1337 Tybeste itself was a cluster of four free messuages with the villeins at *Tybeste Vyan;* Trewinnow also had a pairing of *Meor* and *Vean*. The dispersion in this manor is very marked: the largest cluster was less than half the size of Helstone, and ten places were made up of only one or two houses. Compared with these, the 28 burgages of Grampound in 1296 made it a giant like Camelford in Helstone. (Four places have been identified only tentatively, but it is unlikely that they refer to some place already on the list, and the degree of dispersion is unaffected by the uncertainty.)

Trematon, the final manor to be examined, also had a small enclave (of two messuages) in another parish, and the analogy with the transpontine portion of Tybeste is close, for Little Ash in Trematon (p. 16 above) was the landing place of the Tamar ferry in Devonshire; this ferry was a seignorial monopoly (worth £7 8s. in 1296–7: about as much as the mill and three times the burgage rents of Saltash). Otherwise all the manor lay in St Stephen's parish; and again the church had no messuages near it. In addition to the thirteen rural clusters there were two boroughs: by 1300 Saltash had 118 burgages on the cliff overlooking the Tamar ferry; and there was a petty borough at Trematon castle, probably wholly within the bailey like the small

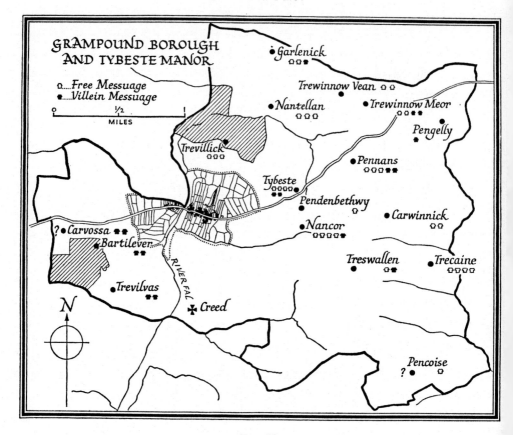

FIG. II

TYBESTE MANOR

Distribution of free and villein messuages in the early fourteenth century. The shading shows
the area of two farms in the 1819 Duchy survey.

castle boroughs of south and mid-Wales, or, indeed, like the Norman borough
at Launceston. But, judging from the rents paid, it had fewer than a score of
burgages in 1300.

It was because of this *novus burgus* at the castle that the old manorial centre
was called Old Trematon. There is no possibility of confusion; for two miles
separate them. Old Trematon (with its large cluster of thirteen houses and
its mixed Saxon and Cornish name) resembles Helstone; a second cluster,
almost as large, was to be found at South Pill (*sc.* South Pool), but this was
almost exclusively villein, whereas Trematon was predominantly free. (Fig.
III.)

The tables and the maps distinguish the legal status of the land-holders.

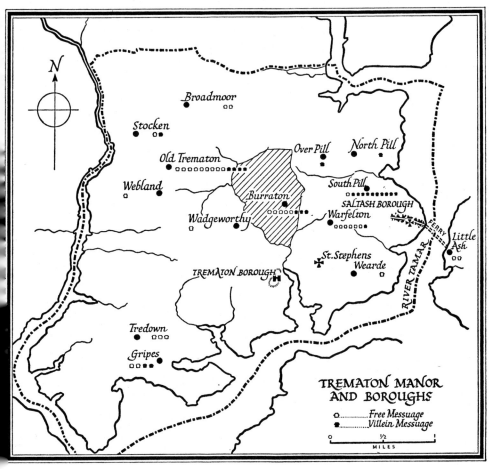

FIG. III

TREMATON MANOR

Distribution of settlement in the early fourteenth century.

The area comprised in the holdings at Burraton is shaded.

No entries corresponding to the modern place-names of Notter, Carkeel, Wivelscombe, Earth, Trevollard, Trehan, Shillingham, or Latchbrook appear in the medieval Assession Rolls; nor in the survey of the Duchy properties in 1819. Tithings of Carkeel and Trevollard are mentioned in the 1296–7 accounts. Earth appears as a personal name there and in the survey of 1331.

The main tenure affecting all Duchy manors in Cornwall was 'conventionary'. Thus at Trematon in 1356 52 out of 58 tenants held their lands for a seven-year period, at the end of which a fresh entry or *assession* was made. During the seven years of the *conventio* all these tenants paid rent, were able to attend the manor court at three-weekly intervals, and were eligible for the offices of reeve, beadle, and tithingman.

TABLE IV

TREMATON: DISTRIBUTION OF SETTLEMENT WITHIN THE MANOR

Modern farm name or place-name	ST STEPHEN'S PARISH		
	Free messuages	*Villein* messuages	*Total* messuages
Old Trematon	9	4	13
South Pill	1	11	12
North Pill	0	1	1
Over Pill	0	1	1
Burraton	5	3	8
Warfelton	6	1	7
Ince (=Gripes)	2	2	4
Tredown	3	0	3
Broadmoor	2	0	2
Wearde	1	0	1
Webland	1	0	1
Wadsworth	1	0	1
Little Ash (Devon: east of ferry)	2	0	2
Stocken	1	1	2
Manor total	34	24	58

The 34 free conventionary tenants among these 52, although in a better
position than the 18 villeins, were liable to forfeit their best beast as a heriot
to their lord when they died, "but no goods else." The rent for a free tenement of average size was 4s. 6d. a year. The 18 villein conventionaries on
this manor paid twice this sum for an average house and holding and had all
the liabilities of a free tenant, with the additional forfeit of all goods at death.
A third small group of villeins (at Trematon there were six) paid 5s. 6d. rent
but were tied to the manor for life in addition to the ordinary villein liabilities and to tallage by the lord at his will; their tenements passed to their
youngest son: these were the villeins "of blood," *de stirpe*.

At Tybeste the services were similarly defined and the villein rents were
at the same level; the free rents were twice these of Trematon and equalled
the villeins'; the villeins *de stirpe* here paid 8s., again higher than at Trematon. The entry fines at the renewal of the convention every seven years were
equivalent to just over three years' rent in 1356 for the free conventionaries
and about twice for the villeins.

In each class of tenancy the acreage assigned to a messuage was not uniform, but considering the differences in geographical position the averages
shown for Tybeste and Trematon in Table V are very close.

TABLE V

AVERAGE ACREAGE PER HOLDING, 1356 (ENGLISH ACRES)

	Free conventionaries	*Villein conventionaries*	*Villeins de stirpe*
Trematon manor	19½	16	16
Tybeste manor	18	19	22

Finally, the size of settlement clusters has been set out for the three types: settlement clusters of wholly free messuages; settlement clusters of wholly villein messuages; and settlement clusters of mixed tenures.

TABLE VI

SIZE OF SETTLEMENTS, ACCORDING TO TENURES

A. WHOLLY FREE (17 places)

	No. of places with:					*Over*
	1 *mess.*	2 *mess.*	3 *mess.*	4 *mess.*	5 *mess.*	5 *mess.*
Helstone	0	1	1	1	0	0
Tybeste	2	2	2	2	0	0
Trematon	3	2	1	0	0	0
Total	5	5	4	3	0	0

B. WHOLLY VILLEIN (22 places)

	No. of places with:					*Over*
	1 *mess.*	2 *mess.*	3 *mess.*	4 *mess.*	5 *mess.*	5 *mess.*
Helstone	3	3	2	3	4	0
Tybeste	1	4	0	0	0	0
Trematon	2	0	0	0	0	0
Total	6	7	2	3	4	0

C. MIXED TENURES (18 places)

	No. of places with:										*Over*
	1 *mess.*	2 *mess.*	3 *mess.*	4 *mess.*	5 *mess.*	6 *mess.*	7 *mess.*	8 *mess.*	9 *mess.*	10 *mess.*	10 *mess.*
Helstone	0	2	1	0	0	0	0	1	1	0	1
Tybeste	0	1	1	2	2	0	0	0	0	0	0
Trematon	0	1	0	1	0	0	1	1	0	0	2
Total	0	4	2	3	2	0	1	2	1	0	3
Total of all types	11	16	8	9	6	0	1	2	1	0	3

The total number of messuages concerned is 203, scattered in 57 different places. Just under half these places (27) were made up of a single messuage or a pair of messuages; one-fifth of the places consisted of a single messuage; only one-eighth of the places (7 out of 57) consisted of more than five messuages together, and three of these seven were the largest agglomerations, of 13, 13, and 12 messuages respectively. No difference between typical sizes of the wholly free and wholly villein clusters is apparent. As was stressed earlier, the absolutely isolated messuage turns out to be very unrepresentative: only 5 per cent of the total messuages were so placed and only one-fifth of all the places considered were so composed.

At this stage in the study of medieval agriculture and settlement in Cornwall the full implications of the evidence presented here can only be dimly discerned. The five parishes analysed here do not exhaust the evidence, for there were Duchy manors at Tintagel, Stoke Climsland, Helston in Kerrier, Moresk, Rillaton, Liskeard, Tywarnhaile, Restormel, Calstock, Tewington, Penlyne, and Trefrize: similar analyses could be made for these places, giving a further geographical sample.

It is clear that a good deal of work in the field and among local records in Cornwall will be necessary. The present author will not have the opportunity for these, but now that these deep-rooted little communities have been identified, those who are more fortunately placed than in Leeds can visit the farmsteads to see whether any of the medieval messuages survive, perhaps as no more than a barn or out-building to a more recent farmhouse. Fields near these farms needs to be examined for remains of houses of the old communities surviving only as earthworks. The evidence of field-shapes and field-boundaries must also be brought in to reconstruct the acres, Cornish and English, assigned to these messuages. Only then shall we know how they stood in relation to the movement of colonization and conquest of the waste, and begin to see how the little agrarian units produced the pennies for the *fines, perquisita, et relevia* of the manorial accounts.

These multifarious *tre-* settlements must also be studied alongside the settlement pattern of medieval Wales and the border brought realistically on to the map by the recent studies of Mr G. R. J. Jones. In their names these multifarious *trevs* seem to reach back safely into pre-Saxon Cornwall, although there is yet no sure way of linking (for example) the 96 different messuages in Helstone of 1331 with the 53 holdings enumerated in the Domesday account of that manor.

The old assumption that scattered settlement was divorced from open-field arable has been shaken by Mr Jones's evidence, where co-aration has been shown to be quite compatible with a landscape that today seems all dispersed farmsteads. Professor Balchin, in one of the few modern sketches of Cornish settlement, reminds us that Domesday Book records in Cornwall "just under a hundred manors with two ploughlands or less," and he continues: "It is clear that these entries can only refer to small hamlets or *trevs* that had no relation to an open-field system, quite apart from the fact that the names in themselves are quite un-English." Mr Jones has shown that a form of open fields could exist in quite un-English surroundings, and further work in Cornwall, marrying field-work and documents, may make it necessary to modify Professor Balchin's assertion. The early publication of Mr Gover's study of Cornish place-names would be a further assistance.

NOTE. This article embodies a paper read to the annual conference of the British Agricultural History Society in April 1961. It has not been revised to take account of subsequent publications, the most important being: W. G. Hoskins, *Provincial England* (1963), pp. 15–52; and G. R. J. Jones, 'The Tribal System in Wales: a reassessment in the light of settlement studies', *Welsh Hist. Rev.*, I, 1961, pp. 111–32. O. G. S. Crawford's copies of Charles Henderson's tracings of Cornish estate plans are now deposited in the British Museum (Maps 199 d.60).

NOTE ON SOURCES. Data in the text, figures, and tables derive from the following P.R.O. documents:

1296–7	E.119	Ministers' accounts (ed. L. M. Midgley, Camden Soc. 3rd ser., LXVIII, 1945).
1300	E.152/8	Extent.
	E.142/6–7	Survey.
	C.133/95	Extent (calendared in *Cal. I.P.M.*, III, pp. 456 sqq.).
1300–1	E.372/146 m.30	Accounts.
before 1307	SC.6/816/9	Accounts.
1327	E.179/87/7	Lay Subsidy.
1331	E.142/41	Survey.
1337	E.120/1	Caption of seisin.
1338–9	SC.6/816/11	Accounts.
1347–8	SC.6/812/3	Accounts.
1352–3	SC.6/817/3	Accounts.
1356	E.306/2/1	Assession roll.
1371	E.306/2/2	Assession roll.
1377	E.179/87/29–35	Poll-tax receipts.

The Duchy of Cornwall Office, Buckingham Gate, London, has assession rolls of 1333, 1364, and 1371, as well as rentals and surveys continuing intermittently into modern times. A series of plans with keys was made by S. Elliott in 1819. Other plans of Duchy properties are at the County Record Office, Truro. Acknowledgement is made of permission from these offices to consult records.

OTHER NOTES. The areas given in the documents are usually in acres Cornish and acres English. Cornish ferlings are equated with holdings of from 9 to 11 acres English; and half-acres with areas from 18 to 20 acres English.

PLATE 3

DOWNTON, WILTS. (pp. 53-5). View E. along the street of the new borough (*c.* 1208).
The old village of Downton is beyond the river, top centre, near the church and the earth-
works of the bishop's castle are in the trees, top right. Compare Fig. 71, p. 54.
(Crown Copyright Reserved)

THE SIX NEW TOWNS

OF THE BISHOPS OF WINCHESTER, 1200-55

I

THE six towns whose plantation is studied in this article are Hindon (Wilts.), Newtown in Burghclere (Hants.), Newtown *alias* Francheville (Isle of Wight), New Alresford (Hants.), Downton (Wilts.), and Overton (Hants.). Their location is given in FIGS. 69 and 78, and in Appendix I grid-references are given for these towns and the other properties of the bishop in this area.

Of the six towns, the first three were planted in open country a mile or more from any previous settlement; the sites of the others were each separated from a pre-existing village by a river and were legally and administratively distinct from their old-established rural neighbours. In one case, New Alresford, the planted town has the distinctive prefix to mark its novelty and separation from Old Alresford, just as earlier town-foundations had given rise to a twin nomenclature at Old and New Windsor and Old and New Woodstock. The migration of the bishop and city of Salisbury to a new site by the Avon meadows also resulted in an 'Old' Sarum and a 'New' Salisbury. In the bishop of Winchester's two Newtowns the name also embodied the novelty of the foundations.

The bishops' six urban plantations were part of a continuing English tradition, too long to set out fully here.[1] It is sometimes thought that the plantation of towns in England begins with Edward I and derives from his experiences in Gascony, where he had moved among the many *bastides* founded by the counts of Toulouse and where between 1250 and 1330 the kings of England granted foundation-charters to no fewer than 101 *bastides*.[2] This same period saw in England and Wales the foundation of at least fourteen new towns as well as the rebuilding of Berwick-on-Tweed (1297) and the re-siting of Winchelsea (1281). This activity by kings, bishops and lay lords in the second half of the thirteenth century may have been stimulated by the success of such earlier plantations as form the subject of this study, but no claim is made for the bishops of Winchester as fathers of English town-planning. The bishops' six new towns were in the same tradition

---

[1] This is the theme of a book, *The New Towns of the English* which I am preparing. For a sketch see . W. Beresford and J. K. S. St. Joseph, *Medieval England* (Cambridge, 1958), pp. 197-228, and M. W. resford, *History on the Ground* (London, 1957), pp. 125-50.

[2] *Bastide*, a convenient word for a planted town, derives from *bâtir* to build. The first in Gascony as Puymirol, founded by the count of Toulouse in 1246; the English series begins with Monségur, artered in 1265. The English kings also renewed or extended the liberties of 17 French foundations on rritory which later became English.

as William I's New Windsor and Ludlow, Richard I's Portsmouth and John's
Liverpool: the tradition may even go back in the royal line—if the grid-plan of
streets is any evidence—to Saxon Oxford, Wallingford and Wareham.

The social and economic forces which encouraged the bishops to augment the
towns of southern England were within the same period inducing other territorial
landlords to plant such towns as Newton Abbot (*c.* 1200) and Chipping Sodbury
(1227), to say nothing of New Sarum. In the same period New Thame probably
arose; in Cornwall semi-rural boroughs like Mitchell; and among the plantations
some like Warenmouth, Northumberland (1247) were to have only a short life
before their sites faded back into the countryside from which they had been
promoted. FIG. 78 shows all the known new towns of the middle ages in central
southern England, and it will be seen that the bishops' plantations lay in a countryside where others had seen and seized opportunity.

The unique feature of the bishops of Winchester's foundations, however, is
the quality of their documentation. The long series of annual account rolls[3] for
the Winchester estates has long been well known to historians, who have used
them for basic studies of the movement of grain prices, the yields of sown corn, the
impact of the Black Death, the progress of commutation and—lately—the levels
of mortality. Since all six of the bishops' towns were laid out within rural manors,
these annual manorial accounts afford an opportunity—perhaps unique in
Europe—of documenting the establishment of a group of new medieval towns.

The bishops' estates lay for the most part within a forty-mile radius of
Winchester, the area shown in FIG. 69. Outside this area the only substantial
properties were the manor of Witney (Oxon.) and the town and surrounding
villages which made up the great manor of Taunton (Somerset). These episcopal
estates were mainly valued for their agricultural produce, their rents and their
manorial payments. Some, like Highclere, Bishop's Sutton and Bishop's Waltham
(Hants.) had a manor house or palace where the bishop could stay on a cross-
country journey or come for the pleasures of the chase. The bishop's income at the
beginning of the thirteenth century also included some small urban properties
in Winchester and Southwark, but only at Taunton does the first surviving
account roll (for the year 1208–9) mention a 'borough'. But this borough, which
brought the bishop £41 8s. 3d. that year, was far from being a new town: it had
belonged to the church since before the conquest and was already substantial
when described in Domesday Book.

Between 1200 and 1255 the bishops were able to augment this inheritance of
one town and forty-three manors in two different ways. They could promote to
borough status an existing settlement which had already shown itself able to
develop non-agricultural economic life—the normal route by which medieval
English boroughs came into existence: the Northamptonshire town of Higham

---

[3] 'Account roll' is used here in preference to 'pipe roll' which can be confused with the royal Pipe
Roll. The bishops' rolls were in class Eccles. Comm. 2 at the Public Record Office; this prefix is omitted
from subsequent footnotes where roll number and membrane are given. The roll for 1208–9 was edited
by H. Hall, *The Pipe Roll of the Bishopric of Winchester* (London, 1903). In the summer of 1959 these rolls
were moved from the P.R.O. to the County Record Office, Winchester. It is to be hoped that this disservice
to all except residents in Hampshire will not be acerbated by re-numbering the rolls and invalidating the
references given by scholars during the last fifty years.

Ferrers may stand as a type-site.[4] On the bishops' estates Farnham (Surrey) and Witney rose this way. The roll of 1208–9 shows the men of Farnham already allowed to pay a lump sum of £7 in lieu of assized rents, fines of land, customary services, heriots, *maritagia*, tolls and market dues. In successive annual accounts

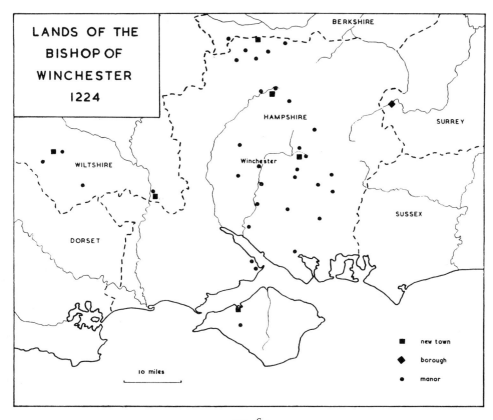

FIG. 69

LANDS OF THE BISHOP OF WINCHESTER, 1224 (pp. 47 ff.)

The six new towns are indicated by squares, the bishop's borough of Farnham by a diamond; the rural manors are listed with map references in Appendix I, p. 73)

this lump sum increased, but only in 1248 was the town granted a charter by bishop William de Ralegh, giving it the rank of borough and wider privileges.[5] At Witney *c.* 1208–9 'a borough was formed by amputation of a part of the township of Curbridge'—189 acres cut from 3,265—making burgesses of those who dwelt along the broad green of Witney village.[6]

---

[4] Overnight, 91 villeins were enfranchised as the first burgesses. *Calendar of Charter Rolls*, 1 (London, 1903), 372-3.

[5] E. Robo, *Medieval Farnham* (Farnham, 1935), p. 173.

[6] A. Ballard in *Oxford Studies in Social and Legal History*, ed. P. Vinogradoff, v (Oxford, 1916), 184. My dating of the borough rests on the entry among the *Purchasia* of 1208–9: 'de Burgo xx s. pro pace habenda' and the expenses that year of three men 'pro libertate novae cartae' (Hall, *op. cit.* in note 3, p. 17); in 1210–11 there was a borough reeve (159270B m.4).

II

In contrast to the promotion of Farnham and Witney are the six manors where the bishops planted new settlements, each a borough from its first day. The first to be considered in detail is *New Alresford*, seven miles ENE. of Winchester near the junction of the rivers Alre and Itchen and less than three miles from the source of the latter. Near the source was the episcopal manor of Bishop's Sutton, acquired in 1136 and soon the site of a palace which was a resting place

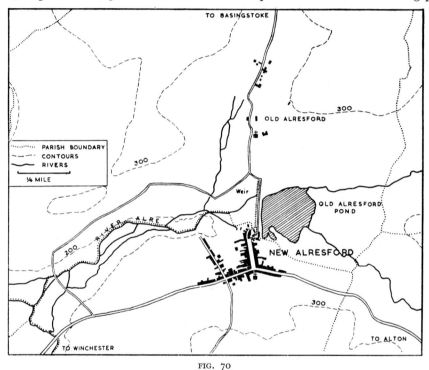

FIG. 70

OLD AND NEW ALRESFORD, HANTS. (pp. 50 ff.)

The new town was planted around a market-place near the head of the canalized river Alre. The Pond supplied water for the canal; across its dam is the road to Old Alresford. The palace of Bishop's Sutton lies 2 miles E., on the Alton road

Crown Copyright Reserved

on the London road and near the wooded hunting country by Alton. The bishop's presence here, together with his household and visitors, was a natural incentive to bring trade outside the palace gate. King John stayed here, and from the king the village obtained a fair and probably its market charter.[7] The real beneficiary, however, was not Bishop's Sutton but Alresford two miles farther west. Bishop Godfrey (1189–1204) opened up the higher stretches of the Itchen above Winchester by canalizing the river. To ensure a good head of water he threw a dam across the Itchen valley and created a great reservoir.[8] This pool, once 200 acres

[7] *Victoria County History, Hampshire* (London, 1908), III, 41-5 (subsequent references to this *History* are abbreviated to *V.C.H.*).

[8] *Ibid.*, pp. 348-54.

in area, still survives as the 30-acre Alresford Pond and across the dam runs the road from New to Old Alresford. This great dam is one of the largest secular earthworks surviving from medieval England (FIG. 70).

In 1200 the bishop obtained a market charter, in 1202 a fair and about the same time the river tolls.[9] But the markets and fairs of John's charters were neither for Bishop's Sutton nor Old Alresford but for a new town at the southern end of the dam, being a broad open market-place lined with houses and abutting on the Winchester–London road with the new church of St. John the Baptist at its head. Why was a new town engineered? What stood in the way of the promotion of Bishop's Sutton?

The answer seems to lie in the Itchen canal. The making of Alresford pond had prevented boats from reaching Bishop's Sutton, if indeed they ever could, since the river rises only a mile from it. Old Alresford village was more than half a mile from the head of the navigation and not on the main Winchester–London road following the Itchen.

We do not need to guess about the events. The monastic chronicle, naming some notable events of the year 1200, recorded:[10]

'Bishop Godfey of Winchester made a new market place at Alresford and the name of the town he called *Novum Forum.*'

A town had been christened New Market, just as in 1227 a new town in Suffolk was to be christened Newmarket. The bishops' town of Alresford is no longer called New Market, only New Alresford, but the documents from the early years of its life have many references to the place as simply 'Alresford Forum'. (Blandford Forum (Dorset), although not a new town, has the same element in its name.) Indeed, the alternative names rather worried the accountant. In 1210–11 he headed his account 'Forum de Alresford' and accounted for 45 burgage plots paying 2s. a year rent and for four others newly taken up that year. From 477 acres of agricultural land, probably that part of Old Alresford south of the Itchen, nearly £15 in agricultural rents were collected. The reeve deducted the expense to which he had been put in making a new fulling mill, pulling down an old mill and filling in the pond. The rest of the money he sent to Winchester. Later, however, with second thoughts all these entries were crossed out and a small piece of parchment stitched two membranes earlier in the account roll. On it, in small handwriting, the same items and sums appear but the heading was now *De Burgo.*[11]

The town, we have seen, dated from 1200. The first surviving roll is from 1208–9, when New Alresford brought the bishop £18 7s. 8d. compared with £96 cash income from the rural manor of Old Alresford. But the increment was not as spectacular as might seem, since £14 derived from the agricultural land attached to the new town. In the first decade of its life New Alresford attracted forty people to come and occupy the *placeae*, the building-plots which the bishop was offering to newcomers.

[9] Tolls: *ibid.*, p. 350; market: P.R.O. C53/2 m. 10; fairs: 159460, 2/2 and *Calendar of Charter Rolls*, III (London, 1908), 349.

[10] *Annales Monastici*, ed. H. R. Luard (London, 1865), II, 252 (Rolls Series).

[11] 159270B m. 11 and attachment to m. 9.

There is no evidence that the bishop provided the houses. As in Edward I's Caernarvon and the Gascon bastides this expense fell on the townsmen. At New Alresford the bishop did provide three public buildings besides rebuilding a fulling mill. These, the chronicler states, were a town hall, a town oven and a boulting house—that is, a place for sifting bran from flour. These three communal buildings emphasized the new community's independence both of Old Alresford and of the manorial obligations, which continued to fall on those who lived in the rural manor. The oven, like the mill, was commonly the lord's monopoly, its use a mark of his seignory and the villagers' dependence. The bishop may well have provided the church, for it was on its patronal festival that the fair was held, but the manorial accounts have no mention of it. Architecturally it could well come from the first decade of the thirteenth century.

The town of 'Alresford Forum' had the simplest of plans: it was the market-place, at one end the London road and at the other the bishop's dam. Just below the dam, to the north-west (FIG. 70) is the head of the bishop's canal and alongside it the town mill. The picturesque fulling mill which now straddles the canal must date from after the disuse of the navigation. The older course of the Itchen before the construction of the dam is indicated by the curves in the parish boundary. The straightness of the final length of canal and the straightness of Alresford's main street are an indication of their deliberateness. Contrast the winding local roads, even the Winchester road in the Itchen valley. Winding rural roads and meandering footpaths—like those from Alresford to the bishop's manors of Beauworth and Cheriton—were the product of slow and piecemeal development in the centuries when field was being won from forest. The market place and the rectilinear *placeae* alongside it remain on the modern map as witnesses to a different historical process, that of deliberation, planning and plantation.[12]

The letting of stall-space and permission to build permanent stalls in the broad main street were additional sources of revenue for the bishop. In 1223–4 this income was £3 6s. 8d., the equivalent of the rent from 33 of the town's *placeae*, while the town courts—with their commercial cases, their registration of land transfer and the fines from the petty crime that accompanied commercial assemblies—also brought in the pence and sometimes more than the pence.[13] In 1264–5 it was £4 9s. 6d., as much as 45 burgage plots would have brought in.[14]

In the fourteenth century, Alresford was one of the ten greatest wool-markets in the country, a collecting centre for the downland east and north-east of Winchester. It is known that wool was shipped down the canal to Beaulieu,[15] and the town's importance as a route centre is stressed by the agreement of 1269, wherein the bishops of Oxford and Winchester joined Henry III in constructing a new road eastwards from New Alresford to Alton, crossing the watershed

---

[12] The burgage plots as distinguishable on the modern map are here 350 ft. long; despite subdivision, it is possible to discern 33 house-and-shop fronts on either side of the *Forum*. At Newtown, I.o.W., plots were 165 ft. long, at Downton the same; at Overton 275 ft. and at Hindon 440 ft. No documentary reference to the size of these *placeae* has been encountered, but those of bastides elsewhere in England and Gascony occasionally occur. Each frontage at Alresford is now about 33 ft. broad.

[13] 159278 m. 1. [14] 159295 m. 17d.

[15] Hall, *op. cit.* in note 3, p. xix.

between the Itchen and the Wey valley, the most direct route from Winchester to London.[16]

There was one other way in which a bishop, like any other territorial land-lord, could gain from the establishment of a new town as an extra marketing centre on their estates. A bishop was both producer and consumer. As a consumer at Bishop's Sutton palace or at Winchester he was keenly interested in provisioning his household and in having plenty of traders with a wide variety of goods offered for sale in competition with each other.[17] As a producer of agricultural goods on his own demesnes he was interested in getting as good a price as possible for what-ever surpluses he wanted to send to market. Adjoining New Alresford were four of the bishop's rural manors. The wheat—to take only one crop—sold for cash off Old Alresford manor averaged 30 quarters a year in the first half of the thirteenth century, and, at an average of 4s. a quarter, was worth £6 a year.[18] The more local market-places and the more fairs there were, the more traders queueing up, the better the price that might be expected.

III

The second town to be considered is *Downton* which lies in Wiltshire just over the county boundary and eight miles SSE. of Old Salisbury. It was a large manor and had belonged to the church at Winchester since the third quarter of the seventh century. South of the parish church of the old village (FIG. 71) are the earthworks of the bishops' castle-residence,[19] and near it was the meeting-place of the Saxon hundred-moot, the tradition still preserved in the farm name. It was alongside this sizable community, very much larger than Old Alresford, that the bishop added a new town almost at the same time as the foundation of New Alresford. The town plans are very similar. Each consists of a single, very broad market-place street with one end at a river crossing and the other making a T-junction with the main road. It is this road, now the main road from Salisbury, which forms the foreground of PL. 3 , while the trees (top right) mark the earth-works of the castle.

In the first large-scale county map of 1773 this part of Downton was simply called 'Street';[20] Stockbridge, another new town of this area (although not the child of a bishop of Winchester) was also often called 'The Street (of King's Somborne)'[21] as indeed was the midland fair-town of St. Ives. If we look for origins or precedents for this very simple form of town plan we might turn (on the

[16] *Calendar of Charter Rolls*, II (London, 1906), 122-3.

[17] All the bishops' new towns except Overton were near an episcopal residence. In the single year 1208–9 the king stayed with the bishop at three of these palaces.

[18] Figures calculated from N. S. B. Gras, *The Evolution of the English Corn Market* (Cambridge, Mass., 1915), pp. 370-400.

[19] While residing here the bishop granted Newtown's charter of 1255.

[20] *Burgus* (as opposed to *forinsecus*) appears in fourteenth-century tax-lists; in 1576, *burgus* (as opposed to *Este Ende and Churche Tithing*).

[21] Stockbridge was probably founded *c.* 1200: P.R.O. C53/2 m. 21; C132/21/12 m. 11. The town of Blandford Forum was also simply called 'this streete' in a survey of 1591: P.R.O. DL/42/116 f. 49.

Winchester manors) to Fareham[22] or Witney, but this is probably too sophisticated. Need we look any further than the end of our noses? That is, to any roadside along which stalls are set up to attract passers-by; or to any village green which commerce turns from green to all the colours of the rainbow when the local people come in to the market stalls and the itinerant traders to the fair booths?

It is as 'the new market of Downton' that the new plantation is first documented. The first surviving account roll, that of 1208–9, is just too late to catch the foundation. 19 *placeae* paid rent *in novum forum* and 11 others were noted as having been let for the first time that year. By 1213–14 there were 72, and in

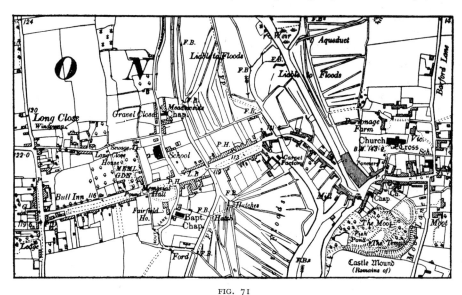

FIG. 71

DOWNTON, WILTS. (pp. 53 ff.)

The new town was planted across the river from the old village where the bishop's castle and the Hundred meeting-place were located ('The Moot'): compare PL. XV. (Sc. 6 in. = 1 mile)

Reproduced from the Ordnance Survey map with the sanction of the Controller of H.M. Stationery Office. Crown copyright reserved

1215–16 the account roll has the separate heading *Burgus de Dounton* for the first time. By 1218–19 there were 89 burgage plots paying rent, two of them occupied by weavers; and a fulling mill paid 40s. rent, as much as 40 burgesses or nearly half the town.[23] The downland sheep, as at New Alresford, were providing occupation in the new town for others than wool-dealers.

Why was it thought fit to tack a borough town on to Old Downton and to set it across the river and away from the castle and village? The shift suggests some fundamental change in route-emphasis from the east bank, where the castle-village lay, to the west bank. It would be interesting to connect it with shifts of route consequent on the migration of Old Salisbury to New Salisbury further upstream

[22] Burgages were being created at Fareham (Hants.) in 1211–2 (159217 m. 4, *Incrementum* and *Purchasia*).

[23] 1213–14: 159272 m. 7; 1215–16: 159273 m. 4; 1218–19: 159275 m. 7d.

but that hypothesis raises difficult problems of dating, since the foundation of Downton borough is nearly two decades earlier than the final move of the bishop of Salisbury from Old Sarum.

By 1225-6 the rent roll of Downton had risen to £5 18s. 4d., and by 1244-5 the bishop's cash income from Downton rents and its court was £19 6s.[24] One aspect of the extra money income which a territorial lord obtained when a new town was planted was the relatively effortless way in which it was earned. This should be borne in mind when comparing the cash yields from the old village and the new town. In 1264-5 the manor of Alresford provided the bishop with £70 and the borough with only £22; the manor of Downton with £110 and the borough with £9. But what a difference in effort, organization and risk! Once the initial land was provided, the borough cost the bishop virtually nothing to maintain. There were no risks of bad harvests to affect his income; no labour problems on the demesne; no marketing problems for the produce of a demesne; simply a collection of rents three or four times a year. To produce the £110 from Downton manor a demesne of 677 sown acres had to be managed; a cattle herd of 101 animals tended; a flock of nearly 1,700 sheep looked after; over 1,300 fleeces shorn and washed. Money had to be spent on property repairs, on buildings, on the village mills, on the bridge. Wages had to be paid and villein labour supervised.[25] The attractiveness of a cash income from a new town is not measured only by arithmetic. To use a simile which a bishop would have understood, it came near to being manna from Heaven.

IV

The third Winchester plantation was at *Overton* in north Hampshire, three miles east of Whitchurch. Here the modern topography (FIG. 72) shows the same double settlement as at Alresford and Downton: an old village with its church and across the river a new market town alongside a main road. On the north bank of the river lie St. Mary's church, the rectory, Court House and Court Farm, all that remain of the original village. A plan of the borough in 1615 is among the estate plans of Corpus Christi College, Oxford. On the south bank, across the bridge, lie the town mill and the five streets which form a simple rectilinear grid pattern. The east-west axis is formed by the road from Whitchurch to Basingstoke, but the market-place was in the north-south road from Kingsclere to Winchester. Overton was the first Winchester plantation to approach a grid plan although this alinement of streets was a common feature of the planted towns. New Windsor, Ludlow, Portsmouth and Liverpool—all anterior to Overton—had it, and at the bishop's seat at Bishop's Waltham, Henry de Blois had remodelled the town to form a grid of nine streets which would not be out of place in a Gascon bastide.

The account roll for 1213-14 shows Overton manor bringing in the usual type of rural rent, a *gabulum assisum* of £19 2s. The next year's roll is defective, but

[24] 1225-6: 159280 m. 2; 1244-5: 159287 m. 2.
[25] 1264-5: 159295 m. 17d.; Downton *manerium*: *ibid.*, mm. 2-3r; *burgus*: m. 3d. The sown area in Downton was 844 if Cowyk Grange is included. Similar areas and stock are found in 1208-9 (Hall, *op. cit.* note 3, pp. xlii-iii) and in 1274-5 (159302 m. 6d.): see Appendices IV and V, p. 214.

the roll for 1217–18 has an entry for Overton *burgus* in addition to the manor, although the roll is too worn to be legible. In the same year a market charter was granted. The roll for 1218–19 is the first to have a completely legible entry for the new town, and it shows 22 burgages each rented at 2s. a year. Fourteen individuals held these plots, one having three, and five others two each. That year one of the bishop's villeins paid 6s. 8d. to have a plot in the town. Four and a half *placeae*

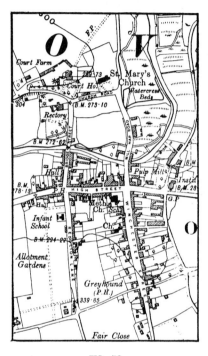

FIG. 72

OVERTON, HANTS. (pp. 55 ff.)

The principal burgages of the new town were in Winchester Street, a broad market-street. Note remain of old village to N., over the river. (Sc. 6 in. = 1 mile)

Reproduced from the Ordnance Survey map with the sanction of t Controller of H.M. Stationery Office. Crown copyright reser

were added in 1219–20 and by 1223–4 there were at least forty occupied,[26] and second market day and fair[27] were granted in 1246.

Some aspects of gain accruing to the bishops have been discussed above one item on the other side of the balance sheet has been omitted until now. Th documentary evidence from Overton fortunately enables it to be quantified. piece of demesne land could not simultaneously grow a crop and a house, an each *burgagium* or *placea* involved some loss of agricultural land from the demesn

---

[26] 1217–18: 159274 m. 5d.; market, P.R.O. C54/19 m. 5; 1218–19: 159275 m. 3d.; 1219–20: 1592 m. 7; 1223–4: 159278 m. 6.

[27] *Calendar of Charter Rolls*, I, 312.

and hence some loss of produce or rent. At Overton the reeve duly set down the loss in his accounts, for the traditional method of accounting would otherwise have made him liable for the old rents at the full amount. In the late fourteenth century the reeve was still making this formal claim for a *defectus* of 36s. from sixteen pieces of land *tractae in burgo*,[28] and the entry can be traced back through the annual accounts. The earliest legible *defectus* is for 1223–4, but part of an entry can be seen on the torn roll for 1217–18.[29] In 1213–14 the Downton reeve had claimed 6s. 'in defectu iii terrarum tractarum in novum burgum' and the 1217–18 roll varies this as 'in dominicum de burgo'. By 1264–5 this 6s. is described as arising from 'ii ferlinlond tractae in burgum' but the 'iii terrae' appear in their usual form in the stock inventory of the annual account where under *Instaurum* the reeve claimed a defect of 16 hens which had formerly been part of the rent from 'iii terrae tractae in burgum' and a 'ferlinlond' let to the fuller of Walton, a hamlet on the west bank of the river. In the account for 1376–7 the 6s. is described most fully: 'defectus redditus ii ferlingarum terrae nativae tractae in burgum'.[30] Similar entries at Witney in 1220 onwards describe *terra Cotstowe* as *tracta in burgum*, and from 1210–11 onwards (two years after charters from the bishop are mentioned) an additional two hides had been *tractae in dominicum*, and these entries suggest an enlargement of the built-up area of the bishop's borough of Witney at the expense of the surrounding agricultural land.[31]

V

The fourth *novus burgus* was planted on the very edge of Hampshire, separated from Berkshire only by the little river Enborne. Facing the bishop's two manors of Highclere and Burghclere[32] was Sandleford priory, named after the ford where the main road from Winchester to Oxford crossed the river. At this crossing, in 1218, the initial 67 building-plots were laid out. The prior of Sandleford prudently took up three of them, and from its situation the town was sometimes called *Nova Villa de Sandelford* and sometimes *Novus Burgus de Clere*. A chapel was built, as at Alresford, for the townspeople and a market charter[33] obtained. The account roll for 1217–18 from the two Clere manors had nothing urban. In the 1218–19 roll there is a bold heading *Novus Burgus* followed by the names of the 52 burgesses who held the 67 *placeae* at a shilling a year. One held five plots, two held three each, seven two each and forty-two people the unitary plot.[34]

As at Overton, the annual account rolls following the foundation year show

[28] 159384 m. 22r.

[29] 1217–18: 159274 m. 5d; 1223–4: 159278 m. 6.

[30] 1213–14: 159272 m. 7; 1217–18: 159274 m. 1; 1264–5: 159295 m. 2 *defectus redditus* and 3d. *defectus instauri*; 1376–7: 159384 m. 5d.

[31] 1210–11: 159270B m. 4; 1220–1: 159277 m. 3; see also note 6 *supra*.

[32] The 'burgh' element in the name derives not from a borough but from the prehistoric earthwork on Beacon Hill. In the early-thirteenth-century rolls the two Cleres appear as a single manor of Cleres. The bishop's palace was at Highclere: cf. plan in G. J. Copley, *An Archaeology of South-East England* (London 1958), fig. 19. Sandleford priory was founded *c.* 1200: *V.C.H. Berks.*, I, 362.

[33] P.R.O. C54/19 m. 5.

[34] 1218–19: 159275 m. 5d; 1219–20: 159276 m. 6; 1220–1: 159277 m. 1d; 1224–5: 159279; 1225–6: 159280 m. 9d; 1264–5: 159295 m. 7d.

the steady arrival of newcomers to take up vacant plots. In 1219–20 two such paid 9d. for their new plot and the accountant noted that they would pay the full shilling in future years. More appear in the rental for 1220–1 and by 1264–5 over seventy burgage rents were paid. In 1224–5 a ditch 1,650 yards long was dug round the town at the bishop's expense and in 1225–6 the bishop had a house of his own built in the town. An account for plastering Sandleford chapel in 1218–19 suggests that the bishop was responsible for the church, the forerunner of the present parish church, which has no medieval features in it.[35]

Apart from the documentary evidence, the late arrival of Newtown on the settlement landscape is attested by another feature, its parochial geography. This feature is important, for elsewhere, when documentary evidence is less ample than for the Winchester estates, it can be the principal indication of a late settlement. As a geographical unit, the parish of Newtown has two significant characteristics: the parish is unusually small, and it is surrounded on all three sides by another parish, giving it a 'bitten out' look. The 475 acres of Newtown must once have formed part of Burghclere which surrounds it on the east and south with a tiny detached portion trapped on the west flank of Newtown; on the north is the county boundary. The small parish area and the bitten-out shape can be seen at many other planted medieval towns, for example at New Windsor, Alnmouth, Boroughbridge, Henley in Arden, Hedon and New Malton. In such cases it was usual for the mother parish to cling tenaciously to its rights and either to deny the new town a church or to give it a quite subordinate status.[35] Such was the position of the churches in the planted towns like Market Harborough and Kingston upon Hull. When at Stratford on Avon the mayor and corporation make their annual pilgrimage to Shakespeare's tomb in the parish church the long progress is a annual reminder of the double settlement: the village of Old Stratford by the church and the new town of Stratford borough, planted by a bishop of Worcester with a neat rectilinear grid focused on the market-place and bridge—but with no church. At Royston, Herts., until an Act of 1540 the late arrival of the town marked by the fact that the town lay in no fewer than five parishes and—as the preamble to the Act[36] stated—'whereof never a Parisshe churche of them is within twoo myles . . . and somme of them be three myles'.

At Downton and Overton there was no new church: the borough continued to use the village church, although the massive architecture of Downton church suggests that it might have been enlarged when the borough was created. At New Alresford and Newtown, as we have seen, there was a new church but the bitten out shape of the new parish bears dumb witness to the late arrival.

The exact site of the burgage plots of Newtown can only be conjectured. This is not because the town was an early failure like Skinburness (Cumberland) or Warenmouth (Northumberland). The bishop's income from Newtown continued to rise through the thirteenth century. In 1257-8 it was £6 15s. 9d. and 1283-4 it was paying a *redditus assisus* of between £7 5s. and £7 8s. a year.[37] The

---

[35] New Alresford chapel was dependent until 1850.

[36] 32 Henry VIII cap. 34.

[37] 1257–8: 159293 m. 24; 1283–4: 159309 m. 9; similar sums a century later (1376–7): 159384 m.

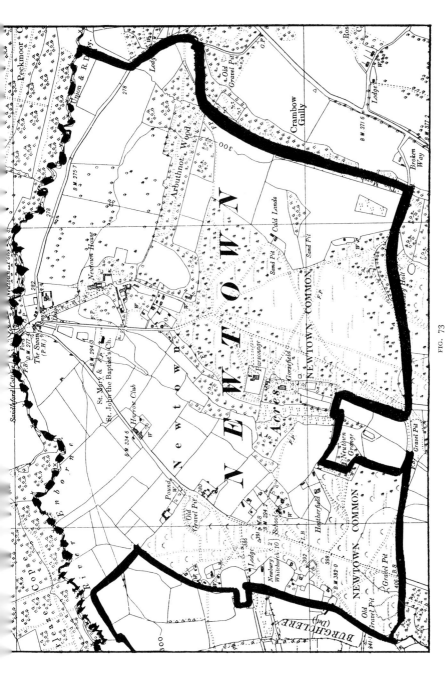

FIG. 73

NEWTOWN IN BURGHCLERE, HANTS. (pp. 57 ff.)

The dotted line is the county boundary; the thick line outlines the small parish of Newtown, cut from Burghclere.
The main street of the borough was where the drive from the ford to Newtown House now is. (Sc. 6 in. = 1 mile)

are no poll-tax returns of 1377–81 extant for Hampshire from which the population after the Black Death could be ascertained, but the rents paid both before
and after the plagues were just over eight pounds. In the Hearth Tax of 1674
Newtown had 64 separate houses and 95 hearths,[38] but to-day the church stands
alone; Newtown House is in its park; by the ford there is an inn and three cottages,
and on the southern edge of the park a group of six houses (FIG. 73). There is no
sign of a market-place or of a grid of streets. The local tradition is that the main
road was diverted from its old course when Newtown House was built, and the old
roadway is certainly visible above the post office. No significant earthworks of a
burgage character have been observed, and there is obviously a great need for
archaeological excavation. As an economic phenomenon the disappearance of a
prosperous market town seems unlikely—although there is always Milton Abbas
to show that history is stranger than fiction—and it may be conjectured that it
was due to the rivalry of Newbury two miles to the north. It will also be noted that
the line of turnpike, the modern main road from Whitchurch to Newbury,
avoided Burghclere and kept west of both the borough site of Newtown and the
church before dropping to the Sandleford bridge. This is the very reverse of the
deliberate diversions of medieval roads into such new towns as Boroughbridge
and Baldock, and its aloof indifference to Newtown indicates that there was
nothing there to interest even a commercial traveller on the turnpike.

VI

Hindon, the fifth of the bishops' plantations, has all the geographical characteristics of the planted town. A few years before the Reform Act the Wiltshire
historian Hoare noted three facts about the town,[39] although he failed to draw the
conclusion from them that the town had been planted: 'Hindon has one long
street'; 'the town does not comprehend above 200 acres of land'; 'the town church
is still parochially dependent on East Knoyle where most of the people of Hindon
are married'.

It was in the fields of East (or Bishop's) Knoyle that Hindon was planted.
The name of the town was taken from a hill, *higna dun*, in the eastern part of
Knoyle parish.[40] The road from Salisbury to Wincanton and Taunton passed over
this hill, and the bishops' route from Winchester to their Taunton estates may well
have lain this way also. Like Newtown in Burghclere, Hindon was planted well
away from its mother village, being 2½ miles from Knoyle.

In the account roll for 1218–19 the entries for Knoyle manor are of the usual
rural type. In 1219–20 there is no explicit *burgus* rental, but the reeve of Knoyle
claimed a rebate (*defectus*) of 6s. 11¾d. for a croft and a virgate and a half 'taken
into the borough and the demesne'. The proprietors, it will be noted, were Adam
and Roger de Hinedon. In the account for 1220–1 there is the heading *Burgus*

[38] P.R.O. E179/176/565 mm. 19-20. Burghclere had 192 hearths. Since this paper was written a
plan of Newtown in 1606, before its depopulation, has been found among the estate plans in Corpus
Christi College, Oxford; a copy is now in *B.M.*, Maps 188.e.2.

[39] R. C. Hoare, *Modern Wiltshire*, I (London, 1822), 181-3.

[40] *The Place-Names of Wiltshire* (English Place-Name Society, XVI, Cambridge, 1939), p. 191.

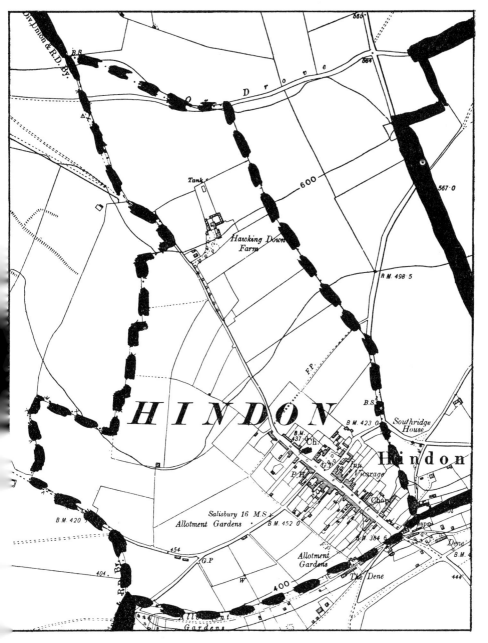

FIG. 74

HINDON, WILTS. (pp. 60 ff.)

...e dotted line marks the bounds of the small parish, cut from East Knoyle. The footpath behind the houses on the W. side of High Street marks the ends of the burgage plots. (Sc. 6 in. = 1 mile)

Hinedon and rents totalling £2 9s. 8d. from it. The borough progressed: in 1224–5 six newcomers were pledged to begin paying the sixpence rents for their plots in the next financial year, the old rents totalling £4 3s.; in 1225–6–7 the total was £4 10s., in 1231–2 £5 16s. 6d. and in 1244–5 £6 4s. 9d.[41] In the middle of the thirteenth century there were just over 150 houses in the town, a few more than at the time of the disfranchisement of the borough in 1832. In the later middle ages the town was moderately prosperous. In 1334 it was assessed at 28s. 9d., not a large sum compared with nearby Wiltshire villages; in 1377 it mustered only 77 poll-tax payers, but from 1378 it elected members to Parliament.[42]

Hindon, disfranchised and lying off the modern main road, would not immediately strike the visitor as a former borough. It still has its long broad street and the houses which front upon it have the characteristic long narrow burgage plots for their gardens, each ending at a half-abandoned back lane by which the burgesses once obtained access to their fields. The parish comprises 212 acres, about half the size of Newtown in Burghclere, and its bounds clearly indicate that it, too, has been cut out from a larger mother-parish. There is no apparent medieval building in the town; the fine stone houses are very uniform and have the appearance of a squire's rebuilding. Some have entrances for coaches and interior yards reflecting the days when Hoare commented that the main street was lined with numerous public-houses. These have vanished with the franchise.

One dated archaeological feature may one day be explored, for the Hindon accounts include one of the few references to any capital expenditure in a new town by the bishops.[43] In 1220–1 the bishop paid for the making of a well 14 fathoms deep (21s.) and for a rope and an iron-bound bucket (1s.). Like Truth it may one day be found at the bottom of the well.

VII

Newtown, Isle of Wight, the last of the Winchester plantations, was founded in 1256. Although shrunk to a town hall and half a dozen houses, it has its grid of streets and burgage plots well fossilized. Once it prospered as a Solent port and indeed so attracted Edward I that he covetously took it from the bishops for himself. The sole Winchester possession in the island was the large manor of Calbourne stretching from the downs northward to the Solent creeks and the marshy and heathy land west of Parkhurst Forest. The bishop had a residence here, built about 1180. This was not in Calbourne village but on the east of the parish at Swainston (441878) and from this house the whole manor was often called not Calbourne but Swainston.[44] The manor took in about 13 square miles and had been part of the endowment of the church at Winchester since 826.

In the account roll of 1253–4 Swainston appears as a rural manor but in the next year's roll there is a short account for expenses in work at a house 'in the new

---

[41] 1219–20: 159276 m. 8; 1220–1: 159277 m. 11; 1224–5: 159279 mm. 2 and 2d; 1225–6: 159280 m. 4d; 1231–2: 159282 m. 6d; 1244–5: 159287 m. 20d.

[42] 1334: P.R.O. E179/196/10; 1377: E179/196/35.

[43] 159277 m. 11: 'in quodam puteo facto de xiiij teisis, xxi s; in corda et buketto cum ferro ligato xij d. Summa xxii s.'

[44] *V.C.H. Hampshire*, v (1912), 265.

borough of Francheville' and in 1256 a charter was issued by Aymer, bishop-elect, to 'the borough of Swainston'. In the account roll for 1256–7 the town's arrival

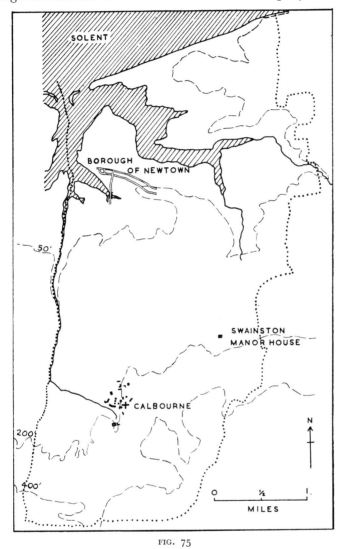

FIG. 75

CALBOURNE PARISH, I.o.W. (pp. 62 ff.)

he borough of Newtown (or Francheville) was planted at the edge of a Solent creek on the NW. tip of the parish. The bishop's manor house was at Swainston, adjoining Parkhurst forest.

marked by the bold heading 'Francheville'. The royal confirmations of this arter in 1285 and 1318 make it clear that 'La Neuton', Francheville and vainston borough were all the same place.[45]

[45] 1254-5: 159296 m. 5d; 1256-7: 159292 m. 9d; charter, *Calendar of Charter Rolls*, II (London, 06), 324; P.R.O. E372/147 m. 40.

The reeves' accounts also show the claim for a rebate on the lost agricultural rents from the land on which the burgesses were living. In 1254–5 the reeve was exonerated from 20s. rent 'terrae de Aretleya tractae in burgum'. Two of the three tenants mentioned by name continued to hold their old land with *placeae* adjoining, so that the haven-side town seems to have been planted around them.

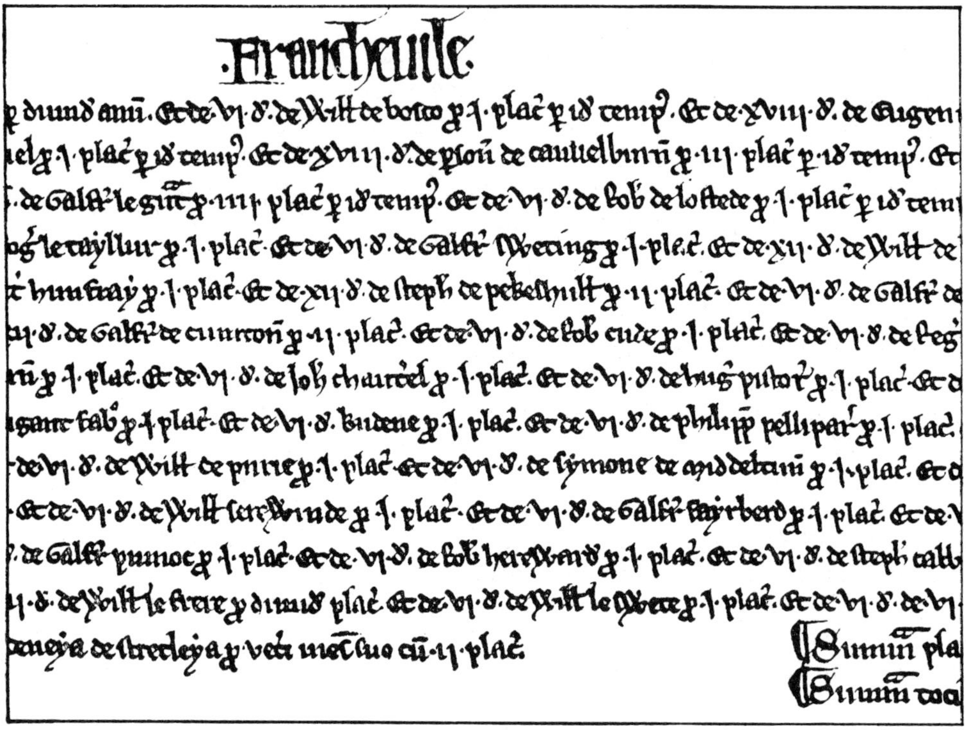

FIG. 76

NEWTOWN *alias* FRANCHEVILLE, I.o.W.

Part of the reeve's account-roll for Michaelmas 1257, with the first half-year's rents for the new burgage plots. Sixpence was paid for a single plot (*placea*), and some burgesses had (cp. ll. 3-4) more than one plot. The first line reads: '. . . per dimidium annum. Et de vi d. de Willelmo de bosco pro i placea per idem tempus. Et. de xviii d. de Eugen(ia de Aretleya pro iii placeis).' The heading is 'Franchevile' (*sic*).

Eugenia de Aretley also rented three of the new burgage plots and Richard de Aretley took up another.[46]

The bishop's rent from each of the initial 73 plots was 1s. a year, but the first account was for only 6d., the foundation coming half way through the financial year. The holdings were not equal: one burgess rented five *placeae*, another four, two took three each, six took up a double plot, 45 the standard plot, and two

[46] 1254–5: 159296 m. 5; 1256–7: 159292 m. 9d.

divided a plot between them. In 1297-8 there were 66 persons occupying 70 burgages.[47] The account rolls, as long as the bishop still held the town, continued to claim for the rebate of the Aretley lands and the *Instaurum* section for the loss of the 40 eggs which had formerly been part of the rent due from this fraction of the bishop's tenantry in Calbourne.[47]

The decay of Newtown may go back as far as the damage in the French raids of the late fourteenth century,[48] but a more enduring obstacle to prosperity was the competition of Yarmouth and Southampton as ports, and also the depopulation of the rural hinterland in the island itself as a result of the great conversions from arable to pasture which brought the Isle of Wight the distinction of England's first anti-enclosure Act[49] in 1488. Despite a fresh charter by Elizabeth I the seventeenth-century town was somnolent. In the Hearth Tax of 1674 only eleven houses were recorded,[50] and twelve in the manuscript plan of 1768 and the manuscript drawings for the first edition of the O.S. map. The *jeu d'esprit* of the neat little William-and-Mary town hall (now owned by the National Trust) tells us more about the economics of a rotten borough than of the silted haven and grassy wharves at the west end of the shadow grid of streets (PL. 4 ; FIG. 77).

In 1284, when bishop Pontiserra was forced to turn all his estates over to Edward I, the town was a much more attractive asset, for even when the bishop paid a fine of £2,000 to receive back his lands, the king clung to Newtown. For ten days in October 1285 Edward stayed in the bishop's manor house at Swainston and, having inspected his new property, issued on the last day of the visit a charter confirming the burgesses in their privileges.[51]

Rural Calbourne at this time had 132 tenants, and the extent of 1297-8, with its long list of demesne services, describes a very different world from that of the burgesses.[52] After reading it, the full significance of the borough name Francheville appears. The new town was the Free Town like the bastide of Villefranche de Queyran which Edward founded in Gascony in 1281. Not for the burgesses the obligation to plough and reap; not for them the obligations of serviture; not for them the cash payments which represented the partial commutation of labour services on the lord's demesne. The greater legal, social and economic freedom of those who took up burgage plots to build upon was the magnet by which populations were recruited. It was an environment which suited and encouraged the bourgeois virtues. It was such an environment that Edward I

---

[47] 1297-8: British Museum, Add. Mss. 6166, f.260; in 1303 the burgesses paid a fee farm of £3 10s. in lieu of rent: P.R.O. C145/62/1.

[48] *Calendar of Inquisitions, Miscellaneous*, IV (London, 1957), 128 and 206.

[49] M. W. Beresford, *The Lost Villages of England* (London, 1954), pp. 103-4 and 147, citing 4 Henry VII cap. 6 and P.R.O. SP12/7/58-9, a survey of 1559.

[50] P.R.O. E179/176/565 m. 1; six of these houses were relieved of tax by their poverty. Calbourne had a total of 138 hearths in the non-burghal area.

[51] Charter: see note 45 *supra*. The forced sale is documented in *Calendar of Charter Rolls*, 1 (1903), 274; *Register of Bishop Pontisserra of Winchester* (Canterbury and York Soc.), 1 (London, 1915), 282 and II (1924), 411, 421, 423, 434, and 671-5; also in British Museum, Harleian Rolls CC21.

[52] Two extents survive: that in British Museum, Add. Mss. 6166 f. 233 sqq. is probably of 1297-8; P.R.O. C145/62/1 is from 1303. They differ in detail but agree on 288 acres of cultivated demesne and on 69 or 70 villeins; in addition there were between 17 and 26 cottars. The labour services and their money equivalent are given in considerable detail. There was pasture of 473 acres feeding 106 kine and 600 sheep.

wished to re-create at Berwick-on-Tweed when he summoned his colloquium of town-planners in 1296. They were to lay out a town 'to the greatest profit of Ourselves and of Merchants'.[53]

It is all the more regrettable that the Winchester documents afford so little information about the recruits who peopled the bishops' six new towns. Here and there the documents mention their occupations: the weavers and fullers, bakers and millers have been noted already. Occasionally one of the bishop's own villeins, like Richard of Waltham, pays to be allowed to dwell in the bishop's borough: but one must suppose from analogous evidence elsewhere that the bishops combined a conservative and a liberal attitude. There was a liberal welcoming hand for those who came from old-established towns with skills already sharpened or in flight from the demesne of other seigneurs.[54] There was a firm conservative and restraining hand on those from the bishop's own demesnes: with a cash payment 'ut audeat remanere in foro' or 'ne placitent apud manerium'.

This combination of old-fashioned demesne farming and new-fashioned free townsmen may seem a paradox, but it was widely found. It may seem surprising that the redemptive influence of the new towns as a solvent of manorialism lagged so far behind the economic influence of the towns as a stimulus to manorial production. One might have supposed that Downton *manerium* would have been full of the most seditious peasant revolts when the villeins looked over the river to the *novum forum*, or that demesne services here would have been amongst the first to be commuted into cash payments. As Miss Levett showed nearly fifty years ago, this was just not so.

'Know all men'—began the bishop's charter[55] to Newtown, Isle of Wight —'that we have given to our burgesses of the borough which is called Franchville all the liberties and free customs which our burgesses of Taunton, Witney, Alresford and Farnham have.'

'All men' might indeed have known, and among them the villeins of Calbourne, but for them the boundary between freedom and unfreedom was a matter of birth, favour or money and its expression was the little stream which marked the borough bounds.

It would be interesting to see the plan of 1636 mentioned by A. H. Estcourt[56]

[53] F. Palgrave, *Parliamentary Writs*, 1 (London, 1827), 49.

[54] The Witney charters of 1210-1 were probably for villeins living in the new borough: 159270B m. 11; also in 1210-11 at Downton 'ij s. de Odone . . . ut possit remanere in foro': *ibid.*, m. 2d; at Fareham, 1211-13: 'iiij s. de Ivone pro burgagio habendo': 159271 m. 4, *purchasia*; Downton in the same year, 'de Helya Bel ut audeat remanere in foro': *ibid.*, m. 5; Fareham, 1213-14: 'j s. de Eva filia Gilberti pro burgagio habendo': 159272 m. 3d, *purchasia*; Alresford, 1213-14, 'de xx s. ne placitent apud manerium': 159272 m. 3d; Overton, 1218-19, 'de dimidia marca de Ricardo de Waltham pro fine vilenagii et pro burgagio habendo': 159275 m. 3d; Newtown, 1225-6, 'xij d. pro manumissione': 159280; 1244-5, Overton, permission to dwell in borough: 159280 m. 13d; cp. H. S. Bennett, *Life on the English Manor* (Cambridge, 1937), pp. 298-305.
At Downton in 1376-7 nearly all the corn stacking and carrying and more than half the hoeing, harrowing, manure carting, sheepwashing, sheepshearing, and haymaking were done by direct villein labour; at Burghclere a quarter of the demesne ploughing was similarly uncommuted: A. E. Levett and A. Ballard, *The Black Death* (Oxford Studies in Social and Legal History, v, Oxford, 1916), pp. 72-141.

[55] Charter: see note 45 *supra*.

[56] Plan by James Mallett, 1768, reproduced in A. H. Estcourt, 'The Ancient Borough of Newtown,' *Proc. Hants. Field Club*, 11 (1890-3), 89-109; there is a plan of 1793 in P.R.O. MR/489, formerly WO78/1648.

in 1893. Estcourt reproduced another plan of 1768 from which FIG. 77 is redrawn. It shows burgage plots, mostly empty of houses, arrayed along both sides of High Street and on the north side of Gold Street, which was the broader of the two. Broad Street begins at the stone bridge over the creek which carried the road to Calbourne and Swainston and there the town hall stands. The plan indicates the ruins of St. Mary's chapel and twelve buildings which may then have been

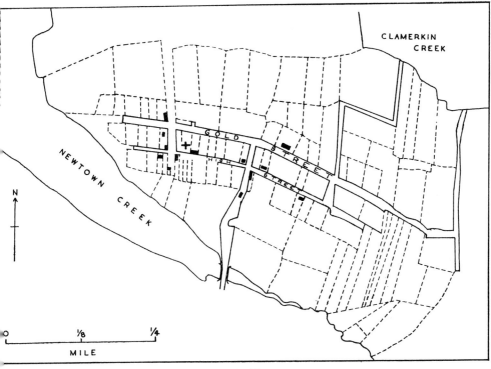

FIG. 77

NEWTOWN, I.o.W.

A plan of 1768, indicating buildings then standing; also the abandoned burgage plots along the streets and some divisions of common fields and marsh. The road over the bridge led to Calbourne. Compare PL.   and FIG. 75

Crown Copyright Reserved

inhabited. At least 42 vacant plots appear, together with the vestiges of holdings in a common field. To the north of the town was a large marsh with salterns, probably the chief employment of the townspeople of that day outside election times.

The provision of a regular and organized trading venue within the borough of Newtown was made more specific by a second charter, this time from the king himself, securing a weekly Wednesday market and an annual fair at St. Mary Magdalen tide. As Alresford began as 'Alresford Forum', so the economic life of Newtown began with its charter for markets and fairs. The season chosen for the annual fair was that of the patronal festival of the new church of St. Mary, which the bishop built soon after 1256 as a chapel-of-ease to Calbourne, where he was patron. This church was in ruins by 1663, but was rebuilt in 1836 by the lay patron,[57] possibly as a gesture of thankoffering for the Corporation's survival in the municipal reforms of 1835.

In 1831 the population was 68 and there were only 39 qualified electors. Three families controlled the votes. In 1835 the *Report on Municipal Corporations* commented:[58]

> 'The houses are merely cottages, of which there are about 14. The town has at some time been considerable as the names of the streets, the sites of which are still known, show . . . There is not an inhabitant capable of exercising any municipal function; there are probably not sufficient inhabitants of intelligence to form a court-leet jury.'

The device on the thirteenth-century seal of the borough had a ship and a leopard: but Francheville's ship had ceased to sail and the leopard no longer leaped. It was a far cry from the days when the tax collectors of 1334 assessed the manor and town at nearly twice the sum contributed by Newport, the capital of the island.[59]

VIII

The greater liberty of action enjoyed by a burgess compared with a villein finds visual expression in the very different form of the entries on the bishops' account rolls for *manerium* and *burgus*. The *burgus* entry is short, often with no more than half a dozen entries: the rents, the arrears, the tolls from the market and fair and finally the profits of justices, the *perquisita curiae*. On the other hand it was not uncommon in the middle of the thirteenth century for the reeve's account for a single manor to cover from four to six feet of closely written parchment, eighteen inches wide. The manorial reeves of Old Alresford, Downton, Knoyle, Overton, Burghclere and Calbourne had to account for rents collected; for demesne services commuted; for produce gathered; for goods transported to market or taken to the bishops' palaces; the wages and expenses of this production; and the changes in the stock of farm equipment, farm animals and grain. The *purchasia curiae*, later entered as *fines et maritagia*, recorded the many payments which arose from the dependent status of the manorial villeins, ranging from entry fines on the inheritance of land to the fine paid for marriage of a villein woman. The heriots, payable on death, were another expression of the same dependence, as were the *annuale recognitiones*, the payments for permission to remain away from the manor as long as the lord bishop would allow. In the short *burgus* entries four categories reflect the economic fortunes of the venture as the years passed: the *redditus assisus* together with the *incrementa* showed how the burgage plots were being taken up the market tolls how successful the venture had been in attracting local dealer

---

[57] This paragraph is based on *V.C.H. Hants.*, v (1912), 265-8.

[58] 1831: *id.*, p. 266; 1835: *1st Report on Municipal Corporations* (1835), Appendix II, pp. 791-6. The smaller and less successful bastides, which once had the Parliamentary franchise, lent themselves easily to electoral corruption; among classic rotten boroughs were the bastides of Boroughbridge and Grampound.

[59] P.R.O. E179/173/6 and 23.

and the surrounding countryside; the fair dues how successful in attracting the wider custom necessary to support the annual congregation; the perquisites of the courts perhaps show less connexion with economic activity, for litigious or criminal townspeople do not necessarily vary in number with economic progress, but large increases in the sums under this head are at least an indication that grass is not yet growing in the streets and market-place.

Apart from the account rolls, the other principal evidence for the burgesses' privileges comes from the survival of charters in which the bishops set down in writing the liberties which they wished their new foundations to enjoy. Not all six towns have surviving charters, although copies may be concealed in the unexamined account rolls of the later centuries. That of Newton *alias* Francheville is known from its confirmation by Edward I in 1285. In 1256 bishop de Valence had taken for a yardstick—as the preamble quoted above shows—the privileges already enjoyed by his established boroughs, and it is interesting to see that New Alresford, then less than sixty years old, was one of the four taken as model alongside the oldest of them all, Taunton. The Taunton charter of 1135-9 is formal and curt, so that to elucidate these privileges one must turn to the charter of 1248 where bishop William de Ralegh put down in writing[60] for the burgesses of Farnham 'all the liberties and free customs hereunder written as they were formerly wont to have'.

What were the privileges which could attract men from other parts of England to come and settle on empty building plots alongside a canal pond and at the edge of a Solent creek? Firstly, the burgesses were to have their own court before their own bailiffs and not to be liable to attend the bishop's court at the village manor house. The court would thus be officered by men elected by the burgesses, understanding commercial practice and sympathetic to the interest of the town. All summonses and distraints were to be made by these officers and not by the manor's. They were to control the price and standard of bread and beer:

> 'to take bread at the baker's house and weigh it and test it, and taste beer in the borough . . . and to have the amercements for beer and bread unless the baker be condemned to the pillory or the brewer to the tumbrel, which punishments are reserved to the bishops'.[61]

The town was to have a yearly fair 'full and without any diminution'. The burgesses were to have 'all the toll which in any manner can arise within their district', although the accounts of Newtown seem to show the bishop receiving the market and fair tolls. The burgesses of Farnham had contracted to make a single annual payment of £12 (fee farm).[62] Such a fixed contractual payment in lieu of rents and tolls marks one more stage in the lord's retreat from a direct share of the risks, headaches and profits of decision-making. It put the bishop into the economic role of a pure rent-collector. The risks, like the profits, had passed to the burgesses, or commercial losses, if they came, did not affect the obligation to pay the contractual sum. Although the Farnham charter permits the fee farm, it does not

---

[60] E. Robo, *op. cit.* in note 5 *supra*.
[61] *V.C.H. Hants.*, II (1900), 285.
[62] *Ibid.*

seem from the Francheville or Alresford accounts that the bishop made such an arrangement in all his towns.

IX

The thirteenth-century documentation for the six towns is good and, indeed superior to that for many old-established towns. Yet it leaves many important questions unanswered. Of municipal records these tiny municipalities have preserved very little. There seem to be none for Hindon and the earliest noted for Downton date from 1660. But of their status as a borough in the later middle age there can be doubt. Downton was reckoned a borough for taxation purpose eight times between 1296 and 1336; it was summoned to the Parliament of 1275 it was reckoned a borough in the *Nomina Villarum* of 1316; it sent representative to 22 Parliaments between 1298 and 1377 and to 16 between 1377 and 1449 Hindon was summoned for the first time in 1378 and on eleven further occasion before 1449. At the Reform Act these petty boroughs went the same way as Old Sarum and Francheville.[63]

The arrival of a borough also augmented the number of communities who were separately represented by their own juries whenever the itinerant judge visited the shire, the countryside at large being represented by a jury for each Hundred. Thus the Assize Roll of 1235 has a separate heading for Alresford Burgus, and it was similarly distinguished at the assizes of 1249 and 1256.[64] When the records of lay taxation begin to be continuous and full at the end of the thirteenth century the distinct status of the new towns can also be seen in their assessment separately at the high rate of one-tenth of the burgesses' movable property, the unenviable distinction afforded to medieval English boroughs.[65]

The names in these tax lists afford a few suggestions of the origin of those who had peopled a town in the first generation of its life, but the evidence of this kind scanty, as also is that of the occupational and social structure. Nor do we know anything yet about the unauthorized flight of Winchester villeins to the competing *bastides* of other seigneurs. No account of the bishops' plantations makes sense unless it is set in the context of an economy expanding at a rate fast enough to permit the successful establishment not only of these six towns but of many other —and these in the interstices of a region where there were very many successful and long-established urban communities. It says a great deal both for the expansion of agricultural production and of population that all these towns could be peopled and their populace kept busy; and at the very same time that the old established towns were also expanding their house- and shop-room. Indeed, the expansion did not stop at the frontiers of England, for the same period saw the colonization of the great empty spaces on the eastern frontier of Europe from the Baltic to the Danube and the multiplication of towns in old-settled parts of Europe like southern Germany and Gascony. In the hinterland of Winchester the

---

[63] M. G. Rathbone, ed., *List of Wilts. Borough Records* (Wilts. Archaeol. and Nat. Hist. Soc., Record Branch, v, Devizes, 1951), pp. vii-xiii and 21-3.

[64] P.R.O. JI/1/775 m. 9; 776 m. 38; 778 mm. 53 and 64.

[65] J. F. Willard, *Parliamentary Taxes on Personal Property* (Cambridge, Mass., 1934), pp. 9-10.

same economic forces produced Yarmouth and Newport (I.o.W.), Portsmouth, Poole, Lymington, Beaulieu and Haslemere, as well as the abortive *bastides* of Newton in Purbeck[66] and Wardour in Sidlesham, near Chichester.[67] There were

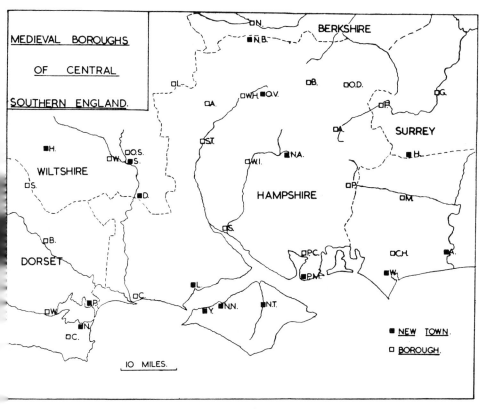

FIG. 78

MEDIEVAL BOROUGHS OF CENTRAL SOUTHERN ENGLAND

Key (planted towns in italics): BERKSHIRE: N. Newbury. DORSET: B. Blandford; C. Corfe; N. *Newton in Purbeck*; P. *Poole*; S. Shaftesbury; W. Wareham. HAMPSHIRE: A. Alton; A. Andover; B. Basingstoke; C. Christchurch; L. *Lymington*; N.B. *Newtown in Burghclere*; N.A. *New Alresford*; OD. Odiham; V. *Overton*; P. Petersfield; PC. Portchester; PM. *Portsmouth*; S. Southampton; ST. *Stockbridge*; WH. Whitchurch; WI. Winchester. ISLE OF WIGHT: NN. *Newtown*; NT. *Newport*; Y. *Yarmouth*. SURREY: F. Farnham; G. Guildford; H. *Haslemere*. SUSSEX: A. *Arundel*; CH. Chichester; M. Midhurst; S. *Wardour in Sidlesham*. WILTSHIRE: D. *Downton*; H. *Hindon*; L. Ludgershall; O.S. Old Sarum; S. *New Salisbury*; W. Wilton.
Corrigendum: Stockbridge, Hants., should have a black square.

so old-established commercial centres at such boroughs as Corfe, Wareham, Blandford, Shaftesbury, Wilton, Ludgershall, Andover, Winchester, Southampton, Christchurch, Chichester, Basingstoke and Guildford. It was among this formidable competitive array that the bishops of Winchester projected their new

[66] Beresford and St. Joseph, *op. cit.* in note 1, pp. 224-6.
[67] *Sussex Record Soc.*, XLVI (1942–3), 340 (1262–7).

towns.[68] There seems to have been room at the top, room at the middle and room at the bottom.[69]

The impact of this urban expansion on the rural hinterland is difficult to measure. How much must one attribute to the arrival of a new local market and how much to the general expansion of population, production and trade in the region? It would also be satisfying to have more information about the engineering of these six projects. Did they spring from a mind like that of bishop Peter des Roches (1204–38), who was born in France, soldiered under Richard I, that royal *bastidor*, fought for the Pope among the towns of Italy, visited Spain and went on crusade,[70] or from that of some lesser official in the episcopal household? Were the towns imitative of work in other dioceses like Salisbury's Devizes or Chichester's Wardour? Did they copy royal plantations like Liverpool and Portsmouth? Were they the child of desperate finances and a search for cash such as seems to have preoccupied bishop de Valence[71] (1251–60)?

Finally, the cloud of ignorance rests on their physical equipment. The documentary testimony —a market-house, some stalls, an oven, a weir, a canal, a fulling mill, some churches, a boulting house, a well, a fourteen-fathom rope and an iron bucket—is rather meagre for six towns and half a century. Here in the enquiry, History and Archaeology may join hands. The householders of New Alresford, Overton, Downton and Hindon may not take kindly to a threat of invasion by spade and trowel, however great their pride in their old municipal institutions. But History has kindly arranged for the decay of the two Newtowns, of Wardour in Sidlesham and of Newton in Purbeck. All one needs is a project for a radar beacon and an atomic pile—and the Inspectorate of Ancient Monuments can begin its emergency dig. In the more realistic meanwhile all disturbances of the soil at the other *bastides* and at the bishop's towns of Witney and Bishop's Waltham would be worth watching closely.

As in all the best intellectual relay races the baton must now be handed on. This particular race is run backwards in time,[72] and moves towards Saxon Oxford, Wareham and Wallingford, for the prospect if one runs forward is meagre. After the foundation of Bala in 1310 there is only Queenborough in Kent in 1363 to keep us going until Falmouth in 1613. It is a long lap. The silence is eloquent, and what it says or seems to say is this: on the one side of the watershed, which must be placed near 1330, is an environment of economic expansion and on the other a long contraction in which the economy was more than sated with towns.

[68] Newtown was flanked by the *bastides* of Yarmouth (founded *c.* 1170) and Newport (1177–84). Across the Solent were New Lymington (*c.* 1150) and Portsmouth (1194). By 1674, when Newtown had 25 hearths, Newport had 1,049 and Yarmouth 124: P.R.O. E179/176/565 m. 1.

[69] At the bottom, see the enterprising lord of Cogges (Oxon.) opposite Witney, who cut up his demesne for building-plots in 1212–13: *Sir Christopher Hatton's Book of Seals*, ed. L. C. Loyd and D. M. Stenton (Oxford, 1950), p. 76, from B.M. Harleian Charters 45/D18; in 1215 the abbot of Eynsham laid out a new borough north of Eynsham village: plan in A. L. Poole, ed., *Medieval England* (Oxford, 1958), 1, 63.

[70] E. Robo, *op. cit.* in note 5, pp. 70-82.

[71] *Ibid.*, pp. 82-91.

[72] A. Ballard, *British Borough Charters* (Cambridge, 1913), p. xci: 'from the earliest times we have to account for boroughs which were artificially created and were not village communities which had acquired a burghal status'.

ven in recovery the Tudor and Stuart economies were well enough stocked with
wns not to feel the need to found any more within England. Only with the
anoverian watering-places and factory-towns do we see Englishmen turning
:ain seriously to the business of laying out new towns in this country.

APPENDIX I

LANDS OF THE BISHOP OF WINCHESTER, 1224

The places are those which head separate accounts in the rolls. In some the manor
:luded adjacent hamlets or villages. The manor of Taunton included 14 villages.
id references locate those places which lie within the bounds of FIG. 69.

rkshire: Brightwell, Harwell, Ilsley, Wargrave, West Woodhay 390630.
ckinghamshire: Ivinghoe, West Wycombe.
oucestershire: Moreton.
ampshire: Ashford 550622, Ashmansworth 415575, Alresford 590337, Beauworth
575260, Bishopstoke 465194, Bitterne 452130, Burghclere 470580, Calbourne
425865, Cheriton 582285, Crawley 425350, Ecchinswell 500600, Fareham
575060, Fawley 458035, Freefolk 490490, Hambledon 646150, Highclere 445588,
East Meon 680220, West Meon 640240, Merdon 420264, Overton 515500,
Ower 472019, Privett 675270, Bishop's Sutton 610330, Twyford 480250, Bishop's
Waltham 555175, North Waltham 562462, Wield 630390, Winchester 480292.
fordshire: Adderbury, Witney.
rey: Farnham 840470, Southwark.
merset: Rimpton, Taunton.
'ltshire: Downton 182215, Ebbesborne Wake 992242, Fonthill Bishop 933330, East
Knoyle 882307.

The New Towns of Alresford, Downton, Hindon and Overton adjoined the
lages of the same name; Newtown in Burghclere was at 478637 and Newtown in
lbourne, I.o.W. at 422908.

APPENDIX II

MEDIEVAL BOROUGHS OF CENTRAL SOUTHERN ENGLAND

These lie within the bounds of FIG. 78. The year given is the earliest reference noted
a borough or burgesses. Domesday boroughs indicated by DB. Planted towns are in
.ics.

·set: Blandford Forum (1307), *Corfe* (by 1288), *Newton* in Purbeck (1286), *Poole*
(*c.* 1248, but probably founded *c.* 1170), Shaftesbury DB, Wareham DB.
mpshire: Alton (1295), Andover (1175), Basingstoke (1228), Christchurch DB,
Fareham (*c.* 1211-12), *New Alresford* (1200), *New Lymington* (*c.* 1150), *Newtown* in Burghclere (1218), *Newtown* in Calbourne, I.o.W.(1255), *Newport*,
I.o.W. (1174-84), Odiham (1204-7), *Overton* (1217-18), Petersfield (1183-97),
Portchester (?1177), *Portsmouth* (1194), Southampton DB, *Stockbridge* (*c.* 1200),
Whitchurch (?1199), Winchester DB, *Yarmouth,* I.o.W. (*c.* 1170).
rey: Farnham (1248), Guildford DB, *Haslemere* (*c.* 1221).
sex: *Arundel* DB, Chichester DB, Midhurst (1295), *Wardour* in Sidlesham (1262-7).
'tshire: *Downton* (*c.* 1208), *Hindon* (1219-20), Ludgershall (1306), *New Salisbury*
(*c.* 1225), Old Salisbury DB, Wilton DB.

APPENDIX III
PROGRESS OF THE NEW TOWNS
data from 1334 and 1377-9

	Assessed lay wealth in 1334[73]	Taxpayers in poll tax, 1377[74]
Old Alresford	445s.	no data
New Alresford	995s.	
Downton manor	700s.	106
Downton Borough	1,100s.	214
Overton[75]	1,090s.	no data
Burghclere	692s. 6d.	no data
Newtown	255s.	no data
East Knoyle	1,500s.	146
Hindon	287s. 6d.	77
Calbourne		22 (1379)
Newtown (Francheville)		196

APPENDIX IV
PROGRESS OF THE BISHOPS' NEW TOWNS
values in 1264-5, 1274-5 and 1375-6

	net rents £ s. d.			profits of justice £ s. d.			markets, fairs, stalls etc. £ s. d.		
ALRESFORD (founded 1200)									
1264-5	15	12	1	4	9	6	2	0	0
1274-5	16	11	0	3	7	10	2	14	3
1375-6	16	12	9	4	12	11	not stated		
DOWNTON (founded *c.* 1208)									
1264-5	6	1	7	2	7	10			
1274-5	6	1	11	3	0	0			
1375-6	6	6	2	4	0	0			
OVERTON (founded 1217-18)									
1264-5	8	1	11	4	12	2	18	4	
1274-5	8	3	11	1	17	0	19	2	
1375-6	8	4	8½	wanting			wanting		
NEWTOWN (founded 1218)									
1264-5	6	19	9	2	0				
1274-5	7	2	5	8	0				
1375-6	7	11	0	7	11				
HINDON (founded 1219-20)									
1264-5	6	4	1½	2	12	6	5	6	
1274-5	6	4	6½	1	7	6	7	4	
1375-6	6	10	4½	2	5	10	8	0	
NEWTOWN, I.O.W. (founded 1256)									
1264-5	2	2	4	8	0				
1274-5	2	9	0	7	0				
1375-6	alienated to king								

[73] Overton and the two Newtowns paid tax of 1/15th of their assessed wealth, the other boroughs at the higher rate of 1/10th. The manors paid at the 1/15th: Hants. data from P.R.O. E179/173/6 and Wilts. data from E179/196/10.

[74] Hants. data from E179/173/41; Wilts. data from E179/196/35. There are no surviving data Hants. in 1377; the 1379 figures are suspect.

[75] It would seem that by the early fourteenth century there had ceased to be a separate settle at Overton village near the church.

APPENDIX V

THE RURAL ORIGINS

	Alresford Manor	Downton Manor	Knoyle Manor	Clere Manor	Calbourne Manor	Overton Manor
wn acreage:[76]						
1208-9	565	831	453	869[77]	—	496
1264-5	386	677	387	383	259	344
1274-5	175	612	199[78]	276	322	317
eep at Michaelmas:						
1208	889	1,764	1,048	1,164[77]	—	775
1264	447	1,697	2,059	242	1,052	1,574
1274	863	1,371	3,128	864	649	2,345
hop's net money ncome, to nearest £						
1208-9	108	140	25	56[77]	—	43
1264-5	69	110	67	60	73	89
1274-5	112	161	100	96	141	149

The variations from year to year when only single years are examined are not ificant: the main interest lies in the level of agricultural production and the contrast 1 the figures in Appendix IV. See p. 195.

ACKNOWLEDGEMENTS

The author would like to thank Dr. J. K. S. St. Joseph for PLS. XV and XVI; Mr. R. E. Glasscock for 59 and for assistance in field-work at Newton and Hindon; Mr. M. J. Mortimore for FIGS. 70, 75 and Mr. D. Ward for FIG. 78; Dr. R. H. Hilton for the reference in note 69; Mr. R. B. Pugh for information t Downton; Mr. J. D. Jones and Father Hockey for information about Newtown, I.o.W. The field- and study of the documents have been assisted by a Leverhulme Research Award and by the Research 1 of the Dept. of Economics, The University of Leeds.

An unpublished paper by Mr. J. Titow shows that 'acre' in the Winchester accounts did not s bear an areal connotation; the reduction at Alresford in 1274-5 and at Overton in 1264-5 and 5 may be due to this practice.

In 1208-9 the two Cleres were undifferentiated: the later figures are for Burghclere only.

This is a minimal figure, the manuscript being too worn to read all the entries. The Calbourne nts are missing from the roll of 1208-9.

PLATE 4

NEWTOWN, ISLE OF WIGHT (pp. 62-8). Some of the High Street (centre) and all Gold Street (left) is grass-grown; the quay (centre) is silted up; the tree-lined hedges emphasize the lines of the old burgage plots. Compare Fig. 77 (p. 67). *(Crown Copyright Reserved)*

5

ISOLATED AND RUINED CHURCHES AS EVIDENCE

FOR POPULATION CONTRACTION

As a utilitarian building a medieval church was a kind of house. As God's house it was better built than any village house, and likely to be ornamented and decorated beyond even a manor house, but essentially it was a house for the parishioners, and its surround, the cemetery, was their everlasting resting place. In this utilitarian equation, church equals congregation ; it must follow then, that *more churches equals more population,* and also that *fewer churches equals fewer population.* These are the equations that make a study of the changing location and total number of churches relevant to medieval demography. The numerical relation between a single church and its congregation was so complex that nothing is to be gained by a study of the actual size of a given church at various dates, more than to say that a very considerable expansion in floor area presupposes some demographic expansion, and that a drastic curtailment of floor area — usually by pulling down or neglecting side-aisles — betokens some demographic contraction. The basic difficulty, in relating a church's size more precisely than this to its parish's population, is that the size of a church varied also with the wealth and social standing of the landowner who endowed it, and further — one would suppose — on the likelihood of his residence in the village ; while in other cases the popularity of a cult, the collegiate status of a church or even its primacy as a Minster could raise a village church in the architectural hierarchy without implying any large local population.

The connection between increasing population and an increased number of churches is a well-known one ; and well documented, since frontier disputes between the jurisdictions of old-established churches and newcomers were endemic, with rival claims for tithes

---

This essay is of a speculative kind, and raises general issues. Detailed evidence would be inappropriate in an essay of this kind. The material is new and is sequential to Maurice BERESFORD and John G. HURST, eds, *Deserted Medieval Villages : Studies,* London, 1971.

and oblations. In the absence or silence of estate documents the chronology of new church foundation provides a rough chronology of rural expansion, particularly at the margin.

The same demographic inferences can be made from the town churches, where new churches developed in the suburbs and extra churches were packed into the old-settled core of a town until parish areas became microscopic, reaching their smallest in the one-street parishes within the City of London. In the completely new towns, the English equivalent of the *bastides* of Gascony, it was not easy for townspeople to have a church of their own since the town area had been cut out of the fields of some existing parish : *nulle terre sans paroisse*, to adapt a phrase. A town with no church, or a town with a church subordinate to some extra-mural village parish church, is clearly a latecomer, and thus even when documents are lacking this junior status is *prima facie* evidence for a *ville neuve* or a *novus burgus*.

II

If a demographic expansion encouraged an increase in the number of new churches and a probable enlargement of the floor area of older churches, what were the fruits of a contrary movement, that is a stagnation or a contraction of population ? Here again, it is better to focus attention at the margin where contraction of settlement was total or near-total.

Its products were deserted villages, of which more than 2,300 are now known in England, and — even more numerous — shrunken villages. Of these historical casualties, some have as full a documentation as one could expect for any English village, although it will be appreciated that the disappearance of a community increases the risk that its documents will have disappeared also. For many others the documentation is slender but explicit. For many more the medieval documentation is slight or totally wanting, and it is in these cases that one must turn gratefully to the archaelogical or quasi-archaeological record of the church of the former community.

What is the range of this type of evidence ? at one extreme there is the church still standing but in isolation from any group of village houses. This is sometimes total isolation, sometimes a church located within the yard of a single farm, and more frequently a church standing in the grounds of a great aristocratic country house, still roofed and still in use not as a normal village parish church but as the private chapel of the house-owner and the mausoleum of his predecessors.

Then there is the ruined church. Like the still-used churches just described, the ruined church can be found in a variety of situations. It may occupy a corner of a field, a nook of parkland, or be incorporated incongruously into a farmhouse or a barn. It too may be found, long neglected, alongside a large country mansion.

Finally there is the church that has nothing left standing above ground. In some cases the memory of a former church has been preserved, so that the Ordnance Survey map has the characteristic words : *church, site of*. There are other churches, however, that have slipped completely from folk memory, so that one has the paradox of a parish name and parish boundaries on the map but without the building that gave rise to the parish. What undoubtedly preserved the memory of a former church, even when all building had decayed, was the fact that around it was the traditional burial place with the respect and superstition that went with the dead. Even when burials ceased, with the total disuse of the church, there were people in the district to carry for a generation or two a memory of ancestors buried there. Thus in Shakespeare's time it was thought profane that sheep and cattle should graze churchyards that had been abandoned for at least a century, and the stories of churches that had become sheepcotes helped to keep alive a strong popular opposition to depopulating enclosure.

After the total decay of a church the grass-grown churchyard was not difficult to incorporate into a field, and the boundary ditch that marked the perimeter of the consecrated area is sometimes all that remains to identify the site ; in long-deserted sites, and particularly on light soils, there is no characteristic difference of ground levels that elsewhere marks out the churchyard area, caused by centuries of successive burials and the displacement of earth thereby.

The most complete destruction, both of wall-footings and of churchyard levels, comes where arable cultivation has taken place. Although the Tudor pamphleteer made much of the voracious, wolf-like sheep that ate up the village and its church on enclosure, the modern archaeologist embraces animal husbandry as his friend and grass pasture as a preserving shroud : his real enemy is now the cereal crop, and the ploughing-up subsidy offered by the Government to arable farmers who bring the bulldozer and the plough to old pastures.

We have set out the categories into which a church can fall after the decay of the community which gave it life, and the categories are equally applicable to the much smaller number of cases where the decayed community was something larger than a village. In the great towns, such as Bristol, Norwich and York, the late fifteenth and early sixteenth century tax collectors were forced to give abatements to compensate for diminished wealth and population. That these claims were not fanciful is witnessed by the many examples of ruined urban parish churches and the consequent amalgamation of parishes. The equation is even more strikingly demonstrated where a town is completely decayed. Thus, the decayed borough, of Old Salisbury is evidenced by nothing less than a decayed cathedral, the excavated foundations being its sum total. The smaller borough of Richard's Castle, on the border of Herefordshire and Shropshire, is evidenced by a surviving but isolated church below the now-wooded mound of the castle from which the Norman borough took its name ; and further down the scale, the only remains of the medieval market centre of Kilpeck Herefordshire, (other than earthworks) is the magnificent Norman church.

III

An important question must now be raised : can we reverse the equation that has been spelled out ? Deserted settlements leave churches isolated or in ruins : yes. But do all isolated or ruined churches signify a deserted settlement ? It might be thought that the question put in this second way had no practical significance in historical or archaeological research. Is there not documentation for *every* medieval community, adequate enough to determine whether or not there was a medieval community and where the settlement lay, without having to bring the position and state of the church fabric into the question at all ?

In truth no such documentation is available for many deserted communities, especially those that were deserted in the twelfth and thirteenth centuries, and those that were never large. Historical research is therefore driven to non-documentary evidence, and to archaeological enquiry. The term " archaeological enquiry " embraces not only excavation — so expensive in money and man-power that the instances will always be few — but field-work, the careful examination of the surface of the ground and standing structures. The fabric of a standing church, isolated ; the ruins of a church ; the earthworks of a churchyard ; the tradition of a church site : these evidences should not be rejected if documents are lacking. But of what are they evidences ? of deserted villages ?

The presence of other earthworks near the church is a crucial element in answering this question, for earthworks alongside a church leave no doubt that there was once a settlement there. But we know that a vanished community could leave no earthworks ; for not all terrains have former roads, former house-sites, and former croft boundaries indelibly marked.

Two types of terrain have been effective in preserving village sites as earthworks : firstly, terrain where building stone was employed for houses in the thirteenth-century and later, leaving house-foundations visible ; secondly, terrain where timber building persisted longer, so that no stone house foundations are visible, but yet the soil is heavy enough to have retained the shape of sunken roads (hollow ways), of former banks and ditches between crofts.

and of the boundary bank between the crofts and the open field selions and furlongs.

It should be added that some destruction by ploughing that has already been mentioned at church sites has afflicted medieval village sites, and there has been much levelling by bulldozers : soil-marks and crop-marks will continue to be observable at these sites from the vantage of the air photograph, but with modern ploughing techniques no one can tell for how much longer the air photograph will help.

But these two types of terrain do not embrace all England, and it is in areas of non-heavy soils and with a persisting tradition of all-timber building that village sites are difficult to detect even when there is the clearest documentary, topographical and cartographical evidence for their former existence. It is in the terrain of these featureless sites that the isolated church will not be accompanied by earthworks. But why should this matter if the equation *isolated church denotes village* holds true ? does not the isolated church in itself prove a deserted settlement ?

Unfortunately the types of terrain where a village site is most likely to be illegible on the ground are just those that fostered rural communities of such a form that certain doubts can be voiced : were there not conditions in which the church would *always* have been isolated from settlement ?

This problem has much concerned me in my researches into the distribution of deserted medieval villages in England, and in the attempts that my archaeological colleague, Mr. J.G. Hurst, and I have made over the last 22 years to locate as many suspect sites as possible. As a result of our experience I feel that it *is* permissible to adjudicate on the isolated church and to determine whether or not it signifies a former settlement site. The crucial factor to be introduced may be called " ecological ", for the validity of the decision (whether it is appropriate in a particular case to invoke the equation, *isolated church equals decayed settlement*) must depend on knowledge and observation of the total settlement pattern in the surrounding district. Fortunately for this ecological approach, a distribution map of deserted settlements in England immediately shows that desertion never attacked a whole group of adjacent villages. Even in those parts of England, such as Warwickshire and Leicestershire, where the local intensity of depopulation attained a ratio of one deserted settlement in five, every deserted settlement has neighbouring villages which have survived. And varied as the agrarian sub-regions of England have been made by the local distribution of soils, these sub-regions embrace a considerable number of parishes. The settlement character of the now-deserted village can therefore be deduced from the settlement character of its neighbourhood, and the validity of the *church equals decayed settlement* equation really hinges on whether the surviving settlements in the neighbourhood of an isolated church are associated with churches.

IV

With this in mind, examples are offered from different regions, beginning with cases where validity can be most certainly claimed, and ending with some cases where the history of local settlement has not yet gone far enough to resolve all doubts.

●

CATEGORY A.

The areas of nucleated settlement in the clay plains and on chalk, with church isolation after enclosure or imparking. (examples : south Warwickshire ; east Leicestershire ; Yorkshire Wolds[e]; Lincolnshire Wolds).

The vast majority of English medieval villages were of the so-called nucleated form (really of many nucleated forms). Where the houses were situated in such proximity with each other it was usual to find the parish church, like the manor house, within the nucleus : often at its centre but not uncommonly at its edge. (Although an edge situation may result simply from a shrinkage of the settlement ; an inspection of the fields beyond the church for house-earthworks will reveal whether the position of the church was originally more central than now appears.) The close conjunction of farm house with farm house, and of manor house and church with farm houses, is a Europe-wide phenomenon, and is plausibly explicable in terms of a group of people brought together for mutual support during the difficulties of colonisation and then for the developed communal routines of open field husbandry. The dwelling places of the villagers were yoked together, one might say, as their oxen were yoked in their plough teams.

This type of agriculture, centred on the plough, the open fields and arable crops, was characteristic of the champion counties of the English lowlands, and in that terrain there is little room for doubt that an isolated church *does* denote a subtraction of settlement, even if the documentation is lacking, and even if there are no visible earthworks of a village near the church. Settlement on the pastoral uplands had a very different distribution of churches. Overall there were fewer churches in the landscape. In the plains one might expect to encounter a church at least every two miles but the terrain of scattered settlement was not one where the same number of families could be maintained (except perhaps in some colonies of mining prospectors). Scattered settlement was not only less densely peopled than nucleated settlement but (again with some exceptions) its *per capita* wealth was also less, so that there were two factors, both operating to reduce the likelihood of church provision. Thus the typical parish of the remoter parts of the kingdom was a large one of many thousands of acres served by a central church, with ultimately many dependent chapels, as settlement multiplied. Thus Halifax and Wakefield churches served two of the largest parishes of the Pennines, Malpas that of an enormous Cheshire parish, and Snaith that of a great area of former marshland on the border of Yorkshire and Lincolnshire. Mother churches of this size and importance were not, of course, isolated but set in a community which became the main administrative, social and economic centre of the parish-region. Such parishes demonstrated that pastoral and late-settled terrain did not always produce the isolated church.

CATEGORY B.

The areas of once-nucleated settlement on poor sands (example : Norfolk Breckland).

Although these village economies were centred as much on the sheep as on the plough, and had open field systems much modified by infield-outfield arrangements, sixteenth century maps and some archaeological evidence point to compact villages. This is important, for no other area of England has a greater frequency of ruined or vanished churches.

CATEGORY C

Romney Marsh.

The local frequency of ruined or vanished churches is second only to that of the Norfolk and Suffolk Brecklands but no old maps are known and very little research has been done on the medieval settlement patterns. Other marshland settlement in Lincolnshire, Norfolk, and south Humberside suggests that nucleation was favoured : in Romney there may or may not have been open farming to bring men close together but the scale of the task of creating and maintaining dykes and drains made collective action a part of self-interest and self-protection.

CATEGORY D.

Possible migrations : nucleated villages with remote isolated churches (examples, Suffolk and Essex green-villages ; Cumberland.)

This phenomenon is far too frequent in Suffolk and Essex to be the product of change and also so localised that the determining factor ought to be easily discerned. It seems incredible that the village church and the nucleated village around its green should always have been so separate as they now appear. The separation is too wide to be explained by a shrinkage of the intermediate settlement from the intermediate fields. The local soils do not bear the imprint of earthworks firmly, and it is an area crying out for archaeological and documentary investigation, but if villages are shown to have once accompanied each of these isolated churches, there remains the mystery of the occasion when such massive migrations to the present nucleated sites were engineered.

Suspect migration sites also occur in Cumberland although in smaller numbers than in East Anglia and without the regular green pattern at the present nucleated site. In one case, Brampton, it is possible that the nucleated site is a quasi-urban plantation of the thirteenth century, and that the old, less convenient, site was then deserted, leaving only the church (in semi-ruin but still surrounded by a cemetery where the town buries).

CATEGORY E

The always-isolated churches of Celtic evangelism.

Once it could have been assumed that village-less churches and church-less villages of Cornwall fell into this category, but I have shown elsewhere that, where documents are available, there is no difficulty in showing that Cornish churches were accompanied by medieval hamlets, and this proves to be in accord with the results of my colleague, Mr. G.R.J. Jones', work on Celtic set-

tlement in Wales and in England. There remain the many isolated and/or ruined churches of Cumberland that have dedications to minor Celtic saints : in
the mountain valleys of the Lake District one might hesitate to claim a former
village to accompany them, but they are also found on the coastal plains. No
house-earthworks have been noticed alongside them but, now that it is known
that early medieval houses — even in the stone-belts of England — were
timber-built, the absence of visible foundations is in itself not conclusive. Cumberland is a county whose settlement history urgently needs the combined effort
of archaeologists and historians.

CATEGORY F.

> *The isolated churches of English* bocage : *Herefordshire, Worcester-
> shire, Shropshire.*

This phenomenon is the most difficult to decipher in the present state of
knowledge. In the late-settled, wooded countries of the west Midlands one
does not have the great single-church parishes of the pastoral uplands. Churches
are not so frequent as in the the arable plains but they are not infrequent.
Yet many of them are not accompanied by any modern settlement. If one
invokes the 'ecological' approach, one finds that existing settlement rarely
focusses on a nucleated settlement, and it is here that concept of a deserted village presents most difficulties. But sites are being identified here and
there in these bocage counties, and the absence of earthworks may simply
arise from the timber structure of peasant farms ; the identified village sites
are new churches.

MEDIEVAL INQUISITIONS AND THE ARCHAEOLOGIST

Only a handful of large-scale plans survive from the middle ages to afford evidence of local topography or of the character and position of single buildings. The archaeologist who looks for documents to elucidate some puzzling structure or topographical feature is therefore driven to written documents; the reverse process, beginning with documents and then moving into the field, is less commonly undertaken, and is perhaps a sufficient indication that the classes of document where detailed information may lurk are not well known among professional archaeologists.

It is obvious, of course, that any documents at the Public Record Office which are listed in the printed index to *Rentals and Surveys*[3] will be informative about physical features which had an economic value; and the machinery of auditing expenditure by the Crown and its officers has also produced a class of documents, conveniently termed *Accounts*,[4] which have been put to good use by the students of building—latterly (with great effect) by the alliance of historians and archaeologists concerned with the King's Works.

Economic interest or curiosity at the Exchequer was also responsible for the great class of feudal enquiries by which the Crown sought to have valued the possessions of its tenants-in-chief or in certain circumstances its sub-tenants. These *Inquisitions Post Mortem* have been well calendared up to 1377 during the last half-century,[5] and there are older *Calendars*[6] of a more summary kind which bridge the gap before a modern series of calendars recommences in 1485. For the thirteenth and fourteenth centuries, in particular, the *extents*[7] which formed part of very many inquisitions *post mortem* are detailed enough to indicate the presence and sometimes the character of the principal buildings which lay on the demesne, from the manor and its precincts to the fulling-mill and the ferry-house. In those thousands of villages for which no manorial accounts have survived the extents may afford the only opportunity of learning the range of physical capital with which the countryside was equipped in these two important centuries.

Because of their close relation to the manorial system and to genealogical research the inquisitions *post mortem* have been known to some field-archaeologists.[8] Much less well-known, because of their miscellaneous nature and disordered archive arrangement, are other feudal enquiries, equally economic in their motive and equally likely to throw a sudden burst of light on some minor topographical feature. A large class is that of *Inquisitions Ad Quod Damnum*,[9] each the result of an order from the Crown to hold a local enquiry to discover what loss to the Crown (if any) would result from some proposal put forward by a private subject or by a corporate body, lay or ecclesiastical.

[3] *List of Rentals and Surveys and other analogous documents* (P.R.O. Lists and Indexes, xxv, 1908).

[4] *List of Foreign Accounts* (P.R.O. Lists and Indexes, xi, 1900);*List of Exchequer Accounts, Various* (*id.*, xxxv, 1912), and other typescript indexes available at the P.R.O.

[5] *Calendar of Inquisitions Post Mortem* (Henry III to Edward III, 14 vols., 1904-54; Henry VII, 4 vols. 1898-1957); the inquisitions of the sixteenth and early seventeenth centuries, much more summary in their form, are indexed in P.R.O. Lists and Indexes, xxiii, xxvi, xxxi, xxxiii.

[6] J. Caley and J. Bayley (eds. for the Record Commission) *Calendarium Inquisitionum post mortem sive excaetarum*, 4 vols. (1806-28).

[7] The *Calendars* indicate whether there is an extent included in the document; only a small minority are printed in full translation.

[8] The call-numbers for the documents themselves, if production of the originals is desired, range from C132 (Henry III) to C141 (Richard III). The file numbers are given in the *Calendars*. The older *Calendarium* uses a now obsolete system of numeration which needs a key, on the shelves of the Round Room, for translation.

[9] This class has the P.R.O. reference C143.

This may not seem a promising way of bringing down to parchment a verbal description of physical features and buildings. But the proposal was often to erect a building
or to make alterations; to construct roads, bridges and causeways; to drain land; to
create or close down ferries; to create parks; or to divert roads and footpaths. In such
cases the building or improvement will be described in the document, both in its
existing state and as proposed to be changed, or the old topography and the new
proposals will be indicated where lines of communication are to be changed or where
new provision, such as bridges or ferries, is under scrutiny. The relevance of such a
class of documents to the dating of buildings both surviving and buried is clear; and
the class of document is equally relevant to the other works of man in town and country
which come in for archaeological examination.

The inquisitions *ad quod damnum* are briefly calendared seriatim in a Public Record
Office *List and Index*,[10] the entry usually giving the date, location and parties concerned
together with a very brief indication of the subject of the inquiry. The full flavour of
such an inquisition can be caught from those for Yorkshire, which have been published
in translation by the Yorkshire Archaeological Society in its *Record Series*.[11] For example
one enquiry in 1255 establishes the date of the diversion from the Roman road which
is such a marked feature of the Tadcaster-York road just north of the site of the deserted
medieval village of Steeton;[12] another records the widening of the city ditch of York
alongside Blossomgate and Micklegate in 1241.[13] Of the unprinted documents one
might instance the enlargement of the chancel of St. Peter's church, Winchcombe
Glos., in 1246, a conduit in Northampton in 1292, a mill-race at Chaddesden, Derbyshire, in 1293 and the new chapel at Henley-in-Arden, Warwicks., in 1369.[14]

The purpose of the assessment of 'damage' by the sworn jury was usually not to
prevent the work being done but to assess the size of the payment which the king might
ask in return for licence to proceed. A number of these licences can be traced via the
inquisitions *ad quod damnum* to the *Calendars* of the Patent Rolls.

The machinery of local enquiry initiated by a writ from the Chancery also produced a number of miscellaneous documents which have been brought together from
parts of six different Public Record Office classes. The fourth volume of the *Calendars of
Inquisitions, Miscellaneous* has just appeared,[15] and although considerably shorter than
its three predecessors[16] it nevertheless contains as good a mixture of archaeological
fodder as they did. What the documents making up this miscellany have in common
that they, too, were the product of an order to describe or value someone's property
someone's proposed work, or the physical and economic effects of some neglect of
property by a tenant or former owner. The contents and fittings of the city house in
London in which the wife of Sir William Windsor, better known as Alice Perrers, had
lived, occupy $3\frac{1}{2}$ pages;[17] another document describes the state of Somerton Castle
Lincs.,[18] and another the size of the ferry-quay at Herringfleet, Suffolk, whence one
crossed to Haddiscoe in Norfolk.[19] The rooms and outbuildings of the manor houses
Findon, Sussex, and Willington, Beds., are detailed,[20] while we learn that the manor
house of Southburton, E.R. Yorks., had four long forms fixed in the ground[21]—a

---

[10] *List of Inquisitions Ad Quod Damnum* 2 vols. (P.R.O. Lists and Indexes, XVII and XXII, 1904-6).
[11] *Yorks. Archaeol. Soc. Record Series*, XII, XXIII, XXXI and XXXVII (1892-1906).
[12] *Id.*, XII, 44-5.
[13] *Ibid.*, 1-2.
[14] P.R.O. C143/1/8; C143/17/5; C143/19/20; C143/368/17.
[15] *Calendar of Inquisitions, Miscellaneous*, IV (1957).
[16] *Id.*, I (1916); II (1916); III (1937).
[17] *Id.*, IV, no. 17; her rural manors appear in adjoining documents.
[18] *Ibid.*, no. 43.
[19] *Ibid.*, no. 47.
[20] *Ibid.*, no. 123.
[21] *Ibid.*, no. 395.

interesting set of post-holes for someone to investigate. Another document dates the final blocking of a manor-house well by stones,[22] and there are many accounts which detail decay and dilapidations within manor houses and their adjacent buildings.

The descriptions are not confined to the manor house. The subject index, which supplements a very full *index locorum et personarum*, has 30 entries concerned with building materials and 55 dealing with various buildings from aviaries through forges, granges, prisons, privies and sheepcotes to wardrobes.

The latest volume brings the series up to 1387. The earliest volume begins in the mid-thirteenth century, and in final recommendation of the contents of all four to archaeologists I append a short note on a few of the documents which have caught my eye.

In 1290 the arrival and departure of Ravenserod on its Spurn Head sandbank are described;[23] in 1313 a good architectural description of a Norfolk manor house;[24] in 1312 of the Scarborough staithes,[25] in the same year of the weirs and obstructions on the Yorkshire Derwent.[26] In 1351 we hear of the complete destruction by fire of the village of Bloxham, Lincs.,[27] now rebuilt; in 1360-1 of the disrepair of York and Scarborough castles.[28] In 1359 there is mention of the slate quarries of the Lake District, among land whose agricultural value defeated the jury: 'It cannot be measured on account of the rocks and crags: if the wood were cut it would not grow again owing to the poverty of the soil.'[29]

A particularly useful group is that which arose from the Scottish incursions into Yorkshire in 1318. There is detail of villages which were wholly or partly destroyed (one or two never to recover),[30] and another document, of great value for the archaeology of settlement, where the jury declare how the abbot of Jervaulx has been forced by economic conditions to 'make towns of his four granges of Newstead, Rookwith, Akebar and Didderston'. Thirty messuages stood in Newstead, 40 in Rookwith and 24 at Didderston.[31] This rare example of new rural settlement on the eve of the Black Death cries out for field investigation.

[22] *Ibid.*, no. 50.
[23] *Id.*, I, no. 1512.
[24] *Id.*, II, no. 143.
[25] *Ibid.*, no. 144.
[26] *Ibid.*, no. 1312.
[27] *Id.*, III, no. 75.
[28] *Ibid.*, nos. 366 and 435.
[29] *Ibid.*, nos. 243 and 363.
[30] *Id.*, II, nos. 385, 453, 455, 489.
[31] *Ibid.*, no. 1797.

7

FALLOWFIELD, NORTHUMBERLAND: AN EARLY CARTOGRAPHIC

REPRESENTATION OF A DESERTED VILLAGE

The authentication of the site of a deserted medieval village and the elucidation of s topography come normally from documents, field-study and excavation rather than om contemporary maps. Only the rare cases, where the destruction of a village dates om the 18th or the 19th century, offer some hope that a large-scale plan of the village ight survive from the period before its depopulation. Thus by chance there are plans f Hinderskelfe (Yorks., N.R.), Faxton (Northants.), Wootton Underwood (Bucks.) nd Milton Abbas (Dorset) as complete settlements unaware of the threat of destruc-

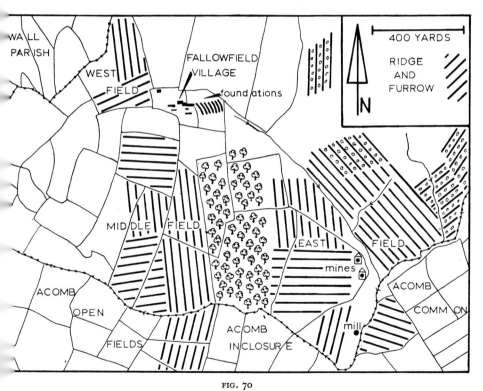

FIG. 70

FALLOWFIELD, NORTHUMBERLAND

Modern field boundaries, with features from plan of *c.* 1583 and visible ridge and furrow

tion.[72] But since the majority of deserted villages had already disappeared by th middle of the 16th century, it is not surprising that the number of cartographic portrayal is so small, for the art of the map-maker did not begin to encompass large-scale estate plans until the decades following 1550. (It is a piece of good fortune that one crud plan[73]—perhaps the earliest depiction of any English village—shows a sketch of th topography of the deserted village of Boarstall (Oxon.) *c.* 1444.)

Even though they were drawn too late to catch sight of the village as living entity Tudor and Stuart large-scale estate-plans may sometimes indicate the site of a forme village. The earliest examples of this type of evidence were previously thought to b the 1586 plan[74] of Whatborough (Leics.) showing the place "where the town (s township) of Whatborough stood', and that of the Jacobean park of Sheriff Hutto (Yorks., N.R.) with the site of East Lilling village included in the pale.[75] Neither these plans, it will be noticed, attempted to show details of village topography. Th Whatborough plan came nearest to this when it drew the boundary bank betwee village and open-field selions, and within the perimeter of the bank added a few sho lines to indicate houses.

Three large-scale plans from Northumberland and county Durham also preser a record of deserted village topography, but in further detail than in the plans alreac published. A plan of East Layton (co. Durham) was recently found among the Bake Baker papers at the Prior's Kitchen, Durham;[76] it was 'measured by Instruments th 14th daye of apryll 1608 by Rob(er)t Farrowe theld(er)', and was on a scale lar; enough to show the shape of the village green, and the empty crofts where the cart grapher wrote: 'the scyte of the howses'. A second Durham village, Whessoe, w surveyed in 1601 during a lawsuit involving Brasenose College, Oxford: documen relating to the dispute survive in Oxford[77] and at the Public Record Office,[78] and the latter there is a plan of the former village site by John Micheson.[79] Again, t empty crofts and their relation to the village green are clearly indicated.[80]

The third plan[81] is of Fallowfield (Northumberland), once a village in the par of St. John Lee but now reduced to one farm (GR/929685) 1½ miles north of Acon and ¾ mile south of Hadrian's Wall. If the date (*c.* 1583) assigned to it in the Briti Museum catalogue of maps is correct, this plan is not only the oldest of the northe trio but three years older than the plan of Whatborough, and therefore the old known case of a Tudor cartographer showing himself aware that he was surveying t site of former village houses.[82]

The contrasts of colour on the original plan are not sharp enough to be reproduc here, but FIG. 69 transcribes the words and symbols of the relevant area.[83] The t crosses at the gables of the second building from the left suggest a principal buildir

---

[72] Hinderskelfe, in M. W. Beresford, *The Lost Villages of England* (1954), pl. ii; Faxton, in Northa Record Office; Wootton Underwood, plan in M. W. Beresford, *History on the Ground* (1957), p. 226; Mil Abbas, in M. W. Beresford and J. K. S. St. Joseph, *Medieval England: an Aerial Survey* (1958), p. 105.

[73] *Boarstall Cartulary*, ed. H. E. Salter and A. H. Cooke (Oxford Hist. Soc., LXXXVIII, 1930); and *V. C. H. Bucks.*, IV, 9.

[74] All Souls College, Oxford, Hovenden maps.

[75] British Museum, Harl. Ms. 6288; Leeds City Archives, Ingram Ms. B.417391.

[76] Baker-Baker papers 72/249, enclosure.

[77] Brasenose College Documents, index vol. xxvii, nos. 1–56.

[78] Public Record Office, DL.44/608; DL.4/41/32; DL.4/42/10; DL.1/195S22 and DL.1/199/O2.

[79] Public Record Office, Maps MR 396.

[80] It is hoped to include notes on the Whessoe and East Layton village plans in a subsequent vol of *Medieval Archaeology*.

[81] British Museum Map Room, Maps 186h.1.2: original at Hatfield House, Hist. Mss. Com *Cal. Salisbury Mss.*, XIV (1923), 304. The prominence of the *mynes* on the plan suggest that it was the product of litigation over the bounds of commons and mineral rights.

[82] What little is known of the village's history will be found in *Northumberland County History*, IV, 8

[83] I am indebted to Mr. Alan Palmer for drawing FIGS. 69 and 70.

ut none of the five buildings is named. Farther to the right (east) the cartographer
outlined with dots eight small rectangles, and wrote: 'old howses foundacions'. To the
outh, these house-symbols met a group of angular trees numerous enough to make up a
mall wood, and to the north were 'stones, rocks and heath'. There is other evidence
hat the land is marginal, for while the furlongs of open-field arable were clearly drawn
o the west, south-west and north-west of 'Fallowefeelde towne', the blocks of selions
n the east and north-east were overwhelmed sometimes with dots and sometimes with
iny rings for 'stones and bushes'.

This area, which the plough had already abandoned in 1583, is now the open
'allowfield Fell, but an air-photograph[84] shows not only the spoil from the little 'mines'
f the old plan but also a large continuous area of ridge and furrow half hidden by
crub and heather. FIG. 70 locates the main features of the 1583 plan by indicating the
1odern field-boundaries and superimposing the names of the three open fields, the
'oodland, the mill, the mines, and the pattern of the open-field furlongs in both Fallow-
eld and Acomb townships. The small circles within the selions to the north of East
ield are those of the cartographer, mentioned above.

There is also ridge and furrow of good quality surviving in air-photographs of the
elds to the north-west of Fallowfield Farm, the selions and furlongs contorted with
1e ploughmen's efforts to master the contours. The modern fields within the area of
1e former Middle Field are now deep ploughed and bear little trace of ridge and furrow,
ut there is a considerable area south of the township boundary in what the plan of
583 indicates as the open fields of Acomb village. The present Fallowfield Farm and
s buildings are quite extensive and probably mask a good deal of the former village
ouses; to the west and south-west a grass paddock has slight earthworks which may
elong to the village; there are also slight earthworks to the east of the farm before the
dge and furrow begins in the southern half of the field. A barn and a house have
cently been erected over part of the site.

RAF 106G/UK/1393/no. 5291.

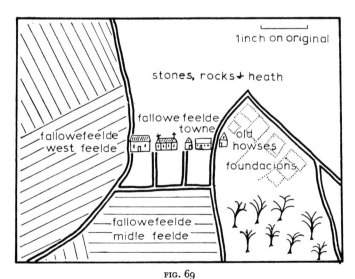

FIG. 69

FALLOWFIELD, NORTHUMBERLAND (pp. 165, 167)
Plan of village *c.* 1583. Sc. 1 in. = *c.* 400 ft.

8

EAST LAYTON, CO. DURHAM, IN 1608: ANOTHER EARLY CARTO-GRAPHIC REPRESENTATION OF A DESERTED MEDIEVAL VILLAGE SITE

A plan of Fallowfield, Northumberland, drawn *c.* 1583 and showing the now-deserted Fallowfield as *old howses* and *foundacions*, was transcribed and commented upon in the previous volume of this journal.[58] This note offers a parallel treatment of a slightly later estate-plan which indicates the site of a former village in co. Durham, also abandoned by the time that the cartographer and his instruments traversed its fields in the spring of 1608.

'The platt of the Lordshype of Layton in the county of durham measured by instruments the 14th daye of apryll 1608 by Robert Farrowe th'elder' forms an enclosure to a volume of miscellaneous records among the Baker manuscripts now deposited at the Prior's Kitchen, Durham.[59] Two folios of the volume refer to the plan: folio 12r contains 'An abstract of all ye pertikuler grounds in Layton with their severall contents measured by instruments by Robert Farrow of Fishborne th'elder in comitatu dunelmi gent. ye 14th of April 1608', totalling 1,013 acres; and the facing folio 11v contains a 'short veu . . . of all ye severall closes as nowe they be severed', together with valuation of each close. The 'short view' places the closes in a different order from Farrowe's *Abstract*, but the names of the majority are the same, and the areas correspond. The 'view' is dated *xxvito martii 1612* and is unsigned. A note by its author refers to Mr. Farrowe's survey and repeats its total for the acreage of the closes. The *platt* (or plan) of 1608 was drawn 'by a Scale of 32 perches In the Ynche' or 1 : 6,336. It measures 21¼ in. by 16 in., and its principal features are transcribed on page 94.

---

54 Groome, *op. cit.* in note 51, p. 6.

55 For example the visitation of 1520 was held in the chapel, *Lincs. Rec. Soc.*, 1938, pp. 164–66.

56 Bridges, *op. cit.* in note 53, p. 178a.

57 Chichele was also of course founder of All Souls (1437) and had some connexion with the foundation of St. Bernard's College, subsequently St. John's. The plans of those and other colleges can be studied in the relevant R.C.H.M. volumes. Ranges of a width less than 16 to 17 ft. are almost unknown at either university. The relative position of the gateway, chapel and hall at Higham Ferrers perhaps recalls the 14th-century arrangement at Pembroke College, Cambridge, except that at Pembroke the chapel is oriented in the opposite direction because the gateway faces west.

58 *Med. Archaeol.*, x (1966), 164–67, figs. 69–70. It is hoped to include a transcript and note on the 1601 plan of Whessoe, co. Durham, in the next volume of *Medieval Archaeology*.

59 University of Durham, Dept. of Palaeography and Diplomatic, Baker Baker Ms. 72/249, and enclosure. The provenience of this volume, containing records of various properties belonging to the Conyers and Baker families, is discussed by Dr. J. M. Fewster, 'Some Conyers Deeds', *Trans. Archit. and Archaeol. Soc. of Durham and Northumberland*, xi (1965), 405. I am indebted to Mr. J. E. Fagg of the University of Durham for this reference, for assistance in examining the record, and for permission to reproduce the material.

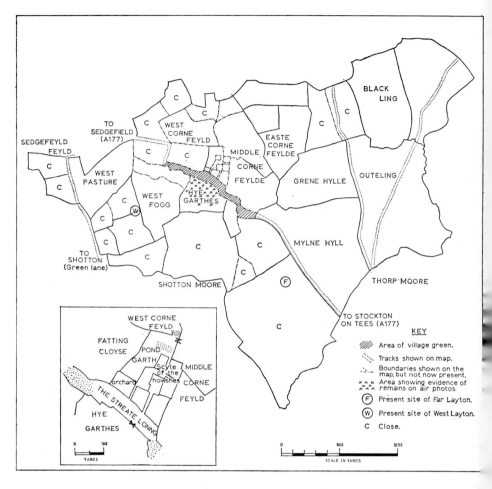

EAST LAYTON (CO. DURHAM)

The accuracy of Farrowe's survey, when it is compared with the modern Ordnance Survey plan, is remarkable, and for the most part the outer limit of the area surveyed is that of the modern bounds of East Layton township in Sedgefield parish. The complicated indentations of the bounds facilitate the identification of particular features, and to aid comparison with the present landscape and with current maps, the positions of two modern farms (which do not appear on the 1608 plan) have been indicated on FIG. 74: *F* is the present site of Far Layton Farm, and *W* of West Layton Farm. The other aid to rapid comparison is the fact that the present main road (A177) from Stockton on Tees to Sedgefield follows a course varying only slightly from the track crossing the old plan from south-east to north-west. The axes of FIG. 74 are those of the National Grid, and the grid reference to Far Layton Farm is NZ(45)/383262, sheet 85 of the 1-in. O.S. map, 7th series.

The references to *severing* and to *severalty* suggest that the closes of the plan had been taken in comparatively recently, some of them from common grazing grounds and some from open fields. The open fields of Sedgefield are shown on the plan as abutting on the north-east of Layton township, and those of Wynyard (a place represented now only by Wynyard Hall) on the east. Shotton and Thorpe Thewles Moors abutted on the southern boundary. East Layton may have had vestigial open fields in 1608, as the names *West Corne Feyld* (sic),[60] the *Middle Corne Feylde* and the *Easte Corne Feylde* infer.

It was between these fields and the main road that the cartographer drew a cluster of small closes, and wrote across them 'scyte of the howshes', with an old orchard to the south-west and the *Pond Garth* on the north-west. These closes abutted on the main road, and at this point the plan shows it perceptibly broadening to form a long, narrow green, which the cartographer identified as *The Streate Lonng*. On the opposite side of the *Streate* there was a large close of nearly 23½ acres, called the *Hye Garthes*, with another, the *Lowe Garthes* (of nearly 6½ acres) to the east. The detail of this area has been enlarged in the inset of FIG. 74.

These fields now display earthworks and crop-marks, particularly on the northern side, and the *garthes* must be those of the former village houses. The NW. corner of the field shows ridge-and-furrow in two oblique air-photographs from the Cambridge University collection,[61] and this is confirmed by an earlier R.A.F. vertical photograph[62] which also shows extensive ridge-and-furrow in the closes that abut on Shotton township, sometimes changing its axis or 'grain' within the bounds of the *closes* of 1608. The moors of 1608 had once been under the plough.

The area marked as the *scyte* of the houses of East Layton is now almost covered by the farm and out-buildings of East Layton. The ridge-and-furrow that Dr. St. Joseph's photographs show to the west of the buildings lies in the area that in 1608 was the *Orchard Close*. The pond of *Pond Garth* can be identified on the vertical air-photograph as a crop-mark. From the main road it is fairly easy to see crop-marks at appropriate seasons of the year in the area of the former *Hye Garthes*. This site has not been excavated or surveyed, and very little is known of the history of the township.[63] The vill was not included in Bolden Book. Depositions in a lawsuit of 1586 stated that the witnesses knew there had been a 'town' (i.e. village) of East Layton earlier in the century.[64] No inhabited building of any kind appears on Farrowe's plan but there was a house, perhaps the former manor, since he noted at the end of his *Abstract* that 'ye garden, house and curtledge are not measured'.

---

[60] The cartographer's spelling was not consistent between one part of the plan and another, nor between the plan and the *Abstract*.

[61] LY 89 and 90, seen by permission of Dr. J. K. S. St. Joseph.

[62] Sortie 541/23, no. 4061 of 16 April, 1948.

[63] *V.C.H., Durham*, III, 323.

[64] Public Record Office, E134, Trinity 28 Elizabeth, no. 16.

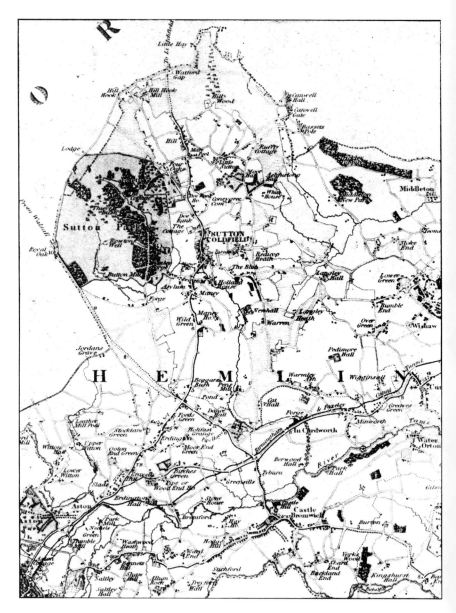

Plate 5. Map of Warwickshire (C. & J. Greenwood, 1821).
Unenclosed common waste land was shaded by the map-makers.

THE ECONOMIC INDIVIDUALITY

OF SUTTON COLDFIELD

ECONOMIC history is a comparatively recent study. The labours of
the first two generations of economic historians produced a series of
broad truths which were invaluable as a framework upon which to base
detailed study.[1] It is only natural that the next generation has turned to
detail.[2] The work of many antiquarians on village history is scanned
again; new work is done on manuscript material hitherto untouched.
The result is to produce an imposing set of exceptions to the general rule.
But this has not discredited the rules: rather the rules have been shown
as reasonable and true as far as they are generalizations, and the exceptions have fallen into place as being the general trend modified by some
geographical, political, personal, or other factor.

Manorial history shows us this process. The first generation saw in it
a slow dissolution from labour-services to money-rents as the centuries
passed: to-day the area in which this held true is seen as distinctly limited.
Many other manors have been found where, even in the earliest records,
part of the village is engaged in duties outside work on the demesne strips,
and many little economies have been discovered where the demesne (and
so labour services) played little or no part. Such manors may be said to
have had an economic individualism by the standards of the 'normal
manor' of (say) the Midland Plain.

It is in this light that a detailed study of the development of the manor
of Sutton Coldfield has importance. And again in the sixteenth century,
when the manor had become a chartered town, another set of very individual circumstances gave it yet another individual character which was to
last (in some aspects) until the present day.

Let us see how the medieval manor of Sutton Coldfield differed from
its neighbours. In Doomsday it is royal, with a large wood within its
bounds, and it borders on the King's Chase of Cannock.[3] Some authorities
have argued that its name is Sutton (South-town) because it is on the

---

[1] W. Cunningham, *The Growth of English Industry and Commerce during the Early
and Middle Ages*, Cambridge, 1915–19; E. Lipson, *Economic History of England.
I. The Middle Ages*, London, 1915.

[2] M. Postan, 'The Chronology of Labour Services', *Transactions of the Royal
Historical Society*, 1937; E. A. Kosminsky, 'Services and Money Rents in the Thir-
teenth Century', *Economic History Review*, vol. v, 1935; C. S. and C. S. Orwin, *The
Open Fields*, Oxford, 1938.

[3] William Salt Archaeological Society, *Historical Collections for Staffordshire*, vol. v,
part 1, pp. 137 and 166 seq.

south of the chase, and was originally a small settlement acting as a
hunting-lodge or outpost. The settlement stands on a long narrow ridge
of Keuper sands running north and south,[1] and the road to Lichfield and
the subsidiary settlements of Maney, Little Sutton and Hill, lie on this
ridge. The Rycknield Street ran to the west about two miles from the
town. The town stands on the slopes of a hill overlooking the ford or
bridge where this Lichfield-road crosses the Ebrook (Saxon Ebroc), and
the homesteads had plots of land running back along a slighter slope
down to a subsidiary stream. It is interesting to speculate whether such
an area of poor soil was deliberately chosen as a royal chase, but the arable
was certainly not of the quality which would encourage a large demesne,
even if there were no other services as an alternative to work on the strips.
As it was, the services of keeping the chase would tend to make the manor
a specialist one—just as the need for men to keep the dykes or to man the
border-defences, or to work the salt-pans in other parts of the country
put the relationship between the lord and the villager on a footing other
than that of agricultural services, and opened the way for the introduction
of a wider personal freedom and a greater tenurial independence.[2] The
nearest modern parallel is the position of the specialists (cooks, wireless
operators, or clerks) in an infantry unit. The majority of the unit will do
its training and manœuvres as a group and the personal freedom of the
individual will be severely limited: the specialists, on the other hand, will
be working at odd hours and often as individuals. Their greater personal
freedom (like that of the tenant at Sutton) was not a privilege granted
deliberately by Authority: it is implicit in the conditions of the job which
they are doing.

The statement of the customs of the manor was certificated in 1329,[3]
but the customs are described as those of the time of the Saxon Athelstan.
The principle services are hunting services, and for the customary tenants
a money-payment was optional (by 1329) for both autumn land-work and
the repair of the mill-earthwork. Whenever the lord came to hunt, those
customary tenants used to drive the wild beasts to a stand according to
their tenure, at the rate of two days' service for a yardland. They used
to buy and sell freely both in and out of the lordship without challenge.
When they died no other heriot than the first beast was paid. Customary
tenants could alienate their tenement in court on payment of a fine only;
and could leave the manor on surrender of their goods. All tenants, free
and customary, had common pasturage all the year round in the outwoods
of the chase and all dead wood for firing. There were fences in the forest
preserves to maintain, traps to be set, and trackways to be cut.

[1] Geological Survey of England and Wales, Sheets 158 and 164 (1 in. sheet).
[2] H. C. Darby, ed., *An Historical Geography of England and Wales before 1800*,
Cambridge, 1936, pp. 165–229.
[3] Public Record Office, Fine Roll, 26 June 1329, Placita Quo Warranto, 13 Ed. I, 780.

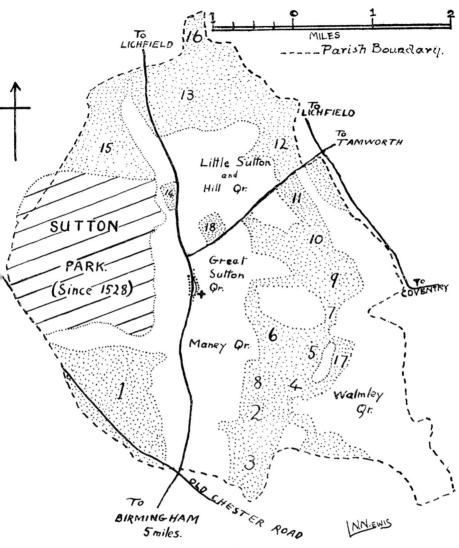

MILES

------ Parish Boundary.

To
LICHFIELD

16

13

15

12

Little Sulton
and
Hill Qr.

To
LICHFIELD

To
TAMWORTH

14

11

18

SUTTON

PARK.

(Since 1528)

Great
Sulton
Qr.

10

9

7

To
COVENTRY

Maney Qr.

6

5

17

8

4

Walmley
Qr.

1

2

3

To
BIRMINGHAM
5 miles.

OLD CHESTER ROAD

N.N.EWIS

FIG. I. SUTTON COLDFIELD.
Eighteenth-century waste.
The key to the numbered Fields is on p. 104.

The forest looms large in this charter, even though the chase had passed by 1309 from the king's hand to the Earl of Warwick. The free market in land appears as early as 1205[1] and there are many subsequent records of sale and exchange of both large and small tenements. The manor's name occurs again and again in the thirteenth- and fourteenth-century records as the Earls of Warwick come into conflict with their neighbours or their sub-tenants over forest- and chase-rights.[2] A market was granted by charter in 1353,[3] another feature distinguishing Sutton from its neighbours.

The end of the Middle Ages saw Sutton still prized as a hunting-seat. In the Patent Rolls between 1446 and 1528 appear 28 royal appointments to forest offices in the manor. It will be remembered that some of these were possible because the Countess of Warwick was a minor, and the others since the manor fell into royal hands on the defection of Warwick during the Wars of the Roses. Among those to be rewarded by a Sutton office was Lord Stanley, who, 'for his labours for the king in time past and recently in the conflict for England' became Master-forester in 1486. It was the royal patronage which later made grants in the manor to Wolsey and to the Dean of the Chapel Royal, one Vesey.

Contemporary eulogists attributed the fortunes of Sutton Coldfield to its citizen John Vesey. Camden described how after Warwick's attainder the manor, being on a most barren soil, fell daily to decay and the market clean forsaken. From this state of affairs Vesey was able to rescue his birthplace. By his personal efforts he built and repaired houses and settled men upon the waste lands.[4] He gave the manor a School, and, most important of all, he obtained from the king a charter giving the town self-government, so that once more Sutton stood apart from its neighbours. Seventeenth-century Sutton flourished as a commercial centre, and its mills formed outposts of the Black-country metal working trade. Eighteenth-century Sutton acquired a new favour in the eyes of the newly prospering manufacturers from Birmingham who saw in Sutton a suitable place to build their country houses some distance from their workshops' smoke. When oligarchic town government came up for nation-wide criticism in the Municipal Corporations' inquiry of 1832 and the subsequent Act, Sutton was one of the few old Corporations to be untouched by the Act. The building of the railway brought to the town the pleasure-seeker from Birmingham who found in the remains of the old royal chase a good rendezvous for a day-trip. The expansion of Birmingham in the late nineteenth century brought Sutton into a new economic role: that of the dormitory town for

[1] Dugdale Society, *Warwickshire Feet of Fines, sub anno.*

[2] *Calendar of the Patent Roll, passim.*

[3] *Calendar of the Charter Rolls, sub anno.*

[4] I. S. Leadam, ed., *Domesday of Inclosures, 1517–18*, London, 1897, p. 664. *Vide* also *ante*, pp. 97-8.

Birmingham workers. In the census of 1921, 10 per cent. of Birmingham emigré workers lived in Sutton, and 60 per cent. of Sutton residents in employment worked in Birmingham. Lower rates and a good grammar school may have assisted the emigration.

To an eighteenth-century observer curiously looking at Sutton Coldfield all these things may have been possible in the future, though he would have considered few of them expedient. But if asked to point out the novel feature of Sutton Coldfield he might well have pointed not to its education, nor its Corporation, nor its retired industrialists, but to what was happening on the waste lands surrounding the town.

The very individual nature of its agriculture brings us back to where we began, to the waste lands which had once been the royal and the ducal hunting-ground.

The waste was not an unimportant part of the medieval manor even where the chief activity of a manor was grain-production. It provided materials for house construction and food for man and beast. Once the work of clearing and settlement was finished and a village had sufficient arable, it would be ringed by a circle of waste. In the fifteenth and six-teenth centuries much of the midland arable land reverted to grass, and so, according to some agricultural economists, to its optimum use. The sheep fed on the grass and the need for wool was expanding, and the brown of the ploughlands turned to green as enclosure quickened. This change aroused bitter controversy and much legislation.

The position in Sutton was happier: and we find the chairman of the Enclosure Inquiry of 1517, Vesey, himself enclosing without hindrance. Many leases of the period allowed men to acquire land on the waste if they would settle there. Most of the Sutton enclosure seem to have been for tillage, not pasture. There was so much waste that there was room for sheep as well as men, and the main Elizabethan problem of depopulation passed Sutton by. The charter gave the Park to the freeholders for pasturage and its area was then larger than it is now, stretching right up to the Birmingham–Lichfield road.

The population of seventeenth- and eighteenth-century Sutton solved the problem of the utilization of the waste in a very individual manner. The charter in 1528 rules that 'any person willing to build and inhabit an house in any part of the waste may enclose sixty acres contiguous and rend 2d per acre a year for ever'.[1] This liberal attitude to useful enclosure is echoed in the 1582 court leet ordering 'that any person may plough the waste if it has been assigned and agreed by three freeholders of the part next adjacent appointed'.[2] But by 1582 there was already a dispute

---

[1] *Letters and Papers of Henry VIII*, vol. iv, pt. 2, g.5083(16), Dec. 1528.

[2] Sutton Coldfield Corporation Records, Box 3. (The classification follows the present author's Calendar, of which a typescript copy is deposited with the Town Clerk and the Birmingham Reference Library.)

between the Corporation (or, more correctly, the Warden and Society) and some freeholders who challenged the enclosure by the Corporate body of some 100 acres of common for its own use.[1] An action in the Exchequer court[2] followed, and the commissioners who made an inquiry formulated a scheme which remained virtually unaltered until the Enclosure Act 250 years later. They ordered:

> 'That it be lawful for the Corporation to leave the plain ground where there was no coppice wood to be converted either to tillage or to pasture for the inhabitants.'

Two-thirds of the available acreage was to be divided by lot among the inhabitants, and one-third to be given to the poorest townsfolk for tillage, and 2*d.* an acre was to be paid. It appears that some 700 acres were balloted for each year in acre lots; and kept for five years. This land then became part of the waste again, and another 700 acres came into circulation. In this way, any given piece of waste would be under cultivation about once every generation: for there were 4,000 acres of waste available for *lotting* under this scheme. These lands became known as 'Lot Acres', and were known under this name until the Enclosure Award extinguished these rights.

The Enclosure Award dealt with 3,331 acres: and most of this was waste. If the 3,000 acres which formed the Park is added, it will be seen that there was something like 6,500 acres of waste, at least in medieval Sutton, out of the parish's total of 13,000. This is a conservative estimate, for there are many references to legal and extra-legal appropriation of parts of the Park in the eighteenth century,[3] and the 29th Report of the Charity Commissioners put the area available for Lot Acres as high as 4,000 acres.

A loose sheet of paper found among the leaves of the eighteenth-century Court Leet order book in the Corporation archives gives a sight of the adminstration of these *Lot Acres*.[4]

> 'Memorandum agreed upon by all the members present at the Hall moot that the fields of commons or waste lands hereinafore mentioned shall be allotted as soon as conveniently may be for crops to all the inhabitants of the part, and to be thrown open again later; and the same shall be lotted for.
>
> 'And that field called Langley Windmill Field and Coneygrey Field shall be for the use of Great Sutton Quarter; and if these fields be not enough the difference shall be made up out of Smith's Field.
>
> 'And that the fields called Over Braddocks Hay be for the use of Little Sutton and Hill Quarter; if that be insufficient then the difference shall be made out of Smith's Field.
>
> 'That Echelhurst Field now Shipton's Bank Field shall be for the use of the inhabitants of Walmley, Beyond the Wood, Ashfurlong and Maney Quarters. . . .

[1] 29th Report of the Charity Commissioners, *Parliamentary Papers*, vol. xxi, pp. 1060 seq.

[2] Public Record Office, Special Commissions, 4684 of 14 Jas. I.

[3] Birmingham Reference Library MSS., 443103 and 424509.

[4] Sutton Coldfield Corporation Records: Box, Ancient Charters, &c.

'That all inhabitants shall have the usual quantity of land as at the yearly setting out of fields.

'That all who draw lots shall pay and shall pay what is usually paid.

'That there shall be no tillage this year for more than three years.

'That the clerks and sergeants of the lordships are to draw like others and not to have those pieces which they choose.'

The field-names and the *Quarter* divisions of the parish do not appear on any contemporary map, but the fields are described in the Enclosure award and have been shown on the map (Fig. 1). The Quarter divisions may be identified from the eighteenth-century *Surveys*[1] of the Town where all entries are made under the different Quarters.

The 3,331 acres lay in a three-quarter circle around the town, extending out to the circumference of the parish boundary. On them lay the settlements of Hill, Little Sutton, and Walmley. Through them ran the roads to Birmingham, Lichfield, Coventry, Tamworth, and Chester, and across them the rough tracks joining Sutton (Great Sutton) and the hamlets. These wastes appear for the last time on the Enclosure Award map, when they were distributed among the owners of land in the parish in proportion to the value of their holding.

Opponents of the Enclosure argued that the poor would suffer by the extinction of these common lands,[2] but in fact the late Poor Law returns cannot substantiate this. This is probably because by this time Sutton was finding another source of wealth in the influx from Birmingham, and the agricultural character of the parish was beginning to defer to the residential.

Two questions remain to be answered, as far as present knowledge can: the first, is this system of Lot Acres unique? Four similar methods of dealing with abundance of waste have been noted: one[3] in the Highlands of Scotland, one[4] in Cornwall, one[5] in Nottinghamshire in some forest manors, and the fourth[6] in Norfolk.

The second question arises from this: we have seen that there was always waste at Sutton and that it was used by king and commoner as each was able. Was the creation of a chase by one king, the preservation of part of it for perpetuity by another king, and its preservation and the peculiar *lotting* of other waste for three centuries due to its unsuitability for other use?

[1] A Survey for 1734 occurs at f. 101 of the 'Court of Record' minutes in Box: Polling Station Number 3 in the Corporation Records. Rentals and Surveys for 1786 are in Birmingham Reference Library.

[2] Petition against the Bill, *Commons Journal*, vol. lxxix, p. 384. W. K. R. Bedford, *Three Hundred years of a Family Living*, Birmingham, 1889, p. 131. Birmingham Reference Library MSS., 424509, f. iv.

[3] I. F. Grant in *The Geographical Teacher*, 1926, p. 480.

[4] G. B. Worgan, *General View of the Agriculture of Cornwall*, 1811, pp. 46 and 53.

[5] J. D. Chambers, *Nottinghamshire in the Eighteenth Century*, 1932, pp. 155 seq.

[6] J. Saltmarsh, *Economic History*, vol. iii, p. 30.

The waste lands lay in a circle within the town as its centre. Plate 5 (p. 96) shows these on a map surveyed before their enclosure by Act of Parliament. The field names can be identified by comparison with Fig. 1. The central core of arable land lies along the Ebrook and its meadows on Keuper sandstone. The waste is higher, all over 400 ft., mainly on gravel or sand. The Park heaths are Bunter and breccia sands, areas of dry woodland heath, and bare soil. To-day degenerated to heath, these lands were once luxurious woodlands.[1] Bunter soils were among the last to be cultivated wherever they occurred in England.[2]

Many commentators, and few of them geologists, noted the barren soils of Sutton. Leland[3] in the sixteenth century, Camden[4] later, and then the Reports to the Board of Agriculture (1794[5] and 1813[6]) all speak of Sutton's churlish and woody soil. It would have been interesting to see whether the nineteenth-century farmer with increased technical skill could have turned the enclosed acres to good arable uses. But the growth of the parish as a residential area and the increasing demands of the Birmingham market turned the farmer to supply other needs, and to-day the new fertility of the once Lot Acres consists not in crops but in housing estates.[7]

Key to Field Names on Fig 1.

1. 'The Coldfield.'
2. 'New Shipton field', or 'Eachelhurst Field'.
3. 'Bury's field.'
4. 'Basset's field.'
5. 'Signal Hays' (and variants).
6. 'White house common.'
7. 'Sidnalls field.'
8. 'New Hall field.'
9. 'Upper and Lower Withy fields.'
10. 'High Heath and Windmill Field.'
11. 'Lindridge Common.'
12. 'Chubbs field and Wheatmoor.'
13. 'Camp Field.'
14. Ley Hill Common.
15. Four Oaks Common.
16. Hawkhurst and Little Hay.
17. Langley Heath.
18. Coneygrey Common.

Other field names were: Chapman's Field, Redicap Field, Bull's Field, Silvester's Field, Powell's Field, Nicklin's Field, Rough Ley, Bradnock's Heys. A full list may appear in the next volume of *The English Placenames Society*.

[1] Wilcox, ed., *Woodlands and Marshes of Prehistoric Britain*, Liverpool, 1933, p. 73.
[2] A. E. Trueman, *Scenery of England and Wales*, 1938, p. 88.
[3] John Leland, *Itinerary*, ed. L. T. Smith, 1906–10, vol. ii, p. 97.
[4] W. Camden, *Brittania*, ed. E. Gibson, 1695, p. 505.
[5] John Wedge, *State of Agriculture in the County of Warwick*, 1794.
[6] W. Pitt, *General View of the County of Stafford*, 1813, p. 144.
[7] A fuller account of the Lot Acres will be found in M. W. Beresford, 'Lot Acres', *Economic History Review*, vol. xiii, 1943, pp. 74–9. See below, pp. 105-10.

LOT ACRES

THIS article describes the abnormal agricultural technique of a particular midland manor. The normal form of medieval organization of the manor was probably only widely found in the midland plain. Only there, where the major alternatives to villein services in the fields were absent, did the map of the manor approach the text-book uniformity of the two or three large fields with the lord's strips running hard by the peasants' in their intermingled holdings. The normal manor has the centre of the picture filled by the open fields: they play the determinant part in deciding the agricultural routine and in them lie the chief sources of economic wealth.[1]

It is equally true to say that no manor ever approached this norm. Everywhere some factor, natural or human, brought some variation. By the sea, by the fens, by the Border and by the hills there existed means of livelihood other than by service at the plough.[2] With the noteworthy exception of the Droitwich salt-pits, the midlands saw comparatively little of such 'abnormal' methods of economic exploitation.

The subject of this study is the township of Sutton Coldfield in the north-west corner of the county of Warwick near to the border of Staffordshire. It is probable that the first settlement in this forest area was in the nature of a royal hunting lodge,[3] for the manor of Sutton lay between the Royal Chace of Cannock and the old Forest of Arden.[4] In the twelfth century the royal manor passed to the Warwick family but they retained it as a hunting seat. The chief services mentioned in early documents are those of the hunt and the preservation of the chase.[5] Here was one alternative service rivalling service in the fields; and the waste had a social value which ensured its preservation even when economically it might have been better to plough and sow. The waste eclipsed the arable in importance in the eyes of lord and peasant, so that the waste was preserved even in the land-hunger of the late Middle Ages. When in the sixteenth century the abandonment of the manor both as a royal hunting

---

[1] The argument of this paragraph is elaborated in C. S. and C. S. Orwin, *The Open Fields* (Oxford, 1938), pp. 1–66.

[2] There is a well-planned account of the major variations from the 'normal' in *An Historical Geography of England before* A.D. 1800, ed. H. C. Darby (Cambridge, 1936), pp. 165–229.

[3] There is a nineteenth-century general history of Sutton Coldfield in [L. Bracken], *Forest and Chase of Sutton Coldfield* (Birmingham, 1860). This account is diffuse and many sources have since been opened. These are listed by M. W. Beresford in 'A Calendar of documentary references to Sutton Coldfield', copies of which have been deposited with the Borough Library.

[4] William Salt Archaeological Society, *Historical Collections for Staffordshire*, v, part 1, pp. 137 and 166 seq.

[5] P.R.O. Fine Roll, 26 June 1329. *Placita Quo Warranto*, 13 Ed. I, 780.

seat and a ducal seat posed the problem of the use of the waste an unusual solution was found.

The abnormal preponderance of waste over arable in a township in Norfolk[1] was solved by 'the division of the arable land...into two unequal parts: a small "infield" cropped continuously; and a large "outfield" of five to ten temporary enclosures from the waste...one broken up each year, cropped for a few years and then reverting to waste'. In a Highland village[2] such allotments from the waste were divided by lot. In Nottinghamshire[3] some forest manors had similar temporary enclosures from the waste for five or six years. All these characteristics were combined at Sutton Coldfield in the system of lot acres.

This local name for the division and allocation of arable from the waste persisted up to the Enclosure Act,[4] when its threatened abolition was seen seriously to endanger the rights of the poorer inhabitants. The petition of the opponents to the bill adds of the lot acres that 'from them the poor derive much benefit and to them the expense of enclosure is greater than the amelioration'.[5] The Rector wrote[6] that 'the proposed enclosure will have a considerable and lasting injury to several hundreds'. The title of a Sutton tract[7] is *General Enclosure Destructive to the Poor*. In 1778, 153 householders had opposed enclosure while 78 had supported it.[8]

The system which the Enclosure Act ended is outlined in the 29th Report of the Charity Commissioners:[9]

The enclosure has put an end to a further source of Corporation revenue from the 4000 acres of waste, of which 700 acres at a time were let among the inhabitant householders in lots of one acre by lot for five years; a small acknowledgement of 6*d*. to 2*s*. 6*d*. per annum being paid. At the end of five years the waste was thrown open and another portion was lotted in the same manner. The land let was usually estimated as worth £1 per acre to the occupier.

This practice varies little in detail between the later description given in 1889 by a Rector recalling the system as he had seen it as a boy[10] and the earlier words of the Chancery decree of 1617[11] which had formalized the practice. Throughout the eighteenth century the waste figures prominently in the order book of the Court Leet;[12] and a loose document[13] found in its pages gives precise details.

Memorandum agreed upon by all the members present at the Hall moot that the fields of commons or waste lands hereinaforementioned shall be allotted as

---

[1] *Economic History*, III, 30.

[2] I. F. Grant, *Geographical Teacher* (1926), p. 480.

[3] J. D. Chambers, *Nottinghamshire in the Eighteenth Century* (1932), pp. 155 seq. There is another parallel in Cornwall, cf. G. B. Worgan, *General View of the Agriculture...of Cornwall* (1811), pp. 46 and 53.

[4] 5 Geo. IV, cap. 14.   [5] C.J. LXXIX, 384.

[6] W. K. R. Bedford, *Three Hundred Years of A Family Living* (Birmingham, 1889), p. 131.

[7] Birmingham Reference Library (hereafter referred to as Birm. Ref. Lib.) MS. 424509, f. iv.

[8] Birm. Ref. Lib. MS. 424509, f. xxxiii.

[9] *Parliamentary Papers*, XXI, pt. 2, pp. 1057 seq.

[10] Bedford, *op. cit.* p. 40. Bedford became Rector in 1850, and wrote this book in 1889. The rectorial glebe included one lot acre (*ibid.* pp. 134–6).

[11] P.R.O. Special Commissions 4684, XIV. Jas. I.

[12] Sutton Coldfield Corporation Records. Boxes 2 and 3. A calendar of these records by M. W. Beresford is deposited in Birm. Ref. Lib.

[13] *Ibid.* Box: Ancient Charters, etc.

soon as conveniently may be for crops to all the inhabitants of this part, and to be thrown open again later; and the same shall be lotted for.

And that field called Langley Windmill Field and Coneygrey Field shall be for the use of Great Sutton Quarter; if those fields be not enough the difference shall be made up out of Smith's Field.

And that the fields called Over Braddocks Hay be for the use of Little Sutton and Hill Quarter; if that be insufficient then the difference shall be made out of Smith's Field.

That Echelhurst Field now Shipton's Bank Field shall be for the use of the inhabitants of Walmley, Beyond the Wood, Ashfurlong and Maney Quarters....

That all inhabitants shall have the usual quantity of land as at the yearly setting out of fields.

That all who draw lots shall pay, and shall pay for the next year what is usually paid.

That all who draw shall put a good and sufficient fence around those that shall happen to their lot keeping the same in good repair until the lands are to be laid out again. There shall be no tillage this year for more than three years.

That the clerk and sergeants of the lordship are to draw like others and not to have those pieces which they choose.

The Court Leet annually laid pains for the infringement of such bye-laws as these.

The tidy precision and legalism of this order was not a spontaneous and rational piece of planning effected at the time of the incorporation of the Borough in 1528.[1] The forfeitures of civil war had brought the manor back to the Crown from the Earl of Warwick. In 1528, Henry VIII granted a charter to the corporate body of the Warden and Society of Sutton at the request of his bishop of Exeter, John Vesey, tutor to Queen Mary.[2] The charter gave the control of the waste to the corporation, but permitted 'any person willing to build and inhabit a house in any part of the waste' to 'inclose sixty acres of the waste contiguous to the house and hold it for ever rendering for it 2d. per year for every acre'.

This was a clear attempt to settle the waste; just as Vesey himself in 1517 had enclosed the waste in parts to build houses for the shelter of travellers, although he had come down to the county as chairman of the Enclosure Commissioners of that year.[3]

The abundance of waste was, as we have seen, partly artificial, and was due to its preservation as hunting ground. But signs are not wanting that its very quantity had from earliest times influenced free settlement and an early land market. By 1205 land was changing hands in small lots;[4] and it was only five miles away that the freeholders of Yardley declared that from time immemorial the inclosure of the waste had always been permitted as long as pasture rights were not affected.[5]

---

[1] *Ibid. loc. cit.* See also *Letters and Papers of Henry VIII*, IV, pt. 2, g 5083 (16) December, 1528). M. Weinbaum, *British Borough Charters*, 1307–1660 (Cambridge, 1943).

[2] The contrasted relations of Vesey with his see and his birthplace are described from the Exeter angle in A. L. Rowse, *Tudor Cornwall* (1941).

[3] *Domesday of Inclosures*, 1517–18, ed. I. S. Leadam (1897), p. 664.

[4] Dugdale Society, *Warwickshire Feet of Fines* (1932), *passim*. Birm. Ref. Lib. MS. 185955 of June 1285—licence to William de Bircleye and his wife to inclose and plough forty acres of waste near the Chase of Sutton, paying annually d. rent at Easter.

[5] Selden Society, *Select Rolls in Eyre*, ed. D. Stenton (1934), p. 449.

The action of Vesey and the charter in disposing of waste was not, then, entirely novel, and it passed without comment in an age very sensitive to enclosures in general. But it was abuse of the charter provisions which led first to a suit in Chancery of 1581[1] and then to an action in Exchequer against the 'unlawful' enclosure of 100 acres of common by the Corporation for their individual use. The commissioners sent to Sutton formulated the scheme of lot acres very much in the terms in which we have seen it described in the eighteenth century, proposing that one-third of the lotted waste should be divided among the poorest, and two-thirds amongst the other inhabitants:[2]

> It should be lawful for the Corporation to leave the plain ground where there was no coppice wood to be converted either to tillage or pasture for the in-habitants...these rules to be kept:
> 1st.   the poorest inhabitants to have one-third of such for tillage.
> 2nd.   the rest to other inhabitants.
> 3rd.   it to be well manured and not to be used for more than three years.
> 4th.   2*d*. per acre is to be paid.

This annual partition, cultivation and restoration of the waste continued until the Enclosure Act. In the award[3] 3331 acres were concerned; there was only one small open field and that at the furthest end of the parish. All but this field and the waste was severally enclosed. Most of the 3331 acres, then, were waste, and waste utilized for lot acres. In addition there is the park, some 3000 acres of heath and woodland given by Henry VIII in perpetuity to the townsfolk of Vesey's birthplace.[4] The area of this was subject to slight diminution by legal and illegal exchange or appropriation,[5] but even to-day the 3000 acres remain in their natural state of waste.[6] Tradition holds that (except for a few years during the Commonwealth[7]) the plough has never been put to the park acres. Thus, in the late eighteenth century (to go no further back) at least 6331 acres out of the parish's total of 13,030 acres were waste. This is a con-servative estimate: for it will be remembered that the Charity Commissioners spoke in 1835 of 4000 acres available for lot acres.

We have so far related the prevalence and preservation of waste to human and social factors. But a study of local geology yields more information. Travellers often spoke as Leland did;[8] he was echoed by Camden,[9] who spoke of Sutton's 'woody and churlish soil', and the same theme appears in the Reports to the Board of Agriculture of J. Wedge[10] and W. Pitt.[11] These reporters were anxious

---

[1] *Parl. Papers*, XXI, 1060. Cf. also the order of the Sutton Court leet of 1582. [Corporation Records, box 3]—'no person shall plough any waste unless it has been limited and assigned by the freeholders appointed for that purpose.'

[2] *Parl. Papers*, XXI, 1063. There were 360 inhabitants in 1721 and 1800 in 1762.

[3] Corporation Records. Abstract in Birm. Ref. Lib. MS. 427518; Corn Rent Map, *ibid.* 427519.

[4] With pasture and commons rights for all freeholders.

[5] For legalized transfer see Birm. Ref. Lib. MS. 443103, 'Bill to empower the Corporation to grant part of the park to Simon Luttrell'. For illegalities see *ibid.* 424509 *passim*, and Corporation Records, *passim*.

[6] Land Utilization Survey Map, Sheet 72 (Southampton, 1934).

[7] I have not been able to trace any written evidence for this, but local historians and pamphleteers of the last century frequently refer to the story.

[8] John Leland, *Itinerary*, ed. L. T. Smith (1906–10), II, 97.

[9] W. Camden, *Britannia*, ed. E. Gibson (1695), p. 505.

[10] John Wedge, *State of Agriculture in the County of Warwick* (1794), *sub loco*.

[11] W. Pitt, *General View of the County of Stafford* (1813), p. 144.

to improve local agriculture, but they had to comment adversely on Sutton soil.[1]

The solid geology map shows a distinct correlation between the Keuper sandstone and the cultivated arable of the award and plan. A drift map[2] shows that the waste is mainly gravel or sand. Along the narrow ridge of Keuper sandstone are strung the medieval settlements of the parish and the one old high road through the parish from Birmingham to Lichfield connecting them. This soil is good foundation; it drains well, gives fertile fields and is used for building. On the Keuper sands, however, the soils have neither the heaviness of the marl regions nor the dryness of the bunter, and give fertile settlements such as Sutton itself.[3]

The Park heaths are bunter and breccia sands:

Stretches of dry woodland heath and bare soil. There is little doubt that this area once bore luxurious woodland, though to-day impoverished and often degenerate to heath.[4]

Dry sandy soils formed by Bunter sandstone were among the last to be cultivated and much heath and natural woodland may still be found in Sutton Park.[5]

We cannot report whether the kings and earls who set aside Sutton Chase for their hunting had observed how poorly agriculture flourished there. We can report with Leland how differently the waste fared at the hands of the squire-archy in adjoining parishes.[6] But it is impossible to give the final verdict to geological determinism: for the choice of those who wished to empark or enclose the sixteenth-century waste was not a free choice. Elsewhere, as accumulated evidence shows, they were able to flout or circumvent the law.[7] But in Sutton the free choice was limited by the facilities of the charter, the technique of lot acres and the ready access to the waste of all freeholders within the borough.

What, after the improvements of enclosure, would have been the fate of this land which had been so long divided as lot acres? The curiosity aroused by this query can never be impartially satisfied. Other neighbouring parishes appear normal in agricultural organization and progress of enclosure. But to nineteenth-

---

[1] 'Fuller understanding of the geographical factor in the enclosure movement clearly awaits regional studies' (W. G. East in *An Historical Geography of England before* A.D. 1800, p. 469). M. Aurousseau, *Economic History*, I, 280, discusses the relation of terrain to enclosed land. But I have not seen discussed any comprehensive relation of the extent of the Royal Forests to terrain. F. H. Baring in his *Doomsday Tables* (1909), p. 202, and *English Historical Review*, XVI, 427, makes it clear that at least in the case of the New Forest there was deliberate eviction of agriculturists from some 150 ploughlands. In other cases one can probably argue that forest was the most economic use of barren soil.

[2] Geological Survey of England and Wales (O.S. Southampton), Sheets 158 and 164 (1 in. maps). A rough correlation of waste and height may also be noticed. All waste is above the 400 ft. contour.

[3] A. E. Trueman, *Scenery of England and Wales* (1938), p. 88.

[4] *Woodlands and Marshes of Prehistoric Britain*, ed. Wilcox (Liverpool, 1933), p. 73.

[5] Trueman, *op. cit.* p. 89.

[6] Leadam, *op. cit.* vol. II, appendix and pp. 394 sqq.

[7] E.g. Erdington (Birm. Ref. Lib. MS. map (1760) 292886); Wishaw (*ibid.* (map of *c.* 1850) 394629). But all the parishes which formed Cannock Chase (footnote 4, *supra*) show much waste. Shenstone (Co. Staff.), which adjoins Sutton on the north, had 1314 acres common waste at enclosure. Handsworth, to the west, had five times as much waste as open field.

century Sutton new alternatives to agriculture presented themselves just as they had in earlier centuries. Then, in medieval times, the woodland had been valuable in yielding charcoal (some authorities favour this as the derivation of 'Coldfield'), then, in the seventeenth century there were six mill pools within the park, each with a sword or button mill; so now in the late eighteenth century the exodus of prosperous Birmingham manufacturers to old or new country houses in Sutton Coldfield heralded the dormitory town and the market agriculture of this present century in the Royal Borough.[1]

---

[1] The Borough is now largely urbanized, particularly along the line of the main road and railway to Birmingham. The park acres are still wood and heath. The agricultural and market character of the town is eclipsed by its dormitory function.

11

RIDGE AND FURROW
AND THE OPEN FIELDS

I

Thirteen article follows Professor Tawney's injunction to historians to lay aside their books in favour of their 'boots'. From observation in the fields, from work on maps of the sixteenth century onwards, from documents and from a modicum of books it puts forward a simple argument. The lay-out of strips, furlongs and fields in pre-enclosure parishes is already familiar to students who have worked on strip-maps or who have seen such printed reproductions as those by Mowat, Fowler or the Orwins. The number of such strip-maps is small, and for some counties non-existent.

It is the argument of this article that the reconstruction and study of the pattern of the open fields in any parish does not depend on the lucky survival of a strip-map or a detailed land terrier of pre-enclosure date. We shall argue that the ridge-and-furrow pattern visible in many Midland fields, and elsewhere, is in fact the pattern of the strips of the open field, fossilized as it were, and unobliterated by the newer alignment of hedges or by the ploughing demands of three wars. This opens up a wide prospect of remapping the appearance of any parish before enclosure—indeed, of remapping a wide area: wherever, in fact, the historian has good boots and a 6 in. Ordnance Map.

Ridge and furrow is a familiar sight to those who look out of railway-carriage windows,[1] and space will not be taken here in describing it. Since the publication of the Orwins' book it is also unnecessary to describe how the strips of the open fields, by the natural movement of soil in ploughing, acquired their ridges and their boundary furrows; or how generations of ploughing the same strips in the same direction between the same bounds gave them even more striking hills and dales. It was between two of these ridges that Swift made Lemuel Gulliver spend his first night in Brobdingnag, and some of the high-backed ridges in heavy clay country almost make the fantasy possible.[2] The sinuous S shape of the strip was first recognized by Maitland[3] as being drawn not with a rod but with a plough; and the yearly movement of the soil by the ploughshare has bitten deeply, almost into the subsoil. Farmers who have tried to exterminate the ridges will tell of the persistence with which even the most cross-ploughed field will acquire its furrows again as soon as the first heavy rain has settled the

---

[1] It is surprising to find so observant a man as Professor Clapham writing à propos of 1886: 'you could see it from no main line now.' The 'it' was 'the patchwork of open fields which had survived until a main line was driven across its shots, headlands and gores'. J. H. Clapham, *An Economic History of Modern Britain* (Cambridge, 1939), II, 449.

[2] Jonathan Swift, *Gulliver's Travels*, pt. 2, cap. 1. Are these the ridges, five feet deep, spoken of by Professor G. M. Trevelyan?—*English Social History* (1944), p. 380.

[3] F. W. Maitland, *Domesday Book and Beyond* (Cambridge, 1897), p. 379.

soil down into its old beds. For the same reason, soil which in one season of the year may look quite level and devoid of traces of ridging will at a later month reveal what centuries of ploughing have done. There will be tell-tale strips of discoloured soil on ploughing days; the colours of ripened corn or the height of the growing crop will vary, and these variations will be in strips; in wet days rain lingers in the old furrows, where, in the winter, snow will remain longest. On a windy day corn will be blown down in strips, not evenly over the field; and the clearest signs of all will be those revealed from air-photographs, when even apparently level soil will show a steady strip pattern.

The equation of this ridge and furrow with open-field strips appears revolutionary to many farmers, and their scepticism induced great caution at the beginning of this investigation. In fact, the equation had been hinted at and quite plainly stated already.[1] But for certain proof we must begin by comparing ridge and furrow with pre-enclosure maps of the same field or fields; we may then apply the equation in other parishes where no maps have survived, and finally outline certain wider problems of agricultural history which this knowledge enables us to pose.

II

Pre-enclosure, or 'strip', maps are to be found in greatest number in the county archives of Bedford,[2] although the Northampton Record Society has almost as many in photostat copies. Maps used in this investigation were drawn from a number of Midland counties and will be referred to by their short titles. Their location is given in the footnote below.[3] The Ilmington map, although only a surveyor's rough working copy, yields the most detail. It is from the late eighteenth century. The sixteenth-century maps from All Souls Library are by far the best of their period in execution and clarity.[4] Unfortunately, the copy of the Whatborough sheet in Professor Tawney's book was badly distorted in

---

[1] A cautious hint of its truth was given me by Mr J. Saltmarsh in 1939. Other witnesses are F. M. Stenton, *Documents Illustrative...of the Danelaw* (1920), p. xliv; Isaac Taylor, *Contemporary Review* (1886), pp. 884–96; W. J. Corbett, *Trans. Royal Hist. Soc.* (1897), p. 67; *39th Report of the Congress of Archaeological Studies* (1932), p. 32. These references were gathered after the main study of maps for this article was completed. None of them in fact, seems to have compared the maps which they knew with the surface of the ground.

[2] The Bedfordshire maps are listed in the two-volume catalogue published by the County Records Committee. The Northamptonshire photographs are at the Record Society, Lamport Hall. The University Library, Cambridge, has a collection of photographs of many Huntingdonshire and some Cambridgeshire maps.

[3] In 1948 only one printed reproduction of a strip-map is available in print, that of Goldington, Beds, in F. G. Emmison, *Types of Open Field Parishes in the Midlands* (Hist. Assoc. 1937), and this, in fact, is not a facsimile but a transcript. Other printed strip-maps will be found in R. B. Mowat, *Sixteen old Maps...of Oxfordshire* (Oxford, 1888); G. H. Fowler, *Records of Bedfordshire, Quarto Series* (Bedford, 1928–36); C. S. and C. S. Orwin, *The Open Fields* (Oxford, 1938); *The Bradford Antiquary* (Bradford, 1888), i. 254; William Salt Society, *Collections for a History of Staffordshire* (Stafford, 1931), p. 61.

The manuscript maps used for this article are located as follows. Whatborough (Leics) 1586 (All Souls, Oxford); Pickwell (Leics) 1616 (Archive Room, City Museum, Leicester); Halton and Colton (Yorks) 1731 (Leeds City Library, Temple Newsam papers); Ilmington (Warws) 1778 (Birthplace, Stratford on Avon); Kinwarton (Warws) 1752 (Birmingham Reference Library, 379051); Whitchurch Tithe Award Map, 1842 and Tredington strip-map 1842 (both Warws.) (Shire Hall, Warwick); Braybrook, 1766 (Northants) (Northampton City Library). The authenticity of the correlation with ridge and furrow can now be demonstrated by the R.A.F. air photographs which became available in 1947. My own comparisons in the field in 1946 were assisted by Mr Peter Ransom, B.Sc., who acted as witness.

[4] Especially those of Padbury and Weedon Weston.

copying[1] and not reliable for comparison with the modern fields or Ordnance Map: but the original map can be correlated.

Such strip-maps as these were large-scale surveys of an area as small as a manor or parish. They were commissioned by landowners, some for projected enclosures; some for lawsuits; and some for better administrative record.[2] They show every strip, name the furlongs into which the strips are grouped, and (in some cases) may be on a large enough scale to write in the owner's name or initials on each strip. The Ilmington surveyor was careful enough to write in the exact width of each strip at each end, and I have seen the same thoroughness in a written Yorkshire land-terrier. There is less satisfaction to be obtained from maps accompanying Enclosure Awards, for they are concerned to show the new lay-out of hedged fields rather than the old order just passed away. The most recent strip-map which I have seen is that of Whitchurch, Warwickshire, made for the Tithe Award in 1842. The jigsaw of strips on this map will be familiar already to economic historians, since an air photograph of a complicated corner of the parish was printed in the Orwins' book. Exactly the same complicated pattern will be found at the junctions of furlongs CIV, CXXXVIII and CVI in the Award Map.[3]

This rather spectacular and lucky identification is backed by a full routine of comparisons in other parishes.[4] The detail on the old maps is good enough for watercourses, village streets, parish boundaries and sometimes roads to be identified. Working from these ascertained points, the detail of the strips can be transferred—to scale—on to a modern 6 in. Ordnance Survey Map. The line of ridge and furrow as observed in the fields can then be plotted on another sheet and the two sheets compared. In such cases as Ilmington, where the strips in the old map were carefully measured, a check can be made by measuring the distance from ridge to ridge: the boundary of the strips was, of course, the furrow, but the work of rain and grass has made the middle of the furrow a rather indeterminate point from which to measure. [See Plates 6 and 7.]

The opening-up of the R.A.F. air photograph collection has made the task of identification and correlation very much easier, although for detailed work the 'boots' are still necessary. These photographs became available after this investigation was completed. The parishes for which the whole strip-map was correlated with ridge and furrow were Ilmington and Kinwarton. Most of Whatborough, Braybrook, Newbold-on-Avon, Colton, Whitchurch, and Allestree have been worked over.

All the strips in the parish do not run in the same direction, but in parallel groups inside the furlongs, some of which run one way and some another. This makes quite rapid correlation of strip-maps with ridge and furrow possible. At the points where furlongs meet, often the points where strips changed direction, the ridge and furrow will change direction. The furlong boundary thus found,

---

[1] R. H. Tawney, *The Agrarian Problem in the Sixteenth Century* (1912), p. 223. The copy of the plan is wrongly dated as 1620 and has also some errors of figures and words from the face of the map.

[2] E. G. R. Taylor, 'The Surveyor', *Econ. Hist. Rev.* (1947), vol. XVII, no. 2, pp. 124 and 131.

[3] The illustration is facing p. 46 in Orwin, op. cit. The Tithe Award map is at Shire Hall, Warwick. The O.S. grid reference for the area of the photograph is 42,680/670.

[4] Allestree (Derbyshire) 1737 (Derby Public Library); Whitchurch (Warws) Tithe Award (Shire Hall, Warwick); since the article was written, the maps for Newbold-on-Avon (Warws) and Thurlaston (Warws) have been loaned to the Northants Record Society for my use. These two early eighteenth-century maps have been compared with air photographs. I am grateful to Miss Joan Wake and the Duke of Buccleuch for this.

it can be easily followed until the next change of direction occurs. Unless detailed measurements are needed, only the number of ridges passed need be counted, and the number of strips can then be marked off later on the map.

Strips are not the only features of pre-enclosure fields which can still be seen clearly enough to be transferred to a map. The lanes and balks which gave access to furlongs show up clearly, and some will still be the line of foot paths and rights of way. Windmill banks can be seen, and many of the marl pits which lined the access-balks. The Braybook and Kinwarton maps show these as pools, which most of them now are. The word 'pits' to describe them has lingered on in Warwickshire at least.

The pits can most commonly be seen at the point where two furlongs met, and can in some cases (as in the West Field at Braybook) be seen to lie roughly in a straight line—the line of an old balk which used to lead from the old line of the Market Harborough lane out into the furlongs of the open fields. Both this balk and the strips here, as one would expect, run through the lines of the hedges laid down at enclosure and emerge unscathed on the other side, precisely in step.

The 'closes' which appear on a strip-map can usually be identified with modern closes, even with the same boundaries in many cases, although amalgamation of small closes into larger modern fields may also be seen. Many of these closes bear signs of ridges: that is, they were once part of the open field before they were enclosed—the significance of this can be considered later.

The enclosure hedge, even when drawn by a nineteenth-century enclosure commissioner or surveyor, may contain signs of following an older furlong boundary: the surest signs are a sinuous curve where the hedge follows the curve of the S-shaped strips. Many of the small closes in West Riding villages, long and narrow, have that shape only because they are consolidated strips, walled around at enclosure. At Ilmington almost exactly 50 % of the modern hedge length follows the lines of older furlong boundaries, which were unfenced. The other 50 % of hedges run where the line of the commissioner's pen ran—across and among the strips.

The equation, whose truth has been argued, also appears valid by an examination of the use of the words 'ridge' and 'ridge and furrow'. In 1586 the surveyor for All Souls College at Whatborough marked the lines of the strips and furlongs on the western half of his map. These correspond with ridge and furrow on the ground. But in the eastern half of the map the surveyor is drawing the enclosures within Sauvey Park. He shows large hedged fields, but writes in one the words:

> theise grounds doe appeare to have bene arrable

and in another:

> this close hath bene also arrable

and in a third uses the significant words:

> theise groundes doe likewise lie ridge and forrow

that is, he used visible ridge and furrow as evidence that the closes had been in the arable fields. 'Grounds' is the common Leicestershire word for enclosed pastures.

A century later the same logical connexion of ridge and furrow with strips can be seen in two other parishes. At Billesdon in Leicestershire the 1674 glebe-terrier[1] has

item the tythe of haye and corne of all such Closes near unto the towne of Billesdon as have not or had not of late yeares anye signe of ridge and furrowe

---

[1] Leicester City Museum, glebe-terriers.

which might argue that the said closes had bene taken out of the antient arrable feildes.

Four years later, there was a lawsuit concerning the tithes of Frankton in War-wickshire.[1] The point at issue was whether certain lands were old enclosure or recently taken from the open fields. The witness is the same: the appearance of the fields—

two thirds of the former common fields in Frankton now lye in very large pastures, so do all the xii yardland tithable to the plaintiff, but with so very little interruption of knowledge by reason that it lyeth still ridge and furrow.

The enclosure had taken place twenty-two years earlier, in 1656.

The word commonly found in Midland land-terriers of the seventeenth and eighteenth centuries is 'land'. The medieval equivalent was 'terrae' for strips which Professor Stenton notes in the twelfth century,[2] and it appears alongside 'seliones' as the word for strips in many medieval documents. In the seventeenth and eighteenth centuries another word sometimes used—'acres'—dies out, probably since this word had now acquired a precise meaning of area which we shall see it did not possess in the medieval terrier. But the word 'ridge' arrives as 'acre' dies out of use. 'Land-ridges' also occurs as a hybrid.

Two strips lying in the fields of Pebworth[3] in 1746 were called 'two whole ridges', but the other 150 strips are called 'lands'. The glebe terrier for Haselor in the same county of Warwickshire describes in 1585 'three and twenty lands *or* ridges'. At Baginton

47 ridges laying in Towne Field

in 1685, appear in the 1693 terrier as

47 *lands* lying in Towne Field.

Ridges appear in the terriers for Loxley, 1585; Leek Wooton, 1616; Willington, 1635; and Leamington Hastings, 1673. These are Warwickshire ridges,[4] but the word is also used in Leicestershire terriers. For those to whom the strips of the open field were an everyday sight it did not seem inappropriate to use the word which described the physical appearance of the strip. It was this physical dis-tinction, created by centuries of ploughing, which enabled one man to know his strip from his neighbour's, even without the help of mere-stones. Such clarity, quite independent of surveyors' measurements, is the underlying assumption of all written terriers which describe the holdings of many thousands in this form:

Begin at Audlies close and go east. The lord one land customary containing half an acre. The Township one land containing half an acre. The lord one land containing one rood. The lord four lands containing one and a half acres. The lord two lands containing two roods. The lord two lands customary containing two roods. W. Barnes two lands containing three roods. A balk.[5]

Much later, in 1620 a very full terrier of the strips in the common fields of Shottery near Stratford on Avon is introduced by the surveyor in these words:[6]

for the better understanding of this book and the contents thereof he that will be pleased to read this little preface following shall not need to doubt in any

[1] P.R.O., Sp. Comm. Exch., E. 178, 6507.   [2] Stenton, loc. cit.
[3] Birmingham Reference Library, 377026.
[4] Shire Hall Warwick, D.R.O. papers.
[5] Grantchester (translation of a terrier of 1352) communicated by Mr J. Saltmarsh. For this point see also J. A. Venn, *Foundations of Agric. Econ.* (c. 1923), p. 8.
[6] Stratford on Avon, Birthplace, Wheler MS. 41.

part. You shall understand the first column from the left hand numbereth all the ridges from one side the furlong to the other according as they are use and belong to the several persons. The second column showeth the persons name to whom each ridge in the furlong belongeth.

Among these several persons were the Hathaways. Over the Avon, a few miles away at Hampton Lucy,[1] the glebe-terrier of a family not unassociated with the son-in-law of the elder Hathaway had used the word ridge for the strips four years earlier.

III

The comparison of strip-map and modern field surface may be convincing, but a word ought to be said about the scepticism of farmers, and its origin. A really sceptical farmer might argue that the examples of strip-maps quoted are by coincidence similar to the pattern of ridge and furrow. He would probably not leave his attack at so weak a point, but go on to argue that ridge and furrow is quite recently made and for a quite simple purpose, drainage; or, in the opinion of some, for increasing the surface area of the land. As to chronology, some farmers will put it as of 'grandfather's time', and others will talk of it as signs of the ploughing up campaign of the Napoleonic wars.[2]

These arguments contain half-truths: the first settlers laid out their furrows, no doubt, with an eye to utilizing the fall of the land for carrying off surplus water. But useful as a ridge may have been as a rough watershed, the total pattern of furlongs is not so totally related to contours that one can see in it a complete system leading water to the main stream or river of the parish. The ridges would have drained a small area, but would not have solved the problem of draining a whole field: that is probably why furrow drainage unaided by artificial drains is called by Clapham 'defective'. Familiarity with ridge and furrow will also show many examples of furrows which ignore contours.[3]

In the same way, the argument from the Napoleonic wars is a true myth based on the transmitted memory of a time when much grassland which had not seen the plough since the fifteenth century was brought under temporary war-time cultivation.

Two kinds of personal observations carried out in his own fields would show a farmer that ridge and furrow is older than grandfather and older than Napoleon. There are many man-made features which dissect a country parish: among these are the railway, older than grandfather; and the canal, often older than Napoleon's wars. Where ridge and furrow is dissected by canal or railway it will be seen to emerge unscathed: it continues, in the same direction, still spaced at the same intervals as it was on the further side. It would be a patient plough-man who would create such symmetry. The ridge and furrow is older than canal or railway. The same continuity 'under' roads and hedges enables one to push back the date of ridge and furrow to before the creation of the road or hedge, and the date of the Enclosure Award will enable a precise date to be given to hedge or newly planned road.

[1] All the Warwickshire glebe-terriers quoted are at the Shire Hall, Warwick.

[2] Sceptical but credulous farmers have seriously put forward to W.A.E.C. officers two fantastic explanations, which were preferred to the one suggested in this article. One said that ridge and furrow enabled reapers to stand in the furrow and cut the corn without bending down. Another said that the distance from ridge to ridge was exactly that of a horse's stride and was of great use in hunting country. The argument that ridge and furrow was designed to increase the surface of the ground was often put forward.

[3] C. S. and C. S. Orwin, op. cit. p. 21, seems to me to place too much faith in the drainage theory; see J. H. Clapham, op. cit. i, 460.

Another way in which a sceptical farmer might be convinced would be an examination of some of his larger fields. Besides seeing ridge and furrow running through hedges, he would be able to see ridge and furrow making its own pattern—the old pattern of the furlongs—within the boundaries of the modern hedge. As he crossed the field, the farmer would see the line of ridge and furrow change direction: usually at right angles. This would be inside the one set of hedges, and is difficult to explain by any modern ploughing process, even during the stress of the Napoleonic wars! Why should a farmer have divided a hedged field into a smaller patchwork?

A study of air photographs would settle the matter. From the air, the frequency with which ridge and furrow continues through hedges is quite unmistakable. Conversely, air photographs of the ridge and furrow surrounding one of the Midland 'lost village' sites shows the ridge and furrow proceeding up to the edge of the village crofts, and then finishing. These sites were abandoned in the century 1460–1560, and the air photograph shows us the medieval village without modern accretions, with the ridge and furrow fossilizing the strips, and the earthworks fossilizing the village and its buildings.[1]

IV

If the argument is accepted, a new range of study opens up. Consideration of open-field problems has usually been confined to those manors with surviving strip-maps (which are few), or to those with unusually full and surviving terriers or extents. Attempts to re-create the open-field pattern solely from Enclosure Awards is a laborious and sometimes impossible task. But if strip and ridge and furrow *are* identical, then a strip-map can be obtained by plotting ridge and furrow on to a large-scale Ordnance Map—the 6 in. or 25 in. scale. The only limitation is the destruction of ridge and furrow by consistent cross-ploughing, although we have shown above that an aerial view will see soil discolorations and penetrate all but the most thorough disguises.

The strip-pattern can be re-created in its essentials without detailed measurement or surveyor's instruments. The main data required is the shape of the furlongs and their size, and the relation of the furlongs to existing landmarks such as hedges and streams. All this can be achieved with a chain or long tape. The ridges themselves can be counted, and marked in conventionally, unless great accuracy is required. A good set of air photographs will, of course, enable the reconstruction to be carried out in the study with fair accuracy.

There is little danger of the furrows of modern drainage or recent ploughing being mistaken for ridge and furrow. Modern furrows are contained within hedges, never overstepping them, and they are very widely spaced in comparison with ridge and furrow. The characteristic S shape of ridge and furrow also serves to mark it apart from any product of a modern plough.

---

[1] Those of Cestersover (Warws) for example (R.A.F. Ref. CPE. U.K. 1925; 2005 and 4003). These were printed in *Country Life*, CIV (1948), pp. 772–3; O. G. S. Crawford, *Air Survey and Archeology* (1924), printed at p. 28 an eighteenth-century strip-map of Calston (Wilts) but not the air photographs of its open fields, although part appeared in his *Wessex from the Air* (1928), plates 23 and 24; in his 'Strip Map of Littlington' (*O.S. Professional Papers*, no. 17, 1937) he used an 1804 map to demonstrate that his air photographs showed the old headlands, but does not mention the strips or ridge and furrow. Ridge and furrow is not visible to me in any of the photographs in his 'Air Photography for Archeologists' (*O.S. Professional Papers*, no. 12, 1929) which deals (apart from lynchets) with pre-Anglo-Saxon field-systems, nor do I see any reference to ridge and furrow in 'Field Archeology' (*O.S. Professional Papers*, no. 13, 1947).

The maps in A. Meitzen, *Siedelung und Agrarwesen...* (Berlin, 1895), 3 vols and Atlas, would afford a basis for similar air and map comparisons on the continent.

I have carried out such reconstructions over several adjacent parishes in the Midlands, with the assistance of Mr Peter Ransom. An even wider reconstruction would be of great use in bringing fresh light on the problem of the geographical distribution of the open fields in the British Isles. Even chance observations convince me that the distribution in the Orwins' book is far too conservative. Any map of distribution which depends on the survival of the positive evidence of documents or maps will be at the mercy of the chances of survival.

Does the presence or absence of ridge and furrow offer any more certain index of open-field distribution? Its presence certainly does indicate that the field in question was at one time under strip. Its absence may mean either that there never has been open field or that the obliterating plough has succeeded.[1] My own experience is that the absence of ridge and furrow particularly in air photographs does fit in with other evidence to confirm that particular fields were never in the open-field arable. This type of land is common near Rugby, where eight parishes run up from the streams to meet in Dunsmore Heath, land which since the earliest written record has been heath and waste. The Heath is a central block into which five parishes converge. The core of the Heath, near to the converging of five boundaries, was as late as 1717 common land for all the parishes.[2] Now if these parishes are examined for ridge and furrow, it will be found that it occurs plentifully: except in those narrow finger-ends of the parishes running over the Heath.

The areas where the existence of open field is most in question are counties bordering on or containing uplands. The counties flanking the High Peak and the Pennines;[3] the valleys of the moorlands of the south-west; the Welsh border; Kent; the Welsh coastal plain: these are the districts where some uncertainty exists. A ridge-and-furrow survey of these areas might yield good positive evidence; and the absence of it is unlikely in these particular areas to be the result of persistent ploughing for obliteration.

Another use to which ridge and furrow can be put is an even more detailed reconstruction of open-field lay-out. All who have worked on open-field reconstruction from pre-enclosure terriers, deeds, tithe awards and enclosure awards will know how much detail of names of furlongs and fields can be rescued from such sources. They will also know how imprecise this information is in topographical location. But, implementing the reconstruction by ridge and furrow (which gives the furlong pattern of the fields), and by paying attention to the field names listed in most Tithe Awards, it is often possible to link together a particular furlong marked from ridge and furrow with a detail in a written document. Thus, in Bilton parish, Warwickshire, the glebe terrier for 1618 detailed some of the strips lying in Severidge with the Lawford brook abutting west and with other proprietors' strips abutting east and west. Clearly, these strips ran north and south, with their long sides east and west. The Tithe Award of 1845 locates Severidge Field, which, examined, yields ridge and furrow running north and south, with the meadowland around the brook to the west. Using a similar combination of a very full parish terrier of Shottery, near Stratford on

---

[1] Of all growing crops, I find market-garden produce the most difficult to penetrate with the eye in search of ridge and furrow. Persistently ploughed land is much less secretive. I have not come across evidence for 'filling up' furrows (G. M. Trevelyan, loc. cit.) unless cross-ploughing is meant.

[2] Buccleuch maps (on loan to Northants Record Society).

[3] From A. Raistrick and S. E. Chapman, *Antiquity*, III, 165–81, it would seem that ridge and furrow penetrates far up Wharfedale. I have myself seen it in the Dales.

Avon, and a modern field-name map,[1] I was able to reconstruct and name Shottery's open fields and identify the Hathaway strips as they lie across the present footpath which leads from the Birthplace to the Cottage.

V

How does the information yielded by ridge and furrow fit in with the traditional picture of the open fields?[2] When I first examined enclosed fields in detail I was surprised at the amount of pre-enclosure landmarks untouched. Not only the ridge and furrow itself, but many remains of balks, headlands, access-lanes, windmill sites, old watercourses and old roads have survived the changes decreed by the enclosure commissioner. Even the boundaries of furlongs (which were, of course, unhedged) were used as convenient lines to follow in setting the course for new hedges. At Ilmington the enclosure surveyor's hedges follow furlong boundaries for all but 50 % of their length. The other 50 % intersect furlong bounds, usually at right angles. The surveyor's purple lines on the Braybrook map follow the same proportion.

Many modern footpaths, deriving from the Enclosure Award, follow balk lines; and it was Dr J. D. Chambers, I think, who pointed out how many apparently irrelevant right-angled turns in old country lanes are in fact very relevant to furlong boundaries. The sober surveyor made the rambling English road.

Many Midland fields to-day are marked by deep holes, usually filled with water. The Warwickshire word for them is 'pitts', and they have provided the name for many fields of the Deep Pits Field, Manor Pits, Church Pits form. Many of these pits lie in a straight line, often at a point where ridge and furrow changes direction: that is, where furlongs met, and balks ran. Thus it would be at the point where traffic passed, but whether it was a marl pit or a watering-place for oxen, I do not know.

Ridge and furrow bears out the erasure of the grass balk *between* Midland strips which is now near a commonplace. It leaves the balk as an access way to furlongs. It throws some doubt on the axiom that drainage determined the direction of strips. One does not have to examine much ridge and furrow before finding neighbouring furlongs whose strips would be quite irreconcilable as far as drainage went. One would expect this to be especially true on marginal or boundary land brought late into the fields: it might prove quite impossible to have assimilated such a new furlong with the directions already existing in neighbouring furlongs and strips.

The point at which ridge and furrow challenges the traditional view is in the size of strips. Where are the acre strips assumed by historians? An acre strip would be 220 yards long, which is roughly the average length of Midland strips. But an acre strip would have to be 22 yards or 66 feet wide. Now 66 feet is too wide for ridge and furrow. The average size is about a third of this, which puts the average area at a third of an acre. Is this confirmed by written terriers and strip-maps?

[1] Stratford Wheler MS. 41.

[2] The study of ridge and furrow and strip-maps deals with a period too late to be able to throw any light on the methodical distribution of strips within the furlong which some writers have seen. Even the earliest maps show so much disintegration and consolidation that they cannot be very good evidence as to whether the demesne was ever in compact furlong parcels (as suggested by Stenton, op. cit. p. lvi). I am sceptical of this, but admit the existence of demesne closes in many seventeenth-century maps.

At Bittesby, a village abandoned in the fifteenth century,[1] every strip in the West Field was measured: the average width was 26 feet, the length just below 220 yards. The limits of width were 39 and 12 feet. Furrows may vary in depth with the soil, but the width is nowhere like 66 feet.

Not all terriers give the area of their strips, but many do. Their main concern was to place the strip in the furlong and to certify its owner. The common use of the word 'acre' for strip (equivalent to the Latin *selion*) may have confused readers and created the myth of the acre strip.[2] Terriers which do give areas are explicit in confirming that the average area was from one-quarter to one-third of an acre. The word *acre* is less popular than *land* to describe strips. The 1620 Shottery terrier[3] lists 2950 'ridges': their average area was 0·38 acres.

The evidence of many other terriers has been gathered and some select references are given in the footnote.[4] The strip-maps confirm. The Ilmington map is the most detailed: the surveyor measured and marked the widths of strips at either end. Here are the widths for Nether Swinsby Furlong. The initials are those of the proprietors, and it will be seen that in one case adjacent strips have been acquired, so that a man holds two 'lands'. In such a case their area is double the standard strip. It may be that the sight of some of these larger 'double' and 'treble' strips gave rise to the acre theory. But such pairs of strips are few compared with the single strip. The examination of ridge and furrow makes it clear that the two lands kept the physical conformation of their origin: they had and have *two* ridges and furrows. Nether Swinsby from the air can be seen to have the same number of ridges that there were lands in the 1778 survey: eighteen.

Nether Swinsby Furlong (1778)

78	2K	80		40	BJ	46
43	HU	49		40	HU	45
45	BP	45		35	HU	43
43	JS	45½		36	BP	44
44	HU	44		37	TS	45
40	EG	41		35	FC	40
38	EG	41		35	JG	42
36	BS	42		34	DSm	41
36	BS	48				

[1] W. G. Hoskins, 'The Deserted Villages of Leicestershire', *Trans. Leics. Arch. Soc.* (Leicester, 1945), XXII, 19.

[2] Perhaps historians have seen on a map a group of strips after consolidation, but have not turned from the map to a terrier. Terriers always indicate how many lands or ridges there are, even in a large adjacent bundle of strips [see the eve of enclosure terrier of 1821 for Halton, Yorks (Leeds City Library, Temple Newsam papers)]. Even so practical a booklet as E. C. Curwen's *Air Photography and the Evolution of the Corn-Field* (1938), pp. 15 and 31, brings forward the ideal strip of one acre, and it creeps into Professor Postan's review of 'The Open Fields', *Econ. Hist. Rev.* (1939), IX, 194.

[3] Stratford, Wheler MS. 41. At Chadshunt, Warws, in 1618, 127 lands covered 50 acres (P.R.O., Sp. Comm. Exch. 4687).

[4] Among references to strips of less than one acre in area may be cited the following: H. L. Gray, *English Field Systems* (Cambridge, Mass., 1915), p. 22; Maitland, op. cit. pp. 379–84; Nichols, *History of Leicestershire* (1795), Framland Hundred, App. p. 115; Stratford, Birthplace, Wheler MSS. 6, fol. 249 (1773); ibid. 39, fol. 2; Birmingham Reference Library MSS. 377026, 388063; Leicester Museum archives 17D 34/14a (1651); ibid. 14b; ibid. 35/29,245; ibid. 35/29,387; Stratford Birthplace, Philipps MSS. 16098; G. Slater, *The English Peasantry and the Enclosure of the Common Fields* (1908), p. 9; Warwick, Shire Hall, map AC/CA/9 (1842); R. H. Hilton, *The Economic Development of some Leics. Estates* (Oxford, 1947), p. 54; Glebe-terriers at Diocesan Registry, York, passim.

PLATE 6

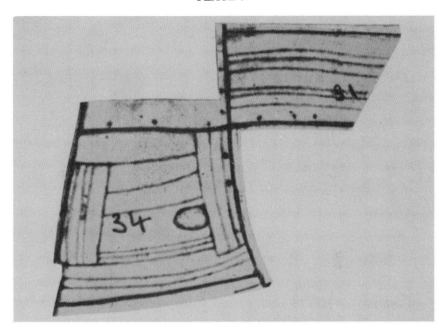

Fig. 1: Part of map of Kinwarton, Warws., 1752.
(Birmingham Reference Library MS. 379051.)

Fig. 2: R.A.F. air photograph no. 1069, U.K. 1333, 7405 of 1946.
O.S. Grid reference: 42/095,590. Crown copyright.

OPEN-FIELD MAP AND RIDGE AND FURROW

PLATE 7

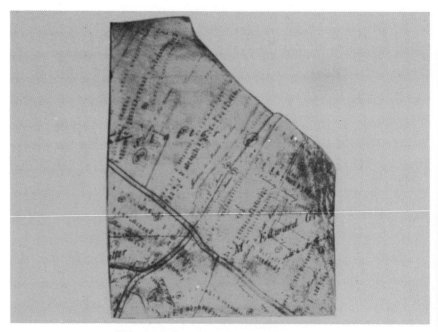

Fig. 3. Part of map of Ilmington, Warws., 1778.
(Birthplace, Stratford on Avon, map portfolio.)

Fig. 4. R.A.F. air photograph no. 106 G, U.K. 1345, 5167-70 of 1946.
O.S. Grid reference: 42/220,435. Crown copyright.

OPEN-FIELD MAP AND RIDGE AND FURROW

Comparison of the map of 1778 with an Ordnance Survey Map makes it clear that these lengths are in surveyor's links: 7·92 in., which puts the average width at 25½ ft. The largest consolidated holding on the map is 4 Hob., being 145 links or 96 ft. wide: an average of only 24 ft. per *land*, or 36 % of the width necessary to create the *acre* strip. Maitland[1] may have the last word:

to tell a man one of his acre strips was not an acre would be like telling a man that his foot was not a foot because it is nine inches long.

VI

The ridge and furrow which we have identified as strips has turned mainly on evidence not earlier than 1550. I once thought it possible that the single strip of that period might have been the result of disintegration of much larger strips of an earlier time, perhaps the time of colonization. But I have found nothing in the physical appearance of strips to support this view; and the larger bundles of strips are clearly the result of consolidating unit strips. A four-unit holding will have four ridges: if this were the original holding, one might expect to find only one ridge. Medieval documents show much consolidation, but little partition. The acre strip appears to be banished even from medieval England. One of the most recent general works speaks of strips 'cut and clipped, divided and sub-divided' but quotes no evidence for it.[2]

There are other unanswered questions from the period of settlement and colonization of Saxon England, for which a further study of ridge and furrow might bring answers. In these pages, ridge and furrow has been used as an index of open-field cultivation. We have not proved that all ridge and furrow now visible in a parish was under the plough *at one and the same time*. The evidence is not of the kind to yield such proof. Ridge and furrow is like a high-tide mark. It shows where the plough has once been; but it does not say when; and it will cover up many marks of earlier (or later) low tides. All it can say is, the tide once came this far: this land was part of the open fields, but it may have been open field when the neighbouring furlong was still waste or common. It may itself even have been abandoned and brought back into cultivation again: but ridge and furrow cannot help to decide this question.[3]

There is another question of chronology: Is very clear plain ridge and furrow a sign of recent enclosure? It must be answered, no. Much land which appears in sixteenth-century maps as closes shows signs of clear ridge and furrow:[4] that is, it had once been in the fields. In other cases we can have the same degree of clarity for ridge and furrow which we know only left the plough early in the nineteenth century. Clarity of ridge-and-furrow definition is only an index of quiescence: such land, once down to grass, has been undisturbed.

Future work on air photographs of ridge-and-furrow patterns may enable one important question to be answered, which so far (since there are so few strip-maps) has hardly been more than asked. It relates to the period of settlement and colonization, and may be briefly put: Is an even, equal set of furlongs a sign of early colonization, and are uneven, jagged, odd-sized furlongs an indica-.

---

[1] Maitland, op. cit. p. 362; also Taylor, op. cit. p. 126.

[2] Henry Hamilton, *History of the Homeland* (1947), text to fig. 6. His 'strips' must be 'holdings'.

[3] See T. A. M. Bishop, *Econ. Hist. Rev.* (1938), IX, 39–40.

[4] The Whatborough map may be cited; as well as the Braybrook map and Brit. Mus. Stowe MS. 795; and such enclosures as those described in P.R.O. Exch. Deps. 4 Car. 1, Mich. 10.

tion of later assarting?[1] If this is so, it should be possible to read from the evidence how the village arable expanded, in what directions, and with what regularity.[2] The assumptions upon which such an answer would be based seem sound.[3]

A village with an expanding population, optimistic about the political or economic future, soundly equipped with capital in the way of good tools and good husbandmen, might think it could safely bring a large area of assart into the fields. Even if the documentary evidence, as Mr Bishop argues, is against communal assarting in favour of individual or family colonization, the same psychological axiom is true. Similarly, the village or family doubtful about the future, in a time of stable or falling population, or in a time of falling demand for the produce of its fields, may have considered that a small increase of area was sufficient for the present. And running through such an interpretation of the evidence must be another determining factor: the individual attractions and repulsions offered by the infinite geographical variations within the parish. Wherever there is a sudden bend in a stream, an outcrop of stubborn soil, a patch of ill-drained marsh, a steepening of the slope or a corner in the parish boundary —there the ploughman will have to temper the shape and size of his furlongs to the demands of nature. The study of ridge and furrow is no more than an attempt to interpret the work of a multitude of such ploughmen.[4]

[1] Dr W. G. Hoskins has suggested to me that a jagged parish boundary with many right-angled turns in it may be a sign that (when the boundary was settled) this was the part of the parish under the plough: the bends being the corners of furlongs and balks. Straight boundaries or smooth curving ones, he suggests, relate to an area where the land was under grass or trees, so that a more regular boundary line could easily be drawn. The projection on the Kinwarton parish boundary on the left-hand side of Fig. 1 and Fig. 2 is in fact following a balk. See also Birm. Ref. MS. 427740 [1495].

[2] Including the advance and retreat of the 'pulsating' village economy. (M. Postan, 'The Chronology of Labour Services', *T.R.H.S.* (1937), 4th series, vol. xx.) Some of the air photographs which show strips, tracks and house sites intermingled on the fringe of the 'deserted' medieval villages may be evidence for this thesis.

[3] Even remembering Maitland's warning: 'if we contemplate strips...the hazard involved in an assumption of their antiquity will increase swiftly when we have left behind us the advent of Duke William', op. cit. p. 362.

[4] This article owes a good deal to discussion with Dr W. G. Hoskins, to the help of Mr Peter Ransom in field-work, and to the assistance of many archivists and librarians whose collections are mentioned in the footnotes.

EXPLANATION OF PLATES 6 and 7.

Figs 1 and 3 are parts of eighteenth-century open-field maps while Figs. 2 and 4 are air photographs of the same areas, taken in 1946.

Fig. 1 shows a complicated intersection of furlongs, with a marl-pit. It is on the parish boundary, which may account for some of the complication. The thick lines show the position of modern hedges. It will be seen that considerable consolidation has taken place within the furlong: there are a number of double-width strips, and some of greater size, but the single, unit strips (such as appear south of the pit) are identical with the width of ridge and furrow.

Fig. 3 covers a wider area. This map was used by the enclosure commissioner and the lines which he has sketched in for roads and hedges can be compared with the modern position of these in the air photograph. The initials of the proprietors are on each strip, and where there has been consolidation a '2' or '3' appears before the initial. The names written in full across the face of the map are those of the new owners of the enclosed fields after the Award. By counting ridges and strips it will be seen that one ridge was the width of one strip: thus, the right hand, 'Shooting to Middle Meadow' Furlong has 25 (3 double, and 19 single); 'Littleton Hill' its 8 singles. The curved line is the disused track of the Stratford-Shipston tramway. The thin lines on the map, which divide the strips, have not reproduced well in the photograph, but the eye will be aided by the initials of the proprietors, written *parallel* to the strips, inside each one.

12

COMMISSIONERS OF ENCLOSURE

THIS essay is concerned with those men who were given by Statute an all-but-absolute authority to enclose and redistribute common and open fields between about 1745 and the General Act of 1845. It deals with Commissioners as professional men tackling problems which were novel in the first generation, and only slowly evolving standards of procedure. Criticism of the partiality (as apart from the cost) of a Commission was rare, so that the questions of proper or improper motive which surround the discussion of many enclosure problems will not arise here. The materials for this investigation are the minutes, accounts, letters and working papers of Commissioners in several Midland counties,[1] and a study of the Commissioners named in all the Acts for Warwickshire, Worcestershire and Staffordshire. The private diary of one Commissioner[2] and the personal account book of another[3] have survived to yield details of work before and after the meetings recorded in the Minutes. The scarcity of these minutes has been frequently commented upon.[4]

The earliest Commissions (1730–60) were very large, and often local, giving something of the appearance of a grand jury of umpires seeing fair treatment of their fellow landowners. When the pace of enclosure quickened, and anxious eyes were cast on the expense of a Commission, a smaller appointment became the rule and the paid professional Commissioner appeared. If landowners could have agreed, an Act and a Commission would have been superfluous. The multiplicity of Acts may be read not only as evidence of dissension on the issue of enclosure[5] among the gentry who flew to Parliament as an arbiter, but perhaps as showing that many who agreed that enclosure was necessary could not agree on the details of property redistribution. A Commissioner disinterested in the lands to be enclosed, but trusted by the owners who had nominated him, might produce an Award about which there might be individual complaints, but which could be accepted as being at the worst equally unfair to everyone.

A Commissioner described his powers in 1766 in these terms:

A Commissioner is appointed by Act of Parliament for dividing and allotting common fields and is directed to do it according to the respective interests of proprietors...without undue preference to any, but paying regard to situation,

---

[1] Cambridgeshire: in University Library, Cambridge, Class ADD 6013–88 and 6955–6; Class DOC 624 et seq. A complete list of these parishes (45 out of the 115 statutory enclosures in the county) is given in *Trans. Cambs. Antiq. Soc.* XL, 78.

Bedfordshire: County Records, Shire Hall, Bedford.

Leicestershire: Muniment Room, The Museum, Leicester.

Yorkshire: Sheffield City Library.

Northamptonshire: Northampton Borough Library.

Staffordshire and Worcestershire: Birmingham Reference Library.

Warwickshire: Birmingham Reference Library; County Records, Shire Hall, Warwick; Birthplace Library, Stratford on Avon.

Buckinghamshire: Drayton Parslow Minutes summarized in *Records of Buckinghamshire*, XI, 256. Buckingham, 1926.

[2] Sheffield, WC/2219.

[3] Warwick, HR/5.

[4] A list is given in *E.H.R.* LVII, 250–63 by W. E. Tate, but is incomplete.

[5] As Paul Mantoux argues, *The Industrial Revolution in the Eighteenth Century*, 1928, p. 170.

quality and convenience. The method of ascertainment is left to the major part of the Commission...and this without any fetter or check upon them beside their own honour confidence (and late indeed) awed by the solemnity of an oath. This is perhaps one of the greatest trusts ever reposed in one set of men; and merits all the return of caution attention and integrity which can result from an honest impartial and ingenuous mind.[1]

The author, the Rev. William Homer of Birdingbury, was a prolific pamphleteer and himself known to have been Commissioner in all the Midland counties. His name appears in Acts for at least twenty enclosures in surrounding counties alone, and the tone of these words from his preface is exactly that of a man self-consciously surveying the importance of his new profession, anxious to set its standards high and to offer guidance to others who would succeed to these duties:[2]

In this age abounding with Inclosures it cannot be an uninteresting subject to canvass the Principles upon which the determination of Commissioners are usually founded. This is now a Science, which in its infancy was confessedly understood very imperfectly. What is here offered is drawn upon a Plan.

And again:[3]

It is the principal design of the writer of this Essay to establish all determinations about Property as much as possible upon certain and invariable Principles.

Eighty years later, the 1844 Commons Committee on Inclosures printed its evidence covering some seven thousand questions to witnesses.[4] Except for minor criticisms of certain Commissioners, there is no evidence of widespread dissatisfaction with the work of the Commissioners.

A contemporary account of the enclosure of Charnwood Forest (*c.* 1840) puts the position fairly:[5]

They executed their very onerous duties with fairness and fidelity although it must not be concealed that a considerable degree of dissatisfaction prevailed at the unparalleled expenditure. A leaning in favour of the principal proprietors has also been imputed to the Commissioners...chiefly in their endeavours to accommodate the Lords by fixing their allotments as near as possible to their respective parks. The reader may satisfy himself as to the general impartiality of the Commissioners by studying the list of claims with reasons for their rejection. The claims of the most influential persons were disallowed: while those possessed of no influence whatever were admitted.

Homer speaks of an age 'abounding with Inclosures', and the world must have seemed like this to a busy Commissioner. It will emphasize the professional pride which we have seen in Homer if we examine the number of enclosures which a Commissioner might undertake.

In 1844, when the main flood of enclosure was almost spent, the Select Committee of the Commons on Inclosure heard witnesses who had been engaged in Commissions. One from Lincolnshire had been fourteen times Commissioner,[6] another, Commissioner, Agent or Solicitor in twenty parishes,[7] and George

---

[1] Henry Homer, *An Essay on the Nature and Method [of] the Inclosure of Common Fields*, p. 61. Oxford, 1766. This is the author called 'Horner' by E. C. K. Gonner, *Common Land and Inclosure*, 1912.

[2] Ibid. p. 1.　　　　　　　　　　　　　　　　　　[3] Ibid. p. 2.

[4] Parliamentary Papers (hereafter called P.P.) 1844, v, Q 3005/6.

[5] T. R. Potter, *Charnwood Forest*, 1842, p. 30.　　　[6] P.P. 1844, v, Q 1328.

[7] *House of Commons Committee Reports*, 1800, IX, 227.

Maxwell told an earlier Committee that from 1773 to 1800 he had been over a hundred times a Commissioner.[1] Christopher Pemberton was Clerk to 45 Cambridgeshire enclosures and his firm's collection of Minutes is now in the University Library.

That these are not boasting or spectacular exceptions to a more moderate rule is shown by the following table:

Table 1

328 Commissioners in 400 Warwickshire, Worcestershire and Staffordshire Enclosures[2]

194 acted in		1 enclosure		49 acted in		2 enclosures
22	,,	3 enclosures		12	,,	4	,,
13	,,	5	,,	8	,,	6	,,
3	,,	7	,,	3	,,	8	,,
1	,,	9	,,	4	,,	10	,,
2	,,	12	,,	3	,,	13	,,
1	,,	14	,,	1	,,	15	,,
2	,,	16	,,	1	,,	17	,,
2	,,	18	,,	1	,,	20	,,
1	,,	21	,,	1	,,	22	,,
1	,,	23	,,	2	,,	29	,,
1	,,	32	,,				

966 Commissioners are named in 400 Acts: an average of over two Commissioners per enclosure. Somewhat similar results could be shown by the tabulation of the 80 Cambridgeshire Commissioners named in 36 Cambridgeshire Enclosures.

Many of these Commissioners are to be found working in other parishes. John Chamberlain was twelve times Commissioner in Warws, Worcs, and Staffs, eighteen times in Oxon,[3] and at least once in Bucks.[4] It was only natural for a landowner looking for a suitable Commissioner to think of those already experienced. The same is true of surveyors, many of whom appear in minute book after minute book. In some cases Commissioners seem to have worked in groups, undertaking as a team[5] (although of course engaged as individuals) work in many parishes. We have families like the Nockolds, three generations of whom were Commissioners; or the Bloodworths of Kimbolton; or such indications of continuity as those seen in the Chesterton (Cambs) papers in 1838 where the MSS. pencil notes[6] make it clear that they were used as a basis for the proceedings *mutatis mutandis* in the Willingham enclosure of 1846, just as Stow-cum-Quy[7] was utilized for Cottenham in 1842.

The Commissioner was usually named in the Act, but the choice lay, not with the Parliamentary Committees who examined the Bill, but with the landowners concerned. This arrangement was given implicit statutory recognition in such a clause as that in the Bottisham (Cambs) Act (1801) which names three persons as Commissioners, and then continues that, if any die, the three principal proprietors are to make the reappointment. At Abberley (1814), if the Commissioner dies the majority in value of the proprietors are to choose a Commissioner.

[1] *House of Commons Committee Reports*, p. 223.
[2] From the collection of Acts at Birmingham, 17240.
[3] Ex inf. W. E. Tate, unpublished thesis.   [4] Buckinghamshire, op. cit.
[5] In Cambridgeshire Hare and Maxwell worked together on three enclosures; Truslove and Custance on eight; Wedge and Custance on five; Thorpe and Custance on three.
[6] Cambridge, ADD 6028.   [7] Ibid. 6032.

At Abbots Morton (1770) the surviving Commissioners are to replace a dead member. At Kingswinford (Staffs) four Commissioners are named, and these four are to choose a fifth themselves.[1] It was common enough for the proprietor of great importance to regard it as his right to nominate a Commissioner: thus the Hathersage Bill states that if the Commissioner John Dowland dies, his successor shall be nominated by the Duke of Devonshire;[2] on 19 January 1824 this provision fell to be carried out.[3] On the other hand, we know from the case of Barton[4] (where some proprietors unsuccessfully tried to have Nockolds as Commissioner) that meetings would reject some suggested Commissioner.

The extant MSS. notes of evidence given to a Parliamentary Committee on the Barton (Cambs) Bill show an agent of one of the parties concerned describing the proprietors' meeting earlier in 1839. It is a great loss that so little other verbatim reporting of evidence before Lords' or Commons' Committees has survived.[5] This note was found among the Pemberton papers.[6]

Mr Adcock called and examined 6th June 1839. He is agent for the Incorporated Society of the Governors of the Sons of the Clergy. He was present at a tithe and enclosure meeting of the proprietors of Barton in Cambridge in February. He had no official instructions, but there stated that he thought the Governors would oppose the project, if it ignored their claims. This later proved to be true. Mr Jackson was appointed Commissioner by the Lords of the Manor, Mr Utton the other. He was not called to another meeting. He did not make any formal objection to the appointments, or vote for or against the Commissioners. At the meeting there were the Lords of the Manor and some proprietors who said very little. There was very little discussion except over the size of the assignments to the Lords, i.e. 1/20th or 1/16th or 1/25th. Mr Pemberton conducted most of the business. There was some discussion of the amount to be paid to the Commissioners and Surveyor.

Professional Commissioners were consulted before Bills went to the Commons, and this tended to give uniformity to the many Private Acts which preceded the General Acts of 1801 and 1845. From the papers of the Yorkshire Commissioner, Fairbank, we know that he was consulted by Sir John Sinclair, President of the Board of Agriculture, who was vainly attempting in 1796 to obtain the third reading of a General Bill.[7]

Proprietors' consultation of Fairbank included an examination of the draft,[8] dining out and spending an evening with some of the promoters[9] and being present at the meetings of proprietors called to discuss the promotion of the Bill.[10] It is clear that a great deal of contentious matter was eliminated and the major proprietors' interests satisfied *before* the Bill went to Westminster.

The Duke of Kingston wrote to the attorney of one proprietor in 1786:[11]

The Duke and several owners desire you will please meet them...in order to consult proper measures for the bringing in a Bill in the next session for inclosing the open field and Commons.

---

[1] Birmingham, 529363. [2] Sheffield, Fairbank MB/237, i.
[3] The implicit right of the great proprietors to reappoint their nominees is shown every time a death occurs while a Commission is in progress. Cf. Cambridge, ADD 6053, f. 48.
[4] Ibid. DOC 622, f. 56.
[5] The accounts in W. E. Tate, art. cit. and in his *Parliamentary Land Enclosures*, Nottingham, 1935, show how useful and at the same time how limited is the information of the Lords' and Commons' Journals. No Committee minutes have survived in the Lords' or Commons' MSS. records and none were printed.
[6] Cambridge, ADD 6022. [7] Sheffield, WC/2219.
[8] Ibid. sub 23 November 1795. [9] Ibid. 28 December 1795.
[10] Ibid. 30 December 1795. [11] Ibid. WC/2240, f. 5.

'The attorney's reply is significant:[1]

It is unnecessary for Mrs S. to see a draft. She only desires that Mr J. Brettle be appointed a Commissioner.

The correspondence which ensued between the Duke's steward and Mrs S.'s attorney is also significant. It shows how the Commissioners were considered as nominees; it moves over to a reminder of the impartiality which the Oath enjoined upon the Commission; and it touches upon the vexed point that Commissioners cost money:[2]

All the proprietors, being aprized of the great expense and delays that would consequently arise by having too great a number of Commissioners did agree that Mr Oldknow should stand as Commissioner for all the parties, and, to prevent an undue preference to be given to any of the parties, Mr Oldknow should name two other Commissioners who had no other connection with any of the parties: viz. Mr Ayre and Mr Stone. Therefore it makes it impracticable for Mrs S. to propose any alteration...and were it not so that, if Mrs S. names her Commissioner, no doubt but the Duke, Mr Broughton, Mr Edge, Mr Saltmarsh, the Vicar and several others would expect to do the same, so that... instead of three Commissioners we should have a dozen? You know too that you told Mr Shering that if the Vicar named a Commissioner you would do so too, but that if he gave up that point you would do likewise. Are not the three Commissioners persons of Honour, Worth and Probity and are not they obliged by the intended oath to make the allotments to the proprietors without favour?

At another meeting of Yorkshire proprietors the draft Bill is approved with the addition,[3] 'that the greatest economy in expenses are to be observed, as otherwise the expenses of the enclosure are likely to be greater than the advantages', and many other proprietors expressed publicly and privately their anxiety to reconcile adequate representation of interests with decent economy in number (and costs) of Commissioners. Sir John Beckett spoke of 'that necessity of representing all interests—which *drives* you to three Commissioners' in his evidence to the 1844 Commons Committee.[4]

Sometimes, a witness told the same Committee,[5] a Commissioner would be chosen from a distance if local feeling was running high. The distance added to the expenses, since three guineas a day was paid for travelling expenses. The letter inviting him to be Commissioner came, said this witness, as a complete surprise: it was from Radnor and he was in Bedford.

An unsuccessful petition meant that the petitioning landowners would have to bear the cost of the application: some idea of this cost is given by the solicitor's bill[6] for obtaining the Badsey (Worcs) Act. Even excluding £225 legal fees, expenses totalled £562 between September 1811 and May 1812. Another £58 went in travelling expenses to meetings of proprietors to obtain their signature of consent, and to London to watch over the Bill in the House. Pemberton's bill for Long Stow[7] totalled £225, including an amount for 'attendances on the members for the County of Cambridge while the Bill was before the Commons and on Earl Hardwick while it was before the Lords...5 guineas' with a note signed by Pemberton: 'many attendances not charged for.'

Pemberton's Bills for soliciting twenty-five enclosures totalled £6215—an average of £248. A Board of Agriculture estimate put the solicitor's cost for an

[1] Sheffield, WC/2240, f. 5.
[2] Ibid.
[3] Ibid. WC/2251, f. 29.
[4] P.P. 1844, v, Q 3631.
[5] Ibid. Q 3697.
[6] Birmingham, 377180.
[7] Cambridge, DOC 645, ff. iv and v.

average bill at £497,[1] but this probably included the usual £200 or more for Parliamentary fees.

The impartiality of Commissioners in their task of reallocation and assessment was essential. The oath inserted in the Acts after 1760 was an attempt to ensure this. There were other attempts to exclude Commissioners with direct interest in the parish. A resolution of the Commons' 'Committee to consider Persons to be appointed Commissioner' ran:[2]

Resolved: there be inserted an oath that the Commissioner is not to be interested in lands so intended to be enclosed or to be steward, bailiff or agent of any person so intending.

Resolved: that the words 'and has not been steward for the last three years' be added.

This was not always observed: the obituary of the first Commissioner for the enclosure of Erdington and Witton[3] described him as: 'Steward of Heneas Legge, of Aston Hall, lord of the Manor of Erdington and Witton.'[4]

We have seen that the expense of a Commission loomed large in the proprietors' eyes, for that sum would be found by an assessed rate on their property. What were those expenses?

There was the cost of promotion, whether successful or unsuccessful. There were the fees of the officers—clerk, surveyor—and the cost of the fencing, hedging and ditching consequent upon the new lay-out of the fields. And there was the Commission's fee. 'There were usually three Commissioners with a fee of three guineas a day each', reports a witness before the Commons' Committee of 1844.[5] In 1800, Maxwell, an experienced Commissioner, said that two sufficed.[6] John Iveson, another witness[7] in 1844, was one of six Commissioners for Charnwood, and often all were present. We have seen that the average number of Commissioners for the 450 enclosures which have been examined was just over two.[8]

The Commissioners' fees were sometimes mentioned in the Act, as was the two guineas for Hathersage,[9] but by no means always. The Board of Agriculture Reports give £344 as the average cost of a Commissioner. The Stow (Cambs)[10] Act laid down three guineas a day, but for fifteen meetings the Commissioner was actually paid £189.[11]

Homer says that:[12]

Commissioners ought themselves particularly to set examples of moderation both in their demands and their expenses, neither to desire to be paid for Commission Days upon which they cannot give attendance on the business, nor to live, when they do attend, beyond their station, nor to make meetings of this kind seasons of jollity for themselves at the expense of the proprietors.

These strictures are echoed by the House of Commons Committee of 1795:[13] 'many complaints have been made of the remissness with which Commissioners

[1] Quoted by E. C. K. Gonner, op. cit.
[2] *House of Commons Committee Reports*, 1801, III, 20.
[3] Birmingham, 326709.
[4] *Aris, Birmingham Gazette*, 7 December 1801.
[5] P.P. 1844, v, Q 2342.
[6] *House of Commons Committee Reports*, 1800, IX, 233.
[7] P.P. 1844, v, Q 3696. But this was a vast enclosure.
[8] Table 1, p. 132 supra.
[9] Sheffield, Fairbank MB 237.
[10] 1839.
[11] Cambridge, ADD 6063.
[12] Op. cit. 108.
[13] *House of Commons Committee Reports*, 1795.

proceed and the exorbitant charges which they sometimes make or expenses which they occasion.' Five years later another Committee reported:[1] 'We have been able to discover no flagrant instance of misbehaviour of a Commissioner' and recommended a fee of two guineas a day, exclusive of travelling day, since Commissioners come 'sometimes from considerable distances where their avocation has carried them'.

One witness spoke of coming fifty miles for an enclosure and protested against the type of contract wherein Commissioners were paid a fixed lump sum: in this case, of two hundred guineas.[2] His colleague had received the same sum, but had travelled only half a mile! To the Committee of 1844 no witness could relate such an agreement within his personal experience,[3] although it had in fact been a recommendation of the Commons Committee of 1801 that a total sum should be named in all Enclosure Acts as a Commissioner's fee.[4]

Even after the General Act there was considerable variety in the fee-clauses, which in some Acts did not even appear at all. Concern for economy in fees moved some petitioners to insert detailed directions into the Act, as at Alstonefield (1834)[5] or Colmworth (Beds) where a detailed Time Book has survived, giving exact times spent on the journey and in the fields.[6]

What were the Commissioners' expenses? One Commissioner spoke of six guineas expenses for a single day; and another that the chief proprietor had made an agreement with him before the Bill for one payment only of £200 and eleven guineas expenses which proved to be insufficient.[7] At Aspley Guise, Beds, the Commissioners' inn-charges of 5s. 3d. a day were met by the proprietors, although the fee was there only 10s. a meeting.[8]

The survival of the private accounts of the Commissioner for Bickenhill, Warws,[9] shows that it cost him about 10s. a meeting for inn-charges for himself and servant. These are not charged in the printed accounts but covered by three guineas allowance 'for each travelling day'. The Commissioner received 183 times three guineas, in fact: that is, three guineas fee for each of the 68 meetings and three guineas for a day's journey to the enclosure and three guineas for the day after the meeting. In many instances the business lasted for more than one day, and the Commissioner's inn at Coleshill was less than five miles from the enclosed fields!

Table 2 takes three busy Cambridgeshire Commissioners and analyses their income and what they did to earn it.

Table 2

Commissioner:	Dugmore	Custance	Hare
Number of meetings	88 [12 years]	443 [22 years]	186 [14 years]
Total remuneration	£1018	£4556	£979
Average fee per day	£12	£10	£5
Average income per annum	£85	£207	£70

These fees are well above the statutory three guineas and probably include travel and subsistence allowances. The total sum was paid to the Commissioners usually not in a lump sum, but in instalments.

[1] *House of Commons Committee Reports*, 1800, IX, p. 1.   [2] Ibid. loc. cit.
[3] P.P. 1844, Q 202.   [4] *House of Commons Committee Reports*, 1801, III, 209.
[5] 4 Geo. IV, c. 15.   [6] Bedford DD/WG/9.
[7] *House of Commons Committee Reports*, 1800, IX, 223-7.
[8] T. Batchelor, *General View of...Bedfordshire*, 1808, p. 221.   [9] Warwick, HR/5.

Each of the recorded meetings in any set of minutes details the business which the Commissioner undertook. Broadly, these vary very little from Cambridgeshire to Warwickshire, although there was no rule of thumb which could indicate how long each detail of the enclosure would take in any one parish.

An enclosure was not to be concluded in one autumn. To survey; or to check an old survey; to value and reallocate; to settle claims and disputes: these were long and arduous labours. Early work of receiving claims took many meetings but could be done rapidly. The later work of valuing and redistributing (with accompanying disputes) was a long task. Many proprietors found that it might be a matter of years, although few offered the Alstonefield incentive to speed by diminishing fees as time passed. Sometimes a forfeit was exacted if the Commissioner was late in the completion of the enclosure. Harwood could not attend a Committee of the House of Commons on the Barton (Cambs)[1] Bill because he had to finish an enclosure engagement by the first of May.

How long did those enclosures take which were not hampered by some such local impediments as the litigation which made the Rhyddlan enclosure last over 40 years[2] or the bankers' bankruptcy at Clun Forest?[3]

Table 3 gives time tables of 53 enclosures whose minutes have been examined.

Table 3

Summary of 53 enclosures[4]

Number of enclosures complete in	1 year		2
,,	,,	2 years	8
,,	,,	3 ,,	8
,,	,,	4 ,,	8
,,	,,	5 ,,	6
,,	,,	6 ,,	2
,,	,,	7 ,,	6
,,	,,	8 ,,	1
,,	,,	9 ,,	—
,,	,,	10 ,,	2
,,	,,	11 ,,	2
,,	,,	12 years or more	8

Commissioners did not have to hold meetings at regular intervals. The adjournments display no regular pattern, and there was no statutory guidance. Enclosures usually began in June, July, August or September (probably to begin after harvest). Of forty-five sets of minutes examined, only eleven began in other months. Good weather and long daylight hours favoured summer meetings, and the cold months were unpopular for journeys to distant parishes. We have seen that the meetings in an enclosure were most frequent at the beginning, when much formal receipt of claims had to be undertaken, so that it is not surprising that Table 5 analysing 659 meetings,[5] shows a significant grouping, with few meetings in the early summer with its growing crops, and many in the autumn.

[1] Cambridge, ADD 6022.
[2] P.P. 1844, v, Q 2248.
[3] Ibid. Q 2493.
[4] Collected from the sources named in n. 1, p. 123 supra.
[5] Ibid.

Table 4

Length of time taken over enclosure and frequency of meetings

Cambridgeshire enclosures		Summary of all known enclosure meetings	
Parish	Dates covered	Total meetings	Average per year
Rampton	1839–1843	29	6
Harston	1798–1801	35	8
Barnwell	1807–1811	37	7
Barton	1839–1840	18	9
Bassingbourn	1801–1814	40	3
Bottisham	1801–1808	31	4
Chesterton	1838–1840	31	10
Comberton	1839–1841	19	6
Connington	1800–1801	5	3
Cottenham	1842–1847	30	5
Eversden	1811–1814	21	5
Fulbourn	1806–1830	37	2
Girton	1808–1814	16	2
Gransden	1813–1826	28	2
Guilden Morden	1800–1814	40	3
Hardwick	1836–1838	40	13
Kingston	1810–1815	24	4
Landbeach	1807–1813	33	5
Longstanton A.S.	1811–1816	32	5
Longstanton St.M.	1813–1816	15	4
Long Stow	1798–1800	16	5
Oakington	1833–1835	36	12
Stow-cum-Quy	1839–1841	15	5
Sawston	1802–1811	33	3
Stapleford	1812–1814	24	8
Steeple Morden	1807–1817	40	4
Stetchworth	1814–1820	26	4
Swaffham	1805–1814	23	2
Swavesey	1838–1839	7	3
Teversham	1810–1818	27	3
West Wickham	1812–1822	44	4
Whaddon	1840–1841	4	2
Willingham	1846–1853	24	3
Waresley	1808–1822	48	4

Table 5

Meetings held in each month

Jan.	Feb.	Mar.	Apr.	May	June	July	Aug.	Sept.	Oct.	Nov.	Dec.
56	54	51	35	38	50	51	66	56	76	68	58

With all the possibilities of delay, proprietors sometimes expressed natural impatience. One wrote:[1]

I must express my wish that the enclosure might not stand over another season. I am afraid that this will be the case unless you take the trouble to remind the Commissioner that he has now been indulged with every reasonable time, and that after such indulgence every delay increases the expense.

[1] Sheffield, F/CP/31/8.

Not all were as lucky as Whaddon,[1] enclosed in three meetings. One optimistic forecast is to be found among the MSS. notes on a proposal to enclose Atherstone (Warws) where the solicitor wrote in pencil:[2]

> Act passed ann 1731 then
> to be surveyed by 2 ffebry 1731
> to be aloted by 2 ffebry 1732
> and to be finished by 24 March 1733

Sometimes Commissioners attributed the delay to proprietors who had not paid their share of the levy. At Leighton Buzzard one Commissioner wrote to the Clerk:[3]

I quite think with you that it is time the Business was brought to a close and I considered we had so settled at our last meeting...'that those proprietors who had neglected to have paid their Rate by a stated time should be proceded against', and as you have since then made several applications...I would take the necessary steps which I consider there is no necessity of our holding a meeting expressly for.

Sometimes the Commissioners themselves were reproached. A solicitor wrote to the Commissioner for Attercliffe (Yorks):[4]

We hope that the enclosure has not encroached too much on your other engagements, but we think it is high time that the business should be closed.

Commissioners were busy men. Apart from the pressure of other enclosure meetings, some Commissioners were clergymen, some land-agents, some surveyors, some stewards. Men who can be called 'professional Commissioners' include Arthur Elliot, whose private diary[5] shows that in the year 1797/8 he spent 105 days holding formal enclosure meetings, and fourteen on consultative work. In eight weeks in 1795 he was engaged in negotiations for the enclosure of eight parishes, and in the next year held 117 meetings for twelve parishes.

To save time, Commissioners held meetings for different enclosures on the same day, usually at the same Inn. To the Commissioner this might seem to save time, but to any one parish it might seem a hindrance, since the meeting would always be outside one of the parishes concerned, and if it were at some central point (such as the Eagle Inn at Cambridge) it would be outside all the parishes concerned. On the other hand if all the meetings were in the parishes concerned, then a Commissioner would spend his time (and the proprietors' money) on the road. Many Acts contained a clause prohibiting meetings more than 6 or 10 miles from the parish.

'It would be a good thing to prohibit Commissioners working more than one enclosure on one day', said Thomas Harrison, himself twenty times a Commissioner, to the Committee of 1800,[6] and to the 1844 Committee another witness said:[7]

Commissioners often find it difficult to give time continuously to one enclosure because of their other commitments.

The Cambridgeshire minutes when examined for simultaneous enclosures, often with the same Commissioners, yield many examples of coincident meetings: the Commissions for Barton and Comberton opened on the same day, and held seven coincident meetings in 1842. Twice in 1814, Thorpe, Commissioner for

---

[1] Cambridge, ADD 6084.   [2] Warwick, HR/35.
[3] Bedford. Uncatalogued MSS., shelf BO.
[4] Sheffield, CP/35/75.   [5] Ibid. WC/2219.
[6] *House of Commons Committee Reports*, 1800, IX, 232.
[7] P.P. 1844, V, Q 199. Elmhirst, the author of *A View of the Agriculture of...Lincolnshire*, 1794, says on p. 84 that he was once engaged simultaneously on nine enclosures.

Kingston, Longstanton and Teversham held meetings for all three parishes on the same day. An inn was a convenient rendezvous, and neutral ground. There is only one meeting at a private house recorded in these 45 sets of minutes.[1]

Did all the Commission attend? There are many cases when the Commission is incomplete. This is usually acknowledged in the minutes: at Whitwick there were three adjournments because only one Commissioner was present, and on three other occasions there is a blank page when no Commissioner came. It must be remembered that the earliest Acts (1730–60) appointed a large Commission. A small quorum was usually designated. At Rothley only four of the five Commissioners were present for over 50 % of the meetings. Alderminster (1726) was enclosed by ten Commissioners, with a quorum of five. Later Acts presupposed a small Commission of professionals, and the Astley Act (1811) rules 'if any Commissioner is absent from the first and second or any two subsequent meetings then he shall be deemed to refuse to act'. I know of no Commissioner who was removed from office: but there were at least one resignation,[2] two refusals to stand,[3] and several Commissioners died in harness.[4]

Proprietors were not compelled to attend meetings. Attendance usually depended on interest. Claims could be delivered by post or proxy.[5] Rampton had twenty-three meetings: at six no proprietors were present; at five over fifteen attended. At these five meetings the business included voting the Commissioners' fees; auditing the accounts; objecting to claims; and considering the result of a lawsuit against one of their number. At Erdington three proprietors heard the award read, although twenty-seven had attended a meeting concerned with a disputed common. The usual formula in the minutes was that 'the award was executed in the presence of such proprietors as attended'.

The reading of the award and its formal enrolment were the Commissioner's last acts. In no set of minutes is there any formal dissolution. It is quite common for the minutes to stop in the middle of a page, or to adjourn to a given date, for which there is no entry. An adjournment *sine die* only appears once, at Salford (Beds). In the Newbold Vernon (Leics) minutes the last three entries are in pencil instead of ink, and then there is a blank.

Since the minutes are in large folio volumes, many pages are left blank. There was no legal compulsion to deposit minutes with the Clerk of the Peace and they seem to have passed into the hands of the Clerk to the Enclosure. Those which survive derive generally from solicitors' offices, where the Clerk had bound them up with a copy of the relevant Private Act, embossed them with the name of the parish and then added them to the office files. There they remained until they passed to the County Records Office or to the Library where they now lie.[6]

---

[1] References to these meetings will be found in the minutes of the parishes named among the Cambridge enclosure papers cited in n. 1, p. 123 above.

[2] Cambridge, ADD 6023, 16 November 1801.

[3] Cardington and Wilshamstead enclosure papers, Bedford, DD/HA/16.

[4] Alexander Watford (Rampton), Jacob Nockolds (Oakington), Martin Nockolds (Chesterton) are some of these.

[5] Leicester, 4D/31/242, is a bundle of proxy claims.

[6] I am grateful to the various archivists and librarians who have helped to track down minutes; to Mr W. E. Tate for answering queries; and to Mr E. Welbourne who first aroused my curiosity unwittingly by stating baldly: 'the only people who gained by enclosures were the Liberals who won a political grievance; the lawyers who gained by the legalism of the procedure; and the Surveyor-turned-Commissioner who lived in the new house overlooking the fields where he made his fortune.'

te 8. Edward VI and the Pope. Other figures in the back row (left to right) are Henry
II, Edward Seymour, 1st Duke of Somerset, John Dudley, Duke of Northumberland
d Thomas Cranmer, Archbishop of Canterbury. *(Unknown artist, c. 1548-9, National
rtrait Gallery)*

13

THE POLL TAX AND CENSUS OF SHEEP, 1549

N March 1549 Parliament granted Edward VI the proceeds of a tax
on sheep coupled with a purchase tax on cloth. It was probably the
shortest lived tax in English fiscal history, being hastily repealed in
nuary 1550 and although some of the tax was collected, it is doubtful
hether it ever reached the royal purse. The records of the collection are
perfect and the proposed national census of sheep failed to be com-
eted.

This list of failures and lost documents may not seem a very promising
ginning. In fact, the failure of the Lord Protector Somerset's attempt
tax sheep is a significant comment on the place of the wool-growing
erest in national politics; the proposal itself is directly related to the long
bate on the place of graziers in the national economy which occupied
blic men all through the sixteenth century; while the surviving docu-
nts, with their information about the size and ownership of a small
nple of flocks in seven counties may be matched by other documents,
yet undiscovered, in local private and public archives.

No tax can be considered apart from the political and social attitudes
those who imposed it, and this tax of 1549 came at an acute moment in
controversies on agrarian policy. It was undoubtedly a product of the
ool of thought labelled 'Commonwealth Men', a group of divines,
iticians, and pamphleteers who were anxious to see the acquisitive
wers of the 'cormorant' landlords limited. In particular, they wanted
age encouraged and the extension of pasture discouraged. A tax falling
sheep and cloth could not fail to be attractive in achieving these ends
social policy, and the Protectorate of Somerset, the young king's uncle,
vided the opportunity.

The tax was resented by landlords and graziers, who were not impressed
the argument that they could easily pass the tax on to the final con-
ners or by the offer of other tax reductions as compensation. The repeal
the tax within the year—and the petitioning of Parliament against it
hin eight months—is a measure of the feeling aroused. The fall of
nerset that autumn and the rise to power of Northumberland brought
end of the whole project.

he circumstances of the sudden repeal have led historians to believe

that the tax was never assessed and never collected. This attitude deriv
from a remark by A. F. Pollard in the longest study of the Protectorate
Somerset which we have. He wrote of this tax:

"This Act never came into force as its operation was deferred f
three years, and before that time arrived Somerset had fallen, and Parli
ment, under the reactionary influence of the 'reformed' Council, abc
ished these taxes, thus relieving the wealthiest classes of any tax on t
wealth which they were acquiring at the expense of the community."

In fact, the Act granting 'the Relief on Sheep and Cloth' makes it qui
clear that the tax was to be levied at once.[2] The period of three years whi
Pollard noticed was the period for which the tax should run, not the peri
for which it should be deferred. The Act ordered that the machinery f
assessment and collection should begin to turn on 1 May 1549, two mont
after the end of the parliamentary session. The collection was to be cor
plete by 1 November. Since the repeal did not take place until the session
Parliament which began that November, there was every reason to expe
until the contrary was proved, that the tax was collected. You could harc
expect the advocates of repeal to raise much sympathy for a burden whi
had never been laid upon them or would not be laid for another thr
years.

With this in mind, I began to search among the records of the E
chequer to see whether there were any assessments or accounts in cc
nection with the Relief. In my first searches I was unlucky: the conte
of the rolls in this class (E 179) are only described in the typescript lists
the Public Record Office in very general terms, so that collectors' accou
for this year, 1549, might on examination prove to have nothing to do w
these taxes on sheep and cloth. The first dozen rolls I examined had
mention of a sheep in them, but at my second attack on the hundred or
rolls for this period I came upon a roll with a quite different appearan
the columns of the calculations necessary to determine a man's liabi
to this new tax. Such accounts have been recovered from five count
Their location is given below,[3] but in order to appreciate what the
sought to do it will be necessary to consider something of the backgrou
to the suggestion that sheep and cloth should be taxed and to summar
the content of the statute authorizing the tax.

It must be made plain that neither in the Act granting the tax nor

[1] A. F. Pollard, *England under Protector Somerset*, 1900, p. 226 n.
[2] 2 & 3 Ed. VI c. 36, *Statutes of the Realm*, IV, p. 78.   [3] See below, p. 152.

hn Hales's proposals for a tax in the previous year[1] can we find any
vert defence of the tax as an instrument of agrarian policy. It was
scussed solely as a revenue-raiser. In the proposals of 1548 it was a
ggestion for a new source of revenue to replace income which would be
st if certain other tax concessions were made. In the preamble to the
ct of 1549 the reasons put forward were the usual ones for any grant to
Tudor monarch: the necessities of defence and the rising expenses of
e royal household. Indeed, in the proposals of 1548 Hales very much
nderplayed the question of incidence. It is a little tax, he argued; it can
passed on to foreign consumers; the burden on Englishmen is so light
at no one will notice it. Yet the context in which the proposals were
ade makes it certain that the deterrent effect of a tax on sheep was both
vious and attractive to Somerset's advisers. It was all of a piece with their
rarian reforms. They could not have been unaware of the effect it would
ve in making sheep-rearing more expensive and therefore less of a rival
tillage. They must have known that the tax on cloth would make cloths
arer and therefore discourage an industry whose growth seemed to have
many undesirable results. The encouragement of tillage and the re-
iction of the large-scale growth of cloth-manufacture were integral parts
the programme of the Commonwealth Men for lower prices and social
stice.[2] The effect of the tax was clearly seen by the unknown author of a
mphlet written just at this time, *Policies to Reduce this Realme of England
to a Prosperous Wealthe and Estate*.[3] He wrote: "Ther coulde have byne
redier waye to cause a great quantiti of the said Ship pastures to be
verted into erable then this Subsidie [i.e. the Relief] uppon Shippe."
deed, he wished that the tax could have fallen more heavily than it did.
Despite the tactful silence of their protagonists, the poll tax on sheep
d the accompanying tax on cloth take their place alongside other Tudor
empts to deter the expansion of grassland and the further enclosure of
ble. The taxes stem from the same policy which sent out the Com-
ssions of Inquiry in 1517–18 and the fresh Commissions in 1548–9, among
om John Hales himself sat. I have elsewhere analysed the results of these
mmissions of Inquiry and the prosecutions which followed.[4] A close
allel to the sheep tax is the Act of 1533 by which it was made an offence

'Causes of Dearth' in *State Papers, Domestic, Edward VI*, v, no. 20, printed in *A Discourse*
he Commonweal, ed. E. Lamond, 1929, pp. xlii-v.
The political thought of this group of men has been sympathetically analysed by A. F.
ard, *op. cit.*, and by Professor R. H. Tawney in *Religion and the Rise of Capitalism*.
Printed from the MS. in Goldsmiths' Library, University of London, in R. H. Tawney
Eileen Power, *Tudor Economic Documents*, 1935, III, p. 327.
M. W. Beresford, *The Lost Villages of England*, 1954.

to keep flocks of more than 2,400 sheep.[1] Any informer could sue for ha
the penalty due to the Crown by the owner of the over-large flock. In so f;
as such informations were laid in the court of Exchequer, I have found
small trickle from 1535 until the end of the reign of Edward VI with iso
lated examples through to the end of the century.[2] This measure was i
the mind of the reformers in 1548. One of Hales's charges to the jury i
the Commission of Inquiry of that year was to report on any violation
the Act of 1533, "if any person hath or doth keep above the number
two thousand sheep, besides lambs of one year's age . . ."[3] But the dire
attacks on the flocks seem to have failed, and in the second Parliament
the new reign the reformers took the opportunity of the call for revenu
to make an attack on the sheep masters from another direction.

Proposals for a direct tax on sheep must have been in the air as ear
as the first autumn of the reign if a paper of 6 October 1547 is correct
dated.[4] This paper took the form of a memorandum to Somerset attempti
to estimate the sheep population, in order to estimate the yield if she
were taxed. The population could only be estimated in a roundabout w
since the only information at ministers' disposal was the amount of t
dues on certain cloths. Having assumed that each cloth contained so mu
wool, the author had to find an equation linking wool and sheep. He ma
two calculations, each based on a different assumption about the numb
of fleeces one would need to get a tod (28 lb) of wool. One alternative ga
him 8,407,819 sheep in 1546, and the other, 11,089,149.

His memorandum then estimated the yield if sheep were taxed, a
it is significant that he took a different rate for different types of sheep,
the Act of 1549 was to do. The reason given was simply that the she
feeding on enclosed pastures gave their master more wool. "Pasture mc
because ther cattell is bothe greater and carieth more wolle, to paie
every sheere sheep thre half pens . . . and for every (Ewe) after two pen
Other sheep, of all kinds, grazing on the commons or the open fall
were to be charged at the flat rate of a penny a head. This was the recog
tion of that superior yield from animals grazing on permanent and enclos

[1] 25 Henry VIII c. 13, *Stat. Realm*, III, p. 451. 'Two thousand' counted in long hundr
of 120.

[2] These informations can be found on the Memoranda Rolls of the King's Remembrar
(E 159) at the Public Record Office.

[3] Strype, *Ecclesiastical Memorials*, II, pt. ii, pp. 359-65, reprinted in Tawney and Pov
op. cit., I, pp. 39-44.

[4] *State Papers, Domestic, Edward VI*, II, no. 13, printed in Tawney and Power, *op. cit*
pp. 178-84.

pasture which lay behind the whole movement to convert arable to pasture in the Midlands at this period.

A second memorandum, known to be by John Hales, was drawn up the next summer, probably for a speech in the Parliament which opened in November 1548. It was headed *Causes of Dearth*, and we shall refer to it simply as Hales's *Causes*.[1] This memorandum also estimated the sheep population and the yield of a sheep tax. It came to a much lower figure than the 1547 calculations. It reckoned on 3,000,000 sheep. This reduction may have been due to some new information at the government's disposal; or it may have allowed for the exemption of the small peasant flocks. Nothing was said about these in the *Causes* but the Act of 1549 treated the small flocks more leniently.

It will be convenient to tabulate the two estimates.

TABLE 1

Type of Sheep		Tax Proposed	1547 (Anon.)	1548 (Hales)
Pasture sheep	Ewes	2d.	2,101,954	750,000
	Wethers	1½d.	2,101,954	750,000
Commons sheep, all kinds		1d.	4,203,909	1,500,000
TOTAL			8,407,819 *(sic)*	3,000,000

Both authors made the same assumption, that half the sheep population was made up of animals grazing on commons and common arable; that another quarter comprised ewes grazing on enclosed grassland; and the other quarter consisted of wethers also on enclosed grassland. The rates of tax proposed were the same in each document.

Different total yields followed from the different sizes of the estimated sheep population. In 1547 the memorandum hoped for just over £35,000 at a flat rate of a penny per head or just over £48,000 at the differential rates set out above. In the *Causes* only £17,187 was expected. Had this been all collected it would have equalled about one-third of the yield of the subsidy for a year. The document of 1547 hoped that, in addition, about twice this sum (£32,253) would be obtained from the levy on cloth.

The interest of these figures is not their accuracy, which we have no means of testing, but their being made at all. They anticipate some of the more sophisticated reckonings which were to appear in the next decades

[1] See p. 139 above, n. 1.

among Cecil's papers.[1] They are themselves useless as a reliable estimate
of the sheep population since they took account only of cloth exported.
They can say nothing about the sheep whose fleeces were giving wool to
clothe English backs.

> "In all this accompte no mention is made of the shepe whose wolle
> was made into Clothe and Cappes spent that yere in the Realme nor
> of skynnes tanned, white lether or parchement. And therfore it maye be
> trulye saied that ther wer more sheepe then is before rehersed."[2]

The second memorandum, Hales's *Causes*, is much nearer to the actual
statute of 1549 than the first. It looked on the poll tax on sheep and the cloth
levy as convenient alternative revenues if the king would abandon his right
to take 'provysions'. The right of the royal provisioners to commandeer
supplies at prices below market level was a widespread grievance, particularly since the royal price-tariff was still that of pre-inflation days: "the
purveyour alloweth for a lambe worthe two shylynges but xii d." Hales alleged that the fear of provisioners and purveyance discouraged food-grow-
ers, and a new and 'certain' tax was looked for, whose arbitrariness would
not deter the 'breeding of victuals'.

> "This certayntie myght be thus gathered: that the kyng myght have
> of every sheepe kept in the comen feldes one peny, of every Ewe and
> Lambe kept in severall pasture two pens, and of every other sheere
> sheepe kept in pasture, thre halfpens."

This would yield, he calculated, £17,187 10s., "which it is thought will
do somwhat, albeit not sufficient, towards the provysions of the kynge
householde."

In addition, Hales proposed a new levy on cloth manufactured in the
kingdom at the rate of 5s. on a broad cloth and 1s. 8d. on a kersey, with
double custom on cloths exported. (A tax on home-produced cloth at the
rate of $3\frac{1}{3}$ per cent "of the pryce and value of all woollen cloths made for
three years" was actually incorporated in the Relief of 1549.)

In exchange for these two new taxes Hales proposed that purveyance
should be abolished from Christmas 1548 except for genuine purchase
for the Household at current market prices. (He also proposed to relieve
towns of their traditional *fee farms*, and to relieve tenants of the Crown
from their obligation to do homage or to pay for non-performance.) I

---

[1] The significance of these calculations has been stressed by Lawrence Stone, *Econ. His.
Rev.*, 2nd ser., II, 1949, pp. 29–32.

[2] Tawney and Power, I, p. 182.

conclusion, the *Causes* attempted to analyse the incidence of the tax on sheep and cloth: the gentlemen will be pleased to avoid the charges of homage; the tax on cloth will be easily passed on to the consumers: "The clothier can have no losse therby, ffor he will recover it in his sale which is after the rate of two pens in the yarde of clothe." In a word, it was to be the dream of all statesmen, a tax to which no one (except foreigners) objected. Inspection of the cloth, which Hales assumed would go alongside collection, would also improve quality, he argued; merchants will gain in repute from this, and the customer would be delighted "when one garnement beying made of good and true clothe shall least [i.e. last] twise as long as garnements do at this tyme." (The despondency among clothiers when the demand for cloth should be thus halved was not considered!)

Restrictions on sheep-masters were also envisaged in another measure which Hales was proposing at this time, one of three Bills to bring down prices and cure rural distress. The draft Bill has been preserved.[1] It proposed, *inter alia*, that guild and chantry land should be protected in the same way as in the Act of 1536 which had attempted to force the purchasers of ex-monastic land to maintain tillage upon it;[2] Hales also suggested that any one keeping more than a thousand sheep on enclosed pastures should turn out one fifth on the fallow common fields each May, there to manure the villagers' strips of arable until Michaelmas.

[1] *State Papers, Domestic*, v, no. 22, printed in Lamond, *op. cit.*, pp. xlv-lii.
[2] 27 Henry VIII c. 27, *Stat. Realm*, iii, p. 578.

II

IT is in this atmosphere of proposals and estimates that Parliament discussed and approved the Bill which became 2 and 3 Edward VI c. 36. From a suggestion, the poll tax on sheep became law; the cloth levy was imposed; and instead of rough estimates of the sheep population, the Act set up the machinery to take a census of sheep in every parish, only eleven years later than Thomas Cromwell's attempt to number the parishioners by the recording of baptisms, marriages, and burials.[1]

The grant of supply to the King did not take any of the conventional forms. The usual *subsidy* (or tax on personalty) was not granted, nor the *tenth-and-fifteenth* (the old, and now conventionalized, local tax). Instead, in view of the danger in which the realm stood, the faithful subjects offered a *Relief* to be paid annually for the three years following.

In view of the close concern which this Relief was to have with sheep, there is a grim irony in the metaphor of sheep and shepherds in the preamble to the Act, akin to the tone in which the Prayer *for Landlords* in the Edwardian Prayer-Book was to ask that landlords should remember themselves to be "Thy Tenants."[2] This preamble to the *Act for the Relief* in 1549 calls on God to protect "this lytle Realme and us His poore Servants and little flock, takinge to his charge and defence our little Sheparde." The servants were modest about their grants, "besichynge his Grace not to cast his eies uppon the smalness of this our simple present."[3]

Despite the abandonment of the term *subsidy* in favour of *Relief*, the principle of assessment was not basically different in so far as it dealt with the assessment of personal property for tax. Those whose property exceeded ten pounds were to pay one shilling in the pound upon it. Aliens were to pay twice this rate if they possessed property at all: otherwise poll tax of eightpence. It is necessary to dwell on this part of the Relief of 1549 because the assessment of the amount a man would pay for his sheep was related to the amount he would already have paid on his personal property. The property on which the tax fell was specified in the Act. Stocks of merchandise and sheep were particularly mentioned. Thus

---

[1] Cox, *Parish Registers of England*, pp. 2–3.

[2] Reprinted in Tawney and Power, *Tudor Economic Documents*, III, pp. 62–3.

[3] *Statutes of the Realm*, IV, pp. 78 sqq. All the following quotations are from this Act unless otherwise acknowledged.

sheep-owner or a clothier would be assessed at 1s. in the pound (5%) on the value of sheep or cloth. The novel proposals in the second part of the *Act for the Relief* laid much more specific taxes on sheep and cloth.

The principle was the one we have seen in Hales's *Causes*, and a connection can be inferred from the entry in the Commons' Journal: "The Bill for the Relief of Subsidy of Goods, Sheep and Cloths for three years—to Mr. Hales." The three categories of sheep, on each of which a different rate was to be paid, were:

1. Ewes kept on enclosed ground for the greater part of any year, whether the enclosed ground were marsh or pasture: "that is to saye, groundes not comen nor comenlie used to be tilled." The tax on these ewes was three pence a head.

2. A tax of two pence a head on wethers and other shear-sheep on these same enclosed grounds.

3. A lower rate of three halfpence on all sheep on the commons or on enclosed tillage lands.

These rates were higher than Hales had proposed in 1548. The Act also made concessions to the small sheep-owner, although opponents of the Bill were later to argue that "it is to your poor Commons having but fewe sheep in number a great charge."[1] Men with fewer than ten sheep were only to pay a halfpenny a head; those with from eleven to twenty were only to pay a penny a head.

These concessions are the more curious when we take into account another important clause. A sheep-owner only became liable to pay any of the poll tax due on his sheep if his obligation exceeded the sum he had already paid that year on goods. A man whose sheep-tax totalled 10s. would pay nothing unless his relief on goods had been assessed at less than that sum. If his sheep tax did exceed his property tax, then he was only to pay the difference. It is this feat of subtraction before the sheep-owners' obligation was finally known which produced the ruled columns of some of the surviving collectors' accounts, headed:

"Ye sums dew unto the kyng hys maieste for ye furst part of ye releyfe of the pole of sheyp, deducting the releyfe for goods a fore unto ye kyng payd."[2]

This said very briefly what the statute said longwindedly. The Hunts collectors arranged their figures in six columns tracing the logic of their calculations.[3]

[1] Preamble to 3 and 4 Edward VI, c. 23, *Stat. Realm*, IV, p. 122.
[2] Public Record Office, E 179, 122, 143. [3] E 179, 122, 144.

1.	2.	3.	4.	5.	6.
The mens Names	Nombre of Sheepe	Place where they goe	Money due for theym	Whereof payde for goods	Remayneth unpaid.

In another Hunts roll tabulation is replaced by prose.

> "Somersham: cc iii^{xx} ii sher sheyp kept by John Castell ye elder, yeoman, most parte of ym yz on the comens."[1]

Castell, having already paid 23s. to the subsidy on goods earlier in the summer, had now to pay only the difference between that sum and the 37s. 9d. due for his sheep-tax: 14s. 9d. (It will be noticed that the sheep are being counted by the old 'long hundred' of six score, so that if the collectors wish to indicate a hundred sheep they will write v^{xx} and not c. Castell's entry makes this clear. He had 302 sheep by the long hundred (not 262 as the figure may first appear to read) and at three halfpence each (being "on the comens") 453d. or 37s. 9d. was due.

Such a double assessment and subtraction were not administratively difficult. The Act assumed that the Commissioners who assessed the poll tax on sheep locally would include many men who already served as assessors and collectors for the Relief on goods in the spring. The assessment on goods was to be completed by 20 March 1549, and the tax was expected at the Exchequer by 6 May. The Commissions authorizing the assessment of the poll tax on sheep were to go out five days earlier and the Exchequer wanted the returns from the counties in its hands by 10 October and the payments by 1 November. The second and third instalments were to follow on the same dates in 1550 and 1551.

Another clause in the Act attempted to provide additional means of catching defaulting graziers. The Commissioners had already been told to empanel the parish priest and other honest villagers to help them: for the poll tax on sheep they were to conduct an annual census in June.

> "Yerely durynge the seyd thre yeres on the Tuesdays after the feast of the Nativity of St John Baptist, there shal be a generall survey made of all and singular Sheepe in every Parishe, Village and other place .. chargeable to the payment of this Relief of Sheepe. Every sheepe shalb taken for a Sheer sheepe that is at the tyme of the survey of the age of one yere or more, albeit the Sheepe be not at that time shooren."

The census was thus appointed for 25 June 1549. In his self-defence written later that year, Hales gave no account of the reception of the Relief but, describing the debate on his unsuccessful Bill to force sheep-master

[1] E 179, 122, 143.

to keep a proportion of cattle, he referred to a proposal for a Census of sheep similar to that found in the Relief.

> "I had thus devysed that the parson or Curat of every parisshe (to whom belongith the tithes) and two honest men shulde yerelye surveye everye mans pasture and shulde not onlie present who dyd transgress this lawe, but who did also observe it."[1]

This proposal was badly received. "This was it that byt the mare by he thomb. Men passe not moche howe manye lawes be made, for they see very fewe put in execution." We do not know how Parliament was persuaded to accept a similar device in the Act for the Relief. In that stage of the development of an independent spirit in the Commons we cannot be certain that a proposal incorporated in a vote of Supply to the Crown would have been resisted implacably. The concessions on purveyance in 1548 may also have quietened opposition.[2]

In the event, the most effective opponents of the census seem to have been the census-takers themselves. If the North Riding returns represent what the parish priest and the honest men of the village found that mid-summer, they must have been men who did not know a sheep when they saw one. Only four or five villages in each wapentake were represented at all, and in these the flocks consisted of a hundred sheep or less.

The entries in the Lords' and Commons' Journals for this period are so short and formal that we cannot tell how the proposals were received in debate. I am inclined to think that the concession allowing a man to count the payment of the relief in goods against his sheep-tax was an amendment introduced to appease the opposition. No such suggestion had appeared in Hales's proposals of the previous autumn. Its effect would be to favour the larger property-owner. If his property tax already came to a large sum it would act as a shield against a further charge on his flocks. A man paying a property tax of 40s. could keep a flock of 160 ewes on enclosed pasture (or 320 ewes on the commons) without becoming liable to a penny of sheep-tax. A man assessed on his property for 10s., on the other hand, became liable to sheep tax as soon his ewes exceeded 40 or 80 respectively. (Flocks of fewer than twenty, as we have seen, paid at a lower rate.)

---

[1] *A Discourse of the Commonweal*, ed. Lamond, 1929, p. lxv.
[2] In the same month that the Relief was granted, Purveyance was abolished *for three years* 2 & 3 Ed. VI, c.3; and fee farms were diverted from the Exchequer *for three years* and applied to local schemes of poor relief and public works by 2 & 3 Ed. VI, c. 5. Since Relief was granted for three years, this savours of a *quid pro quo*.

Parliament rose on 14 March 1549. On 25 June the census of sheep was due
to be taken. All that spring and summer the agrarian discontents mounted.
Hales strove to dissociate himself and his reforming friends from the
violence of the rioters. His opponents blamed his concession as an encouragement to the peasants to attack their landlords. In September, Hales
sent the Lord Protector his long *Defence against Certain Slanders*. The first
payment of the sheep tax was due at the Exchequer by 1 November.

By that day Somerset was in the Tower and his rival, Northumberland
in the ascendant. Hales had fled abroad for safety. The whole policy of
agrarian reform seemed discredited, and on 16 November the new session
of Parliament heard "the Bill exhibited by divers clothiers of Devon for
remitting the Act of Relief for Making of Cloths,"[1] and on the 18th the
Commons began to discuss the "last Relief for Cloths and Sheepe."

This news would not have surprised Hales. In his *Defence* he related
the opposition which he had found when he toured the Midlands with the
Enclosure Commissioners. Juries had been bribed or packed: landlord
hoped that a fine would be the end of the matter, as it had been before; his Bill
had been roughly handled in the Commons. "Perchaunce you wolde have
saied that the lambe had byn cummyted to the wolfe to custodie." Only
that February the Lord Protector's brother, the Lord Admiral Seymour
had expressed views which many of his fellow peers must have shared
The Marquis of Dorset reported that "a little before his apprehension the
Lord Admiral, talking of a subsidy granted to the King of 2d. (*sic*) yearly
for every sheep, declared that he would never give it."[2] Now, within a month
of the first collection of the tax being due, the Commons were cautiously
seeking permission to debate its abolition. Their caution did not stem
from any affection for the tax: the difficulty was constitutional. On 1
November

> "Mr Speaker with the King's Privy Council of the House and twelve
> others of the House shall be suitors to know the King's Majesty
> pleasure by his Council if, upon their humble suit, they may treat
> the last Relief for Cloths and Sheep at four of the clock afternoon."[3]

There could have been few precedents for a Parliament seeking to back
out of a subsidy only just granted for three years. On 20 November the
Speaker reported that the Commons might "treat for the Act of Relief

---

[1] *Commons' Journals*, I, p. 11.

[2] *Defence against Certain Slanders*, reprinted in Lamond, *op. cit.*, pp. lii-lxvii; Seymour
words: *Hist. MSS. Comm., Salisbury*; I, 1883, p. 71.

[3] *Commons' Journals*, I, p. 11. Subsequent dates are from the same source.

having in respect the causes for the granting thereof." The Council was reminding the Commons of the concessions they had received by the abolition of purveyance, and pointing out that the money had to come from somewhere, if not from sheep. On 30 November the Commons sent twelve members to attend the Lords for the 'Answer of the Relief'. Nothing appears about this in the Lords' Journal, but on 11 December a new Bill was introduced which reached its third reading in the Lords by 17 January. It became the statute, 3 & 4 Edward VI, c. 23: "An Acte concerninge the release of the braunches in the laste Acte of Relief for the payment for sheepe and cloths. Also a graunte of a Subsidy to be paid in one year." The poll tax on sheep and the levy on cloth were dead.

The preamble to the Act gave reasons for the repeal of the taxes.

> "(The) Relief of Sheepe is to your poor Commons havinge but fewe sheepe in nomber a great charge, and also so comberouse for all your Commissioners and Officers named and appointed for executing the same, that they cannot in manner tell how to serve your Highness therein accordinge to their duties."[1]

The cloth levy had also proved "comberouse," it was alleged, so that "such graunts shalbe from the said fourth day of November in [1549] deemed and adjudged voide." The 4th of November is not a date which appears in any of the earlier instructions for collection, so that it may be the date of the petition from the Devon clothiers which the House had heard on 16 November. The petitioners had then been told that they would receive an answer at the return of the Knights of the shire, that is, at the session's end. They were probably well pleased with the news their members brought them, a pleasure clouded only by the news of the extra grant which had been made to recompense the little shepherd for his loss of revenue.

> "Another grant, not as any recompense or satisfaction for your most bountiful and liberal release and discharge of your said humble subjects concerning the said Reliefs on Sheep and Cloths . . . but as a token and knowledge of our faithfulness and loving and willing hearts."

More prosaically, Parliament had granted an extension of the Relief on Goods; a fourth instalment was to be paid in April 1552. This is quaintly described by Professor Mackie in the recent volume of the *Oxford History of England* as a "small subsidy."[2] It was, of course, between £40,000 and 50,000, the size of each of the three previous instalments.

---

[1] *Statutes of the Realm*, IV, p. 122.   [2] *The Earlier Tudors*, 1952, p. 500.

Before examining the surviving records of the assessment and collection of the short-lived taxes, a brief comment must be made on the common view, which derives from A. F. Pollard, that Northumberland's rise to power in 1549 marked a wholesale reaction and the end of opposition to enclosure. Pollard did not altogether resist the temptation to ennoble the character of Somerset by blackening that of Northumberland.

There is no need to proceed to the opposite extreme and whitewash Northumberland, or to deny that his policy was more sympathetic to sheep-masters than to those who suffered at the hands of sheep-masters. Yet the record of anti-enclosure measures during his period of office does not entirely support Pollard's thesis. Pollard stated that Northumberland's Parliament of November 1549 set to work to make the yoke of the commons of England less easy and their burden less light. In support of this view he said: "It proceeded to override all the laws passed against enclosure under Henry VII and Henry VIII."[1] Professor Mackie echoes this: "During the rest of the reign there was no further talk of agrarian reform."[2]

These statements are incorrect. An Act passed in the second of Northumberland's parliaments made it an offence, in the tradition of the Act of 1489, 1515, and 1536, for any one to convert land to pasture if it had been under the plough since 1509.[3] Moreover, a new Commission of Enquiry was set up. Its returns were to be sent to Chancery and thence to the Exchequer to remain on record. It surely cannot be suggested that the Commission was to make these dangerous enquiries in order to do nothing. Nor did Parliament turn its back on all discussion of enclosure matters, as Professor Mackie says. Only a week after the issue of the repeal of the Relief had been raised, the Commons discussed a Bill "for having a Number of Sheep and Farms," no doubt the old issue of over-large flocks and the engrossing of holdings. Three days later they discussed a Bill "for the Commons, Sheep and Farms." On 4 and 13 January they debated a Bill "for the re-edifying of Decayed Houses."[4]

Nor did the prosecution of enclosers cease. I have set out below the number of enclosure prosecutions heard in the Exchequer during the two Protectorates.[5] These are not intended as measures of all anti-enclosure activity: the prerogative courts were also at work hearing similar cases but they do show that in this particular court—where the principal attack

---

[1] Pollard, *England under Protector Somerset*, p. 271.

[2] Mackie, *op. cit.*, p. 506. He quotes one Act but ignores 5 & 6 Ed. VI, c. 5.

[3] 5 & 6 Ed. VI, c. 5; *Statutes of the Realm*, IV, p. 134.

[4] For all these dates see the *Commons' Journal, sub diebus*.

[5] Cases appearing in E 159 and E 368 (P.R.O.).

ınder the Henrician statutes had been directed—there was no real differ-
ınce between the time before and the time after Somerset's fall. However

TABLE 2
Annual figures of enclosure cases in the Court of Exchequer.

Year	For having too-large flocks and engrossing holdings	Other enclosure offences
Somerset's Protectorate		
1547	6	10
1548	11	11
1549	8	14
Northumberland's Protectorate		
1550	16	12
1551	3	16
1552	0	9
1553	1	5

r Northumberland went in persuading graziers to support him against
ɔmerset's measures, it is clear that he had not succeeded in barring the
ɔponents of graziers from the courts.

The surviving returns for the Poll Tax on sheep do not cover the whole
ıuntry, nor even the whole of that part of the country where the largest
ıcks were to be found. This imperfect survival of the collector's accounts
characteristic of this class of records of the Exchequer, where the only
:terminant of what survives is pure chance. There was no contemporary
ıcentive to destroy some records yet keep others. The tax was repealed
ɔm 4 November 1549 and any one who had avoided the tax need have
ıd no fears that the record might be used against him in the future.
Although the Act of repeal relieved taxpayers of their obligations
ɔm 4 November there is every reason to believe that the Exchequer
ınt further and actually remitted the sums already paid. In any event,
penny from this tax is enrolled at the Exchequer, while the county
yments from the Relief on Goods of the same summer are fully recorded
the usual style.[1] This is very odd, in face of the eleven surviving accounts

I have examined enrolled *Views and States of Account* (E 368, 327, Easter term, States,
5, and Michaelmas term, States, m. 9, duplicated in E 102, 317) as well as the *Enrolled
sidies* (E 359, 45). The first collection of the Relief on Goods began to be enrolled during
ter Term, anno tertio. The sums given are exactly the same as in the county collectors'
:ipts in E 179 with no additions for the Relief on Sheep or the Relief on Cloth. The
t tax to appear on the rolls is the second collection of the Relief on Goods one year later.

described below which show that eleven Commissions did return thei accounts and their money into the Exchequer as they had been ordered These accounts show that in seven counties at least the Commissioner had not had the difficulties described in the preamble to the Act of Repeal "They cannot in manner tell how to serve your Highness therein according inge to their duties."

I have not been able to trace an order for the repayment of these monies although such an order may exist. It is therefore possible that the eleven surviving accounts (dated from July to October) represent the only Commissions who had made their returns before the fall of Somerset and the new Parliament put a stop to the work. Hearing of the petitions against the Reliefs (and knowing the temper of the Commons) the others may have thankfully decided to hold their hand and make no return to the Exchequer until an order came. It never came. Whether the eleven Commissions had their collections returned we do not know; whether they redistributed the tax we shall not know unless new documents in connection with this tax come to light in the provinces. In any event, the Exchequer accounts show that the king received nothing.

The collectors' accounts come from five counties. The Public Record Office references for these are: Devon, E179/99/315; Hunts, E179/122/14 144, and 146; Notts, E179/159/178, 182, and 185; Oxon, E179/162/27 Yorks, E.R., E179/203/251; N.R., E179/213/209; W.R., E179/208/21 Only for Huntingdonshire are they are anywhere near completeness. A the four Hundreds of that county have returns, made in September There are signs at the bottom of the Normancross roll that a second, no lost, membrane was formerly stitched to it. The North Riding of Yorkshire's return seems to be as full a return as the Riding ever made, but t entries are so meagre that the collection must have been superficial. Or one hundred of Oxfordshire has an extant return. Nottinghamshire ha three rolls detailed enough to suggest a less superficial assessment.

The rolls vary in legibility and clarity of lay-out. Like all Exchequer accounts of this period, they range from the clearest tabulation to the me unarithmetical prose. In Devon the collectors failed to describe the shee giving only a total sum due from each taxpayer. In the other counties t size of the flock is either given explicitly or can be worked out from t sums due from the three categories of animals. Thus, it is no help at all know that Robert Trobrigge of Crediton paid "pro ovibus suis, ul xii^s prius solut' pro bonis suis, 6d."[1] But the sums of money given for ea

---

[1] These and the other quotations following come from the appropriate county rolls wh references have been given above.

sheep-owner in the Buckrose area of Yorkshire are accompanied by a note of the category of sheep. Thus, the flock at Skirpenbeck, assessed at £3 5s., was in the three-halfpenny category, so that the size of the flock—520 sheep—can be worked out.

The Act had distinguished between sheep which spent most of their year on enclosed pastures and sheep spending their time on open fields or common pastures. Hales, it will be recalled, had thought that there were about equal numbers of each type. In the small sample offered by these returns the majority were sheep grazing on the commons, but since these paid at the lower rate there was the temptation to declare a flock as a commons' flock. Rare is the occasion—as at Stainforth in the West Riding of Yorkshire—when a taxpayer was put down for both kinds of sheep. The Commissioners elsewhere seem to have been satisfied to make a simple sum of it: John Castell's 262 sheer sheep at Somersham, Hunts, went "moste parte of ym on ye comens."

In Nottinghamshire the sheep were often described as going "in severall pastures and severall marshes." While it is probable that the use of the word marshes does reflect the importance of the low carrs of the Trent valley as grazing grounds, there is the chance that the local Commissioners were standing strictly by the terms of the Act, which used the term "severall pastures and severall marshes." In another Nottinghamshire entry, the sheep on the commons were described more fully in words which do not derive from the Act and which seem genuinely descriptive: "goyng all ye yere in ye comen faldes feld" at Bunney, and at Flintham "in ye comon falowe feld." Instead of "on the commons" or "*in communibus*" the sheep not grazing within hedges were often described simply as "feyld sheep."

The Commissioners had to report any flock-owners who were living out of the county. In the East Riding, for example,

> "Yt ys presented that Sylvester Eade late dwelling in the Chepe in London and nowe dwelling in Stamforthe in the countie of Lincolne hath goinge in common at Mulforthe . . . eyght hundred sheepe."

Eade's flock was grazing over the site of the former village of Mowthorpe, in the Yorkshire Wolds half way between Duggleby and Kirby Grindalythe. In the Huntingdonshire returns the list of "them that hathe sheyp in the sayd hundred . . . and dwellythe owte of the shyre" had 22 names, as compared with 188 owners living in the county. Of these twenty-two men, all (except two Londoners and a Kentish man) lived in adjoining counties. How large were the flocks on which tax was paid? Taking the 414 instances which these returns offer we find the size distribution set out in Table 3. One useful method of approach is to group the flocks according to their size, and then see what size of flock was the most common. For example, eight of the 414 flocks for which we have details consisted of twenty sheep or fewer; sixteen flocks had between 21 and 40 sheep in each and so on . . . . In Table 3 the number of flocks in each size group has been expressed as a percentage of all the 414 flocks. Thus the eight flocks numbering twenty sheep or fewer accounted for 2 per cent of all the flocks. Forty-eight per cent (or nearly half) of all the flocks had 140 sheep or fewer. The sample is such a small one that, outside Hunts and Notts, it would be foolish to draw any general conclusions from it. The median size of the flocks in the various county returns are also given for interest below.

TABLE 3

Percentage of flocks in each size-group of flock.

Size-group	%	Size-group	%	Size-group	%
0–20	2	141–160	12	281–300	5
21–40	4	161–180	6	301–400	5
41–60	6	181–200	5	401–500	3
61–80	5	201–220	2	501–600	1
81–100	5	221–240	5	601–700	0
101–120	13	241–260	2	701–800	1
121–140	13	261–280	1	800 +	1

The locale of the 414 flocks for which information is available is set out in Table 4. The only extant certificate for Devon has no details of flock-size. The median size of the whole group was 142 sheep. The median size of each county is shown in Table 5.

TABLE 4

Locality of the 414 flocks.

Huntingdonshire (four Hundreds)	186
Oxfordshire (Bampton Hundred only)	52
Nottinghamshire (four Hundreds)	73
Yorks, N.R. and W.R.	61
Yorks, E.R.	42

TABLE 5

Median size in each county.

Hunts	Hurstingstone Hundred	180
	Normancross Hundred	145
	Leightonstone and	
	Toseland Hundreds	125
Notts		150
Oxford	Bampton Hundred	155
Yorks	E.R.	118§
	N.R. and W.R.	110§

In the case of the counties marked § the sample is so imperfect that the figures have very little meaning.)

Set well apart from this general experience of a flock of between 110 and 150 sheep are the flocks of the larger sheep-masters. The largest recorded was 1,550 at Slepe (St Ives). There were also flocks of 1,213 (Warboys, Hunts), 1,203 (Abbot's Ripton, Hunts), and 1,094 (Settrington, Yorks, E.R.). The Huntingdonshire commissioners appear to have been most thorough. They taxed one man who had two sheep on the commons of the borough of Huntingdon. At Ramsey one of the commissioners had 252 ewes and 30 wethers on enclosed pastures, together with 377 field sheep. He duly taxed himself.

Nowhere did the commissioners report flocks near the prohibited size of 2,400, although from other sources we know that flocks of that size existed. As one might expect, the names of the sheep-masters and the location of the pastures include well-known figures and places in enclosure history. A flock of 800 sheep grazed over the lost village of East Lanfield, Yorks, N.R. The sheep-owner at Little Gidding, Hunts, was Robert Derwell. He had 600 sheep on the commons there. In 1594 the Court of Exchequer heard that once "the ffieldes and tilladge grounds belonginge to the said towne of Lyttell Giddinge did lye open and not inclosed."[1] It would be on these fields that the 600 sheep fed. In 1566 Derwell enclosed the fields and destroyed the farm-houses in the village.

"The said fieldes are now enclosed with hedges and converted into severall closes, neyther is there now remaynyng any howses of husbandry nor eny land in Tilladge savinge yt wch is in the occupation of John Bedell, gent., as farmer unto Humphrey Drewell Esq."

[1] E 134, 35 Eliz., Hunts. Depositions of Henry Stretton, aged 68, and Henry Berridge, aged 60.

In Little Gidding in 1549 Drewell was the only flock-master taxed.
There were probably other sheep which escaped, since there were eight
farms then in occupation. It is common to find only one name per village
in the tax returns, as if the Commission were satisfied with one victim.
Occasionally fuller detail is given. At Yaxley, Hunts, William Cony had
flocks of 916, 300, 241, and 200 sheep, all in different Huntingdonshire
parishes. The flock of 916 was feeding in Elton fields. Three other Yaxley
men were taxed: one for 504 sheep; another for flocks of 66 and 75; and
the third for 88 and 45. At Conington, another village as shrunken as
Little Gidding, Thomas Catton had 771 sheep, and Henry Hull 128
Hull also had 150 at Stukeley.

At the foot of the North Riding account there is a short note which
provides the only evidence I have been able to find, other than the mourn-
ful complaint of the Devon clothiers in November, that the Relief on Cloth
was also being collected that summer. On 26 July the Commissioner
for the North Riding wrote as a tailpiece to their roll: "We the Com
missioners aforesaid concerning the releyff of cloths . . . we fynde noth
inge." A short note on this part of the Relief is given below,[1] but as fa
as records of collection go, my present report must be that of the Com
missioners: I find nothing.

The nine months' events just considered came at something of a turning
point in English agrarian history. They mark the most serious of all th
sixteenth-century attempts to check the spread of pasture by legislatio
and administrative action, set as they were alongside other measure
intended to bring down prices and encourage tillage. They failed. Th
riots frightened Somerset's moderate supporters and robbed the reform
ing party of political power. The machinery of inspection and enumeratio
which the reformers hoped to initiate was delicate to handle even in a tim
of political agreement. Neither sheep nor men could be numbered by th
passing of an Act of Parliament. The enumeration of baptisms was t
remain sporadic until the institution of register books in 1598. Bot
muster-rolls and subsidy-lists from this period offer statistical lacun:
which are at once the delight and the terror of the demographer.[2] Even
the first successful census of sheep did not come until 1866 (when ther
were nearly 17,000,000 in England and Wales)—that is, sixty-five yea

[1] Appendix, p. 157 below.
[2] As witness Professor E. E. Rich, 'The Population of Elizabethan England,' *Econ. Hi
Rev.*, 2nd ser., II, 1950, pp. 247–65.

after the census of men—it is nice to remember that as far as the Statute Book is concerned, a census of sheep was ordered two hundred and fifty years earlier than the census of *homo sapiens*.

Although the agrarian policy of Hales and Somerset reads so gloomily, their goal was attained within a few years by the action of external events. Within three years of Hales's flight the whole aspect of the European demand for English cloth had been changed. Looked at from the standpoint of 1600, the mid-century had marked the peak of cloth exports, to be followed by a period of much lower demand, possibly only three quarters of the quantity at the height of the boom.[1] Economic reality pushed the graziers into action which moral sermons and Acts of Parliament had failed to effect. Calculations of profit and loss began to show that the best course of action was no longer the extension of pasture over tillage-land. Corn-growing began again to seem more profitable than wool-growing.[2] The great drive against arable in the Midlands was halted. There were still to be enclosures and the area of tillage would ebb and flow with fluctuations in the prices of grain and wool; but never again would the wolf-like sheep be an increasing menace to corn-growing husbandmen. The language of the preamble to the Act of 1597 may read as if depopulating enclosures were abroad again, but their whole scale of operation was tiny compared with the great enclosures of the early Tudor years.[3] Indeed, there is good evidence that these were halted even before 1549, but they were near enough in men's memories to encourage the fears of the rioters that summer and to encourage the reformers to lunge desperately at the grazier as the prime social enemy.

---

[1] For the figures see F. J. Fisher, *Econ. Hist. Rev.*, x, 1939–40, p. 96.
[2] For a summary of this argument see P. J. Bowden, 'Movements in Wool Prices', *Yorks Bulletin of Econ. and Soc. Research*, IV, 1952, pp. 109–24.
[3] 39 Eliz., c. 2 (1597) *Stat. Realm*, IV, p. 893.

Appendix

A NOTE ON THE RELIEF ON CLOTH, 1549

I have failed to discover any documents recording the collection of this tax, perhaps because I have not been able to plumb the unsorted Miscellanea of the Exchequer. The preamble to the Act of Repeal may have been correct in saying that the Relief was too cumbersome. As in the case of the sheep tax Hales proposed to utilize existing machinery. The Commissioners appointed in the Act were travelling very much the same road in their assessments of the Relief on Goods as the Henrician subsidy; for the tax on cloth the aulnagers were brought in.

Clothiers and aulnagers were instructed to keep duplicate books recording the cloths made and sealed during the year. The Commissioners were to take the clothiers' books and the Exchequer the aulnagers'. From the cloths recorded in the books the levy was to be assessed.

This method of recording the cloths manufactured could have been easily abused. To begin with, the number of clothiers—particularly small clothiers—with whom the Commission and the Exchequer would have to deal was large. Nor was the assumption that the aulnagers sealed every cloth manufactured very realistic. The aulnagers had no recent experience in making accurate and detailed returns to the Exchequer. The aulnage (that is, the old cloth tax) was farmed out for a lump sum so that the Exchequer had not needed a genuine annual return.

We have not the exact terms of the petition against the Relief brought to Parliament by the Devon clothiers in November 1549, but we may read something of its terms in the preamble to the Act of Repeal:

> ". . . which Relief of cloth appeareth now so comberouse to all clothmakers, and also so tedious to the same for makinge of their bookes and the accounts thereof, by reason of the lacke of the Alnagers not alway present when time requireth . . . that in manner they are discourage to make any cloth or to set any men on work about the same."

Tedious and cumbersome it may have been, but it is likely that some attempts were made somewhere to collect the tax, and I have not given up hope of tracing some part of this lost census of cloth production. Even if the central records have gone, there is the chance that some of the Commissioners preserved their copies of the assessments among their family papers.

14

HABITATION VERSUS IMPROVEMENT:

THE DEBATE ON

ENCLOSURE AGREEMENT

'Depopulation hath cast a slander on Inclosure, which because
often done with it, people suspect it cannot bee done without it.'
PSEUDOMISUS, *Considerations Concerning Common Fields* (1654),
p. 39.

T HIS essay attempts an examination of the period between the
Tudor statutes, which sought to preserve tillage and houses of
husbandry, and the Hanoverian statutes which offered the
majority of proprietors in a village who wanted enclosure a means
whereby they could override the conservative minority who were
averse to Improvement. It is the period of Enclosure by Agreement.

Enclosure as such has never been illegal in England but in the sixteenth century there were many Acts of Parliament and much govern-
mental action which looked coolly on the results of certain enclosures,
particularly those which changed land-use or brought a diminution
in householders.

Nor has there ever been a time when the statutes allowed general
enclosure without conditions. The Enclosure Acts of the eighteenth
and early nineteenth centuries were not a blanket approval but a long
series of local Acts permitting local proposals; even when in 1845
the scrutiny of the few remaining enclosure proposals was delegated
to Civil Servants each case had still to be taken on its merits.[1] What
of the period before even local Enclosure Acts were available to those
who could afford them?

Ideally, one ought to be able to chronicle the stages by which
official opinion, the practice of the courts and the votes of the legis-

[1] The first truly General Enclosure Act of 1836 demanded the agreement of the
majority of proprietors; the General Act of 1845 set up permanent Commissioners in London.

lature moved from the suspicion and hostility shown by the Acts[1] of 1597 to the benevolent neutrality of the Hanoverian Enclosure Acts. Because there are no full records of Parliamentary debates and votes in the seventeenth century there are only brief occasions scattered through the period when anything like the mind of Parliament can be discerned. The records of the law courts at Westminster and in the provinces are much fuller but their bulk is an equally formidable obstacle to historical judgements since they have been so little calendared and indexed. But even if a coherent account of the encloser-at-law could someday be written it would be hopeless to look for coherence in official policy or unanimity in the voice of the legislature.

Men took up different stances towards enclosure because the issue raised fundamental tests of social attitude. The enclosure debate of the sixteenth century, as the author of *The Agrarian Problem* and *Religion and the Rise of Capitalism* taught us, passed beyond a contest between those who wore the badge of corn and those who wore the badge of sheep. There were heavy overtones of social approval in the very roll of the word 'husbandman' and they were times when 'grazier', like 'brogger', seemed to be simply a translation of the Mammon of Unrighteousness. The long debates produced a clash of voices because the fundamental issue of the common weal and private profit was one on which men were not unanimous.[2]

Some aspects of the transition from suspicion of enclosure to neutrality or approval are indeed illuminated by regarding it as one stage in the triumph of self-love over social: but it is only a partial illumination. It is also necessary to see the transition in other lights. This essay will consider approval of enclosure agreements successively as: a refutation of the slander summarised in the quotation at the head; a concession to the realities of variety in local agrarian practice; an aspect of faith in the market mechanism and a distrust of regulation; finally, a search for an administrative device whereby enclosure could be 'Regulated'.

[1] 39 Eliz. I cc 1 and 2.
[2] Contemporary *Notes* on the two Acts of 1597 set 'a trifling abridgement to gentlemen' against 'the misery of the people and the decay of the nation's strength': *Hist. Mss. Comm. Salisbury*, xiv (1923), p. 27.

I

The most formidable obstacle to any shift in public opinion towards tolerating enclosure by agreement was the slander which the pamphlet by Pseudomisus sought to refute. Once upon a time enclosure had brought depopulation: was not that the effect, if not the aim, of all enclosures? In November 1597 it was this conjunction of enclosure, conversion of tillage to grass and decay of households which animated the speech by Bacon and initiated the two statutes which mark the final attempt to legislate for the status quo. Although two bills were needed to cover the issues, the reformers' purpose was single. One member noted the ears of the sheepmasters hanging at the door of the Commons but others could have remarked the ghosts from deserted villages haunting the Parliament chamber; and although some critics feared that the sheepmasters had wrung too many concessions in the course of the bill's passage it was these ghosts who triumphed.[1]

When the villagers of Croft, Leicestershire, objected to the terms of an enclosure agreement in 1632 their complaint was summed up in these words: 'the ayme and ends tend to a generall Inclosure and consequently to a Depopulation'.[2]

It was this chain of 'consequently' which had to be broken before enclosure by agreement could become possible, but it was natural in a Leicestershire village encircled by deserted villages that the consequence seemed inevitable. It was not long afterwards that Sir William Dugdale, on the other side of Watling Street, rode from country house to country house collecting for his *History of Warwickshire* and managed to identify most of the deserted village sites of that county without recourse to air photographs. The debate was being carried on in a countryside whose scars seemed fresh.[3]

J. E. Neale, *Elizabeth I and her Parliaments, 1584–1601* (1957) pp. 337–351 and sources there cited.

Public Record Office (hereafter, P.R.O.), P.C.2/41 f. 506: 6 April 1632; the enclosure agreement dated from 1629.

The Antiquities of Warwickshire was published in 1656 and Dugdale seems to have drawn his own maps, on which depopulated places are indicated by a symbol: P. D. A. Harvey and H. Thorpe, *The Printed Maps of Warwickshire* (1959), p. 15.

The protagonists of enclosure had therefore to advocate a 'Regulated Enclosure' with some arbiter to leash the over-greedy:

'to prevent depopulation under some grievous penalty and to leave the decay of tillage at more liberty.'[1]

It was necessary to find a way of marrying Improvement and Habitation and this policy was advocated by the author of *A Consideration*, aroused by the anti-enclosure rising of 1607 and the government commissions of enquiry:

'By redressinge the fault of Depopulation and Leaveinge encloseinge and convertinge arbitrable... the poore man shalbe satisfied in his ende; Habitation; and the gentleman not Hindered in his desier; Improvement'[2]

John Norden, a public advocate of enclosure for Improvement, nevertheless regarded depopulating enclosure as

'the bane of a commonwealth, an apparent badge of Atheisme and an argument of waspish ambition or woolvish emulation.'[3]

The fears of depopulating enclosure were an unconscionable long time in dying. They appear in private comment as well as in public pamphleteering. In 1668 the tithe collector at Pickering, Yorkshire, criticised a local enclosure proposal—

'I should think the Chancery should hinder inclosure because it will make a greate depopulation, above 150 families will be undone.'[4]

Two years after Pseudomisus' pamphlet, John Moore's *Scripture Word Against Inclosure* showed a Leicestershire parson still appealing to the ghosts from the deserted villages:

'They say there may be an inclosure without decay of Tillage of Depopulation... They would not have a Spade called a Spade'.

The core of his opponent's case was this:

To inveigh against Inclosure in generall as if it were the proper cause or occasion of depopulation and decay of tillage is not ratio-

---

[1] *Hist. Mss. Comm. Hastings*, iv (1947), p. 323 (undated but 1613-23).

[2] British Museum (hereafter, B.M.), Cott. Mss. Titus CII f. 165; FIV f. 319; Lans. Mss. 487 f. 21; printed in W. Cunningham, *Growth of British Industry and Commerce*, iii (1917), pp. 898-9.

[3] John Norden, *Surveiors Dialogue* (1607), p. 224.

[4] Yorks. Arch. Soc. Mss. DD32, Marshall to Osborne, July 1668. I am indebted to Mr. A. Harris for this reference.

nall; and that to hinder all Inclosure for the future is neither a necessary nor a sufficient means to prevent or to reforme those evils'.[1]

These two pamphleteers came from Leicestershire and made the air thick with local village names, the deserted villages convincing Moore that he was right: and the villages which had survived an enclosure by agreement comforting his opponent's case. But it is significant that the village names cited by Moore were predominantly old desertions, and if fears of depopulating enclosure seem to have faded to nothing by the end of the seventeenth century it could only have come about by a genuine absence of new depopulations. In debate, evanescent words and actions could be explained away and glossed over but newly decayed villages would have been impossible to refute.

II

If the opposition to enclosure was partially disarmed by fewer and fewer deserted villages, what of the traditional suspicion of conversion of tillage to pasture, even conversion which stopped far short of a depopulation? Had not one statute of 1597 made it an offence to decay a house of husbandry? And had not the other revived the practice of putting

> 'land having once been tilled into a perpetual bondage and servitude of being for ever tilled?'[2]

The increasing toleration of a changing land-use was a most important aid to the toleration of enclosure by agreement. The more liberal attitude towards conversion from corn to grass sometimes derived from a general liberal sentiment approving the right of individuals to decide what to do with their own property; this aspect is well known and can be summed up in Raleigh's words in 1601:

> 'I do not like the constraining of them to use their Grounds at our

---

[1] Moore, rector of Knaptoft, published his first pamphlet in 1656. The opposing quotation is from [J. Lee, parson of Catthorpe], *A Vindication of the Considerations etc.* (1656), p. 17.

[2] *Hist. Mss. Comm. Salisbury*, vii (1899), p. 542.

wills but rather let every man use his Ground to that which it is most fit for, and therein use his own Discretion.'[1]
But a toleration of conversion also arose from a belief in the virtues of local agricultural specialisation, and, like many contemporary statements on free trading, the advocacy stemmed not from theory but from practical interest and self-interest. Indeed, Raleigh's next sentence went straight from the study to the field.

'I know land which if it had beene unplowed (which it now is because of the Statutes of Tillage) would have been good pasture for Beasts,' and he was prepared to see the principle of local agricultural specialisation developed as between England and the continent. He almost preached comparative advantage. For that microcosm of a continent, the English counties, the same view had been put in the Tillage debates of 1597 when it had been successfully argued that the statute ought not to embrace Shropshire[2] since that county's soils made it fittest to be grass and the 'Dayrie house to the whole Realme'; for had not the same Providence arranged that the soil of neighbouring Herefordshire made that county 'the Barne'?

It is the progress of this sentiment of local specialisation which we must now examine, and the victory of the sentiment in Stuart England rested on very substantial advances even under the Tudors. There never had in fact been a complete bondage and servitude of being for ever tilled. On paper the Acts of 1489 and 1515 might read that way, but in enforcement the Crown was weak. When the Act of 1536 gave strength to enforcement it also admitted the principle of local limitation; fourteen counties only were affected by it: roughly, the Midlands and the Isle of Wight (which had set the pace by having its own Act in 1488).[3] The Tillage Bill of 1597 came from the Commons already limited to 25 counties and the Lords added a proviso[4] exempting land converted from tillage to grass within two

[1] H. Townshend, *Historical Collections* (1680), p. 188.
[2] A. F. Pollard and Marjorie Blatcher, 'Hayward Townshend's Journals', *Bull. Inst. Hist. Res.*, xii (1935), p. 16: 17 Dec. 1597.
[3] For the legislation and prosecutions before 1597 see M. Beresford, *The Lost Villages of England* (1954), pp. 102-33.
[4] House of Lords Mss., engrossed Acts, 39 Eliz. I, c. 2; the counties exemption is in the hand of the Commons clerk on the parchment Bill, while the Watling

miles of Watling Street all along its course from the end of the Chiltern downs at Dunstable to Chester, a local concession in the interest of finding fodder for the drovers' herds on their journey south; there is a suggestion that Huntingdonshire had been left out of earlier Acts for the same local reason.[1] The Houses of Husbandry Act had no local exemptions but the provision for the exempt counties in the Tillage bill converted one M.P. (in his own confession) from Saul to Paul. An M.P. who did not see the light on the road to Damascus was the member for Ludlow borough who wanted Shropshire in the bill; the county members cried him down.[2]

Some recognition that local circumstances might make conversion not always a sin against the common weal can also be seen in the limited areas where enforcement of the Acts of 1489, 1515 and 1536 took place; and the Act of 1556 which appointed a Commission with permanent clerks to enforce the existing agrarian legislation gave the Commission express latitude:

> 'they may use theyr discretions in temporing and qualifeing. . . In some places of this Realme yt ys not necessary the purview of this Estatute extende and bee fully executed.'[3]

Local husbandry practices were accepted also in the Act of 1536 which gave the Crown until the day of reconversion half the profits of land illegally converted to grass. But the reconversion was qualified:

> '. . . from pasture into tillage agayn, according to the nature of the soyle and course of Husbandrye used in the Countrey where any such Landes doe lie.'[4]

The Tillage Act of 1597 likewise recognised that in some districts grass replaced tillage not permanently but as part of convertible husbandry.[5] 'The course of husbandrye used in that parte' is a Lords'

Street proviso is in the paper format which the Commons were insisting on for Lords' amendments at this time (Sir. S. D'Ewes, *Journals of all the Parliaments 1680*), pp. 535 and 576-7.

[1] B. M. Lans. Mss. 487 f. 219: proposal to include the London to Berwick road.

[2] Pollard and Blatcher, *art. cit.*, pp. 15-6.

[3] 2 & 3 Ph. and Mary c. 2.

[4] 27 Henry VIII c. 22.

[5] A 'politic' clause: *Hist. Mss. Comm. Salisbury*, vii (1899) pp. 541-3.

revision of the original Bill[1] which had had simply 'custome'. The same Act also continued the tradition of the Act of 1563 in not penalising the conversion of land to grass when it fed a man's own horses, draught oxen or domestic kine. In 1597 it was safe to decay tillage in one place if equivalent areas of grass were ploughed up elsewhere on the estate. This flexibility was approved by the villagers of Eagle (Lincs.) in 1656. Like the villagers of Croft they looked around at their neighbours' example but saw no deserted villages after enclosure:

> 'most of the land now tilled is more proper for grass, and that moor ground now eaten as common is fitter for corn as if proved by experience amongst our next neighbours.'[2]

Durham witnesses in a case of 1608 deposed that the enclosure of the common moor of Gainford had increased tillage,[3] and an advocate of the enclosure of Sedgemoor urged that more and not fewer employment opportunities would result.[4]

Local variations in soil were increasingly argued as a defence by those prosecuted for conversion in the 1630's. Thus Sir Thomas Burton of Frisby, Leicestershire, ordered by the Privy Council in 1631 to sow two yardlands of enclosed land with corn, protested

> 'the soile is a cold claie and not so fitt for Corne as grasse.'[5]

It is not surprising that the odd little Act of 1608 which may claim to be the first English pro-enclosure Act permitted some enclosure by agreement in six Herefordshire parishes on exactly these grounds:

> 'they doe differ in the manner of their Husbandrie from many partes of the said Countie and other Counties in the Realme.'[6]

At the other extreme there were local circumstances which made the northern Border counties vulnerable to the old type of depopul-

---

[1] see f.n. 4 p. 164, above.

[2] quoted in *Lincs. Notes and Queries*, x, p. 248.

[3] P.R.O., E. 178/3749.

[4] Adam Moore, *An Apologie for His Majesties Royall Intention*: B.M. Add. Mss. 48111 (Yelverton Mss.). He was probably identical with the author of *Bread for the Poor* (1653) wherein common fields were declared a 'common prostitute'.

[5] P.R.O., S.P. 16/187 no. 80; other defences of this kind in Joan Thirsk, *English Peasant Farming* (1957), pp. 166-7 and 184-5.

[6] 4 Jas. I c. 11.

ating enclosure at the very end of the sixteenth century. Since the mid-century there had been concern about the decay of husbandmen here.[1] There is the well-known letter from the Dean of Durham pleading for the inclusion of the northern counties in the Tillage Act of 1597:

> 'Of all places those most needed to be looked to. The depopulations are not, as supposed, by the enemy but private men have dispeopled whole villages.'[2]

Northumberland was added to the bill during the Commons debates[3] and the Lords added Pembroke: but Northumberland was not protected for long. In 1601 it was agreed to continue the Tillage Acts but Northumberland was excluded from their provisions.[4]

III

It might be argued that these statutory recognitions of variety in local practice amounted to official toleration of a Regulated Enclosure, if only silently. This point of view is strengthened by examining the machinery by which statutes were enforced. The Act of 1556 admitted that agrarian legislation need not be 'fully executed' and, as in much Tudor legislation, a general prohibition was a prelude to personal exemptions. The dog wagged its tail for a bone while it barked.

Some bought royal pardons, such as that the encloser of Cotesbach received from James I at the instance of a courtier.[5] For others, the

---

[1] e.g. surveys of 1584: S.P. 15/28 ff. 232-74.

[2] *Cal. S.P. Dom. 1595-7*, p. 347.

[3] It cannot have been a Lords' addition, *pace* J. E. Neale, *op. cit.*, p. 345, for Lords' amendments had to be on paper (see n. 4, p. 164 above) and 'Northumberland' is interlineated in the parchment Act, House of Lords Mss; 'Pembroke', however, is on the paper sheet of amendments.

[4] 43 Eliz. I. c. 9 s. 2; the exemption was urged on the grounds that the plague had swept away whole villages locally: D'Ewes, *op. cit.*, p 674

[5] P R.O., C. 66/1618 no. 22; in 1601 a Mr. Dormer sought to have his licence endorsed by Act: the Commons agreed by a majority of 43 but the proviso is not in the Act, 43 Eliz. I c. 9. Other pardons and dispensations to individuals are: C. 66/1020 mm. 29-30 (1566, following the Bucks. Enclosure Commission, E. 178/424;) C. 66/1013 and 1024; C. 66/1787 (1608); and C. 66/2452 no. 46 (1628).

Commissions to Compound and the legal underworld of the common informer gave opportunities to enclose and convert for anyone who could afford to pay. In its most open form the payment was a composition for fines after a confession of past sins. In its most covert form it was a payment to a blackmailing informer in order to seal his lips. The royal revenue benefited a little and the legal middlemen a great deal.

The prerogative powers of suspending and dispensing contributed in a double way to the eventual toleration of enclosure by agreement. In so far as they allowed local and personal circumstances to be taken into account they helped to weaken an unqualified opposition to all enclosure and all change in land use. But their most powerful educative force was one which their originators could hardly have intended: abuse of these powers in the hands of the common informer and their use as a means of non-Parliamentary revenue-raising considerably discredited the principle of restriction by statute or Privy Council.[1] Coke welcomed the repeal of much agrarian legislation in 1624 as

> 'unnecessary statutes unfit for this time. . . snares that might have lien heavy upon the subject.'[2]

The process of discredit (by which shields had become snares) can be seen even before the debates of 1621. In 1597 some feared that the Tillage Laws would simply open the doors to dishonest informers but the official view was that genuine informers would operate; of the informers-by-patent the Queen, it was said,

> 'naturally likes them as little as monopolies or concealments;'[3]

the private common informer in the provinces would be encouraged to act by 'love of justice or faction or emulation.'

an ill-assorted trinity of incentives. In February 1618 a Commission of judges and others was appointed to grant exemptions from the Tillage Acts.

---

[1] M.W. Beresford, 'The Common Informer, the Penal Statutes and Economic Regulation', *Ec. Hist. Rev.*, x (1957); below, pp. 209-26. Informers operated chiefly in Exchequer (E 159) but see also e.g. K.B. 27/1429 (1611, Mich.), mm. 'Rooper' nos. 114, 116, 146 for cases before King's Bench.

[2] Sir. E. Coke, *The Third Part of the Institutes* (1644), pp. 191-4.

[3] *Hist. Mss. Comm. Salisbury*, xiv (1923), pp. 27 and 37.

'The rigor of the statutes may be mitigated according to these present tymes and occasions... Lands which have heretofore bene used in tillage for corne and grayne have of late tymes out of their tryall and experience had of the unaptness and unfruitfulnes thereof for tillage bene turned from tillage into pasture for the mayntenaunce and keepinge of cattell whereby they have in some sorte incurred the penalties of the lawes.'[1]

From these technical offences only the informer had wrung benefit: 'no benifitt redounded to the common wealth nor profitt unto Ourselves but secretly and under hand benifitt made to and by the Informers more to the molestation of our subjects than any to the reformation that the lawes intended.'

A document headed 'Motives and Reasons of the Commissioners for Pardons for Decay of Tillage' claimed that two thousand informations had been thwarted by the Commission's dispensations,[2] and in March 1620 a similar patent was issued to the judges, learned counsel and others. This second patent was revoked in 1621 at a time when the repeal of the tillage laws seemed imminent,[3] but the first patent may be 'Mr. Edward Ramsey's patent' which the Commons debated[4] but did not condemn in November 1640.

The revival of anti-depopulation Commissions during Charles I's period of non-Parliamentary government displayed a familiar mixture of paternalism and pickpocketry. A few oppressors of the poor and would-be depopulators were no doubt penalised or deterred but the victims seem to have been mostly landowners who had enclosed by agreement and infringed the Acts of 1597 (unrepealed in 1624) by some small diminution of the area of tillage or the number of farm-houses.[5] A convenient list of the victims is set out in a document which begins

[1] C. 66/2134 m.1d; C. 66/2150 no. 17.
[2] B. M. Harl. Mss. 7616 f. 6; 7614; f. 127.
[3] *Commons Journal*, i, p. 573; S.P. 14/187/94: the patent concerned parks and warrens for which compositions had been allowed also by a patent of 19 May 1615: Hist. Mss. Comm., *3rd. Rep. App.* (1871), p. 15.
[4] S.P. 16/472 ff. 16-7: 23 Nov. 1640.
[5] The commissioners' allegations and the victims' estate records must be compared where possible: as in M. E. Finch, *Five Northants. Families* (Northants. Record Society, xx, 1956) pp. 158-63.

in 1635 and ends in the Easter term of 1640 with prosecutions which were annulled when Parliament at last met and the Commissions were condemned.[1] It was remembered in Laud's impeachment that 'he did a little too much countenance the Commission for Depopulations.'[2]

The patents show the Commission in its dual role. In March and April 1635 the Commissions were appointed to enquire into depopulations since 1588 in Lincoln, Somerset and Wiltshire.[3] But in May the tone charged:

'patent to release and determine all offences concerninge depopulations and converting arable land to pasture within this Realme and also to compound with Fynes with such offenders as the Commissioners shall thinke fitt to be pardoned.'

In September 1637 another patent for fines and pardons gave the Commissioners discretion in deciding how much reconversion and rebuilding be demanded of one of these repentant sinners: one such pardon was that to William Boughton for offences in Warwickshire, granted on July 12, 1639. After the payment

'his Majestie doth dispence with him for the continuance of the same houses and lands.'

Thus by 1640 conciliar action to maintain tillage had been discredited by the company it kept; but even if it was unlikely that any law would be passed to enforce enclosers to maintain the area of tillage, Parliament had not yet expressed any positive approval of enclosure and had taken no steps to facilitate a Regulated Enclosure. It is ironical that in a period very conscious of Parliamentary sovereignty it was not Parliament but the courts of Chancery and Exchequer which provided the eventual means of lawful Regulation: when Parliament began to approve local Enclosure Bills in the eighteenth century more than a hundred years had elapsed since its solitary approval of the Herefordshire enclosure agreements in

---

[1] C212/20; one proposal of 1631 suggested rebuilding St. Paul's from the depopulation fines for Leics., Lincs. and Northants: S.P. 16/187/95.

[2] S.P. 16/499 no. 10 also censured the Privy Council's committee on depopulations.

[3] All these patents occur in the papers of Lord Keeper Coventry: Birm. Ref Library Mss. 604190, arranged by date.

1608; and many of the early Hanoverian enclosure Acts were simply Parliamentary approval of existing agreements registered already in Chancery or Exchequer.

Section V of this essay will discuss the facilities which developed in Chancery and Exchequer but, first of all, the missed opportunities in Parliament deserve comment.

IV

It has not been noticed hitherto that a permissive clause was deleted from the Bill which formed the basis of 39 Eliz. c. 1 'Against the Decaying of Towns and Houses of Husbandry'. The bill caused a long debate in the Commons Committee and when it reached the Upper House the Lords produced 31 written objections to it. The bill was re-written and re-titled after a conference of the two Houses and the final version which came down to the Commons for re-consideration was very different.[1] In form, it was made up of one large and one very small membrane in the hand of the Lords' Clerk (clauses I-IV of the printed Act) stitched to another large membrane, in the hand of the Commons' Clerk, containing clauses V onwards. Clause VI allowed exchange of land between lord and tenant or tenant and tenant 'for the more better and commodious occupyinge of husbandrye' when deficiencies in the acreage of land going with a farm had been made up from the surplus of another farm with more than the statutory minimum. At the end of clause VI, but struck out, is an even more liberal permission which can still be read underneath the cancellation.

---

[1] D'Ewes, *op. cit.*, pp. 537 and 542: 14 and 26 Jan. 1598. The Lords changed the title of the Act from 'for the Increase of People' to 'Against the Decaying of Towns etc.' The original bill is in House of Lords Mss., 15 December 1597. This Bill and the Tillage Bill reached the Lords together on 17 Dec. (*Lords Journal*, ii, p. 212). The Tillage Bill passed all its stages in both Houses by 23 Jan. but the Decaying of Towns took until 8 February, the eve of the royal assent, to pass the Commons in its revised form. Despite this it was numbered c. 1 and the Tillage Bill c. 2. The preambles to the original 'Increase' Bill and the Act are worth comparing; originally there was a rhetorical flourish akin to that which survived in c. 2, a Baconian ring.

'It shalbe lawfull for anie tenant of anie howse of husbandry with the consent of the Lord of that soyle and of such other Lord as hath Common or interest therein from tyme to tyme hereafter, to inclose into severaltie the landes whiche shalbe put or belong unto his howse of husbandry or any parte thereof.'[1]

The provenance of this part of the document is uncertain. Although in the hand of the Commons' bills of that session it is not a relic of the original bill, for that document survives elsewhere. It does however form part of the new bill which went from the Lords after the Conference, for it bears the order *soit bailee aux Commons*: perhaps it is the acceptable residue of a draft which the Commons brought to the Conference?

In this Parliament of 1597-8 there were two other attempts to give freedom to enclose but they do not seem to relate to this deleted clause. On 20 January 1598, in the midst of the discussions between the two Houses over this bill, it is recorded that the Commons rejected

'a bill for the most Commodious usage of Lands dispersed in the Common Fields.'

but no more is known of it than its title. When the revised Husbandry Bill arrived from the Lords there was a last minute attempt to amend it on 30 January

'that a Man maie inclose soe much Lands as himself listeth soe it be for the mayntenance of his house.'

but it was defeated as

'a gapp to Lett more Sheepe in.'[2]

Alongside this abortive permission to enclose by agreement may be set the single Act of 4 James I c. 11, a timid authority to six Herefordshire parishes to enclose one third of their commons by agreement.

---

[1] House of Lords Mss. engrossed Acts. The Commons hand has a strong left slope on the flourishing small 'd' and will be found in the engrossed cc. 2 and 4-7 of the session The Lords hand is quite different and will be found on the paper amendments (see f.n. 4 p. 45 above), on the provisos sewn to the Commons Bills by the Lords (e.g. c. 6). All c 8 (Deprivation of bishops) is in this hand: it was one of the bills which originated in the Lords (*L.J.*, ii. pp. 198-200).

[2] Pollard and Blatcher, *art. cit.*, p. 22 from BM. . Stowe Mss. 362 f. 17b; D'Ewes, *op. cit.*, p. 584.

The Act had no immediate successors but the psychological climate of 1607 and 1608 was not very tolerant of the word 'enclosure', over which blood had been freshly spilt in the agrarian riots.

A plan for a general permission to enclose was put to James I by John Shotbolt in his 'Verie necessary considerations for the Weale Publique'. (The document[1] is undated but this may be the Shotbolt who obtained a patent for a road-repairing machine in May 1619). He felt that public opinion had become less hostile

'the vulgar or common sorte of people. . . might nowe bee per-suaded and make a generall Triall of the contrary course, that is freely and willingly to assent to a speedy and generall Inclosure in all partes of the Kingdome and bee humble Suitors to his Majestie not onely to yeild his Royall assent thereunto or to tollerate the same but rather to endeavour by all means possible to sett so good a business in hand for soe generall Inriching to all sortes and every particular.'

Shotbolt declared himself an enemy of depopulation:

'most Unchristianlike it tooke not alone ye Bread from ye Mouths but ye Mouths from ye Bread.'

For him, enclosure was not the first step towards a change in land-use but a means to more efficient arable production. The glebe would gain by being consolidated, and the king might act as a model land-lord and set an example by allowing a general enclosure on the royal estates.

In essence Shotbolt's plan was for

'a mutuall consent for a generall Exchaunge (not altering either tenure or title but place along)'

and perhaps as early as 1623 Adam Moore's *Bread for the Poor*[2] urged a Grand Committee in each county for 'just proceeding' in an agreed enclosure.

An abortive bill of 1621 for the improving and better ordering of Commons was based on the idea of local Commissions and may have been connected with Shotbolt's project although it did not embrace

---

[1] B.M. Royal Mss. 18A/XXV; a project dated 27 March 1610 was also for a general enclosure: S.P. 14/120/10.
[2] Published 1653 but 'penned thirty years since'.

enclosure of open field land.[1] In 1621 the Commons was neutral between the liberal and the conservative policies for it also rejected a Depopulation Bill,[2] and had the King not ended the session abruptly the Acts of 1489, 1515, 1536 and 1563 would have been repealed.[3]

The author of *England's Great Happiness, a Dialogue between Content and Complaint* (1677) made his pro-enclosure speaker (*Content*) say:

'I confess I know no statute that gives full power to enclose all the Common Fields in the Kingdom but in my weak judgement there are several that do encourage it.'

He cited the Acts authorising the enclosure of fenland for improvement and the preamble to an Act of 1664 which he dubbed *Trade Encouraged*.[4] This Act permitted export of corn when its price fell below 48s. a quarter and in its preamble it praised tillage and commended the enclosure of wastes and their improvement

'if sufficient encouragement were given for the laying out of cost and labour to the same'

—the 'Encouragement' being in fact not an Enclosure Act but an Act to widen the market for corn. Despite *Content*, a vague commendation of improving wastes was some distance from an act encouraging the enclosure of common fields. Bills to give encouragement had recently failed. A Lords' bill of 1665 proposed to allow the owners of unprofitable wastes to petition the Lord Chancellor or the Chancellor of the Duchy of Lancaster asking for a Commission to divide the commons. It did not survive beyond a first reading.[5] In 1662 and 1663 the Commons rejected bills,[6] of which there survive no details, entitled 'Common Fields' and 'For the Improvement of Commons' and we may guess them to have been in the same vein as

[1] House of Lords Mss., 7 March 1621.

[2] W. Notestein *et al.*, eds., *Commons Debates of 1621* (1935), iii, p. 307.

[3] The 1563 Tillage Act was repealed in 1624; Coke also believed (correctly, I think) that the Acts of 1597 also died in 1624 by non-continuance but the Statute Law Revision Act of 1863 tidily repealed them.

[4] 16 Chas. II. c. 15; Acts such as 15 Chas. II c. 17 (Great Level of the Fens, 1663) and 19 and 20 Chas. II c. 8 (Forest of Dean, 1668) extinguished common rights in the cause of Improvement.

[5] Text of the Bill: House of Lords Mss. 20 Jan. 1665.

[6] *C.J.*, viii, pp. 423, 439, 466 and 486.

the Lords' bill of 1665. Another bill, which failed after its Committee stage in 1666, indicates the means whereby for nearly two generations local agreements had been finding legitimation independently of Parliament.

'Within these forty fifty and sixty years last past there have beene within this Kingdom multitudes of Enclosures of Commonable Grounds Wastes Heaths fermgrounds and Marishes by consent of partyes therein Interested made or ordered to be made, and the same uppon due Consideration thereuppon had been found to bee for the generall good and soe have been declared confirmed and established and decreed by decrees made in the Chancery or Exchequer Chamber or Duchy Court to generall satisfaction and contentment.[1]'

The bill proposed to give certainty to the legitimacy of these decrees by a retrospective blessing on all decrees for the previous sixty years. It did not propose any new machinery for future agreements but it did argue that the confirmation of past decrees would encourage other property owners who were considering an enclosure: yet the suggestion that a confirmatory Act was necessary was a tactless way of encouraging resort to decrees in the future.

In fact, confidence in the legitimacy of agreements registered in Chancery and Exchequer was strong in the 1660's and few decrees were brought in question. The early enclosures by Private Act were closely modelled on this well-established procedure of Decrees.[2] Many Acts simply ratified decrees, and even where there was no decree the early Acts were more akin to instruments for registering agreements among local proprietors rather than for overriding the obstinate opponents of Improvement.

---

[1] House of Lords Mss. 30 Oct. 1666.
[2] e.g. 4 Wm. & Mary (Private) no. 40 (1694) confirmed a Chancery decree for Hambleton (Rutland) of 1653 which had been brought into question: there may have been a genuine grievance of the villagers here (*Cal. S.P. Dom.* 1653, p. 330: petition against the purchaser of delinquent lands). 7 & 8 Wm. III (Private) no. 55 (1696) concerned Maidwell (Northants.) where there had been Chancery decrees of 10 May 1676 and 1 July 1692. A decree of 1716 for Huttons Ambo (Yorks), was confirmed by Act as late as 1805. As E.C.K. Gonner pointed out (*Common Land and Inclosure* (1912), pp. 187–8) there was an overlap in time between Acts and Decrees as a fashionable means of enclosing.

In general, enclosure by decree was enclosure by agreement, even where some pretence of disagreement was necessary before the court of Chancery could have jurisdiction.[1] Many enrolled decrees began by expressions of general local approval which were not cast in stereotyped form and sound more spontaneous than the legal phrasebook.

> 'It would be convenient and pleasing to all men... and might be both good and profitable to all those who were desierous to live as paynefull men in theire callings,'[2]

declared the proprietors and commoners of Brandesburton (Yorks. E.R.) in their agreement of January 1630, one of the earliest to be registered in Chancery.

> 'It would raise and turne to a far greater benefitt to every of them then (sc. than) the enjoyinge of it in comon besides the generall good that would thereby accrewe to the commonWealth,'[3]

declared some Norfolk proprietors in 1627; while Endymion Porter, lord of the manor of Aston Subedge (Glos) claimed that his purchase of the manor at a stiff price had been encouraged by tenantry and freeholders assuring him that they wanted a general enclosure. They

> 'did much incourage and drawe him to proceed therein protestinge that if hee should have a hard bargaine thereof yett they would make him a good gainer thereby if he would agree to a generall incloasure to be made of the lordshipp'[4]

At another enclosure

> 'every man's part exceedingly improved in value;'

and at Thurcaston (Leics.)

> 'the said Inclosure tended soe much to the good of the common wealth and particular benefit of the said Parrishe... soe good a worke should not fayle.'[5]

When Charles I's Privy Council began to denounce and harry enclosure they had to meet the objection that agreed enclosures were

---

[1] In Leics. Dr. Thirsk identified 13 enclosures 1640-60 of which 'at least six' were by agreement. From these, three disputes arose. (*V.C.H. Leics.*, ii (1954), p. 218; C. 78/526 no. 8; C. 78/1214 no. 5.)

[2] C. 78/605; decree of March 1635.

[3] C. 78/273 no. 5.

[4] C. 78/273 no. 7: decree, Dec. 1629.

[5] C. 78/308 no. 21: decree, Dec. 1635.

harmless to the common weal. In March 1631 they described Leicestershire enclosures as

'very hurtfull to the commonwealth although they beare a fayre
shewe of satisfaction to all Parties... but we well know what the
consequences will be, and in conclusion all turne to Depopulation.'[1]

Where Chancery decrees speak of dissatisfaction over an enclosure
the language must be construed carefully. It was a necessary fiction
that a dispute existed, otherwise the jurisdiction of the Court might
not run. The fictitious element appears near the surface in very many
decrees, such as that of Bilton, (Warws), in 1661 which recited the
agreement of 1657, alleging that the defendants were refusing to
perform it; but no defence was entered—'they confess it'—and the
agreement was duly registered.[2]

Where the defence is more fully and vehemently stated or the
plaintiff more querulous it may be guessed that there was genuine
disagreement. At Aston Subedge Endymion Porter's purchase had
not been followed by the agreement which the villagers had promised
him.

'some of them sometyme yeilded to a generall Incloasure yett
some other of them at the same tyme yeilded only to a particuler
Inclosuer and some others refused to yeild to any Incloasure, and
some other of them were not present at any of the said meetings
or propositions nor gave their consent.'[3]

This was just what Adam Moore had encountered in Somerset

'the vehement desires of the discreeter sort to proceed having been
still crossed and cooled by the willful opposition of vulgar Spirits.'[4]

At Aston Subedge, the court of Chancery appointed a local commission of enquiry who admitted the difficulty of ever obtaining
complete consent, and on the report of a majority consent the Court
confirmed the agreement with small amendments—but nearly five
years after the suit began.

'We finde most of the defendants contented... In a cause of this

[1] P.C. 2/40 f. 385: 7 March 1631.
[2] C 33/218 f. 263d: 3 July 1661.
[3] C. 78/273 no. 7
[4] Adam Moore, *Bread for the Poor* (1653).

nature concerninge a multitude we find it a matter difficult to please all.'[1]

It would need examination of a very large number of decrees and also examination of local estate records before any balanced judgement could be made on the proportions of fictitious and genuine disputes. In the cases so far encountered where there was disagreement the court was always told that there had been an initial agreement from which some parties had then retreated; it was on the equity of enforcing the agreement that the jurisdiction of the court rested.

The agreements which were brought to court for registration had very often been the result of long negotiation between the proprietors, the rector and sometimes the bishop. Endymion Porter had negotiated with all these at Aston Subedge. It became usual for the actual allocation of enclosed fields to be put in the hand of arbitrators appointed by the parties, and both in function and name these men anticipated the work of the enclosure commissioners appointed by eighteenth century Enclosure Acts. It was on the basis of commissioner-arbitrators that Shotbolt's proposal to James I had rested

> 'where men cannot agree betweene themselves Commissioners of worthe both for mindes and estates to be in all places selected to mediate all differences and questions in that kind... an unspeakable benefitt to the wholle Comonwealthe in generall.'[2]

At Aston Subedge the villagers appointed two commissioners, the parson one and Porter, as lord of the manor, the fourth. (The local commission of inquiry appointed by Chancery after the dispute was therefore a commission of appeal from commissioners.)

The numbers of commissioners to draw up the awards was sometimes large (again, like some of the early enclosures by Act), as at Brandesburton

> 'there beinge fifteene in number ympannelled;'[3]

and the awards could be voluminous. One decree recited 112 separate articles of the award by the six commissioners[4] but the majority of

---

[1] C. 78/273 no. 7.

[2] B.M., Royal Mss. 18A/XXV.

[3] C. 78/605 no. 3.

[4] C. 78/598 mm. 31 sqq.: Rillington, Yorks; decree, 9 July 1660.

decrees were shorter than this.

Surveyors also appear: at Aston Subedge Porter had met the full costs of a survey. At Claxton, (Yorks), the agreement of c. 1638 provided that

> 'a division should be made and the lands soe lyeing dispersed should be layed together to be inclosed in severalty and a proportionate part of the soyle of the waste should be sett forth in lieu of the right of common to be inclosed likewise in severalty. An expert surveyor shall be chosen to make the said division'.[1]

V

The exact date of the first Chancery decree concerned with an enclosure agreement is not yet known, there being 279 rolls for the period 1603-49 alone and their indexes inadequate for a search of this kind. The decrees and orders registered in books have to be sought in volumes of up to a thousand pages each, two volumes a year for most of the same period and just as inconveniently indexed for this purpose. (The note at the end of this essay offers some guide to the indexes.)

There is some evidence which suggests that the early 1630's saw the formal development of enrollment of agreements in Chancery. In 1631 the Privy Council threatened further action against Midland enclosers and demanded that promises not to decay houses nor lessen tillage upon enclosure should be embodied in a Chancery decree at the landowners' expense.[2] It was in 1633 that the wide approval of the court of the palatinate of Durham began to be extended to agreed enclosures. Miss Leonard traced 28 enclosure agreements registered there between 1633 and 1700, twenty of them relating to open fields, some 25,000 acres of the county.[3] The earliest date mentioned by Gonner is 1614 (Claypool, Lincs.) but he gave no reference[4] and this

---

[1] C. 78/598 no. 2: agreement, 1638; decree, 1659.
[2] P.C. 2/40 f. 540; also *Hist. Mss. Comm. Hastings* iv, (1947), p. 214.
[3] E. M. Leonard, 'The Inclosure of Common Fields in the Seventeenth Century', *Trans. Royal Hist. Soc.* new ser. xix (1905), pp. 111-14.
[4] E. C. K. Gonner, *op. cit.*

case cannot be traced in the index. Nor is it clear whether 1614 was the date of the agreement or of the enrollment.

The considerable lapse of time between an agreement and its enrollment at the end of a Chancery suit makes the date of the earliest enrollment of only minor interest. A decree made in May 1630 dealt with an agreement of about 15 years earlier;[1] another case on the same roll hinged on an enclosure 50 years earlier; a third agreement, known to have been made c. 1615 formed the basis of a suit begun in 1665 with its decree[2] in 1667. A fortunate minority was less afflicted with the law's delays: one agreement was made in 1662, the fields enclosed in 1663 and the decree confirmed the agreement[3] in 1664.

It will also be found that statements about enclosure by agreement also appear on the decree rolls in disputes of another kind which appear from their language to have been genuine and not fictitious suits. These concerned the quantity and quality of the glebe land which had been allocated by a local enclosure, the church's strips having lain promiscuously with the other open field lands. Just as the parochial surveys of glebe land in this period[4] often allude to the date of an enclosure (and sometimes to disputes) so the Chancery cases involving glebe may often give the date of an earlier general enclosure by agreement. One of 1580 is mentioned in a suit[5] concerning the glebe of Hardwick which was heard in 1630.

Being principally concerned in this essay with the provision of opportunities to legitimise enclosure agreements it would be wrong to see too much significance in the beginning of formal enrollment in Chancery. That court had been used as a means of establishing title long before 1630: how often cannot be said in view of the limited character of subject-indexes to the tens of thousands of cases. At Toddington, Beds. in 1589 a suit[6] was 'to establish an inclosure' and

---

[1] C. 78/360 no. 4.

[2] C. 78/669 no. 13.

[3] C. 78/669 no. 18.

[4] M. W. Beresford, 'Glebe Terriers and Open-field Leics.', *Tr. Leics. Arc. Soc* (1949), pp. 77-126; D. M. Barrett, ed., *Ecclesiastical Terriers of Warws. Parishes* (Dugdale Soc. xxii (1955).

[5] C. 78/360.

[6] C. 2/Cc12/34.

the great twenty-sheet plan of the manor drawn by Ralph Agas in 1581 may have been commissioned for this purpose.[1]

Even more utilised than Chancery was the jurisdiction of the court of Exchequer, the most prolific documentary source for the progress of sixteenth century enclosure, legal and illegal. There is no need to rehearse here the many occasions when illegal enclosures brought their perpetrators before the barons of Exchequer. But Exchequer was also the means whereby new titles to land after enclosure were established and the partial indexing of Exchequer judicial records in this period make them more accessible than those of Chancery

The first beneficiaries seem to have been the tenants of ancient demesne, the old Crown lands, and those brought under the Crown by the Reformation confiscations. (The separate jurisdiction of the courts of the Duchy of Lancaster gives analogous documentation for the Duchy estates all over England.) The logic seems to have been this: local commissions, rather like the medieval inquiries *ad quod damnum*, were ordered by the court to investigate whether the Crown's interests would gain or lose by projects of all kinds. High among these projects were revenue-raising steps like the enfranchise-ment of copyhold and the establishing of questionable tenancies. But villagers were also willing to pay for the enclosure of their estates and the Crown, as lord of the manor, had a private as well as a public interest. Many thousands of acres of common rights, parti-cularly in the northern uplands, were extinguished in this unob-trusive way.

Thus, the villages of Raskelf and Sessay (Yorks., N.R.) inter-commoned on what is still rough scrub at Pilmoor. Raskelf was a royal manor and the enclosure decree of May 1580 declared[2]

'it were as benyfyciall or more commodious for her Majesties tennants of her lordshipp and manner of Raskall that the defendants lordshipp and manner of Sessay should be devyded and kepte severall. . . then (*sc.* than) to lye in comen without soveraine.'

In Northamptonshire, on Duchy land, the tenants of Irchester, Rush-en and Raundes made an expensive composition with the Crown in

B.M. Add. Mss. 38065.
E. 123/7 f. 95; E. 159/379 m. 326.

June 1618 for the security of their copyholds; five months later the agreements recited that

> 'the said manor doth for the most parte consiste of Arable groundes which lye promiscuously dispersed and intermingled, with the freehold and customary lands'

and asked for a commission to reallocate the field lands at the same time that the common wastes were being enclosed. This was granted:

> 'that they should have liberty of inclosing and Exchaunging his or their customary esteates.'[1]

For this liberty the tenantry of Rushden paid £ 2,166, those of Raundes £ 1,640 and those of Irchester £ 723.

Parts of the waste of Easingwold (Yorks., N.R.) were enclosed by decree the next year[2] but the records both of Exchequer and the Duchy show that cases of this kind had been considered favourably in the previous reign; thus, part of Bradford (Yorks.) moor was enclosed[3] in 1590. The registration of agreed enclosures in Chancery was no more than an extension to other proprietors of a facility which tenants and freeholders under the Crown had long known in Exchequer.

Finally, there is a parallel in the court of Exchequer to the incidental revelation of the date of agreed enclosure by subsequent disputes over enclosed glebeland in Chancery. The court of Exchequer after the Reformation had jurisdiction over tithe disputes similar to that of the bishops in Consistory Courts.[4] An enclosure, particularly if a change in land use or an improvement in land values was expected, raised issues of great interest to the owners of tithes and to tithe-payers. The opportunity was sometimes taken to commute tithes for an annual sum or to give the Rector a piece of enclosed land in lieu of tithe. Consequential disputes in the courts frequently caused witnesses to describe the date and terms of the agreed enclosure.

---

[1] D.L. 5/27 ff. 1285, 1308-9; D.L. 5/28 ff. 50-6, 68-73, 73-78; E. 314, Northants. nos. 36, 44-5.

[2] D.L. 5/28 f. 151d.

[3] D.L. 5/18 f. 776 and 20 f. 354.

[4] for example see J. S. Purvis, ed., *Select XVI Century Causes in Tithe* (Yorks. Arch. Soc. Record Ser., cxiv (1949).

VI

Thus, enclosure by agreement was facilitated by the death of some old prejudices; by the discrediting of regulation by unsavoury agents; by the registration of a good legal title to newly enclosed fields; by the acceptance of local variations in land-use as normal so that the countryside could be now 'a Barne' and now 'a Dayrie howse' in response to market forces. A century after the member for Shropshire had used this figure of speech in the debate of 1597 English agriculture was dancing to a recognisable tune:

'Men are not to be compelled by penalties, but allured by profit, to any good exercise,'[1]

and in place of Tillage Acts the legislature was considering Corn Laws and Corn Bounty Acts.[2]

There was one final change before freedom to enclose and freedom to choose crops could have their head. The fears and prejudices aroused by enclosure had not all derived from misgivings about depopulation and Habitation. The decaying houses of husbandmen betokened fewer yeomen of England and weakness in the face of the Queen's enemies without: but the decay of tillage betokened shortages of corn for all Englishmen. As Shotbolt[3] had put it, decay of tillage not only diminished the number of mouths in the countryside but also took bread out of everyone's mouth, whether in countryside or in towns. These sentiments resurged in years of bad harvest when even those districts with large grass acreages thought regretfully of the displaced ploughs and resurrected old grievances. The proclamation of July 1607 asserted that the rioters of that year were not justified by any dearth of corn but the evidence runs the other way.[4] Conversely, abundance of corn induced the experiment of repealing the tillage laws in 1593: and in 1618 the patent appointing a commission

---

[1] The dictum comes from Henry Jackman's speech of 1597 quoted in J. E. Neale, *op. cit.* p 343.

[2] The contribution of protection and bounties to enclosure and improvement was stressed in the *Dialogue* of 1677 quoted above, p. 55.

[3] B.M. Royal Mss. 18A/XXV, f. 3.

[4] E. F. Gay, 'The Midland Revolt of 1607', *Trans. Royal Hist. Soc.*, new ser. xviii (1904), p. 213.

to give exemption from the Tillage Acts justified itself by the same
argument: regulation made superfluous by abundance.

> 'Tillage is become much more frequent and usual. . . corn is at
> reasonable rates and prizes. . . woodland and plains have been
> converted to tillage whose nature serves them most aptly.

> There is noe wante of corne lande att this tyme but want of
> pasture and cattle for much woodland and barren grounds are
> become fruitfull corne landes in steed of pasture.'[1]

But despite Bacon's belief in 1592 that

> 'high corn prices invited and enticed men to break up more corn
> ground and convert it to tillage than all the penal laws could ever
> by compulsion.'[2]

the market mechanism could not be trusted even after 1618. In 1630,
a year of poor harvests and high corn prices, the Privy Council
again attacked enclosure in familiar terms:

> 'of evill consequence and example as at all tymes especially at this
> tyme of dearth it being a greate occasion of feare in the common
> sorte of people that such conversion being suffered will occasion
> more scarcitie hereafter;'[3]

and with the noise of bread riots in their ears the Council succumbed
to the temptation to blame everything on the engrossing middleman
and the depopulating encloser. The Council moved away once more
from faith in an unregulated market mechanism and, although the
common informer was not revived, a Committee of the Council on
Depopulation appeared and gave rise to the local Commissions. The
liberal view was temporarily in eclipse again.

That it prevailed by the end of the seventeenth century was
partly due to the bad taste left behind by the agents of a regulated
economy in the 1630's. Yet bad harvests did not cease with the execution of Charles I: as late as 1709, a year of very bad harvests, the
price of wheat reached a height surpassed only twice in the whole
eighteenth century (1799 and 1800) and then during a war-time

---

[1] C. 66/2134 m. 1d; also C. 66/2150 no. 17.
[2] quoted, without reference given, in W. H. R. Curtler, *The Enclosure and
Redistribution of Our Land* (1920), p. 123.
[3] P.C. 2/40 f. 199: 30 Nov. 1630.

inflation. But in 1709 14,000 more quarters of wheat were exported than imported and 77,000 the next year.[1] It was a far cry from the bill of 1598 which had proposed to ban all export of corn until twelve months after each harvest when it could be seen if anything could be spared for foreigners.[2]

It was not sufficient for the advocates of general enclosure by agreement to be able to promise Habitation; it was essential that Improvement should show itself in improved supplies of food which kept pace with the rise in population. We might have worse evidence of the effect of agricultural Improvement[3] than the fact that in two years (1710-12) which Professor Ashton[4] puts 'among the worst of the (eighteenth) century' no one wanted to hang the graziers or have the enclosers in the ditch. The issue of Habitation versus Improvement seemed dead and English farming seemed to be able to offer both.

---

[1] Data from T. S. Ashton, *Economic Fluctuations in the Eighteenth Century* (1959), pp. 181 and 183.

[2] House of Lords. Mss. *sub* 21 Jan. 1598.

[3] 'Improvement' must include distribution as well as production. Imperfections of transport, wholesaleing and retailing had to be smoothed before full advantage could be taken of local specialisation; a little is known of the transport history of the seventeenth century but studies of the mechanism of internal trade are badly needed.

[4] T. S. Ashton, *op. cit.*, p. 141; the two years ran from summer 1710 to summer 1712.

A NOTE ON THE SOURCES FOR ENCLOSURE AGREEMENTS IN THE PUBLIC RECORD OFFICE

This note is not an exhaustive guide: it says nothing of agreements among estate records[1] in private and public custody; nor of the evidence from tithe causes in the bishops' courts; nor of the references to enclosure in the successive terriers of the parish glebe. It is a commentary on the references to agreed enclosure among documents at the Public Record Office and on the indexes which are available there.

Chancery

Agreements can be found fully recited or summarily approved by Enrolled Decree[2] (class C78) or by a Decree registered in the Entry Books of Decrees and Orders (class C33). The *Enrolled Decrees* form a large class which are imperfectly indexed except by surname of the plaintiffs. If this name is known the manuscript indexes at Long Room Shelf L should be searched. There are ten volumes[3] of these in semi-chronological order, given to overlapping and thus mirroring the interior confusion of the decree rolls themselves. All that can be safely said is that C78/1 contains a decree from 26 Henry VIII; that the decrees of Elizabeth's reign seem to begin at C78/15, the end of the reign being reached near C78/111; C78/214 is unequivocally from Charles I and C78/389 from 1649. A volume also shelved at L in the Long Room is an alphabetical *index locorum* to the ten volumes of manuscript Calendars but it is far from exhaustive: Brandesburton (C78/605 no. 3 (1630)), Miss Leonard's main example, does not appear in it, for example.[4]

The *Entry Books of Decrees and Orders* comprise two series, 'A' and 'B'. Before 1629 there was no logic in the division of cases between the two series, but after 1629 the 'A' book of each year covered cases where the plaintiff's surname lay between A and K, and the 'B' book the remainder of the alphabet. The 'A' books make up the odd numbers of the class, C33/1 onwards, and the 'B' the even numbers from C33/2. A list of books identified by years will be found in the Chancery Class List shelved at 24/26B in the Round Room.[5] There are separate indexes to each year of each series but the index is solely by plaintiff's names.[1] No place-index has been found.

---

[1] e.g. the Brudenell documents cited by M. E. Finch, *op., cit.* p. 162

[2] One of these decrees is discussed by G. N. Clark *Eng. H.R.* xlii (1927) pp. 88 sqq. (C 78/586 no. 1: 12 Feb. 1662).

[3] These are numbered Index 16950-9. Index 16950 has additionally a Calendar for the reign of Elizabeth.

[4] Index 16951 (Eliz. to Chas. I) has a partial index of cases concerning manors at pp. 309-17 and 321-4.

[5] Thus Book B of 1661, Miss Leonard's reference *(art. cit.)* for the Bilton decree is now C. 33/218.

Duchy of Lancaster

The *Decrees and Orders* form Class DL5 and are calendared by counties in a manuscript volume shelved at 27/82G in the Round Room. The adjoining manuscript calendars to *D. L. Special Commissions* and *Depositions* should also consulted.

Exchequer

Decrees in the court of Exchequer were not separately enrolled but some could be entered on the Queen's or Lord Treasurer's Remembrancer's Rolls (E159 and E368). Enclosure cases are more common on the former.[2] Most Exchequer decrees found their way not to the Memoranda Rolls but to the *Entry Books* (E123 to E131).[3] There are two Index volumes which attempt to cover the principal cases in the above classes involving land, and in addition a series of indexes and calendars to each class. The first of the two general indexes is Adam Martin, *Index to Various Records preserved in the Court of Exchequer*, published in London in 1819. Martin's index is alphabetical mainly of place-names with a few personal names. It is shelved at 7/136 in the Round Room. Hutton Wood's *Index* is a manuscript index covering very much the same ground but arranged county by county; the order within the counties is not alphabetical.

Other manuscript indexes follow individual Classes of Exchequer documents and, unlike Martin and Wood, aim to be complete. They overlap somewhat but can be listed as follows.

Round Room volumes 7/1 to 7/15 cover the *Entry Books of Decrees and Orders* (Classes E123-5) from Elizabeth to the Commonwealth. These index volumes are of plaintiffs' names.

Round Room volumes 7/16 to 7/19 cover the *Entry Books of Decrees* (Class E126) from 1604 to 1697 in the form of a detailed calendar.

Index volumes 16854-60 form a calendar to the *Entry Books* in chronological order but give the surnames of parties with no other data.

Index volume 16879 ('Vanderzee's Index') is a Calendar to the *Entry Books* from 1558 to 1675; the particulars are brief and where the same ground is covered by Round Room volumes 7/16 etc. the latter are to be preferred.

---

[1] Thus Index 1538 is to the 'A' book of 1630 (C. 33/159) and Index 1539 to the 'B' book of that year (C. 33/160). These indexes, term by term, do not more than place all the surnames of the same letter in one group.

[2] Thus, the Raskelf commons decree of 1580 is on membrane 326 of the K.R. M.R. for Mich. 22 Eliz. (E. 159/379).

[3] Thus, the decree for Ingleby and Barwick commons is in the Entry Book of Decrees and Orders for Mich. 26 Eliz. (E. 123/10 f. 215); those for the Forest of Galtres in 1632 and 1634 in E. 126/4 ff. 46-7 and 155.

In the course of Exchequer proceedings it was common to appoint local commissions to put specific questions to local juries and to return depositions. While a few sets of depositions were enrolled on the Memoranda Rolls (E159) each term the majority were simply filed away and form the class E134 to which there are Calendars on the shelves of the Round Room. Ancillary to these are the *Depositions Taken before the Barons* (Class E133) to which there are good manuscript calendars at Round Room 7/119C-E. Another manuscript calendar at Round Room 7/118R leads to the interesting class E134 Misc., a collection of 2,361 sets of depositions. The commissions sent to the provinces, often with the questionnaires attached, form class E178. As with the parallel classes, D.L. Special Commissions and Depositions, these Exchequer classes are extraordinarily informative in their verbose questions and answers.

Miscellaneous

Enclosure cases in *Star Chamber* and *Requests* may sometimes turn out to be over agreements or alleged agreements.

The varied classes which have been drawn on for the printed *Index of Rentals and Surveys and Other Analagous Documents* (P.R.O. Lists and Indexes no. xxv (1908)) are also rewarding in attempting to trace the progress from open to enclosed land. To these may be added the *Close Rolls* (C54) which aided Dr. Thirsk in her dating of some early Leicestershire enclosures (*V. C. H. Leics.*, ii (1954), pp. 254-9) e.g. Nether Broughton, 1651; C54/3668 no. 19.

15

THE LAY SUBSIDIES
PART I. (1290-1334)

In the late twelfth century a novel standard of tax assessment began to be used: not taking into account the number of ploughlands or the number of knights' fees a man possessed, but reckoning that part of personal wealth which could be distinguished as *movables.* It is, of course, an indication that the economy was no longer one where land formed the only index of wealth; its novelty also emphasizes the cost of foreign war, the main occasion of such Parliamentary grants; the novelty also produced interesting administrative innovations both in assessment, collecting and auditing. From the point of view of the local historian these innovations are chiefly important for the distinct and voluminous class of records which they produced, and the records themselves for the evidence which they afford of the distribution of personal wealth among the more well-to-do laity.[1]

Up to and including 1332 there were sixteen principal grants of tax to be assessed on personal property for which surviving documents may be found.[2] The year of grant is usually mentioned at the head of the account which the collectors returned to the Exchequer, but the interval between grant and collection sometimes means that a different date is given on the outside of the roll and in the detailed *Lists,* county by county, on the shelves of the Round Room at the Public Record office. The degree of survival of these tax returns varies very much from county to county, and no county has a complete set of assessments surviving from all sixteen grants: 1290, 1294, 1295, 1296, 1297, 1301, 1306, 1307, 1309, 1313, 1315, 1316, 1319, 1322, 1327, 1332.

---

1   The documents form part of class E. 179 at the Public Record Office. They have a series of County Lists, in typescript, which may be consulted there or which may be photo-copied at the usual charges. The numbers of these volumes are 7/26 to 7/36C. The first two list Clerical Taxes, 7/28 begins with Beds. to Cumb. and 7/35 has Warws. to Yorks. 7/36 has Wales, Cinque Ports, Royal Households, Divers Counties, Miscellaneous, Unknown Counties and Addenda. All these unsorted or unidentified files are valuable. [The Lists have been sub-sequently published by The List and Index Society.]

2   There is a very full treatment of all the grants up to and including 1332 in J.F. Willard, *Parliamentary Taxes on Personal Property* (Cambridge, Mass., 1934.)

The fullest documents from the process of taxation are the 'Particulars of Account' which report to the Exchequer the values at which local assessors have set the movable property of the individual taxpayers. The names of the taxpayers are arranged by vills and boroughs, and the county covered hundred by hundred or wapentake by wapentake. At the end of the roll is the county total, but there is no need to consult the original records if a county total is all that is required, for these sums were printed by Professor Willard.[3] The county totals, the names of the collectors, together with the record of any arrears or concessions made at the Exchequer appear again in the great rolls of the Enrolled Subsidy to which there is now also a typescript index in the Round Room (Press Marks: 6/24D).

Interest in genealogy has, fortunately, produced a good crop of county *Particulars* among the publications of local Record Societies during the last half century.[4] Indeed, the list is too long to be given here. Even so, no county has all its Subsidy Rolls in print. The existing volumes do mean, however, that a student may easily obtain a view of the form which the rolls of a given year's collection take, and so the more easily begin to tackle the unpublished rolls of his own area. Several of these volumes have excellent *Introductions* in which more than local matters are discussed.[5]

The usefulness of the subsidy rolls does not end with the hundreds of thousands of property owners' names which they furnish. Being concerned with wealth in the form of property other than land, they are material evidence for the local distribution of such property among lay men. Within a vill, and even more strikingly within a hundred or wapentake, there were marked inequalities among the property which the assessors came to tax. The lord of the manor can often be identified by the size of his assessment. Thus in Seamer, Yorkshire,[6] in 1301, Henry Percy paid 5s. 1½d. while the names below his on the list paid sums from 10d. to 2s. 9d. Within the country as a whole, the counties

3   J. F. Willard, *English Historical Review*, xxviii (1913), 517-21, xxix (1914), 317-21, and xxx (1915), 69-74.

4   E.g. W. F. Carter, ed., *The Lay Subsidy Roll of 1332* (Warws.), Dugdale Society Publications, vi, 1926; F. H. Dickinson, ed., *Exchequer Lay Subsidies 169/5* (1327), Somerset Record Society, iii, 1889; W. Hudson, ed., *The Three Earliest Subsidies for the County of Sussex in the Years* 1296, 1327, 1332, Sussex Record Society, x, 1910.

5   There is a discussion of the Northumberland rolls for 1296, but without a full text of the rolls, in F. Bradshaw, *The Lay Subsidy of* 1296 (Archaeologia Aeliana, 3rd ser., xiii (1916), 186-302.) The introductions by J. F. Willard and H. C. Johnson to *Surrey Record Society*, xi (A and B) (1932) are particularly useful.

6   W. Brown, ed., *Yorkshire Lay Subsidy of* 1301 (Yorks. Arch Soc. Record Series, xxi (1897), 57: from E. 179/211/2.

exhibit considerable differences between the total property assessed in an average vill. The remote north in particular is marked by small totals. Many taxpayers in south eastern England were each assessed at sums equal to the whole payment from vills of Northumberland and Lancashire. If the total tax paid is divided by the area of the district concerned, the density differences as one moves from the south-east to the north-west are striking and local historians who make similar maps for small areas within their county would find the results provocative as well as informative.

It is not possible to use this class of document as a direct source of information about total population in the various vills and boroughs. Quite apart from any deliberate evasion, the assessments were not intended to cover every property-owner. At each collection in the years mentioned above (except 1301) the grant defined a minimum value of property with which the assessors were to be concerned. Thus in 1297 no one whose tax assessment would have worked out at less than a shilling was to be mulcted; in the London roll of 1319 there are names crossed out as not possessing the minimum of property upon further enquiry. In 1301, when there was no minimum, the collectors accounted for sums as small as twopence and threepence. It must also be remembered that the assessments were not concerned with clerical property, and in order to avoid the payment of the tax taking away a piece of capital equipment necessary for the taxpayer's livelihood or station certain valuables were exempt: thus the armour and riding-horses of knights were exempt in 1290; and in 1294 and 1295 the treasure of merchants.[7]

The heading of every Lay Subsidy roll will include a statement embodying a fraction: in 1301 a fifteenth, in 1319 a twelfth may be encountered. On occasions, as in 1294, 1295, 1296, 1306, the roll will mention two fractions, and this became the common practice. What are these fractions? They arise from the fact that the sum levied was directed to be a named fraction of a man's movable property (after allowing for minima and exempt goods). Thus the assessors had first to give a total value and then to divide it by the appropriate fraction. According to Parliament's estimate of the urgency of the situation and the taxable capacity of the subject, the fraction would vary from grant to grant. Thus Edward III got a twentieth in 1327 and a fifteenth in 1332. Where two fractions are named on the same roll the explanation is that after 1294 it became more common to levy the tax at a different rate in urban and rural areas. Thus of the two fractions of 1332 (1/10th

---

7   The whole subject of exemptions is dealt with in J. F. Willard, op. cit., chapters iv-vi.

and 1/15th), the smaller applied to the generality of rural townships and the larger fraction was taken from the goods of those who lived in 'boroughs.' The places reckoned as 'boroughs' in this connection do not correspond with places defined as boroughs by other tests (such as charters, burgage tenure, etc.), and all that one can say about them is that the collectors regarded them as having sufficient craftsmen, traders and shopkeepers to qualify for a rate of tax higher than that appropriate for countrymen.[8] (This in itself is an interesting commentary on economic development.) The larger fraction was also taken from those who lived on the 'ancient demesne' of the Crown in the countyside. Places selected to pay the larger fraction are usually placed in separate sections of their county roll; sometimes they appear within their own hundred with a sidenote indicating the fraction. Any calculations of the taxed-wealth-per-acre type must of course take into account this double fraction. A tax payment of two shillings (when a tenth and fifteenth was granted) reflects 20s. 'wealth' in a town but 30s. in the county at large.

The subsidy rolls also provide something of a Directory to the rural settlements of England, even fuller than provided in that other by-product of taxation, the *Nomina Villarum*[9] of 1316. They enable the bounds of the early fourteenth century hundreds and wapentakes to be perceived, and they offer proof of the existence (and of the minimal population and relative wealth) of hundreds of settlements which were to perish in the next two hundred years.[10] A succession of rolls for the same county will often indicate what townships are implied when later documents speak only of a head township and its members (or hamlets). The reductions in taxation which followed from local or national disruptions are indicated in some later rolls which will be discussed subsequently.

II

In 1334 a revolution, unperceived at the time, took place in the system of tax assessment. The Crown found it expedient, and perhaps most efficient, to cease to concern itself with the wealth of individuals. Through its officers it negotiated with the local communities for a payment from each vill and borough which justly reflected the local

8   J. F. Willard in *Historical Essays in Honour of James Tait* (1933), 417-35.
9   Printed, by counties, in *Feudal Aids and Analagous Documents*, 6 vols. (1899-1921).
10   I used the rolls extensively for this purpose in my *Lost Villages of England* (1954).

capacity to pay.[11] How the vill distributed the sum among its inhabitants was not the Crown's concern,[12] and the rolls which found their way to the Exchequer ceased to carry any information other than the names of the townships and the sums due from each. The names of taxpayers virtually disappear. Only one condition was imposed on the negotiators: the sum from each place in 1334 was to be *at least* that paid in 1332, when a tenth and fifteenth of the conventional type had been last imposed. Comparison of the local rolls show how the 1332 and 1334 sums differ. I have elsewhere given the name 'village quotas' to these sums agreed upon in 1334.

The circumstances of the agreements gives some hope that they were considered as realistic and fair and acceptable by contemporaries. They clearly do not reflect *total* wealth (for they are close to the sums of 1332), but they were intended to reflect the *relative* wealth of places, and that information is one which historians cannot dispense with. It is fortunate that this information is available at a point in time very near the high water mark of medieval colonization, when the plough in some areas had pushed as far towards the margin as it was to go for nearly five hundred years, and before the great changes of the post-Black Death period.

What contemporaries could not have envisaged was that the assessments of 1334 were to become the basis of future collections, with only minor adjustments if a major calamity (such as the erosion by the sea of a village) occurred. When the next grant was made, in 1336, the collectors were simply instructed to collect the sums of 1334; and subsequent grants (until the mid seventeenth century) were on the same local basis, with the same sums[13] as in 1334. Thus, for this particular tax, the local shares became fossilized in the proportions of 1334 for three hundred years; and while most of the realism is taken out of documents from any collection after 1334 there is one small benefit to historians. As in earlier years, there is imperfect survival of the local documents from the 1334 collection; but the gap can be filled from 1336 or a subsequent collection. A useful single volume is an Exchequer compilation of local assessments (E.164/7) made probably

11   *Calendar of Patent Rolls*, 1334-1338, 38-40.
12   For the system at Birmingham, Birm. Ref. Library Mss. 569340; for Ilketshall, Suffolk, B. M. Add Mss. 40067; for Oxford, H. E. Salter *Medieval Oxford* (Oxford Hist. Soc., c, (1936), 133-41.
13   There was a similar fossilization in the assessments which formed the basis of clerical taxation. The Taxation of Pope Nicholas in 1291 remained unchallenged until Henry VIII's re-assessment in the Valor Ecclesiasticus, except for the revision of 1318 forced on the northern dioceses by the depredations of the Scots.

in the early fifteenth century, but it has a number of internal omissions and misreadings and thus needs checking against other rolls.

The assessments of 1334 as expressions of local wealth have already been utilised in a few local studies,[14] but there is a good deal more to be done, especially on minute local checks on their internal consistency and on the mapping of the data which they afford. The county totals, together with some local abtements and statements of arrears, continued on the Enrolled Subsidy roll,[15] and it is here rather than in the Particulars themselves that one must look for the realities of payment if there is any question of a serious local adjustment before 1349. After the Black Death the adjustment of local payments acquired a more complicated procedure, and the records which result from these changes will form the subject of a later article. As the fifteenth-and-tenth became fossilized and unable to adjust itself to rises and falls in local prosperity it became necessary to devise new, supplementary taxes to tap local wealth in other ways, and the records of these also demand separate treatment.

14   W. G. Hoskins in Hoskins and H. P. R. Finberg, *Devonshire Studies* (1952), 212-49; W. G. Hoskins and E. M. Jope in *The Oxford Region* (A. F. Martin and R. W. Steel, eds.) (1954), 111, with map; H. C. Darby *The Medieval Fenland (1940); F. Bradshaw,* art. cit.; E. J. Buckatzsch, *The Geographical Distribution of Wealth, 1086-1843, Economic History Review,* 2nd ser. iii (1950), 180-202; M. W. Beresford, *op. cit.,* tables 4-10 and 17: M. W. Beresford, *The Taxation of Ongar Hundred in V. C. H. Essex,* iv (1956), 296-302, Wilts; *V. C. H. Wilts.,* iv. (1959), pp. 294-314. R. E. Glasscock of the Queen's University, Belfast, is engaged on mapping the returns.

15   Durham and Cheshire have no subsidy rolls for the period considered. Northumberland, Cumberland and Westmorland were not assessed in 1334 on account of the disturbed state of the border; assessments survive from 1336.

THE LAY SUBSIDIES
PART II. (AFTER 1334)

In 1334, as we have shown, the assessments of taxable wealth took the form of village-by-village quotas replacing the individual valuations of lay property such as were made in 1332. In 1336, when Parliament next granted a Fifteenth and Tenth, no fresh assessment of quotas was made, the only change being the inclusion of Northumberland, Cumberland and Westmorland, which had been too disturbed to be assessed in 1334. Consequently, most subsequent documents deriving from the collection of this tax contain lists of place-names, arranged by Hundreds within the counties, and against each place a sum of money, its quota as agreed in 1334. What had been intended as a temporary administrative convenience became permanent, and until the end of Charles I's reign these quotas of 1334 remained the basis of local contributions whenever Parliament granted a Fifteenth and Tenth.[2] Grants were made on 42 occasions between 1334 and 1634.

Fossilized in this way, the later accounts might seem of little use to the local historian. In fact, they have a double utility: the attempts to modify and supplement the yield from this stereotyped tax produced interesting evidence of local wealth and changes in prosperity during subsequent centuries; while the very repetition of sums, collection after collection, makes it possible to determine what the quotas of 1334 were for those counties whose rolls from 1334 (and even later collections) are missing or illegible.

There is no class of document at the Public Record Office which can illumine the division of a village 'quota' among the villagers; we do not therefore know whether the tax remained linked to particular tenements or whether there were realistic re-assessments within the villages and towns at intervals.[3]

A useful list of the occasions when a Fifteenth and Tenth was granted and collected will be found in the published *Reports* of the

---

1 The Hundred within which a place fell can most easily be determined from a good 19th century Topographical Dictionary (e.g. that of Samuel Lewis or James Bell). Medieval Hundred boundaries were sometimes re-drawn and do not always correspond to 19th century usage: see here the local *V. C. H.* volumes, if published.

2 e.g. roll of 1445 is headed 'de anno octavo regis Edwardi tertii': E. 179/202/113.

3 A fresh allocation between Oxford parishes was made 1432-40: H. E. Salter, *Medieval Oxford* (Ox. Hist. Soc., c (1936), 133-41; in York a re-allocation was made in 1492 *(York Civic Records*, ii, 84) for 'some of the said parichez which er fallen in extreme ruyne and decay'; it was sometimes complained that hamlets were ignored: *Cal. Inq. Misc.*, iv No. 107 (Somerset, 1380).

Deputy Keeper of the Public Records[4]; the county and borough totals[5] are to be found among the Enrolled Subsidies (class E359); the collectors' rolls among the files of E179 to which there is access via the typescript *List* on the shelves of the P.R.O. Round Room. As with the earlier Subsidies, its arrangement is by counties with an important final section of *Divers Counties* containing a fascinating miscellany of unsorted, incomplete, undated or partially legible documents (shelf 7/26-36; see also 6/24D for the Enrolled Subsidies: E359/1, 2, 4A, 5, 7, 8A, 8B, 8C, 10, 14 and 1B; also E364/1, mm. 5-6).

It is always necessary to read the collectors' statement at the head of their rolls if village quotas are being sought, for there were a number of occasions when Parliament granted less or more than a whole Fifteenth and Tenth, and in such a case the sum appearing against a village name will be less or more than the 1334 quota: a village assessed at 20s. would pay 40s. if a double Fifteenth and Tenth were granted (as in 1404), and 30s. if one-and-a-half Fifteenth and Tenths were granted (as in 1380). With the advent of the village quotas, personal names of villagers rarely appear after 1334 in the main series of collectors' accounts[6] (or 'particulars'), with the exception of Kent and Sussex, where the presence of barons of the Cinque Ports (immune from taxation) necessitated mention of individuals[7]; similar difficulties with the exempt tinners in the stannary districts of Devon and Cornwall brought personal names into the documents.[8]

---

4   *Second Report of the Deputy Keeper of the Public Records* (1841), App. ii, 134-89 and *Third Report* (1842), App. ii, 6-104.

5   The totals for 1334 appear at E. 359/8a; the county sums are printed by J. F. Willard in *Eng. Hist. Rev.,* xxx (1915), 69-74.

6   The presence of names sometimes indicates that the roll is wrongly dated in the P. R. O. List, e.g. E. 179/166/2 is really the Shropshire roll for 1332.

7   e.g. Kent, 1334: E. 179/123/12. The names of barons of the cinque Ports and moneyers of Canterbury living elsewhere in Kent and Sussex are conveniently set out in the Exannual Roll: E. 363/4 mm. 41-4.

8   e.g. E. 179/95/29. Lists of tin-miners' names are enrolled at E. 363/4 mm. 24d, 25, 31 and 33. When a Subsidy of aliens began in 1439 it, too, yielded lists of names; the P. R. O. *Lists* distinguish such county accounts; the enrolled totals are at E. 359/28, 30 and 32-3.

II

Alongside the rigidity of conventional assessments which the Lay Subsidies developed after 1334 one must take notice of two types of supplement and revision: on the one hand are the reliefs and abatements which were sought by places suffering economic disaster, and on the other the attempts to invent new forms of taxation of lay wealth which would counterbalance the arthritic condition of the Fifteenth and Tenth. From Edward III to the Civil War the local quotas remained virtually unchanged, but these three centuries saw considerable changes in local prosperity. Some towns and villages were rising fast: consider only Coventry and Exeter or the cloth-making villages of East Anglia, Yorkshire and the southern Cotswolds.[9] Other places, and some whole districts, went the other way: Old Winchelsea had been washed away by the sea, but New Winchelsea (like some other ports) was in its turn the victim of shifting sands and retreating waters as well as attacks from pirates and the French; border raids brought intermittent destruction both to the Scottish and the Welsh Marches[10]; the Black Death struck heavily at all England, and − in a few cases − removed a village for ever[11], less cataclysmic were the local visitations of fire[12] or flood[13]; more serious was coastal erosion, such as removed the prosperous Yorkshire borough of Ravenserod as well as a score of East Riding villages[14]; and the exhaustion of some natural resource such as a vein of ore or the exhaustion of over-cultivated, under-fertilized and over-populated marginal soils.[15] When part of a village's fields had been enclosed into a royal park, that too provided a reason for a reduction in the village's quota to the Subsidy.[16]

---

9   W. G. Hoskins, 'Provincial Towns in the Early 16th Century', *Tr. Roy. Hist. Soc.,* 5th ser. vi (1956), 1-19.

10   e.g. E. 179/166/48 (1406) and E. 179/166/65 (1427); and on the south coast the French: *Cal. Inq. Misc.,* iv, 128 and 206 (raids of 1378).

11   e.g. Tusmore, Oxon: *Cal. Inq. Misc.,* iii, No. 258.

12   Spondon, Derbys., destroyed by fire and released from Subsidy of 1340: Rymer, *Foedera* (Record Ed.), ii, pt. ii, 1133; Bloxham, Lincs. (1350), *Cal. Inq. Misc.,* iii, No. 75.

13   Norfolk flood relief 1336: details in E. 359/8a and E. 159/125, Mich. *recorda* m. 6.

14   E. 359/10, collections of 1344 and 1346 for Frismarsh (1344) and Ravenserod (1346); see also *Cal. Inq. Misc.,* ii, Nos. 1828, 1914 and 1988.

15   e.g. *Nonarum Inquisitiones* (Record Commission, 1807), 326-40 (Bucks.) − but the circumstances of this tax assessment put a premium on a good local excuse for a fall in the value of a parish; see also E. M. Yates, 'Medieval Assessments in N. W. Sussex', *Trans. Instit. Brit. Geog.* (1954), No. 20, 75-92.

16   H. G. Johnson, ed., *Surrey Taxation Returns* (Surrey Record Soc., xi (1932), 151 (Nonsuch Park, 1545; Byfleet, 1429).

Alongside these economic changes which called for downward revision of some 1334 quotas was another force which produced first a multiplication of Fifteenths and Tenths, and then newer forms of taxes on lay wealth. This force was the persistent growth in royal and State expenditure, particularly on war, reinforced in the sixteenth century by the long inflation, a rise in prices which hit particularly at revenues which were fixed in money terms: thus, a village assessed at 20s. to the Fifteenth of 1334 was in effect giving the king the equivalent of nearly four quarters of wheat; in 1545 the same sum represented only one and a half quarters, and by 1600 would have bought the queen only four-sevenths of one quarter.

The result of such pressures as these can be seen in the new Subsidy of Henry VIII and in attempts, which do not concern us here, to revise the rate of imposts on exports and imports.

III

The simplicity of the subsidy accounts is clouded for the first time in 1338 when the collectors were told to collect the tax (where possible) in kind, at the rate of a stone of wool for every two shillings of tax, but the village quotas themselves were simply those of 1334 again, and the documents merely tell us which places were able to pay in wool.[17] The taxation of clerical property lies outside this article, but the documents arising from the Ninth of 1340-1 are indicative of more than clerical property,[18] for they contain some very interesting statements about local losses from fire and flood as well as some striking assertions about losses from infertility of the soil since the basic assessment of clerical property in 1291.

In 1351 the Statute of Labourers provided that the fines levied on employers and employees who infringed its terms should be pooled and the money distributed by local Justices to those communities which had been particularly severely hit by the Black Death, the pandemic which was still far from extinguished. The survival of documents from the distribution of relief in 1352-4 is incomplete, but almost all have been listed or transcribed by Professor Putnam.[19] As with the Nonae

---

17   G. Unwin, ed., *Finance and Trade under Edward III* (1918), 151; in 1341 and 1347 Parliament granted 30,000 and 20,000 sacks of wool (e.g. E. 179/169/17 and 141/15).

18   The complications of this assessment of a Ninth on the laity of a parish are set out in the Introduction to the Record Commission edition of 1807 (f. n. 15 *supra*), but there are many more unprinted parish accounts; see the summary lists cited in f. n. 4 *supra*.

19   B. H. Putnam, *The Enforcement of the Statute of Labourers* (1908).

Rolls of 1340-1, it is likely that self-interest led both to some exaggeration and to favouritism, but the extreme cases where no relief or total relief were granted are surely worth serious attention. Thus, in the East Riding of Yorkshire, two villages which no longer exist, East and West Flotmanby, obtained exceptional relief.[20] The documents to be sought are the collectors' rolls[21] of 1352-3-4; in rare cases the lists of fines have also survived[22], so that one can see from whom was taken and to whom given. No further relief of this kind was given in the collection of 1357, but fines levied by courts on fugitives and felons were similarly pooled and allocated in relief of distressed villages.[23] The next grant, that of 1372, was normal; and for the next sixty years collections continued, still on the basis of the 1334 quotas.

Two other taxes with documents in class E.179 were concerned with parishes rather than with vills. Taken together with the lists of vills in the ordinary Subsidy accounts and the list of vills[24] compiled for the Exchequer in 1316, they afford the raw materials for a topographical dictionary or gazetteer of medieval settlement. In 1371 a tax of 32s. 3d. was imposed on each parish but hurriedly raised to 116s. when it was discovered that England had many fewer parishes than the king's advisers had believed; the enrolment of this tax provides a unique opportunity of seeing how many parishes were reckoned to be in each county.[25] The other parish tax, that of 1428, has an even more useful by-product for local historians, since places with fewer than ten householders were exempt from it. The county rolls therefore set out the places which had these very small populations, occasionally citing the actual numbers.[26] The microscopics of medieval settlement are clearly of two kinds: the shrunken, depopulated settlement of the nucleated village county and the never-large scattered hamlets of the bocage.

The local impoverishment at which some of the exemptions in 1428 hint is more explicitly mentioned in the grant of a Fifteenth and Tenth in 1433, when from the 1334 quotas Parliament allowed a rebate of

---

20   E. 179/202/53.
21   The 1334 quota is usually stated, then the relief from the wool, and then the sum remaining due.
22   e.g. E. 137/49/1.
23   e.g. E. 179/211/27; county and borough totals E. 359/4; 8b, m. 1; 14, mm. 48-9.
24   Text in *Feudal Aids* (5 vols., 1891-1920).
25   e.g. E. 179/141/15; all counties enrolled in E. 359/8b, mm. 20-1; e.g. Rutland, 44 parishes; Lincs. 627.
26   Printed, by counties, in *Feudal Aids*.

£4,000 to be distributed among those 'poor vills, cities and boroughs desolate, wasted, destroyed or very impoverished, or otherwise too heavily burdened with the tax.'[27] These rebates continued in subsequent grants and were raised to £6,000 in 1445. Thereafter, until its death in 1641, any grant of a Fifteenth and Tenth carried with it these rebates and brought in about £30,000. In the earlier collections, the reliefs allowed to villages are not the same in successive years. Some villages never received a rebate nor is there any uniformity in the proportion of rebate to tax.[28] These variations suggest that some principle of allocation was being followed at least up to 1468. Thereafter, of the rolls which have been examined, the reliefs seem to have become fossilized (like the quotas earlier), and continued unaltered at each collection. The original principle of allocation of relief was that of neediness, although it would be strange and unmedieval if personal interests and local pressures were always excluded. The commissioners who allocated the reliefs were often, perhaps always, the local members of Parliament.[29] It can easily be seen how borough members would like nothing better than to return bringing gifts, but county members had more need to exercise judgments of Solomon: so many vills, so many mouths to feed, so many palms to bribe.

In addition to these occasions when impoverishment was widespread enough to gain Parliamentary recognitions the Subsidy documents may also indicate exceptional conditions arising from some local calamity. Some examples of these have been given above (footnotes 10-16), but the collectors' rolls are not the most likely place in which to trace them The collectors' duty in medieval accounting practice was to state what was traditionally due from the vills: the petitions are more likely to be found on the Memoranda Rolls of the Exchequer[30] and the successful result noted among the Enrolled Subsidies.[31]

---

27   These words (from E. 179/184/86 of 1435) derive from the statute, *Rot. Parl.*, iv. 425a.

28   e.g. the boroughs of Devon as set out in W. G. Hoskins and H. P. R. Finberg, *Devonshire Studies* (1952), 228-33.

29   e.g. E. 179/280, writ of 31 Henry VI (1452).

30   e.g. E. 368/150, Trin. *recorda*, 1 Richard II, Hayling Island.

31   e.g. E. 359/8b collection of 10 Edward III, Norfolk.

IV

Early in Henry VIII's reign the pressure of expenditure caused anxious search for a more realistic and fair tax. The Tenth and Fifteenth continued, but Parliament added to it a new Subsidy with a fresh basis of assessment. In the fifteenth century there had been attempts to tax the greater landed incomes,[32] but studies of the results do not indicate very great efficiency in execution.[33] The new Subsidy of Henry VIII was based on three alternative assessments of a taxpayer's capacity: it was levied either on the capital value of property; or on landed income; or on wages.[34] The assessment rolls, where they survive, provide a directory of the upper, middle and lower-middle classes and are near enough to earliest parish registers to serve as some basis for genealogical tree-planting.

In its turn the Henrician Subsidy became less and less realistic; it was difficult to prod local assessors into fresh assessments, and they all too frequently returned sums from a previous collection, sometimes even with the same names. Dr. Hoskins, who has probably used these Subsidies more profitably than anyone, writes of those of 1524-7 and 1543-4 as being the most informative.[35] The local collectors' rolls are incomplete in their survival, but the final enrolment of the Subsidy records totals from counties and from most boroughs and towns.[36]

These totals afford one of the few opportunities between 1334 and the Hearth Taxes of setting out the counties and larger urban communities of the kingdom in order of merit from the tax-collectors' point of view; other statistical statements of the Tudor period (such as the Returns[37] of 1545 and the bishops' returns[38] of 1563 and 1603) afford only partial coverage of the populations which they attempt to number.

32   In 1404, 1411, 1435 and 1449.
33   T. B. Pugh and C. D. Ross *Bull. Inst. Hist. Research*, xxvi (1953), 1; and *Econ. Hist. Rev.*, new ser. vi (1953), 185.
34   *Statutes of the Realm*, iii, 230-41; there was an enforced 'Anticipation' in 1523; see Hoskins, *art. cit.* Local rolls vary in thoroughness: e.g. E. 179/211/100 and 212/106 seem to be omitting many property owners and wage-earners in Richmond (Yorks.) area.
35   art. cit., *supra*.
36   Totals at E. 359/41. mm. 1-20; an example of a county roll in print is *Bucks Record Society*, viii (1944), ed. A. C. Chibnall and A. V. Woodman.
37   E. 301; see *Surtees Society*, xci and xcii (1893), ed. William Page.
38   B. M. Harl. Mss. 594-5 and 618.

The post-Reformation assessments, if realistic, would also take account of the transfer of property from clerical to lay hands at the dissolution of the monasteries. It must be remembered that the medieval Lay Subsidies up to 1332 were based on assessments of certain kinds of lay property, and after 1332 on village assessments. The clergy were assessed and taxed separately[39], the equivalent of the 1334 quotas being the assessment of clerical incomes made in 1291 revised for the northern Province in 1318, and thereafter not thoroughly re-assessed[40] until the *Valor Ecclesiasticus*[41] of 1535. Thus the assessable wealth of clerical property in any given district must be extracted from the rolls of the collectors of the Clerical Subsidy[42] or (more conveniently) from the *Taxation of Pope Nicholas*.[43] Property passing into clerical hands after 1291 should be included in the Lay Subsidy.[44]

At the time when the Henrician subsidy was becoming as conventionalized and formal as a court dance[45] the continuing inflation was robbing even its adequate sums of their purchasing power. To raise revenue, kings and queens looked further than the modest local estimates of the Subsidy collectors and the shrinking yields of ever multiple Fifteenths and Tenths. In doing so they became involved in political and constitutional crises such as those over monopolies, retail licences, penal statutes and import duties. These indirect taxes, like their contemporary the Poor Rate, fell on the men and women of London and the provinces, but the records of their collection lie outside the class of the Lay Subsidies. Within this class, to conclude, there do lie the fragmentary returns from a small number of fiscal measures which there has not been space to discuss and which never had the attempted comprehensiveness of the Lay Subsidies: such as the abortive poll-tax on sheep of 1549 and the purchase tax on cloth of that same year.[46] The subsidies on aliens from 1439 onwards are also worth examining.

39   J. F. Willard, *Parliamentary Taxes on Personal Property* (Cambridge, Mass., 193 93-109 and 125-7.

40   Partial re-assessments exist from 1523-6: H. E. Salter, ed., *A Subsidy in 1526 (C Hist. Soc., lxiii (1909)*, i-ix.

41   *Valor Ecclesiasticus* (Record Commission, 6 vols. 1810-34).

42   These are also in Class E. 179 and have county lists on the shelves of the Round Room.

43   *Taxatio Ecclesiastica* (Record Commission, 1802).

44   Willard, *op. cit.*, 106-9.

45   Lord North wrote to Burleigh in 1589: 'there is no man assessed before me but known to be worth at least in goods ten times as much as he is set at, and six times more land'. (H. M. C. *Salisbury*, iii, 429).

46   M. W. Beresford, 'The Poll Tax and Census of Sheep, 1549', *Ag. Hist. Rev.* i. (195 9-15, and ii. (1954), 15-29. See above, pp. 137-57.

THE POLL TAXES OF 1377, 1379 AND 1381

Faced with a crisis of war expenditure, the last Parliament of Edward III's reign made him a grant which the *Chronicle* of St. Alban's rightly called 'unheard of'. A new tax was imposed at the flat rate of a groat (4d.) a head. Nearly all lay men and women were liable: only those under 14 years of age and those who regularly begged for a living were exempt.[1] In addition, the beneficed clergy were to pay a shilling and the unbeneficed their groat. Like the lay beggars, the mendicant orders were free of the tax.[2]

This article is mainly concerned with the 4,322 documents which record the collection of this poll tax during the spring and summer of 1377; only a little will be said at the end about the two poll taxes granted to Richard II in 1379 and 1381. These latter were not levied at a flat rate but graded socially, thus making it impossible for us to work out total numbers from any statements of sums paid. By 1379 and 1381 there was also notorious evasion, making it necessary for some counties to be subjected to a revised assessment,[3] and the documents of these years are also fewer than those of 1377. If total populations are not the goal of research, the 1379 and 1381 documents do afford useful information about other members of families than the head of the household, including servants. Occupational details are the most valuable: the 1381 data are the most complete, but there is good coverage for 1379 in some parts of the country (e.g. Yorks. W.R.) These matters are being studied by Dr. R.H. Hilton to whom I am indebted for assistance. It is a pity that the energies of Record Societies have been concentrated on these two poll taxes, and only recently have

---

1   For the background to the taxes and some of the repercussions, Sir Charles Oman, *The Great Revolt of 1381* (1906).

2   The P. R. O. *List* mentioned below treats the Clerical Subsidies separately. The arrangement here is not by counties but by dioceses and archdeaconries. For a summary and references see J. C. Russell, *British Medieval Population* (Albuquerque, U. S. A.) (1948), 131-140. The clergy recorded as taxpayers numbered 30,641 compared with the lay taxpayers of 1,355,555 in the same area (England, with Cheshire and Durham excepted).

3   P. R. O., C. 66/309, m. 33d: to go, if necessary, 'de villa ad villam ... et loco ad locum'.

figures from 1377 begun to be published.[4] Only Wiltshire yet has the
figures for the whole of the county in print. Elsewhere the student
must consult the original files at the Public Record Office or order
photostat copies or microfilms from Chancery Lane.

The list below gives an indication of which counties have been
fortunate in having their poll tax receipts (or acquittances) survive.
Thirteen volumes of a *List* in alphabetical order of counties date and
identify the thousands of files which make up the class (E.179) of *Lay
Subsidies*, ranging from the early thirteenth century to the Hearth Tax
of Charles II. This *List* is on the open shelves of the Round Room at
the **P.R.O.** and (like all indexes there) may be photo-statted or
microfilmed to order. The List is arranged alphabetically by counties,
and within each county the files are arranged chronologically. At the
end come the unsorted files described as *Divers Counties*. By no means
all the unsorted documents are fragmentary or illegible, and it is to be
hoped that more careful examination will eventually allocate these
receipts to their county. Meanwhile anyone wanting to make a
complete study of a county or to search exhaustively for the receipt
from a particular place will neglect the unsorted files at his peril.

At first sight a file of poll tax acquittances is a little formidable.
Two or three hundred separate small membranes fastened together on a
string and sometimes entangled with seals and tags can be daunting,
especially when the handwriting is small, the documents faded or torn.[5]
To read faded ink, the P.R.O. has the ultra-violet lamp, but even torn
membranes are not beyond redemption. The poll tax receipt follows a
common form and there is a double chance of reading the name of the
vill and the number of taxpayers. The name of the vill often appears on
the back of the document as well as in the text of the indenture, while
on the face of the document the number of taxpayers can be seen in
two places: the record of the number of heads (*capitibus*); and the
statement of the sum paid (in shillings and pence or in marks). If the

---

4   The figures for much of Leicestershire are tabulated, together with other population
data, in *V. C. H. Leics., iii* (1955). Unfortunately the author passed by the numerous Leics.
receipts in the Divers Counties files (esp. E. 179/240/256-7 and 259). The figures for Ongar
Hundred of Essex are set out, together with other population data in *V. C. H. Essex*, iv (1956).
The figures for Ploughley Hundred of Oxfordshire can be found *passim* in the various parish
accounts of *V. C. H. Oxon.* (1957); it is a great pity that these were not tabulated in one place,
as for example the lay subsidy assessments, *ibid. V. C. H. Wilts. iv* (1959), pp. 294-314 has the
1334 subsidy and the 1377 poll tax data set out vill by vill. For a map based on the county
totals see H. C. Darby, ed. *An Historical Geography of England* (1936), 232.

5   The *P. R. O. List* does not normally detail what places are contained in each file,
merely the county and/or hundred. The list is in 13 volumes − 7/26-36C.

'heads' part is lost or illegible, the division of the sum by fourpences will yield the number of taxpayers. For Staffordshire there is also an enrollment of the sums paid in each vill,[6] but in general there is no other way to seek a missing receipt except the unsorted files. The so-called 'Great Enrollment' on the Enrolled Subsidy (E.359/8b) gives separately the sums paid by the cities and larger boroughs, but for the country at large gives only the totals of counties.[7] Durham and Cheshire, being exempt jurisdictions, are omitted from this roll and from most of the files in E.179.

For each vill (or, occasionally, group of vills) an indenture of acquittance was returned to the Exchequer witnessing that the representatives (*probi homines*) of the vill had paid to the Exchequer collectors a sum made up of as many fourpences as there were men and women over the age of fourteen, genuine mendicants excepted. It is these documents which make up most of the poll tax files in class E.179. Their language is usually Latin, but those for some of Northumberland are in French.[8] It was not normal for the acquittance to give any further information about the taxpayers, and the only names to be given were those of the *probi homines* (usually two per vill) and the constables. The receipts from 1379 and 1381, the tax not being at flat rate, have lists of names and sums paid by each taxpayer. In 1377, however, possibly as a result of suspected malpractices, some counties have lists of taxpayers alongside the receipts (Oxfordshire,[9] for example) and Northumberland has names throughout. There is similar information for parts of London, Rochester, Oxford, Carlisle, Colchester and Hull.[10]

Once located and deciphered, to what uses can the figures of 1377 be put? The local receipts are obviously not much use in checking or revising the various estimates of county and national population which have been made. Their principal use is to further the study of the local distribution of population in England of the late fourteenth century, the generation which had hardly had time to recover from the Black Death and the succeeding pandemic.

---

6   E. 179/177/19.

7   Printed in Russell, *op. cit.*, 132 and 142 with some errors of transcription. It is necessary to warn students that the impressive statistical tables of this work are sometimes based on elementary misreadings of the original documents. Extremely useful as an indication of poll tax documentation, the book needs checking in every instance against the original documents (esp. Chapter 6 and pp. 150-6, 251-5, 265, 273-8).

8   E. 179/158/29 and 32. File 33 is in Latin.

9   E. 179/161/38 (Pyrton Hundred).

10   The references will be found in the P. R. O. *List* cited.

It must be pointed out at once that the poll tax documents only tell us about the number of taxpayers in those vills for which a receipt survives. The poll tax data are not a census. They omit the under-fourteens and also the unknown proportion of people who managed to escape assessment. We do not know how much evasion there was in 1377: it was severe in 1379 and 1381 when the tax had lost its novelty.[11] We can only assume that the degree of evasion did not vary very significantly from district to district. Anyone who finds this assumption difficult to accept must of course reject the use of poll tax figures of 1377 for anything except establishing minimal populations.

Accepting the assumption, it is still some distance from recorded taxpayers to an estimate of total populations. What percentage of the population was under the age of fourteen? In a largely rural society with a low expectation of adult life, we must expect that the percentage was higher than in England of the modern period and the censuses. Anyone who seeks a rough and ready estimate of the total population of a vill in 1377 might risk taking Professor Russell's 'multiplier'[12] and add fifty per cent. to the number of recorded taxpayers, on the assumption that one-third of the population was then under fourteen. Thus, to take an example, the recorded poll-tax payers, 401 in number who are returned as living in the crowded market-side parish of St. Sampson in York would only be two-thirds of the total population of the parish, according to Russell's figures. Adding another fifty per cent. would give us an estimated total of 601. The roughness and readiness of this method must again be stressed, but it may help some people to feel more vividly the conditions of the late fourteenth century if they can arrive at the order of magnitude of their village's population. Some will be surprised how few its fields then supported, and others — where population has retreated — will marvel that their fields were once so full. (Since the 1377 populations lived in an England much reduced by the plagues it would be necessary to make a further allowance if one wished to estimate the populations of the pre-plague years, the high-water mark of medieval colonisation. For those who like conjecture there is again a Russell multiplier[13] of 1.5, so that St. Sampson's 601 in 1377 would be 901 before the Black Death).

Leaving aside these estimates of total populations from recorded

---

11   The number of taxpayers in the West Riding had fallen from 48,149 in 1377 to 23,029 in 1381.

12   Russell, *op. cit.*, 143.

13   *ibid.*, 260-70.

taxpayers, there are perhaps fewer pitfalls if one is interested in comparisons between places. So long as there is no reason to think that one village had a very different proportion of under-fourteens from another, one can compare the recorded taxpayers of *A* with those of *B* and feel the result has some significance. A village in Northumberland, with its average of thirty-five taxpayers, was clearly in a quite different economic environment from a village in the plains of Buckinghamshire, where the average village had well over a hundred taxpayers. A good deal of medieval economic history has to be invoked if one wishes to attempt an explanation of such diversity, but the exercise is rewarding.

Another way of by-passing some of the above methodological difficulties is to concentrate not on totals or relative numbers but on relative densities. A great deal of economic and social history is again brought to a focus when we see that the taxpayers in St. Sampson s, York, were crowded. eighty to an acre. In the nearby parish of All Saints, Pavement, they were seventy to the acre, but just outside the walls of the city the village taxpayers of the Ainstey showed a typical rural density of 0.034 to the acre, or thirty-four per thousand acres. If this comparison highlights the different conditions of town and country, what of the differences within the countryside itself? The average for the whole West Riding, excluding the largest towns, was less than a half that of the Ainstey, while the average density for Norfolk and Suffolk was nearly twice that of the Ainstey. It is also interesting to see that despite the great cities at on end of the scale (London, 23,314 taxpayers; York, 7,248) and the hamlets with five, six or seven taxpayers at the other[14] there is a considerable 'bunching' in the size-distribution near a population size of from sixty to ninety taxpayers. Exactly why so many English villages had settled down at about this particular size has yet to be explored.[15]

Finally, a few words about the documents from 1379 and 1381. A number of these are in print,[16] and from them the student may learn their characteristic appearance and more easily approach the unpublished files. The degree of evasion forbids even the tentative card-castle of estimates suggested above for 1377. All they offer are the names of whatever taxpayers did not escape the collectors', net, together with a statement of the taxpayer's occupation in the 1379

14   E.g. The five 'keepers of the grange' at Ouston, Warws. (E. 179/192/4a).

15   For the size of settlements in different regions see Russell, *op. cit.,* 306-12 and M. W. Beresford, *The Lost Villages of England* (1954), tables 7-10 and 18.

16   The West Riding returns for 1379 were printed by the Yorks. Archaeological and Topographical Association in 1882; the Essex returns for 1381 will be found in Oman, *op. cit.,* and those for York were edited by J. N. Bartlett, *Trans. East Riding Antiqu. Soc.* xxx (1953) 1-91.

record, when the amount to be paid was socially graded. Thus a genealogist will find even the incomplete rolls useful, and the social historian will be able to make out a little of the social inequalities and the occupational structures revealed so fragmentarily and so tantalisingly. But perhaps one should be grateful for the smallest of mercies in the survival of documents, and one can at least know the minimum number of people following particular occupations and observe the minimum degree of specialisation which marked off the large towns from the general run of rural vills.[17]

With a little experience the student will easily learn to distinguish the documents of 1377 from those of 1379 and 1381. The P.R.O. *List* itself sometimes errs, so that perhaps the following general suggestion may assist.[18] In general, a document where everyone pays the flat rate of 4d. can be assigned with confidence to 1377. Where a document has names, occupations and unequal payments it probably comes from 1379. In 1381 there are unequal payments, but the recording of occupations is less common. The most satisfactory identification both for dates and for location where a document lacks a specific statement is, of course, from the collectors' names which are always recorded in the county's portion of the Enrolled Subsidy (E.359). The revised typewritten *Calendar* of this Subsidy has now appeared on the shelves of the Round Room, and through it Dr. N.J. Williams had made the future task of those who labour in the subsidy rolls a much easier one. Miss Margaret Midgley has in preparation for publication a revised List of extant poll-tax receipts for 1377-1381.

17   See Bartlett, *op. cit.*, table 3.
18   E. 179/200/22, for example, consists of receipts similar in form to those of 1377, but pretty certainly from the parish tax of 1374 (cp. 179/120/41).

16

THE COMMON INFORMER, THE PENAL STATUTES

AND ECONOMIC REGULATION

> Lawgivers have many times fortified their Laws with Penalties
> wherein Private Persons may have Profit, thereby to stir up the
> People to put the Laws in Execution.
>
> Davenant, *Essay on the Ballance of Trade* (1699), 55.

I

THE common informer's power to make money from the misdeeds of others was abolished only in 1951.[1] An age of police detectives and public prosecutors has seen opinion harden against private enterprise in this field.[2] In 1934, when the Commons were debating the matter, an M.P. defined the informer as 'the complete sneak', unconsciously echoing the opinion of an aggrieved Tudor leatherworker,[3] 'hyt was a knaves part to sue ony man upon (the king's) most gracious actes and statutes'. Many acts and statutes once encouraged zeal for the law by offering a share in the penalties. The temptations and abuses in this system were realised by the authors of an interesting draft statute (c.1534) which proposed a special court and an array of district attorneys[4] to replace common informers, who only began suits when matters of *meum* and *tuum* were involved or else through 'malice, rancour and evill will'. Coke's view,[5] just over a century later, was that the informer 'doth vex and pauperise the subject and the community of the poorer sort, for malice or private ends and never for love of justice'.

It was the marriage of justice with malice or avarice which helped to discredit common informers in the eyes even of those who were not lawbreakers. When innocent and guilty alike were put in peril of a fine, some discredit was bound to fall on the principle of economic regulation, and the Crown could not avoid some share of unpopularity since its own share in the penalties made it a slow convert to schemes of reform. Economic offences were those most zealously pursued, so that the informations provide details of an immense number of transactions in manufacture and trade in the period when the informers were most active, from 1550 to 1624; they were then a chief instrument for the enforcement of economic legislation and the indirect taxation of the kingdom: after 1624, virtually exiled from the courts at Westminster, they remained at Assizes and Quarter Sessions as semi-official guardians of good order, with a tawdry bag of poaching, bastardy and theft.[6] Until this

---

[1] 14 & 15 Geo. VI c. 39.

[2] L. Radzinowicz, *A History of English Criminal Law* (1956), II, 140–55.

[3] *Select Cases in Star Chamber*, ed. I. S. Leadam, (Selden Soc. XV 1910), 220.

[4] 'Sergeants of the common weal': SP 1/28/24–41, cited by T. F. Plucknett, *Tr. R. Hist. Soc.* n.s. XIX (1936), 119–44. The economic significance of this project is pictured in the seal, with its plough, two hand-cards, a hammer and a spade 'signifying that by the good industreye of draping of clothes and of marchauntes ffishers maryners myners and handy craftis the greate bourdene of the Common Weale of this Realme ... hath bene alweys susteyned'.

[5] Sir Edward Coke, *Institutes*, III (1644), 194.

[6] e.g. *North Riding Record Society*, i–ix (1884–92), passim; there were occasional projects and reforms after 1660; SP 29/23/12; SP 29/37/92; SP 29/221/78; 4 Wm. & Mary c. 18.

provincial underworld finds its economic historian it is a sad anticlimax from the time when almost every Parliamentary session saw an indignant proposal for the restraint of informers' abuses.

II

Table I displays the number of informations laid in the court of Exchequer for selected Michaelmas terms[1] between 1519 and 1659. It indicates an expansion between 1551 and 1562 and a sudden contraction in 1617–20. The contraction will be discussed later in this article for it owed a good deal to the behaviour of informers in the preceding years. The period of expansion had its roots in the last decade of Henry VIII's reign, although Henry VII's 'Council Learned in the Law' is known to have taken a fatherly interest in penal statutes,[2] and it was on the medieval penal statutes augmented by the tillage acts that Empson and Dudley were set to work as 'masters of the forfayts' in 1503–6:

> Englishmen dyd litle pass upon the observacion and kepynge of penall lawes ... made and enacted for the common utilitie and wealth. There shoulde be few noble men, merchaunts, farmers, husbandmen, grasyers nor occupyers but they should be found transgressors.[3]

Of 115 penal statutes still in force in the middle of James I's reign,[4] one fifth came from Henry VIII's Parliaments, all but three from the last thirteen years of the reign. Edward VI added 11, Elizabeth I, 30 and James himself at least 19. Another *Abstract*, that of Thomas Pulton, found a publisher in 1577 and eight editions were needed by 1603 to keep up with the legislators. In the 1581 edition, with 367 pages of small quarto, twenty-three topics appear on the contents page in 'A', 'B', and 'C' alone. The medieval penal statutes,[5] beginning in the mid-fourteenth century, had dealt mainly with customs and bullion offences; the Tudor extension to other economic transactions caused one speaker in the Commons debate[6] of 1601 to say that no previous age had known so many 'penal and entrapping laws' and Chief Justice Coke to call the 'swarms of informers' a comparatively recent plague of Egypt.[7]

The mid-sixteenth century confidence in the informer finds expression in Bishop Latimer's *Last Sermon* (1550) with its unfamiliar approval of Empson and Dudley.[8]

> For God's sake make new promoters! There lack promotors such as were in King Henry the Seventh's days ... to promote transgressors, as rent-raisers, oppressors of the poor, extortioners, bribers, usurers.

It was this breed of informers whom an abortive scheme of c.1534 would have elevated into something like a public office, and Mr Elton has suggested that the scheme came from the Latimer circle.[9] In 1552 the Privy Council went so

---

[1] At all periods Michaelmas was the busiest of the four law terms: in 1548 it saw 54% of the year's informations in Exchequer and in 1618, 41%.

[2] DL 5/2 and 5/4, cited by E. Somerville, *E. Hist. Rev.* LIV (1939), 427.

[3] E. Hall, *Chronicle* (ed. 1809), 499–502; 4 Henry VII c. 20 was against collusive informers; in 1509 1 Henry VIII c. 4 said that a great number of penal statutes were 'only lately enforced'.

[4] Thomas Ashe's Abstract: H. of Lords, Stanford MSS. 111/1.

[5] e.g. 23 Ed. III cc. 1–5.

[6] H. Townshend, *Historical Collections*, (1680), 287: 5 Dec. 1601.

[7] E. Coke, *op.cit.* III, 191.

[8] Hugh Latimer, *Sermons*, (ed. Canon Beeching), 242.

[9] G. R. Elton, 'Parliamentary Drafts', *Bull. Inst. H. Res.* XXV (1952), 123–4.

Table I. *Number of informations laid in Exchequer, 1519–1659*

Michaelmas term of selected years

Year	All informations	Customs import & export offences	All other offences	Market offences	Wool Dealing
1519	44	14	30	0	—
1529	41	33	8	0	—
1539	88	58	30	1	—
1543	36	17	19	0	—
1544	55	22	33	1	—
5	128	30	98	7	—
6	93	26	67	3	—
7	238	45	193	23	—
8	87	32	55	3	—
9	102	35	67	20	—
1550	176	82	94	35	—
1	229	52	177	108	—
2	222	88	134	59	—
3	103	78	25	11	—
4	174	58	116	68	37
5	130	34	96	63	30
6	225	45	180	142	58
7	115	48	67	42	24
8	99	60	39	27	12
9	23	4	19	13	0[a]
1560	—	—	—	—	15
1	—	—	—	—	59
2	672	53	619	353	39
3	—	—	—	—	0[a]
4	588	107	481	195	24
5	535	158	377	203	54
6	246	62	184	80	21
7	663	244	419	182	136
8	661	187	474	123	50
9	—	—	—	—	0[a]
1570	234	116	118	35	14
1	—	—	—	—	25
2	—	—	—	—	30
3	—	—	—	—	25
4	349	77	272	110	3
5	354	165	189	55	8
6	—	—	—	—	3
7	—	—	—	—	10
8	—	—	—	—	26
9	268	57	211	112	27
1580	316	90	226	130	12
1	209	109	100	48	4
2	155	60	95	39	3
3	311	131	180	112	5
4	555	130	425	166	21
5	508	158	350	55	9
6	615	140	475	320	27
7	557	108	449	261	4
8	379	95	284	122	16
9	477	146	331	247	38
1590	—	—	—	—	34
1	—	—	—	—	7
2	—	—	—	—	45
3	—	—	—	—	5
4	574	69	505	369	94
5	547	88	459	341	57
6	789	125	664	536	30

Year	All informations	Customs import & export offences	All other offences	Market offences	Wool Dealing
1597	513	148	365	269	54
8	519	95	424	341	58
9	371	117	254	141	33
1600	619	146	473	346	32
1	479	108	371	284	38
2	363	115	248	226	26
3	78	25	53	27	8[a]
4	411	80	331	144	11
5	475	97	378	260	41
6	—	—	—	—	10
7	—	—	—	—	4
8	809	275	534	416	66
9	581	135	446	359	11
1610	—	—	—	538	14
1	746	168	578	—	99
2	—	—	—	—	67
3	861	109	752	666	18
4	668	97	571	446	25
5	867	78	789	711	341
6	766	62	704	452	185
7	235	59	176	149	14
8	291	77	214	145	23
9	144	81	63	41	0
1620	95	49	46	25	0
1	85	72	13	5	0
2	97	42	55	44	0
3	64	41	23	5	0
4	29	26	3	0	0
5	27	20	7	0	
6	29	25	4	0	
7	13	11	2	0	
8	26	13	13	2	
9	16	14	2	1	
1630	39	27	12	11	
1	44	29	15	0	
2	37	21	16	5	
3	34	18	16	3	
4	24	13	11	0	
5	15	10	5	0	
6	28	22	6	0	
7	23	22	1	0	
8	33	25	8	0	
9	—	—	—	0	
1640	17	17	0	0	
1	10	7	3	1	
2	11	11	0	0	
3	9	7	2	0	
4	18	17	1	0	
5	14	14	0	0	
1653	123	81	42	0	
4	166	138	28	0	
5	—	—	—	0	
6	148	125	23	0	
7	92	83	9	0	
8	114	97	17	0	
9	66	63	3	0	
Total	24,649	6,805	17,844		

a. In 1559 and 1603 informing in all offences was virtually at a standstill with the new reign, and in 1563 and 1569 the Michaelmas term's law business was stopped by plague.

far as setting up a Committee of Ten to encourage informers' (promoters) who were genuine lovers of the common weal and to meet before and after each law-term to report progress.[1] Nothing more has yet been found of this Committee, but it must have looked approvingly at the increase of informations laid in the next few years (Table I). The Committee's instructions were critical, however, of some informers, those less high-minded who were working 'parteleye for theire owne singular gayne, parteleye for malice, corrupcion and other devilisshe affection'. It was such men at whom the abortive reforming bills of 1543–7 had been aimed,[2] and the awakening suspicion of the free-lance informer probably explains the experiment in the next decade of commissioning informers by patent.[3]

The sudden increase in bulk of the Memoranda Rolls of the Exchequer is mainly due to the multiplication of enrolled informations.[4] A year of Henry VIII's reign rarely produced more than a hundred membranes a term but the Elizabethan clerks were driven to bind their annual crop into two separate— and still large—rolls. 1562 produced 1,050 membranes of *recorda* and 1608 had 1,501, the largest proportion being allegations of economic offences in a *Qui Tam* action, claiming for the informer the share of the penalty which the particular penal statute had promised.

Contemporary reformers always considered the Exchequer as the court where the informers were most active[5] and this is supported by a cursory examination of contemporary rolls from Queen's Bench and Common Pleas.[6] Informers were also at work at Assizes and Quarter Sessions, but the imperfection of these provincial records[7] makes it impossible to display comparable figures. There were good reasons of self-interest, however, which led a common informer to Westminster and to Exchequer. Protected by distance from the cooler verdict of a local jury an informer could make wild allegations against a provincial merchant or manufacturer in the hope that innocent and guilty alike would prefer to pay him a composition rather than to incur the expenses of a journey to Westminster and litigation. It was by banishing the informers from Westminster to the provincial courts that the Act of 1624 finally broke their power, sending them, as Coke put it,[8] back to their former trades, their occupation gone.

III

The 24,649 informations of Table I have been classified into eleven groups,[9] three important classes of which (customs, marketing, and wool-dealing) are displayed also in Table I, cols. 3, 5 and 6. They appear again in Tables III–VI

---

[1] SP 10/14/16–17; C 66/847 m 33d.

[2] *Lords J.* I, 252, 269 and 284.

[3] p. 232 below.

[4] P.R.O., class E 159; loose bundles of informations, E 148 and E 207/39. The informer's name is followed by 'qui tam pro domino rege quam pro seipso sequitur…' 'Common informer', as Cecil once noted (B. M. Lands. 58/59) appeared in no statute: cp. 7 Henry VIII c. 3, 'any *common person* may sue.'

[5] *A description of the courtes*: B.M. Add. MS. 48020 and SP 12/110/19; Harl. MS. 1303 and 6050; Lands. MS. 171/408; E 163/19/17; SP 14/32/22; SP 46/15, ff. 186–200.

[6] In Mich. 1611 King's Bench had 99 informations and Exchequer 746.

[7] Some provincial figures for informations (on apprenticeship alone) are assembled by Mrs M. G. Davies, '*The Enforcement of English Apprenticeship, 1563–1642*,' (Cambridge, Mass. 1956) a study which appeared after this article was written.

[8] E. Coke, *op.cit.* IV, 76.

[9] For the subject-matter of each group see Appendix *infra*. For each information, the *recorda* membrane had a marginal summary which was copied into the contemporary Agenda Books and Repertory Rolls to form an index.

where the annual fluctuations within the period are examined. The character of the offence alleged is important in this analysis, for peak-years were not always brought about by informers fastening on the same type of offence. An examination of the type of offence alleged in informations also demonstrates the wide range of economic transactions which Parliament consented to leave vulnerable to the attentions of a common informer.

Table II. *Informations: summary analysis of offences alleged, sample terms 1519–1659*

offence	no. of cases	
1. customs and foreign trade	6,805	26%
2. marketing	11,809	43%
3. manufacture	1,458	6%
4. agrarian	892	4%
5. labour code	917	4%
6. exchanges	208	1%
7. political Lent	364	1%
8. usury	1,219	5%
9. ecclesiastical	1,114	4%
10. guns, archery, horses	220	1%
11. miscellaneous	1,237	5%
Total	26,243	100%

These offences comprise the 24,649 offences in Michaelmas terms (Table I), and those from 29 other terms in this period not included there.

Not all the penal statutes were equally esteemed, even by the bench of judges, but when in 1604 they drew up a list of penal statutes 'fittest to be put into execution' it consisted mainly of economic offences.[1] After the reforms of 1624 [2] only a fraction of these remained actionable at Westminster but the emphasis remained economic.[3] When an Exchequer official in 1690 drew up a list of model informations[4] he assumed an even smaller range, but still mainly economic:

> importing and exporting goods prohibited or uncustomed; loading or unloading goods before Customs inspection; avoiding ulnage; exporting wool; unlicensed sale of wine; non-repair of bridges.

Even in their most active period (1550–1616) the common informers had lean years and fat years. Did the fat years see every type of offender more vigorously pursued? or were the vipers and caterpillars of the commonweal made fat on a particular diet? Table III shows that the answer is complex. In it, (comparing the lean years 1557 and 1609 with the fat years 1562 and 1613) customs offences loom large but are not very different in absolute numbers. Only in 1557–62 did allegations of illegal methods and standards of manufacture contribute much to the boom in informing. Recusancy and offences concerned with employment were good for a small increase in a fat year but the greatest swell of traffic came from market offences: an eightfold increase from 1557 to 1562 and a further 80 per cent added between 1609 and 1613.

[1] SP 14/10/42, including illegal imports and exports; forestalling and engrossing; depopulation; destruction of woods and timber; alehouses; the assizes of bread and drink; Political Lent; vagabondage; the Statute of Artificers.

[2] p. 225 below.

[3] 21 Jas.I.c 4; recusancy; failure to pay tunnage and poundage; customs frauds; illegal export of gold, silver, powder, munitions, wool, woolfells and leather.

[4] B.M. Harl. M.S. 6050; E163/19/17.

Table III. *Informations laid in Exchequer*

Subject-matter in lean and fat years compared:

Michaelmas terms of 1557 and 1562; 1609 and 1613; 1616 and 1617

	1557	1562	1609	1613	1616	1617
Total number of informations, all subjects.	115	672	581	861	766	235

Classification by subjects:

	1557	1562	1609	1613	1616	1617
1. Customs:						
metal and metal goods	7	2	3	12	6	1
textiles and wool	9	8	39	22	14	14
skins and hides	8	8	16	5	3	0
miscellaneous	9	8	68	64	33	38
food and wine	15	27	9	6	6	6
total	*48*	*53*	*135*	*109*	*62*	*59*
2. Market:						
ingrossing grain	11	55	112	401	111	91
other ingrossing	0	12	50	29	9	3
illegal sale of animals	2	53	130	194	84	34
sale outside markets and fairs	2	88	20	18	33	5
forestalling	0	0	27	3	28	1
regrating	0	36	4	3	0	0
other illegal sales	3	70	5	0	2	1
illegal wool deals	24	39	11	18	185	14
total	*42*	*353*	*359*	*666*	*452*	*149*
3. Manufacture:						
cloth illegally	2	40	11	7	15	0
leather illegally	5	82	14	9	2	0
total	*7*	*122*	*25*	*16*	*17*	*0*
4. Agrarian:						
cutting wood	0	7	6	2	6	0
enclosing	0	0	3	5	5	1
too large flocks of sheep	0	2	3	2	0	8
too few milch kine	0	0	0	0	0	1
total	*0*	*9*	*12*	*9*	*11*	*10*
5. Labour code:						
not apprenticed	0	2	5	10	5	0
breach of service	0	11	0	0	0	0
total	*0*	*13*	*5*	*10*	*5*	*0*
6. Exchanges	*5*	*18*	*7*	*3*	*4*	*0*
7. Political Lent	*0*	*3*	*3*	*1*	*0*	*1*
8. Usury	*3*	*0*	*14*	*7*	*11*	*0*
9. Ecclesiastical	*1*	*51*	*12*	*28*	*201*	*3*
10. Guns, Archery, Horses	*0*	*8*	*2*	*4*	*1*	*12*
11. Miscellaneous, not classified	*9*	*42*	*7*	*8*	*2*	*1*

What of the transition from fat to lean in 1616–7, when the total number of informations in the Michaelmas terms fell from 766 to 235? Table III shows customs offences almost indifferent to this change of weather. There were 303 fewer allegations of marketing offences; the other principal absentees were the harriers of recusants and non-resident clergy; illegal manufactures and usury lost their fascination for informers but these offences were not numerous to begin with.

Table IV. *Informations in Exchequer*

Peak years (Michaelmas term) for various type of offence alleged

Offence:	Customs	Marketing	Manufacture	Agrarian	Labour	Exchanges
Year:	1608	1613	1568	1584	1564	1595
Number of Informations that year:	275	666	163	173	68	21

Offence:	Political Lent	Usury	Guns, Horses, Archery	Ecclesiastical
Year:	1585	1574	1617	1616
Number of Informations that year:	173	90	12	201

There is not space to set out the annual experience for each class of offence, but Table IV indicates the peak Michaelmas term for each and the number of cases entered in that term. There were also short bursts of enthusiasm for single statutes: not sowing hemp on every sixtieth acre of tillage; not perambulating parish bounds;[1] using a hot-press; polluting streams by washing linen (in Lincolnshire) or tin (in Devon). In these cases, as in the Labour and Usury offences of Table IV, there is usually a new statute or a proclamation to explain the interest. It will also be noticed that two large categories which together touched people's pockets and consciences (Marketing and Recusancy) reached their peak between 1613 and 1616, the period when serious reforms began.[2]

IV

Table I has shown that customs and foreign trade offences were the mainstay of the informer before the expansion of the mid-sixteenth century, and they remained almost the sole employment for Exchequer informers after the reforms of 1616–24.[3] Between 1551 and 1624 they had accounted for between a quarter and a third of all the informations. In this class of allegation the private informer is often difficult to distinguish from the official and semi-official informer[4] who was part of the accepted machinery of customs enforcement, and in order to avoid exaggerating the activity of the free-lance, column 3 of Table I separates the customs offences, column 4 giving the totals for all remaining classes of allegation.

Customs informations had one distinction, their seriousness of purpose.

[1] e.g. E 159, 8 Eliz. pt. 2, Trin. *recorda* mm. 272–3.
[2] p. 222 below.
[3] In 1636 one victim was Sir John Mun, son and publisher of Thomas, accused of 'colouringe of straungers goodes': E 165/38.
[4] e.g. Martin's patent, C 66/950 m. 7 (1560); like Mr Elton's Whelpay, he was a haberdasher and was still at work informing in 1588 (E 159,31 Eliz., Mich. *recorda* m. 415).

Mr Elton, noting that in the day of the informer Whelpay (1538–43) there was often no record beyond the first enrolment, has suggested that the customs information was often no more than a manoeuvre in forcing a victim to compound or to pay blackmail.[1] The generality of Tudor and early Stuart informations do follow exactly this pattern of a bare enrolment,[2] but in the customs informations after 1547 the pursuit is to the death, that is to a sworn appraisal of the forfeited goods and the award to the informer of his share in the penalty.[3]

Table V. *Informations laid in Exchequer*

Types of Foreign Trade offence in fat and lean years for informers.

The lean years (1566 and 1605) are shown in italics, the fat years (1567, 1568, and 1608) in roman type.

Types of goods concerned in the offence	Years Michaelmas term				
	1566	1567	1568	*1605*	1608
metal and metal goods	*0*	1	2	*11*	5
textiles and wool	*14*	15	31	*14*	32
skins and hides	*5*	7	10	*11*	14
miscellaneous	*30*	43	49	*40*	73
foods and wine	*13*	178	95	*21*	151
Total	*62*	244	187	*97*	275

Customs informations were also nonconformist in reaching their peak in different years from other economic offences. A busy year like 1613 did not show any unusual interest in the shipping of wrong goods to the wrong places at the wrong time of night from the wrong lading-points. In a lean term for other types of information (like Michaelmas 1602) the steady ground-swell of customs informations provided one third of the enrolments. After the reforms they were to provide more than half (56 per cent in 1619 and 52 per cent in 1620). When the exceptionally busy years for customs offences are examined it will be seen (Table V) that the illegal import or export of foodstuffs, principally the export of grain, were the chief contributors. In years like 1567–8, 1575, 1608, and 1611 these offences excited particular attention. Since many penalties were in proportion to the value of an illegal transaction, informing was more profitable in time of general dearth. The same incentive will be seen at work (below) in the cognate home-market offences of ingrossing and covert dealing in grain.

[1] G. R. Elton, 'Informing for Profit', *Camb. Hist.* J. XI (1954), 149–67.
[2] The membranes of E. 159 rolls being blank after the 'super quo' at the end of the enrolled information; M. G. Davies, *op.cit.* 146, reckons 80% of the apprenticeship suits inconclusive. The abortive informations emphasize the prevalence of compounding.
[3] The closely-written membranes of the customs cases often extend to the dorse and usually stand together at the head of a term's roll. An unpursued information is, of course, an *ex parte* statement not necessarily true in every particular (cp. E. Kerridge, 'The Returns of the Inquisitions of Depopulation', *E.H.R.* LXX (1955), 224). Unhappily, a jury's acquittal in turn does not always mean that the allegation was wrong: Sir Miles Corbett, informed against for having more than 2,400 sheep, was acquitted (E 159/393, Mich. m. 254) but his private sheep accounts show that he had some 5,000 that year. (K. J. Allison, 'The Wool Supply ... in Norfolk ...' (Leeds Ph. D. thesis, (1955), 270–1).

V

Marketing offences were the common informer's main support in the days when the sun shone on him, and the shrunken totals of the cloudy days of 1617–24 emphasise their importance to him. No other single class of offence is so large and the year-to-year variations were wide (Table I, col. 5). Why such sensitivity? As with customs offences, high prices were always a stimulus to informers. Busy market-places always produced more potential offenders but a year of very high prices would stimulate precautionary hoarding, speculative cornering and popular suspicion of the middleman, thus making it easier to gather news of offenders.[1] The Act of 5 and 6 Edward VI c.14 against regrators and engrossers set the penalty in proportion to the value of the illegal deal. Even allowing for exaggeration in the allegations, it is plain that the big honey pots attracted the wasps and the large deal was the one which it paid best to expose in court instead of privately compounding without laying any information at all.

In years of busyness or dearth there was another reason why the records of informations are swollen; the craft of informing needed no seven-year apprenticeship. It was a free trade, and a notorious dealer could not safely make an out-of-court compact with one informer if another could bring him to court a week later. An offence was blocked against further informations only if a fine had been levied or a composition lawfully made; strictly speaking, only with the court's consent. An out-of-court composition was a cheap way out for small offenders but it left notorious dealers vulnerable sometimes to the renewed attentions of the same informer, repentant with righteousness. To come openly to court might be better than eternal blackmail.[2]

Table VI shows the popularity of various marketing offences. It will be seen that 1567–8 and 1608 were years when illegal wool-dealing and breaches of the price- and quality-statutes were the most popular, while in 1608 and 1613 engrossers of grain and regrators of animals were the principal targets. The harrying of the wool-dealer has recently been treated by Dr P. J. Bowden[3] and column 6 of Table I must be read in conjunction with his account of the enforcement of the Act of 1552 and in particular the successive licences to Simon Bowyer,[4] Edward Hoby,[5] and Viscount Fenton[6] as sole informers. The Michaelmas *recorda* of 1615 carry 185 informations claiming £555,000 in fines for wool illegally sold.[7] As will be seen below, this was not the best time for informers to call attention to themselves; and the Privy Council intervened to

---

[1] The peak-years 1594–5, 1598 and 1600 went with high wheat prices; 1562 did not. The last decade of large-scale informing was embittered by no less than five of Thorold Rogers' 'years of exceptionally high wheat prices'. Where fines varied with the length of the offence it would pay to watch and wait, introducing a time lag; M. G. Davies, *op.cit.* 108–42, relates the ebb and flow of informations to some local economic conditions.

[2] The proper procedure: E 123/8/31; impropriety: E 133/2/241–2 and 284: 'he never made the Courte privye nor dyd signyfe to the Courte when his seuyte dyd depende of any composicion'; suits 'faintly pursued' were proscribed by 4 Henry VII c. 20, but the 'fee'd informer' was all too common: 'almost all the Dyers Company are with their consent informed against ... by which combination the suits are renewed and continued from term to term, every one of the Dyers paying (the informer, Hunt,) £ 4 as an annual rent' (*Cal.S.P. Dom. 1580–1625*, 511).

[3] P. J. Bowden, 'The Internal Wool Trade in England during the 16th and 17th Centuries', (Leeds Ph. D. thesis, 1952).

[4] B.M. Lands. MS. 48/67; 51/95; 65/201; *Acts. P.C. 1591*, 65–7.

[5] C 66/1570 m. 25, challenged in 1606: *C.J.*, I, 303.

[6] C 66/2069 m. 7.

[7] E 159/449, Mich. mm. 57–219d, besides 156 smaller claims.

Table VI. *Informations laid in Exchequer*
Market Offences alleged in lean and fat Years

Michaelmas terms

Type of market offence:	1566	1567	1568	1605	1608	1613
ingrossing grain	17	0	0	58	205	401
other ingrossing	3	0	0	57	30	29
illegal sale of animals	19	0	0	76	106	194
sale outside markets and fairs	9	9	4	16	4	18
forestalling	5	1	0	12	4	3
regrating	0	0	1	0	1	3
other illegal sales, price and quality	6	36	68	0	0	0
illegal wool deals	21	136	50	41	66	18
Total	80	182	123	260	416	666

stay and then to squash the informations against all but 'obdurate and continuing' offenders.[1] Only 14 wool informations were laid in Michaelmas term,
1617.

VI

The very range and quantity of informations laid between 1550 and 1616
might seem reason enough for the popular dislike of informers. Yet the reforming proposals did not come solely from chastened sinners fresh from an
appearance in Exchequer. The notorious abuses of dishonest informers were
sufficient to people a whole season of Jonsonian comedies. Mrs Davies has
recently given a conspectus of corrupt practices,[2] making it unnecessary to
document the abuses further; sin is painfully repetitive.

The importance of this corruption lies in the strength it gave to the agitation
for revision of the whole corpus of the penal statutes; it also began to make
Parliament side-step the informer on any new statute by assigning half-
penalties to specific charities. Law-makers were finding that the intended
policemen, guardians of the common-weal, had dissolved into first-class
members of the criminal classes, as in a Kafka nightmare.

No effective action was taken by King or Council until 1616. Informers
were retained, despite their critics, partly no doubt because of the revenue the
Crown received from the other half (or some fraction) of the penalties: they
punished sin and they helped to fill the royal purse, at once blessing him that
gave and him that took. The informer was a partner of the Crown: but it was
an inefficient partnership for the Crown[3] whose income from penalties was
small alongside the court fees and the informers' chance of making money by
out-of-court, unrecorded blackmail.

The cost of expurgating sin, often in proportion to the value of the goods
concerned, could also vary with the length of time the offence had continued:
the number of months an art had been exercised without apprenticeship[4] or
the years an over-large flock of sheep had been kept. In addition there was the

---

[1] *Acts P.C.*, *1615–6*, 356 and 512; *ibid, 1616–7*, 24–6; *ibid, 1619–21*, 293–4; Table I, final
column, *supra*, p. 224, shows the effect.

[2] *op. cit.* 40–77.

[3] 'Little or no benefit hath redounded unto Us by any of the said Informations': C 66/2233,
m.1d. (1620). Exchequer accounts do not sufficiently distinguish the fines from penal statutes.
F. C. Dietz, *The Exchequer in Elizabeth's Reign* (1923), 17, n. 5 shows totals of £1211 in 1560
and smaller sums of from £25 to £791 later in the reign.

[4] Eleven months was the maximum penalty period under this statute; others permitted a
further look backwards.

cost of appearing in London. 29 Elizabeth I c.5 allowed subjects in the remoter provinces to answer by attorney, but lawyers could be as expensive as travel. It was on this element of expense if an information was contested that the worst abuses of informing rested.[1] Even innocent parties might think it better to come to terms quietly. Strictly, these 'compositions' should have been reported to the court and recorded,[2] but all contemporary complaints and projects for reform strongly denounced unlawful compositions, and one notorious Jacobean promotion, the patent of Sir Stephen Proctor in 1610, began its life innocently enough as a public-spirited pursuit of these unlawful compounders, and Bacon seems to have been taken in. He declared the suit to be one

> of extreme diligence ... To point and trace out the particular and covert practices, shifts, devices, tricks and (as it were) strategems ... is a discovery whereof great good use may be made for your Majesty's service and the good of your people.

As befitted the author of *Henry VII*, Bacon protested that he would have had nothing to do with the suit if it had resurrected another Empson and Dudley, but as it stood it would be better at restraining abusive informers than twenty statutes.[3]

Proctor was too thorough and too imitative.[4] Within six months of his grant[5] the complaints of his own blackmailing tactics raised a storm, and James was forced to abandon him to the Tower, the Commons threatening to withold supply unless Proctor was degraded. The Bill[6] against him had in its preamble an interesting general principle:[7]

> the greatest pressures and grievances to any people in a well-governed common wealth do grow by this: when by colour of authority, show of justice and in direct (execution) of penal laws the subjects are oppressed and injuriously dealt with.

VII

James I's ill-judged grant to Proctor was almost the last in a long series of patents whereby the common informer was partially put, as it were, in commission.[8] Single patentees or a group (and their deputies) had been given the

---

[1] A set of costs of incurred by one William Leese, against whom the informer had failed to procede to trial, has survived from the days of Privy Council scrutiny in 1619; E 163/17/17. 'Imprimis, his jorney and horsehyre to London and backe againe 14s; his charges on attending here three days, 10s; his Counsell's fee, 11s; his Attorney's fee 3s. 4d; this bill makinge, 6d; the ratinge of the same, 2s; a subpoena for costs 2s 6d; in toto, 43s. 4d.' See also M. G. Davies, *op.cit.* 56, 278–80.

[2] Some licences; E 122/233; E 165/38; the patent of 1594 (C 66/1438, m. 38) to William Smith was to take forfeit for unlicensed compositions.

[3] B.M. Harl. MS. 7020; SP 14/47/57; Lands. MS. 167/144–50; 168/41; 811/103–32.

[4] £ 4,456 was raised in the Michaelmas term; SP 14/47/105.

[5] C66/1820 m.20: 'collectour of all somes of money payable by reason of any Informacon ... for any forfaiture grounded upon any penall lawe (since 1588)'.

[6] *C.J.* I, 399–544 and *L.J.* II, 635–651 passim; the engrossed Bill of Pardons (H. Lords MSS.), has a last clause sewn to its foot; 'and also exempted out of the said General Pardon, Sir Stephen Proctor, knight'.

[7] H. L. Suppy. MSS., *sub die* 14 July 1610 and MSS. Bills, 5 July 1610; SP 14/54/32.

[8] The idea of a few commissioned informers appeared in the draft bill of c. 1534 (*supra*) and the Commission of Ten in 1552 (C 66/847 m. 33d). Shepparde and seven others were commissioned in 1558; C 66/924 m. 23, revoked, *Acts.P.C. 1558*, 200; echo in Requests 2/104/13. Man'srti patent of 1560 (C 66/950, m. 7) made him an informer throughout the realm. In 1566

sole right to lay informations under particular statutes or parts of statutes or in particular districts.[1] The patents for informing against wool-dealers have already been mentioned. At first, these grants seemed a cheap way of ensuring that offenders were actively pursued and that the Crown did get at least some payment, but the patentees' privileges were easily abused. A sole informer was in an even stronger position for blackmail than a host of competing private informers. In 1597 Cecil noted that[2] 'Her Majesty ... naturally likes them as little as concealments or monopolies'. The comparison was pointed: like monopolists, the commissioned informers could be plausibly justified as usefully serving the common weal with no direct charge to the revenue; they also undertook searching and supervision functions which the Crown was ill-equipped to organise: but the subjects saw only the abuses and the charge.[3]

Parliament was not able to take effective action to regulate informers until 1624, the year of the Acts against monopolies and concealments. The long rearguard action weakened the moral and political strength of the Crown. Two main arguments for retaining the informer so long are illustrated in marginal notes of objection, probably by Cecil, to a reforming bill[4] of 1571: the bill would weaken the execution of good laws which as *pater patriae* the monarch has the duty to see enforced; but reform also 'forgets the Queen's prerogative, customs etc.' The suspending and dispensing power had become an issue because the commissioned informer was usually delegated powers of compounding with offenders to purge past sins. Yet how easily could the patentee, riding the countryside like some latter-day Pardoner, be construed as someone who was offering licences for sale to permit the offence to continue! As a Norwich merchant ruefully confessed[5]

> For my trade of buying of wool, because the statute of the land is against it, it hath cost me for licences since my occupying began at least £200.

In 1604 the judges had unanimously decided in *The Case of The Penal Statutes*[6] that all grants to private persons either of the benefit of fines on penal statutes or of the power to dispense were 'utterly against law'; in 1606 an M.P. with a

---

Cecil was offered a plan for local commissioners for usury, tillage, engrossing corn, apparell, unlawful retainers, non-residence and plurality, unlawful games and failure to breed horses in parkland: SP 14/190/46; SP 15/13/42. In December 1566 the Commons censured a commission to enforce penal statutes; the Queen took the censure ill: Conyers Read, *Mr Secretary Cecil* (1955), 370. 'The oppression of the informers not amended', noted Cecil at the session end: SP 12/41/36. The widespread use of official searchers to enforce economic legislation was a kindred administrative device; e.g. C 66/1026 no. 2761, one man to be Sole Searcher for offenders against artillery and unlawful games.

[1] The following have been noted, and the list may still be incomplete: 1570, Horsey, wine licence offences (C 66/1062 m. 9); c. 1574, various patentees, customs, bowstaves, usury, cutting timber, assize of fuel, leather, export of corn, wood and victuals, keeping sheep (*Acts P.C. 1571–5*, 280, 371, and 396); 1576, Bailey and Blount, cap-making (C 66/1137 m. 25; E 163/13/20; *Acts P.C. 1578–80*, 26, 352 and 384); 1577, Bowyer, wool-dealing, (*supra* p. 230); 1589, Astley and Windebank, cutting oaks (C 66/1329 m. 12); 1591, Kirke and Carter, hemp (C 66/1371 m. 42); 1594, Byneon and Bennett, gig-mills (C 66/1415 m. 11); 1595, Cornwallis, unlawful games (C 66/1448 m. 34; cp. C 66/1137); 1597, Hoby, export of ordnance (W. H. Price, *English Patents of Monopoly* (Cambridge, Mass. 1913), 146–7).

[2] *Hist. MSS. Comm. Salisbury*, XIV, 28; SP 12/107/42; 43 Eliz. c. 1 § 8, confirming recent patents, excluded licences.

[3] E 133/2/241 (1575): the informer Veale had laid 71 usury informations for the deputies of the commissioners Macwilliams and Colshill (C 66/1084) but failed to make proper composition; 56 other offences were alleged.

[4] SP 15/20/22; E 175/6/25–7 may be this bill.

[5] *Hist. MSS. Comm., Var. Coll.* III, 96.

[6] SP 14/10a/6 and *Hist. MSS. Comm. Salisbury*, XVI, 349–50; B.M. Lands. MS. 104/53.

Gilbertian sense of humour proposed a Bill[1] presaging the penal code of Titipoo —anyone informing against an unlawful dispenser could claim half the penalty; in 1610 James I's self-denial, published in *The Book of Bounty*[2] had included the promise never again to entertain suits for the benefits from penal statutes, but in subsequent years the judgement of 1604 was side-stepped by grants to commissions[3] acting in the King's own name. Only in 1617 did any effective remedies against informers' abuses come into play.

<h1 style="text-align:center">VIII</h1>

Six main lines of attack can usefully be distinguished, but all had been present in various private and official projects for the previous half-century.[4] Nearly a decade before the final reform in the statute of 1624 the Privy Council began to take action. With the assistance of J.P.'s, allegations of notorious abuses were collected and the offenders summoned to the Council board.[5] Secondly, a register of fines and compositions in Exchequer was begun. This technique had formed part of Proctor's office[6] but the recording continued in the office of Charles Chambers[7] and one of the register books has survived.[8] It is doubtful whether the office was very efficient, for when the Privy Council wanted to know how many informations had been laid in 1621 it had to appoint a commission to collect the data.[9]

A third and more effective action came from direct intervention by the Privy Council. The barons of Exchequer were ordered to stay or to squash informations laid under certain statutes. The penal statutes which had contributed full measure to the boom in informing between 1608 and 1616 were those against which the Council began to move. There was often a double motive: not only had the enforcement by informing become outrageous but the subject-matter of the penal statutes no longer commanded universal support. It was bad luck for informers that they hung at the coat-tails of restrictionists in wool-dealing, general marketing and the Shrewsbury cloth trade[10] just when their pursuit of recusants and interlopers in the Cockayne scheme was incurring disapproval in powerful quarters.[11]

Thus in April 1616 informations against wool-dealing were stayed on the

[1] H. Lords MSS. *sub die* 17 April 1607.

[2] Long summary in *Commons Debates of 1621*, ed. W. Notestein *et al.* (New Haven, 1935), VII, 491–6; SP 14/37/72–6 are drafts.

[3] e.g. C 66/2134; C 66/2176 *dorse*; SP 39/10/29 (July); *C.J.* I. 309; *Hist. MSS. Comm. Sackville (Cranfield)*, III (proofs seen by permission) *sub die* 14 May 1606; SP 14/20/23.

[4] Principal projects: E 163/15/32; SP 10/14/16–17; SP 12/288/3; SP 15/20/22; B.M. Lands. *MS.* 152/31, 166/286, 168/40; 172/241; *Hist. MSS. Comm. Hastings*, IV. 323; *C.J.* I. 225; *L.J.* II, 411, 660; H. Lords MSS. bill of 17 April 1606.

[5] *North Riding Record Society*, II, 86; *Acts P.C. 1617*, 408–10; *ibid, 1619*, 42,63, 65, 85, 114, 128–9, 196, 227, 275; B.M. Harl. MS. 7608, f. 212–3; SP 14/112/14; SP 14/121/169; 18 Eliz. c. 5 and 31 Eliz. c. 5.

[6] B.M. Lands. MS. 168/71–3; 172/41; cp. E. 123/26/341.

[7] C 66/1750 and 2220; SP 14/109/119, 110/131 and 111/74; *Acts P.C. 1611–3*, 231; E 159/470 Eas. *recorda*.

[8] E 165/38; an earlier volume to which Mrs Davies (*op.cit.* 35 n.36) gives an obsolete reference cannot now be traced by officers of the P.R.O.

[9] C 66/2233 m. 1d.

[10] T. C. Mendenhall, *The Shrewsbury Drapers and the Welsh Woollen Trade* (1953), 163–89.

[11] SP 14/115/30 and C 66/2233 m.1d.: Commission to enquire into abuses of recusancy informing; SP 14/177/24: 'to avoid trouble through informers'; *Acts. P.C. 1616–7*, 16, 18–9; *ibid, 1620*, 225.

same day as those against the East India Company.[1] The next week saw a ban on those who harried London retailers of cheese and butter.[2]

> if those statutes should be strictly put in execucion at this time it would cause them to leave of that kinde of trade.

In December 1617, informations on the statutes of employment and the importation of playing cards were stayed.[3] French and Dutch immigrants were freed of informations under the apprenticeship laws;[4] informers against grain-shipments, victuallers, butchers, and innkeepers were attacked;[5] while two new patents sought to free some of the victims by offering a gilt-edged pardon against which no informer could hope to resurrect a vexing past. A large royal commission of privy councillors and judges was to administer compositions for tillage offences.[6] A second grant, to Spence and others, was designed to arrest abuses by informers working on the apprenticeship clauses of the Act of 1563; the commissioners were to grant pardons in the king's name and keep three-fourths of the fees.[7] This grant sailed very near the wind. In March 1621 the Commons condemned the Tillage Commission and James revoked it in July,[8] but by that time there were bills before the House which provided other—and more effective—ways of combating informers' abuses. Table I has shown how effectively these actions by the Privy Council (or others yet untraced) exiled the informer from Exchequer: the Michaelmas informations of 1619 numbered only one sixth of those in the same term of 1613. The three reforming statutes which followed in 1624 (each of them a bill in the abruptly-ended session of 1621) may therefore appear as an anti-climax, a formal bolting of a stable door. But so long as informers were kept at bay only by Privil Council disapproval there was no security; a change of wind, feared Coke and his supporters, might well bring back the plagues of Egypt.

The Statute of Monopolies, the first of the three measures, had 'dispensations with penall lawes and the forfeyture thereof' in its title. 'Graunts of the benefite of any Penal Lawes, or of power to dispence with the Lawe, or to compound for the forfeiture' declared contrary to law in the Book of Bounty,[9] were now proscribed by statute.[10]

The second reforming statute was the climax of a long agitation for sifting the corpus of statutes to eliminate the 'obsolete' penal laws,[11] and it should be read alongside those other statutes[12] of 1624 which reformed ancient processes

---

[1] *Acts P.C., 1615–6*, 512; *ibid, 1616–7*, 26.

[2] *ibid*, 524; (statute, 3–4 Edw. VI. c. 21).

[3] *ibid*, 409–10.

[4] SP 14/131/12.

[5] SP 14/112/12; 113/26; *Acts P.C., 1619–23*, 42, 65, 85, 128, 196 and 227.

[6] C 66/2134: some who have converted and improved their lands are 'subject to suits and troubles by common informers'.

[7] C 66/2176 dorse (cp. relief to J.P.'s who had omitted to prepare wage-schedules in 1566, C 66/1034 m. 37; and similar projects in SP 14/24/71–3; SP 12/93/26).

[8] SP 14/120/61; 122/10.

[9] SP 14/37/72.

[10] 21 Jas. I c. 3 § 1. Coke, *op.cit.*, iv. 194; 'the Dispenser . . . blowne up and exterminated', but see Price, *op.cit.* 171–5 for later commissions.

[11] 21 Jas. I. c. 28; the 'sifting'; *L.J.*, II, 550–1; H. Lords MSS. *sub die* 18 July 1610; B.M. Lands. MS. 160/338–49; H. Lords MSS., Supplementary Papers no. 1; SP 14/52/72.

[12] 21 Jas. I c. 2, 'for the generall quiet of the Subject agaynst all pretences of Concealments'; c. 8, processes; c. 12, pleadings; c. 13, jeofayles; c. 14, informations of intrusion; c. 16, limit-ation of actions; c. 23, transfers to superior courts; c. 25, forfeitures; c. 26 recoveries. See also G. E. Aylmer, 'Attempts at Administrative Reform, 1625–40', *E.H.R.* LXXII (1957), 232.

of the law open to abuse, culminating in a statute of Pardons (cap.35) 'more extensive than former Pardons ... Loving subjects have fallen into the danger of divers great Penalties and Forfeitures'. A long Statute of Repeal (cap.28) was a fine bonfire of controls. Many of the statutes effected were well-known to informers and their critics.[1] Fifty concerned economic offences, the most important being the Wool Dealers Act of 1552 and all the Tillage Acts earlier than 1597.

There is no doubt that many of these 64 acts were obsolete and that loving subjects had been in peril from them. Consulted in 1610, the judges had recommended, *inter alia* that the penal statute of 1542 *For Crossbows* should be repealed: 'guns are nowe verie serviceable'; Coke's favourite example,[2] the statute of 1363 on chicken prices, had been passed before the great inflation when 'the price was but ii d. a capon'. 'Times are not as they have been, and therefore the necessity of time makes a necessity of alteration of laws', argued Sir Edward Hoby in a Commons debate[3] of 1601, and at the head of the *Brief Collection* of penal statutes its compiler wrote[4]

> many of the said statutes through the alteration of tymes and change of mens Manners are att this Day very hard to kept.

This relativist approach showed a good historical sense, but it lent cover to the belief that the common informer had flourished by keeping an antiquarian's eye on unrepealed absurdities. Tables III, IV and VI have shown that in fact informers were most busy in pursuing offences which were 'obsolete' in a much more subjective sense: an old statute squaring ill with a new economic philosophy. It was not only the price of capons which had changed, but men's ideas. The hostility to the regrator of cheese and the wool-middleman had been weakened by events. In 1621 the tillage laws seemed to some schools of thought as obsolete as the licensed search for concealed lands, with opportunities for informing but no utility to the common weal.[5] A powerful triple alliance thus moved against the informer: the critics of obsolete laws from 'the time when Gascoigne was under the obedience of the Crowne of England'[6] those who had lost faith in statutory restrictions as a remedy against a stop in trade or the high prices of a bad harvest year; and those whose liberalism was more elemental, an antipathy to customs-officers and the wish to do what one liked with one's own.

IX

The course of the 'Bill for the ease of the Subject concerning the Informacions uppon Penall Statutes' makes it plain that the king and council had turned against the informers. It was introduced on 6 February 1621 and spoken to by Coke.[7] James promised in March that it should not lapse with the session; it would be his 'carefullest study' in the summer vacation; on May 30 he gave it

---

[1] The statute also freed country weavers from restrictions; it permitted the export of corn unless the price exceeded 32s a quarter, and relieved occupiers of ex-monastic lands from keeping the tillage and households of 1536; retailers of butter and cheese, 'much molested by informers', were freed by 21 Jas.I.c.22.

[2] See n. 10, p. 223 above.

[3] Sir S. D'Ewes, *The Journals of all the Parliaments* (1682), 622.

[4] H. Lords, Stanford MSS. 111/1.

[5] B. M. Harl. MS. 7614, f. 127; 7616, f. 6; Notestein, *op.cit.* VII, 328 and 511–2.

[6] Judges' opinion, 17 Feb. 1610; SP 14/52/72, f. 204.

[7] For the course of the bill in 1621; Notestein, *op.cit.* II, 44; IV, 207; SP 14/122/10; *C.J.* I, 584, 593. The Bill was revived in the session of 1624 and passed all its stages in 21 days.

public appoval. The Lords were a little more cautious of change, but after nine weeks' negotiations Coke threatened withdrawal of supply and an amended Bill was accepted on December 3. The *Journal*[1] records a Latin pun of thanksgiving at the news: 'sit nomen Domini et dominorum benedictum!'. Coke's own comment was drawn feelingly from the treatment of disease: the Bill was *medicina movenda*, the Monopolies Bill *promovenda*.[2]

The medicine was very simple[3]; an Act of 1588 had barred the Westminster courts from hearing informations on a few statutes, allocating these only to quarter sessions and assizes.[4] The new bill made a rule of this exception, leaving a very narrow range of offences still actionable at Westminster.[5] All other informations would have to be laid before local courts and local juries, and the tariff of distance and expense which had for so long protected the common informer now vanished.

The penal statutes thus emerge, not as efficient weapons of despotism, revenue-raising or economic planning but rather as a political irritant; a means of private profit and lawyers' fees; and an irregular charge on manufactures and trade; in short, a leading example of the discredit into which need so often drove official economic policy. *Meum* and *tuum* had indeed been harnessed, as the Bill for Conservators had hoped, but *Rancour* and *Evill Will* had come in with them. There were many reasons why the Parliaments of 1621, 1624, and 1640 did not meet great depressions and commercial crises with a return to the code of regulation which had been so popular in 1552, but not unimportant was the discredit which had recently fallen on one of the few available instruments for enforcing a policy of economic control: the common informer claiming his share of a penalty for the breach of a penal statute.

---

[1] *L.J.* III, 178.

[2] Notestein, *op.cit.*, II, 521.

[3] 21 Jas.I.c.24.

[4] 31 Eliz. c. 5; informations on unlawful games, non-provision of arms and apprenticeship had to be heard in local courts, but see Davies, *op.cit.* 26–7 for doubts; the side-note on § 2 in *Statutes of the Realm*, IV, 801 is ambiguous. As subsequent practice amply shows, it did not (*pace* Kerridge, *art.cit.* 224) confine the laying of informations to the county where the offence had been committed.

[5] Cf. n. 3, p. 214 above.

APPENDIX

The penal statutes grouped by the classification employed in Tables II-VI

1. CUSTOMS AND FOREIGN TRADE
   a. metal and metal goods   bell-metal, 2 E. VI, c. 37; brass, 33 H. VIII, c. 7; tin, 15 R. II, c. 8.

   b. textiles and wool
   c. skins and hides   these cases rested mainly on grants of customs.

   d. miscellaneous   horses, 5 Eliz, c. 19; white ashes, 2 Ed. VI, c. 26; bow-staves, 13 Eliz, c. 14; horns, 7 Jas. I, c. 14.

   e. food and wine   corn, 13 Eliz, c. 13; wine: customs grants.

2. MARKET OFFENCES
   a. ingrossing grain   5 Ed. VI, c. 14.
   b. other ingrossing   5 Ed. VI, c. 15.
   c. illegal sale of animals   3–4 Ed. VI, c. 19; 27 Eliz, c. 11; horses, 2–3 P and M, c. 7.
   d. sale outside market or fair   5 Eliz, c. 14; 3–4 Ed. VI, c. 19.
   e. forestalling   5 Ed. VI, c. 14.
   f. regrating   5 Ed. VI, c. 14.
   g. other illegal sales   corn badgers, 5 Eliz, c. 12; poultry, 37 Ed. III, c. 3; measures, 17 Ric. II, c. 7; cloth prices, 4 Hen. VII, c. 8; wine prices, 28 Hen. VIII, c. 14; hat prices, 4 Hen. VII, c. 9; butter and cheese, 3–4 Ed. VI, c. 21; price-fixing, 2–3 Ed. VI, c. 15.

   h. illegal wool deals   37 Hen. VIII, c. 15; 5 Ed. VI, c. 7.

3. MANUFACTURES
   a. cloth   24 Hen. VIII, c. 2; 33 Hen. VIII, c. 17; 26 Hen. VIII, c. 6; 5 Ed. VI, cc. 6, 8, 22, 24; 4–5 P and M, c. 5; 1 Eliz, c. 12; 18 Eliz, c. 16; 1 Jas. I, c. 17; 3 Jas. I, c. 17; 4 Jas. I, c. 2.

   b. leather   2–3 Ed. VI, cc. 9, 11; 24 Hen. VIII, c. 1; 1 Jas. I, c. 22; 3 Jas. I, c. 9.

4. AGRARIAN
   a. cutting wood   35 Hen. VIII, c. 17; 27 Eliz, c. 19.
   b. enclosure, engrossing   27 Hen. VIII, c. 28; 5–6 Ed. VI, c. 5; 2–3 P and M, c. 2; holdings etc.   5 Eliz, c. 2; 39 Eliz., cc. 1, 2.
   c. flocks of more than 2,400   25 Hen. VIII, c. 13. sheep
   d. too few milch kine in respect   2–3 P and M, c. 3. of sheep

5. LABOUR CODE
   a. not apprenticed   5 Eliz, c. 4; 39 Eliz, c. 12.
   b. breach of service, wages etc.   5 Eliz, c. 4; 7 Jas. I, c. 3.

6. EXCHANGES   5 Ed. VI, c. 19; 2 Hen. IV, c. 6.

7. POLITICAL LENT   5 Eliz, c. 5; 33 Eliz, c. 7.

8. USURY   37 Hen. VIII, c. 9; 13 Eliz, c. 8.

9. ECCLESIASTICAL   clergy not to lease land, 21 Hen. VIII, c. 14; simony, 31 Eliz, c. 6; recusancy, 3 Jas. I, c. 4.

10. GUNS, ARCHERY, HORSES   27 Hen. VIII, c. 6; 33 Hen. VIII, c. 5; 4–5 P and M, c. 2; 25 Eliz, c. 17; 6 Hen. VIII, c. 13; 1 Jas. I, c. 27.

11. MISCELLANEOUS   garbling spice, 1 Jas. I, c. 19; tin-washing in streams, 23 Hen. VIII, c. 8; unlawful games, 33 Hen. VIII, c. 9; barbers 'and surgeons' signs, 32 Hen. VIII, c. 42; pinners, 34–5 Hen. VIII, c. 6; cables, 27 Eliz, c. 11; cordage, 35 Eliz, c. 8; apparell, 1–2 P and M, c. 2; non-sowing of hemp on one acre in sixty of tillage, 24 Hen. VIII, c. 4.

These are the acts most commonly cited in informations; most appear in Ashe's *Brief Collection* and in the various lists of good and bad penal statutes submitted to the judges and Privy Council.

17

THE BEGINNING OF RETAIL TOBACCO
LICENCES, 1632-41

" THE drugge called Tobaccoe " held a unique place in the fiscal system of early Stuart England. It was a foreign and a novel commodity, so that the Crown's power to tax and control its import went unquestioned. Its popularity spread to all social classes and its rate of consumption seemed unaffected by the strictures of moralists and the imposts of the Customs House. Those, like James I, who disliked the new fashion as a corruption of the age, could have the gratifying thought that the royal revenue was being supplemented at the expense of the wilfully self-indulgent.

Yet the prohibition of unlicensed retailers in 1634 was more than an attempt to improve morals by proclamation. It formed part of Charles I's search for new sources of revenue during the eleven years of non-parliamentary rule, and in consequence both the principle and the machinery of licensing came under fire when Parliament had to be called in 1640. Like other Stuart licences (such as those for retailing wine and ale and for trading in wool) the system provided an indirect, clumsy and unpopular method of raising indirect taxes on articles of popular consumption, but the opponents of the licences were more conscious of the high prices which the licencees charged than of the advantages of collecting the country's indirect taxes without the expense of revenue officers. The usefulness of the retail tobacco tax could not be ignored even by Charles' opponents, and after his execution it returned in the form of an excise duty.[1]

I.

Early references to imposts on tobacco are all concerned with the tax on imports. James I had erected a monopoly of imports to make the collection of the tax easier to supervise and to favour the Virginian planters. Tobacco from Spanish colonies was proscribed in 1624 after many years of discriminatory duties and import quotas,[2] but the principal

---

[1] For the early history of tobacco see F. W. Fairholt, *Tobacco* (1859) ; for the Virginia trade and the import system G. L. Beer, *Origins of the British Colonial System* (New York, 1908) c. 6 ; for reproduction of many of the early printed references to the importation and retailing, Jerome E. Brooks ed., *Tobacco, Its History Illustrated by* . . . *the Library of George Arents, Jnr.* (New York, 1937) 4 vols. and index vol. These works, like that of C. M. Mackinnes, *The Early English Tobacco Trade* (1926), are almost wholly concerned with importation.

[2] R. Steele, ed. *Tudor and Stuart Proclamations* (1910), i, no. 1423.

threat to the monopoly came from tobacco grown on English soil. This was first prohibited in 1619, but frequent proclamations testify to the difficulty of enforcing the ban, especially in the West Midlands.[1]

It was not until 1632 that the Crown turned its eye to the licensing of the retail trade, although a projector connected with the London Perfumers' Company had submitted a similar plan[2] to James I's Commissioners for Projects[3] in 1613. This plan estimated that there were 6,000 London dealers and 12,000 more in the provinces, but it is likely that as yet these numbers were only a projector's pipe-dream. Other evidence suggests a rapid growth in consumption between 1613 and 1632. As tobacco passed from being a medicine to a pleasure its sale spread from apothecaries to retailers of all types. Pamphleteers began to comment on the new " tobacconists " with the Blackamoor hung outside their shop. Between the first edition (1601) and the second (1616) of *Every Man In His Humour* Ben Jonson changed a reference to an apothecary to a " tobacco-dealer ", but in the provinces specialist tobacco retailers were few.[4] In 1634 the Vice-Chancellor of Cambridge told the Privy Council that[5] " apothecaries and grocers are in respect of their trade fittest to be lycenced."

With more shops and more consumption, Charles was more attentive than his father to suggestions for a regulated trade. In 1630 one John Bayly propounded a scheme,[6] but at the time nothing came of it. In January, 1631, the Privy Council asked its legal members to comment on a petition from Endymion Porter and others which seems to be a counter-petition to a scheme emanating from the London grocers and apothecaries, probably Bayly's. Porter cast doubts on the effectiveness of the grocers' scheme, designed only to secure themselves the monopoly of the London trade, and in April, 1632, the two Chief Justices and the Attorney General reported in favour of complete regulation.[7]

> We doe conceave that by ye ungoverned selling and retayling of tobaccoe by all, great abuse and excesse is occasioned, whereupon we hold it most just that his Majestie in his princely care of ye weale of his Subjects doe ordaine good meanes for reformation ; and yt wee know no law to ye contrary, but at his good pleasure he maye ordaine good courses to be holden for reforming of those excesses and abuses.

---

[1] *Ibid.*, no. 1516.

[2] Captain Grice (or Le Grys) proposed a ban on all except licensed dealers who should buy a licence for £5 and pay an annual fee to the Crown of £1. B(ritish) M(useum) Add. MSS. 10038, ff. 76 and 78.

[3] Add. MSS. 10038 (from Sir Julius Caesar's papers) is a bound collection of these half-sad, half-mad ambitions.

[4] These details are taken from the elaborately documented account of the growth of retailing in J. E. Brooks, *op. cit.*, i, p. 49 and ii, p. 21.

[5] P(ublic) R(ecord) O(ffice), P(rivy) C(ouncil Register) 2/44/153.

[6] P.R.O., S(tate) P(apers) 16/180/32.

[7] P.C. 2/41/526–8.

The combination of zeal for the well-being of the subjects with willingness to allow them to commit as many abuses and excesses as they could
afford is characteristic of royal policy in many other directions ; it can
be seen, for example, in the preambles to the contemporary Commissions
declaring enclosure to be a social evil but giving Commissioners power to
compound with any delinquents for substantial fines. It is this ambivalent
attitude which has made it so easy for successive historians to cast Charles
I in rôles varying from the paternal to the pickpocket.

The judges' scheme suggested the sounding of provincial J.P.s to see
where licences might usefully be granted, and this was embodied in an
order of April 30, 1632, of which item 6 reads :

To ordaine that a definite quantity be yerely brought into the Realme.

The reaction of the members of the Virginia Company to the proposal
to restrict supply is not known. In 1622 and 1625 the old Company had
insisted on freedom in the retail trade, [1] but their silence and the use of
their name by Bayly in 1630 suggest that they were not averse to a
restriction of output which would raise the price they could command,
particularly since they had disposed of their Spanish competitors in 1624.

A few replies from provincial J.P.s have survived[2] and others may
perhaps be found among unpublished Quarter Sessions records. At
Almondbury two mercers and an oildrawer were given approving certifi-
cates by the constables, while at Huddersfield they could recommend only
one mercer, " so little tobacco is there used ".[3]

More than a year later, on October 13, 1633, a long proclamation
announced the result of the negotiations and inquiries. It recited the evils
of the excessive taking of tobacco, described the king's solicitude for his
subjects' welfare and his resolve to regulate the trade to save them from
their own self-indulgence. It reported the receipt of the names of worthy
persons certified by their local J.P.s and the issue of licences to these
persons. All other retailing after February, 1634, was forbidden.[4]

II.

A breviate among the papers of Lord Keeper Coventry states that 199
licences passed the Seal before March, 1634 ; the figures given below are
derived from an examination of the Patent Rolls which become prodigious-
ly swollen at this period by the enrolment of the licences.[5] The *annus
mirabilis* was still to come. In 1634–5 the projectors saw the retailers

---

[1] Beer, *op. cit.*, p. 160.
[2] e.g. *Report of the Historical Manuscripts Commission*, ix, App. p. 307 (Great Yarmouth) ;
viii, App. p. 436 (Leicester) ; *Somerset Notes and Queries*, 2nd ser., no. 97 p. 364.   (Wells
Corporation).
[3] *C(alendar) (of) S(tate) P(apers) D(omestic), 1632*, p. 390.
[4] Steele, *op. cit.*, no. 1661 ; S.P. 45/10/167.
[5] Birmingham Reference Library MSS. 604015, No. 2.   [Earl of Coventry MSS.].

queueing for their licences and complaints against interlopers not yet above a whisper.

A second proclamation of March 13, 1634, announced that many fresh applications were still being received and that the Commissioners had granted these. It justified the expensive procedure of formal application and issue of letters patent on the ground that the King had to have an estimate of the amount being sold by his patentees in order to watch the effect on the balance of payments :

> that his Majestie may prevent too much of the Stocke of this Kingdom being sent from out this Realme in payment thereof.

Finally the proclamation offered a share in the penalties to any informer who brought news of unlicensed dealing.[1]

The first licencee was one Henry Shelley. In translation his licence[2] reads :

> The King, etc., for six pounds, thirteen shillings and four pence paid into the hands of the Receiver of monies for enrollment of letters patent, grants to Henry Shelley the licence to sell imported tobacco either by retail or in small amounts during his whole life time at his home (at present in the parish of the Savoy). Our prohibition contained in our proclamation shall not stand to the contrary and he shall yearly pay to us, our heirs and successors the sum of £6/13/4 in lawful English money.

TABLE I.—*Number of Licences Enrolled*[3] *on the Patent Roll*, 1633–41.

Regnal year.					Separate licences.
March, 1633–1634	.	.	.	.	39
,, 1634–1635	.	.	.	.	1,462
,, 1635–1636	.	.	.	.	427
,, 1636–1637	.	.	.	.	164
,, 1637–1638	.	.	.	.	209*
,, 1638–1639	.	.	.	.	235*
,, 1639–1640	.	.	.	.	56*
,, 1640–1641	.	.	.	.	1
Total .	.	.	.	.	2,593

* Goring's patent also in force : see pp. 135–9 × *infra*.

The first 1,928 licences brought in a total of £12,460 in initial payments ("fines") and the expectation of a yearly rent of the same amount.[4] A Committee of the Privy Council had been set up in February, 1634, to

---

[1] Steele, *op. cit.*, No. 1674 ; S.P. 45/10/172.

[2] P.R.O., Patent Roll (C66) No. 2640 (9 Charles I, part 26) No. 40 dorse.

[3] The cases are too numerous to give individual membrane references. They will be found grouped on the following Patent Rolls : 9 Charles I pt. 26 ; 10 Charles I pts. 5, 18, 21–3, 25–9, 31 35, 37 and 41 ; 11 Charles I pts, 5, 16, 19, 23, 28, 35 and 40 ; 12 Charles I pts. 9 and 23 ; 13 Charles I pts. 7, 14, 17, 34 and 43 ; 14 Charles I pts. 1, 6, 8, 16 and 28 ; 15 Charles I pt. 23 ; 16 Charles I pt. 4 [P.R.O., C. 66/2640 sqq.).

[4] Birm. Ref. Lib. MSS. 604015, Nos. 1–129.

deal with tobacco offenders,[1] and in March the Privy Council received a list of 109 names of alleged interlopers against whom the Committee sought warrants.[2] So stimulated, the business of granting licences went on, as a correspondent of Strafford reported,[3] " apace ". In April licences were reported to be going well in Oxford, while in October the Vice-Chancellor of Cambridge was complaining to the Privy Council that he had not been allowed the patronage, and the system of free bidding had given licences to unfit persons.[4] The Council revoked the original licences and returned the licencees their money. The Vice-Chancellor was promised the nomination of any successors on death or withdrawal, and the Council guaranteed that no more than six Cambridge licences would be granted. Oxford and Cambridge were again in step.

In November, 1634, the grant of the new office of the Receiver of Fines and Penalties upon Tobacco Licences was passed by the King.[5] The account books for this Office (until its absorption in the Goring empire in 1637) have survived among the Customs accounts.[6] They show the following receipts :

						£
March-September, 1633	.	.	.	.	.	4563
September, 1633–March, 1634		.	.	.	.	4875
March-September, 1634	.	.	.	.	.	4356

The final audit of March, 1636, showed that another £13,410 was paid over from the Office to the Exchequer in the next eighteen months, so that the annual income from the licencees was just over £9,000. The initial payments for new licences were now very few.

Even before the creation of the Office a small trickle of complaints and disputes had begun to reach the Council, and in 1635 a few more cases of unlicensed dealing are known from the surviving records,[7] but the papers of the Committee of the Council which dealt with tobacco matters have not been preserved, and disputes are only known if the matter at issue got as far as the Privy Council. In March, 1635, for example, the Commissioners for Tobacco sent a list of 109 interlopers whom it wished the Council to apprehend by warrant.[8] In June, 1636, appeared the first of a number of Commissions from the Court of Exchequer authorising local inquiries into unlicenced dealing. The interrogatories attached to the depositions begin[9]

---

[1] C66/25 February, 9 Charles I (1634).
[2] S.P. 16/263/83.
[3] Garrard ed. *Letters of Strafford* (1739), i, 206 and 263 ; S.P. 16/263/20.
[4] S.P. 16/266/18 ; P.C. 2/44/153.
[5] P.R.O. Index 6810 (Docquet Book, November, 1634, f. 4, no. iii).
[6] E. 122/218/25, i–iii.   Mr. N. J. Williams kindly suggested that I might profitably search this miscellany.
[7] P.C. 2/44/169 and 213 ; *C.S.P.D. 1634–5*, pp. 395–6.
[8] S.P. 16/263/83.
[9] P.R.O. Special Commissions in the Exchequer (E. 178) No. 5557.

Inprimis have you knowne any person or persons since the thirteenth of March one thousand six hundred thirty and three to sell or utter tobacco by retaile directly or indirectly contrarie to his Maties. late proclamacions?

TABLE II.—*Exchequer Commissions of Inquiry into Unlicensed Dealing.*

County.				Date.			P.R.O. Reference Sp. Comm. Exchequer (E.178).
Northants .	.	.	.	June, 1636	.	.	5557
Glos. .	.	.	.	Aug. 1636	.	.	5315
Cornwall							5239
Devon				Feb. 1637	.	.	5239
Northants							5557
Worcester City							296
Devon				Aug. 1637	.	.	5239
Cornwall							5239
Devon				Sept. 1637	.	.	5239
Cornwall							5239
Durham .	.	.	.	March, 1638	.	.	5284
Carmarthen	.	.	.	June, 1638	.	.	5933
Yorkshire .	.	.	.	Sept., 1638	.	.	5793*
Devon				Sept., 1638	.	.	5239
Cornwall							5239
Norfolk .	.	.	.	Oct., 1638	.	.	5534
(New Buckenham only)							
Oxfordshire	.	.	.	Oct., 1638	.	.	5594
Cornwall				Nov., 1638	.	.	5239
Devon							5239
Northants .	.	.	.	Feb., 1639	.	.	5557
Northants .	.	.	.	April, 1639	.	.	5557
Sussex	.	.	.	July, 1639	.	.	5685
Pembroke .	.	.	.	Aug., 1639	.	.	5932
Devon				Sept., 1639	.	.	5239
Cornwall							5239
Devon				Nov., 1639	.	.	5239
Cornwall							5239

* Includes list of 140 retailers in York city and 77 in Hull, each arranged by streets.

The evidence in these depositions indicates a widespread provincial market in unlicensed tobacco. The witnesses had bought pennyworths and two pennyworths from petty shopkeepers or pedlars[1] or had seen their neighbours hurrying by with small packets which they had obtained from some small country grocer.[2] Many of these unlicenced dealers claimed that they had bought their stock from licencees, yet they were prosecuted when they resold it. The Commission's sitting at Helston in September, 1637, was disturbed by the ingress of angry townspeople who supported the unlicensed traders.[3]

Even as early as August, 1636, the Commisioners had to report that witnesses were refusing to appear, or remained silent under questioning.

[1] E. 178/5534.
[2] E. 178/5685.
[3] E. 178/5239.

The most effective riposte was that of a Carmarthenshire apprentice, John Hughes, who refused to incriminate his master, Thomas Lewis, by saying whether or not he had sold tobacco from his shop. " I am bound in recognizances of £500 my master's secrets not to reveal ", he said. " Will the Commissioners indemnify me if I answer the interrogatories ?" The Commissioners did not answer, but reported the words of the apprentice to the barons of the Exchequer.[1]

At New Buckenham (Norfolk) an unlicensed dealer ingeniously turned the letter of the law against the patentee. Simon Reynolds had letters patent authorizing him to deal in the town of New Buckenham. Now the town of New Buckenham had been founded late in the Middle Ages, being planted at the edge of the parish of Old Buckenham. As a consequence, the bounds of Old Buckenham passed very near the last house in New Buckenham town. John Dourghty had therefore accepted money for tobacco at his house in the town, but his customers took delivery at a gate in Cole Field in Old Buckenham parish, a mile from its church " not above a stone's caste from New Buckenhame across the procession way ".[2]

The cases which came before the Privy Council were usually less straight-forward than the simple cases of unlicensed dealing prosecuted in the Exchequer. There were joint patentees who had then fallen out, such as the London grocer and the local dealer who had shared the Warrington patent until they quarrelled saying that " twoe thereby in the said Towne cannot live ".[3] There were complaints from the patentees in towns where great fairs were held that their monopoly was being broken by the arrival of London traders at the fair, flourishing their patents and claiming that these entitled them to deal everywhere where they " usually dealt "; and arguing that they had been coming to the fairs to sell tobacco for years past, so that it was a place where there were " usual dealings ".[4] In 1636 the Privy Council was issuing blank warrants authorising a patentee to search pedlars' packs.[5]

The retail tobacco trade soon showed the characteristic pattern of provincial dealing in any commodity for which a monopoly had been farmed : stern letters from the Council, anxious patentees, enterprising interlopers, less fortunate interlopers in prison, and active contraband dealing to link the unlicenced retailer with the smuggler who was avoiding the import monopoly and the customs duty. It was a system which led to irritation of consumers, harassed by the fear of being caught with un-licenced tobacco and begrudging the share of the licencee's fee which they felt was being added to the shop price. A pessimistic commentator[6]

---

[1] E. 178/5933.
[2] E. 178/5534.
[3] Birmingham Reference Library MSS. 604015 No. 89 (February 27, 1637) P.C. 2/48/325 , 341 and 636 ; *C.S.P.D. 1637*, p. 153.
[4] *C.S.P.D. 1635*, p. 384 ; P.C. 2/51/174 ; *C.S.P.D. 1640*, p. 92.
[5] *Calendar of Treasury Papers 1557–1696*, p. 3.
[6] *C.S.P.D. 1635–6*, p. 551.

observed in 1637—"there is less tobacco spent since the licences by a third part", but the figures brought together by Mr. Rive[1] show a mounting home consumption, with London imports averaging 1,800,000 pounds weight a year between 1637 and 1640. He estimated annual home consumption at no more than 600,000 pounds in the years 1632–4. Crown, licencee and retailer were riding on the crest of a wave. Despite the murmurs against the monopoly, Englishmen continued to increase their purchases from retailers. Secure in the judges' opinion, Charles could afford to smile at the objections to a monopoly, and with no Parliament in session since 1629 there was no higher authority to challenge him and overrule the judges.

III.

On March 16, 1637, the king issued Letters Patent giving wider powers of inquiry to a body of seven Commissioners.[2] Previously, any aggrieved patentee had petitioned the Sub-Committee of the Privy Council set up in[3] February, 1634, to deal with offending interlopers, and the action taken had been on behalf of the Council. The provincial Commissions of Inquiry had been issued from the Exchequer by due process of law. The new Commissioners were authorised to act independently and were vested with the powers of summoning unlicensed dealers ; of inquiring on oath who retailed contrary to the proclamations and who was selling in towns where there was no patentee ; and of binding over offenders by recognizances that they would no longer sell without a licence ; false informers were to be sent to the Council.

One of the Commissioners was Lord George Goring, already associated with the licences to export butter and to make gold and silver thread. He was also interested in the farming of the import duty of tobacco.[4] Three months after he had been appointed a Commissioner, Lord Goring was tendering for the right to farm the issue of tobacco licences.

If a note of the proceedings at the Committee on Trade is correctly dated, the farm had been under discussion nine months earlier : the note begins with an estimate of £12,490 16s. 8d. as the yearly revenue from the licences already issued by letters patent. A tender was put in by a group of " Spanish merchants " offering £12,000 a year for the farm of the licence revenue and £11,000 for the farm of the import duty. Lord Goring's tender offered £10,000 for the first year and £20,000 a year afterwards, over and above the existing revenue.[5] He was ordered to bring his offer

---

[1] Alfred Rive, " Consumption of Tobacco since 1600," *Economic History*, i, p. 57 (1929).
[2] Patent Roll 12 Charles I, pt. 13, No. 1, printed in Rymer, *Foedera*, xx, p. 116.
[3] Patent Roll, 9 Charles I, February 25, 1634.
[4] *Dictionary of National Biography*, xx, p. 248.
[5] *C.S.P.D. 1635–6*, p. 551. (I think this paper may be dated one year too early. There is no other reference to the setting up of an Agency as early as 1636.) It is not clear whether the " Spanish merchants " were Spaniards or Englishmen trading with Spain and the colonies.

in writing. In July, 1637, his patent was entered on the Patent Roll.[1] Associated with him were his son, George Goring, Sir Drue Deane and Sir John Latch.

These four men were to form an " Office of Agency" to issue licences and to take fines for compounding with offenders. A rent of £11,000 per annum was to be paid by the Agency to the King. The Agents were to recoup themselves from the licence fees up to this total ; any additional revenue was to be divided between the Crown and themselves in the proportion of two to one. As it stood, the Agency's profit seemed small, no more than its third-share in the two hundred pounds or so by which the annual revenue might be expected to exceed £11,000. But it was from the fines for compounding with offenders that the real profit was expected. An Agency with a share in the penalties might be expected to be more zealous in pursuit of interlopers than either the local patentees or the busy Committee of the Privy Council. Indeed, the over-busyness of the Councillors was mentioned in the grant as the reason why the King was setting up a separate Agency.

The recital of Goring's grant included a summary of the earlier history of licencing and a characteristic statement of the King's motives for regulation.[2] Here his two rôles, the paternal and the pickpocket, are in close juxtaposition :

> and to permit none but meete persones and men of sufficientie to sell or utter any tobacco by retale ... his Majestie ordered the justices to certifie in what Townes and places it might be fitt to suffer selling and retaling of Tobacco and how manie in each place meete to be licenced to use that trade ... consideringe that the ventinge and sellinge of Tobacco by retale would be of greate profitte to such meete persons as should be licensed thereunto and that some improvement and increase of his Majesties owne revenue might well be made out of such licences without any impediment at all to the reformation intended ...

Against the profit to " meet persons " and the increase of the King's revenue can be set the paternalistic opening of the enrolment :

> Whereas the plant or Drugge called Tobacco scarce knowne to this Nation in former tymes was first brought into this Realme in small quantities and taken to be used here as medicine ; but in process of tyme, to satisfy the inordinate appetite of many, it was brought in great quantitie and taken for Wantoness and in excess, which excess causing an excess of drinckinge and many other inconveniences to the great impareing of the health of divers of his Majesties subjectes and depraveing of their manners, his Majesty, out of his care for his

---

[1] C. 66/2770, No. 1 (13 Charles I, pt. 21), 1637.

[2] The quotations are taken from the enrolment of the grant on the Memoranda Roll of the King's Remembrancer in the Exchequer : E. 159/477/Trinity *Recorda* m.68 sqq. (1637).

people, was at length enforced to thinke of some meanes howe to prevent the evil consequences of the inordinate use thereof and for the better repressing of all such excesses and preventinge of future inconveniences ... is nowe resolved to reduce the venting selling and uttering of Tobacco into some good order ...

This is a curious argument whose conclusion would hardly seem to follow from the premises. If tobacco smoking was wantonness, then its repression was for the good of the commonwealth ; but to use it as a source of revenue was to give an impecunious king a vested interest in increased consumption. In fact, wherever a decrease in consumption is reported in the State Papers it is not applauded as the triumph of abstinence and sobriety and a portent of improved public health : on the contrary, it is complained of as diminishing the revenue. On the occasions where the king took action to limit the amount of tobacco his motive was not to decrease the depravity of his subjects but to save Virginia and his own customs duties from the dangers of over-production and lower prices.[1]

The Goring Agency was empowered to take over the register book of the previous assignees. This must have been the book kept by Edward and William Carne, who had been appointed the Receiver of Fines and Penalties in November, 1634, soon after the institution of the licence system.[2] The Agency undertook to pay them their £200 a year and 20s. portage in each £100.[3]

Armed with the list of licencees the Agency was set up at an office in Tower Street[4] and began its investigations. The scope of its activity cannot be judged by the small number of prosecutions which appear on the Exchequer rolls. Out-of-court settlements left no trace in the records. Fortunately the Exchequer record does contain the enrolment of the names of the local retailers who had taken out the 2,093 licences already issued :

> a schedule contayning the names of the respective persons licensed to sell Tobacco by retayle in any place or places within the Realme of Englande and Dominion of Wales together with the names of the places where the said persons are licensed ... theire termes graunted ... and the annual rates reserved.

The list of names[5] occupies both sides of thirty-one membranes, each nearly two feet long :

> all which severall persons are respectively licensed to sell tobacco as aforesaid and hold theire said licences for the terme of theire respective lives.

---

[1] Fairholt, *op. cit.*, p. 319.

[2] Docquet Book to Privy Seal, November, 1634 ; grant of December 20 recited in E. 159/477, Trin. m. 68, sqq.

[3] S.P. 16/440/April grants. (In March, 1639, the Carnes surrendered their right to this income in favour of Pearce Deere and Timothy Butts.)

[4] *C.S.P.D. 1639*, p. 201.

[5] E. 159/477, *loc. cit.*, the membranes following m. 68 being unnumbered.

The geographical distribution of licencees is shown in Table III below.

Table III.—*Distribution of Licences and Amount of Rents Received*, 1637.

County.	Number of licencees.	Total sum due in annual rents.
England :		£ s. d.
Beds. . . .	15	90 6 8
Berks. . . .	24	155 6 8
Bucks. . . .	20	118 6 4
Cambs. . . .	33	99 13 4
Ches. . . .	33	65 13 4
Cornwall . .	116	437 9 0
Cumberland . .	29	92 13 4
Derby. . . .	33	118 0 0
Devon . . .	162	752 16 8
Durham . . .	25	76 6 8
Essex . . .	48	276 10 4
Glos. . . .	92	491 4 4
Hants. . . .	46	235 6 8
Hereford . .	21	120 6 8
Herts. . . .	35	215 10 0
Hunts. . . .	11	53 6 8
Kent . . .	90	486 13 4
Lancs. . . .	59	288 0 0
Leics. . . .	29	136 13 4
Lincs. . . .	63	243 6 8
London (City) . .	84	926 13 4
Middlesex . . .	119	667 14 4
Norfolk . . .	97	446 16 8
Northants . . .	34	137 3 4
Notts. . . .	28	126 10 0
Northumberland .	11	88 6 8
Oxon. . . .	29	169 13 4
Rutland . . .	4	24 6 8
Salop. . . .	33	160 3 4
Somerset . . .	101	435 6 8
Staffs. . . .	46	180 13 4
Suffolk . . .	74	367 6 8
Surrey . . .	58	342 0 0
Sussex . . .	44	199 0 0
Warws. . . .	33	166 6 8
Wilts. . . .	72	302 0 0
Westmorland . .	18	62 16 8
Worcs. . . .	29	174 16 8
Yorks. . . .	92	315 13 4
Total . . .	1,990	£9,846 17 8
Average rent c. .		£5 0 0
Wales :		£ s. d.
Cardigan . . .	5	20 4 0
Carmarthen . .	5	30 10 0
Denbigh . . .	8	40 0 0
Flint . . .	4	15 10 0
Glamorgan . .	15	70 0 0
Monmouth . .	19	97 3 4
Montgomery . .	5	30 16 8
Merioneth . .	7	33 16 8
Radnor . . .	5	19 0 0
	73	£357 0 8
Total for England and Wales . . .	2,063	£10,203 18 4

Notes to Table.

1. There is no entry for the three other Welsh counties.

2. The totals have been calculated from the rents given for each licence in the schedule. The average of £5 per licence is the same in England and Wales, but the cities, the metropolitan suburbs and the seaports had retailers prepared to pay well in excess of that sum.

3. The number of licences issued by the time the schedule was drawn up is not very different from the number (1,928) enrolled on the Patent Roll and set out in Table I above.

4. The expected annual income accruing to the Agency is seen to be somewhat less than the estimates made by Goring (p. 135) and may account for the efforts which were soon made to lower the price at which licences were sold (p. 140).

5. An early list of five Oxford licences is given in P.R.O., SP16/266/18 (April, 1634).

If the number of licencees has any relation to the local consumption of tobacco, it is clear that the most active retail trade was in the two metropolitan cities (including the suburbs of London) and in the western ports. The large number of licencees in the villages of Cornwall and Devon suggest that the habit of smoking, brought in to the chief western ports by the sailors who had made the Atlantic crossing, soon spread to the smaller fishing villages. London's high score must have come partly by reason of its sailors and partly by reason of the concentration of fashion and wealth. To smoke was an increasingly fashionable way of consuming wealth.

The average fee for a licence was £5, but the sum written into the model licence enrolled at the Exchequer was £10. One patentee had bid £30 to be the sole retailer in Southampton, and the trade at Leeds had tempted a retailer to offer £25 for a similar status. The eight retailers at Plymouth had paid £12 10s. each. A licencee in Bury St. Edmund's had paid £6 13s. 4d. to authorize him to sell " on the scite of the late dissolved abbey " but this was not the strangest shop. Another licencee had authority to sell from a tent set up at the gate of Hampton Court palace.

IV.

During 1638 the local inquiries under Exchequer authority continued to be heard ; and both the Privy Council Register and the State Papers contain a number of disputes with licencees and interlopers. The trade in licences seems to have been flagging. In December Goring asked and obtained permission from the Privy Council to lower the price at which licences were sold in any district where no offer had yet come forward.[1] 1639 was a more unhappy year for the Agency. It is true that the Virginians had agreed to restrict their crop to 1,500,000 pounds for that year and to 1,200,000 pounds for the next two years, but only the retailers and the producers reaped the benefit of the artificially maintained price. There are signs that the Agency was failing to cope with interlopers.[2] In March the Privy Council asked the Solicitor-General and the Attorney-General to investigate what remedies could check the abuses which orders and proclamations had failed to suppress. They reported that the number of licences ought to be restricted and local men preferred ; they also approved the suggestion that patentees should be encouraged to sub-let their privilege to other dealers and concluded with the time-honoured resolution in favour of another proclamation.[3]

This was issued on March 25, 1639, paying particular attention to the sale of tobacco by pedlars dealing far from their home town,[4] but within

---

[1] P.C. 2/49/603 ; *C.S.P.D.* 1638–9, p. 170.
[2] *C.S.P.D. 1638–9*, p. 192 ; *1639*, p. 201 ; P.C. 2/49/322, 518, 604, 617.
[3] P.C. 2/50/132.
[4] Steele, *op. cit.*, no. 1800 ; *C.S.P.D. 1639*, p. 149.

a few days the opponents of the Agency were able to profit by a real or imagined misunderstanding. On the last day of the month the King withdrew thirty patents to which there had been popular objection. The seventh of these[1] was entered in the Council Register as " the Commission for compounding with offenders touching tobacco " and a proclamation to this effect was published on April 9, 1639. At first sight this would seem to cancel Goring's Agency, since one of its powers was that of compounding with offenders against the retail monopoly. Tobacco dealers up and down the country rejoiced, but on May 26 the Council explained that quite a different patent had been cancelled : that to Sir Henry Spiller and others to compound with those who were caught importing uncustomed tobacco or who had been growing it in England contrary to the former proclamations.[2] On August 11, the Council authorised a proclamation (issued on August 19) declaring that Goring's patent was in full force.[3]

Yet business was still bad in the licence trade. On August 18, 1639, the Council authorized Goring to lower the price of the Londoners' licences.[4]

In November the Privy Council was treating non-appearance before the Commissioners as contempt of the Council, and in December it was again necessary for Goring to obtain an order from the Council declaring that licences were for a dealer's usual place of business and could not be used to justify selling at distant fairs.

In May, 1640, Charles dissolved the (Short) Parliament which he had been forced to summon. The weakened position of the Agency was set out in an order of the Council[5] dated July 1 :

> whereas it was this day represented to the Board by the honourable the Lord Goring that of late tymes there have beene brought complaints to a very great number concerning the business of Lycences for selling of Tobacco to the Councell Board and the late house of Commons assembled in Parliament, by reason whereof, and some other difficulties and defects arising and growinge in the cours and mannaging of that business—His Majesties rents upon that business are very much decayed and likely to be utterly lost and the promiscuous sale of Tobacco to returne into use, togeather with ye inconveniences to his Majestie and to his people sett fourth in his Majesties proclamacions . . .

By the end of July it was becoming doubtful whether the relief for which the King's subjects were agitating could be made to stop short of the

---

[1] P.C. 2/50/209.
[2] P.C. 2/50/398 ; *C.S.P.D. 1639*, pp. 149 and 230.
[3] Steele, *op. cit.*, no. 1808, printed in Rymer, *Foedera*, xx, p. 348 ; P.C. 2/50/590 : *J.S.P.D. 1639*, p. 469.
[4] P.C. 2/50/602. Goring was made a Privy Councillor in August.
[5] P.C. 2/51/611.

abolition of the whole system of retail licences. The American planters and the powerful Grocers' Company of London both petitioned[1]

> to recall the Proclamacions and Lycences under the great Seale for retayling of Tobacco, and that the Trade myght be left free as heretofore.

The Council also received :[2]

> the petitions of divers the said Pattentees desiering that they might enjoy the benefit of theire Pattents

and after a general discussion, the tenor of which was not recorded, the matter was referred to the Law Officers and two judges, while all men were enjoined to continue to obey the proclamation until an opinion had been received.

The Grocers' petition is probably the same as that considered by the freshly elected Commons on November 23, 1640, and preserved among the Lords MSS.[3] This was cast in the most liberal terms, appealing for free dealing as a general principle of right action—a complete reversal of the attitude taken by the grocers in 1632. As in so many of the Commons' grievances the particular irritations were being welded together into a general statement of opposition to the royal policy :

> whereas freedom of trade is the life and one of the principall liberties of the Subjectes of this kingdome and Tobacco the cheife Commodity of your petitioners trades, some, envying the prosperity of this kingdom and seekinge to enriche themselves—though by the spoyle and ruine of multitudes of familyes—have upon pretence of regulating the said Commodity and answeringe some yerely revenew unto his Majestie (obtained a grant of a monopoly).

Charles I also had to bear the odium of the monopoly of the Irish tobacco trade which Strafford had exercised. This matter was debated by the Commons on November 20, 1640.[4] Both Commons and Lords continued to receive petitions from those who had been fined, imprisoned, bound over or vexed by the Agency whose general powers to act as a judicial organ were questioned in the same months that the prerogative courts as a whole were being attacked. Since the Commissioners had been able to have non-appearances treated as contempt of the Privy Council (with appropriate penalties) their proceedings were associated in men's minds with the unpopular powers of Charles I's Council.[5]

As late as May, 1639, interlopers who " cried down the patents " were faced with the Attorney- and Solicitor-Generals' renewed opinion that the patent authorized the Commissioners to bind over offenders to obey the proclamations ;[6] but in the autumn of 1640 and the spring of 1641 the

---

[1] P.C. 2/51/671.
[2] *Ibid.*
[3] House of Lords MSS. November 23.   (These MSS are indexed by their date alone.)
[4] *Commons Journal*, ii, p. 32.
[5] *C.S.P.D., 1639–40*, p. 326.
[6] *C.S.P.D., 1639*, p. 212.

interlopers were hoping for a reversal of this opinion and redress for their past tribulations by petitioning Parliament with complaints of unlawful imprisonment,[1] fraudulent oppression[2] and extortion.[3] The paralysis of the Agency in face of the imminent summons of Parliament is clear from the petition of Edward Joslyn:

> in regard the Parliament was then approaching, the said Allen (the licencee) forebore execucion.

The Goring agency figured in the general Parliamentary criticism of Charles' economic policy, although the chief tobacco grievance was Strafford's Irish monopoly. Sir Harbottle Grimston[4] said of Laud (probably in the debate of November 18, 1640):

> he might have spent his time better (and more for his grace) than thus sharking and raking in the Tobacco-ship.

Laud was also attacked in an anonymous pamphlet[5] of 1641, *A pack of Patentees Opened, Shuffled, Cut, Dealt and Played*, yet when the expulsion of the monopolists was debated in February, 1641, Lord Goring's son managed to keep his seat:

> The member for Portsmouth satisfied the Committee and the House that he was not concerned in the farm of the tax on tobacco.[6]

It might be thought that the Agency was in question here, but the tenor of the debate of November 20, 1640, and the other reference to tobacco in the *Journal* for February 2, 1641, make it clear that only the Irish monopoly of importing and retailing was at issue. George Goring persuaded the Committee that he was abroad when his father obtained the grant and that his name had been included without his consent.

Indeed no formal revocation of the patents has yet been found. G. L. Beer[7] cited two cases in 1645 and 1646 which suggest that licences were still being taken seriously, and their decline seems to have come more by the lack of an effective central supervision after 1641. But like so many of Charles' sources of revenue, the retailer's licence was to return in the respectable guise of an excise tax.[8] It would be useless for an antiquarian-minded tobacconist to turn back to the months of the Grand Remonstrance,[9] item 28 of which complained of:

> the restraint of the liberties of the subject in their Habitation, Trades and other Interests

---

[1] Lords MSS., March 3, 1641; Dawney's petition.
[2] *Ibid.*, January 25, 1641; George's petition.
[3] *Ibid.*, parchment documents, no. 175; Joslyn's petition.
[4] *Mr. Grymston's Speech in Parliament* (London, 1641) cited in J. E. Brooks, *op. cit.*
[5] Thomason Tracts, (B.M.) i, 56.
[6] D. Brunton and D. H. Pennington, *Members of the Long Parliament* (1954), p. 57 citing *Commons Journal*, February 2, 1641. See also W. Notestein, ed., *D'Ewes Journal* 1923), p. 321.
[7] *Op. cit.*, p. 346; *Hist. MSS. Comm., Reports*, v, app. 1, p. 587; and vi, app. 1, p. 149.
[8] The import duty on tobacco became an excise duty in 1643: G. L. Beer, *op. cit.*, p. 346 no. 3.
[9] Rushworth, *Collections*, iv, p. 441.

or to item 115 which noted with approval that :
    the monopolies are now all supprest.
    The authority to levy a tax on all who sell tobacco now rests squarely
on Parliamentary authority.[1]

---

[1] Excise Licences Act, 1825 : 6 Geo. IV, c. 81 §2.

18

THE DECREE ROLLS OF CHANCERY AS A SOURCE

FOR ECONOMIC HISTORY 1547 -*c*. 1700

A NY reasonable assessment of the progress of historical research takes care to emphasize that patches of light and patches of darkness owe their distribution not so much to insight and blindness among the craftsmen as to the presence or absence of documentary evidence, the tools of our trade. Sometimes, however, research is frustrated not by scarcity but by abundance, and nowhere has this been more true than in those records of litigation preserved at the Public Record Office which remain uncalendared, unlisted, or unindexed. Needs are so various that, while one historian may make satisfactory progress so long as there exists a contemporary index by names of litigants, another's researches are frustrated unless there is an index of places concerned, and another type of research may make no progress through such a voluminous archive without a listing to give some indication, however rudimentary, of the matters at issue. In the seventeenth and eighteenth centuries much litigation in the Courts of Exchequer and Chancery was touched off by matters that are central to the concern of economic history, although means of access to the information embodied in the legal records quite fail to match the importance of these evidences for historical inquiry. Here and there, listings have been achieved which illustrate the range and significance of the subject-matter in a limited number of cases and for limited years: such is the List and Index of *Exchequer Commissions*

[1] This article is concerned with the origins and results of a listing of the subject-matter of cases from decree rolls of the Court of Chancery, carried out as a source investigation project sponsored by the Economic and Social History Committee of the Social Science Research Council. The lists were produced by Mrs Jennifer Booth and Mr Richard Conquest under my general oversight, and liaison with the Public Record Office was maintained through Miss Daphne Gifford, a Principal Assistant Keeper, to whom the investigators and I are grateful for encouragement and facilities. The lists compiled by the two investigators were collated and typed by the P.R.O. between June 1976 and May 1977, and are now available to researchers in the Public Record Office; the Institute of Historical Research, University of London; the British Library, Lending Division, Boston Spa; and in the S.S.R.C. office. Some 12,000 cases are listed, from 749 rolls distributed as in Table 2, below, p. 244.

for the Tudor and Stuart period, long in print[1] and supplemented by the type-script list of "Barons' Depositions";[2] such, for later years, are the superb miscell-anea of Chancery Masters' Exhibits.[3]

It has long been known, principally through Miss E. M. Leonard's work at the beginning of this century,[4] that the Court of Chancery had a special role in the history of the English enclosure movement through its willingness to accept and adjudicate actions relating to land title where enclosure and redistribution of holdings had taken place. In a period when the motives and methods of enclosure were still displaying considerable variety there are instances of Chancery actions in which the litigants were genuinely in combat: but in the majority of cases the combat of the initial pleadings is soon revealed as a posture, the alleged dissent between the parties passing into amity before the enrolled record concludes with a judgement setting out, sometimes in topographical detail as minute as any later parliamentary enclosure award, the agreed titles of the parties to their newly enclosed holdings.[5] Such fictitious lawsuits seem designed to produce only that

Table 1. *Distribution of Enclosure Agreements noted in Listing, by Roll Numbers*

Roll numbers	Number of agreements	Roll numbers	Number of agreements
1–120*	3	751–800*	0
121–200	29	801–900*	0
201–300	30	901–1000*	4
301–400	48	1001–100*	0
401–500	44	1101–200*	0
501–600	40	1201–250*	7
601–700	39		
701–750	16	Total	260

Note: Because of the complex chronological order of the rolls the earliest decrees, let alone the earliest agreements, are not necessarily in the low numbers of the sequence. The earliest agreement seems to be that for Condover, Salop. made in May 1550 and enrolled in 1586 (C.78/85, no. 15); an agreement for Walton d'Eivill, Warws. made in 1560 was the subject of an action commenced in 1630 (C.78/422, no. 6).

* Sequence sampled, see Table 2 for frequency.

Table 2. *Distribution of 749 Rolls Examined in Listing*

One-in-ten sample	One-in-five sample	Sequentially
Nos. 1–120		
		Nos. 121–750
	Nos. 751–1000	
Nos. 1001–1230		Nos. 1231–250

[1] P.R.O. *List and Indexes*, no. xxxvii (1912); the depositions forming the related class E.134 are made accessible via a pasted collection of extracts from Deputy Keepers' printed *Reports* that can be found on the shelves of the Round Room of the P.R.O.

[2] Class E.133.   [3] Classes C.103–C.114.

[4] E. M. Leonard, 'The Inclosure of Common Fields in the Seventeenth Century', *Transactions of the Royal Historical Society*, n.s. xix (1905), 101–46. The cases there cited arose from "months of searches in the decree rolls and decree books"; at the same time she carried out what seems to have been a complete examination of analogous cases in the court of the bishops of Durham.

[5] A complete transcript of C.78/586, no. 1, was printed by G. N. Clark, 'Enclosure by Agreement at Marston, near Oxford', *English Historical Review*, xlii (1927), 87–94. The Chancery procedures are not illustrated in Joan Thirsk and J. P. Cooper, eds. *Seventeenth-Century Economic Documents* (Oxford, 1972).

public declaration of title which the formal enrolment of the court's decree afforded, although the majority of the other judgements preserved on the Chancery decree rolls are concerned with actions over property that were combative, lengthy, and often legendarily expensive.

Although it is now seventy-five years since Miss Leonard drew attention to these enclosure agreements registered in Chancery, it had not proved possible to determine when this convenience was first developed for those who had locally agreed upon an enclosure; nor—more important—how many of these enclosure agreements were enrolled, and what places were involved. Unless some record of the litigation has been preserved locally[1]—and this was rare—the bulkiness of the unlisted rolls made them virtually inaccessible to local and regional agrarian historians. In the summer of 1973 the S.S.R.C. initiated source investigation projects that would open up sources for wider use, the first of which was an analytical listing of the Chancery decree rolls over the years when enclosure agreements were most likely to be found[2] (Tables 1 and 2.)

I

The source investigation projects were designed as a facility for research workers in general, and although my proposal[3] for a decree rolls listing was based on my earlier experience of the utility and frustration of the source,[4] it was not related to any continuing research of my own in enclosure history. Therefore this article is not an attempt at a substantive contribution to agrarian history, but a signal to other researchers that an important archive source is now more accessible—the (not uninteresting) archival form of the rolls is touched upon only insofar as it explains their previous impenetrability—and to assist newcomers to this source.

The substance should be of interest to economic historians with interests beyond agrarian history. Although the interest in the decree rolls began with enclosure cases, the option of searching for enclosure cases alone was rejected early in the formulation of the project in favour of a complete listing of cases in the rolls studied, giving the dates, names of parties, matters at issue, and the places concerned. With disputes over real property making up so much of Chancery litigation at that period it is not surprising if the elements of economic history exposed go beyond matters of tenure and descent, purchase and inheritance, mortgage and debt, to economic enterprises closely connected with land, especially the extraction and working of coal, stone, and mineral ores. Given the close connexion between landed wealth and trade there is litigation over money in home and overseas trade, individual and corporate. No subject index to the

---

[1] E.g. the decree for Birdsall (E.R. Yorks.) preserved among the papers of Ingram of Temple Newsam (Leeds City Archives, T.N./BL/A13: agreement of 1665; A14: award of 1692).

[2] The Committee also funded the calendaring of P.R.O. E.112, Exchequer Bills and Answers, for the period 1660–1714 under the supervision of Dr D. W. Jones of the University of York.

[3] I was a member of the Economic and Social History Committee at the time and submitted a discussion paper on the possibility of projects. After taking the advice of referees the Committee approved this project. In September and October 1974 Mrs Jennifer Booth and Mr Richard Conquest began work on the listing, each working half-time. In May 1975 Mr Conquest withdrew to accelerate the completion of his Ph.D. thesis, and the money so freed enabled Mrs Booth's appointment to be continued until the end of May 1976. I am grateful to Mrs Booth for help with this Report.

[4] M. W. Beresford, 'Habitation versus Improvement', in F. J. Fisher, ed. *Essays in the Social and Economic History of Tudor and Stuart England* (Cambridge, 1961), pp. 40–69. See above, pp. 159-88.

listing has yet been made but it is hoped that the form of each entry in the list will enable researchers to test for their interest by scanning.[1]

II

Something of the range of matters of interest to economic historians is indicated by the examples brought together in the final section of this article, but initially some account of the complex make-up of the decree rolls themselves is necessary, both to assist those who may be encouraged by the listing to make their own explorations and to show what barriers existed before the facility of the listing.

There are some 2,257 rolls in the P.R.O. class C.78, nearly all of them well preserved and legibly written. Chancery rolls normally have chronological sequences, sometimes complicated by the six clerks' offices simultaneously at work on a roll each. Many such rolls already have a P.R.O. list in which the year or years covered by a particular roll can be immediately ascertained. There was no such list for the decree rolls, and when I first began to examine them for the essay I contributed to the Tawney *Festschrift* it was immediately clear why no list had been attempted. It is true that the rolls with the lowest numbers in the sequence dated from the later years of Henry VIII's reign and that the highest numbers came from the early eighteenth century. But between these poles the sequence was remarkably tantalizing. Broadly, the lower the number of the roll the earlier the date; but as soon as any consecutive group of rolls was examined confusion was confounded. Had the Chancery clerks conspired to keep the contents privy until Domesday they could hardly have done better.

Although the later years of Elizabeth, for example, were reached in roll no. 75, cases from 38–44 Elizabeth (1595–1602) occupy all roll no. 232, and cases from 43 Elizabeth (1600–1) are found as far in the sequence as no. 308, although intervening rolls have cases from as late as 13 James I (1615–16). Cases from James I's reign occur more than 300 rolls further on, and all roll no. 707 is made up of cases from 10 Charles I (1634–5), although meanwhile other rolls in the sequence have gone past the Restoration. A case from 1 James II (1685–6) appears on roll no. 1228 alongside a case from 15 Charles I (1639–49), and cases from Charles II's reign are found in rolls with as low a numbering as 610 and as high as 1204. Within this maze a glimpse of order can appear briefly (rolls nos. 156–60, for example, all commence in 1 James I and nos. 171–6 in 6 James I), but there are no regular patterns of six such as might arise from each of the Six Clerks' offices maintaining its own sequence.[2]

The confused chronological sequence penetrates even individual rolls. An

---

[1] The form of an entry in the listing is:
C.78/713, no. 13   22 Nov. 21 Chas. II
Oliver Pocklington and Dean & Chapter of Peterborough *v.* Nicholas, Earl of Banbury and others.
Tithe and boundary dispute in manor of Irthlingborough, Northants.
C.78/714, no. 12   13 Oct. 14 Chas. II
Charles Richardson *v.* John Nicoll and others.
Factorship for selling soap.
Cases where enclosure agreements occur are signalled by having the county name in capital letters. For indirect evidence of enclosure, not signalled, see p. 249 below.

[2] The class C.79, Decree Rolls Supplementary, seems to have an equally diverse chronology although predominantly post-Restoration (from an examination of rolls 1–4 by Miss Gifford); P.R.O. Index 16960.

example has been given of the very unusual situation where a roll has all its cases from the same year, and another is roll no. 200, dated 12 James I (1614–15), but in general each roll proved to cover a wide range of dates: no. 105 spans nine years, no. 331 seventeen, and no. 642 thirty-seven.

The make-up of the sequence was a considerable barrier to one of my principal purposes in the essay, the determination of the earliest date that the facility of Chancery was opened for registering agreed enclosures: my tentative conclusions were based on sampling one roll in ten over that part of the long numerical sequence that Miss Leonard's citations suggested might contain more enclosure cases than she had noted.

It is unlikely that the Chancery clerks of that day did without some form of index. The usual practice, to judge from other types of roll, was to copy the heading or rubric of each case (giving the parties' names) consecutively into books or on to rolls making up "docquets". Docquets for decree rolls have indeed survived: they are unsorted but a first examination carried out by Miss Gifford indicates that they come from the very end of the sequence with which the investigation was concerned, and are incomplete.[1] No modern *index locorum* or *nominum* had been compiled.

Apart from their chronological confusion and their large number, there were other impediments to research carried out by scanning the rolls for particular subject-matter. The typical roll consists of some 40 parchment membranes (each about 45 cm. by 20 cm.) sewn at head and foot to make a long strip perhaps 20 m. long, which has then been wound into a tight roll. A single roll contains on average 15 cases although at extremes there is a roll with one case only, and another with 42 cases.[2] To scan any large bound volume brings its own occupational fatigues for the muscles of eye, wrist, and fingers; medieval and Tudor rolls (such as the pipe rolls and the Exchequer memoranda rolls) where the membranes are laid on top of each other and stitched together at their heads bring into play other muscles, but there can hardly be a more complex physical exercise in historical research (outside fieldwork) than handling long continuous rolls—a process involving the simultaneous winding-on of a partly read roll and unwinding of the next few inches, grappling with two spring-like coils of parchment that have to be weighted down at each interval to free the hand for writing. Since no more than a foot of roll can be comfortably exposed at any one time, the average roll demands 80 of these operations, in which even elbows and nose have been seen at work.

The dates and names of parties given in the listing derive from material in the first few lines of each enrolment where the Bill initiating the action is recited. The claims and counterclaims of the litigants are usually wordy, although the practice of common form assists distillation of the essential facts for the short statement of subject-matter needed in the list; the place or places concerned can usually be found in the course of the recital of the Bill and replication. Neither place nor subject-matter will be found in the contemporary rubric on the left-hand margin of the roll; nor all the names of the parties when several were joined in the action.

---

[1] The docquets make up class C.96; the 72 bundles are indexed in P.R.O. Index 16960 by the initial letter of plaintiffs' names; Index 16951–9 refers in the same way to the class C.78.

[2] C.78/596, C.78/399.

The numbering of the cases in the list follows that on each roll, although it should be noted that these numbers, while not modern, are not contemporary with the enrolment, since the case on the first and earliest-dated membranes of each roll, that found at the heart of the roll after unwinding, was given the highest number of that roll, the case numbered "1" being that at the head of the completed roll. Within some rolls the clerk accidentally passed over a case in his enumeration.[1] The back of the head membrane was often used as a cover, and the roll number inscribed on it in Latin in a contemporary Chancery hand. The rolls themselves form a complete sequence, although no. 395 could not be found during the listing, and no. 663 was then in too poor a condition to be handled.[2] In cases where the outer membrane had become torn or the ink on a membrane faded or worn, it was usually possible to reconstruct the lost information from repetitions later in the recital. The clarity of the handwriting made the number of totally indecipherable names or dates very few.

III

Although as now available the typed list is a unity, it was constructed from listings made by two investigators, Mr Richard Conquest and Mrs Jennifer Booth. The rolls were not searched in strict sequence, since in the early stages of the investigation it was not known from which years each roll derived, and in an attempt to penetrate the disorder an interval listing was undertaken, first every tenth roll and then every fifth. The early rolls in the numerical sequence proved to have no enclosure cases, and the later rolls also showed the movement slowing down at a time when private Bill legislation was beginning to offer an alternative path for registering agreed enclosures (Table 1). It was already a well-known fact in enclosure history that some of the earlier Acts were simply to confirm agreements, including some already enrolled in Chancery, as if to make assurance trebly sure.[3] In the central and larger part of the numerical sequence, as Table 2 shows, the searches extended to every roll. (It is thus not impossible that an occasional enclosure case may still be found in the unexamined rolls in the sequence nos. 1–120 and, of course, in the higher numbers with presumed dates later than 1714.[4])

The issues before the court in "enclosure" cases were usually those of disputed titles to the post-enclosure distribution of land, be the challenge to their legitimacy real or fictitious. An enclosure, however, with its obliteration of old property rights and the establishment of new ones, was an event calculated to raise side-issues that could produce genuine contention such as the Court of Chancery regularly took within its jurisdiction, just as the Court of Exchequer acted where crown lands or tithes were involved.

It would therefore be prudent for anyone pursuing a suspected local enclosure

---

[1] C.78/166, between cases 18 and 19; C.78/376 between cases 1 and 2.

[2] The missing roll may in fact be the number assigned to a sack of miscellaneous documents before their removal for storage at the Ashridge repository (ex. inf. Miss Gifford).

[3] E.g. 4 Wm and Mary (Private), no. 40 (1694), confirmed a Chancery decree for Hambleton, Rutland, made in 1653.

[4] A (partial) enclosure at Wigston Magna, Leics. known from W. G. Hoskins, *The Midland Peasant* (1957), p. 108, though not there given a P.R.O. citation, occurs in C.78/73, no. 7; two of the decrees cited in *V.C.H. Leicestershire*, II (1954), 254–9, were numbered 1335 and 1581, showing that agreements can be expected in the rolls beyond the listing limit of no. 1250, arbitrarily fixed by the funds available.

in this period to follow up all references in the list for suits involving landed property in that place. Disputes over what are loosely called "the customs of the manor" have certainly produced oblique evidences of this sort, the customs proving to be matters of common husbandry, grazing, woodland, or other common rights within a manor. The enclosure of the glebe has already been used as an indication of date for early partial or total enclosure of the commons in a parish,[1] and the Appendix shows that Chancery cases over glebe can also provide oblique evidence for enclosure in this period. The character of the two cases cited does not exclude the possibility that this type of action also could be collusive. More study may indeed show that there was an element of fictional conflict in this type of case also: there are certainly signs in "customs-of-the-manor" cases before the Court of Exchequer that they were designed to register recent changes negotiated with the tenants of royal manors.[2] Disputes over tithes, although not often resulting in Chancery proceedings, have produced a good number of oblique references to early enclosure.[3]

The immediate gain to agrarian history is the bringing to light of 260 agreements distributed between counties as in Table 3. Leicestershire is seen to be the county with the largest number, closely followed by Northamptonshire and Lincolnshire. These midland counties, always at the heart of the enclosure debate, are not unexpected in the list; nor is the presence of Warwickshire, although its number is smaller: Yorkshire, virtually untouched by anti-enclosure measures in the classic period of strife, has a remarkable number of concords.

Since Leicestershire is a county where the agrarian history of this period has been worked from a number of other sources, it provides an opportunity of measuring the quantity and quality of the new information from the 30 decrees of Table 3. Seven of these were already known to Dr Thirsk when she compiled her summary list of pre-parliamentary enclosures for the *V.C.H.*[4] using the classic county history of John Nichols and modern work by Parker, Hoskins, and myself; two other decrees were listed there from rolls much higher up the numerical sequence than the S.S.R.C. listing was able to go.[5] The other 23 decrees now listed give more precise dates than the range of dates (e.g. Sysonby, 1600–50) that the sources known in 1954 would allow (Sysonby, 1626: roll 270, no. 2). No

[1] M. W. Beresford, 'Glebe Terriers and Open Field Leicestershire', in W. G. Hoskins, ed. *Studies in Leicestershire Agrarian History* (Leicester, 1948), pp. 77–126, and other studies of Bucks. and Yorks.

[2] M. W. Beresford in Fisher, above, pp. 181-2. In the centuries before the period of Dr E. J. Evans's *Contentious Tithe* (1976) there are many unstudied disputes over tithe, both in the ecclesiastical courts and in Exchequer. For the former see an example in J. S. Purvis, ed. *Select Sixteenth-Century Causes in Tithe* (Yorkshire Archaeological Society Record Series, cxiv (1949)), and for Exchequer, *Report of the Deputy Keeper of the Public Records*, ii (1841), app. ii, pp. 249–72. In 1600 a surveyor of the royal manor of Settrington, Yorks. E.R. envisaged an agreement being registered in either Chancery or Exchequer (H. King and A. Harris, eds. *A Survey of the Manor of Settrington* (Yorkshire Archaeological Society Record Series, cxxvi (1962)). In the event an agreement was not made until 1668 and a decree enrolled in Chancery in April 1670: C.78/692, no. 6.

[3] An enclosure, by shifting property boundaries and usually altering the balance between arable and pasture, was always likely to arouse disputes over the tithes payable on the yield of the soil and the increase of animals, particularly after the passage of time when even the oldest inhabitants were forgetting the old order. "The tithe barn is fallen down," noted Archbishop Sharp of one of his parishes in 1700, "the town they tell me has now no inhabitants but the parson and the shepherds" (Borthwick Institute, York, Bp.Dio.3, p. 124: Kilnwick Percy, Yorks. E.R.).

[4] *V.C.H. Leicestershire*, ii (1954), 254–9.

[5] Eastwell, C.78/1335, and Long Whatton, C.78/1581.

Table 3. *Distribution of Enclosure Agreements
noted in Listing, by Counties*

Beds.	3	Norfolk	16
Berks.	4	Northants.	26
Bucks.	7	Northumb.	1
Cambs.	12	Notts.	3
Ches.	0	Oxon.	8
Cornwall	0	Rutland	2
Cumb.	1	Salop	3
Derby.	5	Som.	5
Devon	5	Staffs.	9
Dorset	5	Suffolk	2
Durham	1	Surrey	1
Essex	2	Sussex	5
Glos.	10	Warws.	19
Hants.	0	Westmld.	1
Herefs.	2	Wilts.	8
Herts.	1	Worcs.	0
Hunts.	7	Yorks.	23
Kent	2	Montgom.	1
Lancs.	1	Monmouth	2
Leics.	30	Uncertain	1
Lincs.	24		
Middx.	2	Total	260

list of agreements for Warwickshire or Northamptonshire had been attempted.

Finally, now that the names of parties are given in the listings, it will be possible for those interested in particular cases, whether of enclosure or other matters, to follow those names through the classes of Chancery documents that do have contemporary or modern indexes by names; the pleadings are usually recited quite fully in the decree roll but the depositions, where traceable, should be a useful supplement.[1]

IV

To turn from enclosure, overseas trading brought litigants into Chancery chiefly to resolve disputes over debts, especially those of partnerships dissolved by insolvency, disagreement, or death. Accounts were particularly likely to be disputed, and, since they had to be proved, their content found its way to the record, sometimes in considerable detail. Thus the Foleys deliver iron, but do not get paid (1639);[2] a trader's accounts for cinnamon from Barbados and the West Indies come into court;[3] apart from the accounts of innumerable partnerships, the court considered those of the supervisor of the glassworks and ash houses at Newcastle upon Tyne (1651),[4] the salary of a factor at Blackwell Hall (1660),[5] the hiring and passage money of plantation workers for Barbados (1644),[6] and the accounts of a joint stock in a voyage to China (1672).[7] Factorships and apprenticeships in foreign trade frequently generated friction in the Spanish trade

[1] Mrs Booth, at the end of her searches of the rolls, followed up the names of parties in 207 of the enclosure actions, but found only 39 cross-references in other Chancery classes; no matters of substance emerged in these particular cases that were not known from the decree. (E.g. C.78/168, no. 8 (Newport, Essex), leads to C.3/283/73; C.78/277, no. 4 (Hawton, Notts.), to C.3/306/118 and C.9/20/28.) The relationship of the decree rolls and the decree books (class C.33) needs further investigation.

[2] C.78/626, no. 7a.

[3] 632, no. 3: in this and the subsequent footnotes the class number C.78 is omitted.   [4] 522, no. 5.

[5] 572, no. 3.   [6] 735, no. 13.   [7] 800, no. 3.

(1618);[1] the Portuguese trade (1624);[2] in silk at Aleppo (1637),[3] in wool there (1663),[4] and in velvet (1613),[5] pitch, hemp and flax (1576) elsewhere.[6] Mortgaged lands in Boxted, Essex, were expressly said to have provided capital for the cloth trade in 1625,[7] and in 1612 Sir Horatio Palavicino was sued for a debt of £100,000 for goods traded into the Low Countries although the sum is suspiciously round,[8] as is the number of one thousand workmen said to be employed by a Lavenham, Suffolk, clothier in the same year.[9] There are accounts for the purchase of (white) Christian slaves to free them from the infidel Turk in 1629[10] and for the purchase of black (presumably Christian) slaves for the Guinea trade in 1641.[11]

A ship in the Calcutta trade was insured, but not against litigation (1560);[12] and the lighthouses at Dungeness and Winterton Ness brought their toll-owners into Chancery (1623 and 1630).[13] Domestic trade and transport so lack documentation in this period (as Dr Chartres has recently shown) that almost any piece of information is intellectually marketable, whether in rough iron,[14] cheese and butter,[15] wool,[16] salt,[17] buffalo hides,[18] cottons,[19] or gentlemen's suiting.[20] Again, to stay with Dr Chartres, the inn-holder and the inn-holder's widow were frequently in Chancery, especially on matters of tenancies and sub-tenancies.[21]

More often the lines of domestic trade have to be read, like vapour trails, from evidence about production. Production within the domestic system does not occur frequently, nor do issues arising from retailing, where the litigants (even if able to afford Chancery) would not be of the standing to require or afford a formal enrolment of a decree. The extractive industries, because of their uncertainties and their close connexion with land and landowners, were especially litigious to the level of decrees. Disputes over ironworks have been noted from one end of England to another, from Millom, Cumberland,[22] to Horsted Keynes, Sussex;[23] and coal from Lambton, Durham (with provision of machinery and workmen's houses),[24] to the Somerset field at Stratton on Foss;[25] saltpetre at Nantwich (1568)[26] and salt at Droitwich (1561)[27] are quite expected, but less common is a dispute over the techniques of making earthenware pots (1621)[28] and the accounts of a clerk of the furnaces (Iping, Sussex, 1634).[29] Accounts for building a brick manor house at Theydon Mount, Essex (1601),[30] a new deanery at Wells in 1612,[31] a workhouse at Shrewsbury (1652),[32] and new work for Brasenose College in 1660 will be noted.[33]

No litigious Shakespeare has emerged from behind the arras, but the tangled finances of play production do find themselves exposed in two decrees, one concerning John Hemmings, his fellow-actor, a mortgagor of the Globe Theatre in 1611,[34] and the other a posthumous investigation of the partnership held by Thomas Green in the Players' Company of the late Queen Elizabeth.[35] The

---

[1] 203, no. 4.   [2] 219, no. 6.   [3] 366, no. 8.   [4] 698, no. 6.   [5] 152, no. 5.   [6] 95, no. 1.
[7] 412, no. 14.   [8] 191, no. 14.   [9] 146, no. 1.   [10] 312, no. 11.   [11] 463, no. 5.
[12] 20, no. 33.   [13] 268, no. 18, and 240, no. 4.   [14] 332, no. 2.   [15] 343, no. 5.   [16] 485, no. 1.
[17] 390, no. 3.   [18] 340, no. 18.   [19] 527, no. 6.   [20] 292, no. 4.
[21] E.g. Golden Eagle, Cannon St: 290, no. 13; Golden Anchor, West Smithfield: 299, no. 6; Red Lion, Cambridge, 311, no. 15.
[22] 353, no. 7.   [23] 168, no. 15.   [24] 616, no. 7.   [25] 437, no. 7.   [26] 30, no. 10.
[27] 368, no. 8.   [28] 244, no. 14.   [29] 416, no. 6.   [30] 124, no. 3.   [31] 131, no. 4.
[32] 488, no. 3.   [33] 587, no. 1.   [34] 227, no. 5.   [35] 297, no. 11.

economics of literature also occur in the suit over the costs of printing the fourth edition (1631) of Knolles's *Turkish History*[1] and of 300 Welsh bibles in 1646.[2]

The alleged misuse of charitable funds gave specialist employment to the commissioners for charitable uses, after the Acts of 1597 and 1601, but besides their own decrees the Chancery itself was much concerned with the affairs of orphans, widows, almshouses, apprentices, schools, and the like. In 1656 a suit concerned every one of the town charities of Warwick.[3] At the highest levels of education, a scheme to establish a lectureship in history at Cambridge was reviewed by the court[4] (in March 1641, just in time for the English Revolution) and one for a chair in moral theology in 1682.[5] The bursars of colleges had their accounts questioned and reviewed not infrequently, but perhaps the most exotic element from higher education is the suit of ejection that a predecessor of Lord Briggs had to take to end a sit-in by the late master's widow so that he could take up residence in the master's lodgings of Gloucester Hall, Oxford: a justly neglected episode in economic history.[6]

[1] 378, no. 8.   [2] 479, no. 12.   [3] 563, no. 6.   [4] 471, no. 17.   [5] 980, no. 4.
[6] 712, nos. 1, 19.

APPENDIX

Specimen Oblique References to Enclosure

C.78/360, no. 6: decree of 5 May 1629. Hardwick, Northants.

John Gaynard, rector of Hardwick, *v.* Francis Nicoll. In 1585–6 an agreement was made between Lord Mordaunt, now deceased, and Francis Nicoll, deceased, and Henry Reade, then rector, concerning the glebe of 24a. 3r. 4p. at the time of a "general enclosure". After the present rector's institution he claimed that he could not distinguish the glebe lands from others. The defendant admits the claim and a commission is appointed to partition the lands, and on its certification a decree issued.

C.78/360, no. 4: decree of 25 November 1629. Kingthorpe, Northants.

Mabel Morgan, widow of Francis Morgan, *v.* Samuel Clarke, doctor of divinity, incumbent of Kingthorpe. About 1614 Francis Morgan carried out an enclosure by assent of the freeholders and inhabitants, including in it the four acres of glebe. Defendant requests a commission to examine whether the enclosure was prejudicial or beneficial to the living. Both sides agree to a commission, and on its certification a decree issued.

19

THE UNPRINTED CENSUS RETURNS

OF 1841, 1851 AND 1861 FOR ENGLAND AND WALES

The first Census, taken on the night of 10th March, 1801, was planned at a time of considerable uncertainty about the total population of Great Britain. Everywhere, from the new streets of London suburbs to the new mills of the North, there was plenty of visible evidence that population was increasing daily, but no clear evidence of how fast or whether the rate of increase was greater than in the past. The numbering of the people was thought useful by the Army and Navy: for it was the period of the wars against Napoleon and invasion scares were in the air. Had not the landing of a small force in South Wales caused a wave of panic that closed the doors of the Bank of England? Those who paid the ever-mounting poor rates and those who administered the Poor Law were also concerned to have solid fact in place of conjecture. For was it not the age of Malthus, who saw the poor breeding like rabbits with hunger and death the certain rewards for fecundity? It was also the time of the first Income Tax, the first crop census, and the first surveys by the Board of Ordnance. This official passion for collecting data was not disinterested.

In its nature, a complete Census had to be organised in small local units. No Civil Service existed to carry out the counting of nine million heads. The basic counting, by parishes, was entrusted by the Home Office to Overseers of the Poor or other substantial householders. Supplementary questions, concerned with the baptisms and burials recorded in the parish registers since 1700 and the marriages since 1754, were addressed to the parish clergy in England and Wales; but in Scotland—perhaps symbolically—to the Schoolmaster.

Two printed volumes summarise the data collected in 1801 and present the total population of counties, parishes and townships. Part One of the

Enumeration Abstracts (published 1801) concerned England and Wales. Part Two (published in 1802) covered Scotland. A third volume (also published in 1801) summarised the information gathered from parish registers for the purpose of estimating past populations and the rate of increase. Similar enquiries were made in 1811, 1821 and 1831. *Abstracts* were published in 1812, 1822, and 1831-3.

These printed totals are indispensable for local historians concerned with the numbers of people in their township, parish or county. For a number of counties they have been brought together in tabular form in volumes of the *Victoria County Histories*, often with useful comments on changes of boundary that took place between census years and on amalgamations of townships and parishes. To ignore boundary changes of this kind would, of course, bedevil the evidence.

With successive ten-yearly Censuses (only 1941 being allowed to lapse) the questions asked and the tabulation of results have become more and more complex. Anyone who wishes to see the range of information in the printed *Census Reports* and to obtain the proper reference numbers for finding these volumes among sets of Parliamentary Papers in libraries (or for ordering copies of particular sections from libraries which undertake photo copying) must consult a magnificent official pamphlet published in 1951 and written by L. M. Feery of the General Register Office, Somerset House. Its full title is *Interdepartmental Committee on Social and Economic Research : Guides to Official Sources No. 2, Census Reports of Great Britain, 1801-1931*. This gargantuan title affords library-cataloguers a fine range of choices. It will not be catalogued under the author's name, having the anonymity of a committee paper. Its cost on publication was 3s. 6d. and it can be ordered from H.M. Stationery Office under the code 70-561-2. No recommendation to purchase can be too strong.

The printed volumes of Census Reports are concerned with totals for places. But for 1841, 1851 and 1861 the student has access to documents from which the totals were built up. Their utility is not to check the arithmetic of the final tabulators but to offer detailed information about individuals and individual households as they existed on these three Census nights. These files have been moved from their original home at the General Register Office to the Public Record Office where the Long Search Room specialises in their production. The remainder of this article is concerned with the content of these documents, their utility for historians, and the system of indexes that is available at the P.R.O. for those who wish to read the documents or to have them photo copied by the various means available.

For 1841, 1851 and 1861 the documents available are the *Enumeration Schedules*. In 1841, for example, the country was first divided into the 2,193 Registration Districts that had been fixed when civil registration of births, marriages and deaths was begun by the Registrar General in 1837. These were then sub-divided into Enumeration Districts in such a way that no District had fewer than twenty-five or more than 200 inhabited houses. The individual enumerators, 35,000 of them in all, covered these Districts, and for the first time in 1841 it was judged that the literacy of the population was sufficient for forms to be distributed to householders in the same way as in current Censuses. These forms were then collected and checked by enumerators and the information was copied by them into printed books of blank forms, each about 9″ by 12″. It is these books, in the handwriting of the enumerators, that form the *Enumeration Schedules* available for study. To find a particular house or street, therefore, it is necessary to know the Registration District and Enumeration District in which it lay: otherwise a scrutiny of successive volumes would be necessary. (Aids to locating streets within Districts are described below.)

In the documents of 1841 there are six basic pieces of information for each household. These are arranged horizontally across the page in the original forms, but for convenience are set out here vertically.

1. *Place* (Street-name where appropriate; occasionally house-number; house-name for all large houses.)
2. *Houses, whether Uninhabited, Building, or Inhabited* (A vertical stroke in the appropriate column with *U* or *B* for empty or half-built houses.)
3. *Name of each Person who abode therein the preceding Night* (One forename and the surname.)
4. *Age and Sex* (A column for each sex. Age rounded to nearest five years.)
5. *Profession, Trade, Employment or of Independent Means*
6. *Where Born* (A column to be marked Y for yes, if born in the same county as residence on Census night. No, if outside; a separate column if born in Scotland, Ireland or Foreign Parts.)

The columns of each page were totalled and these totals then brought together on another page.

What are the principal uses to which this mass of personal information may be put? There will be those whose prime interest will be in the identification of persons in some form of genealogy. If the parish is a small rural one, the search for an individual ancestor suspected to be living there would not take long. In the large towns it would be a long quest down the pages unless the street or district were known; and in the case of common names like James Smith there could be no certainty in blind searches. In succeeding lines the names of the rest of the family will be given, and here even one James Smith may be distinguished from the hundreds if it is known that he had children with particular names. The ages given for the head of the household, wife and children also narrow the search a little. Thus, I find a John Smith in Hyde Terrace, Leeds, but also see that he was then aged forty (i.e. born in 1801), his wife five years younger and their children seven and one. (Actual, unrounded ages for children under 15 are given.) Their christian names being also given, a genealogist might find his needle in the urban haystacks.

Since county and 'foreign' origins are distinguished, another piece of the jigsaw can be completed. The John Smith cited above, for example, was born in Scotland. The details of occupation would also help to narrow down the search. Where the name is less unusual or the address known the Occupation column will be rewarding in its own right. One must allow for a little self up-grading, perhaps, but there is no mistaking successive entries such as Banker, Female Servant, Solicitor, Woollen Manufacturer. This John Smith has got himself a good address. The contemporary meaning of the occupational terms, with a discussion of the local pattern of occupations, will be found in two volumes of *Abstracts : Occupations* published in 1844 as House of Commons Order Paper nos. 587-8, and the pamphlet cited above devotes thirty-eight pages to this topic.

There will be local historians concerned, as I have been myself lately, not with the history of the individuals as such, but with the history of houses and streets. The Census documents can prove that a particular house was or was not built in 1841, 1851 or 1861 (or that it was in course of erection). They tell if it was empty and hence explain why it might not have been in a local *Directory* of that year. They tell how many houses were in a particular street, and sometimes of streets with changed names. In streets that are un-numbered in *Directories* they suggest in what order the houses may have been placed. And since *Directories*, even in the largest towns, were not published annually the Census gives a foothold for what otherwise might be a five or six year leap in tracing a house or its occupants.

The history of a house is not simply its date of building. The size of family for which new houses were intended, or the size of families that an old house was sheltering is a very significant piece of local social history. Indeed, work on these original *Enumeration Schedules* is the only way that information about the size of families residing together can be obtained, even for large units and the whole kingdom, for the published *Abstracts* did not concern themselves with this statistic. Size of family residing together in one house and the age-structure of the household are not, of course, those of the whole family. Children could have left home, be on holiday elsewhere or away at boarding school. But the age structures of these truncated and 'artificial' groups were significant. The local shopkeeper and the local employer were not unaffected by them.

The age of children living at home, the age of children at work (and the occupation seen fit for young children) can of course be ascertained: as well as the age-structure of an early Victorian household. In the house now occupied by the Department of Education of Leeds University, for example, John Sykes and his wife had children aged 15, 15, 8, 7, and 6. But this was not the whole household; there was a paternal grandmother and a young governess and four female servants.

Indeed, the servants of these households of 1841 are an important element in social history, quite apart from anyone (like myself) pursuing ancestresses among them. The ratio of servants to members of the family Above Stairs is an interesting piece of arithmetic to perform. If this is set alongside different occupations we learn a little more, and it may surprise some to discover that servants were normal in what look today (after the passage of 120 years of wear and tear) as very mean houses indeed. At the other end of the social scale one might work out the numbers and distribution of men (and women) of Independent Means, and in the meaner streets work out a ratio of lodgers. Taking in lodgers to support you was the other pole from you supporting servants. The sub-divided house with more than one family shown by the enumerator is another important social feature. It will be seen by 1841 that many old houses at the centre of towns had become tenements, and realistic figures on levels of population per square yard can be worked out by joining the Census figures for particular houses to the house areas shown on the contemporary large-scale ordnance survey plans or from the houses themselves where they survive.

The empty house, new or old, was a familiar feature of nineteenth century England whenever speculative building and the numbers and levels of people's incomes had failed to match each other. The printed *Abstracts* reveal how many houses were empty in each place in 1841—a comparatively prosperous year—but the documents under discussion enable these to be located in particular streets of a town. Indeed, it is the penetration behind the generalised statistics for a whole parish or a whole town that gives this class of document its greatest utility. To catch the flavour of a single street; its range of occupations; the possible 'foreign' origin of some; the houses empty and the houses a-building: this is the basic material of local social history and it throws light on more than local trivia. These are major clues to different social structures in different parts of England when economic change had in one place exiled the hand-loom weaver while elsewhere he could still make a living; where some parts were made up of people who were virtually born round the corner and others peopled by immigrants from parts really 'foreign', Scotland and Ireland. After all, on Census Night 1841 were not 5,016 persons enumerated as passengers in railway trains? No one (as far as I know) has analysed the composition of these travellers, their trains at an everlasting signal stop in the Census documents. It would be an interesting exercise.

The personnel gathered within the residential institutions of Victorian England are also revealed by the Registrar General's all-seeing eye: palaces— and the Palace itself—poor law institutions, barracks, ships in harbour, public schools, asylums, homes for fallen women, colleges of ancient universities and of the University of Durham, doss houses, clergy training schools and residential hotels are all assembled as if the world had come to an end on these Census nights and the recording angel had already begun his work, but got no further than age, sex, occupation and place of birth. But for social historians that is quite a long way.

The *Enumeration Schedules* of the 1851 Census were compiled by similar methods to 1841 but the questions asked and the form of the documents are more elaborate. The printed page was elongated to take the extra columns. The information available in these columns is as follows:

1. *Name of Street with Name or Number of House* (Numbers become the normal thing in towns and greatly aid matching with the *Directories*; and with the un-numbered streets of 1841 when families appear in both Censuses.)
2. *Names and Surnames* (More than one name often given; also some initials.)
3. *Relation to Head of Family (including Servant).* (This column removes ambiguities in 1841 such as whether a Jane Smith is the Householder's wife or the sister of a widower or of a bachelor.)
4. *Condition: Married or Unmarried, Widower or Widow*
5. *Age and Sex* (Actual age was asked for on this occasion.)
6. *Rank, Profession or Occupation*
7. *Where Born* (The actual place is now specified.)
8. *Whether Blind, Deaf or Dumb*

These documents of 1851 can be put to all the uses suggested above for 1841, with some important additions, and improvements. We have ages to the nearest year. The numbering of houses is a great boon in identifying people and houses within streets. The identification of members of a household is clarified by the statement of relationship with the head. Under Occupations, employers were asked to state how many men they employed, and in the case of master farmers the acreage they worked. This information, although sometimes avoided, is a very useful supplement to the limited information available about the size of particular factories in the mid-nineteenth century; and about non-factory groups of masters and work-people.

The statement of actual place of birth is an enormous boon. It provides much more refined information about internal migration which, as Professor Redford's *Labour Migration in England* showed, was so important in an industrialising and expanding economy. These documents of 1851, after all, come from the year of the Great Exhibition.

The genealogist will also be grateful for the news of places of birth. It will suggest to him where, an appropriate number of years earlier, he must begin to search parish registers for a record of birth and parents. Since so many people had migrated townwards in the previous generation, these clues back to country parish registers are of great utility. In some cases, of course, it sends the chase overseas. I note that the manager of the Leeds Gas Works was born in Manchester forty-five years before 1851: but his neighbour Charles Louis Wurtzburg, wool merchant, was born in the same year in Hamburg and his wife in Berlin; yet their eldest daughter had been born in Leeds, Yorkshire.

In 1851 additional schedules were delivered to houses where schools were carried on. Return of these was on a voluntary basis but more than 68,000 were returned. In 1854 a special Report (*Education: England and Wales*) was issued as Command Paper 1692. The ordinary Schedules indicate whether particular children are *Scholars*. Schools can be identified by the occupation of the Master or Mistress; and an abnormal number of 'Scholars' highlights residential schools.

In 1851 details of places of religious worship were collected by the enumerators, again on a voluntary basis. These are summarised in *Religious Worship, England and Wales*, Command Paper 1690 of 1853.

The Schedules of 1861 became available for study towards the end of 1962. Despite the passage of a century, a period usually regarded as safe for the revelation even of State secrets, it required the questioning and pressure of M.P.s to have the documents transferred from Somerset House to the P.R.O. It is sad to report that their physical condition is much inferior to those of 1841 and 1851. Pages are loose, bindings weak and many volumes are too damaged to be produced for readers. Others seem to be missing completely. This negligence by their former guardians at Somerset House, successive Registrar Generals, is hardly credible in a repository that the public in general imagines to be the safe custodian of the paper records of their passage through this life. One is reminded of the comments of William Prynne when he went to the White Tower in 1661 to find the public records in 'desolation, corruption, confusion in which (through the Negligence, Nescience or Sloathfulnesse of their former Keepers) they had for many years past layen buried together in confused Chaos under corroding putryfying Cobwebs, Dust, Filth, in the darkest corner . . . as mere useless Reliques'.

These *useful Reliques* of 1861 follow the same form as those described above for 1851 and it will not be necessary to set out again the columns of the Enumeration Schedules.

Although pencil was much used by Enumerators it has stood the passage of time very well and in general does not lose clarity when copied photographically. Research workers unable to cope with the strait opening hours of the P.R.O. (will amateurs ever succeed in getting an evening opening akin to that of the British Museum Reading Room?) will be dependent on photographic copies. But unless they are prepared to place orders for the whole of a Registration District they will need to pay at least a short visit to the Long Room to locate the documents and identify the page or pages which they require for the study of their street or district. If all that is required is information about one family, the data can probably be extracted on the spot.

It would be quite wrong to expect the officers of the Photographic Department at the P.R.O. (always extremely helpful) to look up the volume and page reference for a particular house in a particular street. The assistance available from manuscript or typewritten Indexes on the shelves of the Long Room will now be outlined; these useful volumes have not been published but can be photographically copied in whole or part. A librarian, for example, considering the acquisition of a set of his local census documents (such as the small Library at Ilkley has energetically obtained) might well consider having pages of these Indexes copied as well.

The P.R.O. call-number for the Censuses of 1841 and 1851 is H.O. 107. To discover which box within this class contains the Enumeration Schedules for a particular place one should go first to the Index volumes shelved at A93A and A93B. These are actually the printed *Enumeration Abstract* of 1843 (House of Commons Order Paper No. 496) bound in two volumes with the box numbers added against each place. If the location of a place within its county and hundred are already known it is a very short task to find its page in the *Abstract* and from this the box number. If the location is not exactly known, there is a second set of Index volumes, shelved at A94A-D, which take another printed volume, *The Alphabetical List of Parishes and Places*, published by the Board of Inland Revenue in 1897, and add to each place-name the appropriate H.O. 107 reference both for 1841 and 1851. Thus we learn that Abbas, Hampshire, appears in box H.O. 107/403 in 1841 and in H.O. 107/1673 in 1851.

The Indexes for 1851 akin to the *Abstract* for 1841 at A93A-B are in three volumes shelved at A93C, A93D and A93E. Their contents are arranged similarly.

By 1851 the size of the largest towns was such that many boxes would need to be consulted to cover the houses in any Registration District numbered in the *Abstract*. Alphabetical street-indexes have therefore been compiled for a number of towns. These are also on shelf A. Page one of A95F, for example, gives the reference for the various boxes and volumes that contain the details for Halifax streets from Abbots Royd to Albion Street. The following towns have street indexes:

ASHTON UNDER LYNE	95B	CHELTENHAM	*
BATH	95C	CHESTER	*
BEDMINSTER	95B	CLIFTON	95E
BIRKENHEAD	*	COVENTRY	*
BIRMINGHAM	95D	DEVONPORT	95S
BOLTON	95B	EXETER	*
BRADFORD	95D	GATESHEAD	*
BRIGHTON	95C	HALIFAX	95F
BRISTOL	95E	HUDDERSFIELD	95F

HULL	95E	PRESTON	95U	
HUNSLET	95H	READING	*	
IPSWICH	*	ROCHDALE	95O	
KIDDERMINSTER	*	ST. HELENS	*	
KINGS LYNN	*	SHEFFIELD	95V	
KINGSWINFORD	*	SHREWSBURY	*	
LEEDS	95H	STOKE ON TRENT	*	
LEICESTER	95G	SOUTH SHIELDS	*	
LIVERPOOL	95G	STAFFORD	*	
LONDON	95I, J, K, L	STOCKPORT	95O	
MANCHESTER	95N	STOKE DAMEREL	95S	
NEWCASTLE ON TYNE	95NN	STONEHOUSE, EAST	95S	
NEWPORT Mon	*	SUNDERLAND	95W	
NORTHAMPTON	*	SWANSEA	*	
NORWICH	95Q	TOXTETH PARK	95G	
NOTTINGHAM	95H	TONBRIDGE	*	
OLDHAM	95R	WAKEFIELD	*	
OXFORD	95N	WARRINGTON	95O	
PLYMOUTH	95S	WORCESTER	*	
PORTSMOUTH	95T			

* Incomplete index available on request at the counter of the Long Room.

For 1861 the only Index yet available is by Registration Districts (A96L and A96M). To find a given street within one of these Districts it is necessary to send for the boxes one by one. One Leeds District, for example, occupies ten boxes. There is an ominous note in the Index advising reference to a list kept at the Long Room counter which sets out the documents tactfully described as Unfit for Production. Even a brief experience has shown me that this confession of negligent guardianship is an understatement and it is possible to fill in a slip and have it returned with a note that a volume (R.G. 9/3388) was missing when its fellows came to the P.R.O. from Somerset House. Thus seven Enumeration Districts are gone for ever. The P.R.O. call-number for 1861 Census documents is R.G.9.

A reference number accurately copied on to a slip will eventually produce a cardboard box bearing that number. Within the box should be found all the volumes of the Enumerators' Schedules for the particular Registration District. (Subdivision of the largest files into two boxes is sometimes encountered.) Each volume covers one Enumeration District. It has a page which sets out its contents by describing the boundaries of the area that it comprises. H.O. 107/1349, for example, has within it a volume with the following data on its prefatory page.

County of York   Parliamentary Division *West Riding*
Wapentake *Skyrack*
Parish   *Leeds*
Township   *Leeds*
Borough Corporate of *Leeds*
Within the Limits of the Parliamentary Boundary of the Borough of *Leeds*

Within the Municipal Boundary of *West Ward*
Superintendent Registrar's District *Leeds*
Registrar's District *Leeds West*
No. of Enumeration District 18
Description of ditto: 'Includes that portion of the West Ward comprised within the boundaries: commencing at the Corner of Woodhouse Lane and Cankerwell Lane taking the West side of Cankerwell Lane and the North and East sides of the Leeds and Otley Road to the point where the same enters Woodhouse Moor, then taking the South side of the footpath and road leading from that point into Woodhouse Lane by Mr. Tottie's House, and taking the South-West side of Woodhouse Lane to and terminating at the point first mentioned'.

A contemporary town plan will usually afford sufficient topographical detail to recognise the interior of an area so described. It is important to note, finally, that since the boundaries of these Districts followed the centre of streets for some of their course, a street may be divided between more than one District. It is not only that a long street may be crossed by an Enumeration District boundary but that each side of a street might be in a different Enumeration District. An important town street might have to be sought in perhaps four or six books. A really important street which formed the boundary of a Registration District would have its documents not only in different books but in different boxes (with different call-numbers). This explains the multiple reference numbers for some streets in Town Street Indexes A95B to A95V (above).

The printed books which the Enumerators of 1841 filled in were already paginated, so that a page number, an Enumeration District number and a call-number (Registration District) should be a precise reference (e.g. H.O. 107/1349, *District* 18, *page* 28 should lead one to the household of Thomas Boyne, tobacconist, who by 1841 had built himself a residence in Woodhouse, Leeds, that he appropriately called Virginia Cottage. It is now occupied by the Warden of a University Hall.) The 1851 books of Schedules seem to have three systems of pagination, with some possibility of confusion. Thus, one page of H.O. 107/2321 (Leeds, West, 1851) is numbered 163 in pencil; 6 in print and 1042 by a mechanical number-stamper. Those who cite references or wish to order photographic copies should state which system they are following.

POSTSCRIPT: Since this article was written, two further index volumes have been added to the shelves of the Long Room at the P.R.O. They have press-marks A96N and A96O and consist of the *Population Tables* of 1861 (Command 3056 and 3221) annotated for some counties in red ink.

20

BUILDING HISTORY
FROM FIRE INSURANCE RECORDS
An autobiographical fragment

1

With documentary sources, as with one's friends, it is never easy to recall exactly when mere acquaintance passed into familiarity.[1] I am somewhat shaken to see from its footnotes that when I wrote my chapter for the Chapman symposium[2] in 1969-70 that I made no use of fire insurance policies for the dating of house-building, relying mainly on conveyances, estate-plans, rate books, press advertisements and family papers; the same range of sources employed over a far wider geographical area in Christopher Chalklin's recent study.[3] My love affair with insurance policies is therefore relatively recent, and that of an ageing researcher, not to be compared with the amatory techniques of others who were using them for industrial history well before 1971.[4] I have been an old man in a hurry, a scanner rather than a scholar; and these practical notes from a scanner will be superseded if the S.S.R.C. project for an index to the main registers is ever realized.,

Until then even the scholarly will have to scan, if they wish to use policy registers for the history of particular buildings, builders, and built-up areas, since the oldest company with surviving records, the Sun, issued nearly 700,000 policies between 1710 and 1799 and passed the million by 1823; the Royal Exchange policy registers do not survive before 1753 when 29,200 policies had already been issued and are not extant for 1759-73: by 1823 that company had issued nearly 350,000 policies.[5] It is not, however, the sheer bulk of the evidence, covering

---

1   All manuscript references, unless indicated, are to the Guildhall Library, London E.C.2.

2   S.D. Chapman, Ed. *The History of Working-Class Housing* (1971), 93 - 132.

3   C.W. Chalklin, *The Provincial Towns of Georgian England* (1974).

4   A brief survey by J. H. Thomas was published in 1968 (*History*, liii, 381-4).

5   Calculations from the Guildhall Library catalogue, MSS. 7252-3 (Royal Exchange) and 11936-7 (Sun). Incidentally, the Hand-in-Hand policy registers, which are largely confined to London and the home counties, contain well over a million policies for their full extent (1695-1865), and these are indexed by name and (incompletely) by place (MSS. 8674-84).

both London and the provinces, that chills endeavour but the total absence of any surviving indexes, whether by place or by name of the insuring party.

In the space allowed me I must assume that the reader is familiar with the general structure of the insurance business from Dr Dickson's[6] and Professor Supple's[7] histories of the two leaders, and with the general descriptive and evaluation character of registered policies from the use that Dr. Chapman[8] and Dr Jenkins[9] have made of them in their study of the textile industries; including some reference to houses built by factory masters.

2

My first encounter with an insurance policy was for a different form of housing, in the East End of Leeds, an industrial town where hardly any of the manufacturers built houses specifically for their workpeople, [10] the provision being left to private and speculative developers. This policy was contained in a bundle of conveyances for Goulden's Buildings, six pairs of back-to-backs.[11] Policy survival is not common: I cannot recall more than four such policies in the ten thousand bundles in the Town Clerk's strong rooms. Knowing from Dr Chapman's work that registers of policies from the Sun Company were available at the Guildhall Library, London, I sought out the entry for Goulden's Buildings to see whether any others from this locality had been insured in May 1797. A second group of houses in York St was insured by Goulden in the policy next following and I could see other Leeds entries on the pages adjoining and elsewhere, as I browsed idly through the volume. At that stage I realized the magnitude of the labours that Dr Chapman had organized to seek out his cotton manufacturers in what seemed to me totally unordered entries.

6   P. M. G. Dickson, *The Sun Insurance Office* (1960).

7   Barry Supple, *The Royal Exchange Assurance* (1970).

8   Notably 'Fixed Capital Formation in the British Cotton Industry', *Econ. Hist. Rev.*, 2nd ser., xxiii (1970), 235-66; 'Industrial Capital before the Industrial Revolution', in N. B. Harte and K. G. Ponting (eds), *Textile History and Economic History* (1973), 113-37, esp. table 5.4.

9   'Early Factory Development in the West Riding of Yorkshire', in Harte and Ponting (eds), op. cit., 247-80, esp. App. 10.1.

10   One exception was the remote site of John Marshall's first water powered mill on Adel Beck.

11   'Twelve new tenements' insured for £200, May 1797: policy no. 667012, registered in MS. 11937, vol. 19. The houses are illustrated in C. W. Chalklin and M. A. Havinden (eds). *Rural Change and Urban Growth, 1500-1800* (1974), pl. 16, p. 284.

Recalling that Dr Chapman had also cited Royal Exchange policies, I put in a slip for a volume of that company's registers for 1797, the same year as the Sun volume that I had scanned. I saw at once that the Royal Exchange registers had one distinct advantage, for I found a page with an entry that had a bold 'Leeds' in the left-hand margin, and other place-names similarly attached to each entry, although predominantly of East Anglian and south-western market towns — the centres of activity of the Royal Exchange agents at that time. My curiosity aroused, and always more of a scanner than a scholar by temperament, I soon developed a technique for allying eye, wrist and thumb to the natural springiness of the stiff bound volumes, passing rapidly through the pages and applying the brakes only when 'Leeds' loomed like the turn-off sign on a foggy motorway journey. The Leeds policies that I first encountered were more concerned with industrial premises than with houses — a result, I was to learn later, of the late appointment of the Royal Exchange agency in 1784 to a town where there had been a Sun agent since 1737.[12] It was not long before I realized that the marginal 'Leeds' was an agency indication and that policies from surrounding towns of the West Riding had the same rubric, although (as table 1 shows) the agency business was predominantly in Leeds itself.

The Leeds entries, although identifiable with patience, did not occur very frequently in the Royal Exchange registers and it was clear from the Guildhall Library catalogue that the Sun registers were much more voluminous, and might therefore repay effort. I returned to the Sun and sent for another volume from the same year as the Goulden policies. Some way of shortening effort, however, was essential, for my experience in vol.19 had taught me that it would be impossible to read every policy in order to see whether the place-name 'Leeds' appeared in the second or third line of each closely-written entry. There were certainly no place-names in any margin, only personal names. These did not seem to bear any relation to the name of the insured, for there had been no 'Goulden' against policy 667012 but 'Kitchingman'; the same 'Kitchingman' was written against the next policy from Leeds that I encountered; although I did not immediately see the the significance of the name as that of an agent, it did seem worthwhile to search for it, and when it recurred it was indeed at the left hand side of another Leeds policy.[13] As I found years previously in the Exchequer Memoranda rolls, there is all the difference in the world when scanning

12   MS. 11935, vol. 2, 21 Oct. 1737.
13   Kitchingman had been appointed agent a month before the Goulden policy: MS. 14386, 13 April 1797.

an unindexed record if the eye can avoid the labour of reading every word of a line and concentrate on the place where a key-word regularly occurs, optimally where the clerks had used marginal rubrics in a large hand as the insurance company clerks were clearly also doing. Thenceforward it was simply the thumb and elbow motion as before, with the eyes glazed until the appearance of a 'Kitchingman' enlivened them.

At this stage, both in the Sun and Royal Exchange registers, I was given further encouragement by noticing that a 'Leeds' or a 'Kitchingman' policy was often one of a small group from the same place, successively entered; it was even more noticeable for those places and agents where much more business was coming in than from Leeds: Exeter, Edinburgh, Manchester, Liverpool, and numerous country market towns of southern England. Thus the chance of missing the key name in a rapid scrutiny was reduced by the reiteration of the name, sometimes over many successive pages for the busier agencies. These 'bunched' entries for non-Leeds agencies also made it possible to leap-frog them by fingering the pages by trial and error to see where the succession ended: none of the intervening pages had to be scrutinized. The clerks were particularly addicted to bunching the policies from head office and London agencies, and I learned to leap-frog London with provincial supercility. Conversely, for someone interested exclusively in City and West End buildings, the same bunching would greatly ease the scanning operation.[14]

The bulk of the London policies was such that the Sun tried the experiment of separate volumes for the office at Craig's Court, Charing Cross as early as 1726 but reverted in 1731 to an omnibus system, the 'Old Series', used until the General Committee resolved in May 1793 'that henceforward a Country Department be set up with separate Books'.[15] The volumes compiled, identical in form and binding with those registering the London Policies, were boldly marked CD (Country Department)[16] as opposed to CC (Craig's Court or Charing Cross) and were given a freshly numbered sequence although the run of policy numbers was retained, whichever department issued them.[17] With my

---

14　In the Old Series of Sun registers the policies from London Head Office were distinguished by the absence of an agent's name in the margin: as many as 50 successive pages are not uncommon.

15　MS. 11931, vol. 7, 30 May 1793.

16　MS. 11937, commencing with vol. 1, policy no. 618401.

17　The Town Department volumes continued as vols 396-733 of the Old Series (MS. 11936). Some volumes in this series earlier than May 1793 are wholly devoted to London policies (e.g. vols. 363, 368, 373 and 382).

specific interest in a provincial town, it was fortunate that my scanning apprenticeship began in a period when the provincial business had been filtered from the London: it was only later that I had the confidence to move backwards into the undifferentiated Old Series.

The Royal Exchange did not differentiate Town from Country business although this company's one attempt at segregation produced a volume of outstanding interest and significance to industrial historians when from Christmas Eve 1796 to 9 January 1801 all the important policies dealing with textile manufactories were entered in a separate volume, although again retaining a single numerical sequence.[18] Dr Chapman's footnotes show that he made very little use of this volume, perhaps because it is numbered separately from the main sequence: its range of manufactories in all branches of the textile industry at that crucial stage in their transformation would make it a good candidate for publication in full, and its many cross-references lead to policies issued jointly with the Sun, the Phoenix and other companies of the day.

3

At this point my researches into conveyances and rate assessments at Leeds had gone far enough for me to project a complete study of its East End.[19] In particular I had become interested in the speculative building and estate development instigated by the town's terminating building societies on the one hand and by Richard Paley on the other. It would augment the information from the more conventional sources if more Leeds policies could be found. Further progress was made possible by the School of Economic Studies allocating me one of its two research assistants, and the appointment of Brian Barber. It was his transcripts of the Leeds policies from volumes 1 to 58 of the Sun CD series and volumes 17 and 18 of the Royal Exchange 2nd series, begun in January 1971, that demonstrated to me the bulk and potential of this source for the building history of a single town, and in particular the linking of houses known from photographs and estate plans to the same houses as they appeared in conveyances, enrolled deeds, rate books and sale particulars, an invocation of a past townscape. The years covered by Paley's activities in Leeds, culminating in his bankruptcy and death, set the initial limits to our searches: 1777-1807.

After the end of Brian's tenure I continued myself with earlier Sun policies: volumes 262-395 from the Original Series and to vol. 76 in the

18   MS. 7253, vol. 32A.
19   M. W. Beresford, 'The Making of a Townscape' in Chalklin and Havinden (eds), op. cit. See below, pp. 263-74.

CD series, together with 1-16 and 19-36 in the Royal Exchange volumes, aided at a later date (October 1974 - March 1975) by the assistance of Stephen Blake in sampling the earlier years of the Sun Agency in Leeds in preparation for a paper 'A Prospect of Leeds, 1737-1807' for the Economic History Society Conference in April 1975. The work was expedited for the period after 1799 by generous access to a list that Dr Jenkins had compiled, being the numbers of all policies issuing from the Yorkshire agencies of the Sun from 1793. This had been produced by the same methods that I had been employing independently and we first met as scanners facing each other across the great oak tables in the old Guildhall Library. Thus the product of one scanning was able greatly to expedite the searches of someone else, and in turn I hope that my own card index of personal names encountered in Leeds policies will save any future research worker on a Leeds topic having to do his own scanning. No doubt the scanners have passed over some entries unwittingly but that will be remedied only if the projected machine-indexing of the registers is ever achieved.

Table 1. Leeds policies among policies scanned in registers

Years	Number of policies scanned			Number of Leeds† policies noticed		
	Sun	Royal Exchange	All*	Sun	Royal Exchange	All
1738	2,800	—	2,800	11	—	11
1763-6	39,900	—	39,900	123	—	123
1777-83	105,800	—	105,800	198	—	198
1784-1807	225,700	144,500	370,200	1,496	355	1,851
Totals	374,200	144,500	518,700	1,828	355	2,183

* another 141,000 Sun policies and 5,000 Royal Exchange policies were contained in registers from these years destroyed by fire and damp before deposit in the Guildhall Library: these fall mainly in the four years 1783, 1795, 1799 and 1800.

† 'Leeds' policies are those for premises within the townships that made up the parish and borough. The Leeds agents issued policies in other local towns: some 200 of these were noticed in the Sun registers in the years 1763-6 and 1777-1807.

In proportion to the whole number of policies scanned, over half a million, a harvest of 2,185 policies for one town (as set out in table 1) may seem meagre and not very encouraging for others. Yet the wealth of information for building history, as I hope to show elsewhere, is quite out of proportion to the number of policies. I have no space here to demonstrate the range of Leeds insurances, from £10 cottages in the back yards of the main streets, through back-to-back terraces and courts to the West End squares, the houses-cum-finishing shops of the Gentlemen Merchants, and the town's first suburban country house, Denison Hall, insured for £3,000 in 1785; yet even in 1807 there were new policies being written for sums as small as the £100 insurances typical of 1737 and 1738. Researchers from other towns should be encouraged also by the fact that the Leeds agency was never in the first rank. In 1778 Exeter, the most lucrative Sun agency, did six times as much business as Leeds and Edinburgh five times as much. An estimate among the Chatham papers made at the end of the century, gave Hampshire as much insurance business as Lancashire, and both were surpassed by Kent.[20] It must be confessed, however, that the search would be even more difficult in respect of a town that did not have its own agency; Bradford historians are ill-served, for example, and an area where a local company got an early grip on business might have little reward for searchers in the registers of the London-based Sun and Royal Exchange. Yet it is the good fortune of of researchers that these two early-established London companies did succeed in invading so much of the provinces.

Nor are urban historians the only ones to gain from the establishment of local agencies, the essential key to any labour-saving use of the registers, for the rural provinces of eighteenth-century England were not empty of insurable properties, domestic and industrial, and it was no accident that so many small market towns had their own insurance agents. Nor, in the economy of the day, was insurable urban property confined to the industrial towns, the market towns and the metropolis: the seaports apart, there were the spas; and Scarborough already had its own agent when the first Leeds agent was appointed in 1737 and it had a greater premium income than the county town of York.[21]

4

A researcher not concerned with London will, therefore, first need to know whether and when an agency was established in the place that interests him. Royal Exchange agents have to be sought by turning over the pages of registers, but the place-name itself is the straightforward

---

20   Public Record Office, Chatham MS. 30/8/187, f. 232.
21   MS. 11937, vol. 7.

name to seek. The Sun register margins adopted the agents' names as·
identifications, and this choice might seem to force one to read a large
number of policies to see the catchment area of each name; in fact
there are short cuts, since the Sun deposit at the Guildhall Library
includes other classes of record than the registers. For the late
eighteenth and early nineteenth century there is a register of agents
linked to the names of their guarantors and the amount of their
guarantee.[22] Earlier agents' names are recorded in the minutes of the
fortnightly Committee for Country Insurance.[23] These record every
payment as it was received from an agent, so that a national conspectus
of agents in any given year can be gained by reading fewer than 26
pages of manuscript, clearly written and indented from the formal
minutes; even more quickly from the quarterly tabulation of agents
who were in arrears, a situation so widespread and tolerated that most
agents' names will appear in any given year.

The same fortnightly entries can shorten the search in a different
way. When first encountered, I did hope that these payments by the
Leeds agents would correspond in date to the entry of a block of Leeds
policies in the registers, which are in chronological order. But there was
no correspondence of dates, due to the practice of settlement in arrears
which gave the local agent a useful supplement to his 5 per cent
commission by giving him monies between the time when the policy
was issued and the time of their remission to London, a use of monies
very similar to that enjoyed by many provincial agents for the
collection of government taxes, and – in the case of the larger agents –
providing useful sums for short term employment.

Yet settlements were eventually made, if not in the quarters after
they became due, then in the next following. It is possible, therefore,
from the Committee book entries to obtain an idea of the quantity of
one agent's business and its movements up or down, either roughly by
annual totals ignoring the lag created by arrears and irregular payment
dates, or more precisely by examining the arrears statements and
assigning a payment back to the quarter-day when it had fallen due, as
shown in table 2.

What is the relevance of this arithmetical operation to a scrutiny of
the registers? An upward movement of any size in the premiums
remitted from an agent could only have arisen from new policy business
or from the renewal of an old policy with augmented risks, and it was

22　　MS. 14386. See also MS. 14109 (1842-81).
23　　MS. 11935. Agents' names can also be found in the cash books, MS. 12019, wit'
payments for local fire losses. Students of losses should consult MS. 11932 and the Committe
minute books, esp. MS. 11931.

precisely new business and augmented renewals that the policy registers recorded. Simple renewals do not seem to have involved the issue of new policies. It is usually said that annual renewal was automatic in any event, and scrutinized by the company after seven years. There is no evidence from the registers of any such rewriting of policies after seven years as far as ordinary domestic houses were concerned; those who insured business and industrial premises and their contents were of course frequently issued with new policies in respect of changed risks from new machinery, new processes or different amounts of stock held within the building, and it would be unlikely that any active business would survive seven years without the need for a variation in the risks insured. Smaller variations – of address, of partners, of a mortgage – did not occasion fresh policies but endorsement slips which were recorded in a separate series of registers which are not too bulky to search.[24] They have their own interest for the historian of economic change.

The quarter when an agent began to remit substantially more than previously is the time when it would be most worthwhile to begin examining the policy registers. In my work on Leeds before 1777, with 207 volumes of the Old Series registers to choose from, I concentrated on those years when a graph of the quarterly remittances showed its steepest upward slopes, as a week-end mountaineer might make for Snowdon or Scafell, however inviting the crags seemed that lay first at hand. The Snowdonian years for Leeds turned out to be those from 1763 to 1766, as table 2 shows, an interesting commentary on the local post-war situation and in no way due to the energies of a new agent, since these years fall midway in the period of his office (1754-66).

Table 2. **Leeds agent's remissions to London, 1763-5**

8 April 1763	£ 75	(due September 1762)
9 December 1763	£ 86	(due March 1763)
25 May 1764	£ 116	(due September 1763)
17 August 1764	£ 89	(due Christmas 1763)
21 December 1764	£ 57	(due September 1764)
31 May 1765	£ 82	(due Christmas 1764)
4 October 1765	£ 81	(due March 1765)
20 December 1765	£ 98	(due September 1765)

Source Guildhall MS. 11935, vol. 5 (James Wilkinson's payments).

24   MS. 12160.
25   From 1784 there is an overlap: see the Catalogue.

5

If a search through the policies of a particular year is envisaged, the Guildhall Library catalogue gives the date-ranges of each volume: a printed copy will be found in the drawers of the London Collection Catalogue at L64.9, and a typescript list is available from the Manuscripts Department desk. The drawer Catalogue includes the other categories of Sun and Royal Exchange deposits usually with date range but without further details, as well as the records of other fire offices. A search for a policy whose number is already known is most likely to be carried out by someone who sees a printed reference to a policy: or finds a reference to its number in his scrutiny of the endorsement books or in the registration of a subsequent policy. For postal photocopy orders it obviously saves the Library staff considerable time if the volume number is given when it is known; regular users will certainly acquire their own photocopy of the relevant portions of the catalogue.

To locate the appropriate volumes for policies of a particular year or to locate a policy whose number is known, the Royal Exchange series presents no difficulties since the catalogue gives the day, month and year of the first and last policy in each volume, and the early policies (apart from the one specialized industrial policy volume) are in one continuous chronological sequence. For the Sun, however, table 3 shows an idiosyncratic overlap of policy numbers between volumes.

Table 3. Extract from Guildhall Library catalogue, Sun Registers, Old Series: MS. 11936

Vol. 150	1763-4	202801 - 205800
Vol. 151	1763-4	203001 - 206000
Vol. 152	1764	206001 - 209000
Vol. 153	1764	206201 - 209200

There are usually blank pages at the end of a volume, so that ther was clearly an over-riding policy of beginning each volume with a policy number ending in -1 and ending it with an -0, and within each volume the policies were entered in a strict numerical and chronological order. The idiosyncrasy arose from two clerks working in parallel, with two registers always in use. I assume that each clerk was given a ration of 200 printed policies, already numbered in sequence, which he used up as orders came in from agents and the insurances were to be entered in the register. Thus on Monday, 16 January 1764, when Clerk A had come to the end of vol. 150 with policy 205800, he could not open the waiting vol. 153 with policy 205801 since that number had already been used up by Clerk B who ended volume 151 the previous Tuesday with policy 206000 and began volume 152 with policy 206001 on Wednesday, reaching 206141 by Monday. Clerk A, therefore, took up the next unused bundle of 200 policies and began to enter policy 206201; he finished that bundle at 206400 on 24 January and then had to follow up with 206601 since Clerk B had already started work on the numbers from 206401.

Overlaps of this sort demand careful use of the registers at the opening and closing months of a year if a search is intended to begin or end with the year. If one is tracing a particular policy by its number, the Library catalogue is not quite sufficient to locate it for reading or for photocopying since it may lie in either of two adjoining volumes: as for example, policy 206472 which, from the policy numbers given in the catalogue must lie in either vol. 152 or vol. 153. It lies actually in vol. 152, the work of Clerk B on 27 January 1764.

6

Each researcher has his own quarry, and the information in the policies is sufficient for many appetites to come; and passing beyond urban building history.[26] This short paper is designedly a guide into the sources, not a guide for their use, although undoubtedly it will be easier to test the realism of valuations for private houses than it has yet proved for factories. Sale prices are known from conveyances, and at different parts of the social ladder more and more people were living in houses similar in value to their neighbours. For the gentleman merchant and his widow, it was the Act of Uniformity imposed in the schools of taste that ranged similar houses alongside each other in Terraces, Rows, Parades, and Squares. For the low wage-earners who made up the

---

26   The country house, the farm house and the non-textile country industires would particularly repay study.

tenantry of the new back-to-back streets it was a uniformity imposed on landlords by building costs in relation to expected rent levels, an array of brick houses five-and-a-half-yards square. With practice, as with Dr Chapman's mill types,[27] it is possible to deduce a house's character from its insurance valuation; and, with the insured values far lower than those of mills,[28] the premiums were smaller and the temptation to undervalue seriously was less.[29]

A small postscript may be added for those unable or unwilling to use the head office registers in the Guildhall Library for their local history researches. A certain number of agents' registers have survived locally, and these will be listed and their locations given in a work expected to be published by Heinemann in 1976 — Edwin Green's and H.A.L. Cockerell's *The British Insurance Business 1547-1970: an introduction and guide to insurance archives in Great Britain.*

27 Chapman, op. cit., note 8 above: Type A, £1,000 - 2,000; B1, £3,000; B2, £5,000; C, over £10,000.

28 In 1785 the largest house in Leeds was insured for £3,000, as much as a B1 Chapman mill; Thomas Lee's new house in Boar Lane had been insured for £2,000 in 1765. New houses in the West End after 1779 ranged from £200 upwards, the highest noted being £720 in 1792: MS. 11936, vol. 386, no. 399339.

29 2s. per £100 was usual for houses; as late as 1807 as many as one quarter of new Leeds agency policies were for £100 or less.

21

PROMETHEUS INSURED: THE SUN FIRE AGENCY

IN LEEDS DURING URBANIZATION, 1716-1826

Prometheus, the god of fire bound in the service of industrial power through the steam engine, was received into the pantheon of the Industrial Revolution with David Landes' votive offering of 1969;[2] and might have been there earlier, had not the old term *fire engine* given way to *steam engine* in common usage: a god of steam is harder to find in mythology. "Fire" and not steam engines were blamed in 1803 for the deterioration of the West End of Leeds: "from the Erection and Construction of a great number of Fire Engines and other Erections for carrying on Manufactures the Mansion House (sc. Manor House) would be a very unhealthy Place of Residence and in no respect eligible for the said Christopher Wilson who is wholly unconnected with trade".[3]

Fire was no stranger to industrial Leeds even before these engines. The finishing of woollen cloth rather than weaving was the town's speciality and several finishing processes necessitated the application of heat: in a minor way at pressing shops, and in a major way with dyeing and the manufacture of soap and other detergents. The town also had its brewers, bakers, seed-oil crushers, tallow-makers, distillers, and smiths, all potentially incendiary; nor were inn- and stable-keepers unaware of accidents kindled by neglect or inflamed customers. House chimneys, much more numerous than industrial chimneys, showed Prometheus in domestic chains but even here an accident or neglect could start a blaze. Although there is no record of disastrous fires in Leeds akin to those of the E. L. Jones annals,[4] in 1725 the museum catalogue of the town's first historian, Ralph Thoresby, listed "a Piece of Ceiling of the Hall in this House . . . burnt to a perfect Cinder in the Night . . . yet no further damage done, kept as a Memorial of a watchful Providence",[5] and in 1816 Whitaker, Thoresby's editor and reviser, noted the increased danger since builders had turned from English oak to imported timber: "the refinement of insurance, unknown to and scarcely needed by our ancestors a century ago,

[1] An early version of this paper, with illustrations of many of the buildings mentioned, was presented at the 1975 Conference of the Economic History Society at Bodington Hall, Leeds. The task of extracting policies was shared with Dr Barber and Dr Blake, successive research assistants appointed by the University of Leeds. Dr Jenkins kindly loaned me a numerical finding-list of West Riding policies, deriving from his own researches, which I utilized to extend the examination of Sun Registers from 1807 to 1826. At the Guildhall Library, London, Mr Cooper and his staff were generous in facilities.
[2] D. S. Landes, *The Unbound Prometheus: Technological Change and Industrial Development* (1969).
[3] *Acts Local and Personal, 43 Geo. III cap. 57*, releasing Wilson settled estates.
[4] E. L. Jones, 'The Reduction of Fire Damage', *Post-Medieval Archaeology*, II (1968), pp. 140-9.
[5] D. H. Atkinson, *Ralph Thoresby* (Leeds, 1885), I, p. 267; the fire occurred before 1689.

provides now against the inflammability of resinous woods . . . oak was a stubborn log, if dark and unsightly".[6]

The general development of this "prudent refinement" has already been treated by the historians of the Sun and Royal Exchange, the two principal London-based companies,[7] but there has been no study of the numerous provincial agents appointed to solicit business, collect and remit premiums, organize protection and salvage, receive claims, and eventually pay out approved losses, the company rewarding them by commission.

These fire agents have a place in business history akin to those who collected taxes or sold stamps: a part-time agency was ancillary to another trade or to the developing profession of attorney,[8] and an agent had a similar use of others' monies between collection and remittance. The Sun company was the first to establish a Leeds agency in 1737, and its local pre-eminence was maintained for nearly a century. The fortnightly entries in the Sun Committee Books[9] enable the Leeds remittances to be calculated: in 1737/8 they were £21, and as this small northern market town urbanized and industrialized they rose to a peak of £4,660 in 1809 (Tables 1 and 2), a sum 50 per cent greater than the remittance from the Liverpool agency and equal to 60 per cent of Manchester's.

The details of ownership, insured property and its value were taken from the policies and entered into head office registers on a daily basis. The surviving Sun and Royal Exchange registers[10] were utilized in Dr Chapman's pioneer studied of cotton mills and subsequently of the West Country woollen industry;[11] they were a principal source for Dr Jenkins's studies of Yorkshire textile mills[12] especially in establishing comparative values for the fixed capital insured, although they are not unimportant in identifying and locating small-scale enterprises not otherwise documented and recording partnerships not otherwise known,[13] and well-known industrial revolutionaries such as Gott and Marshall appear, if not pre-natally, then pre-historically.

Outside the textile industries the policy registers have been only sporadically utilized by historians,[14] principally through the absence of indexes to the 1·3 million policies issued by these two companies before 1824. The discovery that certain marginalia differentiated the policies from each agency emboldened a complete scrutiny of the Sun registers from 1721 to 1826 and the Royal

[6] T. D. Whitaker, *Loidis and Elmete* (Leeds, 1816), p. 80.

[7] P. G. M. Dickson, *The Sun Insurance Office, 1710-1960* (1960) (hereafter, Dickson, *Sun*) and B. E. Supple, *The Royal Exchange Assurance: A History of British Insurance, 1720-1970* (Cambridge, 1970) (hereafter Supple, *Royal Exchange*).

[8] As in M. Miles 'Eminent Practitioners', in G. R. Rubin and D. Sugarman, eds. *Lawyers, Courts and Industrial Society*, (1982).

[9] Sun Committee Minutes (hereafter CM): Guildhall Library, London (hereafter GH) MS 11935.

[10] Sun registers from GH MS 11936 for the Old Series (hereafter OS) and 11937 for the County or Country Series (hereafter CS). Royal Exchange registers (hereafter RE) from GH MSS 7252-3.

[11] S. D. Chapman, 'Fixed Capital Formation in the British Cotton Industry', *Econ. Hist. Rev.* 2nd ser. XXIII (1970), pp. 256-60; *The Devon Cloth Industry in the Eighteenth Century* (Devon & Cornwall Record Society new ser. XXIII (1978)); and 'Industrial Capital before the Industrial Revolution' in N. B. Harte and K. G. Ponting eds. *Textile History and Economic History* (Manchester, 1973), pp. 113-37.

[12] D. T. Jenkins, *The West Riding Wool Textile Industry, 1770-1835* (Edington, 1975) and 'The Cotton Industry in Yorkshire, 1780-1900', *Textile History*, X (1979), pp. 75-95.

[13] As in G. Shutt, 'Wharfedale Water Mills' (unpublished M.Phil. thesis, University of Leeds, 1979).

[14] As in I. Donnachie, 'Sources of Capital and Capitalization in the Scottish Brewing Industry', *Econ. Hist. Rev.* 2nd ser. XXX (1977), pp. 269-83.

Exchange from 1774 to 1807 to identify the policies issued by the Leeds agents, and particularly those for properties within the town itself.[15] It was the very range as much as the number of its industrial establishments that characterized the growing town in the 1780s: and the growing business of the fire agents, especially in this decade before the giant mills, rested on this variety in clientele.

The property insured by the agents' clientele went beyond the buildings of industry and their contents to a wider group characteristic of urbanization, from private houses to inns, shops, warehouses, and public buildings. An important part of Chapman's and Jenkins's work was to identify and measure the insured value of fixed capital needed in different categories of enterprises in wool and cotton, from the giant to the pygmy. Insured values must be approached with caution, as they both showed, but it is now possible in one industrial town to assemble at least rough categories in a ladder of insured values (Tables 6 and 8) for a full range of urban buildings and their contents: from the giant woollen mill complex of Wormald and Gott, visited by emperors and insured in 1801 for £64,800,[16] down to the one-room houses and cellar dwellings in the Boot and Shoe Yard, notorious among sanitary reformers after 1833 and insured by their first owners for between £10 and £12 each.[17]

I

Whitaker's date for the beginning of "refinement" in Leeds was accurate: the first local policies were taken out at the Sun's London office on 5 November 1716, no better day for inaugurating anti-incendiarism than Guy Fawkes's, especially in the year after the 'Fifteen when loyal anti-Tory fires burned brightly: the first prudent insurer was the Tory alderman William Cookson who had been recently imprisoned in Newgate for supposed Jacobite sympathies.[18] Until 1721 the value of an insurance was not recorded in the Sun's register but it is thereafter clear that the policies being issued for Leeds properties were for clients of the same class as Cookson, founder of a dynasty of Dr R. G. Wilson's Gentlemen Merchants. *Annus Mirabilis* was 1724 with 17 new insurances covering £8,200 of property but by 1728 and 1729 no new insurances appeared[19] and there were only two in 1730, supporting the current pessimism of the company's itinerant inspectors: "in Yorkshire the Business of Insurance is little Known or regarded, in most of the Towns".[20]

This situation was changed after a local agent was appointed on 21 October 1737; "this Committee being of the opinion that it will be to the Advantage of this Office to appoint an Agent at Leeds in the County of York, they propose, Mr John Wilkinson. Recommended by Mr (blank)",[21] and in November the *Leeds Mercury* advertised that

[15] Explained in M. W. Beresford, 'Building History from Insurance Records', *Urban History Yearbook*, 1976, pp. 7-14. See above, pp. 263-4.

[16] CS 40/719778, July 1801: for £32,400 but an equal amount with the Royal Exchange, RE 32A/184918.

[17] OS 300/459986, May 1792.

[18] OS 6/7533.

[19] OS vols. 7-13.

[20] Dickson, *Sun*, p. 69.

[21] CM 2, 21 Oct. 1737.

Mr John Wilkinson of Leeds being appointed Agent for the Sun Fire Office, application may be made to him for new insurances on houses or goods. And on producing the last receipts (sc. from London) he is empowered to receive yearly payments on the insurances already made. Proposals may be had gratis.[22]

There were already Sun agents in the north of England at Newcastle, Manchester, Lancaster, York, Hull, and Scarborough. Leeds was only one of several additions to the list in 1737: Royston, Poole, Bristol, Chichester, Ruthin, Durham, Gloucester, and Chester, although at the same time agents at Dorchester and Colchester were in financial difficulties and Peterborough's was insolvent.

Table 1. *Premiums from Northern and Other Provincial Agencies of The Sun, April 1737- April 1738*

	£		£
Newcastle	251	Exeter	487
Liverpool	94	Andover	445
Manchester	87	Winchester	380
Scarborough	226	Great Yarmouth	268
York	182	Norwich	260
Hull	93		
Leeds	21		

Source: Sun CM 2.

An agent in Leeds, little more than a small market town, had less potential business than the fashionable spa at Scarborough or the county town at York, and still less than an agent in a country town of southern and eastern England with much residential property and public buildings to be insured together with a catchment area rich in country houses, inns, breweries, and corn mills. Alongside the sums in Table 1 the £21 remitted in Wilkinson's first full year was meagre, and the remittance was only £69 when his nephew James took over the agency in 1754.[23] The remittances first went into three figures two years later and by 1766 were four times those of 1754, but at the younger Wilkinson's bankruptcy in 1766 he was dismissed.[24] As with provincial revenue agencies of government, the Sun accepted that remittances would be in arrears but an agent's delays, profitable in giving him the use of short-term monies to supplement his five per cent commission, could be fatal for the Company if he became insolvent. The Sun never recovered £265 of the £279, equal to about four quarters' premiums, due at Wilkinson's bankruptcy.[25]

The first year of James Walker, drysalter and pawnbroker, was vigorous for he remitted £387; in 1775 he reached £670 but when he died in 1777 the sum was only £382. He had issued only six policies the previous year and most of his small earnings from the agency would have been his commission on older policies at their annual renewal. He had no competition from any other company's agency in Leeds and virtually none from other Sun agents in

---

[22] *Leeds Mercury* (hereafter *LM*), 15 Nov. 1737; Wilkinson was a merchant.

[23] Dates of agencies and sums remitted from CM 2-16: fidelity bonds were expected of agents but the rule was not strictly enforced: the first Leeds agent to have a bond (£100) recorded was James Wilkinson (CM 3, 25 Jan. 1754).

[24] CM 5, 23 May 1766.

[25] Ibid. 6 Nov. 1767.

Yorkshire where the only new appointment since 1737 had been at Sheffield. Business in Wakefield, the West Riding county town, was left to the Leeds agent until 1795 and in 1777 Joshua Hartley took over an agency that already handled one quarter of the Sun's business arising from all three Ridings of Yorkshire.

Hartley himself had become insolvent as a merchant and small millowner five years before obtaining the agency but his standing must have been good: he paid off his creditors and showed as much energy on behalf of the Sun.[26] In 1778 he issued 31 new policies and 24 more in 1779, bringing remittances back almost to Walker's best year. In 1782 the duty placed on policyholders raised government revenues but for a while depressed the insurance business.[27] The agent collected the duty so that the record of remittances cannot thereafter be used as a precise indicator of agency business since it did not distinguish premiums from duty remitted and duty was not proportional to premiums (p. 387 below). There is no doubt, however, (Table 2) that the Leeds agency was still able to find new business. In 1796 James Kitchingman, "gentleman", took over an agency whose remittances were more than twice those of 1783, and which had survived intensified competition locally. Before 1784 the Royal Exchange insured no property in Leeds although it actively insured houses, factories, and warehouses in the cotton counties.[28] A rival local fire company was founded in Leeds in March 1777 at the Leeds Bank office but closed down in July 1782 "on account of the intended duty" and the Sun's directors reluctantly agreed to Hartley's request for policyholders in the defunct company to be allowed the remainder of the year's premium if they transferred to the Sun; as a public relations exercise the Sun bought its rival's fire engine and presented it to the town.[29]

Table 2. *Progress of the Leeds Agency, 1740-1826*

	Leeds Remittances Annual Average	Highest Annual Remittance of Period	Total London and Provincial Offices	Leeds Percentage		Annual Average	Highest in Period
A. Before Insurance Duty, 1782					B. Remittances Gross of Duty, 1783-1826		
	£	£	£ '000			£	£
1740-9	33	40 (1749)	0.24	0.13	1783-9	723	875 (1789)
1750-9	84	122 (1759)	0.33	0.25	1790-7	1331	1632 (1796)
1760-9	269	392 (1768)	0.57	0.47	1798-9	1498	1630 (1798)
1770-9	514	670 (1775)	0.94	0.55	1800-4	2655	4128 (1804)
1780-2	516	580 (1782)	0.12	0.46	1805-9	4125	4660 (1809)
					1810-15	4181	4581 (1810)
					1816-19	3986	4291 (1817)
					1820-6	3620	4272 (1820)

Duty: 1782-97, 1s. 6d. per £100 insured, *not* proportional to premiums; 1798-1804, 2s.; 1805-1815, 2s. 6d.; from 1816, 3s. With remittances usually in arrears a duty imposed at midsummer would not inflate figures greatly until the next calendar year.
Sources: Leeds: CM 2-11; other offices: GH 11963, vols. 2-5.

[26] He had owned a rasping and chipping mill in the Meanwood valley (*Leeds Intelligencer* (thereafter *LI*), 13 Oct. 1772, 12 March and 17 Aug. 1773, 16 Jan. 1776). His nieces received legacies to recompense them for their father's losses in supporting his brother "in 1772" (York, Borthwick Institute, Prerogative Court wills, March 1797).

[27] Dickson, *Sun* pp. 98, 302; Supple, *Royal Exchange*, does not give annual figures in Tables 5.1 and 7.1, but Fig. 3.1 shows a dip after 1782.

[28] The Royal Exchange began a specialized register for such policies, now RE 32A received at the Guildhall Library in 1953 but seemingly overlooked in Chapman's searches for his 1970 article.

[29] *LM* 18 March 1777; GH 11931/6 fo. 167 and 11932/12, 10 Oct. 1782.

More competition was felt when the Royal Exchange appointed a Leeds agent[30] in September 1784, the Phoenix of London in 1786 and the Manchester Fire Office in the same year.[31] The Royal Exchange agent issued £13,200 of policies in his first year[32] but it was not a serious threat (Table 2). Indeed, as Dickson and Supple have shown, the two companies collaborated to take on some of the new high-risk industrial business, 41 such policies being issued between 1784 and 1807.

Table 3. *Sun and Royal Exchange: Leeds Policies Registered, Annual Averages, 1784-1807*

	Sun	Royal Exchange	R.E. as % of Sun
1784-9	47	7	15
1790-9	73	19	26
1800-07	93	19	20

Source: OS 319-397 and CS 1-79.
Note: this table exaggerates the R.E. share since 22 of the 156 volumes of Sun registers from these years are lost or damaged.

One result of the new agencies of 1784-6 was an outbreak of large advertisements in the Leeds newspapers[33] but the Sun's local position was dominant until after the war. An estimate made for Chatham in 1788 assigned £3·62 million of insurance to Yorkshire, of which 60 per cent was in the Sun;[34] one third of the Yorkshire remittances came from Hartley's agency.

When the Sun's special agent, Philip Bewicke, came to Leeds during a tour of inspection in 1806 his comments were glowing: "the business in Leeds has trebled since Mr Kitchingman has been the Agent, no office does much business there compared with the Sun".[35] His remittance of £3,474 in 1806 was in fact double not treble Hartley's peak and it included duty at an increased rate, but there was better still to come. In the years 1807-11 the remittances exceeded £4,500 and in 1818 Kitchingman's remittances, although lower than the golden years, still exceeded £4,000.

The growth of business, if spectacular, had not been uninterrupted: the upward trend faltered in the last year of Walker and Hartley's tenures, possibly through their illness; there was a sharp fall in 1797, and Kitchingman's remittances of 1807-11 although high did not seem capable of further increase.[36]

His son, agent from 1819 to 1839, was able to maintain them until 1823 but they were halved by 1825. Urbanization and industrialization had not ex-

[30] He was Lucas Nicholson, town clerk, solicitor, and banker, an interesting cluster of part-time occupations that reinforced each other (*LI*, 12 Oct. 1784 and 17 March 1820). When bankrupt in 1812 he resigned as town clerk but was succeeded by his son with whom he then shared the insurance agency. This still did not match the dynasty of Sun agents at Manchester where James Platt was agent from 1783-92, his widow from 1792-6, and her family for the next 41 years.

[31] *LI* 21 Feb. and 6 June 1786.

[32] RE 8-9.

[33] *LI* 13 Feb. and 13 March 1787: five years later a Standing Order of the Sun told their agents to "be known to the County in general by a public advertisement in the Country Newspapers, twice before every Quarter Day" (GH 11935B vol. 2, 11 Oct. 1792).

[34] P.R.O. 30/8/187, fo. 232.

[35] GH 11935A, vol. 1, fo. 18 (1-4 Nov. 1806).

[36] Kitchingman senior was dismissed for insolvency: CM 10 fo. 100.

hausted their propensity to increase insurable properties but the agency could not escape competition from within and without: Sun agents were now appointed at Bradford, Huddersfield, and Halifax;[37] nationally the advent of new companies brought further falls in an already declining premium revenue,[38] and the names of new agencies proliferated ominously in the Leeds directory.[39]

II

The "Advantage of this Office" anticipated in 1737 had certainly been achieved, and the "Refinement of Insurance" saluted by the town's historian in 1816 had attracted a wide clientele unrefined and refined.

The landed aristocracy, having London solicitors and bankers, could insure in London: the Ingrams insured Temple Newsam[40] for £3,000 in 1769 but the Leeds agent handled no insurance for Harewood House until 1821 (house £8,000 and stables £1,500)[41] and for his highest premiums had to look to industry rather than land; but "Gentlemen Merchants" from Leeds with country houses continued the connection they had established in Briggate. Gledhow Hall[42] was insured "unfurnished" for £1,660 in 1776, Nun Appleton House[43] for £3,500 in 1789 and Osmondthorpe Manor[44] for £3,000 in the same year. Farnley Hall,[45] the home of Turner's patron, was the most highly insured house at £15,000 with £2,000 for "pictures and prints framed and glazed as per Catalogue deposited at the office".

The public buildings of Leeds were also less remunerative for an agent than those insured at the Charing Cross and City offices, but there was a prehistory of that Civic Pride on which Asa Briggs centred his essay on mid-Victorian Leeds.[46] The Church of England seems to have trusted in God to deliver them but the Unitarians at Mill Hill[47] insured against Acts of God for £300 in 1779 and the following year the Methodists their chapel and adjoining houses at Quarry Hill[48] for £1,000. There was no Town Hall before 1858 but the magistrates insured their meeting room in Kirkgate for £200 in 1785. Theatres had a poor fire record, and Tate Wilkinson's theatre of 1771 in Meadow Lane was insured for £1,000 but only against fires at performances.[49] The General

[37] In 1779 Hartley began the practice of advertising dates when he would visit these towns; a Sun agent at Skipton picked up some cotton business but cotton mills in Airedale, Wharfedale, and Nidderdale were insured in Leeds. The Huddersfield and Halifax appointments were abortive.

[38] Dickson, *Sun*, p. 99; Supple, *Royal Exchange*, fig. 8.1.

[39] There were sixteen in 1817: E. Baines, *Directory, General and Commercial* (Leeds, 1817), p. 191.

[40] Original on show at house; GH register for 1769 defective.

[41] CS 136/982923.

[42] OS 172/240217.

[43] OS 365/561430.

[44] OS 358/552475.

[45] CS 191/1142753: the catalogue, like the plans of mills frequently mentioned, is now missing from the Company records; Fuseli's 'Ghosts' is specifically mentioned in a policy elsewhere: OS 381/608404 (Houghton Hall, Norfolk).

[46] A. Briggs, *Victorian Cities* (1963), ch. 4. For the capital values of public buildings see K. Grady, 'The provision of public buildings', (unpublished Ph.D. thesis, University of Leeds, 1980); most of those in his gazetteer have policies.

[47] OS 274/412760.

[48] OS 281/424539.

[49] OS 207/300499.

Infirmary "in a field not quite finished" was covered for £1,500 in 1770 and for £2,000 when completed.[50] The workhouse trustees were more cautious: it was 1809 before they insured,[51] by a vote of 9:3. No policy has been found for the older cloth halls but the Tom Paine Hall in Albion Street, with the Music Hall over, had a policy for £1,000 on its completion in 1793.[52]

At one time or another all the best people could have been encountered at the agent's, for of the 85 "persons paying tax on male servants" in 1780, 66 (77 per cent) had policies;[53] of the 168 names in the Leeds section of the *Northern Directory* of 1781, 100 (59 per cent) occur in the registers.[54]

Of 72 "principal merchants in the home and foreign trade" in 1782 only five seem to have been uninsured.[55] Policies exist for all the local owners of Savery and Newcomen engines between 1790 and 1800;[56] for all the known customers of Boulton and Watt at the same period;[57] and in 1793 the mayor, his deputy, the recorder, all twelve aldermen, and 20 of 24 town councillors held policies.[58] The succeeding pages consider, in the context of industrialization and urbanization, the range and value of the properties insured by the agents' clientele.

III

Fire insurance began in Leeds with private houses and their contents but when policies become detailed it is clear that the larger proprietors of Leeds—unlike York or Scarborough—had counting-houses, workshops, warehouses, and stables integral with their homes and insured in the same policy; the workplace and home of retailers were similarly covered by single

Table 4. *Lower Ranges of Policy Values in the Period of Growth, 1760-1809*

| Years | £0-200 | Number of policies registered in each range | | | | | Total policies registered |
		£201-400	£401-600	£601-800	£801-1,000	over £1,000	
1760-7	19	47	44	21	18	37	186
1770-9	15	45	35	24	23	51	193
1780-9	44	81	70	43	53	203	494
1790-9	84	151	117	62	89	315	818
1800-9	36	132	93	67	85	438	851

Percentage of policies in each range

Years							
1760-9	10	25	24	11	10	20	
1770-9	8	23	18	12	12	26	
1780-9	8	16	14	9	11	41	
1790-9	10	18	14	8	11	39	
1800-9	4	16	11	8	10	51	

Sources: Sun OS 130-395 and CS 1-90; RE 1-61.

[50] OS 198/286590 and 268/461808.
[51] Leeds City Archives, LO/Q2, 4 Jan. 1809.
[52] RE 26/133484.
[53] P.R.O. T 47/8; all 51 of those in Leeds paying duty on silver plate (1757-62: T 47/5) and carriages (1753-66: T 47/2-4) appear in the registers.
[54] *Bailey's Northern Directory* (Warrington, 1781), pp. 221-5.
[55] Names from J. Singleton, 'Extracts from an old Leeds merchant's memorandum book', *Proceedings of the Thoresby Society*, XXIV (1919), pp. 31-8.
[56] J. Tann, *The Development of the Factory* (1970), p. 91.
[57] Birmingham Reference Library, Boulton and Watt MSS., engine books and order books.
[58] Names from *Universal British Directory* (1793) p. 536.

insurances. These town-centre premises dominate the smaller insurances of Table 4. The share of the under-£400 insurances, although declining after 1770, was still one-fifth at the peak of growth in 1808-10, when half the policies registered were for less than £1,000.

An increased propensity to insure is likely but unmeasurable:[59] the increase in houses within the town is a certain contribution to increased business (Table 5).

Table 5. *Houses in Leeds Township, 1740-1831*

	Number	Average annual growth (%)
1740	2,364	
1740-2		1·2
1772	3,347	
1772-93		4·8
1793	6,691	
1793-1801		0·4
1801	6,682	
1801-11		1·9
1811	8,187	
1811-21		3·6
1821	11,191	
1821-31		4·3
1831	16,065	

Sources: 1740 Leeds City Archives DD 204/3; 1772, *Proceedings of the Thoresby Society*, XXIV (1919), p. 34; 1801-31, census reports.

Individual house values were much less than £1,000 since policies often included contents and more than one building: the first agency policy[60] of £300 insured a brick, timber, and tiled house in Boar Lane, a principal street, for £200 and a warehouse 'adjoining to the north' for £100; the second,[61] also for £300, insured a pair of houses in Briggate, another main street, each at £150. The house of the merchant Lee at the corner of Boar Lane and Briggate, illustrated in the margin of Cossins's town plan of 1725, was insured[62] in 1747 for £200 and this remained the upper limit for the insured value of a house until houses in Kirkgate were insured[63] for £300 in 1753. In January 1758 the merchant Martin Brown insured Holbeck Lodge, a little out of town, for £800—the same value as a house "new built" in Gay St., Bath[64]—as part of the town's first large composite insurance[65] of workshops, drying houses, and stocks of "wool, canvas and bags"—£4,300 in all.

Some insured properties were declared "newly built", like the Molyneux house "near the Free School",[66] £300, in 1760; others were older houses with owners converted to insurance by prudence or the example of their betters. No new streets were built in Leeds between 1613 and 1771, so that the new houses from Table 5 in this period lay "backsydes" as tenements or cottages

[59] Supple, *Royal Exchange*, pp. 103-5.
[60] OS 48/75482.
[61] OS 48/75483.
[62] OS 80: Aug. 1747, numbers illegible.
[63] OS 105/140819.
[64] OS 121/145835.
[65] OS 121/160904.
[66] OS 130/285972.

covering former crofts, garths, folds, or yards behind the houses of the main streets or the arterial roads. The "16 cottages under one roof in a field" insured for £15 each in 1775 were in fact a terrace behind a house on the Wakefield turnpike, later Gray's Walk;[67] and the widow Wilson's twelve Kirkgate properties insured for £13 each in 1780 were clearly not frontage houses.[68]

The third policy issued by the agency, in December 1737, shows another way of augmenting dwellings. George Priestley, sheargrinder and common councillor, insured for £100 one house fronting the Lower Headrow where he lived, for £50 a second house behind, and for £100 a "malthouse now converted into tenements at the upper end of the yard to the north".[69] Private houses were converted, especially older houses whose owner no longer lived in Leeds: in June 1738 Thomas Ellwood of Kendal insured for £160 "a house in three tenements" at Hill House Bank, the weavers' hamlet to the east of town;[70] Francis Iles of Tadcaster insured "a house in three tenements" at the Bank in 1758 together with eight houses in Kirkgate "adjoining each other", that is yard property.[71]

Just as the town rate books increasingly contained multiple entries of high and low value properties adjoining but with the same owner, so the policy registers have longer and longer entries from multiple ownership as successful investors developed infill properties in different parts of the town. In 1751 a policy for nine houses was still exceptional.[72] The first to exceed ten was Jeremiah Dixon's £3,000 policy of 1761.[73] The father of Joshua Hartley, the Sun agent, owned and insured 15 houses in 1777,[74] and Widow Iles 27 at £9 and £10 each in 1780,[75] although opportunities for multiple ownership of new houses were limited until the advent of new street development after 1790.

The early business of the new Royal Exchange agency in 1784 was concentrated on tradesmen's and industrial premises but its policies included the beginning of a new development, the streets of the East End erected by speculative builders, owner-occupiers, small investors, and the building clubs. Successive policies of June 1787 insured not only nine unfinished larger houses that the Greater Building Club was erecting on the south side of St. Peter's Square[76] but nine cottages (actually each a pair of back-to-backs with a cellar dwelling below) of the Lesser Building Club in High St.[77] Ten similar houses of another club in Union St.[78] were insured in December 1789. In November 1790 fifteen smaller houses in High St. were insured for £20: all were Club houses and probably one half-back house of a pair.[79] The Sun had insured Club houses since November 1788[80] as well as such speculative housing as the

[67] OS 240/356938.
[68] OS 285/429774.
[69] OS 48/75484.
[70] OS 50/77400.
[71] OS 122/161427.
[72] OS 92/124958.
[73] OS 136/180929: a Briggate inn, and sixteen scattered dwellings.
[74] OS 262/392791.
[75] OS 283/427718.
[76] RE 13/102207: £50 "unfinished"; £100 finished: RE 17/114228.
[77] RE 13/102208: £30 "not yet finished"; £50 finished: RE 17/114230.
[78] RE 17/114232-3.
[79] RE 20/119327. OS 357/550198: Union St; Hill House Club: OS 369/553499.
[80] OS 319/667012.

twelve back-to-backs of Goulden's Buildings[81] (£18 each) adjoining the parish burial ground, and the one-roomed houses of Johnson's "Square", (£14) subterranean on the slope of Quarry Hill. None of the new streets were millside houses erected by industrialists for their workers.[82]

From 1767 Leeds had its West End,[83] but if Park Square resembled Grosvenor Square, Park Row a Bath terrace, and the villas of Little Woodhouse a miniature Hampstead, there was a characteristic difference made explicit in the insurances: there were still commercial and handicraft buildings behind these residential façades even the largest, Denison Hall.[84] Earl Cowper's tenant built a "cotton spinning and packing house" in the grounds of Woodhouse Lodge;[85] St. Peter's Mill was built in the grounds of Belle Vue not a hundred yeards from the windows of Denison Hall;[86] and at Portland House, built in 1788, the Elams, principal cloth exporters to America, insured "the north-west and south-east wings used as a warehouse".[87]

The full range of East and West End houses is displayed in Table 6. Only two residences standing in 1826 had been insured for more than £2,000, both built before 1786. The Georgian streets of the West End [6B] had a narrow range of architectural style and size within more modest limits of value, £720-£1,600, not dissimilar to the older main street residences [6A] with workshops and warehouses. The detached villas [6C] were in the same range of values. Even the best of the post-war streets elsewhere in Leeds, with small front gardens [6D] were in a quite different range. The more prevalent terraces of gardenless "through" or "back-to-back" houses had values similar to their prototypes in the East End initiated by the building clubs but superior to levels and (or depths) reached in the one-room yard houses and cellar dwellings [6E and p. 382 above].

IV

Industrial policies, especially after 1790, brought more striking increments to premiums than even the largest premises of Table 6. Commission was the principal "Advantage" of an agency[88] although other business might accrue when clients came to pay premiums: the Sun office was in Briggate at Kitchingman's wine and spirits shop and the Royal Exchange in Commercial Court at the offices of Nicholson, solicitor, banker, and town clerk. Since smaller domestic policies were often renewed without re-registering, the period of increase in numbers registered (Table 7) was also one of higher average values: £1,162 in 1782 rising to over £2,000 in 1796, 1800 and 1806, each a

---

[81] CS 27/691783.

[82] Gott had "7 cottages in the mill yard" (CS 4/627124) but had no property in the back-to-back streets erected near his mill. Isolated establishments like Scotland Mill or the Pottery had a few employee houses (OS 208/302865).)

[83] 2 Park Row: OS 303/461805.

[84] RE 11/95834.

[85] Herts. County Record Office, Cowper MS 4949.

[86] CS 2/620326 and 130/959960.

[87] OS 269/404618.

[88] Initially five per cent of premiums; probably ten for new policies by 1826: Supple, *Royal Exchange*, pp. 51 and 134.

Table 6. *House Insurances, Leeds Centre and West End*

Name and location	Year of insurance	House stables	Insured values, £ Commercial & industrial premises	Contents	Policy no.
A. *Town Centre*					
*Lee, Boar Lane	1765	2,200	500	500	OS 164/225988
Rider, Albion St.	1799	1,400	—†	200	CS 28/695193
Bischoff, North St.	1805	1,050	650	3,100	CS 66/778288
Hey, Albion St.	1797	1,020	—	270	CS 20/672935
Pottgeisser, Briggate	1796	1,000	1,650	—	CS 13/654202; 654655
Wilson, Manor House	1796	700	2,400	—	CS 13/654202
B. *Park Estate, Terraces and Squares*					
*Markland, Park Row	1782	1,600	200	900	OS 303/461804
Armitage, 5 South Parade	1794	1,500	200	800	CS 8/636170
Dunderdale, 5 Park Place	1800	1,450	—	850	CS 33/703832
Entwistle, Park Place	1789	1,400	—	1,000	OS 362/558467
Widow Busk, 4 South Parade	1792	1,400	—	1,100	OS 386/599397
Cattaneo, 3 South Parade	1782	1,300	—	6,550	OS 303/461806-7
Bolland, Park Square	1809	1,200	—	550	CS 86/837247
Dunderdale, Park Row	1777	1,000	250	3,000	OS 262/392792 & OS 264/398364
Bischoff, 1-2 South Parade	1790	1,000	100	1,200	OS 366/569216-7
Cotton, 18 Park Place	1789	1,000	—	400	OS 364/562787
*Elam, 8 Park Place	1802	1,000	600	—	CS 44/728172
Pullan, 8 Park Square	1800	999	—	600	CS 34/705775
*Lee, Park Place	1792	850	—	150	OS 387/603993
Gatliff, East Parade	1792	720	—	1,180	OS 386/599339
C. *Detached Houses, Little Woodhouse and Peripheries*					
Denison, Denison Hall	1785	2,600	500	3,000	RE 11/95834
*Lee, St. James Lodge	1801	1,400	2,000	6,000	CS 40/719154
*Rhodes, Beech Grove	1804	1,300	—	800	CS 63/771349
Elam, Claremont	1782	1,000	—	—	OS 303/463351
Wainwright, Simpson's Fold	1793	1,000	—	—	OS 392/611808
Coupland, Little Woodhouse Hall	1795	1,000	—	—	RE 30/149597
Shepley, Woodhouse Grove	1789	800	—	200	OS 364/561114
Hebblethwaite, Hillary House	1796	800	400	1,800	CS 13/653477
Turner, North Town End	1789	750	250	—	OS 386/599160
*Blayds, Park Lane	1785	700	—	1,000	OS 328/503477
Wainhouse, Belle Vue	1793	670	350	730	CS 2/620636
*Oates, Belmont	1786	600	300	3,200	OS 339/521500
Pottgeisser, Park House	1787	600	—	—	OS 347/538125
Rhodes, Campfield House	1788	600	60	540	OS 357/549569 & 364/56513
Elam, Portland House	1788	—	600	—	OS 357/549557
D. *Houses with Small Gardens*					
Queen Square	1817		150		CS 119/935357
Grove Terrace	1825		200		CS 149/1032123
Bedford Place	1826		166		CS 165/1070574-5
E. *Through and Back-to-Back Terraces*					
Union St.	1801		7 @ 57 each		CS 40/719938
Lady Lane	1807		12 @ 87		CS 76/808560
Union St.	1810		12 @ 42		CS 90/842796
Providence Row	1811		10 @ 70		CS 94/857218
Charles St.	1814		11 @ 82		CS 110/905113
F. *Cellar and Yard Houses*					
Headrow	1802		6 @ 25		CS 45/731153
Marsh Lane	1802		14 @ 15		CS 45/731155
Vicar Lane	1802		13 @ 15		CS 45/731156
Old Infirmary Yard	1803		18 @ 33		CS 55/749847
Hill House Bank	1803		23 @ 18		CS 55/749628
Hill House Bank	1806		40 @ 15		CS 73/793666

* See also Table 8.
† "wool warehouse and house under one roof".

year when Leeds policies of over £300,000 were registered, a sum that would be larger were not Sun registers lost and damaged.

Table 7. *Policies Registered from the Leeds Agents of Sun and Royal Exchange, 1750-1826*

Annual average		Annual average	
1750-9	8	1790-9	92
1760-9	23	1800-9	96
1770-9	25	1810-19	77
1780-9	47	1820-6	102

There are no R.E. policies from Leeds before 1784 and few after 1807; the averages exclude 1759, 1768-9, 1773-4, 1776, 1783-4 and 1811, years when Sun registers are diminished by loss or damage.
Sources: OS 88-395 and CS 1-156; RE 1-61.

The agent could expect that only his incompetence or a sharp blow to his clients' fortunes stood in the way of jam today and jam at each annual renewal. A single large premium was more easily collected than the same sum in smaller premiums, and the largest policies were the least competitive since experience of large risks drove the major companies to share such insurances.[89] The insurance of Gott's town workshops and warehouses in 1787 was shared;[90] the "range of buildings unfinished" in January and April 1793 was solely a Royal Exchange insurance[91] but the Sun returned to join in the £16,000 insurance of mill, machinery, steam engine and stock in 1794[92] and thereafter to the £65,750 of 1819.[93]

Since no one has extracted policy values for the whole country, a national league table cannot be constructed to put Leeds in its place although some larger giants than Gott have been noticed. The Duke of Bedford insured for £80,000 at Woburn and the £9,400 policy for Leeds's largest brewery[94] was dwarfed by £100,000 at Hanbury's in Spitalfields;[95] the town's Moot Hall "or Sessions House with shops under" at £400[96] was a pygmy alongside the London Mercers' Hall at £50,000,[97] the Aire Calder Navigation building at £15,000[98] alongside the London Dock Company's £85,500[99] and no Leeds merchant insured stocks as valuable as Francis Haywood's £40,200 in five Manchester warehouses.[100] Chapman's northern league of cotton manufacturers[101] c. 1795 is headed by the Peel and Douglas complexes at £191,600 and £80,950 but Bank Mill, Leeds did rank sixteenth at £11,600. The midland league table for that year[102] has three leaders tying at £15,000 but one of them

---

[89] Dickson, *Sun*, pp. 87-96.
[90] RE 13/104520.
[91] RE 25/131905 and 26/133485.
[92] RE 26/139242.
[93] CS 127/950611-2.
[94] OS 391/609334-5: Green and partners, Hunslet.
[95] Dickson, *Sun*, p. 76: policy 740180 in missing volume.
[96] CS 45/431157.
[97] OS 419/721055.
[98] CS 19/671203.
[99] OS 430/764535.
[100] RE 21/128862.
[101] Chapman, 'Fixed Capital Formation', pp. 256-8.
[102] Ibid. pp. 263-6, and for Scottish insurances pp. 262-3; for brewery values see I. Donnachie, 'Sources of Capital and Capitalization in the Scottish Brewing Industry', *Econ. Hist. Rev.* 2nd ser. XXX (1977), pp. 269-83.

(Denison at Nottingham) had once played in a Leeds jersey, and in 1796 Marshall and Gott were each insuring at over £25,000, setting them sixth had they been eligible for the national cotton league.

At the time when Bank Mill, Leeds' first cotton mill, was insured[103] in 1791 (£7,000) the largest policy was held by Oates and partners for their "warehouses with utensils" and their residence, Belmont, "in a field near Little Woodhouse" insured[104] for £7,300 in 1789. This was a traditional cloth finishing establishment using neither steam nor water power. Next in value were similar new-built premises occupied by Lloyd and Cattaneo (£7,850) in South Parade, and Denison Hall (£7,300) a larger new-built residence but with warehouses and outbuildings for finishing. Among the remaining policies exceeding £5,000 the only manufactory was the Leeds Pottery:[105] Sir James Ibbetson's policy (£6,300) was for Denton Hall and a variety of property in the town centre;[106] Sir William Milner of Nun Appleton's was also for residential property (£6,000);[107] the Navigation had a £6,200 policy, £5,700 for its three Leeds warehouses by the bridge;[108] the mercer Wrigglesworth's shop in Briggate (£5,400) was another non-manufactory.[109] While three of the five £5,000 policy-holders were woollen merchants, one was a linen merchant[110] and another a grocer.[111]

The steam engine, so crucial in the long run for increasing the size of manufactories, first appeared in a policy in 1789 when Ard Walker insured a "fire engine for raising water only";[112] a second was insured at Browne's Hunslet scribbling mill in 1790 but in a small policy[113] totalling only £500 which was the value of the Markland engine in a £7,000 policy[114] of 1791, raised in 1795 to £1,500 in a £11,600 policy;[115] while Gott's steam engine was insured for £1,200 in 1794.[116]

In December 1796 the Royal Exchange opened its remarkable separate register of industrial policies,[117] and by 1799 there were thirteen Leeds textile mills with insured steam engines: premises of this kind comprised half the 24 insurances of £10,000 and above registered between 1796 and 1826, including the nine largest in value (Table 8).

The new engines were to augment insurance not only by their own value and the larger premises needed to house powered machinery but also by the combustible risks they brought.[118] After a fire in February 1796 which cost

[103] RE 21/127048.
[104] OS 364/564239; increased to £10,000 in 1791 (OS 374/579959) and £13,200 in 1796 (CS 17/663067).
[105] OS 344/530638.
[106] OS 236/349891.
[107] OS 365/561430.
[108] OS 303/461813.
[109] OS 280/422505; Turk's Head in the yard behind.
[110] Fenton, Mill Hill: OS 388/603621.
[111] Green, in Shambles and riverside warehouse: OS 139/186728 of 1761, the earliest policy to reach £5000.
[112] OS 364/562205: valued at £100 in an oil and cotton mill, Hunslet (£1,000).
[113] RE 20/119326.
[114] RE 21/127048.
[115] CS 8/636966.
[116] CS 4/627124 and RE 26/139242.
[117] RE 32A.
[118] Loss registers (from 1819): GH MS 11937A; earlier losses in MSS 11932 and 12019.

the Sun £1,000,[119] Marshall's insurance rose to £25,020 covered in the Sun, Phoenix, and Royal Exchange equally.[120] The engine itself contributed only £450 but £8,550 was for the risks in an adjoining warehouse without power. Like the merchant-finishers[121] the mill-owners insured large values of stocks or "stocks and utensils". Gott's policy of £60,500 in 1819 included £18,400 stock at Bean Ing and £22,500 at Burley Bar, his town warehouse.[122]

Agents found the increase in large industrial premises doubly advantageous: as all the companies developed categories of ascending risks and rates, premiums—and hence agents' commissions—rose more than proportionately to the sums insured. In June 1796 Gott and his partner Wormald insured their town houses, furniture, clothes, and plate for £1,550. The premium was 2s. per £100. For £50 of glass and china, more at risk from maidservants than fire, a higher premium of 5s. per £100 was required.[123] Bean Ing was insured the same day for a sum twenty times as large[124] but earning about fifty times the commission, for although about half this insurance was at a rate of 2s. or 3s. and £4,100 paid at the glass-and-china rate, £11,100 paid at 7s. 6d. and £750 at 10s. 6d.—a total premium of £81. The average premium per £100 was 2·1s. on the house policy but 5s. for the mill policy and a rate of 10s. 6d. was far from the ceiling. Marshall was then insuring at 21s. for £6,000 of his risks[125] and by December[126] at 25s. on £15,100; even his warehouse rate was 3s. more than normal, "from proximity to the mill" and the premiums for the whole £25,020 policy averaged 19s. per £100.[127]

V

The consideration of commissions earned on these larger premiums and on the very much larger number of small insurances brings together the two elements of this short study: the history of two London companies increasingly able to organize the insurance of combustible property located from London by delegating most of the promotional and payment work to part-time towns' agents, a delegation not itself free from risk; but prospering also from the growth in the number and value of insured premises and contents as industrial towns such as Leeds increased their stock of houses, shops, inns, warehouses, and craft workshops. Thus, Table 8, an overview of the Leeds insurances exceeding £10,000 has three policies traditional in the character of the capital investment they protected, even if novel in the high values: Brown's £11,000 policy was entirely for warehouse stocks and the Navigation's warehouses (£15,000) were built for holding stock; Baron (£11,500) undertook no manu-

[119] GH 11932 vol. 15, 28 April.

[120] CS 17/663500 and RE 32A/154906.

[121] As late as 1815 Rhodes insured £6,000 in stocks at premises adjoining his house, Beech Grove, and £18,000 at new premises without power of any kind: CS 112/910952 and 124/949160.

[122] CS 127/950612; 950611 insured an additional £5,250 of domestic property.

[123] RE 31/151661.

[124] RE 31/151662; CS 14/656502: £29,550.

[125] RE 31/151655 equally with the Phoenix.

[126] RE 32A/154906 and CS 17/666500, equally with the Phoenix.

[127] The highest rates at Bean Ing were always on the drying rooms, using stoves, and premises adjoining the engine-house.

facture, and the town charity trustees, at £10,000, out-landlorded the wealthiest owners of Table 7.

Urbanization,[128] however, was seen as much in terraced streets as in West End villas; and industrialization in pygmies as much as in the giants of Table 8. The economic historian, whose God is not always that of the big battalions, must be grateful that, when private records are lacking, the policy registers have survived to document such a wide range of capital investment, to be set alongside data already known from the policies of cotton and woollen mills. Since insurance was not universal and registers have suffered their own attacks by fire and water,[129] these records cannot form a basis for a calculation of the

Table 8. *Policies of £10,000 and over, Leeds Insurances, 1716-1826*

Value £	Date	Name	Place	Occupation†	Policy number
65,750	1819	Gott	Bean Ing	woollens	CS 127/950611-2
33,550	1822	Graham	Kirkstall; Burley	woollens	CS 139/998918
27,400	1825	Ingham	Hunslet*	woollens and machinery	CS 150/1032894-7
25,020	1796	Marshall	Holbeck	flax	CS 7/663500
23,500	1825	Rhodes	Beech Grove; Woodhouse Carr	woollens	CS 150/1032216
22,650	1817	Titley, Tatham, Walker	Water Lane	flax	CS 117/930976-7
19,450	1807	Lee	St. James Lodge	woollens	CS 79/810654
18,400	1806	Fisher, Nixon	Holbeck; Boar Lane	woollens	CS 68/784442/3
16,000	1796	Markland, Cookson, Fawcett	Bank	cotton, woollens, worsted	CS 13/653223
16,000	1826	Hives, Atkinson	Bank	flax	CS 158/1050702
15,000	1797	Aire Calder Navigation	Riverside*	warehouses	CS 19/671203
14,550	1801	Brown, Williams	Woodhouse Lane	woollens	RE 32A/184148
14,510	1799	Brooke	Hunslet	woollens	RE 32A/169295 and 171514; RE 36/169296-7
14,000	1821	Blayds	Park House; Hunslet; Oulton Hall	woollens	CS 138/988147
13,650	1815	Hudson	Mill Hill	corn and fulling	CS 112/903929
13,200	1796	Oates, Phillips, Wilson	Park Lane; Belmont	woollens	CS 17/663067
13,100	1809	Paley & Co.	Knostrop	soap	CS 86/837252
12,100	1806	Sowden, Hodgson	Kirk Ings	oil and corn	CS 70/786451
11,150	1801	Baron	Headrow	draper	CS 40/717565 and 717937
11,000	1800	Smith, Shaw, Read	Kirkgate	woollens	RE 40/183744
11,000	1815	Brown	Woodhouse Lane	merchant	CS 113/912808
10,749	1804	Wilkinson, Holdforth, Paley	Bank	cotton	CS 57/758808-9
10,400	1794	Nevins, Gatliff	Hunslet	woollens	RE 32A/155018-9
10,000	1802	Pious Use, charity trustees	Town centre	property	CS 47/731153-7

* including property outside Leeds.

† "Merchant" and "merchant-manufacturer" cannot be clearly distinguished; only the main products are given here.

[128] Considered by various authors in D. Fraser, ed. *A History of Modern Leeds* (Manchester, 1980) esp. chs. 2-7.

[129] Fire—Prometheus Unbound—has destroyed all the RE registers for 1759-73, 32 of the 277 Sun OS registers from 1758-93, and 15 of the 156 CS registers from 1793-1806. Normal archival risks probably account for the non-survival of other companies' registers from this period; for these: H. A. L. Cockerell and E. Green, *The British Insurance Business, 1547-1970: An Introduction and Guide to Historical Records* (1976).

total value of capital invested in a town's buildings:[130] but with the investors in private housing, the members of cooperative building clubs, the retailers, the clothworkers, the cloth finishers, the founders, the machine makers, and the smiths they permit sight of entrants over thresholds as low and significant as those already known from the cotton districts: even though the frequent disappearance of names, especially from partnerships,[131] emphasizes that a threshold was an exit as well as an entrance.

[130] Premiums not being pro rata to sums insured (p. 289 above), agency remittances cannot lead to total values insured.

[131] Much information lies in the Sun's Endorsement Books, recording ownership variations: GH MS 12160.

Plate 9. The First Surviving Plan of Leeds (1560)

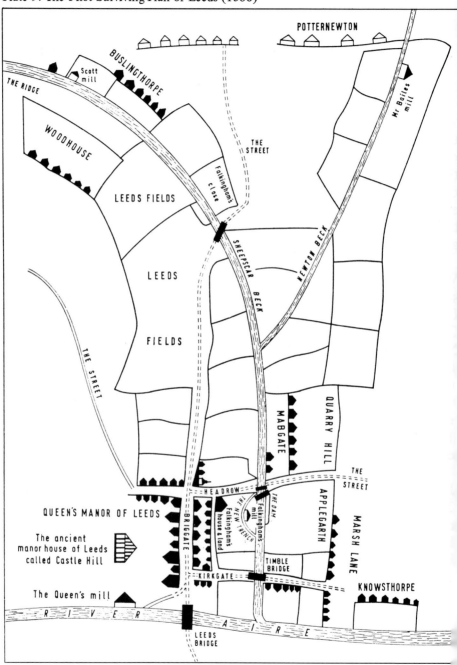

Produced as evidence in a law-suit over mill rights, this crude plan nevertheless shows houses in the manor of Leeds (indicated here in black). These are concentrated on Briggate ('Bridge-gate', i.e bridge street). The 'ancient manor house' stood well to the west on Castle (now Mill) Hill; Note the outlying hamlets of Knowsthorpe, Buslingthorpe and (Great) Woodhouse.

22

LEEDS IN 1628: A 'RIDINGE OBSERVATION'
FROM THE CITY OF LONDON

THE SURVEY which is transcribed at pages 302-7 below was made by two Londoners in the autumn of 1628. Although brief mention was made of the extensive parish of Leeds, with its out-townships and chapelries, the concern of the survey was the manor of Leeds and the principal object was to assess its current worth to the lord of the manor and its economic potential. That worth was made up partly of payments from those who occupied land, demesne and copyhold, and partly of payments arising from manorial jurisdiction surviving from the middle ages.

The survey of Leeds in 1628 is paralleled by similar surveys of other West Riding manors (detailed on p. 301) which are to be found in the same manuscript volume among the archives of the Corporation of London.[1] These surveys of fourteen manors were made in September and October 1628 by two representatives of the City of London, Alderman Nicholas Rainton[2] and the lawyer, Arnold Child.[3] Their enquiries were assisted by formal assemblies of local juries in courts of survey, to whom an array of questions was put in the traditional way. The questions that were put can be identified[4] but fortunately, both for readability and informativeness, the results of the journey of enquiry were presented to the city in a form that—for the most part—was literary rather than legalistic.

A great deal of ground had to be covered by the two Londoners, from the Pennine manor of Marsden near Huddersfield to Cridling near Doncaster; and they found some ignorance and some suspected concealment in the answers that they obtained from the courts of survey. For this reason alone their personal observation had to be invoked to make their report to the City effective and, as historical evidence for the state of Leeds in 1628, it is good fortune for us that the two observers, modestly

---

[1] Corp(oration of) Lond(on) R(ecords) O(ffice), R.C.E. Rental 6.16; subsequently cited as 'Rental'.

[2] Alderman Sir Nicholas Rainton or Raynton (1569–1646); haberdasher; alderman from June 1621; sheriff, 1621-2; lord mayor, 1632-3, knighted, May 1633; master of Haberdashers Co., 1622-3 and 1632-3; president of St Bartholomew's Hospital, 1634–46; committed to the Tower by Charles I, May 1640.

[3] Nothing has yet been noted about Child except his membership of Grays Inn.

[4] Rental, unnumbered fo. 98.

calling their report a mere 'ridinge observation',[5] were men of affairs with an eye to significant economic assets and changes; but additionally that their report was vigorous, personal and lively in its language. The description of old St Peter's, two years before St John's was opened to relieve the pressure of population on pews, is typically vivid:

a verie faire church, built after a Cathedrall structure and having one side therof double Iled, is soe besett with scaffold (i.e. wooden gallery) over scaffold so as noe place is voide to hear ye Minister,[6]

but the furthest flight of literacy fancy came in the gratuitous comment in the survey of Marsden that the boulders in the Pennine stream were too large for any cart to carry away, and that the fall of the stream produced waterfalls equal to the famed cataracts of the Nile. At Leeds a smaller stream, the mill leat of Scott Hall in the Meanwood valley, even took the survey from impersonality into the first person singular and plural.

We understood that Sir Henrie Savell was verie angrie and a little troubled in that we looked upon the Mill. If the Mill be not the Citties the watter that drives it (I am sure, is,) and usurped from his proper current.[7]

Their survey was wholly verbal although the art of cartography had been applied already in 1560 to make the topography of Leeds plainer than words could achieve.[8] The 1628 survey is therefore in a tradition of verbal description and assessment which can be said to go back to Domesday Book itself. Since that early survey together with the most important of its medieval successors were transcribed and translated by John Le Patourel for the Thoresby Society[9] in 1957, it seemed a fitting tribute to a colleague and friend to make the 1628 survey my contribution to this *Festschrift*.

Neither the Leeds survey of 1628 nor the considerable number of contemporary surveys of other manors in the same archive have yet appeared in print. I encountered them by accident some twenty years ago when I was pursuing the cartographic work of John Norden, surveyor and author of the *Surveiors Dialogue* (1607). Somewhere I had noted that

[5] 'We could not suddenly learne out in this our ridinge observation': Rental, fo. 44 p. 139 below.

[6] Rental, fo. 38; pp. 302-3 below.

[7] Rental, fo. 41; p. 304 below.

[8] Public Record Office; the maps, often reproduced, arose from orders of the Duchy court: D.L.42/97 f. 5 and f. 16d; 16 November and 14 December 1559. Like the 1628 survey, this map extended to the hamlets of Knowsthorpe and Woodhouse as components of the in-township.

[9] John le Patourel, ed., *Documents relating to the Manor and Borough of Leeds, 1066-1400* (Publications of the Thoresby Society, vol. xlv, Leeds, 1957).

some surveys made by him and his son were preserved among the papers of the Royal Contract Estates of the Corporation of London. My own interests at that time did not include the history of Leeds so that, when I noticed a survey of the manor in one of the paper volumes at the Corporation of London Record Office, I did no more than order a photocopy, idly transcribe it as a distraction from my work for *History on the Ground*, and then present a copy to my colleagues Gordon Forster and Gordon Rimmer who were activists in Leeds history.

In 1960 Professor Ashton's study of the *Crown and the Money Market*[10] elucidated the character of the Great Contract between Charles I and the City from which these surveys derived but he was not concerned with the properties as such and did not cite the surveys. As far as I know, the Great Contract series of surveys has not been used by any historian, and the few phrases cited by Mr Forster[11] in *Leeds and Its Region* in 1967 are the only ones to have seen print.

Why should the Corporation of London have a survey of Leeds among its archives? why should the City in 1628 have commissioned two travellers to make shrewd assessments of northern manors, from Pennine hamlets to the small market town of Leeds with hardly more than 500 households: just incorporated by the king, it is true.

The volume containing the fourteen West Riding surveys is the work of one hand, probably that of the lawyer Child, for the record tells us that after the sixty-four days spent with Alderman Rainton in Yorkshire (surveying the manors in the Honour of Pontefract and in Sheriff Hutton) the lawyer worked for twenty-four days in London 'transcripting'. Other surveyors, including John Norden the younger, produced similar reports on manors in other counties, from Cornwall to Kent. What the scattered manors had in common was that they were at that moment recently acquired by 'the Lord Maior Commonaltie and Cittyens of London': and by 1641 they were disposed of. The riding observers were in fact scrutinizing assets recently acquired from the king in settlement of his debts to the City, assets which the City was anxious to turn into cash at the earliest convenience and not to hold as investments.

These acquisitions and dispositions arose from the Great Contract, the administration of which has left a range of documents in the Corporation archives, quite apart from the surveys. From these documents Professor

10 R. Ashton, *The Crown and the Money Market, 1603–1640* (Oxford, 1960).
11 G. C. F. Forster, 'From the Foundation of the Borough to the Eve of the Industrial Revolution', in *Leeds and Its Region*, ed. M. W. Beresford and G. R. J. Jones (Leeds, 1967), p. 136.

Ashton has elucidated the history of the transaction, and the next five paragraphs derive from his study.

The contract which was made by Charles I with the Corporation of London in 1627–8 was . . . a gigantic repayment operation whereby the King conveyed certain lands to trustees of the Corporation in payment of the principal and outstanding interest on the loans of 1617 and 1625 and of a further advance [in 1628] of £120,000.[12]

In the autumn of 1627 Charles I had offered to repay the outstanding loans made from the City in 1617 and 1625 by offering the Corporation its choice of royal lands, valued at twenty-five times their current annual rental. With no allowances for the unpaid interest outstanding, this proportion was unacceptable to the Corporation. The eventual agreement provided for a valuation at twenty-eight times the annual rental, covering the principal and interest of the two earlier loans and the further advance of £120,000; just under £350,000 in all. Royal lands to the annual value of just under £12,500 were therefore selected, and among these was the royal (former Duchy) manor of Leeds (or strictly, the manor of Leeds Main Riding since there was an outlying portion of Leeds–Holbeck manor forming an enclosed pocket at the heart of the in-township near the parish church and not then in the Crown's possession).

The survey's attempt to ascertain the current value of the manorial rights and its curiosity about the potential of unexploited assets within Leeds fall into place in this context. Indeed the difficulty that the two surveyors had in eliciting information about these values gives point to Professor Ashton's comment that the apparently tough bargain of reckoning the Great Contract estates as worth twenty-eight times their annual rent arose from 'the fact that many of these lands were being let at uneconomic rents'.[13]

The loans of 1617 and 1625, repaid by the transfer of the Great Contract estates, had been made in the collective name of the City but in monies in fact largely advanced by the City Livery Companies, great and small. In 1628 the new owners did not intend to administer these scattered estates as a source of income. A sale for cash, as rapidly as prudent, was the aim. The Livery Companies were under the additional pressure of Charles's anxious demand for the promised new loan of £120,000 to pay for the expenses of the La Rochelle expedition. For the City to find one purchaser for a whole manor was not always possible,

[12] Ashton, p. 132.
[13] Ashton, p. 135.

and although the sale of the manor of Leeds (p. 132 below) was negotiated with one man, it was purchased by a group of six.

The process of redeeming the king's old debts and collecting the new advance occupied the spring of 1628: in the late summer, as a prelude to the local sales, came the organization of the regional surveys. The evidences that survive among the Great Contract files are of three kinds: firstly, the references to the appointment of surveyors and to their objectives in the minute books of the Corporation committee; secondly, the surveys themselves: and lastly the records of the bargaining for sale of the manors and the deeds of conveyance by trustee for the City to the new owners.

The title of the volume that contains the Leeds survey expresses its occasion and aims.

Observacions upon the 14 Mannors within the Honor of Pontefract in the Countie of Yorkshire taken upon a short viewe thereof in September 1628 by Nicholas Raynton Alderman of London and Arnold Child of Grays Inne Esq. at what tyme they kept Courtes in those severall Mannors and tooke the atturnement of the Tenants there in the behalfe of the right honorable the lord Maior Commonaltie and Cittyens of London by one especiall Commission to them directed by the Assignees in Trust the 25 day of August 1628. Hereunto is annexed the fynes assised by us in those Mannors now due but not payed as also the Copy of their Verdicts, all of them excepting [manuscript defective] their Rentalls are annexed to them.

The fourteen manors had as their unifying feature membership of the Honour of Pontefract, that great medieval lordship vested in the Crown as duke of Lancaster.[14] Of the extensive territory of the Stuart borough of Leeds—the ancient parish—only the manor of Leeds Main Riding appears in the survey but it will be seen from the list on page 134 that other local manors at Rothwell, Scholes, Roundhay, and Barwick in Elmet were also surveyed by Rainton and Child. The survey of Scholes is particularly interesting for its archaeological description of the former manor site:

quadrangle moted round about; and in that quadrangle stood the house. The Motes are now dried upp bearinge grasse which is usuallie mowed everie yeare, as alsoe another square peece of grounde parcell of the $2\frac{1}{2}$ acres which was formerly the yard or garden, close to the earthed mote . . . called *Fallhouse*,[15]

---

[14] This subject is treated in the Introduction to Le Patourel, *Manor and Borough*.
[15] Fo. 63.

a situation not very different from Leeds where

> the Mannor house . . . stoode by the riverside moted rounde about with a dike now almost quite earthed upp lett by coppie of court rolle.[16]

The two surveyors derived their authority to visit the manor and hold a court of survey from a Commission issued by the trustees of the Royal Contract estates and copied at the end of the volume.[17] The difficulties they had in obtaining information by the old processes of manorial courts of survey are very apparent from their report; and not only in Leeds.

Since a formal court of survey was part of the technique of assessment it was necessary to have a lawyer as one commissioner but, even without such a court, an assessment of the economic worth of a manorial estate hinged so much on the legal status of the various tenants that someone, like Arnold Child, learned in the law would have been essential to an effective enquiry. In the resolution of conflicting statements about tenure the lawyer had one advantage over the jurors at the court of survey, although Child seems not to have found it very easy to use. It is clear from the report that he took up to Leeds a rental sworn at a Duchy court of survey in the second year of Edward VI's reign (1548–9) and also had access to the cartularies (or *Couchers*) in the Duchy office at the Savoy,[18] with their references to 'old' and 'new' demesnes and to burgages that he recognized as significant although clearly puzzled by them: not surprisingly when only two years earlier the borough charter of Charles I had thought the medieval burgages and burgess rights unworthy of mention.

Child was recommended to the corporation's 'Committee for the sale of the lands latelie purchased of the Kings Majestie' and appeared before that Committee on 19 August 1628.[19] Two days later a second name, that of a proved man of affairs, was put forward.

> The Committee did prevail with Alderman Raynton to undertake for the Mannor in the honour of Pomfrett and Sheriff Hutton . . . Mr. Chylde to accompany him thither for a Noble a day for soe long as hee shalbe out upon this occasion for hi travaile and paines, his Charges for himselfe his Man and horses to bee also born and £6 allowed towards the furnishing himself with Horses.[20]

The Alderman was to have £10 allowed for horses, and 'they reste well contented . . . and would take their Jorney thither sometyme in th

16 Rental, fo. 41; p. 304 below.
17 Rental, unnumbered fo. 97.
18 Rental, fo. 42; p. 305 below.
19 Corp. Lond. R.O., R.C.E. Committee Minute Book, 1627–32, fo. 61.
20 Ibid., fo. 62.

next weeke'. The Commission of authority was issued to them four days later.[21] On 21 October an account of their activities was received and read to the Committee,[22] and the whole business was concluded in sixty-four days. On 15 December Rainton was paid £169. 2s. and Child £26. 13s. 4d.[23] Child's remuneration included that for the twenty-four days he had spent making a transcript not only of the survey but of those extracts from the manor court rolls that appear in the unnumbered folios following the fourteen manorial surveys, and also of the Articles that were put to the jury at the courts of survey. Some of the answers to these articles were also transcribed in the same volume but not those from Leeds, but some later folios of the volume may have been lost; it has no binding nor cover.

The 1628 survey of Leeds attempted no total valuation, perhaps daunted by the admitted uncertainties when the local informants, even on oath, were so ignorant, silent or evasive. Four individual valuations were thought important enough to be given marginal entries in the otherwise blank right-hand columns: £4. 5s. for the Marsh and Parrock grounds (fo. 42); £100 for the coal mines, £70 for the revenues arising from the office of bailiff, and £30 from the tolls for weighing wool and tallow (fo. 43); and £139. 1s. 8d. for the entry fines of that year (fo. 44).

The Corporation had accepted the manor of Leeds in the Great Contract at a valuation based on an annual rental of £54. 4s. 2d.: about £1,500 by the convention of the twenty-eight years' purchase.[24] The Commission to Rainton and Child authorized them not only to survey but to seek out potential customers in the West Riding to treat for part or whole of each manor:

declare to the Tennants of the severall Mannors as well Lessees as Coppie-
holders that the said Committee are purposed to sell to everie Tennant aswell by
lease as by Coppie the lands they hould (if they desire to buye the same) or to others
that will.[25]

At Leeds it was the 'others' that tendered. In January 1629 it was reported that the manor had been sold entire, neither to leasees nor copyholders but to Richard Sikes. The sale took place 'in the presence of divers of the

[21] Rental, unnumbered fo. 97.
[22] R.C.E. Committee Minute Book, 1627–32, fo. 67.
[23] Ibid., fo. 86.
[24] Ibid., fo. 55: 'Leedes: Rents £54. 4s. 2d.; Money Paid: £1517. 16s. 11½d.; Rents
erved: £58. 5s. 2¼d.' The sum for Leeds was exceeded in the Honour of Pontefract only
Rothwell (£1,876) but the three Cottingham (E. Yorks.) manors brought in £7,600, and
whole lordships of Middleham and Richmond £20,376.
[25] Rental, unnumbered fo. 97.

Tenants' although it is not clear whether they had been there as witnesses or as unsuccessful bidders.[26]

The Corporation made a good bargain, for Sikes paid £2,710. 8s. 10d. the first instalment within six days and the whole sum by the end of June This was an 80 per cent increase on the price put on the manor when the king had surrendered it the previous year. It was increases of this kind indeed, which angered the king when he discovered them and which led in 1632 to a royal commission of enquiry into the Great Contract dealings.[27]

Although Richard Sikes was the sole purchaser named in the committee minute book, the actual conveyance on 6 May 1629 was to a group o six: William Skelton, William Marshall, John Thwaites, Henry Watkinson, John Wade, and Richard Symson.[28] Some of these names reappear when the manor was conveyed in one-ninth shares on 30 January 1655 and it was one of these ninths that Thoresby possessed in 1714.

With the sale of 1629, documents about the manor of Leeds cease to appear in the Corporation of London archives, and the royal sale of the previous year had ended the long interest of the Crown and the consequent documentation in the archives of the Duchy of Lancaster. A accidental consequence of these incidents in public finance in 1628–9 therefore, is something of a Dark Age in the history of Leeds for the second half of the seventeenth century redeemed only by the beginning of the Corporation records. It is the more fortunate that on the eve of the period two such shrewd and lively travellers made their 'ridinge observation' of the town.

On the 'observation' itself no detailed commentary is offered here. I language flows freely and there are few difficulties of idiom or technicality. It is economy of space that prevents further commentary here: an further commentary, that sought to take up the facts and judgements of the two observers one by one, would need to be a very long one, for the text has many passages of prime importance both for what they relate the situation in 1628 and for their implications in the comparatively Dark Age of the history of Leeds. Now in print, it is expected that the 162 survey will be frequently cited, for just as the survey itself refers back the records of the Duchy in the mid-sixteenth century and earlier, so, for the historian of Leeds, its details lead him forward, revealing element influencing the situation revealed not only in John Cossins's map of the town in 1725 but also in Netlam and Francis Giles's map of 1815.

[26] R.C.E. Committee Minute Book, 1627–32, fo. 91.
[27] Ashton, *The Crown and the Money Market, 1603–1640*, pp. 145–53.
[28] Leeds City Archives, LC/TC 5258, bdle 4.

Note on the contents of the volume, R.C.E. Rental 6.16

after blank folios are 17 unnumbered folios [85–91] containing notes of surrenders *(sursumredditiones)* of customary lands in Leeds from January to Michaelmas 1627: these included cottages, closes, cowhouses *(helmes)* and a fulling mill.

f.98 unnumbered] 'Articles to be enquired of' [numbered 1–12]

f.101 unnumbered] Answers to the Articles, beginning with Beghall but nwards omitting Leeds.

Note on the transcript

The transcript follows the original in its paragraph divisions, its use of older lettering to begin some paragraphs and its generous use of round rackets; inconsistencies of capital letters, spelling and punctuation have not been corrected; abbreviations and contractions, except £.s.d., have been extended. The narrow page of the original and the broad margins made for a short line of writing: to economise space the transcript is continuous; the beginning of each folio is indicated thus [42]. Occasional marginal notes on the left-hand side of the page are printed in italics at the end of the paragraph against which they are set in the original. Five right-hand marginal notes total the sums of money mentioned in the including paragraphs and have been omitted.

The manuscript is the property of the Corporation of London with hose permission it is here transcribed. It can be consulted at the Corporation of London Records Office, Guildhall. Once numbered *R.C.E.no.60*, now has the call-number *R.C.E. Rental 6.16*. The help of the Deputy keeper of the Records, Miss Betty R. Masters, and her senior assistant, Mr J. Sewell, is gratefully acknowledged.

[37] YORKESHIRE
The Mannor of LEEDES called the Mayne Rydinge

LEEDES is an Ancient Markett Towne some 10 or 12 miles Northwes'
beyond Pontfract, and 6 miles Northward beyond Wakefeilde (anothe:
great Markett Towne). It standeth pleasantlie in a fruitefull and enclose(
vale; upon the North side of the same River of Eyre, over or beyond ;
stone bridge, from whence it hath a large and broad streete (paved witl
stone) leadinge directlie North and continuallie ascendinge. The house
on both sides thereof are verie thicke, and close compacted together
beinge ancient meane and lowe built; and generallie all of Tymber
though they have stone quarries frequent in the Towne, and about it
only some fewe of the richer sort of the Inhabitants have theire house
more large and capacious: yett all lowe and straightened on theire back
sides. In the middle of the streete (towards the upper end wheare th
Markett place standeth) is built- the Court or Moote House (as the
terme it) and from thence upward are the shambles, with a narrow street
on both sides, much annoyinge the whole Towne; yett for theire Conven:
encie, and wante of roome, not to be avoided, or placed elsewhere. Th
Kinges Mannor (now the Citties) is called the Mayne ridinge lying
rounde about the Towne of Leeds; scarce anie waie a mile from it, som
parte of it streacheth over the river of Ayre, lyinge on the South side (
the stone bridge, conteyninge [38] about 20. or 30. acres on which is bui
soe manie or more houses, now copihoulds divided all into small parcell
and excellent ground, meadowe and pasture. George Shires hath abo\
3. acres thereof on which is newly built a faire house payinge 4s. p(
Annum rent. It is conceived this is parte of the Demesnes called the Ha
Ings as the verie name still Imports. Robert Sowden houldeth anoth(
parte thereof with a house alsoe, purchased of Mr Samuell Casson la'
Alderman of Leeds.

THIS Mannor is all enclosed and lieth in verie small parcells as son
halfe an acre, some 2 acres some more, manie lesse havinge hous
scattered frequentlie and throughout the whole Lordshipp, by reason (
theire great Clothinge on which trade the whole Towne, cheefely, and in
maner wholie dependeth.

THE parish of Leedes stretcheth itselfe farr beyond the Mannor eve
waie invirroninge the same rounde about, and conteyninge therein s
free chappells and soe manie preachinge ministers, and yett the Church

Leeds (which is a verie faire church built after a Cathedrall structure and having one side thereof double Iled) is soe besett with scaffold over scaffold, so as noe place is voide to heare ye Minister. *6. free chappells in Leeds parish.*

The ground in this Mannor is all generallie good and certenly in that place cannot be lesse worth than 4 nobles and 30s. an acre and I am verily persuaded [39] they are lett at a dearer rate; Though we could learne little of the tenants, who generallie as it were in a subtle combination, mixt with feare would have concealed, and obscured even palpable thinges.

Upper woodhouse and Nether Woodhouse are parcell of this Mannor and lye Northwest from the Towne of Leeds some parte close adjoininge. *Woodhouse a member of Leeds.*

Knowsthropp (or rather Knaves-Thorpe) lyeth about a myle East from the Towne and is the more fruitefull place, where dwelleth but 4 coppi-houlders houldinge about 80. acres apeece

Theire names are

1   Richard Sikes a burger of Leeds
2   Adam Baynes
3   John Cowper and
4   William Stable

4 tenants of Knavesthorp a member of Leeds.

These have onlie a common pasture betweene themselves lyinge beneath Knowsthorp upon the river Eyre: very rich ground conteyninge about 16. or 20. acres (as we conceived) and over the river on the South side of this Common where the forde goeth over, lyeth the stayner (but in Rothwell parish) a peece of pasture in Common to them alsoe and conteyninge about 7 acres for which they paie yearly to the Kinge 9s. they have a late coppie of it made by one Tusser as we were Informed. *Knowstrop Common. The stayner in Rothwell parish.* [40]

THE other common and wast belonginge to this Mannor are called Woodhouse Moore conteyninge as we conceive about 50. or 60. acres this is Light grounde and lyinge upon a high hill haveinge manie small cottages rounde about and adjoininge upon it. In this Common hath beene a Cole myne, now not used; yett in lease with these mynes of Knowsthrop payinge for this 20s. per annum ut infra. *Common called Woodhouse Moore 50. or 60. acres. Colemyne not used in lease with others of Knowstrop.*

THERE is another Carr or Common called the high rigge bending
Northward in a steepe descent but verie short and shrubby ground, an
withall ['somewhat', deleted] barren this peece conteyneth about 20. c
30. acres. *Common called the high rigg 20. or 30. acres.*

THERE is allsoe another little Common called Woodhouse Carr whic
is a Myrie peece of grounde conteyninge about 6. or 8. acres. An
through this Common runneth a Becke or smale streame upon the Nor
side of which becke called Laury Bankhill, on the west side or end of it
built a water Mill, close by the becke side. It is a Corne Mill and stande
as we veriely conceive and beleeve, upon the Common or wast of th
Mannor; and encroached thereon formerlie. This Mill is lett by Lease
one John Cowper (a coppihoulder of Knowstropp in this Mannor) f
the rent (as he saieth) of 22 £ per annum. Sir Henrie Savill kt ar
barronett havinge [41] grounds adjacent receiveth the rent therec
Howsoever, the watter that drives this Mill is taken out of the form
Beck or streame and diverted from his course about 2 furlonges above t
Mill of purpose (cutt in a straight trench) to drive the same. We unde
stood that Sir Henrie Savell was verie angrie and a little troubled in th
we looked upon the Mill. If the Mill be not the Citties the watter th
drives it (I am sure, is,) and usurped from his proper current; whi
beinge taken awaie and reduced, the Mill as to the use thereof utte
ceaseth. quaere whose Mill this is.

   Sir Arthur Ingram knight hath the Corne Mills of Leeds in fee farr
and hath also a litle Mannor (as it is saide) within the Mayneridinge
Leeds called Kirkegate and Holbeck; it was formerlie Churchlan
belonginge to a certaine religious house in Yorke and dissolved by kin
Henrie the 8th. *Corne Mills in fee farme to Sir Arthur Ingram.*

THE parkes parte of the Ancient Demesnes were lately purchased fro
the Mannor in feefarme doublinge the rente which before was 4 £.
Annum now in the possession of one [blank] Jenkinson. *The parkes in
farme modo Jenkinsons.*

THE Mannor house of Leedes stoode by the riverside moted rour
about with a dike now almost quite earthed upp lett by coppie of co
rolle formerly Cassons Lande. *Noe Mannorhouse. The place where
stoode granted by Coppie of Cort Rolle.* [42]

THE demesnes we could not heare of said only they are now held as
Tenants saie by Coppie of Cort rolle in the tenure of severall persons.

See the Coucher booke which speaketh of old demesnes, new demesnes
urgage etc. and alsoe a certeyne rentale of Leeds brought up with us
ade by 12. of the tenants there upon oath in ye 2d. yeare of Edward 6th
herein the kings rent of the demesnes (with the parke aforenamed
einge parte thereof) came unto 28 £.4s.8d. quaere how these lands are
evested and altered now in tenure. *vide le Coucher. a Rentall made in ye
nd yeare of Edward 6th which speaketh of much Demesne.*

HERE is a ['litle' deleted] peece of ground called the Mersh and the
arrock (a litle peece of grounde with greate old oakes about it) stand-
ge in the Mersh paieing yearlie to the kinge 4s. James Sikes houldeth
e Parrock and other the Marsh which was grounde lately taken out of
e wast as we were informed it is worth 4£ 5s per Annum it is about 3
res. *Wast improved called the Marsh paying 4£.5s. per Annum.*

HERE are diverse fullinge Mills other then what Sir Arthur Ingram
th which formerlie were demesnes now lett by coppie of Cort rolle as
e were informed. *Fulling Mills formerly demesne.*

HE Colemynes of Knowsthorp in Leeds are possessed by Adam Baynes
hn Cowper and others graunted by leese [43] for 4 markes per Annum
gether with the Colemines in Woodhouse Moore worth 20s per Annum
ore. This Colemyne for the neernes ['vicinitie' deleted] thereof to the
pulous Towne of Leeds yealdeth a good revenue and cannott (as we
niecture be lesse worth then 100 £. per Annum it cost the lessees, as
emselves saide about a dozen yeares past an Income or fyne of 200 £.
r xxi yeares in revercion after six yeares then in beinge, soe there are
out 15. or 16. yeares behinde. *Colemynes in lease for 15. or 16. yeares to
me payinge 3£.13s.4d. per Annum to ye Kinge.*

IE Baylyweeke of Leeds with the Common Oven there Sir Arthur
gram hath, for about 15 or 16 yeares yett to come, it is executed by one
exander Metcalfe gent valet per Annum 70 £. *Bayliweeke and Common
n for 15 yeares yett to come.*

IE weighinge of woole and Tallow possessed by Thomas Metcalfe gent
der the rent of 13s. 4d. per Annum worth 30 £. per Annum, how long
lease is we could not learne.
This weighinge is challenged by the Corporation of the Towne as
perly belonginge unto them by a Statute in that case provided, see the
tute. *nota.*

THEIRE grounds in respect of the tenure lye verie confused and blende together in smale parcells and can hardly be discovered without [44 invidious search and Inquisicion and the people unwillinge or ignorant t discover how much and by what tenure theyhould.

THEIRE rents consideringe the place, are smale as some 4d. an acre an some 2d. an acre; how much of each would require a curious searcl *Redditus regi 4d. an acre per Annum. 2d. an acre per annum.*

THEY saie amongst themselves that the Coppiehould rents in tha Mannor come unto about 25 £. per Annum and 17 £. per Annum or there abouts free rents, besides 4£. 3s.2d. per Annum of free burgage tenui which the Bayly collects, thother the Grave of the Mannor year gathereth.

Here are alsoe newe and increast rents how much and for wha collected we could not suddenly learne out in this our ridinge observa tion.

THE number of the Tenants in this Mannor of all sortes are about 28 besides 250. resiants (sic) which are householders. *number of the tenan 280. besides 250. resiant.*

THE fynes assessed in this Mannor amount unto 139£. 1s.8d. all d since the 3rd daie of Januarie not likely yett to be payed for ['for' delet and reinstated]. *fines due see the abstract thereof 139£.1s.8d.*

THEY pretend theire fynes to be certaine, and have not paied anie longetyme, quaere the Cause, and if those belong not to the Cittie. *fir certeyne as they pretend.* [45]

THEY have a composition, or gratuitie to the late Queene Anne (w held this in dowrie) for theire peace and quietnesse as they saie. Th delivered upon oath in writeinge (since the Court we kept there at t Atturnement of the tenants) upon retturne of theire verdict, that the fynes are and ever were certaine. Which beinge an answeare to a questi not asked, nor anie waie prepounded to them, we forbore to accept t same in theire verdict, but retturned it againe as voide; least by c acceptance thereof it might be supposed their fines were, as th delivered, to ye prejudice of the ye Cittie.

THE Towne of Leedes is lately encorporated by Kinge Charles into an Alderman yearly ellected out of 10 Burgers and 20. Comoners assisstants. The names of ye Burgers (though perhaps here impertinent) I have inserted vizt.

Sir John Savill knight and Baron of Pontfract who was theire first Alderman and continued but a while

Robert Benson an Attorney at lawe now Alderman

John Harrison gent late Alderman

Samuel Casson Atturney at law ['late' inserted] Alderman

Richard Sikes Clothworker

Benjamin Ward Clothworker

Thomas Metcalfe Marchant

Joseph Hillarie Merchant

(blank) Hodgson gent

Seth Skelton gent

46 blank]

23

THE MAKING OF A TOWNSCAPE:

RICHARD PALEY IN THE EAST END OF LEEDS, 1771–1803

For his first book, published in 1935, William Hoskins chose a long title but one which brought together a past topography, a past society, and a past economy, a fusion of subject matter that was to characterise all his later writing. The essay which follows, written a generation after *Industry, Trade and People in Exeter, 1688–1800*, also happens to have a long title with a similar mixture of elements (as is appropriate for a tribute volume) in its study of a leading figure in an early but formative stage in the transformation of the urban environment when industrialisation came to Leeds and its region.

Among modern urban historians the informative use of studies on a scale large enough to embrace the individual house and street was pioneered by Professor Dyos.[1] *Victorian Suburb* was published in 1961, and the history of townscapes will never be the same again. Alongside work on the local contribution of building to the overall level of the English economy, initiated by Weber in 1955, some beginning has now been made on the no less intricate but wholly local problem of the timing, the motives, the movers, and the strategy of urban housing development in terms of the size, shape, and social standing of particular houses and particular streets. Here, rather than with aggregates, are the foundations of historical explanation.[2]

As with the builders of factories, the history of domestic housing cannot be written wholly in terms of the giants. Recent studies of insurance inventories have shown that new mill building in industrial areas of the Midlands and the North could involve the raising of a capital sum very different from the expenditure of a Gott, a Strutt or an Arkwright. Estate development did have its giants, and we now know something of their strategies from Sir John Summerson and Professor Olsen's work on Georgian London, and from Mr Chalklin's survey of the provinces: but the characteristic protagonists, who sold and purchased fields and then built speculatively upon them, were far from giants. Initial development on this small scale within the yards, gardens, and burgage plots of old towns had been indicated by Dr Kellett, among others, in his study of Glasgow from 1780 (published in 1961), and it will be found as a reiterated theme in the studies of the early years of industrial housing in England brought together in the symposium, *The History of Working-class Housing*, edited by Dr Chapman. It is odd that Manchester, where the transformation began earliest and most rapidly, has so far failed to stimulate academic curiosity of the kind that gave rise to Mr Taylor's study 'The eighteenth-century origin of the Liverpool slum'. If the word *slum* did indeed come into English use in the 1820s, the houses that it described in the industrial North were then no more than a generation old. It was therefore their character, their density and their setting, rather than their aged dilapidation, which marked them out: and these attributes (in Leeds at least) arose from entrepreneurial decisions made no earlier than Richard Paley's land purchases on the eastern edge of Leeds in 1787, and the first promotion of a terminating building society in the town in the same year.[3]

I

No new street of houses was built in Leeds between 1634 and 1767. The inactivity is remarkable. In 1634 John Harrison had built New Street at the North End of Leeds as an adjunct to the new church of St John's, the new vicarage, and the new almshouses with which he endowed that fashionable and expanding quarter of the town centre. On the best estimates, the population of the in-township had risen between 1634 and 1767 from 5,000 to 16,000. This additional population was absorbed in traditional ways: by tenementing of large houses near the centre; by new infill building in the burgage plots of Briggate, and in the crofts and garths of the five other old streets that made up the clothing town; and by infill of farmyards or *folds* along Marsh Lane, the arterial road towards York.[4]

Nor was the tardy resumption of street building in 1767 an East End matter. While a tentative but eventually unsuccessful attempt was made to create a West End[5] of new streets and squares from 1767 onwards, no new streets were built in the north or east quarters of the town, whether for artisans or labourers, until twenty years later when the population was nearly 22,000. There can be no doubt. Quite apart from the positive dating evidence from the conveyances, placing no street before this date, there is the cartographic evidence: John Tuke's map of 1781 shows no street[6] (other than in the West End) that was not already there in John Cossins' map of 1725.

The working-class cottages[7] that eventually made up most of the East End did not come in a single wave of speculative building. The first were built by several near-contemporary terminating building clubs, and it was not until the advent of Richard Paley that one can discern an organised attempt to meet the new need by speculative development of streets and courts in high density, back-to-back housing. Significant as this development was in the long run for the sanitary history of Leeds, it must be noted that its early vigour was no more successful than the West End development in achieving a rapid completion. When Paley was bankrupted in 1803 there were vacant building plots in every street that he had essayed, and four of the large fields that he had acquired on the edge of the East End were bare of streets, even though one of them contained the first two steam-powered cotton mills in the town. In his two most developed closes, McAndrews Garden and Forster's Close, there were nearly three acres of unsold building ground in 1809. Nor was the position much better in 1815, as the first large-scale plan of the town shows; and it was 1823 before the assignees of the Paley estate succeeded in disposing of the final acres.

Thus for the whole of the first generation of steam-power in Leeds, from 1790 to 1820, there was abundant land near the factories, half-developed and certainly available as 'building ground' although Fowler's map of 1821 was the first printed map to sketch in hypothetical street-lines with such a caption. The demand for new houses was limited by population increase and influx, the acceptable average level (judging from the ratios both in 1771 and 1801) being not far from one house for every additional 4·5 persons. Demand was also limited by income so that the working-class 'cottage' was typically the back-to-back house, one room up, one room down, the whole needing a ground area of some 30 square yards. In the not untypical area of streets and courts developed by Paley (Fig.

11.4b), where there were 272 dwellings on the 12,500 square yards of McAndrews Garden, the extra ground needed for access by streets and courts reduced the overall density from 46 to 30 square yards per house, or about 105 houses to the acre.

Since by 1793 Paley had accumulated some 38 acres of potential building ground in the East and North Divisions of the in-township, demand would have had to increase by some 3,800 houses for all the plots to be taken up, assuming 100 houses to the acre. In the event, the average annual increase for the whole in-township between 1772 and 1801 was about 112 houses, and the average was certainly no more than 120 between 1801 and 1811 when the Census figures are available. Paley's hopes, which proved fatally optimistic, may have been inflated by seeing 200 new houses a year from 1790 to 1795 and 180 a year from 1800 to 1805. Yet even if that rate had been maintained through every year of the trade cycle, it would have taken nearly twenty years to drain the reservoir that he held. Even had Paley been able to build more factories, there would still have been much vacant land. The four factories that he did build (Bank Low, Bank Top, Cawood's Foundry and Marsh Lane Flax Mill) covered 2,700, 1,570, 1,800 and 250 square yards respectively, or 1·3 acres in all. By 1831 the total number of new industrial establishments in the whole East End was no more than 29, many of them smaller than the Paley mills.[8]

The assignees of his bankrupt estate after 1803 were only a little better placed, for the annual average for 1811–21 was 320 new houses. Even set against the greatest rate of increase for the whole nineteenth century, that of 540 per year between 1821 and 1831, Paley's building ground was extensive, and of course there were at all times fringes of the old built-up area where other developers were bringing land on to the market. Paley's ground was well placed, as Fig. 11.1 shows, but he did not enjoy a monopoly of strategic sites.

In the economic history of nineteenth-century Leeds the decade 1821–31 was perhaps the most critical. It was the decade of the first passenger railway, the first gas works, the first significant public buildings programme, the first smoke abatement cases, and the first invasion of the West End by working-class streets. This rapid and massive accumulation of houses where there had once been fields, and of sewers where there had once been streams, was to culminate, a year after the 1831 census, in a cholera epidemic. Intermixed high-density industrial and building development on this scale may have been within Paley's vision and ambition forty years earlier, but in fact the local economy of his day, although on the move, could not yet achieve movement of that magnitude.

A critical editorial in the *Leeds Mercury*, noting the contribution of piecemeal development to sanitary problems, once commented that in Leeds the whole street plan 'looked as if the town had used an earthquake for an architect'.[9] Paley's original plans had nothing as fortuitous as this. He did not want to be bounded by the limits of small fields and small purchases, and his initial streets, yards, and courts were designed as coherently for his clientele as the West End was for another part of the social spectrum. He could hardly have anticipated that in the 1930s more of the original East End would survive than the West End, nor that some of his working-class cottages would still be occupied in 1955, that is 122 years after Robert Baker had condemned them in his cholera report to the Leeds Board of Health in 1833.[10]

II

Whether in East End or West End, coherence and strategy in street development were difficult to achieve without owning several adjoining fields, for the enclosure of the common fields of Leeds on the north and east of the town had characteristically produced small fields of no more than two or three acres, while the former manorial park on the west, which had once possessed the unity of demesne ownership, had been broken up at disparking. Physical division of the old park was accompanied by multiple ownership, no single proprietor in Leeds being wealthy enough to take on the whole of the demesnes. The assembly of selions into the long, narrow fields of the north and east was indeed a step in building up a compact property but it went no further: at enclosure (the post-medieval date of which is unknown) there must have been many proprietors to be satisfied, for the characteristic pattern discernible from the late seventeenth century onwards was of the one-field owner. Why was there not the agglomeration which elsewhere in England went alongside farming developments of the seventeenth and eighteenth centuries? It is probable that the single-field owner-ship was retained in Leeds because fields of the in-township were an annexe to industry: they were of particular value to freeholders who were occupied in the finishing trades, needing tenter grounds with light and air away from the confined yards of their town centre workshops. Any field plan on a scale large enough to show detail is likely to have tenters sketched in.[11] By the late eighteenth century even the large vestigial grass common, the Moor, was prized by the freeholders as much for its tenter rights as for its grazing.

Singly-owned fields of this size were appropriate to small-scale development, and indeed in the 1820s and 1830s they were to succumb one by one to small-scale developers,[12] producing some of the worst features of insanitation for the 1840s. But, in the 1780s, when the first developers were hoping to achieve large-scale projects, it was necessary to find willing sellers who would dispose of something larger than the tenter garths. In 1755 the Ibbetson estates at the Leylands had been freed from entail and put on the market, but they were made up of scattered fields. ' So situated that there is now a Fair Prospect and Opportunity by granting Building Leases, to make a great Improvement of the same', claimed the preamble to the Estate Act,[13] but the Leylands – a notorious slum name at the end of the nineteenth century – were not developed in fact until after 1815. Yet, as it happened, there were two other medium-sized settled estates, one in the East and one in the West, which had achieved a measure of agglomeration and which were not unwilling to sell building ground at the key moment.

The Wilsons' project, in the West End, was possible only because from 1717 Richard Wilson I invested the proceeds of legal office and a good marriage in a deliberate but slow accumulation of land, restoring the former unity of the Park estate and going beyond it.[14] His motive was probably not a building development but to make a fit setting to the west of the old Manor House were he lived, and which his son rebuilt as a residence in 1765. But building leases began to be granted on the town edge of the accumulated estate by Richard Wilson II in 1767; in the next year a large plot for the building of the Infirmary; and just before his death in 1792 Richard II had contracted to sell a plot of land near Bean Ing for the Gott mill. The family had abandoned the Manor House for Bristol.

In the East End also, the first developers found an estate, only a little smaller than the Park estate of the West End, that was ready to sell off building ground which included quite large fields at the very edge of Vicar Lane, Kirkgate, and Lady Lane, the three streets to the east of Briggate, the old central market street of the town (Fig. 11.1). This estate, by coincidence also a Wilson estate (although of a quite different family), was sub-manorial, being based on North Hall near the bridge that took Lady Lane over Timble Beck towards Quarry Hill and York. It lay on both sides of the Beck, where water fulling mills and dye houses were already sited, even in 1715 when landscape engravings emphasised the sylvan nature of

Leeds as viewed from the east.[15] These settled estates of Ann Wilson had been freed from entail by Act of Parliament[16] as early as 1765. There were no takers for twenty-two years after the Act until in 1787 the Crackenthorpe Gardens Building Society bought enough ground to allow an interconnected group of three streets to be laid out north of Kirkgate and east of Vicar Lane.[17]

This first development by a terminating building society was quickly followed by four others, all in the East End. But the major and further development of the East End for working-class cottages was to be undertaken by private speculative building, virtually all of it by one man, Richard Paley, 'soap boiler and chapman', in an elaborate ambition that ended with his bankruptcy in 1803 and the transfer of his estate by the Commissioners of Bankruptcy to assignees who were to sell it piecemeal in the interests of Paley's creditors.

My first apprehension of Paley's role in the development of the East End of Leeds arose from frequent encounters with his name and those of his assignees when I was working over the deeds of the properties in the York Street Unhealthy Area, purchased for clearance by the Corporation in 1892. Some of the bundles included manuscript and printed *Abstracts of Title to Lands to be sold by Richard Paley*, and his name frequently occurred at the beginning of *Schedules* even when there was no actual statement of title surviving from the late eighteenth century. Soon after, I began to meet his name in the Town Rate Books where I was tracking down the owners of cottage properties in the 1790s, and by good fortune this was the very time when the City Archivist was taking a further consignment of documents from a Leeds solicitor's collection, including the papers of Paley's assignees in bankruptcy.[18] I am grateful to the City Archivist, Mr Collinson, for permission to work over these papers in advance of their cataloguing. The papers include many deeds and mortgages from the years when Paley was accumulating his estate, and other transactions are documented in the West Riding Registry of Deeds. The property advertisements in the *Mercury* and the *Intelligencer*, the two Leeds newspapers, afford further evidence; the clearances of recent years and the accompanying purchases have now brought other property deeds of that period into the hands of the Corporation, including maps of Paley's Skinner Lane project; three other maps, two manuscript and one printed, have also been found in the miscellanea of the solicitor's collection mentioned above.

Richard Paley's progress towards the first purchases of 1787 must now be charted. Apart from brief references to his partnership in

Plate 10. The East of Leeds, I. Dufton's Yard, looking north (1901). From a series of photographs taken for the Commons Committee hearing property-owners' objections to designation as an *Insanitary Area*. The Yard is a court at the rear of back-to-back houses, entered from Somerset St. by a tunnel (left). The principal open sewer of the town was 25 yards away conceivable that some of the young children shown could still be living in 1974.

Plate 11. The East End of Leeds, II. Back York Street, looking west (1901). On the left is the chimney and wall of a saw-mill; across the narrow street the doors and windows c six pairs of back-to-backs. Goulden's Buildings, insured with the Sun by William Gould 'bricklayer', for £200 as 'twelve new tenements' in May, 1797. Paley sold the land in Ja uary 1797. (See arrow at 11a on Fig. 11.1, p. 318 below.)

the Bowling Iron Works, his name will not be found among the chronicles of the industrial revolution, although he may fairly lay claim to that often mis-used adjective of historians, 'neglected', since he was not only the pioneer of speculative building for the working classes of Leeds, but also the builder of the town's two first steam-powered cotton mills, earlier than the woollen mill of Gott or the flax mill of Marshall. These, and his provision of a new foundry for the Leeds engineer, Cawood, lie beyond this essay, and the loss of all accounting records makes it impossible to disentangle Paley's business affairs.[19] Which of his ventures provided capital for which we shall never know. But his biography, as far as contemporary newspaper notices go, begins with an infusion of capital from an endowment of worldly goods openly celebrated and published in every marriage service.

III

In June 1771, at the age of twenty-five, already a soap-boiler and already in Leeds, he was married, and the *Leeds Intelligencer* noted the fact tersely:[20] 'last Monday was married at Otley Mr Paley Soap Boiler of this town, to Miss (Mary) Preston of Merebeck nigh Settle, an agreeable lady with a fortune of £1,000', and in June 1772 the *Intelligencer* reported that his first child, a daughter, was christened at Leeds Parish Church.[21]

Richard Paley himself was born at Langcliffe near Settle in the Craven limestone area of the West Riding, where his father, Thomas, inherited a small estate centred on Langcliffe Scar Farm. Born in 1746 and dying in 1808, Richard was almost an exact contemporary of his celebrated cousin, the theologian William Paley (1743–1805). As a younger son, William's father had left the family estate in Craven for a career in the Church, becoming a minor canon of Peterborough and only returning to the Settle area to become headmaster of Giggleswick School. As a younger son also, Richard Paley left Settle some time before 1771 to become a soap boiler in Leeds. In July 1772 the Poor Law apprenticeship register shows him taking Elizabeth Frances.[22]

No record of any property transactions by Paley has been found earlier than a house purchase at the industrial village of Hunslet, south of the river, in November 1773. In April 1775 he leased an extensive property at Kirk Ings, next to Leeds parish churchyard, (15 on Fig. 11.1) and running south from Kirkgate to a riverside wharf in the basin above the Navigation locks.[23] By that time Leeds had become a merchanting and finishing centre for cloth rather than a place of manufacture, with a plentiful use of soap in the finishing processes.[24] The Kirk Ings property had a house on Kirkgate, built by the old Leeds merchanting family, the Cooksons. It was from a widow Cookson that Paley took the forty-year lease, and began to improve the warehouses, malthouses and soaphouses. In February 1776 the improved property formed the security for a loan from his father, redeemed in March 1779 but mortgaged again in May 1779 'with buildings erected and about to be erected'.[25]

If his wife's dowry had helped him to come to Kirk Ings, so centrally situated, this second dip into the family purse enabled him to move his manufacturing to a country site, purchasing some fields at Knostrop in November 1780. Here he built a house, and after massive purchases of further land in 1787 he built the soap works that were to be known as *Gibraltar*,[26] although retaining the Kirk Ings base where the firm's counting house stood 'containing every requisite Convenience for a large family; with the compleat Warehouses, Dressing-Shops, Drying-house, and Tenter Ground'.[27] In the same year, 1787, his investment interests significantly widened: besides his Knostrop purchase, he took a quarter share of £700 with the Sturges in the Bowling Iron Works partnership; bought a riverside mill at Wakefield for the associated Fall Ings works;[28] and – taking on for the first time the role that stimulated this essay – he re-entered the property market in the East End of Leeds, not to extend his work premises nor to build his family a town house, but to participate in the building of new streets of working-class houses.

If Leeds did not have a true West End before the developments on the Wilson's Park estate, it had long had essential elements of an East End, like all industrial towns situated on rivers bringing traffic westwards from the sea. Additionally, Leeds Bridge posed a barrier to further westward movement of traffic larger than barges, and the head of the Navigation was built east of the Bridge in 1699. The south bank was low and marshy at the Navigation terminus, and wharfside development was initially restricted to the north bank. Apart from wharves, warehouses and the processing industries, the north bank eastward of the Bridge was the site for important water-mills, both corn and fulling; while only a few yards east of the parish church the Timble (or Adel) Beck joined the Aire. For more than four miles from the higher ground north of Leeds this Beck was lined with mills – Marshall's first flax mill lay on it in Adel – and in its last mile the dyehouses began to accumulate on either bank. A plan of 1772 shows further dyehouses crowded around the junction of

Beck and river between Leeds and the weaving hamlet of Hill House.[29]

The Timble Beck, crucial to the development of the first industrial East End, flowed north and south before joining the Aire, and no roads followed its bank: the two arterial roads going east to York and Pontefract crossed it at Lady Bridge and Timble Bridge. These two bridges lay at the eastern end of the Headrow and Kirkgate respectively, and from bridge to bridge there was still open ground on either side of the Beck; south of Timble Bridge there was also open ground to the east where the causeway carried a road to the hamlet of Hill House (22 on Fig. 11.1).

Within two years, 1787–89, all this open land between the bridges,[30] east and west of the Beck, was owned either by one of the building clubs or by Paley. A military occupation could hardly have been better planned, although the diverse membership of the Clubs and the different composition of their trustees make collusion unlikely. If there was a unifying factor, apart from the attraction of the proximity to existing streets, it lay with the trustees of the Ann Wilson settled estates to whom much of this land belonged; Paley's own purchase of three houses in St Peter's Square (5 on Fig. 11.1),[31] products of the Greater Building Society, was probably no more than an ordinary investment, although it is true that he laid out his streets to link with Duke Street and St Peter's Square, and to the west of the Beck he took from the Wilson trustees the spare land that the Crackenthorpe Gardens Society was not using for its three parallel streets, an area on which Paley built before April 1791 'twelve several cottages . . . with the cellars under the same on the said piece of Ground bounded on the north by a New Street late other part of the Said Crackenthorpe Garden called Ebenezer St'.[32]

The chronology of Paley's purchases, re-sales, mortgages and redemptions is reserved for Appendix I. A summary of sales in Table 11.1 shows that between 1788 and his bankruptcy he sold more than ten acres in parcels of varying size. After 1803 his former estate provided the chief reservoir of land for development in the East End of Leeds, and his assignees conveyed some 32 acres before they wound up his affairs in July 1823, fifteen years after his death.[33]

These figures include the Knostrop estate, purchased between 1780 and 1787 for the Gibraltar soap works; this property lay well east of Leeds in open country and will not be considered further here. Apart from the domestic and industrial base at Kirk Ings, Paley's building developments can be said to begin with the contract in October 1786 for the purchase *inter alia* of a close at Black Bank and a close at

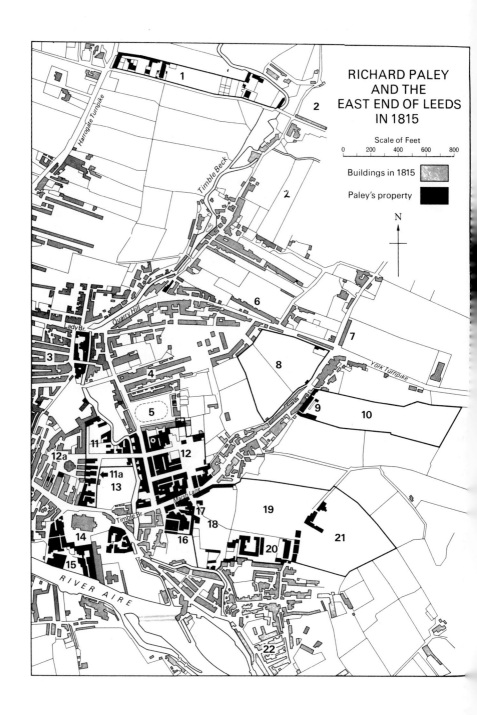

RICHARD PALEY
AND THE
EAST END OF LEEDS
IN 1815

Scale of Feet

0   200   400   600   800

Buildings in 1815

Paley's property

N

TABLE 11.1 *Summary of Paley's and assignees' sales, 1788–1823*

	Number	Area sq yd	Houses thereon
1788	2	346	—
1789	—	—	—
1790	2	2,115	—
1791	—	—	—
1792	3	2,744	1
1793	6	14,130	2
1794	1	423	—
1795	6	5,756	—
1796	8	7,777	15
1797	7	3,927	4
1798	2	714	6
1799	2	1,433	—
1800	8	8,159	2
1801	6	3,831	5
1802	1	424	14
1803	—	—	—
Total	54	10·7 acres	49
1803–23 (Assignees)	110	32 acres	356

Coneyshaws.[34] It may be significant that the former had recently been advertised as suitable for purchase by a building club,[35] and that the first terminating building societies in Leeds were being formed at this time (Fig. 11.1 nos. 3, 12 and 22).

The chronology of purchases can be followed in Appendix 1, but the most significant in terms of the building styles discussed below were those of Forster's Close (1787), McAndrews Garden (1787) and White Cross Close (1792). For the industrial developments near Marsh Lane the crucial purchases were those of Skinner's Croft (1789) and Well Houses (1789).[36]

Early experience at Kirk Ings would have taught Paley the advantages of leasing, improving and mortgaging, but since there

Fig. 11.1   The East End of Leeds, 1815, with Richard Paley's developments, 1775–1803. Base: Francis and Netlam Giles' plan of 1815; Paley's closes and houses located from deeds and maps cited in the text. 1 Skinner Lane (White Cross Close); 2 Mabgate Green and Cotton Mill; 3 Crackenthorpe Gardens Building Society; 4 Lesser Building Society (High St.); 5 Greater Building Society (St. Peter's Sq.); 6 Union Row Building Society; 7 Union Place Building Society; 8 Ridsdale Purchase, 1792, (north); 9 Paley's Galleries; 10 Coney Shaw; 11 Forster's Close; 11a Goulden's Buildings (see pl. 13, p. 289); 12 McAndrews Garden; 12a St James' Church; 13 New Burial Ground; 14 Parish Church and Yard; 15 Kirk Ings and Wharf; 16 Cawood's Foundry; 17 Marsh Lane Flax Mill; 18 Ridsdale Purchase, 1792, (south); 19 Sigston's Closes; 20 Skinner's Close with Bank Top and Bank Low Cotton Mills; 21 Low Cavalier Close with Well Houses; 22 Hillhouse Building Club (East King St., and East Queen St.)

was virtually no leasehold land available in Leeds his estate development had to take the form of purchases, improvement and resale of
freeholds. He was also a landlord of house property, as Table 11.2
shows, and the 'To Let' advertisements are too consistent for this
role simply to have been forced upon him by difficulties in selling.
Indeed the reverse, since 'For Sale' advertisements of houses did not
appear in any quantity until his financial difficulties on the eve of
bankruptcy in 1803.

The last year for extensive sales of plots was 1801: in 1802 he had
sold only one plot,[37] and at this time he was still carrying the two
large mortgages,[38] totalling £15,000, renewed in February 1800. In
February or March 1803 he remitted £5,000 to London for the local
collector of Excise but failed to find acceptance for his bill;[39] he
publicly disowned agreements made by one of his servants;[40] his
former partner Dade, died at this time;[41] large mortgages were
obtained from bankers at Malton, Huddersfield, and Pontefract in
March, and despite another mortgage and a public offer of sale for the
Knostrop estate in April,[42] he became bankrupt on 21 May 1803 at
the suit of the Huddersfield and Pontefract mortgagees.[43]

In the absence of any general business records it is not known which
of his enterprises forced him into a crisis of liquidity; the soap-
making firm certainly continued to function after the bankruptcy,
directed by his son, and there had been no massive land purchases
since 1793. The dissolution of the cotton-making partnership with
the Wilkinsons in 1795 had been followed by a group of mortgages[44]
totalling £17,425; at that time also the cotton mill was put up to let,
and interested parties were invited to seek details of building ground
for sale. Ironically, the last two acquisitions before Paley's own
bankruptcy were the result of the insolvency of others: in 1799 a
house in York as a result of the default of a grocer; and in 1798 closes
at Richmond Hill and cottages at Hillhouse from the bankruptcy of
his former associate at Kirk Ings, the brewer Thomas Appleyard.[45]

IV

So far in this essay a purposive purchase plan has been assumed. It
can be documented. The premeditated yet casual nature of Paley's
first partnership with Thomas Dade, a timber merchant also from
Knostrop, is set out in a note which the assignees' solicitor prepared
for the instruction of counsel in 1807 when the interest of Dade's heir,
Edmund Maude, was being extinguished in a cash-and-land
compensation payment.[46]

Mr Paley long previous to his Bankruptcy and Mr Dade in his lifetime [i.e. also before 1803] became Joint Purchasers of Sundry Estates in Leeds which were Conveyed to them as to an undivided Moiety to Mr Paley and his Heirs and the other Moiety to Mr Dade and his Heirs. Mr Dade's Moiety was between himself and his Partner Mr Maude although conveyed solely to Mr Dade.
Mr Paley and Mr Dade purchased the above Estates with the sole View of parcelling them out in Building Lots, and from time to time proceeded to sales of sundry parts thereof, sometimes dividing the purchase Monies equally and at other times the whole received by each without ever coming to an account with each other. Mr Paley agreed verbally to become the Purchaser of a Plot of Ground part of the Joint Estate and has proceeded to erect Sundry Buildings upon it without any conveyance from Mr Dade, and Mr Paley has also erected Sundry Buildings upon other parts of the Joint Estate.
Mr Paley is indebted to Dade and Maude [Dade's sole legatee] by Trade and by the Sales of the Joint Estate, even excluding those parts built on without contract. Mr Maude is willing to convey the unsold part of the Joint Estate and the other parts built on by Mr Paley if he is given the balance of the Trade Account.

The Paley-Dade joint (or indistinguishable) property formed only a small part of the estate which the assignees were then endeavouring to sell off, but the survey and valuation that were made for them are most useful evidence of Paley's intentions, for this area lay nearest to the town, and by 1803 its street development had been taken further than anywhere else in the whole Paley estate. The fortunate survival of maps[47] from the partition of 1807 and from 1809 enable the incomplete development to be shown in detail (Fig. 11.4a and b), and its housing character will be discussed in a later section.

Away from the two beckside fields (Forster's Close and Mc-Andrews Garden) where the Paley-Dade purchases lay, Appendix I shows further housing development on land bought solely by Paley, mainly between Marsh Lane and the industrial hamlet of Hill House but with three other fields near the junction of Marsh Lane and York Road. The accumulation of houses on the whole Paley estate can be seen in the surviving town Rate Books, where owners and occupiers were distinguished, and these data make-up Table 11.2.

By 1790 Paley, whose town properties in 1787 did not extend beyond the soap-house, maltkilns, and residence at Kirk Ings, owned forty houses, virtually all in the East Division and rated so low that they must have been working class cottages. In the Rate Book of 1795 he was assessed on twice that number, and by 1800 on treble; and these were the houses that he had retained – others, not appearing against his name in the Rate Books, had been built for immediate resale; and most of those who bought building plots from him had also built on them. The period of greatest development shown in

TABLE 11.2   *Paley in the rate assessments, 1790–1805: number of houses*

	Total Number	Kirkgate Division	East Division	North-east Division	Elsewhere
1790	40	2	35	3	0
1795	83	16	57	10	0
1800	123	25	71	26	1
1805	262	18	172★	71	1

★13 others had already been sold by the assignees, 1803–5.

Table 11.2 was between the Rate Books of 1800 and 1805, and everything attributed to Paley or his assignees in the 1805 Book must have been built before the bankruptcy of May 1803. Indeed, between 1803 and 1805 the assignees had already disposed of thirteen cottages and nearly three quarters of an acre of building ground not assessed to them in 1805. The Census of 1811 shows that 136 houses were built since 1801 in the East Division of the town; that is, the area between Marsh Lane and the river. From our evidence, 114 of these had been built by Paley in the first two years of that decade.

Paley was also rated on his commercial and industrial properties, and on the vacant ground that he had accumulated but not yet developed. Four surviving Rate Books between 1790 and 1805 allow us to take stock of the overall situation.[48] As might be expected, the total value of the building ground fell over time as it was converted into buildings, more than compensated for by the steady rise in the assessed value of the new buildings. The overall values rose fastest between 1790 and 1795 although the peak was reached in the 1800 assessment: the lower assessment of 1805 is a result of the sales of some assets by Paley himself on the eve of the bankruptcy, and by the asignees after November 1803 (Appendix 1 and Table 11.3).

More striking than this absolute growth is the place that Paley swiftly took among the property owners of the town. Even in 1790, after only three years of property development, his total assessment of £164 ranked fourth among the property owners of Leeds, outdone only by three families, Nevile, Wilson, and Denison, who then had nearly a century of merchanting or the professions behind them. (The high assessments on the Aire-Calder Navigation and on the Town Charities estates are excluded from these rankings.) In the

TABLE 11.3 *Paley in the rate books; 1790–1805.*

	DIVISIONS												
	Kirkgate		East		South		North East		Mill Hill		Total Land	Total Buildings	Total
	Land	Buildings	Land	Buildings	Land	Buildings	Land	Buildings	Land	Buildings			
As Owner													
1790	10.10.0	17.19.0	55.10.0	57.14.0	—	3.10.0	20. 0.0	8.15.0	—	—	86. 0.0	87.18.0	173.18.0
1795	9. 0.0	121.10.0	79. 0.0	209. 2.0	—	3.10.0	22.10.0	148.18.0	—	—	110.10.0	483. 0.0	593.10.0
1800	3. 0.0	82.13.0	72.10.0	270. 5.0	—	3.10.0	17. 0.0	183. 3.0	—	—	92.10.0	539.11.0	632. 1.0
1805	—	56. 0.0	26.17.0	299.15.0	—	—	13.10.0	137.10.0	—	5. 5.0	40. 7.0	498. 0.0	538. 7.0
Rented													
1790	—	33. 8.0	7. 0.0	5. 0.0	—	—	15. 0.0	10. 0.0	—	—	7. 0.0	38. 8.0	45. 8.0
1795	—	32.15.0	48.10.0	5. 0.0	—	—	15. 0.0	—	—	—	63.10.0	47.15.0	111. 5.0
1800	—	32. 5.0	24.10.0	1.10.0	—	—	10. 0.0	—	—	—	39.10.0	33.15.0	73. 5.0
1805	—	57.15.0	29.13.0	—	—	—	10. 0.0	—	—	—	39.13.0	57.15.0	97. 8.0

Source: LCA. LORB 34–7: Rateable value in £.s.d.
Largest single industrial rating for comparison:
Nevile, King's Mill (corn and oil) (1790) 400 5 0
Wormald and Gott, Bean Ing Mill (cloth) (1795) 133 0 0
   "   "   (1800) 207 0 0
   "   "   (1805) 217 0 0

assessment of 1800 Paley had climbed to second place, falling short of Nevile by a mere £49. In the 1805 Rate Book the entries for Paley's assignees give a total only £34 less than Nevile's, and there had been disposal of land and buildings by the assignees in the two years since the bankruptcy.

The Rate Book evidence effectively displays the cottage property accumulated by Paley; although the undeveloped building ground is itemised in the Rate Books, the best view of its extent is obtained on a map such as Fig. 11.1, based partly on conveyances and partly on the maps of the central area made for the assignees in 1807, 1809 and 1810. Its base, drawn from the Giles's map of 1815 indicates the contribution of Paley to the total East End, and shows not only his ambitious strategy of purchase but also the small proportion that had been taken up for high density building by 1803, and the relatively small further development between 1803 and 1815 resulting from the assignees' sales. Fig. 11.1 also shows his important industrial buildings: the two steam-powered cotton mills at Bank Low and Bank Top, the Marsh Lane Flax Mill, and Cawood's New Leeds Foundry.

A third view of the semi-developed estate is afforded by the topographical detail in the massive mortgages of 1795–96, the renewals of 1800 and the final mortgages of March 1803 (Table 11.4). Like the Rate Book entries, these descriptions often located a property by naming the earlier owners, so that the names of Ridsdale, Wilson, Elsworth, Eamonson and Rogerson still haunted the documents. The solicitors acting for the assignees continued to preserve their documents in parcels corresponding to these names, and this system of filing had a practical point when it was necessary

TABLE 11.4   *The Paley mortgages, 1795–1803*

	Location	Origin of land	Composition
(b) (c)	Timble Bridge	ex Hall	Four messuages near the Calls and Old Church Yard.
(b) (c)	Kirkgate	ex Wild	Royal Oak Yard.
	Marsh Lane	ex Lee	Messuages; newly erected but vacant flax mill with steam engine and 1½ acres adjoining; messuages and gardens on north side of Marsh Lane, bottom.
(a) (c)	Marsh Lane	ex Ridsdale	Dryhouse with tenters, warehouse; tenter ground and ropery,

			2¾ acres adjoining; messuage with carpenter's shop on north side; stable and cowhouse.
(a) (b)	Marsh Lane	ex Ridsdale	6 acres, north side of Marsh Lane, top.
(c)	Marsh Lane	ex Elsworth and Eamonson	Brickyard, 6½ acres, on east and south-east side of Marsh Lane and 62 newly erected messuages.
	Hill House Bank	ex Baynes	Two newly erected cotton mills with steam engines; nineteen newly erected messuages and ¾ acre adjoining.
	Hill House Bank	ex Wilkinson	Thirty-four newly erected messuages and 4 acres adjoining.
(b) (c)	Northall Bridge	ex Mrs Wilson	Messuages, warehouse and shops.
(b) (c)	Hill House Bank	ex Mrs Wilson	Sigston Close, 5 acres.
(b)	Well Houses	ex Rogerson	Nineteen messuages and 3½ acres adjoining.
(b) (c)	Sheepscar (Skinner Lane)	ex Denison	Ten newly erected messuages with workshops, warehouses, stables, and garden, with 4 acres adjoining.
(b) (c)	St Peter's Square	ex Sykes	Messuages with stables and gardens on east and south side of Square, with shares in communal central garden.
	York Street	ex Sykes	Eleven messuages.
	Marsh Lane	ex Goulden	Four newly erected messuages; thirteen messuages.
	Mabgate	ex Elsworth	Three cottages.
(a)	Marsh Lane	ex Hudson	Messuages.
	Timble Bridge	ex Dade	Forty-one messuages.
(a)	Kirk Ings	ex Cookson	Remainder of lease, made 1775.
	Fall Ing, Wakefield	?	6½ acres and messuages, lease of 1792.
	Bristol	?	Potash manufactory, newly erected.

(a) Items re-mortgaged between February 1803 and the bankruptcy. The Knostrop properties were mortgaged to Lumb 18 April 1803 for £5,000; see also Appendix 2 for industrial premises mortgaged 8 March 1803.

(b) Items mortgaged and redeemed in the £15,000 mortgage of 1 March 1796–24 September 1796, which also included the Knostrop properties.

(c) Items mortgaged and redeemed in the £10,200 mortgage of 17 May 1793–26 September 1795.

to draw up Abstracts of Title for the information of prospective purchasers and of conveyancers. Summaries of the content of all the mortgages[49] will be found in Appendix 2.

V

After this brief aggregate view we now pass to consider in more detail the characteristic houses erected by Paley on land that he developed between 1788 and 1803. A number of his cottages were packed into the *Folds* of Marsh Lane but there were two areas particularly worthy of consideration that show him introducing the interior court form of development to the East End. One of these lay on the Harrogate turnpike near to Sheepscar and Mabgate water-mills (Figs. 11.2 and 11.3) and the other occupied most of Mc-Andrews Garden, between Marsh Lane and St Peter's Square (Figs. 11.4a and 4b).

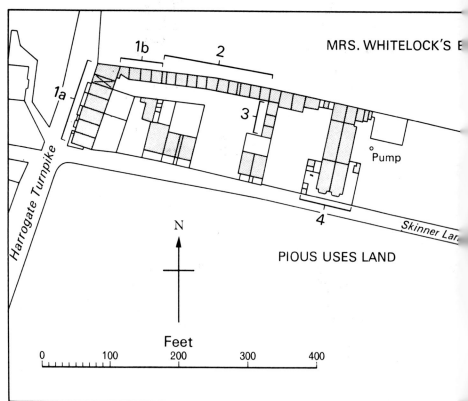

Fig. 11.2   White Cross and Fish Pond Closes, developed by Paley, 1792–6. Houses and shops facing Harrogate Turnpike with entrance passage to Brown's Yard (1a); twin bay-windowed merchants' houses and workshops (1792) (4);

The axis of building club development in Leeds was usually a new street frontage. In only two cases, Union Row and Union Place, both small-scale terraces, was this street frontage an existing road. The clubs who required a greater area took up closes into which they had to drive their own roads, thus creating Nelson Street, Ebenezer Street, George's Street, High Street, King Street, Queen Street, and St Peter's Square. These streets formed frontages for terraces of back-to-back houses, sometimes with cellar dwellings below.

Interior courts are found only occasionally, where streets did not run exactly parallel and there was room to spare behind the terraces for an infill of small groups of similar houses, back-to-back or blind-back, facing into an interior court and reached from the street by a tunnel or series of tunnels. If we are thinking of standards customarily acceptable to incomers, it should be remembered that

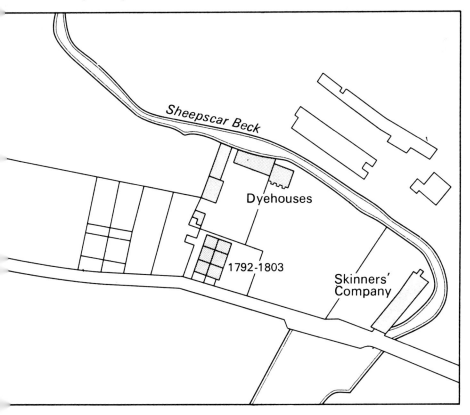

Skinner Lane (created 1793); blind-back houses in Brown's Yard (from 1796) (1b, 2 and 3). Industrial premises leased by the Skinners' Company lay between the Beck and Skinner Lane. Base: plans in LCD 12929 (1803) and 8899 (1815).

interior-facing courtyard housing of this kind was exactly what had been produced during the previous generation of infill in the burgage plots and innyards of Briggate and Kirkgate; and it was already the style of Birmingham and Liverpool streets.[50]

Indeed, since only its first stage was reached in his lifetime, the courtyard developments by Paley after 1793 at the newly purchased White Cross Close (Fig. 11.2) could easily be mistaken for such a burgage infill, entered through a tunnel beneath a pair of superior houses erected on the east side of the Harrogate turnpike, were they not too far from the town to be on a burgage plot, and the circumstances of their origin so well documented. It is clear that Paley intended to build a set of interior courts accommodated to the long, narrow shape of the Close, just as he was filling up the more rectilinear shape of McAndrews Garden with interior tunnel courts between the south side of St Peter's Square and Marsh Lane (Figs. 11.4a and b).

In White Cross Close each of the fourteen houses built between 1792 and 1803 had one room only on their ground and first floors.[51] They were blind-back, that is without entrances on their north sides, and had their only door facing southwards into a common yard since the next close northward was not in Paley's possession and, indeed, was still undeveloped in 1815. The whole group of houses was later

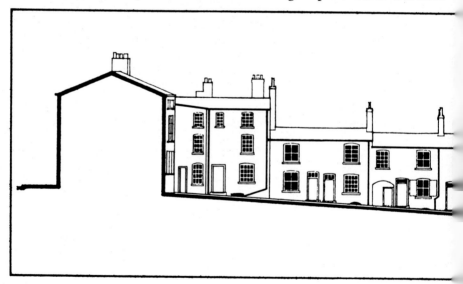

Fig. 11.3   Brown's Yard: elevation of blind-back houses, 1796–1803. Scale drawing by R. Stuart Fell, from photographs before demolition in 1956.

known as Brown's Yard (Fig. 11.3) but its original name, as the 1815 map shows, was New Row; the few houses that had then been achieved on the southernmost side of the close were then called South Row. The length of this close and its neighbour, Fish Pond Close, some thousand feet, made it impossible to continue a yard indefinitely eastwards, and for access to the eastern part of the close it was necessary for Paley to create his own road all along the southern edge of the close and to build a bridge giving access to Mabgate at the eastern end of it. Thus was Skinner Lane born.[52]

Earlier than the White Cross Close development, the conjunction of the Greater and the Lesser Building Society's houses at St Peter's Square and High Street shows that (in 1787 at least) there was as yet nothing deterrent for those buying quite large houses if they had back-to-back houses (and even cellar dwellings) close by them.[53] Similarly at Skinner Lane, the non-repellent character of the blind-back houses designed for New Row is shown by the fact that from their earliest days they were neighbours to a superior pair of houses erected by Paley himself and offered to let in 1793 as 'Convenient and New-built . . . with Warehouses, Dressing-Shops, and Tenter Ground adjoining, pleasantly situated at Sheepscar near Leeds, and very suitable for a Merchant or Cloth-Dresser',[54] while further east Paley was offering to sell building land from the adjacent

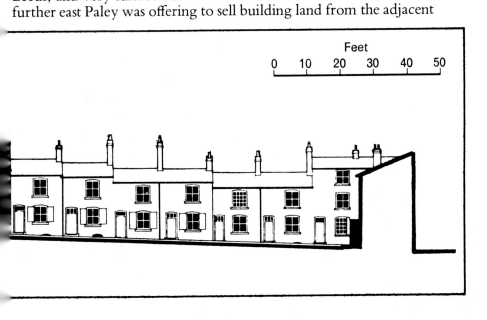

Fish Pond Close, 'eligibly situated'. A plan in a conveyance of 1815 shows that this pair of houses had ornamental gardens and orchards on their eastern side[55] (Fig. 11.2, no. 4).

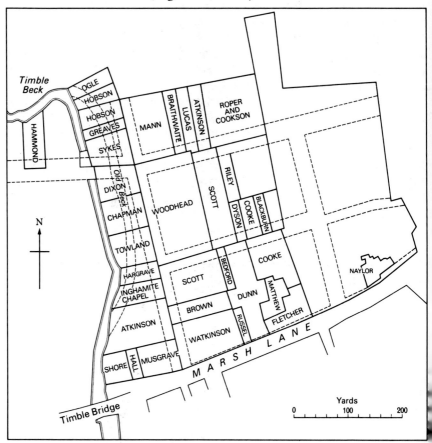

Fig. 11.4a   McAndrews Garden: Paley's Purchase (1787) and division into building plots (1788–1801). The names of purchasers are shown on each plot. Source: plans of 1807 (LCA, DB 233) and 1809 (DB Map 119).

The Paley development of courtyards in Marsh Lane began earlier than at Skinner Lane, and Fig. 11.4a shows the building plots into which Paley divided McAndrews Garden for the sales that began[56] in January 1788 and were still incomplete at the bankruptcy. The last recorded sale[57] was more than two years before the bankruptcy, and, as Fig. 11.4a shows, there had been no takers for the eastern part of the York Street–Off Street block nor for what one would have thought would have been two attractive corner sites at Brick Street–Marsh Lane and Duke Street–Off Street. Although so much nearer the centre of the town than Skinner Lane, the York Street and Off Street development shows the same hesitant development. Incomplete in the partition and sale plans of 1807 and 1809, it had gone very little further by the time that the 1815 map was drawn.

If the first Figure (11.4a) shows the varied sizes of plot for which takers were forthcoming, the second Figure (11.4b) in contrast shows the virtually standard house-size with which the thirty-five plots were filled, each five by five yards, the same area as the cottages of the building club streets. It also shows, facing each other across York Street, two completed examples of the long interior court with a tunnel entrance; two others, incomplete, on the north side of York Street; and shorter courts between Duke Street and the diverted course of the Timble Beck. The longer courts had from fourteen to eighteen houses within them, and the shorter courts, two or three.

Along the main frontages of Off Street, Duke Street, and Marsh Lane the standard back-to-backs were built two deep, and any remaining land within the plot was filled up with an appropriate number of blind-backs. Immediately north of the land in this Figure, it will be remembered, Paley himself owned three superior houses built at the south-east corner of St Peter's Square and included in Fig. 11.4b; on a plot in York Street bought in 1796 by Roper, Cookson and Co. the partners had erected another superior house together with a warehouse; the other non-cottage development was the small chapel of the Inghamite connection in Duke Street, built on land purchased from Paley in 1797.

Of a third type of Paley building we unfortunately know very little. On the Ordnance Survey map of 1850 'Paley's Galleries' appear on the south side of Marsh Lane; they were later absorbed by the goods yard extensions to Marsh Lane station and their deeds are not available for study.[58] Yet their name and hints in other conveyances suggest that they were built by Paley,[59] and they certainly appear on the assignees' sale plan of 1809. They were taken over by the railway too early for photographs, but from photographs of other Leeds properties the 'galleries' were probably wooden platforms giving access to first-floor, single-room, houses back-to-back.[60] Two- and three-storey single-room back-to-backs with interior tunnel-staircase entrances were certainly built here-and-there in Leeds in the 1820s, although disparaging comment on London model building schemes shows that Leeds shared the usual provincial distaste for multi-storey tenements, perhaps from their similarity to barrack and prison styles.[61]

By a later development that Paley could not have envisaged, the tunnel character of the courts between York Street and Off Street was accentuated when the extension of the railway station westwards from the old terminus at Marsh Lane to a central station thrust an embankment across the courts by neatly excising two houses from either side of each yard and further enclosing the courts by the archway that carried the tracks across the yard of each court.[62] Built in 1796 and 1797 at an overall density of 138 houses to the acre but then no more than 80 yards from grass fields, these working-class cottages in their triply tunnelled courtyard were to be a central issue in the long debate on slum clearance that divided informed opinion in Leeds during the last quarter of the nineteenth century.

VI

A complete entrepeneur of his day, Richard Paley was also the pioneer of foundry and mill building in Leeds earlier than Gott or Marshall, a fact that has escaped attention hitherto, probably because he was building for cotton and flax and not for wool. The absence of fame has been fortunate in one respect, for Gott's Bean Ing mill was recently swept away by a Corporation anxious to demonstrate that the 'Motorway City of the North' was truly in the second half of some century or other: yet three Paley mills were still standing un-noticed at Whitsun 1974. Paley's industrial activity can be treated only briefly in this essay, for it was not significant as an influence on housing location until nearly a decade after his bankruptcy and death. When James Watt junior came to spy out patent infringements[63] at Paley's mill in 1796 he had to approach on three sides over open ground (18, 19 and 20 on Fig. 11.1) like a raider on a medieval town, and even in 1815 working class streets on Paley land were no nearer Bank Low and Bank Top Mills (20 on Fig. 11.1) than they were to Bean Ing; the development by 1815 south of the Bank mills was not on Paley land.

It was Paley who brought the steam engine to the East End of Leeds, thus giving it a conjunction of mill chimney, mill effluvients, back-to-back courts, cellar dwellings, burial grounds, inadequate water, inadequate sewerage and inadequate drainage that was to figure large in the criticisms of the East End of Leeds made by Robert Baker and others in 1833, 1839 and 1842. It was to be an ugly and deadly conjunction of streets and steampower but it must be stressed that there was no actual conjunction in Paley's lifetime. Paley had owned the land, and could have built streets cheek by jowl with the mills.[64] No doubt he would have done so in time, but his first choice lay with more conservative sites adjacent to Marsh Lane, Timble Beck and the new housing of the Building Clubs, and in 1803, after fifteen years of property development, he had not built streets alongside the two Bank Mills. Mill Street did not come for twelve years more until the assignees in bankruptcy succeeded in selling

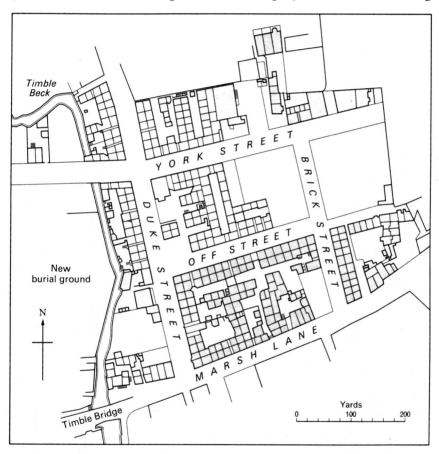

Fig. 11.4b   Building plots as developed with back-to-back houses and interior courts (1788–1803). Source: as for Fig. 11.4a, and 1850·O.S. 5 feet = 1 mile plan.

part of the building ground in November 1815. Thenceforward there was an East End with houses and mill chimneys thoroughly inter-mixed, and St Peter's Square stood among them as incongruously as the incomplete Park Square in the West End. The unhappy conjunction was finalised when the gas works (1818) and the first railway station (1834) were sited in the same group of fields, to which other mills had meanwhile come.

It was an essential feature of deteriorating working-class housing standards in the 1830s and 1840s that the properties were simultaneously accumulating and ageing. Each of these processes, products of the passage of time and of urban development, brought their contribution to urban deterioration and to the Sanitary Question. The significance of Paley's East End development, therefore, is not so much that he filled the greater part of two closes with high density working-class housing but that he set a pattern for speculative development in Leeds which contemporaries accepted and which later generations followed. As we have seen, the state of demand for this type of property by 1815 did not extend this pattern very far, even where employment in the new mills was close at hand: but after that date, and especially in the 1820s, it was the pattern to be followed by those who developed the remaining parts of Quarry Hill, north of High Street and east of St Peter's Square; by the developers of the southern end of the Leylands, north of Lady Lane; and by some of those who eventually took up the parcels of ex-Paley land put on the market piecemeal by the assignees in bankruptcy between 1803 and 1823.

Paley did not originate the back-to-back house in Leeds although it was the form of working-class housing with which he and his sub-developers peopled the East End. The first back-to-backs were being built by members of at least three different Building Societies while Paley was acquiring Forster's Close and MacAndrews Garden. The Building Societies did, however, align their front houses along streets. Within McAndrews Garden and Forster's Close Paley and his sub-developers built back-to-backs but on plots shaped so as to exploit every square yard of the interior space between the grid of streets (Figs. 11.4a, 11.4b). As a result, whole lines of houses were set end-on to the street just as Brown's Yard was set end-on and not frontaging Skinner's Lane. Interior courtyards with only a tunnel entrance to the street had been created, the Paley pattern, high density housing with additional sanitary hazards.

In the first half of the nineteenth century it was common to name streets as well as courts and yards after the landowner or the speculative builder who had developed them. Many of those who had purchased plots from Paley or his assignees were so commemorated on the large-scale OS plans of 1850. After the bankruptcy there seems to have been an understandable wish to forget Paley himself, and Leeds has never had a Paley Street. However the 1850 OS plan did bear his name. A row of thirteen back-to-back houses with 97 inhabitants on the south side of Marsh Lane near the railway terminus was then called Paley's Galleries. They were soon to be demolished to make way for railway sidings so that we have no photographs, but from a description of them in 1848 they were back-to-backs piled vertically as tenements with wooden galleries serving the upper storey and cellar dwellings beneath.[65] For one who had tried so hard to maximise the density of housing in the East End of Leeds the survival of his name at the Galleries was not an inappropriate memorial.

APPENDIX 1   *Outline chronology of Richard Paley 1746–1808 and his assignees in bankruptcy, 1803–1823.*

1746		Born at Langcliffe, Settle.
1771	June	Marriage to Mary Preston of Merebeck, Settle.
1775	April	Takes forty-year lease of Kirk Ings and wharves from *Cookson*.
1776	Feb.	Mortgage on improved Kirk Ings properties from father for four years.
1780	Nov.	First purchases at Knostrop.
1782	July	Purchases two houses at Low Bank.
	July	Leases a brewery in the Calls to Appleyard and shares wharves with him.
1786	Oct.	Contracts to purchase cottages, a close at Black Bank, cottages at Mabgate, and Coneyshaws Close.
1787	Jan.	Large purchases at Knostrop from *Lucas*.
	Feb.	Purchase, with Dade, from *Eamonson*: 4 acres and 41 cottages, Marsh Lane.
	Feb.	Purchase from *Hall*: 4¼ acres of Forster's Close for £1,050.
	April	Purchase from *Elsworth*: 3 acres at Coneyshaws and one messuage in Mabgate for £255.
	Aug.	Purchase of McAndrews Garden from *Ann Wilson* settled estate.
	Dec.	Contributed £700 to £2,800 capital of Bowling Iron Works; purchase of Fall Ings, Wakefield.
1788	Jan.	Plot of 238 sq yd from McAndrews Garden to Hartley.
	May	Plot of 108 sq yd from McAndrews Garden to Hall.
	June	Purchase of remainder of Crackenthorpe Gardens from *Ann Wilson* settled estate.
	June	Mortgage for five years of Eamonson and Elsworth purchases for £900.
1789	April	Mortgage for four years of Forster's Close for £800.
	May	Purchase from *Baynes* of Skinner's Croft, 2 acres, dyehouse etc. for £445.

	June	Purchase from *Rogerson* of close and workshops at Well Houses, Hill House Bank. Elected to Corporation, Sept.
1790	May	Purchase from *Goodall* of 286 sq yd and nine messuages in Marsh Lane.
	May	Purchase from *Wild* of Royal Oak, Kirkgate.
	July	Plot of 975 sq yd from a close near Marsh Lane to Atkinson.
	Oct.	Plot of 1,040 sq yd from McAndrews Garden to Mann.
	Dec.	Purchase from Barnes of Lots xv and xxx from Greater Building Society, St Peter's Square, for £200.
	—	Paley builds two cotton mills with steam engines, one for Wilkinson, Holdforth and Paley, on land purchased from *Baynes*.
1791	Feb.	Purchase from *Hudson* of five cottages north of Marsh Lane for £130.
1792	Feb.	Purchase from *Ridsdale* (Ann Wilson) of two closes, 4 acres Tenter Close), dyehouses etc. south of Marsh Lane.
	Feb.	Purchase of two Yards in Kirkgate.
	May	Mortgage on Knostrop properties of £8,000 for three years.
	July	Purchase from *Denison* of White Cross and Fish Pond Closes for £2,200.
	Aug.	Plot of 106 sq yd to Maude.
	Sept.	Plot of 2,530 sq yd and house in Marsh Lane Close, to Dunn.
	Nov.	Mortgage on White Cross Closes and houses in St Peter's Square for £2,500.
	Nov.	Plot of 108 sq yd from Crackenthorpe Gardens to Goodall.
	Nov.	Purchase from *Lister* of three closes of 7 acres in Marsh Lane, north side.
	Nov.	Fall Ings partnership dissolved; lends ex-partner £1,000 at 5 per cent.
1793	Jan.	Purchase from *Lee* of croft and 41 messuages in Marsh Lane south side, Dufton's Yard.
	Jan.	Plot of 373 sq yd Marsh Lane, south side, Appleyard.
	Feb.	Plot of 1,335 sq yd near Kirkgate. Ministers and Zion chapel trustees (eventually St James).
	April	Mortgage of Hall, Wild and Ridsdale purchases for £8,000 for three years.
	April	Plot of 240 sq yd from Marsh Lane woodyard to Wilkinson.
	May	Mortgage on most of remaining properties for £10,200.
	May	Mortgage of Lady Lane properties for £2,585 for two years.
	May	Takes lease of Harper's water-frizing mill, Mill Garth, for twenty-five years.
	May	Purchase from *Ann Wilson estate* of Sigston Closes for £2,950.
	May	Purchase from *Ann Wilson estate* of Lady Bridge cottages and workshops.
	May	Purchase from *Lucas* of Green End Croft, Mabgate, for £2,000.

	May	Plot of 37 sq yd and two houses from Marsh Lane, north side to Naylor.
	June	Plot of 275 sq yd from Ridsdale's Close to Joy.
	Aug.	Plot of 11,870 sq yd in Mabgate to Wilkinson.
	Nov.	First press advertisement of property to let at Sheepscar (Skinner Lane) and elsewhere.
1793	?n.d.	Mortgage of Well House properties for £2,000.
1794	Jan.	Plot of 423 sq yd from Crackenthorpe Gardens to Smith.
1795	March	Plot of 424 sq yd from McAndrews Gardens to Goodall.
	June	Partnership of J., and J. J. Wilkinson, and Paley dissolved.
	Aug.	Plot of 355 sq yd near Lady Bridge to Simpson.
	Sept.	Mortgage on Eamonson and Elsworth properties for £2,425.
	Sept.	Buys £100 share in Leeds Waterworks Co.
	Sept.	Plot of 80 sq yd in Marsh Lane, Tenter Garth to Tomlinson ex *Green*.
	Oct.	Plot of 236 sq yd from McAndrews Garden to Towland.
	Oct.	Plot of 2,009 sq yd on Kirkgate, north side to Wright.
	Nov.	Plot of 2,652 sq yd near Lady Bridge to Bootham.
		Watt complains of Paley's breach of steam engine patent.
1796	Jan.	Plot of 4,015 sq yd at Skinner Lane to Brown and Sayer.
	Feb.	Plot of 135 sq yd and two houses from McAndrews Garden to Cooke.
	Feb.	Plot of 1,307 sq yd with warehouses at McAndrews Garden to Roper and Cookson.
	Feb.	Plot of 885 sq yd and thirteen houses from McAndrews Garden to Salt.
	March	Plot of 136 sq yd south-west of St Peter's Square to Baistow.
	March	Mortgage on Well House, two cotton mills and thirty other properties of £15,000.
	April	Plot of 144 sq yd from Dunn's Garden to Dyson.
	April	Plot of 867 sq yd to Scott.
	May	Plot of 288 sq yd from McAndrews Garden to Atkinson.
	May	Cotton Mill to let; sale of building ground envisaged.
1797	Jan.	Plot of 288 sq yd from McAndrews Garden to Lucas and Atkinson.
	Feb.	Plot of 514 sq yd in Marsh Lane to Lee.
	April	Plot of 392 sq yd from McAndrews Garden to Braithwaite.
	May	Four houses in St Peter's Square to Rathmell.
	June	Plot of 2,147 sq yd in Marsh Lane, bottom to Woodhead.
	July	Plot of 496 sq yd in Marsh Lane, bottom to Ingham.
	Sept.	Plot of 90 sq yd from Tenter Garth ex *Green*, Marsh Lane, east side to Gledhill.
	—	Holdforth, Wilkinson and Paley purchase a Watt engine from Soho.
1798	Feb.	Acquires from bankrupt *Appleyard*, closes at Richmond Hill and cottages at Hillhouse.

	Sept.	Plot of 466 sq yd in St Peter's Square to Smithies.
	Nov.	Plot of 248 sq yd and six houses in Marsh Lane bottom to Bell.
	Nov.	Paley contracts to build flax mill with steam engine in Marsh Lane for G. and J. Wright.
1799	March	Plot of 1,057 sq yd in Close adj. Sheepscar Beck to Richardson.
	Sept.	Obtains houses in York from trade debt by Johnson (£3,300).
	Oct.	Plot of 376 sq yd on Quarry Hill, north side to Clarkson.
1800	Feb.	Mortgage on remaining estate for £13,000.
	Feb.	Mortgage on Wilson purchases for £2,000.
	March	Plot of 923 sq yd to Goulden.
	April	Plot of 420 sq yd from Forster's Close to Hammond.
	May	Plot of 129 sq yd from McAndrews Garden to Simpson.
	May	Plot of 174 sq yd from McAndrews Garden to Wilkinson.
	June	Plot of 166 sq yd and two houses from McAndrews Garden to Lee.
	Aug.	Plot of 284 sq yd from Forster's Close to Sykes.
	Oct.	Plot of 1,360 sq yd in a Marsh Lane croft, and maltkiln to Musgrave.
	Dec.	Plot of 4,481 sq yd from Forster's Close sold for Burial Ground.
	Dec.	Plot of 222 sq yd in a close, Marsh Lane to Mennill.
1801	Jan.	Plot of 166 sq yd from McAndrews Garden to Wilkinson.
	June	Plot of 953½ sq yd near Lady Bridge woodyard to Woodhead.
	Sept.	Plot of 338 sq yd and five houses from Forster's Close to Schofield.
	Sept.	Plot of 4,491 sq yd from Forster's Close to Blayds and others.
	Dec.	Plot of 553 sq yd in St Peter's Square to Sherbrock.
		Plot of 1,809 sq yd from McAndrews Garden to Watkinson.
1802	April	Plot of 424 sq yd and fourteen houses from Forster's Close to Sykes.
1803	Jan.	First press advertisement for sale of Sheepscar, Mabgate, Lady Bridge, St Peter's Square and Kirk Ings properties.
	March	Malton Bank mortgage.
	March	Huddersfield and Pontefract bankers' mortgage.
	April	Lumb mortgage; Knostrop estate advertised for sale.
	May 11	Probate of Thomas Dade's will.
	May 21	Commission of Bankruptcy; assignment of personal goods; Bank Upper Mill and building lots advertised.
	June 11	First meeting of creditors; some dividends paid.
	Sept.	Further sale advertised.
	Nov. 28	Richard Paley subscribed 10 guineas for relief of poor.
	Nov. 29	First conveyance by assignees: 179 sq yd to Asquith.
1804	Jan.	Further sale advertised.
		Twelve conveyances from assignees.
1805	Feb.	Further sale advertised.
	Nov.	Creditors agitate for change of policy by assignees.
		Nine conveyances from assignees. Paley resigns from Corporation in Sept.

1806	Jan.	Further sale advertised.
	Feb.	Further sale advertised.
	May	Further sale advertised.
	Oct.	Creditors again agitate.
	Oct.	Further sale advertised.
		Eighteen conveyances by assignees.
1807	Jan.	Creditors yet again agitate.
	Mar.	Partition of the Dade moiety in favour of legatee, Edmund Maude.
		Sixteen conveyances by assignees.
1808		Four conveyances by assignees.
	Nov. 24	Paley dies at Knostrop, leaving widow Agnes, and son George as heir.
1809		Plan of central section of estate made for assignees; no conveyances this year.
1810	Dec.	Printed Sale-plan of estate by Oastler for assignees' sale; three conveyances this year.
1811		Six conveyances by assignees.
1812		No sales by assignees.
1813		No sales by assignees.
1814	Dec.	Original Clapham group of assignees replaced by Ikin group.
1814		Six conveyances by assignees.
1815	June	Further sale advertised.
1815		Eleven conveyances by assignees.
1816	Nov.	Further dividend to creditors.
1816		Seven conveyances by assignees.
1817		No sales by assignees.
1818	Feb.	Remaining part of estate advertised for sale.
1818		Three conveyances by assignees.
1819		One conveyance by assignees.
1820		One conveyance by assignees.
1821		Two conveyances by assignees.
1822		Three conveyances by assignees.
1823	Jan.	One conveyance by assignees.
	Mar.	One conveyance by assignees.
	April 12	Last five conveyances by assignees.
	July	Final dividend paid.

---

* The values of purchases and mortgages are incompletely known since the enrolments at WRRD always omitted this confidential fact; original deeds in LCA and LCD do not survive for all transactions.

Appendix 2 *Paley's mortgages, 1776–1803*

Date	Location	Origin of land	Mortgaged to	£	Redemption
4.2.1776	Kirk Ings	Cookson, 1775	T. Paley	?	6.3.1779
1.4.1779	Kirk Ings	Cookson, 1775	J. Crofts	?	?
30.1.1787	Knostrop	Lucas, 1780	J. Lucas	?	?
3.6.1788	Coneyshaws Close and Mabgate	Elsworth, 1787	C. Davison	900	26.8.1793
14.5.1789	Forster's Close	Hall, 1787	W. Hey	800	14.1.1793
25.11.1789	Knostrop	Lucas, 1780	J. Lucas	?	?
27.5.1792	Knostrop	Lucas, 1780	Beckett, Calverley & Co.	8,000	17.12.1795
22.11.1792	White Cross Close	Denison, 1792	Townend	2,500	assignees, 1807
	St Peter's Square	Barnes, 1790			
11.4.1793	Timble Bridge	Ridsdale, 1792			
	Royal Oak, Kirkgate	Wild, 1730	Glover	8,000	5.12.1799
	Forster's Close	Hall, 1787			
	Marsh Lane, 4 closes, of 9 acres	Ridsdale?			
3.5.1793	Northall	Mrs Wilson, 1793	Beckett & Duncombe	2,585	6.4.1795
17.5.1793	Timble Bridge	Ridsdale, 1792			
	Royal Oak Yard	Wild, 1790			
	Forster's Close	Hall, 1787			
	St Peter's Square	Barnes, 1790			
	St Peter's Square	Stephenson, 1793			
	White Cross Close	Denison, 1792	T. Paley	10,200	26.9.1795
	New buildings	Elsworth, 1787			
	New Buildings	Eamonson, 1787			
	New buildings	Goodall & Cookson, 1790–1			
	Kirk Ings	Cookson, 1775			
	Fall Ing, Wakefield	—			
11.6.1793	Marsh Lane	?	E. Wetherhead	?	10.12.1799
23.11.1793	Cavalier Hill Close	Wilkinson, 1792	S. Harvey	2,000	7.2.1800
	Low Bottom Close				
?.5.1793	Marsh Lane,	Mrs Wilson, 1788	H. Duncombe	?	6.4.1795
	Sigston Closes				
	Well House Close	Rogerson, 1788			
28.9.1795	Coneyshaws Close and Mabgate	Elsworth, 1787	R. Goddard	2,310	assignees, 1807
1.3.1796	see Table 11.4, item (b)		W. Dawson	15,000	24.9.1796
12.3.1796	all in 28.9.1795 and 1.3.1796 mortgages		T. Paley	?	22.9.1796
18.4.1796	Hill House and two cotton mills	Baynes, 1789	T. Wilson	1,000	?
28.9.1796	Knostrop	Lucas *et al.*, 1780	J. Armitage	?	?
7.2.1800	Cavalier Hill Close	Wilkinson, 1792	J. Armitage & W. Cookson	1,300	
	Low Bottom Close				
15.4.1800	See Table 11.4	Ridsdale, 1792	Cookson *et al.*	?	19.2.1803
22.4.1800	Northall	Mrs Wilson, 1793	Rhodes	2,000	1.2.1803
	Well House Close	Rogerson, 1788			
15.9.1801	Forster's Close	Hall, 1787	Blayds *et al*	?	?
8.3.1803	Marsh Lane Closes, Wright's Flax Mill, Farmery's Whitesmithy, and Cawood's Iron & Brass Foundry	Ridsdale, 1792	Malton Bank	?	?
12.3.1803	Kirk Ings lease	Cookson, 1775	Seaton, Seaton & Seaton	?	?

Date	Location	Origin of land	Mortgaged to	£	Redemption
18.4.1803	Knostrop	Lucas *et al.*	Lumb	2,000	?
18.4.1803	Marsh Lane, closes Marsh Lane, cottages	Ridsdale, 1792 Hudson, 1791 }	Lumb	3,000	?

Sources: 4.2.76:WRRD, BZ35; 1.4.79: CE546; 30.1.87: CU193; 3.6.88: CX35; 14.5.89: DA186; 25.11.89: DB243; 27.5.92: DI428; 22.11.92: DK449; 11.4.93: LCA, DB233; 3.5.93:WRRD, DN119; 17.5.93: DM256; 11.6.93: DM662; 23.11.93: DN178; 5.1793: DR150: 28.9.95: DS187; 1.3.96: DT251 and LCD 359; 12.3.96: DT306; 18.4.96: DU9; 28.9.96: DW103; 7.2.00: EC55; 15.4.00: ED339; 22.4.00: ED550; 15.9.01: EK118; 8.3.03: EM 462; 12.3.03: EM590: 18.4.03: EN575; 18.4.03: EN623.
WRRD; West Riding Registry of Deeds. LCA; Leeds City Archives. LCD; Leeds Corporation Deeds, Civic Hall.

NOTES AND REFERENCES

Maps. Printed maps are those of John Cossins (1725), John Tuke (1781), and Netlam and Francis Giles (1815); those of Thomas Jeffreys (1770) and John Heaton (1806) are less useful.

1. H. J. Dyos, *Victorian Suburb* (Leicester University Press, 1961).
2. For a recent bibliographical essay, see A. Sutcliffe, 'Working-class housing in nineteenth century Britain', *Bulletin of the Society for the Study of Labour History*, no. 24 (1972), 40–51. An early study of the local strategy of development in Leeds was the M.A. thesis of David (now Professor) Ward, part of which appeared as 'The pre-urban cadaster and the urban pattern of Leeds', *Annals of the Assocn. of American Geographers, lii* (1962), 150–66. B. Weber, 'A New Index of Residential Construction', *Scottish Journal of Political Economy*, II (1955), 104–132.
3. Sir John Summerson, *Georgian London* (2nd edn, rev. Barrie & Jenkins, 1962; Penguin Books); D. J. Olsen, *Town Planning in London: the Eighteenth and Nineteenth Centuries* (Yale University Press, 1964); C. W. Chalklin, *The Provincial Towns of Georgian England: a study of the Building Process, 1740–1820* (Edward Arnold, 1974); J. R. Kellett, *Glasgow* (Blond Educational, 1961); S. D. Chapman, ed., *The History of Working-class Housing* (David & Charles, 1971); I. C. Taylor, 'The eighteenth-century origin of the Liverpool slum', *Trans. Hist. Soc. Lancs. and Cheshire*, cxxii (1970), 67–90.
4. Illustrated in M. W. Beresford, 'The back-to-back house in Leeds, 1787–1937' figs. 3.1 and 3.2 (below, pp. 361, 362).
5. Illustrated in M. W. Beresford, 'Prosperity Street and others', in M. W. Beresford and G. R. J. Jones, eds, *Leeds and Its Region* (British Association for the Advancement of Science, 1967), figs. 41–3. See below, pp. 351, 353, 354.
6. In the transpontine South Division of the in-township the development was similar: infill of yards on Meadow Lane and Hunslet Lane until the building of Kendall Street (1793) and Camp Field (1805–6). Beyond the in-township on the south bank were the industrial villages of Hunslet and Holbeck.

7. 'Cottage' was the contemporary term: see W. G. Rimmer, 'Working men's cottages in Leeds, 1770–1840', *Thoresby Society*, xlvi (1961), 165–99. The usage arose not from neo-rustic romanticism but probably from the unbroken tradition of infill at the farming *Folds* on the town edge; see also maps cited in note, above.

8. Houses in the in-township: 1772: 3,345 (*Publns of the Thoresby Society,* xxiv (1919), 34); 1801: 6,694; 1811: 7,854; 1821: 11,160; 1831: 16,580 (Census); rates of building in the 1790's from Rimmer, *loc. cit.*, p. 187; number of factories *ex inf.* Dr. M. J. Ward.

9. *Leeds Mercury [LM]*, 25 September 1852.

10. Robert Baker, *Report of the Leeds Board of Health* (1833).

11. For example, the plan of Crackenthorpe Gardens before its sale to the Building Society trustees: Leeds City Archives [LCA], DB Map 373 (1784).

12. As late as the Tithe Award of 1847 (LCA) the average size of the 54 fields designated as 'building ground' was only just over $1\frac{1}{4}$ acres.

13. 28 Geo. II cap. 10.

14. R. G. Wilson, *Gentlemen Merchants* (Manchester University Press, 1971), pp. 193–203; but it is wrongly stated there (p. 198) that Richard Wilson I inherited the Parks estate intact; purchases of many closes 'part of the Ancient Park' will be found in 1717, 1729 and 1748: West Riding Registry of Deeds (Wakefield) [WRRD], M19/26; AA326/422; AC169/237.

15. The second of W. Lodge's *Prospects* of 1715, with the southern part of the town in the foreground, has a less idyllic view of the town with a line of dyehouse chimneys on the eastern skyline.

16. 5 Geo. III, Acts Private.

17. Leeds Corporation Deeds [LCD], 320, 334, 423 and 435.

18. LCA, DB 233.

19. Creditors claimed that from £15,000 to £20,000 capital was locked in the soap works and the cotton mill; one assignee declared hopefully that after meeting creditors' claims in full there would be £50,000 to distribute: *Leeds Intelligencer [LI]*, 13 February 1804. For descriptions of the cotton mills see *LI*, 24 October 1796 and LCD, 1615; for the flax mill, *LI*, 19 October 1801; the foundry, *LI*, 11 July 1805.

20. *LI*, 25 June 1771; Paley's partner, Thomas Dade (note 41, below), came from Otley; perhaps Paley had connnections there. In 1800 a Mrs *Agnes* Paley joined Richard in a conveyance: Borthwick Institute, York, R. IV. K57; R. I. 38, f. 356; WRRD EK 118/166.

21. *LI*, 3 September 1772.

22. LCA, DW 514 and 685 for the Langcliffe connections; LO/AR1 for the apprentice.

23. WRRD, BX71/111. Breviates of most of the WRRD deeds appear also in LCA, DB 233.

24. Wilson, *op. cit.*, pp. 37–62.

25. WRRD, BZ35/51; CE545/686; CE546/688.

26. WRRD, CU192/236; DB98/125; DB243/296.

27. *LI*, 28 March 1808 and 18 November 1816 for the Paley offices and home.

28. WRRD, DF596/769; DH491/622; DK613/758; DS185/199; DM256/306; Hilary Long, 'The Bowling Ironworks', *Industrial Archaeology*, v (1968), 171–7; W. L. Norman, 'Fall Ings', *ibid.*, vi (1969), 1.

29. Plan *penes* British Waterways Board, Dock Street, Leeds.

30. Most of it was in use as allotment gardens, as the field names show: McAndrews Garden; Dunn's Garden; Crackenthorpe Gardens; Forster's Close was also known as Old Garden; the conveyance of Ridsdale's Tenter Close in 1792 describes it as part gardens: WRRD, DH455/569; DL692/815.

31. WRRD, DF7/6.

32. WRRD, DG72/106.

33. Assignees' sales: WRRD, EP329/426 (29 November 1803) to HX510/507 (2 November 1823).

34. WRRD, CW85/108.

35. *LI*, 5 December 1786.

36. WRRD, CT417/546; CW441/568; DI603/839; DB143/174; DI464/662.

37. WRRD, EM16/21: 424 square yards and fourteen newly erected houses on part of Forster's Close.

38. WRRD, EC55/860; DN178/238; also LCD5063.

39. LCA, DB 233, 'Counsel's Opinion' 1804: the sheriff was in possession of Paley's property 'to a large amount'.

40. *LI*, 7 February 1803.

41. Dade's will was proved on 3 November 1803: WRRD, EW742/853: it provided for a division of the Paley-Dade joint purchases but this was not achieved until March 1807 (WRRD, FD14/15). On 18 February 1803 Paley conveyed his share to trustees for his heirs, the origin of the 'private estate' of 2 acres remaining to his son in 1809: LCA, DB Map 119.

42. WRRD, EM462/612; EM590/807; EN575/773; EN623/835.

43. 'indebted in the course of trade, for £3,062 2s 3d to 'Seatons', four of whom were still shareholders in Richard Paley and Co. six years later. The Paley files in the Court of Bankruptcy records are not among the small sample undestroyed; Public Record Office B6/11, f. 131 but see C13/57 (ii) no 50.

44. 'Mr Paley having an unusual occasion for a large sum of money' took a loan in the form of £15,000 of 3 per cent Consols (LCD 359: 1.3.1796).

45. Appleyard: WRRD, EA35/36 and EB779/1045; also LCA, DB233; York: WRRD, EB1/1043.

46. LCA, DB 233: 'Note for Counsel', undated.

47. 1807: LCA, DB 233, map with partition deed; 1809: LCA, DB Map 119. A printed map by Oastler was published by the assignees in 1810, showing all the East End properties; there are several copies in DB 233.

48. Rate Books, LCA, LO/RB 34–7.

49. 1795–6: WRRD DS187/201; DT251/289; DT306/360; DU9/10; DW103/109; 1800: EC555/860; ED 339/445; ED 550/744; 1803: EM462/612; EM590/807; EN575/773; EN623/835.

50. Birmingham: *Victoria County History: Warwickshire*, vii (1964), 52–4; Liverpool: I. C. Taylor, *loc. cit.* (see note 3 above), 67–90, esp. fig. 9.

51. LCD 83, 8596, 8879, 10864, 12356.

l

52. WRRD, DM691/826; 692/827; 693/828; LCD, 83.

53. High Street was for 'the Sons of Labour' and St Peter's Square for 'Persons in the Middle Road' according to the *Leeds Guide* (1808); for the physical contiguity of these classes, see Beresford, *art. cit.*, inf.n.4, fig. 3.3. See below, p. 364.

54. *LI*, 4 January 1793.

55. LCD 8899: as fig. 11.2 shows, there was a block of six back-to-backs immediately east of the orchard; these were also built by Paley (LCA, DB97: Wild's Title); north of them were premises leased to the Skinners' Company.

56. WRRD, CX111/146.

57. WRRD, EH205/260; twenty messuages were 'unfinished' at the time of the Malton Bank mortgage, 8 March 1803: WRRD, EM462/612.

58. Being in the custody of Eastern Region, British Rail, and not the British Transport Historical Record Office, York.

59. LCD, 92.

60. Line Fold is the classic photograph (Leeds City Library, Local History Room). The Census of 1851 shows twenty-one separate dwellings in the Galleries; matched with the 1850 OS plan, two storeys are suggested.

61. *LM*, 22 July 1848.

62. Illustrated in Beresford, *art. cit.*, p. 84.

63. Birmingham Reference Library, Boulton and Watt MSS: in-letters, 20 June 1797; out-letters to Paley, 7 December 1795 and 7 February 1796; 'Catalogue of Old Engines', July 1796, p. 102.

64. A few houses had been built by Paley near Bank Mills and Cawood's foundry, but no streets created: see nos. 20 and 21, Fig. 11.1.

65. *LM*, 22 July 1848; for the 97 inhabitants of 1851 see PRO, HO 107/2319/4/5.

24

PROSPERITY STREET AND OTHERS:
AN ESSAY IN VISIBLE URBAN HISTORY

This chapter is a short essay in certain visibles: it indicates a few evidences by which the ye may catch for a moment something of those former ways of life in Leeds indicated by revious chapters. The visible or visual records of the history of Leeds are one of many ategories of evidence on which a historical curiosity may feed, and no category is self-ufficient, whether document, map, newspaper cutting, Blue Book, biography or building. he prominence given here to visuals necessarily rests a little on the author's enthusiasms ut it has two other claims: the inquiring visitor is likely to begin with what he sees, and to sk questions about the visible remnants of the past before he asks questions about less angible things; and the visible evidence is perhaps more easily assimilated by the non-spec-list reader, and even professional historians may learn, for an appreciation of visibles has ot always formed part of their training.

It is sometimes the architectural form of a building that speaks of its place in the society of s day: this is true of buildings such as Holy Trinity Church, Leeds Town Hall, the fragments f the Cloth Hall and the Assembly Rooms, and the small number of workingmen's cottages at survive from the early days of factory industry. It is sometimes the siting of a building r a street which is historically significant. Mr. Forster's chapter* has indicated how the ldition of borough to manor created the isolation of Leeds parish church (St. Peter's, in irkgate) (Woledge, 1945). It is distant alike from the main shopping street (Briggate) and om the banking and insurance offices (in Park Row and adjoining streets), an isolation which ves many visitors to Leeds the idea that the parish church of Leeds is in fact St. John's New Briggate or Holy Trinity in Boar Lane.

Sometimes it is the name of a building or a street which may suddenly catch the attention d take the mind to the time and circumstances of its first naming. The swine of the edieval village have long ceased to be driven along Swinegate, the way from the bridge to e manor house on Mill Hill; and the town mill has long ceased to turn. The marsh of Marsh ne is dry but it remained long enough to deter good quality housing from that area, making the centre of the old East End of Leeds. The *mabels* or whores have gone from Mabgate but eir houses there, just outside the north-east edge of the town, made it the Southwark, if t the South Bank, of Leeds in the time of the first Elizabeth as it comes momentarily to ht in the plan of 1560 (Plate 9). New Briggate follows the line of *New Street*, new at the

Not included in this volume.

time when St. John's church was built there in 1632–4, just beyond the north or *head* Row
of the borough. This new street and church indicate expanding population in that area jus
as surely as the new churches of the nineteenth century suburbs, such as Christ Churc
(1823–6, Plate 12b) or St. George's (1836–8). If it recalls a popular feeling or a public hero
a name may indicate the date of a feature. Thus there are Wellington Bridge (1817–9) an
Victoria Bridge, begun in 1837, the first year of the queen's reign.

Barrack Street leads to the remarkable fragments of the Cavalry Barracks. In 1822 Baine
describes them as 'a spacious building of ominous aspect'. When they were newly erected
this would certainly have been true, for was it not only three years since Peterloo? Th
remnants are now petty workshops and garages: the horse and its rider are departed.

Later names of historical significance are Tramway Street and Education Street, an
neither could belong to any other decade than their own. There is also the evocative Pro
perity Street, a name to match *Hard Times*, the other side of the Victorian picture, the Leec
workhouse at South Lodge. Prosperity Street consists of artisans' houses, the first erected i
1874 when the street was named. By the slump of 1879 one in every twelve building worke
was unemployed, and with only ten houses built, building halted until prosperity shoul
come again. Ten more houses were built in the boom of 1882, but the slump of 1886, th
boom of 1890 and the slump of 1894 were to pass before there was a complete Prosperi
Street (1898–1901) (Beresford, 1961). Leeds has no Crisis Street, but it must have been
near thing.

The first of Baines' *Directories of Leeds*, published in 1817 just after the end of the war wi
Napoleon, has a curious statement in its historical introduction:

> Since the riot of June 1753, no event of sufficient importance for the notice of History
> has occurred in the town.

Napoleon, it is true, had not sailed up the Aire, but Leeds had seen those world-shaki
changes in transport, commerce and industry which Dr. Sigsworth has described in an earli
chapter,[*] and in the period 1753 to 1817 the town's physical appearance had undergone cruc
changes, some of which are displayed below. Thus, History may slip by undetected.

The product of the past, historical evidence, may also be passed by undetected when
takes the form of surviving buildings, sometimes set singly (as in the first railway passeng
terminus at Marsh Lane) or in groups (as in the Georgian terraces of Park Place and Pa
Square). The physical remains of the very distant past acquire a glamour like that which hau
the ruins of Kirkstall Abbey or the still-used Norman fabric of Adel Church, and no spec
effort is needed to draw them to the attention of visitors or historically-minded residen
The less distant past, of great importance to the history of the town and region, can easily s
into oblivion through neglect and destruction of its buildings, lying as they do in a lim
between 'antiquated' and 'antique': old enough to be the attention of developers, and yet r
old enough to have the romantic glamour of Fountains (Plate 12a) or Roman Aldborough. Th
Leeds has tolerated the remains of Marshall's pioneer flax mill being weed-grown by Ac
Beck, and allowed Gott's Mill at Bean Ing to be levelled for a car park. The most import
single monument of the Industrial Revolution in Leeds was obliterated in a week.

*Not included in this volume.

Not even the most zealous preservationist would wish that the wooden houses of a medieval village still lined Kirkgate, for it is unlikely that medieval Leeds was very different from any other market village or petty borough of its day. Its individuality began in that local and regional expansion of wool textiles which Mr. Forster has already described. Since its individuality and its important place in the history of industrial society rested on its marketing, its merchants, its manufactures and its transport facilities, it is proper to look principally for visible remains of this type of activity, and for other tangible signs of commercial and industrial society in the eighteenth and nineteenth century: domestic houses of merchants, manufacturers and their workpeople; and the places of their social congregation—their churches, chapels, hospitals, almshouses, schools, libraries, assembly rooms, court houses, prisons and town hall.

Past ages have been as destructive as our own, and some buildings, such as the Moot Hall that almost blocked Briggate (Plate 14a) have gone for ever; so have the first Infirmary and the first Cloth Hall. The medieval parish church was destroyed in the act of enlarging it, and only a street name behind the Grand Theatre indicates that until 1859 it was the site of John Harrison's Free (Grammar) School. The vicar's tithe barn in Kirkgate was pulled down in 1812 to build the National Schools. Surviving engravings of the Market Building on the corner of Duncan Street and Vicar Lane make one regret its replacement by Edwardian shops but the Market Building itself replaced what was then the Post Office but in origin a fine early eighteenth-century merchant's house, shown as 'Alderman Atkinson's house' in Cossins' plan of Leeds in 1725. Nor was the Alderman's house the first occupant of this valuable site: its baroque facade, as drawn by Cossins, shows that it was erected in the late seventeenth century, and on this valuable central site near the junction of village and borough it would certainly have had medieval predecessors in timber, the type of house that seemed 'ancient, meane and low built' to those sophisticated London aldermen who came north in 1628 to survey Leeds when Charles I was about to pawn the manor to the City of London. What they saw in Briggate was a commercial and manufacturing community still living in houses appropriate to an agricultural market village:

> the houses on both sides thereof are verie thicke and close compacted together, being ancient, meane, and low built; and generallie all of Tymber; though they have stone quarries frequent in the Towne, and about it; only some fewe of the richer sort of the Inhabitants have theire houses more large and capacious, yett all lowe and straitened on theire backsides.

A century later, in 1725, Cossins' plan shows one half-timbered building, the White Swan Inn at the corner of Kirkgate and Briggate, looking as if it has strayed from Stratford-on-Avon. Other inns, shops and private houses in Briggate would certainly have still been timber-built, for there had been no Great Fire as there had been in wooden London, and an early nineteenth century engraving of the Moot Hall (Plate 14a) depicts, facing it on the west side of Briggate, houses that have characteristic protruding timbers on their first floor. One such building still survives on the east side of Lower Briggate in Lambert's Yard, and it is possible that others are hidden beneath stucco facades elsewhere.

The merchants of 1725, it will be noticed, did not spurn a residence in the very heart of the town. The new and elaborate town-houses depicted in the margin of Cossins's plan

Plate 12a. Fountains Abbey *(C.H. Wood [Bradford] Ltd.)*

Plate 12b. Middleton Colliery Railway and Christ Church, 1829 *(N. Whittock)*

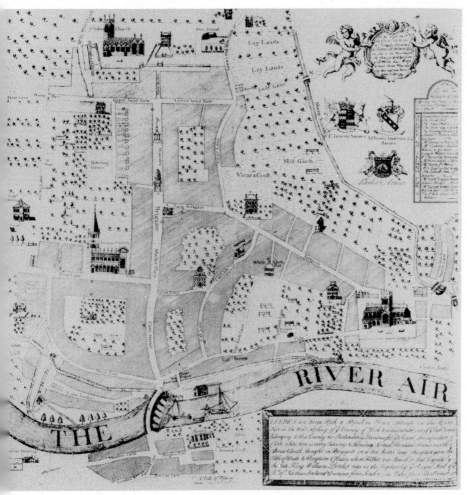

Plate 13. A New and Exact Plan of the Town of Leeds, 1725 *(J. Cossins)*

Plate 14a. The Moot Hall in Briggate, 1816 *(T. Taylor)*

Plate 14b. Leeds Town Hall (1858) and Civic Hall (1933) *(C.H. Wood [Bradford] Ltd*

Plate 15. Aire and Calder Navigation Warehouse (1827-28) *(N. Whittock)*

were nearly all in central streets, and they had their warehouses and counting houses at th
rear. For a merchant, his home and the place of work still coincided, as they did on a lesse
scale for the retail butchers of the Shambles or for a family weaving-enterprise with the loom
in the upper chamber. There were no factories and office blocks deserted by night.

When Sheepshanks House was replaced by the Ritz Cinema, the last of the stone merchan
houses depicted by Cossins passed from sight, although its appearance was captured by th
camera. However, at the foot of Hartley Hill in North Street there is a nearly identical hou.
of the same period, still (for the moment) intact. This is Bischoff House. A quirk of non- <
pre-planning has allowed one-storey shops to be built in its garden, and many passers-▶
are probably ignorant of its existence. But there is a fine, uninterrupted view of its facade fro
the junction of New York Street and New Briggate, and the traffic lights give motoris
frequent opportunity to meditate on the historical significance of its size, style and locatio
for it was one of the first merchant houses to reject the town centre in favour of a slight
detached site. It still combined a home and a counting house, but it was separated from ⟩
neighbours and from Old Leeds by an open space and an ornamental garden.

For the less well-off it was still necessary to live in the central streets, where room for t
expanding population was found by building both residential and commercial accommodati◀
in what had been gardens or *backsides* (Plate 10) of the long, narrow thirteenth-centu
burgage plots, access being obtained by tunnels such as those which lead to some of the in
yards that occupy these plots to-day. Surviving deeds make it clear that *ancient burgages* r
the full length from Briggate to Lands Lane. By the mid-nineteenth century these yards h
become notorious for overcrowding and a high-death rate (Beckwith, 1948). Sanitary ▶
formers of the mid-nineteenth century gave national publicity to these crowded teneme
yards, and conditions in the Boot and Shoe Yard (near the Market in Kirkgate) we
often cited. In 1795 this Yard contained twenty-two cottages, but in 1839 there were thir
four, sheltering 340 persons (Rimmer, 1961). Figure 40 shows pressure building up equa
behind the houses of the Upper Head Row.

Table XVIII   Population of Leeds in-township, 1740–1901

1740	10,000*	1801	31,000	1851	101,000
1754	14,000*	1811	36,000	1861	118,000
1771	16,380*	1821	49,000	1871	140,000
1775	17,121*	1831	72,000	1881	160,000
1790	22,000*	1839	82,000	1891	179,000
		1841	88,000	1901	196,000

Source: Beckwith, 1948; Rimmer, 1961; (* *estimates*). Census reports, rounded.

Table XVIII indicates the population pressing on building and housing resources. The ▮
fruits of economic growth in Leeds did not begin to be gathered before 1783 and perhaps
until 1786 (Wilson, 1966). Certainly Jefferys' plan of 1770 shows very little more building
the centre of the town than Cossins' plan in 1725. But the Leeds merchants earned th

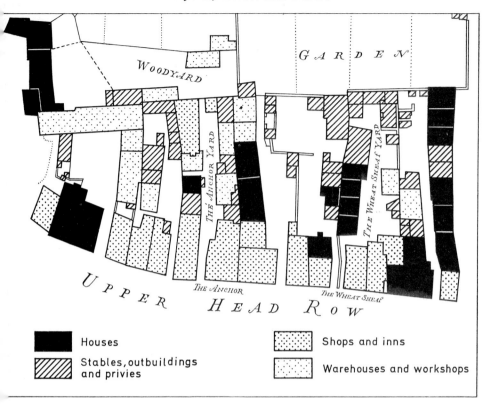

Fig. 40. Crowded building in the gardens and yards of the older streets, 1793

The 'Pious Uses' plan in the Leeds City Archives shows the area on the north side of the Head Row, between ⸻odhouse Lane and New Briggate. Here, on the northern edge of the town, one garden (top right) was intact, ⸻ another (top left) had become a woodyard. Piecemeal building is clearly indicated in the former gardens ⸻ind the houses, inns and shops on the main street frontage. Approximate scale: 1 in. = 25 yards.

⸻osperity by hard work, and they were not tempted to fly away to idle in green pastures and
⸻ral mansions. They still wished to live at or near their place of work. Thus the centre of
⸻vity of Leeds throughout the Industrial Revolution was never far from the junction of road,
⸻er and canals near Leeds Bridge (Plate 13).

⸻It was unlikely that good-class residential building would move east, for that way lay the
⸻lls of Sheepscar Beck, the riverside wharves and the marsh, while towards Quarry Hill and
⸻chmond Hill the sprawl of working class cottages had already begun. Westwards the prospect
⸻s brighter. By 1725 two roads westwards were already built up: Swinegate, near the river
⸻ık, with less elegant properties; and Boar Lane, fit for houses of aldermen, whose gardens
⸻ssins showed running back to join the grounds of Red Hall on the Head Row, making a
⸻en belt that came as far as the very western edge of the burgage plots in Briggate. This green

belt remained intact until Albion Street was cut through in 1792, and the first development of
fashionable new streets in the mode of Bath, Bristol and Bloomsbury took place a little further
west. Here the Wilson family had been busily accumulating an estate since the late seventeenth
century, much of it the former park of the medieval manor house, which had become the site
of their Mansion. Richard Wilson, Recorder of Leeds, had allowed a piece of this land to be
taken in 1757 for the new Coloured Cloth Hall, and his son, also a Richard and a Recorder,
released a plot for the new Infirmary in 1768. In 1767 the first 'new erected messuage' in Park
Row appears among the family deeds, and the east side of the street was complete by 1781.
Sixty-year building leases were taken up in South Parade (from 1776), and in East Parade (from
1785) thus completing a large open Square with the Cloth Hall and Infirmary on the south
side (Fig. 41). Park Place (begun in 1778) was of another pattern, a long row of houses with
large front gardens and a vista south to the Aire meadows and the Park ings. All then seemed
set fair for the creation of a second Square on the Wilson lands, that is, Park Square where
building leases survive from 1788 onwards.

Leeds has been extremely unfortunate in the attempts to develop good-class open residential
squares. The first, bounded by Park Row, East Parade and South Parade, was sacrificed under
the pressure of land-values, and its green interior began to be built over, the first intruder
being the new Magistrates' Court House of 1811. Further north, Queen's Square was begun
in 1806 but never completed to the original design; Hanover Square (projected in 1827),
Woodhouse Square (1830) and Blenheim Square (c. 1831) suffered the same fate. Blenheim
Terrace took eight years, from 1831 to 1839, for completion. St. Peter's Square, in the East
End, did achieve completion (before 1815) but it was ill-placed, degenerated into slums, and
has long since been obliterated.

Two types of ill-fortune dogged such enterprises as squares and terraces, more ambitious
than single house-building. They might be ill-timed, coinciding with slack periods of trade
such as were to thwart Prosperity Street itself; or they might be ill-placed and their situation
soon cease to be elegant. Mills arrived on their doorstep, and the southward vista became
quite unlike what it had been when the windows of Park Place and South Parade were first
curtained. The arrival of industry, and eventually of industrial streets, in what might otherwise have been the West End of Leeds, is of crucial significance in the nineteenth century,
and—ironically enough—it was the Wilsons who made the fatal step. On the western edge
of their estate was a smaller dyer's establishment known as Drony Laith. Its hand-processes
were quite innoxious as well as quite distant from Mill Hill. In 1792, however, the Wilsons
sold a plot of land adjoining Drony Laith to the cloth manufacturers, Wormald and Gott, who
then built Bean Ing mill. This proved far from innoxious; it was not a watermill on a river
goit but a mill with a steam-engine and chimneys and, eventually, a gasworks of its own.

The workshops of the industrial belt of Leeds had always emitted some smoke, but they
did not use coal on the scale of a steam-engine, and they were located east and south of the
town, so that the prevailing winds coming from the south-west took the smoke away from
Briggate and the properties west of it. Gott's mill had a new technology but also a new
position, west of the best residences of the day, and in a democratic fashion it spilled its smoke
on their very doorsteps. As Gott's machines multiplied, the exodus began. In the *Directory*

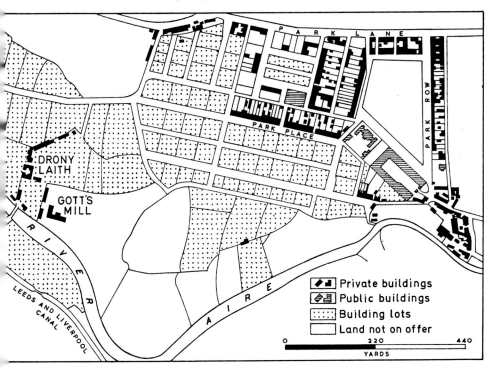

Fig. 41. The West End of Leeds in 1806

Detail from Teal's plan of the Wilson estate 'divided into Lots as the same is intended to be sold'. Note the substantial but incomplete development of the squares, begun a generation earlier. On the west is Gott's new mill whose smoke inhibited the development of the square and rows. The public buildings are, from west to east: St. Paul's Church, the Infirmary, the Cloth Hall and Mill Hill Chapel.

1798 eleven of the thirty-eight members of the unreformed Corporation had addresses the streets of the Park estate, seven of them in East Parade. In directories after 1815 their names are more likely to be found in Headingley or Potternewton or at the detached villas which they had built in the fields of Woodhouse, on a hill-slope and safely to the north. Surviving houses of this exodus are *Claremont* in Clarendon Road, *Belmont* near St. George's, and *Beech Grove* in the University precinct, where it houses the Department of Education.

With the exodus, some building plots in Park estate remained empty. Park Square has the best remaining Georgian houses in Leeds but they do not form a complete unit. Except for the River Authority offices, standing on the site of St. Paul's church (1792), the later buildings are not replacements of good Georgian buildings: they obligingly fill the gaps left by the failure of the Georgian enterprise.

The remainder of the estate met a worse fate. In Fowler's plan of 1821 the area is still marked optimistically as *Building Ground*, but when building did begin it was of a very different quality. In 1824, when the inhabitants of Park Square unsuccessfully attempted to sue Gott for smoke nuisance, these new houses were described as

> houses built as cheaply as possible for labouring people. Two or three of them were partly blown down during the winter (of 1823).

Not only was the area packed with narrow streets, housing Gott's workers, but other new mill building was permitted, even nearer to Park Square than Gott's (Fig. 42). A few of these houses were set around courtyards, imitating the built-up yards of the old town, but the majority were back-to-backs. Back-to-back houses were a response to the need for cheap housing. They are found in a limited number of nineteenth century northern industrial towns, a distribution pattern not yet satisfactorily explained. Thirty thousand were built in Leeds by 1844 (below, p. 357ff.). Fig. 43 shows the price paid for this type of development. The cholera deaths are those shown on Robert Baker's *Sanitary Map* presented to a House of Lords inquiry in 1842, and it will be seen that the death rate was highest, not in the older houses but in houses no more than twenty years old, and in many cases less than a decade old.

This contrast between life in the 1840's south of Park Lane and that in the villas to the north should not surprise us: for this was the industrial society which shocked the young Disraeli, and the two sides of Park Lane were, in a sense, his Two Nations.

Some space has been given to the circumstances in which this particular block of working class housing developed, for it is unusually well documented; south of the river in Holbeck and Hunslet it was matched in quality and exceeded in quantity, and by the time of the first large-scale Ordnance Survey plan (1847), streets of this sort had proliferated. They were found not only in the older area of working-class housing east of the town on Richmond Hill and Quarry Hill but along North Street and Camp Road almost as far as Sheepscar and Woodhouse Carr. Significantly, the same march of narrow streets and back-to-backs accompanied the multiplication of mills and engineering works on the north bank of the river immediately west of the Park estate, along what is now Kirkstall Road and Burley Road.

This westward extension of industry and working-class housing must have been a principal factor in limiting the period of time during which a villa in Little Woodhouse or Carlton Hill provided a sufficient refuge from distasteful sights, smells and neighbours. It was a remarkably short period before the owners sold off their villas and the surrounding fields to speculative builders and themselves took refuge in the out-townships, on Woodhouse Ridge or in Headingley, Meanwood or Chapel Allerton.

As they retreated, the *Building Grounds* and the streets of artisan housing spread themselves. The first signal of this retreat came in 1830 when Newman Cash, the banker, sold off the eastern grounds of his villa, Springfield House, to make room for Springfield Place, the first street in this once-exclusive area to have houses facing each other across very small front gardens, and forced by covenants to mirror each other in architectural style. Thereafter the fields were in perpetual retreat, especially when Mrs. Lyddon's large estate, which had been in Chancery since 1828, was sold off in 1845 for division between the contending heirs. By the 1860's, the new streets had reached Woodhouse Moor, and by the 1880's they surrounded it. Thus, the social pattern of Leeds housing had been radically transformed. A Park Estate

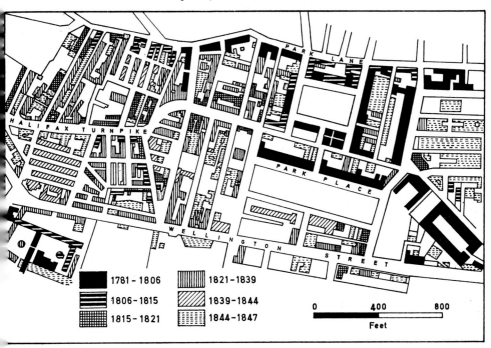

1781 – 1806
1806 – 1815
1815 – 1821
1821 – 1839
1839 – 1844
1844 – 1847

0   400   800
Feet

Fig. 42. The Invasion of the West End of Leeds, 1806–47

Despite the sale-plan of 1806, development did not take place until after 1821, when working-class streets of back-to-back houses intermingled with mills (cp. Figs. 41 and 43). The open square based on Park Row was sacrificed to commercial and institutional building. Gott's mill was extended.

ale plan of 1817 displays a last hope that Leeds might polarise into an industrial and artisan ast End and a wealthy residential West End. These hopes were destroyed, and (like England self) the divisions between the Nations in Leeds became one between North and South. The etter residential properties became concentrated on the northern heights and along the urnpike roads that came in from Otley via Headingley, from Meanwood and from Harrogate. On the other hand the fields served by Kirkstall Road, Burley Road and York Road were overed with a very different style of brickwork: and, of course, south of the river, industrial uilding and working-class housing went in every direction.

At first glance these developments may seem narrow matters, of interest primarily to storians and architects and geographers. But they are ghosts that haunt us from their grave. hey have had a sharp impact on the lives of our contemporaries; whether those who had to se these houses of the 1830's and 1840's as their homes in the 1940's and the 1950's; or ose who contributed through their rates and taxes to the task of slum clearance and replace-ent described in Dr. Fowler's chapter.* And the ghosts will walk for many years after the st of the 78,000 back-to-backs has been reduced to rubble, for the distribution of building

Not included in this volume.

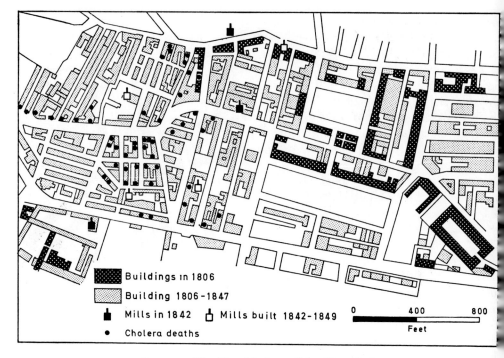

Fig. 43.   The Two Nations of the West End

Robert Baker's 'Cholera Map' of 1842 plotted the distribution of cholera deaths to show the connection with poor housing and sanitation. There were no deaths in the 'good class' houses of Park Square, Park Row and Park Place, yet many in the newer but inferior properties to the west.

for the different social classes of Victorian Leeds has helped to determine the pattern of Leeds society in our own day. The leafiness of the approach roads through Headingley Meanwood or Chapel Allerton is in striking contrast to the scenery along those approach roads that succumbed to the builders of the 1830's and 1840's. Leeds has zones of middle class housing and zones of working-class housing, zones which are not lessened when the working-class housing is re-housing. It is not only the door-to-door salesmen, the cast-off clothes dealers and the social workers who have to pay regard to this zoning, but also those who have to draw boundaries for the catchment areas of Leeds schools in such a way that comprehensives are socially comprehensive.

The antecedent, and indeed the economic basis, of the bricks and mortar of Victorian housing was the multiplication of other buildings, the workplaces: the mills, foundries engineering workshops, tanneries, warehouses and offices of Victorian Leeds. Oddly enough despite the developers, there are more examples of this type of building still standing (and in use) than there are houses contemporary with them. In particular, Water Lane, Meadow Lane and Hunslet Lane are still a largely unexplored paradise for the industrial archaeologist and there is still a good deal of original factory building along the riverside and the Leeds and Liverpool Canal. Fire has recently condemned the magnificent warehouse of the Aire and Calder Navigation (Plate XI), but the terminal buildings of the Leeds and Liverpool canal are well preserved in the shadow of the City Station for those who have the patience to find the entrance, and at Armley the canal bank passes by another of Gott's mills as well as along the edge of the park, now a golf course, that surrounded his mansion. A full survey of these relics of pioneer industrialisation is still awaited; and the ancillary buildings of wholesale distribution and of commerce should not be neglected. The extravagances of Victoriana are coming back into fashion, and nothing was more extravagant than the looting of architectural ideas from many centuries and many countries that is expressed in the Victorian buildings of central Leeds. The factories outside the town centre were usually more utilitarian but there are magnificent fantasies such as Marshall's Mill in Water Lane.

From the 1850's onwards the streets of the old town centre began to be rebuilt piecemeal very much in the same way that yet another rebuilding is taking place under our own eyes. The Victorian rebuilding pulled down the residences, shops and counting houses of seventeenth- and eighteenth-century Leeds and replaced them, sometimes by restrained quasi-classical buildings such as the Bank of England (1862–64), but more commonly by fantasticks such as the Church Institute (1866–68, but imitating the early 1300's); by the insurance companies' quasi-cathedrals in Park Row; and by the various municipal buildings near the Town Hall (Plate 14b).

The building of Brodrick's Town Hall (1853–58) is the subject of an essay by Asa Briggs that admirably demonstrates how building history is economic and social history, and not just architectural history. A similar treatment could be given to the various Infirmary Buildings, perhaps contrasting them with St. James' Hospital; to Marsh Lane, Holbeck and Central Stations as well as derelict cinemas, tram depots and chapels; to the General Cemetery, encompassed by the University precinct; and to the buildings that house the educational institutions of Mr. Taylor's chapter.[*]Nothing is sacred, and nothing is safe from the attentions of History as present merges into past.

[*]Not included in this volume.

SELECT REFERENCES

. Beckwith, 'The Population of Leeds during the Industrial Revolution', *Thoresby Society*, xli (1948), 118–96.
M. W. Beresford, *Time and Place*, (1961). See above, pp. 1-23.
. J. Bonser and H. Nicholls, *Printed Maps and Plans of Leeds, 1711–1900*, *Thoresby Society*, xlvii (1960).
Asa Briggs, 'The Building of Leeds Town Hall', *Thoresby Society*, xlvi (1963), 275–302.
Asa Briggs, 'Leeds: a study in Civic Pride', in *Victorian Cities*, (1963).
. Pevsner, *The Buildings of England. Yorkshire: the West Riding*, (1959), 307–351.
W. G. Rimmer, *Marshalls of Leeds, Flax Spinners, 1788–1886*, (1960).

W. G. Rimmer, 'Working Men's Cottages in Leeds, 1770–1840', *Thoresby Society*, xlvi (1961) 165–99.

G. W. Rhodes, 'Housing Development in Leeds', M.A. Thesis, University of Leeds, (1954).

R. G. Wilson, 'Transport Dues as Indices of Economic Growth, 1775–1820', *Economic History Review* xix (1966), 110–23.

R. G. Wilson, 'Leeds Woollen Merchants, 1700–1830', Ph.D. Thesis, University of Leeds, (1964)

G. Woledge, 'The Medieval Borough of Leeds', *Thoresby Society*, xxxvii (1945), 280–309.

Professor Beresford wishes to acknowledge the help of Mr. J. M. Collinson, Leeds City Archivist and Mrs. Mary Forster, in the collection of material.

25

THE BACK-TO-BACK HOUSE IN LEEDS, 1787-1939

Although condemned as a town in its entire locality at the first glance, [Leeds] may really have only peculiar points of local influence from whence the gross results are derived. Robert Baker, *On the State and Condition of the Town of Leeds (PP, xxvii [HL] of 1842), 23.*

Back-to-back houses were run up in defiance of the universal condemnation of all persons, without the slightest regard to the health and comfort of the inhabitants. Editorial, *Leeds Mercury* (14 October, 1862).

The characteristic feature of working-class housing in Leeds is the prevalence of the 'back-to-back' type of dwelling. Small 'through' houses are being built at the present time in considerable numbers but even in the case of new dwellings in the more outlying parts of the city, the back-to-back plan has by no means been superceded. The continued erection of this type of house forms a marked exception to the general rule followed by the large towns of the country. A. W. Fox, *Report of an Inquiry into Working Class Rents, Housing and Retail Prices (PP, cvii of 1908), 258.*

I

THIS essay is wholly concerned with working-class housing of a type that reformers condemned, though, like Robert Baker, I am aware that the provision of houses for the growing population of industrial Leeds did not result in a town that was one continuous slum. Any detailed local study of reformist critics and their targets might seem to be heading straight for the platitudinous, a reiteration of generalised complaint familiar both to the audiences of the sanitary reformers and to historians of the sanitary movement. Fortunately, the Leeds critical tradition took its tone from Baker, the town's first social statistician.[1] As the quotation at the head of this study indicates, he was well aware that the proper study of housing was a micro-study, an intensely local scrutiny. Baker's house-to-house enquiry, organised for the Statistical Committee of the reformed Corporation in 1837–9, gave him both chapter and verse with which to confound the sceptical and the complacent.[2] In his later writing, especially in the influential *Local Report* submitted to the Lords Committee of 1842, he continued to set the housing problem in terms of particular streets and particular houses. Indeed, Baker's need to convince his readers, as well as his scientific interest in objectivity, made it necessary for him to stress the difference between the good and the bad streets. The ratepayers in

the good streets had to be reminded that the improvement rates were
spent largely on improving *their* environment; while the localisation
of bad and good housing conditions was an important part of his
argument, based on the cholera map[3] of 1833. In his sanitary map
of 1842 he showed that the Angel of Death had left whole streets
in the 'first class' areas untouched, concentrating on certain areas
of the town, almost solidly covered with the red and blue spots that
indicated cholera and contagious diseases of 1834–9. These blocks
of spots were in the areas of worst quality housing, and Baker wanted
the correlation to be driven into his readers' minds.[4] Death, disease,
moral squalor, poverty, high poor relief, and high crime rates were
found under the same group of roofs, making up what increasingly
began to be known as the East End.

II

Alongside the reiterated criticism of particular streets the critical
literature of Leeds housing in the nineteenth century has another
preoccupation, with which this essay will be concerned. Critic after
critic, decade after decade, national as well as local, fastened on a
distinctive form of housing, to condemn the 'back-to-back'. Leeds
was not alone among industrial towns in having back-to-backs but
no other town continued to build them for so long nor fought so
tenaciously to retain them.

No one has yet made a study of their regional distribution but
they were few even in the meanest parts of London, and there were
many northern towns without them. Manchester had 10,000 of them
by the 1890s,[5] and they were to be found in many West Riding
factory towns. Bradford had them : in 1854, the first year of its
municipal building byelaws, 1,079 of the 1,601 plans sanctioned
were for back-to-back houses.[6] Yet when Bradford and Manchester
began to forbid further back-to-backs, Leeds continued to permit
them. Despite the general ban on this type of house in the Housing
Act of 1909, they continued to be built in Leeds until 1937. Abolition was slow, and demolition was slow, so that the back-to-back
was at the centre of the postwar housing problem in Leeds. In the
last few years the clearance programme has demolished virtually
every back-to-back that appears on the Ordnance Survey plan of
1850 but the field-worker in housing archaeology can still (1969)
find back-to-backs built in the 1850s and 1860s.

TABLE 3.1

STOCK OF HOUSES, AND PROPORTION OF BACK-TO-BACKS,
LEEDS BOROUGH, 1801–1920

	All houses	Back-to-backs	
		number	percentage
1801	11,500	less than 1,000	less than 10
1886	61,000	49,000	71
1920	108,000	78,000	71

Sources: 1801 houses, Census; back-to-backs, Rimmer *art cit* in note 8 (p 122), 187 for total of all types of working-class cottages, 1790–1800. 1886: houses, total of 1921 Census less building as in Table 3.3; back-to-backs, Table 3.3. 1920: houses, 1921 Census; back-to-backs, G. W. Rhodes, *Housing Developments in Leeds, 1919–39*, (unpublished Leeds MA thesis, 1954), 11.

But even those who have never seen a back-to-back house[7] will not find it difficult to grasp and appreciate its distinctive feature : the lack of a back door; of a back window; and, indeed, of any through ventilation, since these houses were built so closely and economically together that houses in adjoining streets had their back walls abutting (or shared). You enjoyed a neighbour not only on both side walls of your room but also on the third, the back wall. The symmetry of identical houses set along a street frontage, which had reached its most civilised form in the Georgian squares and terraces, was rapidly degraded into the meanness of 'rows'.

The back-to-back house was small, and initially it had only one ground-floor room and one bedroom above, the 'one-up, one-down'. It was thus part of high-density building development and the search for the maximum rent or the maximum number of saleable houses per acre. Each house, even in the 1850s, was no more than 5yd by 5. The back-to-back thus came to the attention of the sanitary reformers in consequence of the physical and social defects of closely packed living. But it was not just the small size of the Leeds back-to-back that made it a target for critics : as Professor Rimmer has shown, in size the urban 'cottage' (as the back-to-back was so often called) was no smaller than many rural cottages.[8] The new town houses for the working classes that, from the 1750s, were crowded into the innyards, burgage plots, and gardens of the older houses at the centre of the town were of this size also. Nor was the back-to-back unique for its day in the paucity of its provision of water, its drains, and its sanitation. The unique defect of the back-to-back was the absence of through ventilation and the extreme restriction of light, since only one of the four walls of any room was able to have a window. Poor ventilation was more than the inconvenience of unmoving smells. Medical knowledge was becoming increasingly aware of the risk of airborne infection, and of the diseases and deformities that arose from scarcity of light and air.

If the eighteenth-century cottage labourer lived in a small room with poor water and poor sanitation, yet he had his back door : historians of vernacular architecture are coy about back doors, but post-medieval cottages of all sizes seem to have had them, even if they gave access only to a mean yard, a small garden, or a fold yard. Whatever else he gained on coming to live in a back-to-back street, the town labourer lost his back door.

How did the back-to-back come to be accepted as a tolerable way of housing for the urban working classes, when it was part of the tradition neither of mean rural cottages nor of early town develop- ment? The early importation of an alternative, rurally-derived, house type into the industrial districts of Leeds is plainly shown in the fold-yard type of development illustrated in Fig 3.1. This was the type of new housing that Tuke's map of 1781 shows spreading in quasi-ribbon development along the main roads from Leeds to the south, south-east, east and north-east. These 'Folds' stand out on contemporary plans, particularly the first large-scale plan of Leeds (1815), since they gave no straight-line edge to successive frontages, such as the upper-class terraces or the sides of fashionable squares had given. Instead, even such a main road as Marsh Lane varied in width since the groups of houses were stepped back at different distances.

This *Folds* development, which may be approximately dated to the period 1750–80, was accompanied by a second type of urban cottage building, the occupation of whatever vacant space was still left in innyards, gardens and orchards lying behind the houses that lined the streets of the old core of the town, especially Briggate, Kirkgate, Vicar Lane, and the Headrow.[9] Indeed, here, it may be hazarded, lay the unintended transition to the back-to-back in the form of a single cottage with no through ventilation, no back windows and no back door. How? The new housing was obtained by lining the interior walls of an innyard or a garden with cottages : but

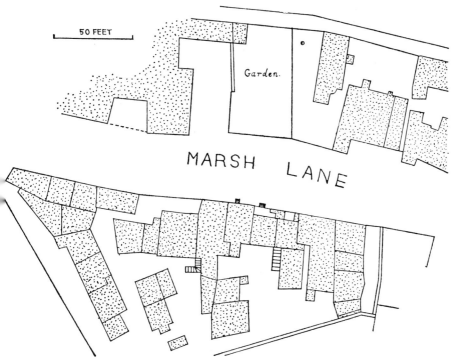

Fig 3.1. Leeds working-class cottages before the back-to-back: infill of two *Folds* on the south-east side of Marsh Lane, from survey of 1793, Leeds City Archives, DB 204/8.

there was usually room for no more than one line along each wall, thus the front—and only—door faced inwards to the yard, the remnants of which made up the yard of a court. Here from the mid-eighteenth century at least, incomers to Leeds were living in houses without back- or side-windows or doors.[10] (See Fig 3.2).

As it happened, all the principal streets of inner Leeds were lined with houses, shops and inns that gave available spaces for development in the long, narrow crofts behind them. In Kirkgate there were the crofts of the original village, in Briggate the burgage plots laid out in 1207, and in the Headrow the new extensions of the early seventeenth century. The town plan of 1815 shows these former open spaces virtually solid with infilled cottages, warehouses, and finishing shops.

Until at least 1781 the spread of roadside Folds and burgage infill was sufficient to meet the demands for working-class housing as population rose, without creating any new streets; and development

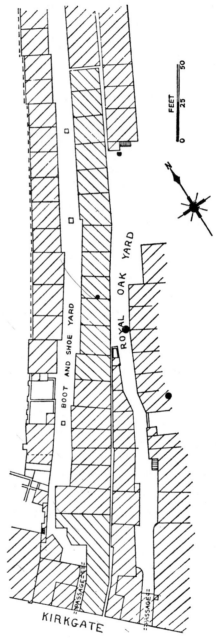

Fig. 3.2. Leeds working-class cottages before the back-to-back: infill of two *Yards* in Kirkgate, with cottages abutting on the Yard walls; the notorious Boot and Shoe Yard and its neighbour were cleared in 1844 under the Improvement Act of 1842: plan from LCD No 69.

in Park Row, Park Place and Park Square was catering for the much smaller number who could afford elegant housing. Tuke's plan of 1781 is a fortunate piece of evidence; for it shows Leeds replete with Folds and central infill, and just initiating its West End, but quite devoid of any new *cottage-streets* north of the river. The West End terraces apart, there was still no straight-line street outside the old burghal core in 1781. A long block of houses on the east side of Mabgate might seem to be such a street but on close examination it turns out to be *Near and Middle Fold*, a ribbon of cottages 200yd long.[11] Despite the name, which suggests a cluster of the Marsh Lane type, these two Folds in Mabgate were made up of two parallel rows of cottages, some with cellar dwellings, side by side for a length of over 200yd; the detail on the 1850 OS plan makes it clear that these were not back-to-backs; for even where the two parallel ribbons were set closest to each other there was a distinct space between the buildings. The ground on which these two Folds were built was not an innyard, for it lay in open country, but it had plainly once been a small, narrow, but long, field.

The techniques of developing such a field, end-on to a thoroughfare, would soon have to be applied more widely, for the main-road frontages within a reasonable distance of the town were becoming continuously built up by 1781, and if the open spaces nearer the town were to be taken over for building it would have to be by the creation of brand new streets opening up their interior and breaking through at some point into the existing thoroughfares.

The first place where such a block of streets was laid out for working-class cottages lay just north of the Kirkgate crofts, east of Vicar Lane but west of Sheepscar Beck, thus adjoining that part of the old town where infill development had already created a working-class area. This development, begun in 1787, created Union Street, Ebenezer Street, George (or George's) Street, and Nelson Street, with the short Sidney Street to join them to Vicar Lane on the west. On the east they abutted on the beck, where the street called Mill Garth formalised a trackway to the mill and the waterside meadows.

The houses which lined these pioneer streets were undoubtedly back-to-back cottages, many of them having separate cellar dwellings underneath. The large-scale OS plan of 1850 clearly marks them as back-to-back,[12] and the shape and position of the houses in 1850 is exactly as on the first medium-scale plan of the town, drawn in 1815, and the dimensions of the building plots and the houses on these two plans are exactly those of the original deeds of 1787–8.

If it is true that these were the first back-to-backs in Leeds, the manner of their creation is the more interesting. They were not a speculative investment by the owner of the field, nor the speculation of some commercial or industrial capitalist; the latter type of investor is exemplified by Richard Kendall's 65 cottages and Paley's 175 cottages (1800–05) in the East Ward.[13] The Union Street back-to-backs were erected by a building club, one of those terminating building societies of the type described by Mr Seymour Price but not actually known to him. Its articles of agreement were drawn up on 3 November 1787, providing for the division of the *Crackenthorpe Garden* into fifty-two building lots. A number of the original conveyances from the building club to the first owners have survived among the deeds that have come to the town clerk in the process of compulsory purchase for clearances. With the deeds of the pair of back-to-backs later known as nos 22 and 26, Union Street, is the will of Sarah Brown, made 11 February 1794 and devising

> two cottages or dwelling houses being the front and back house site in Union Street, Leeds, then occupied by Robert Anderson and William Waddington, next adjoining the tenements of William Brown.

Six other pairs of back-to-backs in Ebenezer Street had five cellar dwellings under the back part of the range, entered from Union Court. Three other pairs, built in Union Street near Sarah Brown's, also had cellar dwellings opening into the other side of Union Court; these originated in the sale of Lots 11 and 12 by the Crackenthorpe Garden Building Club.[14] (See Fig 3.3, top line.)

The Union Street development of back-to-backs was only a few months ahead of another building club, already known to the historian of building societies,[15] though not hitherto dated. On 27 February 1788 an agreement was signed for the Hill House Building Club to purchase *Chamfor Close*, between the Aire and the slopes of the Bank, and divide it into forty-two lots. On these lots back-to-backs were also built, making King Street and Queen Street.[16] It is a curious coincidence that these two areas—the Crackenthorpe group of streets and the Hill House streets—were the first where the Corporation used its powers in the 1870 Improvement Act for the purchase and clearance of insanitary buildings.[17] Piecemeal and slowly the back-to-backs of 1787–8 began to come down,

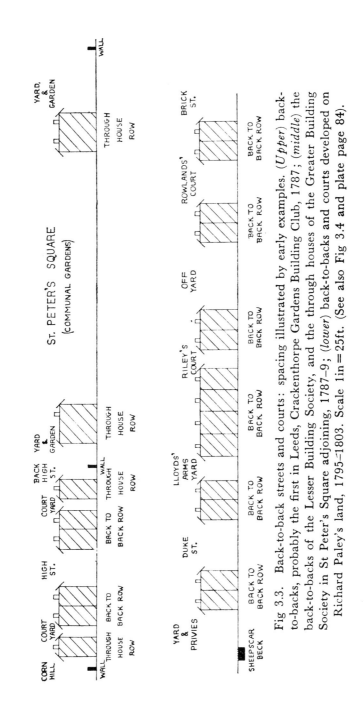

Fig 3.3. Back-to-back streets and courts: spacing illustrated by early examples. (*Upper*) back-to-backs, probably the first in Leeds, Crackenthorpe Gardens Building Club, 1787; (*middle*) the back-to-backs of the Lesser Building Society, and the through houses of the Greater Building Society in St Peter's Square adjoining, 1787–9; (*lower*) back-to-backs and courts developed on Richard Paley's land, 1795–1803. Scale 1in = 25ft. (See also Fig 3.4 and plate page 84).

a century old. It was to be 170 years before this first group of back-to-backs was completely demolished.

III

Between 1787 and 1815, as a comparison of Tuke's plan with that of Netlam and Giles shows, cottage building in streets invaded many more fields on the north, east and south of Leeds, the western development being desperately reserved for better quality building despite the reluctance of purchasers to come so near the industrial precinct that was developing near the river.[18] Professor Rimmer has counted an annual average of 150 new houses in the years 1774–1815, with energetic bursts of 200 per annum in 1790–5 and 900 per annum in 1800–05.[19] If the streets added between 1787 and 1815 are examined, virtually all were of back-to-backs (Appendix II), though development was sporadic enough for many streets to be shown still incomplete in 1815, and the old field boundaries were shown by the surveyors round the empty spaces. If the comparison of maps is continued through the series[20] 1815–26, 1826–33, 1833–44 and 1844–50, the successive additions to the in-township of Leeds again appear as almost all back-to-backs. Of the two outlying hamlets of the in-township, Little and Great Woodhouse, the former was still reserved for better class housing but the old fold-yards and the cottages on the commons encroachments in Great Woodhouse[21] were slowly eclipsed by the much greater number of back-to-backs. While a 'New Town of Leeds' was laid out just over the township boundary in Chapel Allerton as well spaced villas,[22] another *New-town*[23] (at Sheepscar but recently demolished) was made up of single-cottage streets, back-to-backs, and *pace* Professor Rimmer, closed courts.[24]

The widespread progress of back-to-back housing in Leeds from 1787 to 1850 is at the present moment (1969) marked out for all to see : for it comprises that area north of the river that has been cleared and redeveloped in giant flats, and those adjoining acres that have been cleared of substandard housing and await the phoenix that the City Engineer will some day rouse from their ashes and rubble.

The argument so far has suggested how the unventilated, one-up-one-down, cottage spread from the innyards into independent streets, where the rows of cottages were thrust so close together that no space remained between each row, and the back walls of adjoining rows were built to touch each other. If the transition was as smooth as this, it is not surprising that there was no contemporary comment on the birth of the back-to-backs, and no outcry on behalf of their inhabitants.

If the cottages were to be occupied by the working classes, then rents had to be low, and if rents were to be low, then the capital costs per house had to be kept low. This economic pressure towards high-density housing is understandable in the early developments such as Union Street and Paley's York Street estate, taking up land of high value near the town centre : but the back-to-back development continued, as we have seen, far away from the town centre into isolated fields neighboured only by cow pastures and tenter grounds; into the quite remote hamlet of Great Woodhouse; and in the isolated field on Carlton Hill that gave birth to Little London.[25] High land values could not have been the coercion here.

No doubt the spread of back-to-backs was facilitated if people came to accept in outlying areas what they already knew in the inner town;[26] and no doubt, as Baker often argued, the zeal for maximising rents per square yard was infectious among landowners.[27] But the economical beauty of back-to-backs in a property developer's eye was not only their density, yielding maximum rents per square yard, but the neat way into which they fitted into the shape of the vacant spaces available in Leeds as 'building ground' : fields on the eastern edge of the town are designated in this way in printed maps of the town from 1821 onwards but 'eligible building ground' was a commonplace in the advertisement columns of the local press[28] from the 1780s.

The size and shape of the fields comprising these 'building grounds' were important determinants of the type of housing development that took place on them. The open fields of Leeds had been enclosed at an unknown date, probably in the later Middle Ages. Their enclosure produced the characteristic long, rather narrow, fields which can still be seen outside the built-up area in the town plan of 1815 or in earlier manuscript plans of particular holdings. Fields of this size and shape had not been inconvenient for pasture or hay-ground around a developing town, and they were not unsuited to market gardening, while many of the grass fields were also used for rows of tenters. But their small width, in proportion to length,

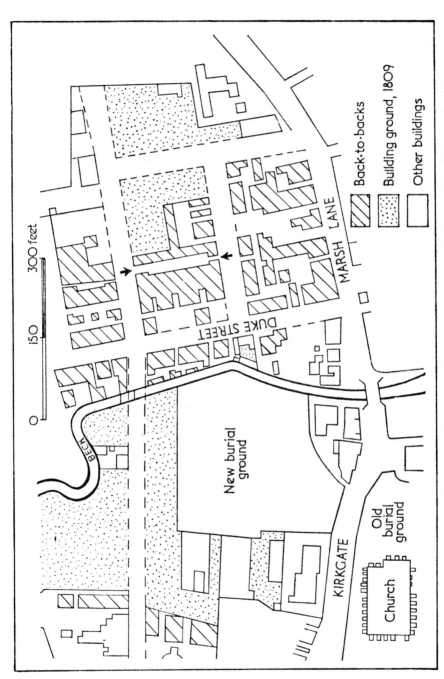

Fig 3.4. Estate development of back-to-back streets and courts in Leeds sold off in small plots by Richard Paley, 1795–1803: from plan following his bankruptcy, Leeds City Archives DB

posed particular problems when it came to laying out houses and streets within such fields.

The typical working-man's cottage of the late eighteenth and early nineteenth centuries was about 15ft square, and the minor streets of Leeds were usually 30 or 40ft wide. Thus a street of single cottages needed a ribbon of land with a minimum width of 60ft (ie 15 + 30 + 15). It will be noticed that in such a ribbon, 30/60ths, or half the surface area was unproductive of house rents : dead ground as far as a developer was concerned.[29] But if, instead of a row of single cottages, a row of back-to-backs was set on either side of such a street, then the 30ft of dead ground would be matched by 60ft of housing, a reduction in 'dead ground' from 50 per cent to 33 per cent. A further economy could be made by not having streets of full width between the back-to-back rows, merely separating them by a courtyard; if access to such a courtyard was given by a tunnel it enabled all the four sides of the court to be built upon, and the use of a tunnel rather than an alley permitted an extra room (which meant extra rent) over the tunnel passage.

The typical field available as 'building ground' in Leeds after 1750 was from 120 to 200 ft wide, and about 600ft long, an area of from 1 5/6 to $2\frac{3}{4}$ acres.[30] In these long narrow fields there was room for more than one parallel unit of back-to-back + street + back-to-back. Some actual distributions will be seen in Fig 3.3. Fields of this size and shape, undoubtedly the parcelled-out furlongs of former open arable fields, can be seen in the 1815 plan on either side of the road—significantly known as Long Balk Lane, later Camp Road—that gave access to the level plateau north of the town, and on either side of the Harrogate turnpike, the principal northward artery. It was on the east side of the latter that the fields known as the *Leylands* became covered with what were to become notorious back-to-backs; the fact that all these fields had their long axis at right-angles to the thoroughfare gave them an additional advantage, for the streets could be led straight in.

The tyranny of the pre-existing narrow fields as the dominating units of building development was accentuated by another inheritance from pre-industrial Leeds. Not only were fields small and narrow but the pattern of landownership was dominated by the smallholder. There were very few large estates,[31] and the largest and most compact, the former manorial demesne of the *Parks*, had already been taken up for the West End developments of the 1780s

and 1790s. The land which earliest came on to the market for
building development was usually simply a single field, the whole
of a man's patrimony, and so the problem of optimising the layout
of new streets was the problem of utilising a single field. Had
developers several adjacent fields to work in, they could have made
cross streets, or the long streets of one field could have been connected to the long streets of the next field. But nothing is more
characteristic of the early piecemeal back-to-back streets of Leeds
than to find their ends blocked by a wall, by a change in level, or
by the sides of other houses in another unconnected street. The line
of blockage is simply the old field boundary. On one side a developer
has set out his streets : and on the other side a different developer
at a different time has set out his; and never the twain should meet.

The extreme of subservience to an existing field—and property—
boundary is demonstrated in the 'half-backs'—lines of cottages only
one room deep but so pressed against the edge of a field that no
room was left for a back alley. The builder, therefore, put up half
a back-to-back house as far as the peak of the roof and then dropped
vertically down what would otherwise have been the partition wall
between back-to-backs.[32] Doubtless in some cases there was the hope
that at a later date the next field might be developed, and the lonely
singles matched off. Certainly the piecemeal progress of lot purchases
and house erection must also have left singles temporarily in mid-air
within normal back-to-back streets. Where a half-back was never
matched off, its vertical wall formed a grim cliff face to a court, or
became the closed end of some alley, court, allotment, cemetery or
factory yard. They were beloved of bill-posters. It was a forbidding
aspect when the only doors of back-to-backs were thrust against one
of these half-back cliffs (see Frontispiece).

Short disconnected streets not only accentuated the airlessness of
the back-to-back environment but were inimical to the development
of through drainage, water and sewerage systems. This is why sanitary reformers took piecemeal building development as a main target
for criticism.

> The land has been disposed of in so many small lots to petty proprietors
> who have subsequently built at pleasure, both as to inward form and
> outward ideas.[33]

In 1844 the sewerage engineer, Vetch, wrote :

> It is to be regretted that, on so great an extent of low ground destined
> so soon to be covered with population, some general plan of new streets

should not be adopted in conformity with good drainage and ventilation.[34]

The piecemeal disconnected streets, leading nowhere in particular and often at right-angles to thoroughfares, were also of little use as highways, and the highway authority was reluctant to adopt them. Fifteen years after Vetch's regrets the Privy Council's Medical Officer wrote of Leeds :

> The principal streets are fewer than is common in other great towns and the interspaces between the principal roads are occupied by dense and often complicated congeries of ill-kept streets and courts, which have but seldom been adopted as highways by the municipal authority, and are in a very foul state.[35]

One of the reasons why the Leeds back-to-backs of the 1870s and 1880s are more pleasing than those of the earlier period is not only the wider spacing laid down in the byelaws after 1866, but also the fact that streets became very much longer, and linked with each other, some of them being sufficiently arterial to have early tram and bus routes along them. Their length was made possible by an important change in the size of the characteristic development unit. By the early 1860s, particularly in the north and north-east, very little undeveloped land lay within the actual township (or 'in-township') of Leeds, and the building grounds were now moving into the fields of rural townships (such as Roundhay, Potter Newton, Headingley, and Chapel Allerton) where there were both larger fields, and (more important) larger estates to be developed as planned entities. Closed-in courts and narrow alleys, like cellar dwellings, are not considered in this short essay, though, as the last quotation shows, they were often linked with back-to-backs in reformers' criticisms. So far, back-to-backs have been considered as the components of 'streets', that is, spaces left between facing doorways that were of the width accepted elsewhere in Leeds as a street; for the pavements, roadsurfaces, drainage and scavenging of these 'streets' was often of the lowest quality, as the last quotation also indicates. But even less attractive were the back-to-backs crowded so closely that there was less than a street's width between facing rows, and made up into so short a cul-de-sac that there was no through ventilation, and the building blocking the cul-de-sac (a factory or a wall of half-backs) also blocked out light and sun. If the development was set behind old-established properties, access to it would be through a narrow passage or by a tunnel, further restricting air, sun and ventilation. Courts and alleys were commonplace in all towns, and in essence they were little different from the infill of the old innyards and burgage plots, but back-to-backs facing into courts of this type in Leeds gave an additional ill-savour not found everywhere.[36]

IV

It can hardly be said that back-to-backs crept in through the back door since that was the very feature that they lacked, but no contemporary comment on their arrival has yet been noted in the Press. Explicit criticism of back-to-backs by sanitary reformers also came later, though the streets cited by Baker in his criticisms of 1833, 1839 and 1842 included many that were made up of back-to-backs.

The notion that it might be necessary to regulate the builder's activity through laws and byelaws was a natural accompaniment of proposals for laws to determine standards of water supply, drainage and sewerage. In his evidence to a Select Committee in 1833 John Marshall, MP for Leeds, put building regulation in such a context:

> It is advisable to have some improvement made in sewerage and regulation of buildings and small tenements . . . for the health of the inhabitants, and for the comfort of the humbler classes, combined with the saving in the poor rate.[37]

In the same year, Baker's report to the Leeds Board of Health devoted seven pages of close print to a list of streets in which there had been cholera deaths. As one would expect, the leaders in disrepute—'most wretched', 'very very dirty', 'wretchedly filthy', 'most confined'—were the crowded courts and yards of the innermost town, such as the Boot and Shoe inn yard; and the decaying agricultural cottages of the Folds: indeed the cholera had begun in Leeds in Blue Bell Fold,[38] 'small and dirty containing about 20 houses inhabited by poor families many of whom are Irish'. But back-to-back streets were also among the leaders: there were eight deaths in Bath Street, eight in Orange Street, eighteen in Quarry Hill, eleven in Richmond Road and eight in York Street (see Appendix 3.2, below).

In the 1839 *Report* of the Council's Statistical Committee nine places were named as 'proverbial' for their squalor: two were innyards (the Boot and Shoe, and the Wellington) and the other seven were back-to-backs, including the pioneers, Union Street, George Street and Ebenezer Street.[39] The five streets named by the Streets Committee in 1842 as 'the worst for typhus' were all back-to-backs, as were three of the four named as 'outstandingly unhealthy' in Vetch's sewerage report of 1844.[40] Similarly the cholera deaths of 1849 and the diarrhoeal mortalities of 1854–8 were severest in the back-to-backs of Camp Field, Mill Street and Quarry Hill;[41] and the prize for squalor awarded by the Privy Council's MOH in 1865 was again Ebenezer Street, unequalled in age and disrepute : 'filthiest street of all'.[42] From 1870 the borough MOH's reports regularly listed the fever streets, and they were generally made up of back-to-backs.[43]

The reports cited so far took as their target the conditions of specific streets but did not condemn the back-to-backs as such, though in his report to the House of Lords Committee in 1842 Baker had used the term *back-to-back* and came near to a general condemnation, both for their size and lack of ventilation.

> The building of houses back-to-back occasions this in great measure. It is in fact part of the economy of buildings that are to pay a good percentage.[44]

Baker did, however, set out figures of costs, rents and working-class budgets to show how a labourer would not be able to afford the rent if house-builders had built houses any larger.[45]

It is a curious irony that, in the very months when Chadwick's *Report on the Sanitary Condition of the Labouring Population* was being printed, a direct attack on the back-to-back by legislation was being defeated. Following on a recommendation of the Select Committee of 1840 on the Health of Towns,[46] a 'Bill for Regulating Buildings in Large Towns' was introduced into the Commons on 7 May 1841 and only minutely amended in Committee on 24 May. The bill did not go to the Lords until the following February, and on its return it still contained its original clause outlawing back-to-backs :

> it shall not be lawful to build any house, except corner houses, on any new foundation unless there shall be a clear space of at least Twenty Feet wide between the back wall of such house and the back wall of any opposite house;

and the marginal rubric was even more explicit : 'Houses Not To Be Built Back-to-Back'.[47] However, the building interests were aroused, and at this late stage the Commons sent the Bill to a Select Committee which met between March and mid-June 1842. The witnesses heard by the committee ranged from reforming interventionists to classical advocates of laisser faire. The 1840 committee's report had tried to assuage fears about regulations:

> the regulations would be framed so as to interfere no further with everyone's right to manage his own property than was necessary to protect the health of the community; nor would they extend beyond what that urgent duty of government justified;[48]

but the majority of witnesses heard in 1842 were horrified at the idea of limiting a builder's freedom. It was this idea of a 'duty of government' that had moved Dr James Williamson of Leeds to say to the 1840 Committee,

> the working classes are now exposed to the evils arising from cupidity and defective arrangements of many of their landlords, and they seem to me to require the protection of some such general enactment.[49]

The witnesses from Leeds in 1842 were of a different mind. Mr Beckett of Kirkstall Grange, who admitted that no other house except his own porter's lodge lay within half a mile of his own, told the committee that the Bill's proposals had 'created a very strong sensation throughout the country', and clearly not a sensation of approval. The town clerk of Leeds also gave evidence against the ban on back-to-backs 'which would drive the lower classes into lodgings' by putting up rents. He advocated a compromise solution: to permit back-to-backs to be built in blocks of eight (ie four front and four back) with spaces between each block in which a privy could be sited. His council had been advised by builders that to follow the bill and give a back yard and privy to each house would have entailed a rise of about 30 per cent in the cost of each house of back-to-back size.[50] (Thomas Cubitt was to say much the same in his evidence of 1844 to the Royal Commission on the State of Large Towns:[51] 'it is a much cheaper mode, and if we prevent it we prevent houses for the accommodation of poor people'.)

After this and similar evidence the Select Committee deleted the clause on back-to-backs from the bill, and the whole bill was dropped after the end of June 1842, ostensibly to await the Poor Law Commissioners' (that is, Chadwick's) *Report*, which was available on 9 July, 1842. In the event, the Public Health Act of 1848 contained no reference to back-to-backs.[52]

In the absence of national legislation to ban the building of back-to-backs it was necessary for urban councils to take powers by specific clauses in local improvement acts that they were promoting, or to pass byelaws under other statutory authority, such as the Public Health Act of 1858. Leeds was decidedly not of this mind. In Manchester, said its town clerk in 1869, 'since 1844 the building of back-to-back houses has been illegal' through the requirement that every new house should have a privy and ashpit behind it (Manchester Police Act, 1844).[53] The town clerk of Liverpool, who had been town clerk at Bradford 1861–6, also gave evidence to the same Royal Commission. Liverpool had used its powers under an act of 1861 to pass a byelaw 'that prevents back-to-back houses'; the town clerk of Halifax also said, 'I think back-to-back houses are exceedingly injurious.'[54]

The former town clerk of Bradford's evidence included his ringside view of the local turmoil at Bradford after the building byelaws of 1860.

> Their effect was to prevent a class of house that had been built until that time, that is to say, back-to-back houses in long rows . . . the effect was to prevent any houses being built of that sort.[55]

The method of the byelaw was to prescribe an open space at the rear and side of each house, so that a block of two pairs of back-to-backs would have been the maximum permitted. There had been considerable local agitation following 1860, based on statements that builders had been deterred, and housing consequently scarcer and dearer.

> I do not think that was the cause of the scarcity, but the agitation led to certain concessions in 1866 that were to a great extent temporary, (for example back-to-backs built on land already laid out as building ground).[56]

James Hole's prize essay of January 1865, which had a public reading before the mayor in Leeds Town Hall, setting off a long debate in the local press, praised the Bradford byelaw of 1860 and bemoaned Leeds'

> want of municipal regulations, especially including one to prohibit the erection of back-to-back houses which have now unfortunately become almost the universal plan for the dwellings of the working class of Leeds, and even for some as high as £20 annual rental.

He was, naturally, even more critical of the old existing back-to-backs. He recalled Baker's criticisms of 1839 and 1842, and added : 'a large proportion of these homes still exists, made worse for twenty years' additional wear and tear'. Hole was driven to conclude that the council needed powers to regulate the type of new buildings erected :

> the utter powerlessness of the working man over the construction and condition of his dwelling justified municipal interference, and the municipal power had as much right to prevent these as to insist on their proper sewerage.[57]

The best that the mayor could do in reply was to adduce the alleged scarcity that regulation had brought to Bradford (a junction of cause and effect that, it will be recalled, the town clerk of Bradford had denied), and certainly to exaggerate :

> in Bradford where this class of houses could not be built, the effect had been so much to increase the rentals that three or four families were driven into one house.[58]

While Manchester, Liverpool and Bradford had been formulating byelaws Leeds had done nothing. There had been improvement acts in 1842, 1848, 1856 but no mention of back-to-backs in them. It was true, Hole admitted, that section 190 of the 1842 Leeds Improvement Act had given the council power to compel a proper privy for each newly erected house, but

> if the cottage speculator chooses to disregard such regulations he may do so with impunity. No summons has been issued for many years for any breach of building regulations. The back-to-back system of house-building has rendered this (clause) all but impracticable.[59]

The tolerance of back-to-backs did not make all property owners in Leeds enthusiastic for them on their own doorsteps. For example, the deeds for the sale of the plot of land on which no 8 Cavendish Road (now part of the School of Economic Studies) was to be built prescribed in 1864 that 'no house of the description known as back-to-back shall be erected on the said plot', nor for the next twenty years was it to bear a public house.[60]

The only effective—and still partial—restriction of back-to-backs in Leeds came in 1866 with the byelaw that took up the proposal made by the town clerk in 1842 : new houses of this type could not be built in blocks of more than eight (four front and four back), and yard privies had to be placed between each block.[61] It is the serried ranks of these blocks, regularly broken by the privy yard space, that still catch the eye of the visitors from the south or from the northern towns that never had back-to-backs.

The continuance of back-to-back building, even in blocks of eight, remained the target for sanitary critics. Articles in *The Builder* in 1869, 1891 and 1897 cited Leeds as an incorrigible friend of the back-to-backs,[62] and a standard textbook on building development, published in 1883 observed sadly: 'I understand that back-to-back houses are still being erected in some northern towns'.[63] In Leeds the Council[64] and builders were unabashed at such comments. In 1888 an official inquiry by Barry and Smith showed that in each of the years between 1875 and 1887 (when 16,070 new houses were built in Leeds) two-thirds of all new houses were back-to-backs. Table 3.3 shows these proportions continuing until 1903, and Leeds was not yet alone in its affection for the back-to-back.

> In all the large manufacturing towns of Yorkshire back-to-back dwellings have been and are still being built to a considerable extent. In Lancashire, the Potteries and the Black Country it has been almost discontinued.[65]

Their report examined cases in Halifax, Morley, Stainland, Todmorden and Keighley: they were able to show, contrary to the arguments of mayors and master builders, that the difference in cost of a through house and a pair of back-to-backs of the same floor area was negligible, but the division enabled two separate tenancies to be created, and the return from the back-to-backs was made about some 20 per cent higher.

At about this time the secretary of the Leeds Permanent Building Society, Fatkin, was giving evidence to another royal commission. About one-seventh of his 9,348 members owned two adjoining pairs of back-to-backs which they had erected on a single building lot 10yd square, living in one of the four and drawing an income from the rents of the other three, out of which they were paying off their mortgage. The fashion in back-to-backs was changing, he said: instead of a kitchen in the cellar, more and more of his members were putting up houses that had a small kitchen alongside the parlour on the ground floor.[66]

These 'superior' back-to-backs were the £20 pa rentals mentioned by Hole in 1865, and described in 1906 by Lupton:

> modern scullery houses which contain a living room on one side of the door, and a scullery on the other, a bedroom over each, and usually a third attic bedroom with dormer windows built in blocks of eight, with rentals of from 3s 9d to 5s 6d.[67]

(Through houses at that time were rented for 5s 3d to 6s, and older, one-up one-down, back-to-backs were then 2s to 3s).[68]

It is significant that in 1898, when the corporation were planning
the houses that they would rebuild in the York Street area after their
first major slum-clearance programme, they wished to put up back-
to-backs, and sent a deputation to the Local Government Board in
Whitehall to argue their case. They failed to convince London.[69]
Indeed official opinion was now so firmly set against back-to-backs
that the Housing, Town Planning Act of 1909, section 43, laid down
the countrywide ban that the Bill of 1841 had attempted.

> Notwithstanding anything in any Local Act or byelaw in force in any
> borough or district, it shall not be lawful to erect any back-to-back houses
> intended to be used as dwellings for the working classes.[70]

The official views of the medical officers of health were undoubtedly coloured by the evidence of disease differentials. A good deal
of such local evidence was brought together in Darra Moir's report
of 1910 :

> even relatively good types of back-to-back, when compared with through,
> have a death rate 15 to 20 per cent in excess, although this is not evident
> when they are in blocks of four only, possessing some degree of ventila-
> tion.[71]

The excessive mortality was found in all types of fatal illness as well
as chronic diseases of the chest and in defective growth.

In 1909 the Leeds Master Builders Association petitioned against
legislative ban on back-to-backs, as might have been expected.[72] Their
arguments were the old ones, that through houses would put rents
beyond the reach of working-class incomes. Darra Moir's report
believed that the rise in rent for a through house of equivalent size
would have to be about 20 per cent if a landlord were to have the
same return on his capital. Rents in Leeds were not in fact high :
the Board of Trade's survey of wages and prices in 1908 had
showed that Leeds ranked as low as thirty-second of the seventy-
three largest towns in England and Wales in respect of its rent index,
and other local prices were also low; Leeds ranked fifteenth among
the seventy-three local price indexes. In absolute terms a two-room
back-to-back could then be rented at 3s to 3s 6d, a three-room from
3s 6d to 4s 6d, a four-room from 4s 6d to 6s, and a superior five-
room from 5s to 6s 6d.[73]

In the event, 1909 did not see the end of back-to-back building
in Leeds : the escape route for builders lay through a provision that
the Act should not apply to streets where the plans had been

TABLE 3.2

LEEDS BUILDING PLANS APPROVED, 1886–1914

	Total house-plans	Villas	Semi-Detached	Through houses	Back-to-back	per cent
1886	1,596	13	10	441	1,132	71
7	1,847	18	16	693	1,120	61
8	2,058	14	8	620	1,416	69
9	2,010	13	12	605	1,380	69
90	1,990	18	26	689	1,257	63
1	1,845		na			–
2	2,097	15	35	664	1,383	66
3	1,923		na			–
4	2,017	9	30	586	1,392	69
5	1,794	21	28	391	1,354	75
6	2,242	12	42	518	1,670	74
7	2,350	21	54	747	1,528	65
8	3,318	21	84	1,033	2,180	66
9	4,596	21	132	1,124	3,319	72
1900	3,549	19	133	1,097	2,300	65
1	2,947	19	88	812	2,028	69
2	2,635	18	140	728	1,749	66
3	3,529	38	177	912	2,402	68
4	3,144	54	134	1,291	1,665	53
5	2,559	21	133	1,403	1,002	39
6	1,553	30	105	735	683	44
7	1,290	33	102	580	575	45
8	1,074	22	87	439	526	49
9	724	19	67	332	306	42
10	903	28	87	411	377	42
1	441	25	78	264	74	17
2	363	37	43	221	62	17
3	276	22	56	134	64	23
4	359	35	71	196	57	16
TOTALS	57,029	616	1,978	17,666	33,001	58

Source: Annual Reports of Building Clauses Committee, Leeds Corporation.

TABLE 3.3

LEEDS HOUSES COMPLETED, 1886–1914

	Total	*Back-to-backs*	*Back-to-backs per cent*
1886	1,103	719	65
7	1,208	783	65
8	1,723	1,084	63
9	1,571	1,179	75
1890	1,728	1,194	69
1	812	552	68
2	1,876	1,212	65
3	1,915	1,258	66
4	1,949	1,308	67
5	1,707	1,134	66
6	1,681	1,229	73
7	1,832	1,396	76
8	2,399	1,633	68
9	2,903	2,034	70
1900	3,059	2,143	70
1	3,030	2,035	67
2	2,201	1,358	62
3	2,572	1,563	61
4	2,923	1,751	60
5	2,442	1,170	48
6	1,748	765	44
7	1,135	504	44
8	919	410	45
9	836	411	49
1910	584	226	39
1	505	122	24
2	350	110	31
3	220	32	15
4	287	26	9
TOTALS	47,218	29,341	62

Source: *Annual Reports*, Building Clauses Committee (1886–98); Building Plans Sub-Committee of Improvements Committee (1899–1914).

approved by the council before 1 May 1909 : the slow completion of streets had long been a regular feature of Leeds housing history, even streets begun in boom years. (I have shown elsewhere how Prosperity Street, a street of back-to-backs, took from 1874 to 1901 to complete, although only made up of sixty-four pairs.[74]) In 1910–14, when 1,946 houses were built in Leeds, a quarter were back-to-back.[75] Then all building virtually ceased for six years and it was 1937 before the last street was completed, so that back-to-backs were still being built in the years when the 150-year old back-to-backs on Quarry Hill were being slum-cleared. (See Frontispiece)

The strength of the back-to-back tradition in Leeds is a part, perhaps the most extreme part, of that 'local influence' in building styles, with which this essay began. The surprise of southern visitors, first seeing the northern hillsides and their regimented streets, is one indication that we are not dealing with a nationwide style of working-class housing. Cubitt declared that he had never built one himself, and they do not seem to have been a feature of the London industrial districts. It has been seen above that Liverpool, Manchester and Bradford had their back-to-backs, but fell out of love with them. Darra Moir's study of 1910, which is concerned with the whole country, cites examples in a very limited number of towns, all northern. Besides Manchester and Bradford, he refers to Shipley, Morley, Huddersfield, Batley, Bradford, Halifax, Keighley, Cleckheaton, Brighouse, Dewsbury, Linthwaite, Heckmondwike, Pudsey (Yorks), and Chester le Street (Co Durham). Barry and Smith's study of 1888 refers to 'discontinuance' of back-to-back building in Lancashire, the Potteries, and the Black Country. The actual examples they cite lay in Halifax, Morley, Stainland, Todmorden and Keighley.

Such an uneven local distribution is difficult to explain. The back-to-back seems to have lingered longest in the wool textile towns but there was no functional role for the back-to-back in the industrial process : the back-to-backs were not built as weavers' chambers, though some in their middle age lived on to be part of clothing sweatshops. Anyway, they existed outside the textile towns. If they seem to be built to match the low purchasing power of their working-class tenants (as the protagonists of back-to-back always claimed), there were many industrial areas with equally low wages and yet not a back-to-back in sight. Nor can they be satisfactorily claimed as the consequence of high land values; in Leeds they were

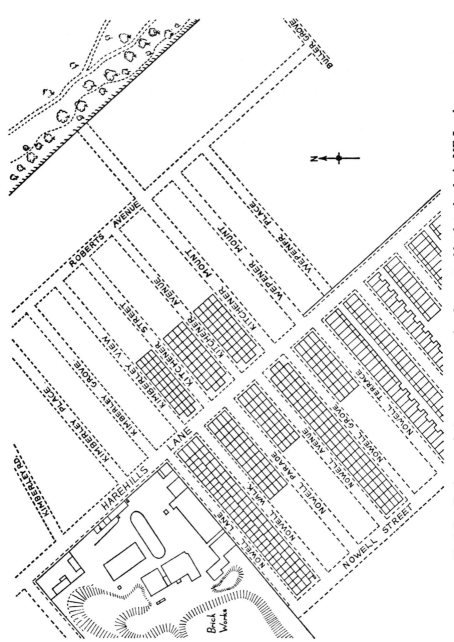

Fig 3.5. Early twentieth-century street development of back-to-backs in NE Leeds.

found on the dear land and on the cheap land; and there is no evidence that land values were systematically higher in those industrial towns that made the most of every square foot of their building grounds by packing in the back-to-backs.[76] Baker characterised back-to-backs as 'part of the economy of buildings that are to pay a good percentage',[77] but, again, there is no reason to think that cupidity or philanthropy among English landowners was distributed in the same way that we find the presence and absence of back-to-backs in industrial towns of the nineteenth century.

Using historical evidence, it has been suggested when and how the back-to-back working-class cottage came to Leeds; and it has been argued that it matched the particular size and position of fields, and the size of ownership units. It will need studies in other towns where back-to-backs proliferated to determine whether the Leeds chronology and typology are universal. But all periods of English vernacular architecture—and working-class housing is a part of the vernacular—have displayed such local and regional differences. In general, the observed differences discussed by architectural historians relate either to function or to the local availability of different building materials. Neither of these can apply to the back-to-back. It had no industrial function peculiar to it; and, while the majority were made of cheap bricks, there were Pennine back-to-backs that used local quarry stone. Driven from a simple economic explanation and deprived of arguments from use and materials, there is nothing left except a rather desperate refuge in 'cultural' factors,[78] of the sort that have produced local differentiation in the demand for fish-and-chips, Yorkshire pudding, Rugby League, and Lancashire hot-pot. Differences of taste, they lie beyond the quantifiables of price, income, density, costs, rents, returns, and land values.[79]

NOTES

1 Robert Baker was medical officer to the Poor Law Guardians, then a councillor, and later a factory inspector. His reports [hereafter cited as *Baker, 1833*; *Baker, 1839*; and *Baker, 1842*] were: *Report of the Leeds Board of Health* (1833); 'Report upon the Condition of the Town of Leeds and of Its Inhabitants, by a Statistical Committee of the Town Council, October 1839', *Journ (Royal) Stat Soc*, ii (1840), 397–422; 'On the State and Condition of the Town of Leeds', *Sanitary Condition of the Labouring Population, Local Reports*, Parliamentary Papers [hereafter *PP*], xxvii, Lords (1842).

2 Leeds Civic Hall, Committee Strong Room, shelf 36: Minute Book of the Statistical Committee; unprinted Council Minutes, iv, ff 525–9.

3 This map, more crudely constructed than that of 1842, was printed in *Baker, 1833* and is reproduced in K. J. Bonser and H. Nicholls, *Printed Maps and Plans of Leeds, 1711–1900, Thoresby Soc,* xlvii (1960), no 72.

4 The map was printed in *Baker, 1842*, in colours. In the more salubrious north-west suburb it is significant that the only streets with spots were the two blocks of back-to-backs: St James St and Little London (Carlton St and Reuben St). The environmental factor was further emphasised by Baker's use of smoking chimneys to locate the factories of Leeds.

5 A. Redford, *The History of Local Government in Manchester*, i (1939), 418.

6 Asa Briggs, *Victorian Cities* (1963), 155.

7 Baker employed the term 'back-to-back' in 1842 (*Baker, 1842*, 5) but it cannot be traced further since the absence of early references from the *Oxford English Dictionary* suggests a narrow experience of the world among Oxford lexicographers.

8 W. G. Rimmer, 'Working Men's Cottages in Leeds, 1770–1840', *Thoresby Soc,* xlvi (1961), 165–99; although it is not plain, the 'cottages' of 1787–1800 were mainly back-to-backs. See note 16, below.

9 Ventilating flues were incorporated by some later builders (*Leeds Mercury,* 20 October 1862). The 1866 building byelaws envisaged pipe or shaft ventilators, but the 1869 bye-laws were less specific: 'means as shall be satisfactory to the Council'.

10 Rimmer, *art cit* in note 8, discussed the infill development, using material from the 1792–4 survey of the Pious Uses (sc Charities) Estates, now Leeds City Archives, DB204/8; the *Fold* pattern can be seen in the plan of a Marsh Lane estate in the same survey.

11 An old-established animal-fold use for the crofts enclosed behind house-frontages of any shape is suggested, not only by the long narrow *Folds* of Mabgate, but also by *Fold* as an alternative name for the Yards of Kirkgate inns: the Wellington Inn Yard deeds (Leeds Civic Hall, Deeds Strong Room [hereafter cited as LCD], no 300) refer to 'eight tenements in the Fold', and call the Yard 'Kay Fold' or 'Peckersgill Fold'. Kay was the owner c 1632, and Peckersgill c 1704.

12 Shown by dotted partition lines within the firm outline of the whole building block. The almost standard size of a back-to-back, 5yd square, is also prominent on the plan. Directories also reveal back-to-back streets by having twice as many house-numbers than there are house-frontages on the plan; courts in back-to-back streets are usually named but their inhabitants not listed.

13 Rimmer, *art cit* in note 8, 187, based in the Rate Books, Leeds City Archives. Paley's development lay between York Road and Marsh Lane (Fig 3.4); and LCD no 1128, twenty-three cottages built in Watkinson's Yard with deeds going back to Paley's sale to William Watkinson, joiner, in 1792).

14   LCD nos 320, 334, 423 and 435. This land had been released for building development by the Anne Wilson Settled Estates Act of 1765.

15   S. J. Price, *Building Societies* (1958), 19–31.

16   LCD nos 604 and 607. In 1789 the St James St Building Club began to operate (LCD no 5706, ii) but its land purchases also date back to 1787. In 1789 the more elaborate 'Greater' and 'Lesser' Building Societies were beginning St Peter's Square and High St on Boggard Closes, Quarry Hill, which they had bought in 1787, the year after their foundation. The former was a quite elegant square but the latter was mainly back-to-backs (LCD nos 945, 1787 and 8433). In July 1786 the Union Row Building Association also bought its plot on Quarry Hill: building on its twenty-two lots was complete by 1796 (LCD nos 1999 and 1893C); these houses were of 'cottage' size but a single row only.

17   In 1869 a sub-committee of the council, considering a clause in the next improvement bill, cited 200 houses and 46 cellar dwellings in Back George St, Nelson St and Mill Garth, ie the town's veteran back-to-backs (Civic Hall, Committee Strong Room, Sub-scavenging and Nuisances [Cellar Dwellings] Committee, minutes, August 1869). When the Social Science Congress met in Leeds in 1871 the editor of *The Builder* (xxix [1871], 778, 817 and 929) took the Ebenezer St courts as the worst example of housing in the host town.

18   The frustrated development of the Wilson (Park) Estate at the West End of Leeds is illustrated in M. W. Beresford, 'Prosperity Street', see M. W. Beresford and G. R. J. Jones, ed, *Leeds and its Region* (1967), above, figs. 43-3 (pp. 353-4). In the course of the smoke-abatement action heard against Gott's mill in 1824 it was stated that 'many houses have been built . . . as cheaply as possible for labouring people. Two or three of them were partly blown down during the winter': *Report of the Trial and Indictment* (1824), 8–9. The status of the intended West End was not enhanced by the building of a gasworks there in 1826.

19   Rimmer, *art cit* in note 8, 187. The *Leeds Intelligencer,* 27 March 1787, reported 'near 400 houses erected' in 1786 and the same number anticipated for 1787.

20   Printed town plans are calendared in Bonser and Nicholls, *op cit* in note 3.

21   This development can be traced in the Denison Mss (Univ of Nottingham, Dept of Mss), eg DeH 20 and 38.

22   The New Town project on land belonging to Earl Cowper was mooted in 1825 as 'this Utopia . . . without manufacturing smoke' (*Leeds Mercury,* 30 July 1825), delayed by a bankruptcy of leading partners, abortively put up in lots in 1828 and offered again in 1839; the earliest sales so far noted in the deeds are of 1848 (LCD no 9172).

23   The more humble New Town project was developed on Griffith Wright's land from 1823 (LCD nos 4564, 4613 and 4954).

24   Rimmer *art cit* in note 8, 186: Mushroom Court, between Cambridge St and Grey St was wholly enclosed, and entered only through tunnels,

with steps to allow for the slope of the hill on which the estate lay (OS five-foot plan, 1850).

25   LCD no 6477, with plan; 10040, and 12543.

26   It could be argued that experience of cottages in innyards that were entered through archways would accustom people to living in closed courts entered through tunnel passages.

27   *Baker, 1842*, 5. 'Cottage property in Leeds realizes about 7 or 7%, and in many cases a much greater percentage . . . It is very well known that property of that description realizes a better rate of interest than property of a higher description': evidence of Matthew Johnson of Leeds, *Sel Comm on Rating of Tenements*, (*PP*, xxi of 1837–8), Q 2325. Similar returns were assumed by correspondents of the *Leeds Mercury*, 16 October 1862, a quarter-century later.

28   'Land in the skirts of the town frequently sells for £300 an acre, and there are instances of ground well adapted to building selling for £1,000 an acre. Of the prosperity of Leeds . . . the many new streets in the town and the manufactories and villas in the neighbourhood erected and being erected are very convincing proof.' Sir F. Eden, *The State of the Poor* (1797), 847–8; also Rimmer *art cit* in note 8, 189–91 for other evidence of land values.

29   Minimum street widths of 36ft appear in the Building Regulations of 1866; alleys were to be at least 12ft wide.

30   The average size of fifty-four fields designated as *Building Ground* in the Tithe Award of 1847 (Leeds City Archives) was just over $1\frac{1}{4}$ acres; streets laid out in the grounds of large houses of the 1790s were similarly confined.

31   Only four landowners had more than 60 acres of field-land in 1847 (Tithe Award); three lay on the eastern edge of the township and the fourth on the western edge.

32   A line of these is illustrated in Beresford, *Time and Place* (1961) plate ii. The influence of a boundary on street lengths is shown by the irregular group near Henrietta St, determined by the jagged township boundary at that point. See above, pp. 1-23.

33   Baker, 1842, 4.

34   *RC on the State of Large Towns and Populous Districts, PP*, xvii of 1844), 9.

35   *2nd Rep of the MOH to the Privy Council, for 1859* (*PP*, xxix of 1860), 134.

36   Among the nastiest, although not publicised like the Boot and Shoe Yard, must have been the inward-facing houses of the *Rows* that filled up the 456sq yd of Camp Field, south of the river and eventually surrounded by mills. Development of these back-to-backs began in 1805–6.

37   *Sel Comm on Public Walks* (*PP*, xv of 1833), Q 607.

38   Blue Bell Fold lay behind 46 East St at the Bank.

39   *Baker, 1839*, 400.

40   *RC on the State of Large Towns and Populous Districts* (*PP*, xvii of 1844), Qq 5761 and 5766.

41 *PP, xxix of 1860,* 133–9 (see note 35).

42 *8th Rep of the MOH to the Privy Council, for 1865 (PP,* xxxiii of 1866), 226–45.

43 The MOH's *Report of the Sanitary Condition of Leeds for 1867* (1868) has a dot distribution map for fever cases, and subsequent *Reports* from the Leeds MOH followed suit.

44 *Baker, 1842,* 5.

45 *Ibid,* 11–13. Baker was not unsympathetic to the economic realities of landlordism, and he particularly praised Croisdale's cottage property management on the Bank, and Holdforth's in Mill St (*Baker, 1839,* 401; *Leeds Mercury,* 2 November 1839; Rimmer *art cit* in note 8, 183).

46 *Rep of Sel Comm on the Health of Towns (PP,* xi of 1840).

47 The original Bill is bound in *PP, i of 1840* as 93–124; the amended Bills as *Ibid,* 125–56 and *PP, i of 1842* 287, 319, 351 and 367. The clause quoted was originally no 17 and later no 20.

48 *PP, xi of 1840,* xv.

49 *Ibid,* Qq 1667–1807: Dr Williamson had been a member of the Council's Statistical Committee of 1839.

50 *Rep of Sel Comm on Building Regulations Bill and Improvement of Boroughs Bill (PP,* x of 1842), 143–9, 160–1 and 306. Eddison himself had shares in a philanthropic company for London tenement building (*Leeds Mercury,* 22 July 1848).

51 *PP, xvii of 1844,* Q 174.

52 The Royal Commission on the State of Large Towns which reported in 1844 and 1845 had also rejected building regulations as a remedy for urban discontents (*PP, xvii of 1845,* 63), and twenty years later, when proposals for building controls in a Leeds Improvement Bill were put forward, an alderman made it clear that local magistrates might have the same ideas on the sanctity of private property that had inspired the Commission of 1845: 'it would be difficult to obtain the sanction of Quarter Sessions to any byelaws interfering with property' (*Leeds Mercury,* 3 February 1865). See also note 61, below.

53 *1st Rep of the Sanitary Comm (PP,* xxxii of 1868–9), 129–30 and 144.

54 The Liverpool byelaw of 1864 made back-to-backs illegal *in courts.*

55 *Ibid,* Q 990.

56 *Ibid,* Qq 2213 et seq.

57 James Hole, 'The Working Classes of Leeds', prize essay of January 1865, reprinted as appendix to his *Homes of the Working Classes* (1866), 125.

58 *Leeds Mercury,* 3 February 1865.

59 Hole, *op cit* in note 57, 128.

60 Univ of Leeds, Bursary deed no 27, seen by permission of the Bursar.

61 'In no case shall dwelling houses be erected in blocks so that any block contain more than eight dwelling houses': Building byelaw no 11 of 1866; byelaw 8 of 1869 reiterated this provision, and banned blocks of more than four half-backs. No printed copy of these early byelaws

has been found but they were enrolled at Quarter Sessions despite fears voiced in 1865 (note 52 above): Leeds City Archives, QS Minute Books, November 1866 and April 1869. See 35–6 Vict ch xcvii, S.23 (1872).

62 *The Builder*, xxvii (1869), 26; lxi (1891), 172 and 326; lxxiii (1897), 22 and 237.

63 F. Maitland, *Building Estates, a Rudimentary Treatise* (1883), 28.

64 But the Leeds MOH, it may be noted, 'objected on sanitary grounds to the erection of back-to-back houses' (Leeds Civic Hall, Committee Strong Room, shelf 11: Building Clauses Committee Minutes, 27 October 1871). The eight-in-a-block byelaw was being enforced at this time (eg plans disallowed, 5 February and 25 March 1870; demolition of an offending building, 14 May 1875).

65 F. W. Barry and P. G. Smith, *Joint Report on Back-to-back Houses to the Local Government Board* (1888), 2.

66 *RC on the Housing of the Working Classes, Minutes of Evidence* (PP, xxx of 1884–5), ii, 371–9.

67 F. M. Lupton, *Housing Improvement: a Summary of Ten Years' Work in Leeds* (1906), 2.

68 The Leeds Industrial Dwellings Co, which owned many blocks of working-class property in Leeds, had a revaluation of its houses in 1889 (LCD no 1988), and its back-to-backs were then letting at from 2s to 3s 8d a week.

69 *The Builder*, lxxv (1898), 567 and lxxvi (1899), 99.

70 9 Edward VII, cap 44.

71 L. W. Darra Moir, *Report on Back-to-back Houses* (PP, xxxviii of 1910), 1.

72 *The Builder*, xcvii (1909), 103.

73 A. W. Fox, *Report of an Inquiry by the Board of Trade into Working-Class Rents, Housing and Retail Prices* (PP, cvii of 1908), 256–61.

74 M. W. Beresford, *op cit* in note 32, 4-9. See above, pp. 4-9.

75 Table 3.3, p. 118.

76 There seems to have been no shortage of building ground in the in-township of Leeds before the 1880s. There was no building upwards, except Paley's Galleries, a sort of vertical back-to-back, described in the *Leeds Mercury* of 22 July 1848 as being as bad as the new tenement flats in the Metropolis, 'completely airless'.

77 *Baker, 1842*, 5.

78 It was, after all, a Leeds MOH who stated publicly that local people actually preferred to live in back-to-backs (*PP*, vii of 1885, 325–7).

79 This essay has grown from work in progress on a total building history of Leeds. Work during 1966–8 was assisted by a grant from the Social Science Research Council, and by the help of Mary Forster and Richard Peppard, research assistants. The minute books of committees and the property deeds in the Civic Hall strong rooms have been consulted by kind permission of the Town Clerk, and with much help from two of his staff, Mr Blair and Mr Senior. The figures have been drawn for me by Mr P. D. Reardon.

APPENDIX 3.1

STREETS FREQUENTLY CASTIGATED BY CRITICS AND CONTAINING
BACK-TO-BACKS

Brighton Court	4 back-to-backs on either side
Camp Field	3 rows of back-to-backs
Cavalier Street	all back-to-backs
Clarkson's Yard	8 back-to-backs, entered through a tunnel
Cross Lisbon Street	some back-to-backs
Dufton's Yard	12 back-to-backs, 6 through
Ebenezer Street	38 back-to-backs, 11 through
Goulden's Buildings	24 back-to-backs in interior court; adjoining grave-yard
Harper Street	33 back-to-backs, 11 through; adjoining markets
Howarth Court	14 back-to-backs, entered through tunnel
Mill Street	31 back-to-backs
Nelson Street	41 back-to-backs, 9 through
Noah's Ark	10 back-to-backs in totally enclosed court but one of the few developments south of the river that came to the attention of reformers
Off Street	53 back-to-backs
Orange Street	40 back-to-backs, 3 through
Paley's Galleries	back-to-backs of several stories, unique in Leeds
Phillip's Yard	11 back-to-backs
Quarry Hill	26 back-to-backs, many through
Riley Court	7 back-to-backs
Somerset Street	29 back-to-backs, 2 through
Spring Street	23 back-to-backs, 4 through
Sykes Yard	14 back-to-backs
Templar Street	49 back-to-backs, 36 through
Union Street	53 back-to-backs, 3 through
Walker's Yard	18 back-to-backs
Wellington Place	12 back to-backs (at least)
Wellington Yard	38 back-to-backs and 15 single cottages (at least)

APPENDIX 3.2

THE FIRST GENERATION: THE 43 STREETS MADE UP WHOLLY OR PARTLY
OF BACK-TO-BACKS BUILT BETWEEN 1781 AND 1815

Bow Street (6)
  Back Bow Street (1)
Brick Street (4)
Bridge Sreet (3)
  Little Bridge Street (1)
*Burmantofts (Street) (4)

Camp Field (10)
  Front Row, Middle Row,
  Back Row
Cankerwell Lane (2)
Cavalier Street (21)
Charles Street (17)

Copper Street (2)

Duke Street (15)
*Ebenezer Street (11)
Ellerby Road
 Ellerby Lane (27)
 Back Ellerby Road

*George's Street (10)
 Back George's Street (6)
Goulden Square
 *Goulden's Buildings (11)
*Harper Street (5)
High Street (7)
 Back High Street
*Hope Street (2)
John Street (1)
Kendall's Buildings
Kendall Street
 Kendall Row (9)
(East) King Street (4)
Leighton Lane
Line Street
 Little Line Street
Lisbon Street
 Lisbon Court
Marsh Lane (55)

*Nelson Street (9)
New Park Street (3)
New Row (3)
Nile Street (2)
 Back Nile Street
*Off Street (10)
Park Court
(East) Queen Street (2)
Randerson's Yard
Richmond Road (25)
St Anne's Lane (5)
*St James' Street (9)
Steander Row (7)
Sykes Street
 *Sykes Yard (3)
Templar Street
Union Street (8)
 Union Row (6)
Walker's Place
 Walker's Row
Walker's Yard
*York Street (30)
 Back York Street
Zion Street (4)
 Back Zion Street (2)
 Zion Square
*Little London—Reuben Street (2)

NOTES TO APPENDIX 3.2

The numbers in brackets after each name are the cholera cases in 1832 (Robert Baker, *Report of the Leeds Board of Health* [1833], 21–7). The 372 cases in these 43 streets made up 28 per cent of the total (1,448) for the in-township.

The list consists of streets, etc, that (a) appear on Netlam and Giles' plan of 1815 and also (b) have back-to-backs indicated on the large-scale (five-foot = one mile) OS plan of 1850. It also includes Reuben Street, Little London, which lay within the in-township but just beyond the bounds of the 1815 plan; Great Woodhouse hamlet, also part of the in-township, lay beyond the area of the 1815 plan but Thorpe's plan of 1821 shows no streets laid out beyond the courts and folds except possibly Pickard Street (which was back-to-back).

Streets marked by asterisks * also had cellar dwellings.

APPENDIX 3.3

THE SECOND GENERATION: 360 OTHER STREETS WITH BACK-TO-BACKS, BUILT
1815–1850
(Back-to-back houses on OS 'Five-foot' plan of Leeds, 1850)

Sheet 1
Smith's Bdgs
Clarkson's Row
Pleasant Green
Pleasant Court
King's Row
King's Court
Graveley Tce
Graveley Row

Sheet 2
Moseley St
Albert St
Chancellor St
Rhodes Sq
Buslingthorpe Row
Scott Hall St

Sheet 3
Hobson's Bdgs
Close St
Mark St
Spenceley St
St Mark's St
Cross Mark St
Asquith St
Cemetery St
Cross Cemetery St
Scotts Tce
Holborn Tce
Charing Cross St
Huddersfield St
Bateson St
Toulson Row

Sheet 4
Lapish St
Pickard St
Pickard Green
Horrock St
Tolson St
Daisy St
Hobson St

Walsh Row
Oaklands Row
Oaklands St
Beckett St
Alfred Tce
Camp St
Meanwood St
Reuben St
Bk Reuben St
Primrose St
Sheepscar Bdgs
Victoria Place
Barrack St
Buslingthorpe St
Buslingthorpe Lane
Buslingthorpe Tce
Chapletown Rd
Wild's Court
Roundhay Rd
Wingham St
Wingham Place
Wingham Tce
White St
Roundhay St
Queen's Tce
Sheepscar Row
Sheepscar Green
Sheepscar Vale
Chapeltown St

Sheet 6
Fenton St
Sunny Bank Tce
Toulson Place
Cankerwell Lane
St James' St
Portland Crescent
Bk Portland Cres

Sheet 7
Carr St
Elmwood Vale
Elmwood St

Cobourg St
Queen's Pl
Barclay St
Whitelock St
Stamford St
Darley St
Lilac Tce
Concord St
Imperial St
Myrtle St
Busfield St
Vandyke St
Byron St
Cannon St
Mason St
Cloth St

Sheet 8
Winnflower Place
Lincolnfield Tce
Lincolnfield Row
Lincolnfield Place
Lincoln St
Hay Mount Place
Hay Mount Bdgs
New Cleveland St
Cherry St
Cherry Row
Pilot St
Rushworth St
Haigh St
Cambridge St
Grey St
Lion St
Tiger St
Violet St
Low Close Bdgs
Providence Bdgs
St Luke's Tce
Upper Cherry St
Green St
Pollard St
Lilac Tce

Concord St
Accommodation Place
Accommodation Tce
Harrison's Bdgs
Farrar St
Boston St
Selby St
Whitehall St
Anglesea St
Beckett St

Sheet 9
Hollis St
Grattan St
Florist St
England St
Dover St
Corporation St
Baker St
Angel St
North Hall St
North Hall Tce
Pimlico St
Burley Rd
Caroline Place
Park Lane
Newcastle St
Durham St
Darlington St
Wortley St
Wellington Tce
Abbey St
Denton St
Thackray St

Sheet 10
Harcourt Place
Marlborough St
Chatham St
Hanover St
Bk Hanover St
Howard St
New Park St
Bk Park St
Park Court
Fountain St
Caroline St
Parliament St

Government St
Somers St
Bedford Place
Chorley Lane
Leighton Lane
Oxford St
Bentick St
Portland St
Portland Cres
West St
Henrey St
Charley St
Forest St
Mercy St
Wellington St
Well St
Bk Well St
Skinner St
Grove St
Lisbon St
School St
Eldon St
Cropper Gate
Wellington Place
Calder St
Airedale Pl
Westminster Pl
Cross Lisbon St
Castle St
Saville St
Little Queen St

Sheet 11
Russell Pl
Merrion St
Belgrave St
Bk Nile St
Nile St
Copenhagen St
Hope St
Templar St
Lower Templar St
Cross Templar St
Bridge St
Livery St
Malt St
Templar's Court
Moscow St

Noble St
Sun St
Star St
Gower St
Brewery St
Bell St
Poland St
Saint St
Time St
Pendulum St
Tulip St
Pink St
Rose St
Little Bridge St
Lydia St
Nelson St
Union St
Ebenezer St
George's St
Bk George's St
East Lane
Harper St
Sykes' Yard
Sykes St
Goulden's Bdgs
Goulden's Square
Dyers St
Somerset St
Upper Somerset St
Little Somerset St
Cross Somerset St
Duke St
Quarry Hill
St Anns Lane
Charles St
Clarkson's Yd
St Mary's Row
Church St
Little Line St
Billett St
Cross Billett St
Shear St
High St
Bk High St
Upper Corn Hill
Little Albion St
York St
Brick St

Off St
Brussels St
Lee's Square

Sheet 12
Linsley Row
Union Row
Boynton St
Hound St
Fox St
Cross High St
Prospect Row
Lemon St
Orange St
Mason's Bdgs
Stone St
Plane St
Stainburn Sq
Vienna St
Vienna Court
Cross Vienna St
Purdy St
Giles St
Chapel St
Carver St
Cross Ebenezer St
Helen Court
York Court
Crispin St
Cato St
Railway St
Grantham St
Madras St
East Field St
Clay St
Glue St
Cross Shannon St
Steel St
Flint St
Forester's Arms Court
Cleveland St
Plaid Row
Cable Row
Shannon Row
Vincent St
Rodney St
Sloe St
Hatfield St

Shaw St
Elm St
Oak St
Upper Accommodation
  Rd
Keeton St
Sugden St
Blackburn's Cres
Cottage St ·
Woodman St
Bath St
Beckett St
East Beckett St
East Grove St
Rock St
Burmantofts
Upper Burmantofts St
Cross Burmantofts St
Barker's Row
Barker's Bdgs
Waterloo St
Pea St
Anchor St
Bean St
Acorn St
Upper Acorn St
Mulberry St
Wheat St
Bread St
Apple St
Windsor St
Edgar St
Plato St
Railway Tce
Accommodation Row
Pleasant Place

Sheet 14
Front Row (Camp
  Field)
Middle Row
Back Row
Stone Row

Sheet 15
Pool Row
Pitt Row

Short Row
Williams Court
Walker's Row
Walker's Yard
Steander Row
New Lane
New Lane Place
Hinchcliffe's Court
Land's Court·
Kendall St
Kendall Row
Waterloo St

Sheet 16
Foundry St
Milk St
Brook St
Lower Cross St
Upper Cross St
Upper Cross Yard
Spring St
Spring Yard
Giles' Bdgs
Ball's Bdgs
Lumb St
Brighton Yard
Brighton Court
Wheeler St
Mill St
Worsted St
Spinner St
Richmond Rd
East Field St
Clay St
Edmund St
Catherine St
Providence St
Cross St
Little Providence St
Dolphin St
Little Dolphin St
Short Dolphin St
Cross Dolphin St
Dufton St
Wrigglesworth St
Copper St
Brass St
Brown's Bdgs

Upper Wrigglesworth St
New Row
Flax St
Kendall's Bdgs
Back Ellerby Rd
East King St
East Queen St
Zion St
Back Zion St
Zion Square
Cavalier St
Upton's Court
Willis St
Morpeth St
Upper Cavalier St
High Markland St

Fawcett St
Cookson St
Sussex Court
Sussex St
Surrey St
Leicester St
Kent St
Elam St
Sheffield St
Bachelor's St
Bachelor's Bdgs
Lower Bachelor St
Ellerby Lane
Walker's Place
Carnation St
Dahlia St

Sheet 19
John St
Orfeur St
Barstow St
Douglas St
Banner St

Sheet 20
Bridgefield Bdgs

NB No back-to-back houses on Sheet 5. Sheets 13, 17, 18, 21–25 cover land outside in-township.

INDEX

.